Margarita Hidalgo
Diversification of Mexican Spanish

Contributions to the Sociology of Language

Edited by
Ofelia García
Francis M. Hult

Founding editor
Joshua A. Fishman

Volume 111

Margarita Hidalgo
Diversification of Mexican Spanish

A Tridimensional Study in New World Sociolinguistics

ISBN 978-1-5015-1695-5
e-ISBN (PDF) 978-1-5015-0453-2
e-ISBN (EPUB) 978-1-5015-0444-0
ISSN 1861-0676

Library of Congress Cataloging-in-Publication Data
A CIP catalog record for this book has been applied for at the Library of Congress.

Bibliographic information published by the Deutsche Nationalbibliothek
The Deutsche Nationalbibliothek lists this publication in the Deutsche Nationalbibliografie; detailed bibliographic data are available on the Internet at http://dnb.dnb.de.

© 2018 Walter de Gruyter Inc., Boston/Berlin
This volume is text- and page-identical with the hardback published in 2016.
Cover image: sculpies/shutterstock
Typesetting: fidus Publikations-Service GmbH, Nördlingen
Printing and binding: CPI books GmbH, Leck

♾ Printed on acid-free paper
Printed in Germany

www.degruyter.com

Margarita Hidalgo

Diversification of Mexican Spanish

A Tridimensional Study in New World Sociolinguistics

ISBN 978-1-5015-1695-5
e-ISBN (PDF) 978-1-5015-0453-2
e-ISBN (EPUB) 978-1-5015-0444-0
ISSN 1861-0676

Library of Congress Cataloging-in-Publication Data
A CIP catalog record for this book has been applied for at the Library of Congress.

Bibliographic information published by the Deutsche Nationalbibliothek
The Deutsche Nationalbibliothek lists this publication in the Deutsche Nationalbibliografie; detailed bibliographic data are available on the Internet at http://dnb.dnb.de.

© 2018 Walter de Gruyter Inc., Boston/Berlin
This volume is text- and page-identical with the hardback published in 2016.
Cover image: sculpies/shutterstock
Typesetting: fidus Publikations-Service GmbH, Nördlingen
Printing and binding: CPI books GmbH, Leck

♾ Printed on acid-free paper
Printed in Germany

www.degruyter.com

Table of contents

Acknowledgements —— xii

Prologue —— xiii

Introduction: Sociolinguistic diversification —— 1
1 Diversification —— 1
2 Diversification: Social stratification —— 3
3 Diversification: Stratification and popularization —— 4
4 Language traditions —— 5
5 Literary and popular language —— 10
6 Language reforms and standardization —— 11
7 After the Wars of Independence —— 15
8 Schools of thought —— 17
9 The case of Spanish: from the beginning to New World Spanish —— 21
10 New World Spanish: spoken and written —— 22
11 The aim of this book —— 26
12 The chapters —— 30
13 Explicative models —— 33

Chapter 1
The origins of Spanish: Spain and the New World —— 35
1.1 The origins —— 35
1.2 The rise of Castilian —— 37
1.3 Repopulation of Andalusia —— 40
1.4 Toledano and Old Castilian —— 42
1.4.1 De-affrication, devoicing and inter-dentalization —— 43
1.4.2 De-palatalization —— 47
1.4.3 Yeísmo or de-latelarization —— 47
1.4.4 Aspiration and omission of /s/ in implosive position —— 48
1.5 Additional changes —— 48
1.6 Spanish initial F-: past and present perspectives —— 49
1.7 Features of Judaeo-Spanish —— 51
1.8 Features from Spain transplanted to New Spain —— 52
1.9 The features of Andalusian Spanish —— 53
1.10 Spanish speakers in New Spain —— 55
1.11 Spanish speakers and the castes in the 16th century —— 57
1.12 Theories on the origins of New World Spanish —— 59
1.13 Koines and koineization in New World Spanish —— 61

- 1.14 The use of dialect features in New Spain —— 63
- 1.15 Conclusions —— 65

Chapter 2
The first speakers of Mexican Spanish —— 70
- 2.1 The first Spanish speakers in Mesoamerica and social stratification —— 70
- 2.2 The Spanish Caribbean experiment —— 71
- 2.3 The *encomienda* in New Spain —— 73
- 2.4 The new system of social stratification —— 74
- 2.5 Origins of the first Spanish speakers —— 75
- 2.6 The New Laws of 1542 —— 78
- 2.7 Spanish speakers in the 16th century: numbers and regions —— 81
- 2.8 The new environment —— 81
- 2.9 The process of socialization and diffusion —— 82
- 2.10 The center —— 84
- 2.11 The Inquisition —— 87
- 2.11.1 Matters of routine in and around the Holy Office —— 88
- 2.12 Spanish and the Holy Office —— 94
- 2.13 The sins recorded by the Holy Office —— 96
- 2.14 Spanish speakers and ethnic groups in the *Abecedario* —— 97
- 2.15 Spanish speakers of African descent —— 101
- 2.15.1 Afro-Mexicans and the process of acculturation —— 103
- 2.15.2 Afro-Mexican enclaves —— 104
- 2.16 Conclusions —— 107

Chapter 3
The Spanish language and its variations in New Spain —— 110
- 3.1 The earliest Spanish documents written in Mexico —— 110
- 3.2 The *First Letter* by Hernán Cortés —— 112
- 3.3 The *Second Letter* by Hernán Cortés —— 113
- 3.3.1 Salient features in Hernán Cortés' *Cartas de Relación* —— 118
- 3.4 Adaptation of Amerindian languages —— 120
- 3.5 Morphology and syntax —— 120
- 3.6 Common verbs in transition —— 123
- 3.7 Verbal clitics —— 124
- 3.8 Stylistic and dialect variations —— 125
- 3.9 Indicative and subjunctive —— 126
- 3.9.1 Imperfect subjunctive in adverbial clauses —— 127
- 3.9.2 Imperfect subjunctive in translation —— 128
- 3.9.3 Conditional sentences with –SE in translation —— 129

3.9.4	Conditional sentences with –RA in translation —— 129
3.10	Extinct and current lexical items and discourse markers —— 130
3.11	Use of Taino borrowings —— 131
3.11.1	Documentation of Taino borrowings in New Spain —— 132
3.12	Pronouns of address —— 133
3.13	General features of 16th century Spanish pronunciation —— 134
3.13.1	General features of 16th century Spanish: morpho-syntax —— 135
3.14	Conclusions —— 136

Chapter 4
Koineization and the first generation of Spanish speakers —— 140

4.1	The first generation —— 140
4.1.1	Spanish space and Spanish institutions —— 141
4.2	The formation of the Mexican Spanish koine —— 144
4.3	The Spanish spoken and written in the 16th century —— 144
4.3.1	Evidence of dialect contact and dialect change —— 146
4.4	Other documents related to Hernán Cortés —— 147
4.4.1	The features of Cortesian texts —— 150
4.4.2	Spellings of common verbs —— 151
4.4.3	Morpho-syntactic features of Cortesian texts —— 152
4.4.4	Position of verbal clitics —— 153
4.4.5	Pro-etymological and anti-etymological verbal clitics —— 154
4.4.6	Variable use of PARA and PA —— 159
4.4.7	The use of imperfect subjunctive —— 160
4.4.8	Pronouns of address: from Cortés' letters to 1555 —— 161
4.4.9	Diffusion of Spanish, discourse markers, and lexical items —— 162
4.4.10	Loans from Taino and Nahuatl —— 164
4.5	The speech of Diego de Ordaz —— 165
4.5.1	Morpho-syntactic features of Diego de Ordaz —— 166
4.5.2	The origins of *voseo* —— 168
4.6	Nahuatl loans in the *Vocabulario de la lengua castellana y mexicana* —— 170
4.7	The explicative model of proto-Mexican Spanish —— 173
4.8	The Gulf of Mexico —— 175
4.8.1	The sibilants in the Gulf —— 177
4.8.2	*Leísmo* in the Gulf —— 178
4.8.3	Use of subject pronouns: *vos, vosotros, vuestra merced* —— 179
4.8.4	Imperfect subjunctive: variations in –SE and –RA —— 179
4.8.5	Lexicon —— 180
4.9	Conclusions —— 181

Chapter 5
How Spanish diversified —— 184
- 5.1 Occupational activities and social networks —— 184
- 5.2 Mining and metallurgy —— 185
- 5.2.1 Mining centers and ethnic groups —— 190
- 5.2.2 Taxco —— 193
- 5.2.3 Pachuca —— 193
- 5.2.4 Sultepec —— 193
- 5.2.5 Puebla —— 194
- 5.2.6 Queretaro —— 194
- 5.2.7 San Luis Potosi —— 194
- 5.2.8 Guanajuato —— 195
- 5.2.9 Zacatecas —— 195
- 5.3 Forms of labor and language contact —— 196
- 5.3.1 Losing the ties to the land —— 199
- 5.3.2 Labor and agriculture: indigenous vs. Spanish crops —— 201
- 5.3.3 The *obrajes* —— 201
- 5.4 Formal education —— 203
- 5.4.1 Education for women —— 206
- 5.5 Additional activities promoting the use of Spanish —— 206
- 5.6 Spanish literature in Spain and in New Spain —— 207
- 5.7 Conclusions —— 209

Chapter 6
Continuity and change: The second generation —— 211
- 6.1 The innovations of the second generation —— 211
- 6.2 Linguistic documents: the Central Highlands —— 212
- 6.2.1 Pronunciation traits —— 212
- 6.2.2 Other pronunciation features —— 213
- 6.2.3 Morpho-syntactic features —— 215
- 6.2.4 Imperfect subjunctive —— 217
- 6.2.5 Pronouns of address —— 217
- 6.2.6 Original letters by Alonso Ortiz —— 218
- 6.2.7 Mixing *tú*, *vos* and *vuestra merced* —— 220
- 6.3 Suárez de Peralta's *Tratado del descubrimiento de las Yndias y su conquista* —— 222
- 6.3.1 Relevant features in Suárez de Peralta's *Tratado* —— 222
- 6.3.2 Object pronouns LES and LOS in the second-generation —— 226
- 6.3.3 Other object pronouns —— 228
- 6.3.4 Verb forms —— 230

6.3.5	Pronoun of address in the *Tratado* —— 230	
6.3.6	*Vuesa(s) merced(es)* —— 232	
6.3.7	Use of imperfect subjunctive —— 233	
6.3.8	Conditional sentences ending with –RA —— 233	
6.3.9	Discourse markers, idiomatic expressions and other features —— 233	
6.3.10	References to ethnicity —— 234	
6.4	Linguistic documents: the Gulf —— 235	
6.4.1	Miscellaneous traits in the Gulf —— 236	
6.4.2	The system of pronouns of address: *tú, vos, vosotros, vuestra merced, su merced* —— 237	
6.4.3	Clitic pronouns as direct objects —— 240	
6.4.4	Imperfect subjunctive: variations of –SE and –RA —— 241	
6.4.5	Lexical items referring to ethnicity —— 242	
6.5	More examples from the second generation —— 242	
6.6	Conclusions —— 243	

Chapter 7
Religion, bilingualism and acculturation —— 249
- 7.1 Religion as a driving force —— 249
- 7.2 Population losses and language shift —— 250
- 7.3 Factors contributing to maintenance: new political organization —— 251
- 7.4 New religion and language maintenance and shift —— 254
- 7.5 Rescuing the past for the future —— 258
- 7.5.1 The second generation and the good memories about Tlatelolco —— 259
- 7.6 Strategies of Hispanization —— 261
- 7.6.1 Religion and the indigenous masses —— 262
- 7.6.2 Hispanicization of the indigenous —— 264
- 7.7 Transculturation and miscegenation —— 265
- 7.8 Language contact, bilingualism, and socio-ethnic groups —— 271
- 7.8.1 Bilingual individuals and bilingual groups —— 272
- 7.9 Ethnicity and socio-ethnic labels —— 274
- 7.10 Hispanization of the Afro-Mexican population —— 275
- 7.11 Conclusions —— 276

Chapter 8
Diversification and stability: 17th century —— 278
- 8.1 Spanish speakers in the 17th century —— 278
- 8.2 Education of Spanish speakers —— 280
- 8.3 Uprooting and integration of the castes —— 281
- 8.4 Colonial Spanish in the oldest Spanish-speaking regions —— 284

8.4.1   The spelling of the sibilants in Castilian —— 285
8.4.2   The spelling of the sibilants in the Central Highlands —— 286
8.4.3   Sibilants in the Gulf —— 288
8.4.4   "Regular" *seseo* —— 289
8.4.5   Residual verb forms —— 290
8.4.6   *Leísmo* in the Central Highlands and in the Gulf —— 291
8.4.7   Inanimate objects and *leísmo* —— 297
8.4.8   Pronouns of address: *tú*, *vuestra merced*, *su merced*, *Usted* —— 298
8.4.9   *Vuestra merced*, *Usted* and *vosotros* —— 299
8.4.10 Change of pronouns in the personal domain —— 301
8.4.11 Imperfect subjunctive with –SE and –RA —— 302
8.4.12 Ethnic groups —— 304
8.5   Literature in Spanish —— 305
8.6   Conclusion —— 306

Chapter 9
The end of the colonial period: 18th century —— 308
9.1   Attrition of peninsular Spanish variants —— 308
9.2   The growth and decline of the colony —— 309
9.3   Spanish emigrants to New Spain —— 310
9.4   Population of New Spain —— 312
9.4.1   The Revillagigedo Census —— 312
9.5   The growth of the cities —— 317
9.6   Education —— 318
9.7   The Bourbon reforms, the economy and ethnicity —— 319
9.8   Language attrition in the Central Highlands and in the Gulf —— 321
9.9   Attrition of morpho-syntactic variants —— 323
9.9.1   Direct object pronouns LE and LO —— 323
9.9.2   Pronouns of address —— 325
9.9.3   Use of –SE and –RA in conditional clauses and imperfect subjunctive —— 328
9.9.4   The use of –SE and –RA in official documentation —— 331
9.10   Lexicon —— 332
9.11   Language reforms, journalism and literature —— 335
9.12   Spanish-accented Nahuatl —— 338
9.13   Conclusions —— 341

Chapter 10
Diversification, attrition and residual variants —— 343
10.1   Attrition-focused variants —— 343

10.2	Optimal residual variants —— 354	
10.2.1	The prepositions PARA and PA —— 357	
10.2.2	Dissolution of hiatus —— 358	
10.2.3	Addition of –s in the preterit —— 359	
10.2.4	Duplicate possessives —— 359	
10.2.5	Amerindian loans —— 360	
10.3	Residual variants belonging to the vernacular realm —— 360	
10.3.1	The diphthong /we/ in various positions —— 365	
10.4	Verb forms —— 365	
10.4.1	The endings –RA and –RA in protasis and apodosis —— 367	
10.5	Lexical items and idiomatic expressions in popular speech —— 368	
10.6	The common denominator: residual variants —— 369	
10.7	Infrequent variants in modern Mexican Spanish —— 371	
10.8	Variants discarded in Mexican Spanish —— 372	
10.9	Modern *Usted* —— 373	
10.10	Conclusions —— 374	
11	**Conclusions —— 376**	
11.1	A tridimensional study —— 376	
11.2	The role of history: direct external factors —— 376	
11.2.1	Creole and semi-creole varieties —— 377	
11.3	From the past to the present: indirect external factors —— 379	
11.4	Peninsular, New World and Latin American Spanish —— 384	
11.5	Stages of diversification —— 385	
11.6	PARA and PA in Venezuela —— 388	
11.7	Diversification of the New World Spanish tree —— 388	
11.8	Final conclusions —— 390	

Appendix —— 394

References —— 401

Index —— 415

Acknowledgements

I want to express my gratitude to those who over the years have been assisting me in the completion of this lengthy project. First, I appreciate the encouragement and patience of my family and my friends for applauding, supporting, and even celebrating my initiatives. Next, I would like to thank Alicia García, Margaret Posner, Lori Palmer, Melody Tune, and Ginger Stockdale, all at San Diego State University, for helping me create tables, maps, figures, and miscellaneous documents needed in the composition of this and other manuscripts. They also helped me to resolve the minor and major technical problems I encountered on a regular basis. I am indebted to Melody Tune for her special assistance during emergencies.

I certainly appreciate the tenacity of my former San Diego State University students who saved class notes, maps, recordings and exams that helped me refresh my memory. During the years of the California bonanza, I was able to travel often to Mexico and to Spain. These research years were extremely insightful since I was able to observe directly the language use and language attitudes of native speakers from whom I grasped *in situ* most of the variants and variations that I have selected for analysis. I am also grateful to the librarians of San Diego State University, the University of California at San Diego, the Henry E. Huntington Library, and the Archivo de Indias in Seville for the expedience and interest in locating the old, rare, and not easily available bibliographical materials that I needed to consult.

Last, but not least I want to thank Salvador González for the feedback he has given me on the content of this book and for formatting and reformatting this and other manuscripts that in the beginning were shapeless and hopeless.

I dedicate this book to my father (1909-2005), who is in Heaven; to my energetic mother, who keeps me going and hopeful; to my brother for listening to my theories and contributing with his own; and to my younger sister for the imaginative language games we played when we were children.

Prologue

I am thrilled for the opportunity and the privilege to share this book with students and scholars of sociolinguistics. After one hundred years of intense query in linguistics, the time is right for the disciples in the field to move on from the fundamental perspectives advanced by Ferdinand de Saussure in his *Cours de linguistique* générale (1916), where he proposed the distinction between synchrony and diachrony. We have advanced to newer conceptualizations proposed by the social sciences in general and sociolinguistics in particular, which in turn will allow us to see the possible outcomes of change in a historical sociolinguistic perspective. Synchronic analysis focuses on description of the regular internal dynamics and mechanisms that govern language behavior in general, while diachrony is concerned with the development and evolution of language through history. The diachronic approach attempts to make sense of history and the processes that are conditioned by speakers' behavior. Sociolinguistics has contributed with an additional dimension that connects social meaning to both language and history.

As linguistic corpora become available to a wider audience, the challenge of looking into authentic texts from the past has turned into a truly gratifying experience that aids in understanding the dynamic relationship between the spoken and the written language. The examination of large subsamples of variants aids in the description of a language system, e.g. colonial Spanish, and in refining the methodology used to corroborate or reject postulates on language evolution, attrition, variation and change across historical periods. The analysis of language data is also conducive to reconstructing the intersections of history, society, and language. Two documents retrieved from the Henry E. Huntington Library have been extremely useful to initiate the historical analysis of the Mexican colony: the first one is the *Segunda Carta de Relación* by Hernán Cortés (1522), published in Seville in the House of Jacobo Cromberger; the other one is a rare inquisitorial manuscript known as *El Abecedario* (1571-1700).

The advantage of the historical sociolinguistic approach at hand lies in the availability of native speakers on both sides of the Atlantic who may still share the intuitions their ancestors had about the use of variants that made history in the history of language. I am hopinig that this book will contribute to gaze at the role of history in linguistic studies. In the beginning, I thought that I was going to have an up-close and private look at the deep roots of the peninsular Spanish tree; now I believe that some features of late medieval and pre-modern Spanish are still alive and well. The exploration of challenging perspectives is making me rise through higher spheres of inquiry and contentment. Having access to original or paleographed manuscripts is an adventure similar to searching for lost treasures in sunken vessels or ancient cities surrounded by mysterious tales and legends. A manuscript belongs to history and the social context in which it stemmed, and cannot be ignored if we wish to understand the content and the form. The literal transcription of manuscripts may vary according to the scholar who found the precious gem in search for invaluable information. Some scholars choose to modernize superficial aspects of a manuscritpt to make it more accessible to readers. For this reason, transcriptions vary from collection to collection; some components can be rescued *in toto*, while others are permanently lost. In the selection of subsamples, I respect the collector's guidelines, e.g. adding or omitting accent marks, using abbreviations for honorifics such as *vuestra merced* (*v.m.*), etc. Coordinators and collectors of manuscripts may have different perspectives when transcribing verb forms; for example, some of them follow the modern rules for accentuation (*él se cayó allí*, 'he fell over there') even when the original manuscript appeared unaccented. Following modern rules of orthography, others only place the accent marks when there is a difference in meaning, as in *yo voto* ('I vote') vs. él *votó* ('he voted').

Introduction: Sociolinguistic diversification

1 Diversification

This book explores the notion of diversification in the context of New World Spanish sociolinguistics. Diversification refers to both the act and the result of diversifying the roles, functions, domains, and even traits of a transplanted language, which may be rejected or diminished by the speakers living in the environment where the transplantation occurred. When a transplanted language is diversified, there are less risks of attrition, shift, or death. By the same token, if the transplanted language is empowered by the speakers (immigrant or native), its chances of survival and growth are much higher. The point of departure is the analysis of the Spanish written, and by inference, spoken from the very beginning of the Spanish presence in the vast region first known as New Spain and later Mexico. While it is difficult—if not impossible—to examine all the occurrences and changes that took place during almost five hundred years, it is feasible and extremely useful to select features that emerged and evolved in different ways. The variety of Mexican Spanish is the second oldest in the American continent, and as such it did assimilate some of the innovations occurring in the Spanish-speaking Caribbean region.

Diversification is encompassing since it covers two-and-a-half centuries of language development preceded only by the early stage of koineization (Hidalgo 2001a: 27-30 and 2001b: 56, 65ff). In the context of diversification the aim of this book is to address, explore and problematize the relationships between external factors and internal changes affecting New World Spanish in general and Mexican Spanish in particular during the entire colonial period (1520-1821). A tridimensional view of history, society, and language may allow a better understanding of the relationships amongst the main components within the colonial setting and serves as the framework to study the historical and social milieu in which colonial Spanish unfolded. While history remains in the background as the independent variable, societal forces are more visible, and appear closer to language data in general and select variants in particular.

The comparative approach is useful to understand or at least to infer some of the differences between Mexican Colonial Spanish and other New World varieties. External factors refer to events that are in principle independent from language phenomena. In the case of New World Spanish we can think of major historical events such as discovery, exploration, conquest, colonization, and emigration, to name a few that are clearly pertinent to the New World, where several European languages were transplanted. Many a time external factors are conspicuous and thus can be identified with more precision than internal linguistic changes. On the other hand, extra-linguistic factors such as gender, age, education, ethnicity or the socio-economic status of a speaker or groups of speakers may be more difficult to grasp in historical sociolinguistic studies as they relate directly or indirectly to language phenomena, e.g. language variation, change, or linguistic occurrences such as borrowing, attrition or erosion of specific features. In the diversification of New World Spanish, the roles of Spanish speakers should be underscored, for they were the agents of spread, transmission, diffusion, change, and some other innovations.

In "El castellano en América" (1901/1954), reprinted in miscellaneous outlets, Rufino J. Cuervo, the pioneer of Spanish-American dialectology, admits that the Spanish spoken in the New World derives from the different peninsular regions, but that as a whole the variety is not similar to any one particular dialect nor is it identical in the regions of the former colonies. Cuervo adds that there is "a gradual diversification of forms, constructions and meanings that may be common to one region or to several regions" (557). This in turn may cause a breach between the Spanish spoken in the New World and that spoken in Spain. The literary language co-exists with the common language while the changes that are generalized in the latter are eventually accepted in the former. The notion of diversification explains the emergence of dialects, primarily those identified as regional; it also aids in explaining the relationship between the spoken and the written language, which in the past were closer than in the present. In fact, the literary language has its origins in the language spoken in medieval Spain.

The development of New World Spanish features selected from colonial texts sheds light on the interaction between external factors and internal evolution, though the outcome of this interaction is not systematic. For this reason, in some cases it is merely addressed, while in others it is explored in depth and problematized. The origins of New World Spanish correspond closely to a stage of koineization, defined by the mixture of various dialects of peninsular origin, for the immigrants to the New World were from every region within Spain. Regions were differentiated by history, demography and dialect traits that in some cases precede the Discovery of the New World (e.g. *leísmo*), and in others are almost simultaneous to it, for instance, convergence of the sibilants ç (affricate voiceless dental) and *z* (affricate voiced dental).

In Mexico koineization was both delayed and accelerated. The earliest arrivals had been in the Caribbean region prior to reaching the shores of the Gulf of Mexico, an event that facilitated the convergence between and amongst Spanish speakers (1519-1555). As a result of continuous immigration and (re)accommodation of speakers of diverse peninsular regions and social strata, koineization proceeded in intervals, and was followed by a thoroughgoing stage of diversification covering the entire colonial period, including a paramount phase of stratification that was critical to propel the restructuring and social transformations caused by colonization. Social stratification fostered sociolinguistic stratification early in the colony, and consequently, the conquest and colonization of the Mesoamerican peoples inverted the roles of the languages in an environment politically dominated by Spanish speakers (Hidalgo 2001a). In different areas of the New World, koineization (1493-ca.1550) must have taken longer and was extended after the 16th century. Diversification could not have occurred without popularization or vernacularization, a process that disseminated the Spanish koine along with the features belonging to the common variety (e.g. frequent verb forms such as *vide* < *ver* ('to see') and *truje* < *traer* ('to bring'). Some of these features later became archaic and were allocated or relegated along informal registers or rural varieties. Since the mid-16th century, colonial activities and lifestyles unfolded along the axis of urban and rural distinction, which in turn contributed to social stratification. In sum, diversification includes social stratification, standardization and popularization, processes that were indispensable for diffusion of Spanish in all domains (including rural, informal, and colloquial). Without a quasi-standardized or a semi-formal standard variety, Spanish would not have reached the prestige it had in the colonial period; by the same token, without a vernacular or vernaculars, New World Spanish would not have been disseminated to tiny spots, isolated regions, and enclaves inhabited by indigenous people and speakers of African languages.

2 Diversification: Social stratification

Social stratification was based on the caste system rather than on the social class structure known in pre-modern and modern times. The system imposed in New Spain was meant to ensure the socio-political hegemony of Spanish speakers over the native population and some other non-Spanish-speaking groups. It represents the basis of colonial social strata, which differentiated and ranked the whole population in corporate units generally defined by ancestry (Old Christian lineage vs. New Christians), marriage (intra- or inter-ethnic), and occupation (manual and others). Social stratification is rooted in the ancestral experience of medieval Spain, where Christians, Muslims and Jews maintained their separateness and distinctiveness via endogamy (Sáez Faulhaber 1993: 97). The religious differences of the Old World were replaced with divisions justified on ethnic practices that were not too effective, inasmuch as mixed unions occurred on a regular basis even during the period that can be considered exclusive to the first generation (1520-1555).

Pioneering many transformations, the *encomenderos* (grantees of Indian labor) were from diverse peninsular regions, social strata, and occupational backgrounds. They formed a peculiar caste for they had been directly or indirectly involved in the foundation of colonies in the Caribbean islands and in the conquest of Mexico. They belonged to the first generation of Spanish speakers who took the credit for enforcing the system of social stratification and for promoting marriages with members of the surviving indigenous nobility; they were in charge of the masses of working Indians who performed many tasks that provided sustenance to the entire population. The second and subsequent generations of children of Spaniards, known as *criollos* or *euromestizos*, belonged with their parents to a privileged stratum. The next group was formed by legitimate *mestizos* and Indians followed by mulattos and blacks who were first enslaved and later slowly manumitted by their masters. Spaniards were bureaucrats and merchants; *criollos* were big landowners; *mestizos* were artisans and small shopkeepers; mulattos worked in urban trades; and Indians were mostly peasants. There were, however, individuals of all races in the several strata, with the exception of Spanish speakers, who almost never worked as servants. Whereas the caste system was the basis of social stratification, the class system was an incipient phenomenon (Sáez Faulhaber 1993: 99-100). The quantitative imbalance between the Spanish-speaking population and the other ethnic groups points to the socio-economic and political privileges of the former. With a very low proportion of European women, Spanish speakers had little or no chance of self-reproduction and resorted to population growth via exogamy. The unions with the indigenous and the population of African descent changed the demographic profile of the vice-royalty where urban areas and Mexico City as their most important residential center, grew steadily. By 1570, one-half of the Spanish-speaking people lived in the vice-royal capital (Velasco 1993:71). The newer economy of Mexico City attracted a high number of immigrants from nearby towns and cities (Pescador 1993:115).

3 Diversification: Stratification and popularization

While koineization might have taken place regardless of social stratum, stratification and popularization are more clearly associated with the new caste division. Once the basic Spanish koine was established in New Spain, other dynamic forces intervened in a more comprehensive process of diversification. Whereas the popular variety of Spanish was spread to all regions, cities, towns, villages and even marginal spots within New Spain, the semi-formal standard was used in the emerging formal domains (official correspondence, education, government, commercial transactions, etc.). This dual process occurred simultaneously. First, the proto-Mexican Spanish koine became firmly rooted in the Central Highlands, where more than one-half of the Spanish speakers resided, where first-generation Spanish speakers used Spanish almost exclusively in most domains, and where they created the Spanish institutions needed for its continuity. Registers of semi-formal standard(ized) Spanish varieties of the times (late medieval and pre-modern) were used. Transmission was effective as the second and subsequent generations continued to use Spanish in the aforementioned domains and contributed to the diversification of the Spanish language by strengthening typical Spanish institutions and introducing new ones (e. g. private religious education, creative literature, and miscellaneous cultural activities). While the educational attainment of the elite of Spanish speakers is beyond doubt, they also used features that at present are considered non-standard. Some of those features that were spread in, around, and beyond the areas of the Central Highlands have been preserved inter-generationally; after language and educational reforms, they have been relegated to informal domains and have become part of the Mexican Spanish koine, rural Spanish, or popular Spanish. Those vernacular features that are no longer frequent or standardized are herein redefined as residual variants.

By 1519, the political division of New Spain was made up of 129 towns located primarily in the Mesoamerican zone of influence where Spanish speakers settled or were active in *encomiendas*, mining sites, agriculture, and some other enterprises. The Indian population of the region and of each locality in particular ranged between the hundreds and the thousands (cf. Gerhard 1993). Nonetheless, the mere presence of Spanish speakers was a factor contributing to the spread of Spanish. The groups of Spanish farmers that appeared in the second half of the 16th century were skillful in agriculture and cattle raising, and were given grants of different sizes, where they could harvest land near a town. Indian laborers were brought to the sites to grow wheat, maize or harvest silk (Chevalier 1952/1963: 54-55). When the activities of the countryside were differentiated and opposed to those of the growing cities, the rural-urban dichotomy became an important axis that even today explains the linguistic variants of Mexican Spanish, in particular, and New World Spanish in general. The resulting koine of New Spain was constantly renewed and (re)adapting vernacular features that either remained in the Central Highlands or were spread to other regions of New Spain.

4 Language traditions

Tradition lingers heavily in the study of Spanish language and literature. The literary model and the relationship between literary language and popular speech cannot be detached from studies of dialectology, or even from sociolinguistics.

Indeed the study of New World Spanish is since its inception associated with the notion of an ideal, archetypal, or prototypical language derived from a well-known community of professional and amateurish writers. This is the point of departure of Rufino José Cuervo (1844-1911), author of major studies such as *Apuntaciones críticas sobre el lenguaje bogotano* [Critical notes on the speech of Bogota] (1867/1907), a pioneer book published at least five times in the late 19th century and at least three in the 20th century. Cuervo's work is not a treatise on the ways of speaking in the city of Bogota, capital of Colombia, but a comparative study addressing point by point, the language issues that in his view should be recognized and pertinent to all Spanish speakers. In order to reach this goal, the famous author resorted to analysis, comparison, reconstruction, exemplification, and inference. All these methods in combination explain to an extent the origin, the uses, and the differences between established norms based on the literary language and the observed usages of the Spanish spoken in the Colombian capital.

Highlighting the grammar model and the ways in which the literary language has shaped and nurtured the popular language, Cuervo's *Apuntaciones* (1914/1954) dwelt extensively on pronunciation, syllabification, pronouns of address, irregular verbs, and origins of lexical items. While it was difficult to keep a distance from the norms of the former, popular speech transpires more spontaneously giving rise to a dialect or dialects, particularly when a language is spoken in a vast region. Cuervo did not disparage the knowledge of dialects; on the contrary, he believed that it was truly beneficial: from one word belonging to a dialect, the researcher can reconstruct the necessary links between the origin, which may not be found in the literary language, and various intermediate versions (73). His ample perspective not only provided a solid foundation to understand language change but also explained the causality of the facts. For instance, some of the forms used by authors belonging to classic periods turned into archaic forms no longer in vogue amongst modern writers or individuals of advanced education. The selection between the popular and the cultured in the common language depends on the gentleness gained from individual upbringing more than from formal education. The different styles can be cultivated according to the author's personal taste, because the relationship between the literary language and the common speech does not permit to break the rules that act as the common denominator (e.g. gender and number agreement in singular and plural). Furthermore, those words that now belong to a popular variety cannot be resuscitated in the formal variety: examples such as *truje, vide, ansi, mesmo, dende* caught his attention because at his time they were still used in popular varieties (Cuervo 1914/1954: 53), and even today they alternate with the equivalent standard variants, i.e. *traje, vi, así, mismo, desde*. An issue of major concern was the lack of universality of language when this is spoken in vast regions; language is not identical to itself in time or space for even small communities are heterogeneous, and speakers use many words and phrases that are not necessarily well known. The diffusion of those rare items depends on whether or not a good number of educated persons might accept them (706-707).

Also in the *Apuntaciones*, Cuervo deals with the comparison between the familiar speech and the literary language, which aids not only in understanding language changes, but also in seeking the causes that generate them. For example, in the early periods of the Spanish language, the verb ending –RA, exclusive of the indicative, was used in the apodosis of conditional sentences as in '*Si tuviera, diera*' (< Latin '*Si haberem, darem*') ['If I had something, I would give']. In medieval Spanish, the forms in –RA prevailed in the two clauses. By the same token the form in –SE, corresponding etymologically to the subjunctive, was being used in the hypothesis. In the Golden Age the use of the endings –RA and –SE were about equal in frequency until –SE began to decline (46-47). At present, the alternation between both forms is supposed to be the rule in modern grammars, as in '*Si tuviera, daría* with the conditional –RÍA in the resulting clause. The repetition of –RA and –RA in both clauses is not preferred in normative styles, but the abuse of –SE and –SE in conditional sentences has been discarded too. The acceptable pattern is the "free" alternation of forms ending in –SE and –RA. The assumption of "free variation" becomes relevant in contemporary studies of conditioned variation.

In his short but insightful article "Las segundas personas del plural en la conjugación castellana" ['Second persons plural in Castilian conjugation'] (1893/1954), Cuervo traces the origins of the verb forms ending in *–ades* and *–edes* belonging to the paradigm of *vos* (with the meaning of 2nd person plural informal). In the 13th century, these verb forms maintained the intervocalic *–d–* (e.g. *érades, íbades, guardades, faredes, partides, passedes, viniérades, quisiéredes*, etc.). By the 15th century, the loss of the intervocalic *–d–* began to occur resulting in the reduced ending *–ees*, which very soon turned into *–és*, as in *avés, querés, serés*, etc. For a period, the full and the contracted forms contended in the writings of renowned authors until the former began to decline and became the minority. Diphthongized forms such as *amáis, sois, tenéis, habláis* alternated with those that were reduced, e.g. *leés, sabés, perdés, sepás, tengás* (139-140). In the 17th century, the playwrights stereotyped the peasants using *habés, sos, tenés*. Finally, when the pronoun *vos* disappeared in Spain, the verb forms associated with it became obsolete in popular speech. For a period of time, *vos* was perceived as being more formal than *tú*, and survived in vast regions of the Spanish-speaking New World. Moreover, these days it is used with reduced forms, as in for instance, (*vos*) *acordás, tenés, sos, cuidás* (147-150), which in turn has given rise to the widespread phenomenon identified as *voseo*, a variant that was not too frequent in New Spain

A topic derived from the use of the 2nd persons reappears in his *Apuntaciones*. Cuervo was concerned with the use of the pronoun *vos*, which in the New World is used exclusively in singular with reduced forms coming from forms with a diphthong, e.g. *vos querés* or *no comás* (292) derived from *queréis* and *comáis*. He recommended the use of the verb forms corresponding to the pronoun. Once an interlocutor begins using *tú*, he / she should be consistent with the conjugations and should not insert *vos*, although Cuervo admits that some writers from Madrid do mix *tú* and *vos* (338-340). Cuervo was appalled by the replacement of *tú* by *vos* and the archaic forms that accompany *vos* such as *amás*, *tenés*, *dijistes*, *tomastes*, *andá*, *comé*, *salí*. Moreover, *vos* is clearly mixed with the object pronoun *te*, instead of *os*, which disappeared in New World Spanish and generated sentences such as: "**Vos decís eso pero te** *aseguro que no es cierto*" (341). ('You say that but I assure you that it is not true').

Rufino Cuervo addressed a major issue of Spanish morphology in a seminal paper initially published in *Romania* (1895). In "Los casos enclíticos y proclíticos del pronombre de tercera persona castellano" ['Enclitic and proclitic cases of third person in Castilian'] (1954), he explains in detail the uses of LO and LE, the clitic pronouns referring to [+ animate masculine singular] objects in manuscripts written between the 13th and the 19th centuries (171-178). Cuervo documented thousands of cases that are summarized below. In the ancestral Castilian system, the object pronouns LO and LA and their corresponding plurals refer to both [+ / − animate] objects; the divergence from this etymological system is noticed in the 13th century when writers begin to use LE for [+ singular masculine animate] objects in order to distinguish between [+ animate] and [− animate] objects. This clitic shift culminated in the 16th and 17th centuries with a clear tendency (62%) to use LE (see Table 1).

Table 1: Use of LO and LE: 1202-1889

Period	LO (%)	LE (%)
1202-1501	542 (33.74)	109 (4.70)
1504-1602	397 (24.71)	490 (21.15)
1606-1700	222 (13.82)	939 (40.54)
1726-1813	88 (5.47)	199 (8.60)
1818-1889	357 (22.23)	579 (25.0)
Total tokens	1,606 (100%)	2,316 (100%)

When the 16th century is separated from the 17th century, it is clear that almost two-thirds of all the clitics are placed under the column of LE while a little over one-third belong in the column under LO (see Table 2). The trend known as *leísmo* culminated in the Spanish Golden Age centuries amongst writers from Madrid (e.g. Lope de Vega, Tirso de Molina, Calderon de la Barca, Miguel de Cervantes, and Santa Teresa). This drift continued into the late 19th century, and was spread to authors from other regions who had been residing for a long time around the Court in Madrid. The tendency to use LE or *leísmo* was associated with an air of culture and elegance that was validated in literature to the extent that speakers who normally used LO in the home domain or in the street, shifted to LE in writing. Cuervo underscored the efficacious prestige of the Court in creating a parallel and consequent awareness amongst those who spoke a different dialect (178-179). Before the 18th century, the use of LO was clearly a minority at 36 percent, while LE accounted for the majority or 66 percent of all tokens computed.

Table 2: Use of LO and LE: 16th and 17th centuries

Period	LO	LE
1504-1602	397 (64.13 %)	490 (34.28 %)
1606-1700	222 (35.86 %)	939 (65.71 %)
Total tokens	619 (100 %)	1,429 (100 %)

Closely related to the use of clitics as direct objects were the verb forms of commands corresponding to the pronoun *vos*, which always take a final *–d*, as in *cantad* (< *cantar*), *comed* (< *comer*), and *venid* (< *venir*). When these affirmative commands take an object, speakers and writers of the times used to transpose /l/ and /d/, as in *dalde, venilda*. In this realm, Cuervo (1914/1954) agrees with those who adduce a grammatical and logical argument saying that *dad* and *venid* are the verb forms and that LOS, LAS, LE function as objects; for these reasons the verb forms must go before the clitics (236-239).

Another topic of discussion in the 20th century was the complex evolution of medieval sibilants represented by the graphemes <s>, <ss>, <ç>, and <z>, whose convergence in Andalusian and New World Spanish is known as *seseo*. In this field, Cuervo not only demonstrated his erudition in *Disquisiciones sobre antigua ortografía y pronunciación castellanas* [Reflexions on old Castilian orthography and pronunciation] (1898) (henceforth *Disquisiciones* 1954: 240-476), but pioneered the still ongoing debate on the uses of the sibilants. The two versions of this essay deal cogently with the diverse origins of <ç> and <z> in different positions (e.g. initial, medial or final), with the general overlap in pronunciation (mostly dental voiceless fricatives), and also with their appearance in texts dating from the 12th to the mid-17th century, when they merged in both writing and speech. Cuervo used the comparative method in order to explain the similarities (and differences) with Hebraic, Arabic, Latin and Castilian letters, and grappled too with the many interpretations of the writers and scribes who maintained the graphemes as separate entities, despite the fact that their pronunciation had merged. At the time, the printers attempted to follow Nebrija's model, but the orthography failed to correspond to the pronunciation or to the etymology. From the mid-16th century and on, the old Spanish orthography was disrupted giving rise to a major split in the regions in which two major dialects emerged: Castilian and Andalusian (253-279). The confusion in pronunciation gradually invaded the writing trends, and even the best authors hesitated between letters and constantly amended their manuscripts (284-285).

5 Literary and popular language

Popular language forms belong to the repertoire of a different variety, which is at present clearly distinguished from the modern academic standard. This distinction may be identified today as diglossia, where variety H(igh) functions effectively in institutional domains and between speakers of advanced education, and variety L(ow), which is used almost exclusively in informal settings and between less educated speakers (Ferguson 1959). This was the situation observed by Cuervo and his 19th century contemporaries when the gaps between varieties must have been wider, given sharp stratification between the groups of Spanish speakers, who after the Wars of Independence, ended up in extreme polarization. On the one hand, the *criollos* and leaders of the independent movements—who in most cases belonged to the intelligentsia of the former colonies—were separated from the mass of uneducated speakers, indigenous and non-indigenous, who formed the class of the new proletariat. For this reason, Cuervo had more than sufficient material to indulge in remarks, explanations, and abundant notions of correctness justified by the uses of the literary language. Spanish-American dialectology and Spanish linguistics had a good start that emphasized a descriptive, comparative approach. Numerous works of historical linguistics, phonetics, and history of the language followed the trend initiated by Cuervo, who in his own way also delved on the connection between external factors and internal changes (Cuervo 1901/1954). According to Cuervo, the most influential factor shaping internal changes and general attitudes was the intervention of language academies (cf. *Disquisiciones*, *Apuntaciones*, "El castellano en América"). Some of the most relevant works of Spanish linguistics tackle to an extent the connections between internal processes and external factors (see for example, Catalán 1956-1957 and 1957; Granda 1978, Lapesa 1985, Penny 2000).

6 Language reforms and standardization

Koineization in Toledo, Spain's cultural capital during the Reconquest period, was instrumental in curbing the spread of polymorphism already present in the northern kingdoms, where hundreds of documents were being archived. The ramifications of the koineization movement are revealed in the practices of the Toledo chancery, which began to influence the literary language. The examination of the external facts and internal linguistic changes in medieval Spanish explains that the Iberian fragmentation brought about by the Reconquest was reduced by koineization and by language reforms that can be interpreted today as language planning and codification. Three key movements in the history of Spanish define the language reforms.

In the 13th century, the first language reform was promoted by Alfonso the Tenth, who had a personal commitment to regulate Spanish spelling under the principles of the Toledo chancery, on a Castilian basis that made significant concessions to Toledo with an almost perfectly phonetic system. It has been assumed that medieval Spanish orthography is a faithful picture of the language as it was spoken in official and cultured circles at Toledo about the year 1275 (Entwistle 1936/1951: 152-157). The personal intervention of Alfonso and the many scribes who followed newer practices are embodied in the *Primera Crónica General* (the history of Spain), the *Grande e General Estoria* (the book of world history), and the *Libro de las Siete Partidas* (a major work on jurisprudence), written in Castilian but no longer in the dialect of Burgos. Despite the fact that the king's guidelines were based on a clear linguistic criterion, the vast production was not uniform. His policy is justified under a simple orderly principle: the prose written in his kingdom should reflect a version of 'straight Castilian' or *castellano drecho* (in modern Spanish, '*castellano derecho*'). Straight Spanish had as a model the taste of Burgos, although it made some concessions to the language of Toledo and Leon. Whenever there was ambiguity or excessive regionalism, the king determined that the forms would follow the speech of Toledo, which served in the process of leveling. In this way, the signs used in the writing system known as *graphemes* were solidly established (Lapesa 1985: 237-242).

Until the 16th century, the transcriptions of Spanish sounds conformed to the norms fixed by the chancery and Alfonso's prose. This planning endeavor enabled the language to be used for didactic purposes at the same time that several problems of lexicography and syntax were addressed. The *castellano derecho* advocated by Alfonso as the norm for the written language definitely prospered and continued in later centuries. It was even perfected by the writers of the 14th century (e.g. Juan Manuel, Juan Ruiz 'Arcipreste de Hita', Sem Tob and Pero López de Ayala). The medieval vacillations of the Castilian prose were resolved throughout the 14th century. Spanish spelling and orthography were consolidated, insofar as the attitude of the writers was oriented towards the establishment of a normative criterion. Some of the controversial cases of spelling and phonetics settled in this period but some others ensued. By the mid-15th century, scribes, notaries, and both professional and amateurs writers were confronted once more with contending norms (Lapesa 1985: 248-251).

The publication of the celebrated *Gramática de la lengua castellana* (1492) by Elio Antonio de Nebrija represents the second key moment in language reforms. It was written after he finished the translation of the *Introducciones latinas* (1486) as he himself indicated in his prologue. The renowned prologue to his former work concluded January 2, 1492, while the printing was completed on August 18, 1492. This coincides with the seizure of Granada, the discovery of America, and the publication of *La Celestina* a few years later (1499), most likely authored by Fernado de Rojas. The end of the 15th century marks a momentous break-off point between medieval and modern Spanish; it also marks the advent of the printing press and the beginning of standardization, a movement that may have contributed to the regularization of the existing koine. The Spanish grammar appeared before the Italian, the French, the English, and the Portuguese grammars. Nebrija's policy and the purpose of his grammar are spelled out in his prologue: Spanish was destined to become an imperial and a national language that would consolidate the recently unified country; it will serve to stabilize the vulgar language of Spain; it will help to fix the rules and to transmit the glories of the past. It will be completely independent from Latin and will also be like Latin (in Quilis 1984: 87). Nebrija addressed his wishes and desires to the Queen of Spain: "after Her Majesty has succeeded subjugating and ruling over barbarian and native peoples whose languages were itinerant, as a result of that subjugation, they will need to understand the laws which the victor imposes on the vanquished. And along with those laws, then, those people could come together to understand Spanish through my grammar book, just as we now learn the rules of Latin grammar in order to comprehend it" (in Quilis 1984: 101-102).

Spanish linguistic imperialism has been identified as one the major goals of Nebrija's grammar primarily because he made it clear in his famous prologue. Codification was the other goal of Nebrija's plan since he wanted to ensure the longevity of Spain's literary production by reducing the variations of the written language and establishing a uniform code. Thus, given his predicament, he codified Spanish in accordance with the classical model and devised structural parallels between Spanish and Latin. In addition, his grammar would facilitate the learning of Spanish by speakers of other languages. Finally, Nebrija envisioned the role of language, politics, and religion in the building of an empire (Milán 1983: 123-124).

The transition to modern Spanish is represented by the codification of Spanish, which did not spread swiftly into all domains. Instead, Spanish usages developed in an irregular pattern from the medieval period until the Spanish Royal Academy was founded in the 18th century. According to Douglas (1982), the introduction of the printing press in Spain had an enormous impact on spelling, for it took only about a generation (1475-1500) for many of the individualistic contractions and manuscript abbreviations such as flourishes and tildes to be discarded in favor of a simpler alphabetic system. Between the beginning of the 16th century and the installation of the Court in Madrid in 1561, many changes took place. First, double letters that had no phonetic significance began to simplify, as in *attender* → *atender; rrey* → *rey*; second, the unpronounced final *d*, as in *segund, algund* disappeared; third, the groups *mb* and *mp* (as in *también* and *compañero*) became stabilized as in modern Spanish. During the reign of Philip II (1556-1598), the most extensive crystallizations of spelling conventions took place, since the doctrine that accepted pronunciation as the principal criterion for spelling was truly relevant in this period. In addition, etymological criteria had its won significance, and the spelling of words was adjusted to this principle, as in *digno* (spelled *dino* in Castile), *escrito* (previously *escripto*), *duda* (previously *dubda*), *católico* (previously *cathólico*). Between 1575 and 1625 some orthographic problems were resolved: stabilization of learned combinations such as -*g(-m-)* as in *aumentar* and *pragmatica*; -*(c)*- as in *acción* and *nación*; -*c(t)*- as in *lector* and *sujeto* (from *subjecto* or *sujecto*). Despite the resolutions, the etymological criteria did not prevail in the change from *quatorce* to *catorce*, in the loss of *b* as in *dubda* → *duda*, and in the change from *ph* to *f* in words of Greek origin such as *filosofia* from *philosophia*. Some other spelling patterns were resolved until 1726 (use of *b, v* and *u, c* and *z*, accent marks, etc.). Between 1516 and 1625, Roman type in printing began to supplant the older black letter type, and in general great strides towards the stabilization of spelling occurred. The introduction and spread of the new bureaucracy—which had begun under Charles V—became fully entrenched under Philip II, who spent his days surrounded by piles of documents. Philip II preferred the distinction between *u* vowel and *v* consonant, which were used interchangeably before 1630, although forms such as *deue* for *debe, sauido* for *sabido*, and *auisaros* for *avisaros* are not infrequent. The Spanish king had the freedom to make unambiguous *b*'s or *v*'s but seemed to prefer an ambiguous graph that looked like half *b* and half *v* in the forms of the verb *haber* and words such as *inconveniente, resuelvo, enviar*, etc. (Douglas 1982: 420-421).

By the time Philip II was in office, the pronunciation of *ç* and *z* had changed and fused into a single phoneme. In printing, this merger between Old Spanish *z (facer > fazer > hacer)* and *ç* or *c*, did not appear until 1620, and resulted in new spellings like *hacer* and *veces*. Thirty years later, it was followed by a shift from consonant *ç* + vowel to consonant *z* + vowel. The resulting spellings were *templanza, alzar*, and *alcanzar*. His spelling reveals a close adherence to the Old Spanish distinction between voiceless *ç* or *c* and voiced *z*, rendering *esperança, Lorenço, Caraçoça, parece*, and *hace*. The king's writing reveals the fusion of *ç* and *z* at an early stage, perhaps because the devoicing of the Castilian *z* to [s] or [ts] had occurred before the late 16th century (Douglas 1982: 421). Classical Latin *h*, a laryngeal or pharyngeal aspiration, was lost in pronunciation as early as Vulgar Latin and sometimes as late as the 12th century in Spain. In the medieval period, classical Latin word-initial F before a vowel became a Spanish aspirate *h*, but the aspiration was lost in writing. Word-initial Latin *g* sometimes became Spanish *h*, as in *hermano < germanu, helar < gelare*, and *hinojo < genuculo*. During the 16th century, *h* was being used for two purposes: (a) to indicate the existence of a no-longer pronounced Latin *h*; and (b) to denote the pronunciation of an aspirated phoneme /h/. Moreover, printed books always showed *h* from Latin (as in *filiu > hijo*), while the use of *h* as in *onra/honra, hombre/ombre* had not been yet established. "The use of the letter H in the forms of the verb *haber* lost ground in the printed books that were published between 1575 and 1625, the period in which Philip's spelling might be expected to exert its influence. In the present tense of the verb, an accent mark often replaced it, as in *é* for *he* and *á* for *ha*" (Douglas 1982: 421). Finally, Philip spelled with *h* words in which Spanish-initial *h* was derived from Latin. The forms of the present tense of the verb *haber* were *he* and *ha*, respectively, but he spelled *abiendo* instead of *habiendo* and *abra* for *habrá, aya* for *haya, abria* for *habría, vbiese* for *hubiese, abia* for *había*. The verb *hacer* was spelled with *h (hareis, ha, he haria)*; probably this spelling was transposed to the forms of the verb *ser (era)*, which in his writing appears as *hera*. He also wrote *hecho* instead of *fecho*, which was the spelling of his secretaries and correspondents. This spelling paralleled that of the usage of published books.

Other changes include the use of *y*, which began to decline to give way to *i*, as in *yglesia > iglesia* and *seys > seis*, a change completed around 1650. The use of written accents was still in the formative stages and the device of using the letter *y* to indicate the tonic value of /i/ in vowels clusters was frequent, showing *leya* for *leía* and *oyr* for *oír*. The king also used *i* as a semivowel (*seis, podreis, informais*), and where *y* appears at the end of a word, the cause may be analogy, as in *rreyno* for *reino*, a form which might have been influenced by his signature *Yo el rrey*

('I the king'). Double *r* in initial position disappeared from most printed books about 1505, whereas trilled *r* following *n*, as in *honra* > *honrra* was spelled either *r* or *rr* until about 1580. Despite the fact that double letters were in vogue, Philip avoided its use as in *assi, fuesse, offrecer, possible*. The simplification (initial *rr, tt, cc*, post-n *rr, pp, ff, ll, ss*) decreased gradually between 1505 and 1726. The use of *qua* [kwa] was used consistently by the king, his secretaries, and the publishers. Because Philip preferred to guide his writing by the patterns of pronunciation, he used forms like *pareceme* instead of *paresceme* and *nace* instead of *nasce*. He also avoided the learned diagraphs *ch, ph, rh* and *th* in words of Greek origin. His name was consistently spelled Felipe after 1600. In sum, the spelling practices of Philip II of Spain reveal his pronunciation-oriented tendency, which was not strong enough beyond the confines of his own study. The 17th century evolved slowly and did not always follow many of the practices described herein (cf. Douglas 1982).

The third key movement in the history of Spanish in Spain was the creation of the Spanish Royal Academy, founded in 1713 during the reign of the Bourbons. This institution accomplished two major forms of codification: lexical and structural. The former is represented by the *Diccionario de autoridades* (1730), while the *Gramática de la lengua castellana* (1771) reflects the prescriptive approach of the neoclassical authors (Milán 1983: 125). It is assumed that diffusion of Spanish rules via updated dictionaries and grammars has indeed accomplished the goals of preserving the linguistic unity of Spanish speakers around the world (cf. www.rae.es).

7 After the Wars of Independence

The work of the Spanish academicians during its first century of life affected the entire Hispanic world, both in Spain and Latin America, but the Royal Academy turned into a foreign institution once the vast majority of the colonies became independent from Spain. Shortly after the movements of Independence, academies were established in 1825 in both Bogota and Mexico (Guitarte and Torres Quintero 1974: 318-319). The separation from Spain is epitomized by the many contributions of Andrés Bello (1781-1865), the grammarian, philosopher, and jurist born in Venezuela, acting diplomat in England, and nationalized Chilean. In his youth, he was acquainted with the most celebrated protagonist of South American independence, Simón Bolívar, and with the illustrious German scientist Alexander von Humboldt.

In the realm of Spanish linguistics, the most impressive of Bello's works is the *Gramática de la lengua castellana destinada al uso de los americanos* [Grammar of the Castilian Language Destined for the Use of Latin Americans] (1847) initially published in Chile and five more times in Colombia between 1860 and 1889 (Torres Quintero 1952: 14-15). It is thus assumed that the country that was most favorably impacted by Bello's school of thought was Colombia (cf. Torres Quintero 1952). Bello's grammar is known for its innovations, both ideological and pedagogical. His prologue is genuine and calls for the dependability of his principles. His lessons are prepared for his fellow Spanish-speaking folks hoping that Latin Americans would change their perspectives on Spanish grammar and the concomitant teaching practices (Bello 1954: 18-20). The pragmatic aspects of the grammar include the reduction of the parts of speech and the removal of the case system inherited from Latin, because the declensions in Spanish did not make sense any longer. The grammar also streamlined the verb moods (indicative and subjunctive) into categories that were more easily understood; in addition, he proposed a new nomenclature for verb tenses, which in combination reflect a universal principle: time is linear and verb tenses show the temporal sequence more logically (anterior and posterior events viewed from a point in time referring to present events). The classification of irregular verbs is still the most useful for teaching Spanish to both native and non-native speakers. Like most modern grammars, it provides plenty of examples from the classics and from real-world situations, since Bello believed that the rules for New World Spanish were based on the use of its speakers rather than on ancient and no longer realistic models.

Before the publication of his grammar in Santiago de Chile, Andrés Bello believed that the interplay between Latin and Spanish was complex, and although he defended the teaching of the former, was not satisfied with the application of grammatical structures of Latin to Spanish. Admitting that Latin might provide some general notions on the structures of language, he had been advocating the teaching of the ancient language as the most necessary area of education, albeit with some reservations, since he underscored that students would not necessarily learn the rules of Spanish. To this end, the Spanish Royal Academy employed the Latin model in the preparation of the Spanish grammar. Assuming that languages evolve within a relatively stable matrix from where the roots derive, and that it would be undesirable to dismiss (natural) language development just in the interest of an old static grammar, Bello's goal was to unify the Spanish language in order to match standard practices around the Spanish-speaking world (1954: 23). His departure from the grammar of the Spanish Royal Academy was a statement of political, linguistic, and cultural freedom of the Spanish-speaking New World and the acknowledgement of its integration and respect for unity within its own diversity (Zubiría 1982: 21-22). Loyal to his predicaments, he wrote a grammar for Spanish speakers living in the New World, those who had a new identity based on newer political and linguistic realities. Because the grammar has indeed responded to concrete educational needs, it has been published more than seventy times in the American continent and in Europe (Jaksić 2001: 150-151).

8 Schools of thought

This book is inspired in the works of historical linguistics, history of Spanish, and dialectology, and is enriched with newer interpretations derived from the field of sociolinguistics. It is a major challenge to explain the traits transplanted to the New World, because it cannot be assumed that Spanish was a static entity with no variations. Thus, searching for the causes of change or the interrelationships between internal change and external factors requires an explanatory model covering: (a) socio-historical and demographic trends, (b) language documentation, and (c) the analysis of select features over at least the three centuries of colonial life. The diachronic analysis renders outcomes that may be more effective showing the development in the three above-mentioned dimensions. In the transplanted environment, language is normally a dependent variable primarily or exclusively controlled by external factors, but internal dynamics are not relegated to having a secondary role. As proposed by Martinet (1953: 5-6), the most challenging question has to do with the genuine weight or pressure that an external factor might have over an internal change. To this effect, the researcher may be tempted to explore in depth the social history of a language by spelling out the concatenation of causes and effects, a truly stimulating endeavor. Searching for the causes may shed light on the significance of the external factors and on the diffusion of select features of say language A, though the intrinsic qualities of a language are not a guarantee that it will do better than competing languages. Other circumstances related to the particular socio-linguistic situations of the time and the territories in which change or diffusion occur might have more impact on language change.

Historical linguists have identified internal changes occurring from the time in which the earliest manuscripts appeared and have traced some of the changes to Latin and Vulgar Latin. Researchers have focused on the regularity of consonantal change, and there is little or no doubt that there is consistency in the internal processes that have taken place. The internal changes of Spanish and other Romance languages are well known, and may or may not be explicitly connected to external factors. In essence, it is the task of the disciples of historical linguistics to find the cause or multiple causes and to join all the dots. Such gargantuan projects may or may not be successful. More than a century of study of Spanish historical linguistics has rendered plenty of results, e.g. the *Manual de gramática histórica española* [Handbook of Spanish Historical Grammar] (1904/1977) by

Menéndez Pidal. Thanks to this work we know sufficient about the internal changes of Spanish and the regularity of sound change, which many times nonetheless have been interpreted as being indivisible particles for they seem to be severed from the external causes that triggered them. Furthermore, researchers have highlighted the consonantal alterations that in the end distinguished Spanish from other Romance languages. Assimilation, dissimilation, metathesis, epenthesis, hypercorrection, acoustic equivalence, and some other processes of change were explained and exemplified by Menéndez Pidal and other authors (e.g. Lathrop 1984; Penny 1991, 2000 and 2012). An inventory of internal changes has provided effective clues to make constructive inferences about the processes leading to change, e.g. in assimilation, the initial process prompts the match of one trait to another similar (preceding or following) feature. Spontaneous changes are motivated by internal causes; in contrast, combinatory changes result from the presence of other phonemes. Following Saussurian principles, it is assumed that these changes are perfectly regular (Saussure 1915/1945: 236-238).

In extracting language data from ancient documents, historical linguistics can reconstruct general language patterns and the rules associated with them. The analysis of data across time and space is thus extremely useful to isolate the main traits of a language and/or the competing variants in a specific period. Assuming that language is constantly changing, historical linguists can observe the pace of change of those variants that acquired a social meaning in their own contexts. Change can be fast or slow, intriguing or dull, simple or sophisticated until one variant prevails over the other. The evidence provided by historical linguistics and the conceivable links to socio-historical factors serve as the point of departure to postulate theories of variation with the focus on a particular community. Such arduous endeavor is not facile for the researcher has to examine the data in discrete units. The work of Romaine (1981) offers the socio-historical approach in linguistics and the methodology to examine the development of relative clause markers in Middle Scots documents (1530-1550), a sample of texts written during the reign of James V. The emphasis lies on the contributing role of variation between WH forms, TH forms, and omission; the relative markers appear as an independent variable characterizing stylistic variation, its connection to time-period, and the internal syntactic constraints on relativization. This type of analysis suggests that the style is the result of a series of processes embedded in a linguistic and socio-historical context where one variant was associated with the written corpus and the other with the colloquial register. The role of history or historical events surrounding the documents in question is less important than the discrete variables under study. This approach appeals to sociohistorical linguistics, whereas historical sociolinguists may emphasize the independent role of history in shaping and explaining language variation and diversification.

Historical linguists assume that the history of a language is a function of the history of its speakers and not an independent phenomenon that can be studied without reference to the social context in which it is embedded (Thomason and Kaufman 1988). The authors "do not deny the importance of purely linguistic factors such as pattern pressure and markedness considerations for a theory of language change, but the evidence from language contact shows that they are easily overridden when social factors push in another direction" (4). The assumptions underlying the concept of a genetic relationship derive from various analyses and interpretations of contact-induced language change. The first assumption refers to the main stimuli of linguistic change over time: (a) drift or the tendency to change due to structural imbalances; (b) dialect interference between stable and strongly differentiated dialects and between weakly differentiated dialects through the differential spread (in waves) of particular changes; (c) foreign interference. The second assumption is that change can occur at any level of the linguistic system and that internally motivated sound change is normally regular. The third assumption underscores the role of inter-generational transmission and/or via peer groups with little or no change over the short run; provided there is a stable sociolinguistic context, transmission will be normal. The fourth assumption reads that when or if transmission is imperfect the resulting system may have massive interference from the structure(s) of the language(s) originally spoken by the transmitter group (8-10).

Highlighting the connection between external factors and internal changes, Calvet (1999: 34-35) advances a model that considers language as a social practice inseparable from its environment. The ecology of language likewise presupposes different levels of analysis. In the eco-linguistic system the co-existing languages are related in a certain way that each of them is assigned to a specific niche. For this reason, a language is subject to the external stimuli to which it is adapted. The reaction to the stimuli is regulated by an internal mechanism, which in turn neutralizes the effects or consequences of change. The responses to the stimuli are self-regulated by the communicational needs of the speakers and the societal functions of language. The question raised by Calvet (123-128) is the following: What are the effects of a given ecology on a language when it is introduced into a new environment made up by social organization, social functions, and social roles? Both language and society are subject to internal pressures, and while language changes under social pressure, language change is not mechanical but results from tensions simultaneously present in both internal structures and external forces. Cases of artificial communities, where speakers of diverse languages intermingle for a period of time, exemplify the type of communication that can emerge naturally in a new environment. In the era of corsairs and pirates, the ships sailing on the Mediterranean shed light on developing linguistic niches, where speakers of various Romance and non-Romance languages lived and worked. The resulting contact code, based on a version of Late Latin, was a mixture of all the languages. For this reason, it presented a reduced syntax but the new composite was constantly adapted and (re)lexified. The vocabulary of such code circulated from ship to ship, port to port and island to island. Ships and sailors were not only the carriers of lexical innovations but played a role in the diffusion of lexicon. In this way, 'pineapple' turned into *anana* in French (via Portuguese but originally from Guarani). Other examples belonging to the international lexicon of trade used by sailors are *banana*, *caiman*, and *hurricane* (Spanish *banana*, *caimán* and *huracán*), etc.

In the present century, the significance of external motivation has taken its place alongside internal impulse, and again contact is considered to have a more significant role in language change. Farrar and Jones (2002: 1-8) discuss the different perspectives that may have justified neglecting extra-linguistic factors pertaining to social characteristics of situations in which speakers interact. First, an explanation for a change will not point to one motivating factor but will invoke a number of interacting factors. Second, the role of the internal/external dichotomy may serve as a descriptive tool for categorizing different factors but it is insufficient as a theoretical explanation, because internal factors are not separated from external factors in discrete camps for the convenience of researchers. Finally, when there is an implicit hierarchy of internal factors and these are weighed against extra-linguistic ones, the assumption leads to believe that the majority of changes a language undergoes are due to internal factors and that for this reason, the search for external or extra-linguistic motivating factors is warranted. Presumably if a lower position is not assigned to external factors, there will be a more ample view of socially motivating factors because thus far it has not been proven that internal factors really do play a more important role in the process of language change.

Historical sociolinguistics proceeds on a uniform principle of development, namely, that the circumstances and the effects observed in the present will most likely approximate those observed in the past. This synthesizing view postulates that the social context and the external factors surrounding language variants can be reconstructed in order to identify the independent variables impinging on variation in a specific period. The difference lies in the type of source material utilized for research, for the corpora of the past are limited in space and the authors of the manuscripts did not have any interlocutors (Conde Silvestre 2007: 41, 53).

9 The case of Spanish: from the beginning to New World Spanish

The advocacy for external factors can be illustrated within the framework of the historical episodes occurring in medieval Spain. When the Muslim armies invaded the Iberian peninsula in the 8th century successfully pushing inland, a series of events initiated meaningful changes that impacted the variety of Hispanic Romance spoken in that territory. This undeniable fact, known as the Reconquest and the reaction of the invaded Christian peoples triggered language, culture and religious contact(s) that have called for an explanation. Language contact occurred between linguistic codes that were genetically unrelated; from this point in time, researchers strive to explain the processes leading to a more balanced environment. The exploration of the processes and analysis of koineization aids in elucidating the external causes of linguistic change in the middle ages because it highlights the dynamic geo-chronological stages that shaped the Spanish language in its original territory. Koineization started in Burgos in the 10th century, continued in Toledo (11th-12th century), and ended in Seville in the 13th century. Identifying the features of each stage leads to making a case for the interplay between extra-linguistic, external, and internal causes. The *Reconquista* is the major external factor responsible for the mixture of peninsular dialects, in turn prompted by repopulation movements, which in the end were conducive to the emergence of a vast southern province (cf. Tuten 2003). Because it turned into the depository of select Spanish traits that evolved in diametric opposition to northern features, Andalusian is the end-result of the *Reconquista*, a statement that leads to the next question.

If language like art is considered a creative activity, then it is legitimate to ask if social structures have impact on language change, language use or language traits per se, or in the emergence of new dialect or dialect zones. These predicaments should apply to a social history of language that would ideally connect every historical event to a major language change or language feature. An integrative model explaining the cause-and-effect linearity or co-linearity of internal and external changes would be advantageous. Because this case study deals with the fate of a transplanted language, it propounds a comprehensive explicative model that elucidates the types of variants that were modified from the transplanted peninsular tree in the new environment. The model excludes the contact with the indigenous languages, except for nouns derived from Amerindian languages; in this study, all the variants were selected from the polymorphic inventory of the peninsular tree. The focus on the first group of variants examined is attrition, for only one variant or a dyad survived in the New World, while the other was either discarded or modified; the second group of variants is known as residual.

Residual variants are defined as those that persisted in two domains: the general colloquial and daily speech of most speakers, and the variants that have been reallocated to varieties spoken in regions or sectors distant from urban, cultural, and educational centers.

10 New World Spanish: spoken and written

In a lesser known essay "Castellano popular y literario" ['Popular and literary Castilian'], published posthumously (1944/1954), Cuervo proffers illuminating and abundant data on the differences between popular and literary varieties. He divides the phonetic distinctions in two major groups: vowels and consonants. The alterations of the former represent a miniscule proportion when compared to the numerous consonantal changes. These alterations do not refer to the changes identifying large regional dialects (i.e. Castilian, Andalusian, or New World Spanish) but to more extreme phenomena that he himself observed in Colombia and other places. This essay is enriched with the reports that were known to him at the time. The phonetic dissimilarities between standard and non-standard Spanish aid in the identification of the features that exist in social dialects, better known as popular varieties.

The inventory of consonantal changes can be further exemplified in the interchange of the alveolar series: /d/, /l/, and /r/ in syllable-final or absolute final position. The examples below illustrate the two sides of the interchange, the most common being the substitution of /l/ by /r/ known as rhotacism (see left Column). The opposite is also feasible, and is known as lambdacism (see right Column). The traits listed below have not been regularly reported in any of the social or regional varieties of Mexican Spanish, but they may have occurred in former stages and in certain specific areas such as the ports of Veracruz and Acapulco.

alcalde	> [arcarde]	*Carmen*	> [calmen]
blanco	> [branco]	*cuerpo*	> [cuelpo]
faltar	> [fartar]	*sacerdote*	> [saceldote]
golpe	> [gorpe]	*matar*	> [matal]
hilvanar	> [irvanar]	*comer*	> [comel]

Other variations in social dialects can be considered more extreme and include the use of /r/ in words beginning with /d/, as in *después* > [repué]; *decencia* > [recencia]; *dice* > [rice]; *añade* > [añare]. Also by loosening the articulators' contact, /l/ can turn into /d/, as in [devantarse] < *levantarse*; [almirar] < *admirar*; [almitir] <

admitir; [liferencia] < *diferencia*; and [melecina] < *medicina*. More radical is the change from /s-/ to /l-/ as in *muslo* > [murlo] (1375-1381) and the vocalization of alveolar consonants (1388), as shown below:

barco > [baico]	*salga* > [saiga]
porque > [poique]	*valga* > [vaiga]
largo > [laigo]	*golpe* > [goipe]
torpe > [toipe]	*papel* > [papei]

One of the most intriguing internal changes has to do with the substitution of initial labiodental /f/ by aspirated [h] in a group of words that by the 19th century were identified as vernacular, for example: [harto] ('full' or 'fed up') < *farto, fartus* or [jieřo] < *fierro, ferrum* ('iron'). While researchers offer multiple insights referring to the history, diffusion and social class distribution of both variants, it has been challenging to explain the extreme distance in points of articulation (/f/ > [h]). According to Lapesa (1985: 280-286) in Old Castile, the aspirated variant [h] turned silent in speech but continued to appear in writing. The hesitation between the two variants indicates that the actual sound was an aspirate, which survived in standard Spanish through 1580. At this stage, /f-/ disappeared and was replaced by [h], which was no longer aspirated but silent [Ø] in Old Castile. As of the 17th century, the aspirate was weakened and lost in Old Castilian but it survived in the Andalusian territory. In the written language [h] had spread to the southern territory re-conquered by the Castilians and from there to the New World. By the 16th and 17th centuries, the criterion of correctness was more open than in the past, and a selection amongst available sounds led to the establishment of regularity in the literary language. The invention of the printing press contributed significantly to regularize the writing, an event that brought to an end the polymorphism of hand-written manuscripts. Aspiration was relegated to rural uneducated speech, especially before the diphthongs *-ue, -ie* (as in *huerte* < *fuerte*), *hue* < *fue*), *hiebre* (< *fiebre*).

In exploring the origins of /f/ > [h] in initial position, Cuervo (1944/1954: 1407-1409) resorted to the opposition and tensions between literary language and the distribution of vernacular features. Old Spanish writers preserved the etymological initial F, and by the time of Nebrija's grammar, the erudite reaction had restored the F- in some of the words that appear with H, which were almost equally divided into those that today are spelled with F- and those spelled with H-, which was silent. Popular speech was however more advanced and has preserved the aspiration in words derived from Latin as in the examples in Table 3, which shows the evolution from Latin to medieval Spanish to modern Spanish and finally to popular dialects. Aspiration of F- in initial position was extended by analogy to additional groups of words. In rural Colombia the aspiration also includes words that did not form part of the traditional group of /f/ vs. /h/, for example, (a) fue > *jue*; fuera > *juera*; (b) afuera > *ajuera*; (c) enfermo > *enjermo*; (d) firme > *jirme*; (e) fácil > *jácil*.

Table 3: Evolution of words with initial F

Latin	Medieval Spanish	Modern Spanish	Dialect
FACTUM	fecho	hecho ('fact')	*jecho*
FOETERE	feder	heder ('to stink')	*jeder*
FILIUS	fixo	hijo ('son')	*jijo*
FĒMINA	fem(i)na	hembra ('female')	*jembra*

Equally interesting and insightful are the observations he made about the variations of /s/ in different positions. In his "Castellano popular y literario", Cuervo (1944/1954: 1413-1415) emphasized the common nature of this phenomenon across the Spanish-speaking world, i.e. southern Spain, Cuba, Veracruz, Colombian coasts, Venezuela, Chile and Argentina. The different realizations of /s/ are applicable to both *c* and *z* given the widespread use of *seseo* in the New World. The most interesting realizations occur in the following cases:

(1) In final position before voiceless consonants, where it is perceived merely as a pause, as in *esto* [e'to] and *usted* [u'té] or disappears altogether, as in *los fósforos* [lo foforoh], *desfilar* [defilar], *resfriar* [refriar]. Plural of words ending in a consonant may be marked only with the vowel *e*, as in *Las mujeres y la fortuna* [la mujere y la fortuna].
(2) Before voiced consonants within the word, aspiration can be partially assimilated to the following consonant having the effect of duplication and opening of the preceding vowel as in *mismo*: [mihmmo], *obispo*: [obihppo], *usté*: [uhtté], *riesgo*: [riehggo].
(3) In final position before voiced consonants there is at least an aspiration marking the difference between singular and plural as in [la letra] [la letrah]; [la madre] [la madreh]; [el niño] [lo niñoh]; [lo diente] [lo dienteh].
(4) In initial and intervocalic positions, it can be aspirated or omitted, as in *suba* [huba], *señor* [eñor], *casino* [cahino], *casa* [caha].
(5) In final position before a word beginning with a vowel, the sibilant appears more closely linked to the following word, as in *los ojos*: [lo sojoh]; *los hombres*: [lo s(h)ombreh]; *los amigos*: [lo hamigoh].
(6) In implosive position before a voiced consonant sibilant /s/ can turn into a voiceless fricative /x/ or /f/, as in examples, *disgusto*: [dijusto]; *rasgar*:

[rajar]; *resbalar*: [refalar]; *resbalón*: [refalón]; *desbaratar*: [efaratar], most likely found in Chile than in other places.

In his *Apuntaciones*, Cuervo (1907) was concerned with language variation across time and space, particularly when a language is spoken in vast territories. For this reason, the uniformity or universality of all the terms is not possible. Diversification entails the change of the original meaning of an item derived from peninsular Spanish into a different meaning assigned in the New World. The change can be drastic or subtle, and only the speakers' subjective interpretations can explain the change (417-418). For this reason, Cuervo explains in detail the circumstances in which items originated. Though his point of departure is the speech of Bogota, he indulges in comparisons with other dialects of the Spanish-speaking world. Regional dialects emerged as a result of language expansion, and one word can have multiple meanings. Divided in subsections, Cuervo offered numerous examples of lexical variations (e.g. articles 579, 585, 616-617) which are uncontrolled, except when some terms are accepted by a considerable number of educated speakers (article 709). Lexical variation across dialects of the same language endorses Saussure's principle on the arbitrariness of the linguistic sign (Saussure 1915/1945: 130-136). The case of New World Spanish illustrates that lexical variation is conducive to distinguishing boundaries between and across regional dialects, where diversification has been truly effective, first in creating confusion and then in resorting to clarification, since the same word can have radically different meanings depending on the region where it is used. The most common example of polysemy is the noun *guaga* with the meaning of 'bus for collective transportation' used in the Caribbeam region, while in the Andes it means 'baby'.

Various explanations may shed light on the external causes that have discouraged Mexican Spanish speakers from using the six extreme features listed above, which were observed by Cuervo at the end of the 19th century and the beginning of the 20th century. Diffusion, stratification, and pressures from academic standards are among the external factors that have contributed to deter the radicalization of Mexican Spanish, except among speakers living in extreme isolation or extreme socio-economic marginalization.

This book highlights words that belonging to colonial Spanish have survived in modern New World Spanish with diverging, similar, or identical meaning(s). The analysis of New World Spanish variants has been facilitated by collections of colonial documents, which aid in the comparison of Mexican Spanish with other varieties, e. g. *Documentos para la historia lingüística de Hispanoamérica, siglos XVI a XVIII* (Fontanella de Weinberg 1993) and *Documentos para la historia lingüística de Hispanoamérica, siglos XVI a XVIII*, vol. 2 (Rojas Mayer 2000). The first of the two volumes includes varied texts from Santo Domingo, Mexico, Peru,

Chile, Argentina, and Uruguay, while the second covers the Canary Islands, Cuba, Costa Rica, Venezuela, Colombia, Ecuador, Paraguay, Mexico, and the United States.

In the identification of linguistic variants and variationist trends, two volumes on New Spain have been selected for analysis: The first one is *Documentos lingüísticos de la Nueva España. Altiplano Central* (Company Company 1994), which covers the Central Highlands; this is complemented by *Documentos lingüísticos de la Nueva España. Golfo de México* (Melis et al. 2008), which includes the Gulf of Mexico. The Central Highlands and the Gulf of Mexico are the two oldest Mexican regions in which Spanish speakers settled on a permanent basis. Other manuscripts on New Spain complement the linguistic corpora needed to examine select variants. The *Second Letter* by Hernán Cortés printed in Seville (1522) and excerpts from the *Abecedario* (1525-1770), a rare inquisitorial manuscript bound in Mexico City by the Holy Office were obtained with permission from the Henry E. Huntington Library. Additionally, subsamples from colonial sources serve to extract language data. The letters by Diego de Ordaz (1529-1530) transcribed by Lope Blanch (1985), the *Tratado del descubrimiento de Yndias* (1585) by Juan Suárez de Peralta, transcribed by Perissinotto (1994), the *Vocabulario en lengua castellana y mexicana y mexicana y castellana* (1555/1571/1970) by Alonso de Molina, and the modernized collection *Comerciantes mexicanos del siglo XVIII* (Yuste 1991). All of them contribute in understanding the historical events of the colonial period and the everyday routines and worries of the common people living in New Spain.

11 The aim of this book

This book aims at discussing the origins of Mexican Colonial Spanish and the components that make it similar to or dissimilar from other varieties of New World Spanish. In order to achieve this goal, I have selected variants that can be traced to the very origins of the Spanish language in the American continent, to wit: Amerindian transfers and borrowings, *seseo*, *leísmo*, *voseo*, and the use of imperfect subjunctive endings –RA and –SE, which have been highlighted by scholars at different junctures. This analysis is noteworthy because these variants were assigned a social meaning in the environment of transplantation. I also examine the gaps between normative Spanish and the residual forms derived from Mexican Colonial Spanish, a term referring to the Spanish variety written (and spoken) in Mexico during the colonial period (cf. Arias Álvarez 2014). Residual variants are those that originally belonged to the semi-formal or informal registers and were redistributed or reshuffled to New World Spanish popular varieties. Residual variants are divided into two sub-types: (1) optimal or general and (2) popular. The first group includes those that are still used by a majority of speakers in colloquial registers, informal domains, etc. Popular variants are those that have reappeared in rural sub-regions or areas of high socio-economic marginality. The study of these variants sheds light on the current gaps between New World standard Spanish and vernaculars. Therefore, the differences are explained by the polarization of socio-educational disparities that have been observed since the earliest colonial times.

Amerindian borrowings into Mexican Spanish are derived from both Taino and Nahuatl. The former are older than the latter, and some of the Taino borrowings were replaced by Nahuatl loans. At some point in time, Taino and Nahuatl loans competed with Spanish but Spanish speakers were responsible for integrating the Nahuatlismos into the Spanish spoken in the 16th century. After Independence from Spain, Nahuatl loans were incorporated into general Spanish and many of them and are still vital today. Transfers from Nahuatl into Mexican Spanish are found in the phonetic realm, particularly in the adaptation of affricates [tɬ] and [ts]. They are vital in the area of the Central Highlands, where the Nahuatl language has had a permanent influence particularly in frequent toponyms (e.g. volcanoes, towns, villages, neighborhoods, and streets), but their vitality decreases as the distance from the Central Highlands increases.

Seseo is the end-result of the convergence of medieval Spanish sibilants that unfolded in the dialects of southern Spain and the most widespread merger that has prevailed in all domains in New World Spanish. Mexican Spanish writers of the koineization period (16th century) used the different graphemes available in peninsular Spanish. *Seseo* appears to be motivated by an internal regular change and a series of mergers that coincided at a point in time between the 15th and the 16th centuries. The use of the grapheme <s> increased gradually after the 16th century, whereas the graphemes <c> and <z>, representing sibilant phonemes, were later restored by language reformers under etymological principles. *Leísmo* is the trend of Castilian origin that did not prevail in New World Spanish. It refers to the use of clitic pronoun LE for [+ animate masculine singular] direct objects. New World Spanish, like Andalusian, preferred the traditional pro-etymological system LO and LA. Spanish-speaking immigrants from diverse peninsular regions intermingled in the New World colonies where the two systems co-existed, and where the pattern of divergence from Castilian was consolidated after having gone through a long process of accommodation. The use of the pro-etymological system increased gradually over the long colonial period. Therefore, in most regions of the American continent *leísmo* was discarded due to its irregular variations. *Voseo* is the surviving use of the pronoun *vos* with exclusive singular meaning in New World Spanish. In the 17th century, *vos* was replaced by *tú* in New Spain, but the former pronoun was transformed in many Central and South American colonies with the resulting variant used as a subject and object pronoun, and reduced monophthongized verb forms in the present indicative and in commands. Singular *vos* and plural *vos* and *vosotros* were infrequent in New Spain perhaps because their meanings and verb conjugations overlapped. In contrast, *vuestra merced* was over-abundant in Mexico, and like in Spain, it was used with 3rd person singular conjugations and the corresponding plural *vuestras mercedes*, until both were replaced by modern Spanish *Usted* and *Ustedes*.

A major shift from the times of Cortés and the *Second Letter* (1520-1522) is observed in the use of verbs in imperfect subjunctive with alternating endings in –RA and –SE. This occurrence is identified in subordinate clauses referring to subsequent events, as in *Le sugerí que le escribiera* or *escribiese* ('I suggested that he write to him') or *Le aconsejó que siguiera* or *siguiese peleando en ese pueblo* ('He advised him to continue fighting in that town'). It is found, too, in conditional sentences such as *Si tuviera algo se lo diera* ('If I had something I would give it to him'). The frequency of forms in –SE is glaring in Cortés' prose and 16th century documents, and remained throughout the 17th only to decrease noticeably at the end of the colony when Mexican *criollos* shifted to variants in –RA, a preference that continues until the present.

Optimal or general residual variants include colonial transfers of lexical items that were also (re)transmitted inter-generationally, e.g. the verb *ligar* ('to tie' or 'bind') with the figurative meaning of 'to flirt' with or 'to have a date', has identical meanings in Mexico and Spain. Other colonial transfers are socio-semantic, e.g. the noun *lana*, originally referring only to 'wool', has been extended to mean both 'wool' and 'money', the latter meaning derived from the lucrative loom industry of the 16th and 17th centuries. With the meaning of 'money', the noun *lana* has spread all over the country, across social strata, and well beyond the Mexican borders. The colloquial word used in Spain for money is *pasta* (derived from the more lucrative mining industry) but unknown in Mexico with this meaning. The second category of residual variants includes verb forms that belonged to the peninsular matrix and were (re)transmitted inter-generationally during the colonial period. After the language reforms and re-codification, they have been relegated to rural and isolated varieties (e.g. verb forms in the 1st and 3rd persons singular of preterit indicative as in *vide*, *vido* from the verb *ver* 'to see', and *truje* and *trujo*, from the verb *traer* 'to bring'). The frequency of the variants in the colonial documents seems to have determined its survival in today's popular varieties and almost exclusively amongst speakers residing in isolated and/or socio-economic marginal regions.

Finally, this book discusses the changes occurring in different New World Spanish varieties and Mexican Colonial Spanish. The analysis of select variants of the latter unravels a myriad of connections between internal, extra-linguistic, and external factors. In most cases, the analysis is based on observed rates of attrition throughout the colonial period. The focus on attrition is glaring in *seseo*, *leísmo*, the endings in –SE and –RA, and *voseo* (see 2 through 5 below).

(1) Amerindian borrowings and pronunciation transfers are clearly the result of language contact. Spanish immigrants, explorers, and travelers were responsible for the spread, (re)trans-mission and diffusion of Amerindian loans.

(2) *Seseo* was a latent phenomenon that debilitated the medieval Spanish internal system, probably generated by the disruption of the Hispanic Romance spoken in the Iberian Peninsula since ancestral times. Having lost the distinction of pertinent features (e.g. voiced vs. voiceless sibilants) in the southern peninsular varieties, the convergence of the sibilants found a fertile ground throughout the process of transplantation to New World soil.

(3) *Leísmo* had a good beginning in New Spain when Spanish speakers were involved in the mining economy, trade, and miscellaneous cultural activities. *Leísmo* declined towards the end of the colony when speakers preferred the ancestral pro-etymological forms more in vogue in southern Spain showing, again, an attitude of convergence with Andalusian speakers. Language academies and language planning must have contributed to regularize this variant in New World Spanish.

(4) The use of verb endings in –RA and –SE is conditioned by both internal and extra-linguistic factors: the contending form –RA progressively acquired subjunctive meaning in direct proportion to the gradual political distance that colonies were keeping from Spain.

(5) *Voseo* stems too from the peninsular tree but it is not uniform in New World Spanish. *Vos* lost its vitality in the colloquial domain and was replaced by *tú*. At the end of the 15th century, the pronouns of address available to Spanish speakers were distributed along the non-deferential (*vos* / *tú*) and the deferential (*vuestra merced* / *su merced*) axis, a system transmitted to the New World, as substantiated in the written language of all colonial centers and adjusted in different ways in the various colonies. According to Penny (2000: 152-153), *vos* disappeared in those colonies that were closer to peninsular Spanish: the Caribbean islands, most of Mexico, Peru, and Venezuela. According to Lapesa (1985: 392, 579), a new use of *vos*, known as *voseo* emerged with the reduced verb forms (e.g. *vos tenéis*, > *tenés*, *vos podéis* > *podés*) and has survived in large areas of Central and South America, and in the Mexican state of Chiapas, which is historically linked to Guatemala. In Spain, *vos* became obsolete during the 17th and 18th centuries.

(6) The use of standardized PARA and reduced PA continues the be subjective, and it is reflected in speech patterns already present in the 16th century. The analysis presented herein is not based on attrition because the two variants alter-

nate in the same contexts on both sides of the Atlantic. In both cases it has the meaning of direction or intention similar to English 'towards' or 'in order to'. This alternation, which appears since the times of Hernán Cortés, has been re-transmitted for centuries in contexts that are identical to those found in the famous *Second Letter*.

12 The chapters

Chapter 1 introduces the reader to the beginnings of the Spanish language history and the period in which Castilian emerged, marked by the repopulation movement in Andalusia and the transplantation of Spanish into the New World. It provides information on the features of Castilian as opposed to those of Andalusian and looks into the different theories on the origins of New World Spanish, to wit: monogenetic, polygenetic and koineization. It puts forward the more encompassing theory of diversification, which was the end-result of the transplantation over three centuries of colonial development. Chapter 2 describes the lifestyle of the first speakers of Mexican Spanish and the role of the *encomenderos* (grantees of native labor) in shaping the new society. The *encomenderos* attempted to enslave the native population but the humanists interposed serious objections, i.e. the New Laws of 1542. The new set of regulations derailed their plans and had a long-term effect throughout the colonial period. In response, the *encomenderos* arranged the importation of African slaves and added to the complexity of an already multilingual / multicultural and multi-religious scenario, where Spanish / Portuguese Jews also played a dramatic role, causing the intervention of the Inquisition. Established in 1571, the Inquisition was partially responsible for the diffusion of Spanish. A rare Inquisition's manuscript known as the *Abecedario* sheds light on the diverse origins of Spanish speakers who migrated to New Spain. Chapter 3 examines the printed letter by Hernán Cortés, where he narrates his early skirmishes in Mexico, an exceptional document known as the *Segunda Carta de Relación* [Second Letter] published in Seville by Jacobo Cromberger in 1522. The *Second Letter* is the point of departure to analyze and compare the abovementioned variants of New World Spanish; this document offers subsamples of Amerindian borrowings and subsamples of alternating variants derived from the peninsular Spanish tree. All the chapters examining language data focus on the continuity and / or the attrition of select variants. Chapter 4 continues the analysis of colonial documents from the first half of the 16th century and examines a good subsample of Nahuatl transfers and Nahuatl borrowings. The Spanish variants selected for analysis in chapters 3 and 4 are representative of the development of New World Spanish in general and Mexican Spanish in particular: (1)

sibilant graphemes *s*, *ç* and *z*; (2) verbal clitic variants LO and LE; (3) pronouns of address *tú, vos, vuestra merced, su merced, Usted*; and (4) imperfect subjunctive endings –RA and –SE. The first generation of Spanish speakers was inclined to preserve the peninsular Spanish variants while anticipating a low-intensity trend of change and attrition that gradually increased over the centuries.

Chapter 5 deals with the occupational, educational, and cultural activities of Spanish speakers. The most significant economic enterprise was mining, which attracted Spanish and non-Spanish speakers to the emerging sites and their surroundings. Spanish speakers founded newer towns, schools, and churches around the mining districts consolidating the compactness of a newer Spanish-speaking community, which was always the quantitative minority but at the same time a powerful group with common attitudes and values. It is proposed that mining, agriculture, the textiles industry, and services were the main labor domains in which non-Spanish speakers were exposed to Spanish. Most of these activities contributed to the diversifying the roles of Spanish and the solidarity of the Spanish-speaking minority. Chapter 6 analyzes the attrition-focused variants used by the second generation of Spanish speakers, who added more components to the process of diversification. Variations to the traditional sibilant system were initiated in the second half of the 16th century, a period in which *seseo* was moderate. The use of the verbal clitics LE and LO remained unchanged from the previous decade with the Castilian variant LE prevailing over LO. In the second generation the singular pronoun of address *vos* [– formal] was more frequent than *tú*. At this stage, the neologism *vuestra merced* had little competition with other pronouns. Finally, the contending forms of the imperfect subjunctive –SE and –RA also show inter-generational variation with a decline of 22 percent in the Central Highlands and minor changes in the Gulf of Mexico. The regression in the Central Highlands may be explained by the fact that the second and subsequent generations of writers did not match the standards of the first generation, i.e. the northerners of privileged socio-educational background who stand out today as the foremost protagonists of the colonization of Mexico.

Chapter 7 deals with the consolidation of Spanish-oriented institutions, particularly the Catholic Church, which was pro-active in incorporating indigenous languages to the tasks of conversion. Spanish language contact with indigenous languages was conducive to bilingualism and /or trilingualism amongst select members of the clergy, reciprocal Nahuatl/Spanish influence, various degrees of acculturation, and Spanish proficiency. In the second half of the 16th century the policy of the Spanish Crown was to separate the indigenous from other groups, and therefore speakers of indigenous languages were congregated in newer native communities administered at a distance from Spanish speakers, which might have resulted in syncretic venues leading simultaneously to language maintenance and language shift.

Chapter 8 discusses the growth of the Spanish-speaking population resulting primarily from miscegenation at the time in which the economy of New Spain enjoyed both stability and diversification of activities. By the 17th century, it is clear that the minority of Spanish speakers enjoyed an enviable quality of life and that the established caste system developed its own projects. This chapter also examines the attrition rates of the selected variants (*seseo, leísmo*, pronouns of address, and the –SE and –RA endings). By the 17th century it was obvious that several generations of Spanish and non-Spanish speakers were exhibiting mixed speech / writing patterns. The 17th century is also known for the expansion of horizons in Spanish and the high quality of its literary production. Chapter 9 highlights the external historical events that had a powerful impact on the administration of the colonies (i.e. the Bourbon Reforms) and the distinct demographic trends prevailing in the 18th century, such as commerce with Spain, urbanization, and the professionalization of miscellaneous services. It continues the analysis of the same variants examined in previous centuries showing the transition to the Independent period, particularly in the sharp decline of those identified with peninsular Spanish (e.g. direct object pronoun LE and the –SE form associated with imperfect subjunctive). In this century, literature and journalism in New Spain differed significantly from the production in Spain, which had lost the luster of the Golden Age, though it was both innovative and versatile.

The summary in Chapter 10 displays the graphic quantitative differences between the sets of variants derived from the peninsular tree and the gradual diminution by century and by region of each variant representing peninsular Spanish. It also exemplifies the two types of residual variants: optimal and popular. The difference between attrition-focused variants and residual variants lies in the type of variation displayed over time. Whereas attrition leads to a permanent change, residual variants were reallocated to contexts of informality or marginality though they maintained the same co-referencial meaning. Chapter 11 closes with a discussion on the origins and effects of diversification in connection with the external factors that may have impinged on attrition. Finally, the Appendix lists a subsample of 221 subjects retrieved from the Inquisition's manuscript known as the *Abecedario*; the origins of the subjects attest to the diversity of ethnic and linguistic backgrounds of New Spanish residents. The sample is interesting because it reveals the spontaneous writing patterns of the notaries and secretaries of the Holy Office and the Spanish variants they used.

13 Explicative models

An explicative model is a useful description, although by no means exhaustive, of observations that make sense in the historical context under study and are useful to understand at least the major components of sociolinguistic phenomena: history, society and language. No single model can account for all the variants and variations as they relate to external or extra-linguistic factors. Each model may nonetheless explain multiple factors affecting internal changes as they become associated to the social context(s) and / or to the intersection of various social contexts and sub-contexts. The explicative model proposed in this book supports the theory of diversification. The notion of linguistic niches proposed by Calvet (1999) and / or the development of domains as elaborated by Fishman (1972a: 78, 81, 83 and Fishman 1972b: 113-117) may explain continuous and uninterrupted diversification of Spanish in New Spain, for diversification was not as extensive or continual in colonies that were not on the spotlight of the metropolis. In Spain's favorite setting permanent domains were built and renewed at all levels of the new colonial society; their emergence delineated the role-relations and contexts of interaction into which the newer groups were organized, and where Spanish (the newer language) was promoted or preferred as the medium of communication in the newer multilingual society. Some smaller or distant colonies from Spain did not have the opportunity to indulge in creative literature and other language-related activities; this explains that the Church, the Inquisition, and the mining industry had a tangential interest and a limited or delayed role in some other colonies.

This book contributes to the analysis of massive language data, both quantitative and qualitative; the varied approaches may be necessary to follow leads and inferences in the specific ambiance where Spanish was transplanted. Linguistic corpora provide the evidence of (re)trans-mission, diffusion, and allocation of language variants and variations. Therefore, the historical sociolinguistic model of diversification is testable in different New World nations, regions, and sub-regions. While this book offers the results of general trends and the necessary theoretical principles and methodological strategies for verification and/or corroboration of the proposals advanced in it, more research is needed to identify the internal linguistic constraints (genres, speech styles, topic, intention, or type of sentence and / or clause) by historical period. The major implication of this case study is that history can not be changed or distorted in order to accommodate it to language data or language findings. The directionality of cause-and-effect events entails the predictability of history as the independent variable; furthermore, the scrutiny of language variants may indicate that social and language occurrences depend on the specificity of historical events or on the shockwaves produced by the events. The tridimensional approach allows us to see the pertinent language data glaring on the surface and the socio-historical reliefs standing out on a dynamic contextual background that is open to renewed interpretations.

Chapter 1
The origins of Spanish: Spain and the New World

1.1 The origins

This chapter presents the most relevant external and internal factors that contributed to the formation of Castilian, Andalusian and New World Spanish. As a result of the repopulation movement advanced by Castilians during the very long period known as the Reconquest or *Reconquista* (711-1492), the new regional variety emerging in southern Spain came to be known as Andalusian, an offshoot of Castilian. In the history of the Spanish language, Castilian, Andalusian and New World Spanish are studied simultaneously because one cannot be entirely separated from the other two. The chronological order strongly suggests that the focus should be on Castilian first, Andalusian next, and New World Spanish last, but not least. The vast majority of studies do acknowledge the rise of Castilian in the first place, and as a result of the *Reconquista* (Reconquest) of southern Spain, the origins of Andalusian are interspersed with those of Castilian. Likewise, the emergence of New World Spanish is inextricably associated with both the history and development of Andalusian, although until recently Andalusian was not a well-known variety. The connection between Andalusian and New World Spanish has not been rejected; on the contrary, over one century of research has validated the preliminary proposals and theories advanced on the origins and development of the latter. The most important external factor impinging on the formation of New World Spanish was the transplantation of a prestigious European language, which was buttressed by the system of social stratification implemented in different New World colonies, the most prosperous found in the Mesoamerican and Andean regions. The system of social stratification had a dual socio-linguistic effect: on the one hand, it promoted the cultivation of an semi-formal standard, and on the other, the use of a vernacular variety unfolded in all the regions, towns, and cities where Spanish-speaking groups had relative and / or absolute power and control over the new colonial society. In this chapter, relevant features of Castilian, Andalusian and New World Spanish are compared and contrasted in order to highlight the patterns of evolution and systematic change, whenever possible.

The first speakers and writers of New World Spanish were born in different Spanish regions and belonged to different social and educational strata. Most of them were adult males who had had the trans-regional and transatlantic experience in their youth. There is more than sufficient evidence pointing to the diversity of peninsular regions from where Spanish immigrants originated but quantities are approximate in all available samples. The analysis of the samples confirms that the proportion of Andalusians was higher than any of the other immigrants from peninsular regions, even if at present none of the regional New World Spanish dialects is identical to any peninsular dialect in particular; moreover, the Spanish from some New World regions shares salient features with both Andalusian and Canarian Spanish. Assuming that Andalusians typically conformed one-third or more of any sample in any given area of the New World, the questions that follow refer to the contribution of Andalusians as compared to the rest of the immigrants, who also had had trans-Castilian experience and contact by the time they arrived in the New World. Does this imply that Andalusian stand out as the sole and most significant contributor to the formation of New World Spanish? In the New World environment, speakers of other Spanish varieties were active participants in building the underpinnings of a new colonial society, but Andalusian must be taken into consideration as a significant component.

While the original features of New World Spanish were similar across the continent at least during the 16th century, regional variation has been reported as a result of contact with indigenous languages, provenance of Spanish immigrants, location of new Spanish speaking communities, and socio-economic development, among other factors. It is thus useful to discuss the differences between peninsular dialects and the features that were passed on to the various New World Spanish colonies. After the partial colonization of the Caribbean islands, Mexico became an extremely active center of mining, agriculture, education, and religious experiments, a focused colony, an ideal place to test the hypothesis on the diversification of a language spoken by a minority of Spanish speakers. Mexico had a large indigenous population, several prestigious native languages, and a minority of Africa-born slaves or African descendants born in the New World. Due to the economic activities around the mining sites, the Mexican central areas attracted both ordinary immigrants and high-ranking officials from Spain, who underscored the relevance of all things being Castilian.

In spite of the regional variations and environmental differences ensuing in the newer areas, it is accepted that the origins of Spanish in the New World are similar, because the basic linguistic layer throughout the sub-continent is the same. The divergences between the regional varieties are spelled out more clearly after the various movements of independence from Spain occurring in the 19th century. Even during the three-century colonial period, regional differences began to be noticed. As a case in point, the Caribbean region and Mexico were considered as a unit inasmuch as the dates of colonization occurred in the early decades of the 16th century. Three main theories about the origins of New World Spanish were advanced in the 20th century: (1) the first one is known as monogenetic for it proposed that New World Spanish was a direct descendant of Andalusian Spanish; (2) the polygenetic theory underscored the diverse origins of New

World Spanish; (3) and the theory of koineization stands out as the synthesis of the former two. A linguistic and sociolinguistic model showing that features of New World Spanish derive from the mixing of Spanish dialects and the addition of lexical items from Taino[1] and Nahuatl is advanced in order to explain how the earliest variety of Mexican Spanish was formed.

1.2 The rise of Castilian

The record of Christian resistance and the rise of Castilian hegemony are epitomized in Spain's linguistic history for the unity of Visigothic Spain was disrupted by the Muslim invasion, an event that placed the whole south and center under the control of the non-Christian culture (Entwistle 1936/1951: 106). In the 10th century, Castile expanded as far as the Duero River (912) and the Guadarrama mountain range (ca. 950), a less extensive territory than what is now known as *Castilla la Vieja* (Old Castile). In the late 11th century, after the conquest of the kingdom of Toledo from the Moors it was necessary to distinguish the newly acquired region south of the Guadarrama as *Castilla la Nueva* (New Castile) from that of the north (Old Castile). The fullest extent of Castile was achieved at the end of the 12th century, when the Reconquista reached the Sierra Morena. Beyond this point, the term Castilian did not apply but the territory to the south was and still is Andalusia (Penny 1991: 25-26). (See Map 1.1 for location of traditional regions, cities, rivers, and mountains).

Following closely the development of the Reconquista, the most distinguishing traits of Castilian emerged in the north. Andalusian nonetheless evolved with differing variations, which in combination make the resulting regional dialect a contrastive unit within the Iberian Peninsula. The discovery of the New World coincided with the publication of Elio Antonio de Nebrija's *Gramática de la*

---

[1] Before the Spanish conquest the Arawakan language was spoken in a number of disconnected areas from what is now Cuba and Bahamas to South America. Taino was known in the Greater Antilles (Hispaniola or present-day Santo Domingo and Haiti), Cuba, Puerto Rico, Jamaica and the surrounding islands. As the first Amerindian language known to by Europeans, it furnished the most widespread borrowings into European languages. The term Cariban refers to the group that includes the languages of the Antillean Carib and other South American indigenous languages. The lexicon of this region is known since the Discovery of the New World because Christopher Columbus himself and the active Spanish-speaking explorers spread select words across continents. In research, however, the borrowings from the Antilles are known as either *antillanismos* or *tainismos*; they seem to have been adopted, often adapted phonetically and morphologically and also documented in Spanish sources as early as 1492 or 1493.

lengua castellana (1492/1984), the first grammar of a European language. A few decades later, Juan de Valdés was also attempting to set the Spanish language standards in his *Diálogo de la lengua* (1535). Both scholars described the Spanish language and the criteria of correction prevailing at the end of the 15th century and the beginning of the 16th century, respectively. The precedent to normalization of Spanish medieval usages can be found in the intense work of Alfonso X the Learned (1221-1284), who was determined to set the rules of *castellano drecho* (correct Castilian) since the mid-13th century. Correct Castilian followed the Burgos model with some concessions to the speech of Toledo and Leon. In the end the speech of Toledo was the basis to the linguistic leveling of the kingdom, and the graphemes used were solidly established. Until the 14th century, the transcription of Spanish sounds adhered to norms fixed by Alfonso's Chancery and writings. By then, Castilian prose had become the vehicle of cultural transmission (Lapesa 1985: 240-242, 245-246). Directing his works from Toledo, the king made history as a humanist and historian. The Reconquista proceeded slowly until the Christian groups succeeded in repopulating the southern region, which had been heavily influenced by the Muslims.

In its earlier stages Castilian was a diasystem, that is, a mixture of dialects with no unified or homogenous structure. It shared traits with other dialects and had certain features not found elsewhere (Lloyd 1987: 273). Manuscripts written in early Old Spanish did not follow standard models until the scribes working for the king Alfonso rectified such situation. Under his reign, the royal Chancery patronized the simulation of the Castilian variety spoken in Toledo. Towards the end of the 13th century, the practices of Toledo began to influence the literary language but no longer represented the dialect of Burgos (Entwistle 1936/1951: 139, 169). Based on the Castilian dialect of Toledo the literary norm favored the older Romance standard at least as spelling is concerned. As a result of the scholarly endeavors of the king, regional traits disappeared in the 13th century. In contrast with other Hispano-Romance varieties, Castilian was the vehicle of a considerable production of scientific, historiographical, legal and literary work. By the end of Alfonso's reign, it was no longer possible to identify a specific regional flavor in the writings of Castilians. The new supra-regional literary standard was based upon the speech of the Toledo upper classes, a variety originated in the Burgos area and extended to Toledo at the time of the Reconquista of New Castile. A standardized Castilian was increasingly used in the documents issued by the Chancery and stood as model of correctness whenever they were read, copied or imitated. This does not mean that the speech of Toledo was readily emulated by the upper classes of other Spanish cities. On the contrary, other Spanish cities developed their own norms, which in the end, contrasted with those of Toledo.

This is the case of Seville, which was the largest and economically most prosperous city of the kingdom (Penny 1991: 15-16).

Alfonso the Learned believed that Castilian was the proper instrument to disseminate the culture that he was gathering and unifying; consequently, he deliberately broke with the tradition that supported Latin in erudite and scientific works. In supplanting Latin with Spanish, one finds the main reason for the large number of definitions. Because Spanish lacked the vocabulary to translate most of the works used, it was necessary to build words, to bring in learned words, or to explain uncommon words to the reader. In doing so, he resolved to name the objects while clarifying their meanings through etymologies, explanations, and descriptions. His method was flexible, since he preferred to follow concrete rather than abstract patterns. Alfonso promoted the idea that nouns were not so much concepts as they were something real, because his words were a reflection of everything in existence. Through his work, the preliminary dictionary of a Romance language can be reconstructed (van Scoy 1940). A random sample of 47 definitions retrieved from the *Siete Partidas* aid the reader in understanding the conception of the Spanish world as seen by the king. His definitions comprise a micro-context of lexicographic nature that can be placed within its referent, a macro-context, where each level corresponds to amplification and progressive extension. The structures utilize a set of symbols where clarity is better expressed by the separation of the parts (Roudil 1970: 162-163).

The Spanish spoken in the Iberian Peninsula showed since ancestral times a clear tendency to geo-chronological stages of koineization. Such process began in Burgos (9th to 11th centuries), one of the oldest northern cities, where immigrants from Asturias, Galicia, Santander, the Basque region and Navarre, as well as Mozarabs (*mozárabes*) from the south settled in the border county of Castile. These immigrants spoke different but mutually intelligible dialects, though the Basques also moved into Castile in large numbers, where they had to learn the Romance variety of the other speakers. Koneization continued in Toledo (11th and 12th centuries), and where a rapid increase in southward expansion and demographic mixing of the Christian Hispano-Romance speakers took place. In Toledo and its surrounding areas *mozárabes*, *mudéjares*, Jews, and Christians lived alongside with new arrivals from Castile, Leon, Asturias, Galicia, Navarra, Aragon, and Catalonia, not to mention the Christian Franks. Toledo is truly significant in the history of Spanish for it laid the foundation for an early standard model. Having its center in Seville leveling and koineization continued in Andalusia in the 13th century (cf. Tuten 2003).

1.3 Repopulation of Andalusia

The repopulation movement in southern Spain was simultaneous with the strides made by the Reconquista. According to González Jiménez (1997), Andalusia was repopulated during the 13th century after the defeat of the Almohads at Las Navas de Tolosa (1212). This allowed the Christian kingdoms sharing a border with Andalusia to work on the territories that they had repossessed. Initiated by Castile and Leon, the campaigns culminated in 1248 with the seizure of Seville. Christian settlers came from regions incorporated to the kingdoms of Leon and Castile but also from Navarra, Aragon and even Portugal. Other territories such as Cadiz and Jerez became part of Castile. The new Andalusia was comprised of the current provinces of Jaen, Cordoba, Seville, Huelva and Cadiz on the Guadalquivir Valley. The new Christian settlers were mostly concentrated in important cities such as Baeza, Ubeda, Jaen, Cordoba and Seville, from where the *moros* (Muslims) had been expelled massively only to resettle in Granada or in northern Africa. In order to repopulate the re-conquered territory, the Spanish Crown distributed lands, housing and other goods to each and all settlers. Large lots included buildings or agricultural installations to members of the royal families, ecclesiastics, cathedral councils, monasteries and military organizations. Other estates known as *heredamientos* (neighborhoods comprised of houses), cereal lands, and parcels for olives were sufficient to cater to the needs of an entire family according to social rank. The beneficiaries of these estates were obliged to occupy the assigned land and comply with military service; in essence all re-settlers were by definition proprietors of either small or medium-size estates.

The new society had to be identical to a Western feudal society from where the settlers originated and where at least two groups were distinguished: the first one belonged to privileged nobility or clergy, while the second one was made up of peasants or artisans, a mass with no privileges. The aim of the Andalusian repopulation movement was to build a new society with no traces of Islamic background. It was a society of free men, proprietors of their own parcels and under no obligation to pay tribute to their lords. Andalusian society was a frontier society, a feature that was logged in the *repartimiento* books (distribution records) in which the settlers were grouped according to rank: members of the nobility, the military, and commoners who owned a horse, a few weapons, and who were willing to go into combat. The complex process of rupture substantially altered the trajectory of a region shaped by the Islamic trends. This heritage appears in forms of agricultural organization such as flour or oil mills or the spatial model of exploitation from where the haciendas derive. There are some other traits of urban infrastructure that are reminiscent of the Eastern culture. In the new repopulated areas, societal space was reorganized in a different manner. The Spanish nobility and the new local bourgeoisie became the landowners around the city of Seville. The base of Eastern-derived agriculture was cereal, a crop precluding other forms of agriculture that required different technology, safer markets, and abundant manpower. The role of cities was reinforced by the repopulation of Andalusia, emphasizing their military and administrative qualities and altering the rural repopulation that was reorganized from the urban nuclei; cities functioned as administrative enclaves of the Christian dominions in which a coherent system regulated the use of natural resources flowing from the city to the countryside and vice versa. In this new environment, the raising of cattle flourished in the entire region. The repopulation of Andalusia forced the Castilian-Leonese society to resettle in a good part of Extremadura, La Mancha and Murcia. This explains why the northern Christians were not able to fill in all the gaps left by the expulsion of the *moros*. Depopulated areas were found near the proximities of the frontier with the kingdom of Granada. The frontier society of the 13th century was readjusted slowly and locally because it was difficult to attract permanent settlers despite the incentives that were awarded since the times of Alfonso. Settlers living in and/or selling castles and villas were tax-exempted. Despite many other privileges, repopulation of the region was not dense (González Jiménez 1997).

Finally, toward the late 15th century, the war and the frontier society came to an end and a new wave of repopulation triggered the much needed demographic growth of some villas, which had been reduced to walled spots. In some Andalusian regions the growth was higher than 300 %. This incited feudal lords to transform their estates into large dominions, where settlers-vassals could establish themselves. The repopulation of Granada followed the guidelines implemented in other regions, but there the newly arrived Christian settlers consisting in about 40,000 families had a difficult coexistence with the *mudéjar* (Muslims who remained in Spain after the Reconquista) majority capitulating at the end and converting to Christianity. After being pressured and defeated more than once, the Muslims of Granada turned into *moriscos* (baptized/Hispanicized Moors). This is in synthesis the origin of Andalusia, a region that prospered after the definitive expulsion of the infidels and the Discovery of the New World. Far from remaining underdeveloped, its economy flourished as a result of the multiplicity of exchanges with the New World. In the spheres of culture and language, Andalusia became a competitor with other regions, particularly Castile (González Jiménez 1997).

Andalusian Spanish was the end result of the mixing of different varieties that medieval Castile had, insofar as the former mirrors the process that transformed into Spanish the language of Old Castile at the end of the Middle Ages. Castilians from all provinces and settlers from Asturias-Leon, Galicia, Biscay, Navarra, Aragon and Catalonia swarmed the re-conquered territories of the south together with Portuguese, French and Genovese, among other foreigners, all speakers who went through the process of leveling. This occurred in two key periods of the Castilian expansion to the south: (a) the 13th century, when Christian warriors seized Muslim Andalusia; (b) the 15th century, when the Catholic kings Ferdinand and Isabella annexed the kingdom of Granada. Both events caused the intermingling of immigrants, who were either linguistically divergent or convergent, a fact which in turn led to cultural exchanges and / or accommodation of different types. Documents from Andalusia point to the heterogeneous demography of the southern varieties of Spanish (Frago Gracia 1993: 54-55). The mixed origins of Andalusian were perceived as a drawback, and consequently, speakers of Andalusian were the victims of condescension on the part of speakers from other regions. Spaniards and foreigners singled out Andalusian Spanish and even argued that within large territories, it was going through internal fragmentation. The scholars of the 16th and 17th centuries believed that Andalusians had different linguistic habits from those observed in other Spanish-speaking regions. Grammarians disparaged both *seseo* and *ceceo* but made harsher remarks on the latter. For example, in Western Andalusia they said *caça* for *casa*, *maça* for *masa*, and the other way around. However, *seseo* was more accepted than *ceceo* (see definition and more examples in 3.2). Despite the narrow-minded judgments, some authors acknowledged the existence of sociolinguistic variants within the Andalusian urban centers, and by the 18th and 19th centuries, there were more than sufficient testimonies on the salient features of Andalusian (Frago Gracia 1993: 112, 119, 121). Spanish language historians and dialectologists have identified and contrasted the features of Andalusian and Castilian from both the descriptive and historical perspectives (cf. Zamora 1967: 287-331; Frago Gracia 1993).

1.4 Toledano and Old Castilian

In its earliest years, Castilian did not show a homogeneous structure but shared some traits with other dialects, and also had certain features not found elsewhere, perhaps because speakers belonging to the lowest and least prestigious class intermingled with the upper class for Castilian society was characterized by a fluidity of social class, in sharp contrast with its later rigidity. As Castile spread its power and its language to the south, devoicing was carried along with it (Lloyd 1987: 273). *Toledano* is the oldest variety distinguishing voiced from voiceless sibilants, while devoicing was spreading to the south of the Guadarrama River. Toledano eventually adapted the innovations of Old Castilian (Lapesa 1985: 371-372). The internal changes of these two varieties stem from a series of mergers that explain the trend of consonant simplification prevailing since at least the late 15th century and most likely unrelated to the Discovery of the New World. The mergers include devoicing, de-affrication, de-lateralization, inter-dentalization, and de-palatalization, the latter two completed in the mid-17th century. In addition, the change from /f-/ > [h] > [Ø] across social groups and regions within Spain sheds light on patterns of evolution that are not inconsequential for the varieties of the New World Spanish spoken today. In this realm, scholars have painstakingly documented the progressions taking place from the 12th to the 15th centuries. Particular attention has been given to the sibilant consonants, which are divided into voiced and voiceless with different points of articulation. Devoicing, the most important change, is derived from the differences between Old Castile with its capital in Madrid to the north of Toledo, which stands out in Spain's multicultural hub during the Reconquista. While *toledano* distinguished between voiced and voiceless sibilants with the northern influences disseminating smoothly toward the south, Old Castilian represented a simplification motivated by the establishment in 1560 of a new court in Madrid, a small village which not only attracted nobility from ancestral regions of Spain but which also superseded Toledo as a center of power and prestige. Madrid became the enclave of the northern pronunciation soon associated to innovations such as the aspiration of word-initial F- derived from Latin. With some resistance, from the new capital this change was spreading to the rest of New Castile, Jaen, Eastern Granada, and Murcia (Lapesa 1985: 372-373).

1.4.1 De-affrication, devoicing and inter-dentalization

It has been proposed that medieval Spanish had six sibilant consonants, divided in three pairs of voiceless and voiced. The model of such distinctive pronunciation was Toledo, the cultural capital of Spain at the time of the Moorish invasion. Table 1.1 shows three voiced sibilants (1, 3 and 5), which went through the long process of devoicing. The dental affricates (1 and 2) changed the manner of articulation and became fricatives, a change ensuing in the north and the northern plateau. Once the sibilants completed the process of de-affrication, the contrast remained between voiceless and voiced sibilants, but was further reduced as a result of the influx of northern settlers to Madrid, who after two or three generations did not distinguish voiced from voiceless fricatives, perhaps because voicing had become a marker. The sharp differences which defined the speech of Toledo were leveled in the new capital. The new voiceless pronunciation found its way in Madrid and elsewhere, and by the end of the 16th century became the norm. It is believed that this change was consummated until the second half of the 17th century, when the articulation resulted in a new voiceless inter-dental fricative, just like modern /θ/ (in writing <z> before <a>, <o> and <u> and <c> before <e> and <i>). In sum, the distinctive voicing phonemes merged with their voiceless counterparts (see phonetic symbols in Column 1).

Table 1.1: Spanish sibilants before the 16th century

Ph.	Symbol	Description	Grapheme	Examples
1.	/ẑ/	Voiced dental affricate	<z>	fazer, razimo
2.	/ŝ/	Voiceless dental affricate	<ç>	força
3.	/ʒ/	Voiced pre-palatal fricative	<g>, <j>	gentil, gesta, jornal
4.	/ʃ/	Voiceless pre-palatal fricative	<x>	baxo, xabón, axuar
5.	/ż/	Voiced apical-alveolar fricative	<-s->	rosa, prisión
6.	/ṡ/	Voiceless apical-alveolar fricative	<ss>, <-ss->	señor, pensar; passar, esse, amasse

The grapheme <ç>, known as *"ce con cedilla"* (phoneme 2) derived from medieval manuscripts and was shared with Aragonese, Leonese, and Galician. Devoicing spread through Toledo, Extremadura, Murcia, Andalusia and the New World. In addition, dental affricate sibilants moved their point of articulation, a change already attested in western Andalusia since the early 15th century and occurring, too, in the northern regions independently of and mostly likely after the emergence of Andalusian. In Toledo, de-affrication of /ŝ/ (phoneme 2) occurred after the de-affrication of /ẑ/ (phoneme 1); as a result, for some time, the opposition of the two was maintained but did not persist after the mid-17th century. Scholars have focused on the opposition between /ŝ/ and /ẑ/ and the loss of the distinction between the two in various regions of Spain. It is assumed that the fusion began to occur during the first half of the 16th century and that it was consolidated as of the second half, despite some endeavors to restore the voiced quality. In southern Spain the lack of distinction between the two pairs of sibilants resulted in the fusion of four sibilants (1, 2, 5 and 6). It has been proposed that in Andalusian, the de-affrication of /ŝ/ and /ẑ/ had occurred earlier than in the northern regions (Catalán 1956-57) thus accelerating other changes. Finally, the coalescence of apico-alveolar phonemes /ṡ/ and /ż/ resulted in one single voiceless /ṡ/, which eventually lost its apical quality. The end result is a pre-dorsal-dental fricative /s/ prevailing in Andalusia, the Canary Islands and the New World (Catalán 1957).

In Castile, the merger of de-affricated affricates rendered one single fricative that forwarded its point to articulation resulting in inter-dental /θ/, a change consolidated about 1630 or 1650, and also occurring at a later stage in Extremadura, Murcia, Jaen, regions of Almeria and Granada. The Castilian pronunciation is based on etymological criteria, and for this reason, it maintains the distinction between the de-affricated inter-dental /θ/ merger (resulting from 1 and 2) and the voiceless apico-alveolar /ś/ resulting from the merger of sibilants 5 and 6. The devoiced merger retained its apical quality in the Castilian varieties of northern and central Spain. For more detailed accounts and interpretations of the sibilant Spanish system, see (Lloyd 1987: 330-344; Penny 1991: 84-91; and Arias Álvarez 1997: 43-59).

In the kingdoms of Seville and Cordoba as well as in the west and south of Granada, the confusion of apico-alveolar sibilants (5 and 6) with the dental affricates /ẑ/ and /ŝ/ coming from 1 and 2 went in a different direction the merger resulting in a single voiceless sound with dorsal-dental or dental articulation of [s]. The elimination of the apico-alveolar sibilants in favor of the dentals or inter-dentalized variants was identified as *çeçeo-zezeo*, inasmuch as the resulting pronunciation originated from abusing the sibilants 1 and 2. In the process of devoicing of the three original voiced phonemes (1, 3 and 5), the sibilants were reduced to one in most of Andalusia, the Canary Islands and the New World, where at present several variants co-exist: one dental [s] and one inter-dentalized [s^θ]. The use of the former variant is known as *seseo* and is represented by the dental convex that became prestigious because it was used by the upper classes of Seville, whereas *çeçeo* was the inter-dentalized variant with a pronunciation not necessarily based on an etymological criterion (Lapesa 1985: 374-375).

The process of devoicing and the readjustment of the point of articulation reduced the original distinctions in most of Andalusia and the New World to one single phoneme with at least two non-distinctive articulatory variants: one coronal (flat or slightly convex) with the tip of the tongue pointing down, and another convex or pre-dorsal with the tongue fully convex and the tip of the tongue touching the lower teeth. The apical concave variant remained in Castilian territories (Zamora 1967: 288; Lapesa 1985: 510-511). By the 16th century the Andalusian innovations spread to the writing norms. In 1549 scribes from Seville used to write *resebí, parese, nesecidad, ofrese, resela*, in lieu of *resçebi, paresçe, nesçesidad, ofresçe, resçela* (< the Old Spanish orthography). The Andalusian spellings are also documented in the Canary Islands and Puerto Rico since 1521, in Cuba since 1539, and in Mexico since ca. 1523-1525 (Lapesa 1985: 375). *Seseo* emerged simultaneously in all the extended Andalusian zones and showed from the beginning intra-dialectal differentiation across regions and social strata. Manuscripts from different dates and provinces proffer sufficient evidence of such polymorphism (Frago Gracia 1993: 228-229ff).

The boundaries and distribution of variants (e.g. aspiration of word-initial /f-/, *seseo, ceceo*, and apical /ś/) recorded before World War II and before the influential role of the mass media are extremely useful to understand the phenomena transplanted to the New World Spanish colonies (see Maps 1.2 and 1.3 for the distribution of the sibilants in Andalusia). According to Navarro Tomás et al. (1933/1975), the distinction between /s/ and /θ/ and the *seseo* and *ceceo* variants appear in syllable-initial position, while many other variations are found in final position. It was commonly believed that the confusion between /s/ and /θ/ (realized as *seseo* or *ceceo*) occurred throughout Andalusia. In order to test this hypothesis, Navarro Tomás et al. (1933) surveyed all the Andalusian provinces, to wit: Badajoz, Huelva, Sevilla, Cadiz, Cordoba, Jaen, Granada, Malaga, Almeria, Murcia, and Las Alpujarras, where they found varying distributions of both sibilants. In Badajoz, for example, the Castilian distinction prevailed amongst educated subjects whereas *seseo* was heard among peasants and workers coming from the towns of the province. Also in Badajoz, they found three variants of /s/: (a) apico-alveolar concave; (b) coronal, pre-alveolar or post-dental flat; (c) pre-dorsal-dental convex. The first variant prevails in most of the province; the coronal variant is heard in the western towns, where the apical pronunciation reappears with relative frequency (Navarro Tomás et al. 1933: 27).

Unquestionably significant for the history of New World Spanish is the dispersal of the three sibilant variations in Seville, the least common being the distinction between /s/ and /θ/, and the most widespread the *ceceante* variant. Between these two, *seseo* is used in the northern and southeastern towns. The social significance of *seseo* and *ceceo* in Seville is even more substantial because the former is more prestigious than the latter. The upper classes from the city of Seville adopted the *seseo* variant. In Seville, sibilant [s] is pre-dorsal dental convex pronounced with the tip of the tongue over the lower teeth with an acoustic effect similar to that of ص and other velarized or emphatic Arabic sounds (Navarro Tomás et al. 1975: 38). The distribution in other provinces is equally interesting, since in most of them the three variants were found. In Murcia, Malaga and Las Alpujarras the authors reported only two variants (39-60). Castilian and Leonese settlers, known for distinguishing *s*, *ç*, and *z*, repopulated the Andalusian provices in the 13th century. Both *seseo* and *ceceo* emerged in the city of Seville and the provinces before the 16th century, but *seseo* was introduced from the north (62-63). The coronal and pre-dorsal variants of Andalusian [s] were influential in the confusion of ç and z with s in this region. Upon the expansion of Castilian to Andalusia, either the pre-dorsal or the coronal variants of the Hispanic-Arabic population that remained in these kingdoms under the Castilian dominion replaced the pronunciation of apical [ś] received from the colonizers' speech. Due to the dental nature of ç and z, these consonants were also confused with Andalusian [s] as soon as they lost their occlusive component (72-73).

1.4.2 De-palatalization

The merger of sibilants with a pre-palatal point of articulation (3 and 4 in Table 1.1.) rendered a new de-palatalized voiceless uvular or velar phoneme. Known as *rehilante*, the voiced palatal /ʒ/ (in writing <g> or <j>) was a groove fricative (similar to English *pleasure* or French *jour*) coalescing with its voiceless counterpart /ʃ/ (as in English *sh*oe or Italian *pesce*). This change was not only typical of Castilian but occurred, too, in Galician and Asturian-Leonese. In Castilian, however, the evolution continued, as speakers perceived the need to distinguish pre-palatal /ʃ/ from the apico-alveolar /ṡ/. De-palatalization was the strategy that made the palatals truly different from other Romance languages and ancestral peninsular dialects. In Spain, words pronounced with a pre-palatal phoneme such as *mexior, dexiara, moxiere, vexiés, oxios* resulted in *mejor, dejara, mujer, vejez, ojos*, which are pronounced with a voiceless uvular or velar fricative transcribed as either /χ/ or /x/, better known as *jota* (Lapesa 1985: 377-378). Needless to say, the phonemes /ʃ/ and /ʒ/ contended for a long time, but towards the end of the 17th century, the velar phoneme /x/ or its Castilian uvular variant /χ/ prevailed, while the pre-palatal phoneme (see 4 in Table 1) was relegated to non-Castilian dialects.

Finally, in regions where aspirated [h] and from Arabic-aspirated sounds turned into /f-/, the velar phoneme /x/ coming from the pre-palatals 3 and 4 also became aspirated and was confused with the former. Early documentation of [h] in lieu of <g> or <j> seems to denounce lower social strata, as in *hentil* for *gentil*, or *hermanía* for *germanía*, or the opposite hypercorrect pronunciation, as in *gerida* for *herida*, or *harro* for *jarro*. Aspirated [h] prevailed in areas of northeastern Spain, Extremadura and Andalusia. From Andalusia it was spread to the Canary Islands and the New World, but it did not turn into the preferred variant in the entire American continent; aspiration occurred mostly in the Caribbean, other coastal regions, and peripheral New World areas (Lapesa 1985: 379-380).

1.4.3 Yeísmo or de-latelarization

Documents from the early 15th century show occasional evidence of sporadic confusion between the phoneme /j/ (generally spelled <y>) and the palatal lateral /λ/ (spelled <ll>). Although the distinction is maintained in spelling, in most dialects of modern Spanish, the two have merged into the same, non-lateral palatal sound, which may range phonetically from a palatal fricative [j] to a sibilant [ʒ], depending on the dialect zone. Thus, for example, with few exceptions, Spanish speakers pronounce *yo* and *llover*; *Yolanda* and *llamar*; *haya* (< *haber*) and *halla*

(< *hallar*) as a central palatal. This phonemic merger is called *yeísmo*, based on one name of the letter <y>. "Although not attested in Spain until the 18th century, this merger probably began in late Old Spanish since all varieties of Judeo-Spanish (separated from Peninsular Spanish in 1492) and most varieties of American Spanish witness its accomplishment" (Penny 1991: 93).

1.4.4 Aspiration and omission of /s/ in implosive position

Final /-s/ was never too tense in the common pronunciation and became lax in southern Spain until it was aspirated. The resulting aspiration [h] was not written because speakers were aware that it was a variant of sibilant [s]. The oldest samples of /-s/ weakening can be traced to 1492 as in *escrivanoØ públicos* and *Juan VásqueØ*, the first one omitted in the noun and the second one in the surname. It is assumed that weakening continued through the 16th century in southern Spain and the New World in manuscripts of Toledo, Seville, Mexico, Arequipa, Panama and Peru (Lapesa 1985: 387-388). In implosive position /-s/ is also aspirated as in *mascar* [mahkar], *los hombres* [loh ombreh]. Aspiration can be followed by omission as in [lah ólah] > [la óla] forms that are common in Murcia and Andalusia (Lapesa 1985: 502-503). According to Penny (1991: 94) weakening of /-s/ shows degrees of intensity on a scale from one to five, the least intense changing from /s/ to /ɹ/ as in desde [deɹde] occurring in northern rural areas. The second most intense in most of southern Spain, northern areas and most of the New World consists of the realization of /-s/ (and of θ where there is a separate phoneme) as an aspirate [h]. The third most intense is the weakening of /-s/ typical of Andalusia. The total loss of /-s/ occurs in Western Andalusia and most of the New World as in *los hombres* [loh ómbre]; *las olas* [lah óla]. Finally the most acute form of weakening is the total elimination in all environments as in *las olas* [la óla] and *las manos* [la máno] occurring in Eastern Andalusia.

1.5 Additional changes

The neutralization of /-l/ and /-r/ or the omission of any of the two is attested in Spain since the 12th and the 14th centuries, and in the New World since 1525 and 1560. Such occurrence does not define New World Spanish but it is spread over coastal and insular territories (Lapesa 1985: 575). Interchange of these two syllable-final liquids leads to some confusions such as *harto* ('satisfied') and *alto* ('tall'); *arma* ('weapon') and *alma* ('soul'), but unlike *seseo*, there is no merger (Penny 2000: 126-127). Other examples include *puerta* > [puélta], *calor* > [calól].

Another feature attributed to Andalusian is the weakening of /d/ in both final and intervocalic position, which is frequent in numerous Spanish words as in *bondad, calidad, cantidad, ciudad, majestad*; and in past participle endings *-ado-* and *-ido-* as in *cuidado* ('cared for'), *limpiado* ('cleaned'), *pintado* ('painted'), *llovido* ('rained'), *teñido* ('dyed'). The series of Latin stops /b/, /d/, and /g/ in intervocalic position turned into fricatives, and the fricatives can be further deleted in some dialects. According to Zamora (1967: 316-317), the deletion of /-d/ and /-d-/ has also been observed in Castilian but it is more frequent and deep-seated in Andalusian varieties.

1.6 Spanish initial F-: past and present perspectives

In his *Gramática de la lengua castellana* (1492), Antonio de Nebrija stated that "the *h* is not a letter, but the signal of the spirit, just a breathing sound" (113). Moreover, the letter H is used to pronounce the first letter of words such as *hago* and *hecho*, and although in Latin it was insignificant, we pronounce it distressing the throat like the Jews and the Moors, from whom we received it (118). In the 20th century Menéndez Pidal confirmed that the Spanish of the 15th and 16th centuries counted on an aspirated *h* in words such as *hazer, humo, holgar*, that is today entirely silent in the written language (1904/1977: 114). A major change consistently addressed in Spanish language history is the evolution of what is generally believed to have been labio-dental /f-/ to aspirated [h]. Latin labio-dental /f/ was adapted as a bilabial fricative [φ], and then into fully aspirated [h]. Juan de Valdés, the author of *El diálogo de la lengua* (1535), explained why the letter H is used in almost all the words in which Latin used F. One of his Italian interlocutors, Marcio, claimed to be stunned by the fact that many Castilian speakers still use the variant [f]. The only justification adduced by Valdés is that such Castilian pronunciation [h] derived from Arabic and that such discrepancy can only be attributed to a difference in knowledge of Castilian, given that Castilian speakers do use the variant [h] because they are legitimate Castilians while those who use [f] merely strive to appear Castilian (Valdés 1535/1964: 73-74).

The change from /f-/ to [h] has also been attributed to the 'revolutionary' influence of the Basque substratum (Otero 1971: 187). Presumably, the absence of /f/ in Iberian languages, particularly Basque, would have reinforced the aspirated component of /f/ (Menéndez Pidal 1968: 201-202; Alarcos Llorach 1968: 254-255). Comparing modern Spanish with other Romance languages, the former contrasts with the latter because in standard speech, the letter F has been replaced by the letter H. In some words, H turned out to be completely silent. One school of thought proposed that the primitive zone of aspirated [h] spread over non-Castilian territories, that is, Cantabria, Biscay, north of Burgos and La Rioja, where several variants co-existed, as in *forma*, *horma*, *orma*, and *porma* (all derived from Latin FORMA). In this zone the variant with [h] prevailed in colloquial speech with variable aspiration, sometimes very firm while others very weak. A second zone includes the southern territory of present-day Old Castile, where /f-/ was strongly rooted but was displaced towards the end of the 15th century because speakers preferred a weak aspiration. The third zone extended through New Castile and Jaen including the territories re-conquered by Castile from 1085 on, where the two variants co-existed. In New Castile /f-/ was restored and imposed ca. 1140. It is assumed that from New Castile it was spread to western Andalusia, Cordoba, Seville, Huelva and Cadiz. In the 14th century aspiration reappeared in non-common rustic words such as *hoto*, *hato*, *heda*, *huron*, *haça*, *herrén*, *hosco*, etc. This zone preserved the aspiration until the mid-16th century when it was lost in the second. Initial /f/ was maintained however in common words such as *fazer* (modern *hacer* 'to do'); *fijo* (modern *hijo* 'son'); *ferir* (modern *herir* 'to hurt'); *fava* (modern *haba* 'white bean'); *folgar* (modern *holgar* 'to rest'); *fierro* (modern *fierro* or *hierro* 'iron'); *fablar* (modern *hablar*) 'to speak', etc. (see Menéndez Pidal 1968: 221-233 and map facing page 233).

The change in question is not overemphasized for it is assumed that the near-perfect phonographic system conceived by Alfonso the Tenth was disrupted towards the end of the 15th century when the retention of /f-/ interfered with the ideal pronunciation. At the end of the 15th century, Elio Antonio de Nebrija reaffirmed the phonetic principle that Castilian should be spelled as it was pronounced, whereas the humanists who intervened in the process of normalization insisted on the use of the etymological criterion. Nonetheless, external events rather than internal changes swayed the seemingly consummated scheme and altered permanently the outlook of the Spanish language. Scholars assume that there were latent changes incubated as of the 15th century due to powerful external forces such as the expulsion of the Jews and the *mozárabes* from the re-conquered territory (1492) and the emergence of Seville as the capital of southern Spain. The pressure was exerted not only on the Castilian dialect as a whole, favored by the chanceries and the heroic songs, but on each individual form derived from Castilian. Each phenomenon has its own peculiar history not identical to any other, but in essence contributing to the eventual outcome. The most thoroughgoing of these phenomena is the substitution of F in writing by H (Entwistle 1936/1951: 159ff).

The traditional view that initial Latin /f-/ was replaced by aspiration as a result of contact with Basque has been questioned by Martinet (1951-1952: 141-143) and also by Penny (1991: 79-82, 91). Penny's point of departure is the modern spelling of two groups of words: Group 1 with initial H- as in FĪCU, FĪLIU, FĪLU,

FARĪNA, FORNU, FACERE, which have rendered *higo* ('fig'), *hijo* ('son'), *hilo* ('thread'), *harina* ('flour'), *horno* ('oven') *hacer* ('to do'), respectively. Group 2 with initial F- as in FŎRTE, FŎNTE, FRONTE, FŎLLE, which rendered *fuerte* ('strong'), *fuente* ('fountain'), *frente* ('forehead'), *fuelle* ('bellows'), respectively. In Old Spanish both groups were spelled with F because they were learned words. The objections to the contact-with-Basque theory read that the development of /f-/ > /h/ is also found in some small Romance territories where Basque influence was unfeasible. The substratum account does not explain why Group 2 words appear with initial F in Spanish. Loss of /f-/ may have to do with the internal evolution of ancestral areas such as Cantabria, where the spoken Latin may have preserved a bilabial articulation (represented by φ), which had been replaced by the labio-dental variant in Rome and in those areas in closest contact with Rome.

As for the regional distribution of /f/ and /h/, at present the aspirate or glottal fricative variant (as in *humu* < FŪMUS, *hambre* < FAMINE and *ahorcar* < FURCU) is restricted in Cantabria, eastern Asturias, western Salamanca, Extremadura, and western Andalusia, regions that are tangential to the main focus of /h/-dropping, namely Madrid. It is also limited to the least prestigious social groups within the abovementioned areas, a pattern that was carried by the pioneering settlers to the New World, who commonly use the aspirate variant regardless of social class. From the second half of the 16th century on, the /h/-dropping trend spread faster among the social elite in both continents. In the New World the result has been the competition between educated /h/-dropping and uneducated /h/-retention, in contrast with Spain, where /h/-dropping is virtually complete. Aspiration survives in New World rural varieties and also in lower-class urban speech. In all cases the same phoneme represents both the descendant of Latin F (as in *humo*, *horca*, *ahogar*) and the product of medieval pre-palatal sibilants as in *caja*, *mujer*, *junto*, *jugar* (Penny 2000: 162-163).

1.7 Features of Judaeo-Spanish

In the remarkable year of 1492 the Spanish kings Isabel I and Fernando II ordered the expulsion of the Jews from the kingdoms of Castile and Aragon by the Alhambra Decree (also known as the Edict of Expulsion). Following the expulsion from Spain, Sephardic Jews settled mainly in the former Ottoman Empire, Morocco, Algeria, and areas of Middle East, like Israel, Lebanon and Syria. The language varieties spoken by the Sephardim have been reconstructed from language data of speakers still living in diverse communities around the world. The variety of Spanish spoken by the Sephardim is known as Judaeo-Spanish, also called *ladino*, which is derived from Castilian with traits adopted from Andalusian Spanish.

After more than five hundred years, *ladino* Spanish has preserved some of the features of 15th century Castilian. As a case in point, Balkan Judaeo-Spanish speakers still use Latin F- as /f/, as in *fazer*, Spanish *hacer* ('to do'), *furmica*, Spanish *hormiga* ('ant'), *fambri*, Spanish *hambre* 'hunger', though Eastern varieties show aspiration or no consonant. The paradigm of 2nd person plural *vos* shows the 15th century variation but with palatalization of final /s/ in the monophthongized forms: /kantáʃ/ ~ kantáis/, keréʃ/ ~ /keréis/. In addition, like in Portuguese, syllable-final /s/ is palatalized, but only before /k/, as in móʃka (Penny 1991: 22). The Portuguese integration occurring in the 16th century resulted in the mergers of apico-alveolar fricatives (phonemes 5-6 in Table 1.1) and dento-alveolar affricates (phonemes 1-2 in Table 1.1) with dento-aveolar fricatives (i.e. *seseo*), but maintained the contrast between voiceless and voiced pronunciation (phonemes 3 and 4). The last pair is exemplified in *dixo* [dijo] 'he said' and *oʒo* [ojo] 'eye', that is, the persistence of the voiced / voiceless distinction (Penny 1991: 22-23), which is glaring in this variety.

1.8 Features from Spain transplanted to New Spain

The simplification of the Castilian consonant system resulted in the split in two well-defined varieties: the first one is the northern-central peninsular territory corresponding roughly to Castile, but extended to the kingdom of Toledo, Murcia, and eastern Andalusia with three voiceless fricatives (apical /ś/, inter-dental /θ/ and uvular /χ/. The second major variety includes most of Andalusia, Cartagena (in the province of Murcia), the Canary Islands and the New World, where the three voiceless sibilants were further reduced to two: (1) dental /s/ and allophonic variations, and (2) post-palatal, velar /x/ or glottal fricative [h] (Lapesa 1985: 381). Features of Peninsular Spanish transplanted to the New World derive from either of the two macro-dialects resulting from the distribution of changes described above. Manuscripts from the 16th century aid in illustrating the features of the different regional dialects when these are not representative of the Castilian officialdom. However, literary texts and other formal documents are evocative of Old Spanish, which is understood as the fusion of *toledano* and Old Castilian. The 16th century may be considered a period of transition between Old and modern Spanish, which coincides with an intense stage of Spanish colonization, when most of the changes had not been completed. Although some of them were still ongoing, i.e. aspiration of initial /f/ represented by [h], devoicing, de-affrication and de-palatalization, others such as the merger of the fricatives and affricates as in Andalusia (*seseo/çeçeo*), the merger of /ʝ/ and /ʎ/ (lateral palatal) as in Andalusia (*yeísmo*), and the aspiration and deletion of /-s/ in Andalusia were advanced.

1.9 The features of Andalusian Spanish

When the New World was discovered the dialect differentiation of the Andalusian varieties was strongly consolidated. The misspellings of graphemes are significant because the Andalusian texts provide the evidence of linguistic peculiarities, attitudes, and socio-cultural strata in both Spain and the New World (Frago Gracia 1994: 91). Devoicing preceded the discovery of the New World and its regional variations can be traced to the 16th and 17th centuries. The influence of Andalusian copyists appears in the cacographic transcriptions they made in manuscripts of non-Andalusian authors, the most noticeable of them being *ceceo-seseo* variants which render forms such as: *abrasado, assendiente, asertar, cabesa, comiensa, concluciones, deceplina, dissenciones, çarsal, caucó, comensó, condisión, deceplina, jues, lucitano, lus, mostasa, paresca, reconosca, resívanlo*. These forms correspond to the following Castilian variants: *abraçado, ascendiente, acertar, cabeza, comiença, conclusiones, disensiones, çarzal, causó, començó, condición, disciplina, juez, lusitano, luz, mostaza, parezca, reconozca, recíbanlo*. Presumably, the Andalusian scribes attempted to correct the original forms leaving sufficient traces of their regional origins. The samples of errors are abundant since the scribes use <s> or <ss> *anegadisas, assendrada* in lieu of *anegadizas, acendradas*. The opposite practice also occurred: *agazajava, baptizmo* in lieu of *agasajaba, bautismo*, etc. (Frago Gracia 1994: 20-21).

Many of the innovations of Andalusian Spanish were incubated in the city of Seville, which emerged as the receptive center of all the novelties coming from the New World, the Mecca of money and merchandise, and the host of all negotiations with Spanish speakers who had been living across the Atlantic. At the same time, because Spanish speakers wanted to evade their unpromising destiny through migration to the New World, they experienced personal and family uprooting. The New World was the salvation board though not all the dreams of success were achieved there either. One of the dreams was to find a position in public service. Spanish speakers believed that by being away from the mother country, they would be free. One of the most important issues discussed by observers of the new linguistic reality is the socio-cultural stratification of the community of Spanish speakers. Various authors pointed out the dialect variations of Spanish within the Peninsula, for instance, Mosé Arragel, Gonzalo García de Santa María, Bernardo de Aldrete and Juan de Valdés, who were not indifferent to the social and geographic variations of Spanish present in the vast Spanish dominions and the expansive influence of the Spanish language (Frago Gracia 1994: 42-44, 49, 95).

The expansion of Spanish was conducive to morpho-syntactic, lexical, and phonetic variation, which in turn had to do with the medieval heritage. The double forms or *dobletes* show the vacillations of the writers in most manuscripts. For instance, the prepositions *e* and *y*; negative *non* and *no*; *ni* and *nin*; synthetic future *verná* and *vendrá*; analytic future and conditional tenses as in *decir lo he* and *decir lo hía*; non-assimilated infinitive and direct object as in *tenerlo* and *tenello*; various imperfect indicative forms, as in *tenía, tenie* and *tenié*; and double imperfect subjunctive forms, with –SE and –RA endings (as in a*masse* and *amara*). Diffusion of some variable forms reappeared in some New World regions, as for example, the use of the article + possessive + noun as in *la nuestra nao; los mis esforzados, la mi Elvira, la mi luna, la mi compañera*; or double negative as in *nadie no le veía*. The use of *cibdad* contrasts with *çiudad* or *ciudad*, whereas *nos* contrasts with *nosotros, vos* with *vosotros*, and *gelo* with *selo*. Spanish was transmitted to the New World with these variations, some of them inherited from medieval Spanish, others from the Spanish Golden Age, and some others from modern Spanish. The differences observed at present are consolidated, although they may have been used in different contexts or restricted by frequency or pragmatics. Spanish speakers were scattered all over the continent and those of some regions lived alongside others from other regions, a fact conducive to the nativization of the New World Spanish lexicon, since at times items restricted to a peninsular region became general or had a wide diffusion in the New World. As a result, lexical items used in the New World aid in the identification of the regional origin of emigrants and the corresponding variety, which highlights the differences against peninsular Spanish (Frago Gracia 1994: 65-68, 70).

At the time of the discovery of the New World, standardization of Spanish was still ongoing but had nonetheless a solid foundation to become diversified and to be used in numerous functions of public life and formal domains. It was on its way to substitute Latin in spheres in which Latin had prevailed. The regional dialects observed today were also observed in the 16th century, and finally, by the end of the 16th century, there was already a colony of Spanish speakers in the New World, that is, about 250,000 who were resolute in pursuing their dreams in the New World colonies. Spanish speakers working in public service, many more working for the Inquisition, and those who by necessity cultivated the art of letter writing contributed with multifarious documents that are at present extremely useful in the reconstruction of the major features of New World Spanish.

1.10 Spanish speakers in New Spain

The earliest sample of immigrants to Mexico (1493-1519) includes those who arrived with Hernán Cortés, Pánfilo de Narváez[2], and with other captains. These three groups make up a total of 743 adult males distributed as follows: 30 % were from Andalusia; 13.1 % from Extremadura; 26.1 % from Old and New Castile; 10.4 % from Leon; 4.8 % from the Basque region; 12 % from all other regions within Spain, and only 8.2 % from Portuguese, Italy or other European countries (Boyd-Bowman 1985: xli-xlii). In the Age of Exploration, a Spanish speaker who immigrated to the Indies in 1511 could reappear as a *vecino* (house or lot owner) in Santo Domingo in 1514, again as a *vecino* in Cuba in 1519, as a conqueror in Mexico in 1520, and then in Guatemala in 1523, only to return to Spain in the interim, and embark once more to the Indies in 1527 with a final destination to Peru in 1534 (Boyd-Bowman 1985: xxxiii). The origin and destination of the Spanish speakers who arrived in Mexico after 1519 are as significant as the whereabouts of the original group. The destination of the 16th-century colonists of known origin is divided in five periods as seen in Table 1.2. The total of 17,278 passengers from Spain leaving for New Spain represents slightly more than a full-third or 34.3 percent of the total of 50,395 recorded destinations to the New World between 1493 and 1600. Table 1.2 also shows that between 1520 and end of the 16th century, 16,400 immigrants settled in Mexico or central Mexico, which was already distinguished from the northern frontier and Yucatan, where only 420 and 458 immigrants were recorded, respectively (Boyd-Bowman 1976: 602).

---

[2] Pánfilo de Narváez was born in Cuellar or Valladolid in 1478 to an upper class family. He took part in the conquest of Jamaica in 1509, and three years later he participated in the conquest of Cuba under the command of Diego Velázquez, who later became its governor. In 1518 Velázquez had sent the young conquistador Hernán Cortés off to Mexico to begin the conquest of the mainland, but the Governor later changed his mind and appointed Captain Pánfilo de Narváez together with a force of over one thousand Spanish soldiers to explore Mexico. Narváez had the mission to send Cortés back to Cuba while taking command of the expedition. Cortés was ahead of his enemies, and in the process of defeating the Aztec Empire, he was forced to leave the capital of Tenochtitlan to return to the coast, where he fought against Captain Narváez. On May 24, 1520, the forces of Cortés and Narváez clashed at Zempoala, near Veracruz, where the former turned out victorious. His victory attracted many of Narváez's soldiers to the campaign undertaken by Cortés, who retained control of the expedition and the vast wealth that came after his triumph.

Table 1.2: Destinations of 16th-century Spanish colonists of known origin

Region of New Spain	1493-1519	1520-1539	1540-1559	1560-1579	1580-1600	Totals	%
Northern Frontier	--	NSF	NSF	NSF	420	(420)	0.8
Mexico	743*	4,022	2,057	7,218	2,360	(16,400)	32.5
Yucatan	--	278	NSF	120	60	(458)	0.9
New Spain	743*	4,300	2,057	7,338	2,840	17,278	34.3

() = Subtotals, NSF = No separate figure available, * Colonists already in Mexico

At the end of the 16th century slightly more than one-third of the Spanish immigrants destined to Mexico were from the province of Seville, which sent 4,000 colonists or more. Seville was followed by Badajoz and Toledo with 1,000-2,000; in third place, the provinces of Caceres, Huelva, Guadalajara, Madrid and Cadiz contributed with 400 to 1,000 immigrants; and finally Granada, Cordoba, Jaen, Ciudad Real, Palencia, Avila, Segovia and Burgos sent each from 200 to 400 Spanish speakers, provinces from predominantly Spanish-speaking regions, that is, they were not from bilingual areas such as Galicia, Catalonia or Biscay (see Table 1.3). As in the rest of the New World, the regional origin of the immigrants to Mexico was mixed, while the representative provinces of Spain included the northern-central and southwestern regions. The most compact group was that of Andalusians but there were also a good number of northerners.

Table 1.3: Emigration to Mexico by province (1493-1600)

Province	Number of colonists
Seville	4,000+
Badajoz and Toledo	1,000-2,000
Caceres, Huelva, Guadalajara, Madrid and Cadiz	400-1,000
Granada, Cordoba, Jaen, Ciudad Real, Palencia, Avila, Segovia and Burgos	200-400

Source: Boyd-Bowman (1976: 603)

There is also information on the occupation and gender of the immigrants. Many of those who were originally from Seville became merchants; others from northern regions resettled in Seville, Triana, Huelva, Palos, Sanlucar and other southern cities from where they transported merchandise between Spain and the New World. Until 1529 the trading centers in the New World were Santo Domingo and Mexico City. Between 1520 and 1529, forty merchants appeared in Santo Domingo, thirty in Mexico City, and eleven more had uncertain destiny. After 1535, forty more merchants settled in the vice-regal capital. In the periods 1540-1559 and 1560-1579, Mexico attracted 108 and 147 respectively, and only 43 in the last period. With respect to gender, in the period 1540-1560, Andalusia outranked the rest of the country sending over half of all women: those who were married, those who were to join their husbands in the New World, and those who were single adults or very young girls; one in every three females was from the city of Seville itself (Boyd-Bowman 1976: 592-598).

Virtually all records or estimates on the emigration of Spanish speakers to the New World confirm the diversity of regional origins. This diversity is glaring in Table 1.4 which shows the precise origin of 1,370 Europeans migrating to New Spain in the 16th century; this confirms the predominance of Andalusians in absolute numbers, followed by Extremadura and the northern provinces of New Castile, Old Castile and Leon, which together make up a total of 438 or 32% of Spanish speakers from monolingual provinces. Andalusia by itself represents 26.4% of the total sample. There is also detailed information on the origin of 123 slaves brought to New Spain in the 16th century (Aguirre Beltrán 1972: 240). Finally, Map 1.5 shows the general patterns of emigration to the New World.

Table 1.4: Origin of 1,370 Europeans in the 16th century

Andalusia	362	Murcia	11	Portugal	30
Extremadura	188	Asturias	10	Italy	20
New Castile	175	Catalonia	7	France	6
Old Castile	129	Navarre	4	Flandes	3
Leon	75	Valencia	3	England	2
Basque region	23	Canary Is.	3	Germany	1
Aragón	16	Balearic Is.	1	Greece	1
Galicia	15	Unspecified	285		

Source: Aguirre Beltrán (1972: 240)

1.11 Spanish speakers and the castes in the 16th century

By the time the Spanish Inquisition was established in New Spain, the Spanish-speaking population was partially mixed with both the native population and the population of African descent, which had been imported via the slave trade. Table 1.5 provides information according to episcopate the most populous being that of Mexico City followed by Tlaxcala, Oaxaca and Yucatan, areas of dense indigenous population. Three decades before the end of the 16th century, Indians

(Column 3) were still the overwhelming majority at more than three million people or 98.7 percent of this particular sample, which does not include Puebla, Guanajuato, Queretaro and other dense indigenous areas of central Mexico (Aguirre Beltrán 1972: 210). According to this classification there are six groups: the group known as "Europeans" (Column 1) includes 6,644 Spanish speakers in 1570, a figure that approximates the subtotal appearing in Boyd-Bowman for the period 1560-1579 (see Table 1.2 above). However, Table 1.5 is useful to see the preliminary results of *mestizaje*, which occurred since the early 1520's. Column 2 indicates the estimate of Africans–most likely born in Africa–while Column 3 contrasts with all the others. Column 4 is the most interesting addition to the New World population since "Euro-*mestizos*" were most likely born in New Spain and raised in Spanish households whereas "Indo-*mestizos*" in Column 5 were individuals of mixed origin but raised in indigenous households or communities; the estimate for these groups is strikingly similar to that in Column 6 or "Afro-*mestizos*". Euro-*mestizos* are also known as "*criollos*" or "*españoles americanos*", a group to be distinguished from Spanish speakers born in Spain. If it is assumed that all mixed groups were Spanish speakers and the subtotals of Columns 1, 4, 5, and 6 are added, the group of potential Spanish speakers may increase to at least 20,000.

Needless to say, other records provide higher estimates for the same year. In this realm, scholars classify the colonial population of Mexico, Central America and the Antilles according to three major ethnic groups: (a) Whites (b) blacks, mestizos and mulattos; and (c) Indians (Rosenblat 1954: 88). The calculation for whites or Spanish speakers comprises those who were born in Spain and the New World in one single group. Estimates vary considerably due to the different criteria used to calculate populations (see also Konetzke 1972/2001: 92).

Table 1.5: Population by castes in 1570

Bishopric	Europeans	Africans	Indians	Euro-mestizos	Indo-mestizos	Afro-mestizos
Mexico	2,794	11,736	1,310,904	8,632	1,992	2,000
Tlaxcala	900	3,278	844,828	944	100	100
Oaxaca	420	532	583,600	256	50	50
Michoacán	1,000	1,955	94,556	247	200	200
New Galicia	1,000	2,630	108,360	530	75	75
Yucatan	350	293	282,612	156	20	10
Chiapas	180	145	112,000	302	--	--
Totals	6,644	20,569	3,336,860	11,067	2,437	2,435

Source: Aguirre Beltrán (1972: 210)

The demographic quantitative weight of each original group is as significant as mobility, occupation, language and/or dialect contacts, face-to-face interaction with other Spanish speakers, training in manuscript writing, and the political or economic wave that unfolds in colonial societies, where the role(s) of immigrants and the dynamic forces prevailing at some point in time need to be taken into consideration. Geographic mobility is thus a variable that has to be factored in the model that explains the formation of proto-Mexican Spanish; to this, we may add the attitudes of the various groups of protagonists in the emergent society.

As a case in point, in the Mexican scenario, the mendicant orders played an important role in assigning prestige to some of the indigenous languages that were widespread in vast regions, e.g. Nahuatl. At the same time the mendicant orders over-asserted the role of Latin in the education of select indigenous groups while Spanish was not competing yet with Latin as the preferred language of the Catholic liturgy, religious conversion, formal education and diplomacy. In the constellation of languages present in the New World, Spanish obtained its own role because it was the language of the colonists who empowered themselves in the New Spanish society. Spanish became prestigious for the early history of the New World is written primarily in Spanish by the same actors or witnesses who in turn conveniently added features from Taino and Nahuatl, the languages available to them since the late 15th and early 16th centuries, respectively. The role of Spanish is manifold: it was used as the preferred colloquial language of the newcomers who also counted on a vernacular. Spanish was written by common individuals, chroniclers, historians, and functionaries of institutions such as the Mexico City Council or the secretaries of the Inquisition. When the need arose, Spanish was elevated to functions of solemnity and formality by the different protagonists who rapidly accessed positions of power and prestige. In addition, oral Spanish was transmitted to every generation of individuals of Spanish descent born in New Spain. Finally, some speakers of indigenous languages and/or African languages acquired or learned Spanish after a few decades of intermingling with active Spanish speakers. In sum, the demographic and language data point to diverse linguistic trends coming from Spain and their uses in the new lands.

1.12 Theories on the origins of New World Spanish

Andalusia and the 'problem' of *andalucismo* in the New World were zealously addressed during the first half of the 20th century. (1) Proponents of the monogenetic theory claimed that New World Spanish was a direct descendant of Andalusian, the southern peninsular variety; (2) the polygenetic theory maintained that New World Spanish and Andalusian had undergone independent processes of evolution and that they were not necessarily correlative. The German philologist Max L. Wagner, advocate of the first position, provoked interesting reactions and replies (1920/1924). For several decades, P. Henríquez Ureña (1884-1946), the advocate of the second position, refuted the monogenetic theory with the data available to him at the time, but admitted that New World *andalucismo* prevailed along the coastal lands, and considered that Andalusian traits resulted from an analogous independent development and not necessarily from an influence from southern Spain. Finally, he discussed the non-existence of Spanish-based creoles in the New World (except for Papiamento), and the geographic distribution of following features: (1) Weakening of intervocalic and final /d/; (2) Velarization of /b/ before the diphthong *–ue*; (3) merger of /y/ and /λ/ (*yeísmo*); (4) realization of /x/ as /h/; (5) velarization of final /n/; (6) fricativization of /rr/ and /r/; (7) lateralization, aspiration, deletion and/or vocalization of pre-consonantal /r/; (8) various points of articulation of /s/ (apico-alveolar, dorso-alveolar, coronal); (9) weakening and stratification of final /-s/, which is regularly aspirated and deleted in the lower classes and consciously maintained among individuals of the upper strata; (10) convergence of sibilants or *seseo*; (11) widespread *seseo* and non-existence of *ceceo*; (12) the use of *vos* as singular familiar pronoun of address that is in some countries more intimate than *tú* and a substitute of the more general informal pronoun. This feature (known as *voseo*), originating in Spain, has survived with variations in the New World (see Hidalgo 2001a).

In addition, P. Henríquez Ureña should be given credit for introducing the topic of immigration and demography by looking into the ship logs of the Archivo de Indias (1509-1533) in Seville, where he calculated the proportion of passangers of each peninsular region. His data showed that 43.7 percent of the settlers were from northern Spain and 42.9 percent from southern Spain, while the rest were coming from other provinces. Taking into consideration the comparable estimates, he classified peninsular regions according to absence or presence of *seseo*, and where such trait exists, he distinguished areas according to aspiration or non-aspiration of final /-s/. The results showed that settlers from regions that distinguished /s/ and /θ/ comprised slightly more than one-half of the total, whereas those that were *seseantes* constituted about less than half. The polygenetic or *anti-andalucista* theory was supported by A. Alonso (1961/1953), who added linguistic data to the existing demographic data. Alonso asserted that several traits attributed to New World Spanish are not linked to *andaluz*, to wit: *seseo, yeísmo*, and neutralization of /-r/ and /-l/. In his view, the identical phenomena in Spain and in the New World, especially with respect to *seseo*, was the result of leveling, a process by which speakers of diverse peninsular dialects gradually eliminated traits of their original provinces in search of linguistic homogeneity and accommodation to life in the New World. Such process of accommodation originated in the desires to belong to a more encompassing group, since Spanish immigrants were relinquishing their former provincial identities while embracing a new one.

1.13 Koines and koineization in New World Spanish

A third explicative model on the origins of New World Spanish puts in bold relief the notion of koines and koineization. The first Spanish linguist who referred to New World Spanish as a koine was R. Lapesa (1956), who was followed by D. Catalán (1956-1957) and P. Boyd-Bowman (1964). The resulting compromise has added the notion of a New World Spanish leveled and adjusted variety to New World conditions but concentrated—although not static—in the Caribbean region. Despite the fact that the Andalusian quantitative weight superseded all the provinces in the total number of immigrants, the region that contributed with the largest number of officials and administrators was Old Castile. The challenge for the disciples of koineization is to identify the features of dialects in contact and the processes that lead to the formation of the resulting dialect or koine. The spread of the southern pronunciation was completed when the New World Spanish-speaking communities were settled and had developed their own lifestyle, while at the same time remained connected to important metropolitan cities such as Seville and Cadiz, centers of intense commercial activities. The distribution of the features listed below varies by region but the basic 16th century layer of New World Spanish is the common speech of peninsular speakers and also a particular predominant (and simplified) dialect: *andaluz* from Seville. Common variants along the tri-continental coastal areas in Spain, the New World, and Africa (i.e. Canary Islands) are the following:

(1) *Seseo* or merger of voiced and voiceless, fricative and affricate, and apical and dental sibilants resulting in the use of one single dental voiceless sibilant /s/. In contrast, Castilian distinguished apical /ś/ from /θ/ and maintained the apical sibilant in the environments where Andalusian had replaced it with non-apical sibilants (see Map 1.3).

(2) *Yeísmo* or merger of voiced palatal, one central /y/ and one lateral /λ/ favoring the central palatal in most regions of the New World. In contrast, with few exceptions Castilian distinguished /y/ from /λ/.

(3) Aspiration and deletion of final /-s/ in implosive and final position, as in *los papeles* > [*loh papeleh*] or [*loh papele*]. In contrast, with few exceptions Castilian did not aspirate or delete /-s/ in any position.

(4) Neutralization of pre-consonantal /r/ and /l/ (as in *arma* > *alma*; *puerta* > *puelta*). In contrast, Castilian maintained the difference between both consonants.
(5) Aspiration of [h] (< initial Latin [f], as in FŪMUS > [*humo*] or [*jumo*]. Aspiration might also appear before the diphthong /we/ and /wi/ as in *fuerte* > [*huerte*]; *fui* > [*hui*]. Castilian restored the silent [h] while Andalusian was aspirating it for a long time.
(6) Weakening of intervocalic and/or final /d/ (as in *pescado* > [*pescao*] *bondad* > [*bonda*]). Both Castilian and Andalusian tend to weaken final /d/ but the frequencies are higher in Andalusian, which in combination with all the above-mentioned traits makes Andalusian salient.

It is assumed that koineization is a contact-induced process that leads to quite rapid and occasionally dramatic change. Through koineization, new varieties of a language are brought about as a result of contact between speakers of mutually intelligible varieties. Koineization occurs in new settlements to which people have migrated from different parts of a single language area. Dialect contact, and with it koineization, is one of the main external causes of language change. The term "external" refers to social factors such as migration, which can reasonably be expected to promote change. In contrast, "internal" factors have to do with aspects of the structure of a particular language (its phonology and its grammar) which, perhaps due to structural imbalances, are predisposed to change. Koineization can take place relatively swiftly—though probably more gradually than pidginization (Kerswill 2006: 669).

Following the assumptions presented herein, it is convenient to proceed to the analysis of extant subsamples of language data for they may contribute to the chronological reconstruction of New World Spanish. In the early stages, the northern-central features were used in writing as attested in the documents of the 16th century. Those Spanish speakers who had proclivity for reading and writing contributed to shaping an semi-formal standard that stemmed from the system of social stratification, since the variety of Spanish spoken and written by those belonging to the privileged group turned into a relatively fluid linguistic model closely associated with the reputation and power of the monolingual Spanish-speaking elite. The concept of a superposed model is based on the respectable variety of *toledano-castellano*, used primarily in the Mexican Central Highlands in restricted domains (courts of appeal or *audiencias*, universities, church). Such variety alternated in a diglossic relationship with the New World Spanish koine spoken and to a lesser degree written over the entire continent by those belonging to the lower social strata, which was made up of both subaltern Spanish speakers and second language learners (indigenous groups and speakers of African languages).

Once established in the new colony, the first generation of Spanish speakers born in Spain and the first generation of Spanish speakers born in New Spain formed a compact group who had countless reasons to profess solidarity and loyalty to one another and to manifest their willingness to accommodate to the new conditions imposed by both the metropolitan projects and the New World environment. Not only were Spanish speakers very far from the native land, but were quantitatively a minority vis-à-vis the large indigenous groups. Spanish speakers counted on peninsular dialects from various regions but *toledano* and *castellano* or *toledano-castellano* were accessible to a group of educated speakers who were able to distinguish in writing the pairs of voiced from voiceless sibilants, the fricative from affricate sibilants, distinctions made in medieval Spanish. There is evidence that this variety was used in New Spain (see Chapter 3).

1.14 The use of dialect features in New Spain

Toledano and Old Castilian did not aspirate sibilant /s/ in implosive position but maintained distinctions that had been lost in Andalusian. While Andalusian had gone too far in the simplification process, Spanish speakers settled in the New World colonies found more than sufficient variants to choose among those that were perceived as being the most appropriate through the process of accommodation. The explanation of linguistic adoption lies in multiple causes (both external and internal): the system of social stratification stands in itself as an independent factor impinging on the perceived prestige of at least a number of select features. Despite the quantity and distribution of speakers (past and present) all over the Spanish-speaking world, final /s/ has not disappeared from the vast majority of spoken registers (formal and informal), but it is stratified in those regions and among those speakers who consciously or not select variants of variable (s), as for example, sibilant [s], aspirated [h] or deleted [Ø]. The first generation of Spanish speakers living in the New World used more, and more frequently, their respective varieties of Spanish for informal communication, which was a primary necessity. The second generation was made up of offspring of Spanish speakers born in New Spain, but also of more recent newcomers from Spain, and children of mixed marriages. The third and subsequent generations were similar to the second one until the first one aged and disappeared.

It is clear that Spanish speakers coming directly from Spain had had the transatlantic experience and many of them had had trans-regional contact while those born in the New World did not necessarily had (re)contact with Spain.

Therefore, the second and third generations of the 16th century were responsible for adopting the features of the different varieties available to the second and subsequent generations. Their choices were determined by both socio-demographics and socio-cultural and political prestige. Assuming that the first generation of adult Spanish-speaking males used Andalusian, *toledano-castellano*, or features representative of additional dialects, the process of accommodation was more intense amongst speakers of the second and third generations. The second and third generations may have been more inclined to adopt *seseo* not only because it had been in vogue in southern Spain but because it had become prestigious in the city of Seville. These external influences must have been crucial in the adoption of *seseo*, but the internal factors may have to do with the loss of pertinent features such as affrication and voicing. With respect to aspiration or deletion of final /s/ and the full-fledged pronunciation, some speakers adopted the full pronunciation of different available variants with preference for the dental articulation which was more prevalent than the apical articulation. Those with higher levels of formal education chose the variants that were the closest to the written norms (pronunciation of final and intervocalic /d/, pronunciation of vibrant or flap /r/ and rejection of the lateral /l/). In Mexico, there were sufficient speakers of Castilian, who in the newer spheres of colonial society, were empowered as miners, *encomenderos*, merchants, educators, inquisitors, and religious leaders. Spanish speakers who were not from Castile or from Castilianized regions and were, in addition, striving to occupy posts of power and prestige most likely accommodated their speech patterns to the norms of Old Castilian or the transitional variety utilized in the 16th century in the domains that were perceived as being formal or that were created in order to convey a discourse of formality.

It is likely that along the coastal areas the traits of the tri-continental koine were more frequently available. Thus, if there was aspiration of /s/ in implosive or absolute final position in the early stages of koineization, sibilant [s] was restored at least in some speech registers during the stage of diversification or even later when standardization reached more individuals and groups of individuals. It is not easy to validate this hypothesis because the existing documents were written by literate individuals who more or less followed the norms of the time. Against the scarcity of documents belonging to semi-literate individuals, the diversity of manuscripts compiled by Company Company (1994) and Melis et al. (2008) is useful to refine the proposals advanced in this chapter. (For detailed discussions, see Chapter 3).

1.15 Conclusions

The point of departure in the history of New World Spanish is the series of changes that occurred in peninsular Spanish following the Reconquista. The phonetic mergers observed in both Castilian and southern Spanish may have been accelerated as a result of repopulation movements, weakening of ancestral ties, and the emergence of newer communities with different attitudes and values. The series of consonantal mergers which took place in Castile may be interpreted in the light of structural principles, for they pinpoint a case of neutralization of oppositions leading to systematic simplification. The mergers were going to occur anyway given the prolonged interaction of external factors and latent internal changes in peninsular soil.

This chapter has also explored the most important differences between the traditional varieties of peninsular Spanish (*toledano* and Old Castilian) and the origins of Castilian and Andalusian, the latter being a descendant of the former. It has repeatedly mentioned those features of Andalusian which were transferred to the New World Spanish coastal regions; it has also provided demographic data on immigration from Spain to the New World in general and Mexico in particular highlighting new interpretations such as the demographic balance of Spanish speakers from northern and southern Spain. Finally, it has discussed the three most popular theories on the origins of New World Spanish, to wit: monogenetic, polygenetic and koineization. Far from discarding old theories in lieu of new ones, this chapter reaffirms the appropriateness of theories and data that have to be reckoned with in order to explain the origins of New World Spanish. While the theory of koineization is fully valuable to account for the origins of New World Spanish, consideration to both internal and external factors are deemed necessary to elucidate the operational definitions of newer developments (stratification, popularization and creolization or lack of creolization). These definitions may be all-encompassing and aid in further clarification of New World Spanish phenomena, whose chronological stages may overlap in significant ways.

In order to explain sociolinguistic occurrences at all speech levels (and even literature), the notion of diversification is in the long term the aggregate needed to describe the growth, spread, expansion and dissemination of New World Spanish and its variations according to location, attitudes, demographic trends, and some other variables. Spanish was not only spoken as a primitive koine but was stratified and popularized among speakers of diverse backgrounds and also across (newer) emerging domains. It was spoken by native speakers and individuals of non-Spanish speaking origin (indigenous, Afro-Hispanic, and all those who were roaming around the new territories that belonged to Spain). The koine was not fully standardized as transplanted from Spain because it was used in a diglossic relationship with a semi-standardized variety; the latter was written by the first and subsequent generations of immigrants who composed thousands of pieces of manuscripts of different genres. The municipal council of Mexico City, the secretaries of the Santo Officio, common letter writers, and many others had ample opportunities to use Spanish in writing. Finally, New Spanish speakers were fond of literature both as amateurs and professionals. All these uses confirm that the transplanted language had all the necessary conditions to be spread and diversified.

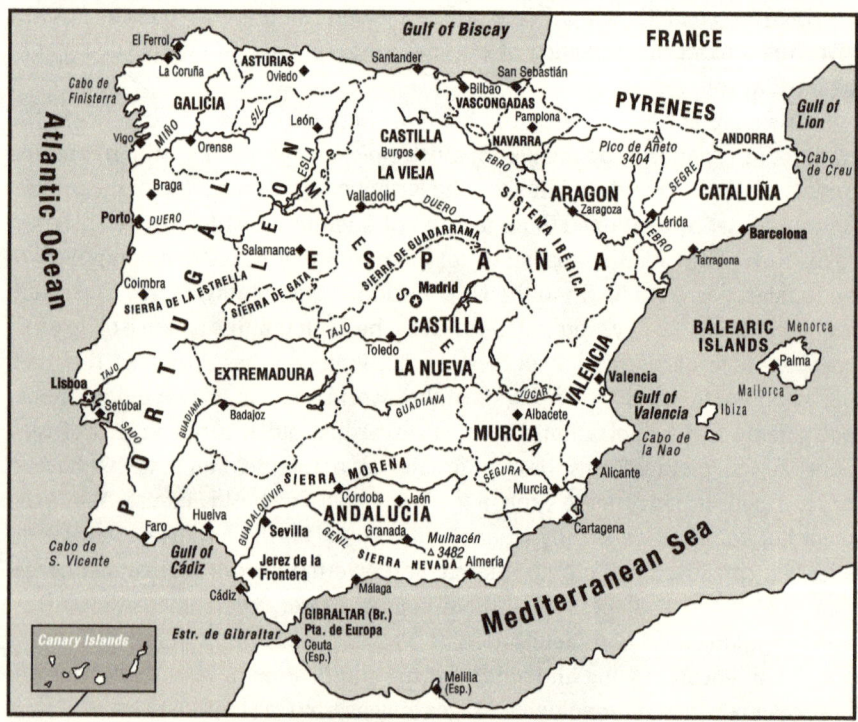

Map 1.1: Spain: Regions, cities, mountains and rivers

1.15 Conclusions — 67

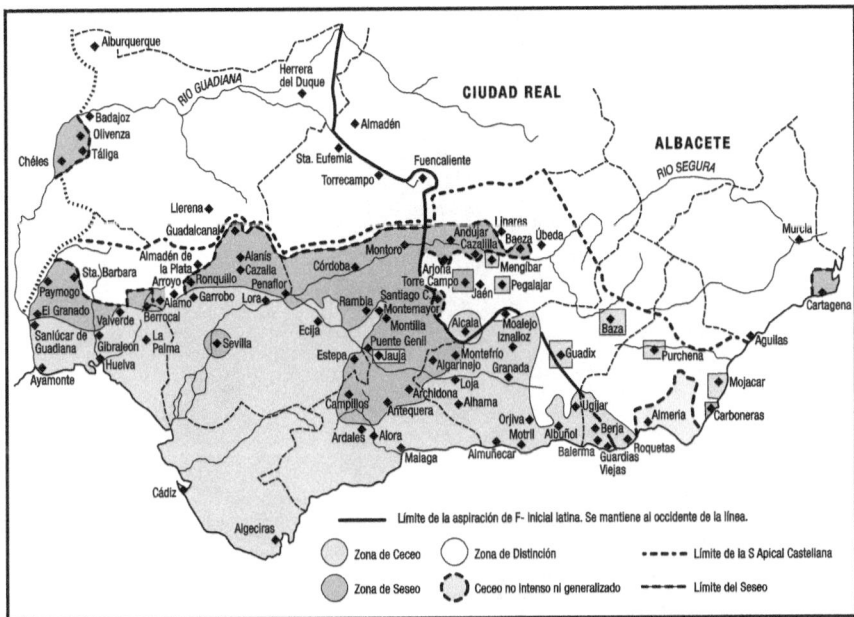

Map 1.2: Boundaries of pronunciation in Andalusian. Source: Adapted from Zamora (1967: Map XXI)

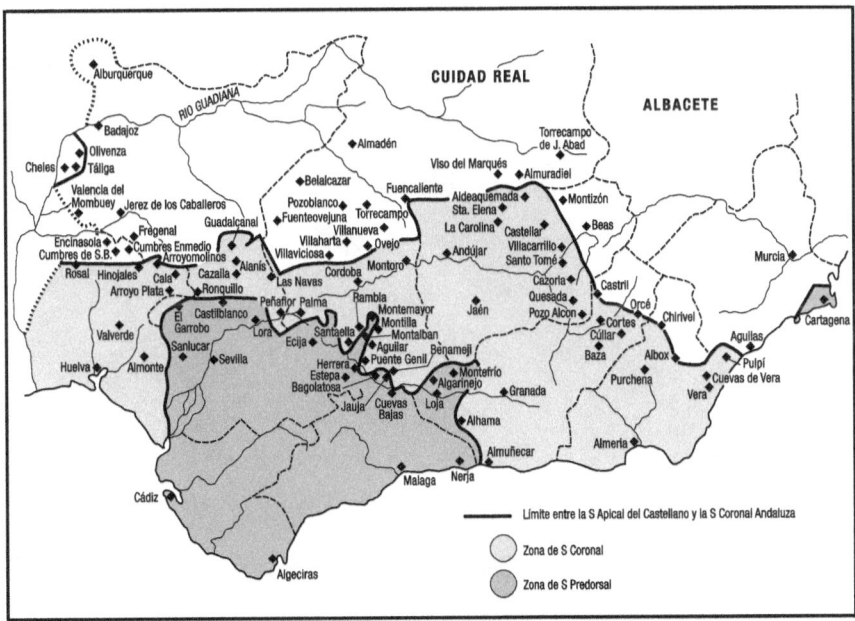

Map 1.3: Variants of /s/ in Southern Spain Source: Adapted from Zamora (1967: Map XX)

68 — Chapter 1 The origins of Spanish: Spain and the New World

Map 1.4: Pronunciation of /s/ and /z/ in the Province of Seville Source: Navarro Tomás et al. (1933/1975: 36)

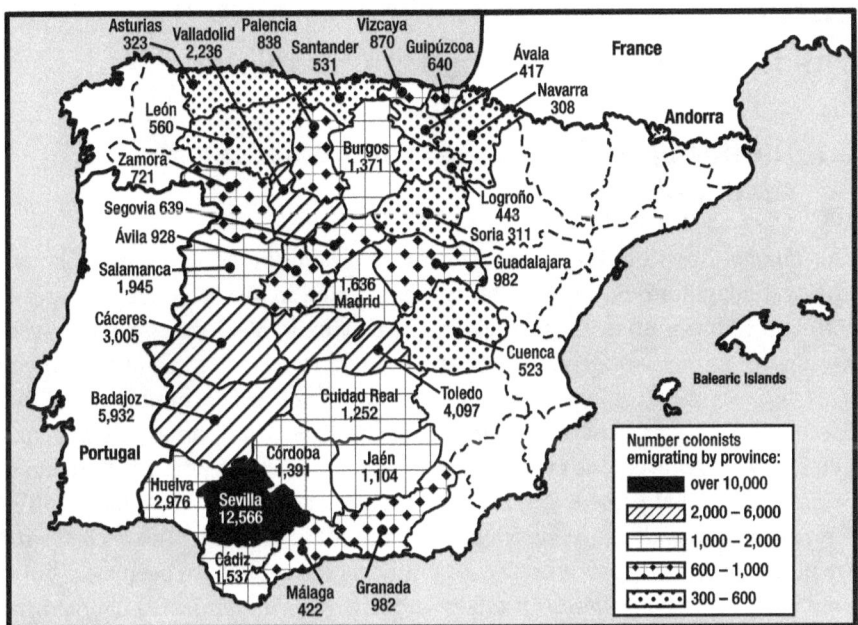

Map 1.5: Spanish emigration to America: 1493–1600. Source: Adapted from Boyd-Bowman (1976: 590)

Chapter 2
The first speakers of Mexican Spanish

2.1 The first Spanish speakers in Mesoamerica and social stratification

This chapter describes the external factors that contributed to the transplantation and adaptation of the Spanish speakers living in Mesoamerica during the 16th and 17th centuries. Spanish explorers arriving in Mexico had a short-lived experience in the Caribbean islands and brought to Mexico some of their practices and recently acquired knowledge of that region; this encounter armed the Spaniards with sufficient understanding of the New World, an experience that helped them to prevent the mistakes they had made in that region. The Caribbean contact is useful at present to grasp the functions of the most important institution, the *encomienda*, and the activities and attitudes about it. The *encomienda* era also explains the formation of new gentry, which could have been more powerful had the *encomenderos* (grantees or trustees of Indian labor) counted on the full support of the Spanish Crown. Nevertheless the woes that betided the early Spanish speakers jeopardized their intentions to enslave permanently the native population. The ambiguous position toward the indigenous, protected by the Christian mission and exploited by the prevailing forces, led to a process of acculturation that turned into a process of gradual assimilation. The opposition to slavery narrowed the social distance between Spanish speakers and speakers of indigenous languages and prevented the formation of socio-ethnic dialects with glaring features of indigenous languages.

This chapter also explores the roles that some of most important institutions played in the transmission of oral Spanish in the environment that ensued after the fall of Tenochtitlan. The significance of this analysis is not redundant given that to date, most scholars have dealt abundantly with the preservation of Mexican indigenous languages, primarily Nahuatl, and some others of central and southern Mexico. Those Spanish speakers who explored the islands were first exposed to Taino, which was appropriated after only two decades of contact. The second Amerindian language known to Spanish explorers was Nahuatl while some others were at least distinguished in the early stages of Discovery. Taino and Nahuatl are however the two languages that directly influenced proto-Mexican Spanish. In addition to Spanish speakers and speakers of indigenous languages, the newer Mesoamerican area received speakers of other European languages as well as speakers of African languages; this unsuspected diversity was ideal for the formation of proto-Mexican Spanish, which was used mostly for daily interaction between Spanish speakers in informal domains. By the time of the colonization of New Spain, Spanish had more than sufficient regional and social variations that were used in the intermingling between Spanish speakers belonging to the first and second generation of immigrants. The interaction of Spanish speakers from diverse peninsular regions and sociocultural strata and occupations led to a process of koineization followed by popularization or vernacularization.

The diffusion of oral Spanish by agents representing the Spanish officialdom is as significant as the (re)transmission at the informal spheres of interaction and intra-familiar domains. Spanish speakers very soon formed a compact group of close-knit networks identified by language, religion, and other norms of societal interaction. Religion was a major component intervening in the identification of socio-ethnic stratification. The semi-formal variety of Spanish used in the Mesoamerican area followed to an extent the prevailing norms of educated or semi-educated Spanish speakers in the domains of religion, education and government. The active agents of (re)transmission were the Spanish speakers empowered by the *encomienda*, the municipal councils, the Inquisition, and the Church, among others. Acts of identity proclaimed in public celebrations and activities conducive to the process of socialization proved to be effective forces of transmission and solidarity amongst Spanish speakers, who were always the minority. While the information on the quantities of Spanish immigrants is not entirely reliable, this chapter illustrates how the qualitative functions of Spanish grew first in informal domains and later in formal domains.

2.2 The Spanish Caribbean experiment

Mexico's conquest and colonization was preceded by the discovery of the Antilles. Spanish explorers were in Hispaniola (present-day Santo Domingo), Puerto Rico and Cuba (mostly Spanish-speaking countries at present) before they reached Mexico. There they clashed with the natives, who were speakers of Taino. All of the men who participated in the conquest of Mexico had been on those islands for different periods of time. Cortés' expedition departed from Santiago de Cuba on July 1519 (see Map 3. 1). Encouraged by the Spanish Crown, the early Spanish explorers had established the *encomienda* system (from the verb "*encomendar*" 'to trust' or 'to commend'), which apparently was legitimized by the *Leyes de Burgos*, promulgated on December 27, 1512 in Burgos, Spain. This was the first codified set of laws governing the behavior of Spanish colonists in the New World particularly in reference to native Indians. These procedures enumerated the regulations for the government of the indigenous peoples, forbade the maltreatment of natives, and endorsed their conversion to Catholicism, albeit they were never truly enforced. Despite the heated debates over the *encomienda*, the Spaniards in charge of the islands succeeded in retaining rights to exploit the land shares and the peoples who were living there. In the Antillean period, Indians were delivered for service in haciendas, mines and farms. The *encomendero* receiving the cacique and his group of Indians had permission to take them to the mines and farming lands. In Hispaniola there were 715 *repartimientos* (sites for labor draft) with 22,344 Indians for service (Zavala 1944: 112, 118). The *encomienda* had the support of the royal powers to enslave the native population from the time of the discovery of the New World through the mid-16th century (cf. Simpson 1929). The difference between the slave trade pioneered by the Portuguese and the experiments of the *encomenderos* resided in the manner in which human traffic was administered. Slaves were carried back and forth from territory to territory, while the indigenous populations remained mostly in their own environment, notwithstanding major disruptions to their autochthonous way of life.

A component of the Iberian identity, the *encomienda* was more than a pragmatic solution for economic and government development, an institution that gave order to social status and religious zeal since it effectively focused the energy of the crusading impulse and encouraged the Spanish Crown's desire for power. For those who participated in battles against non-Christian peoples, the *encomienda* was the replication of familiarity with Iberian socio-cultural structures, where wealth, power and success were not symbolic but real. It was a key element in the conquest and transplantation of the Spanish civilization. In Extremadura and Andalusia, the *encomienda* was a common practice. Therefore, for Hernán Cortés and his men, such form of organization served manifold purposes: it recreated something of the existence they had known in their homelands and exploited the resources of the conquered land. While details differed depending upon geography and location, the shared characteristics between the Iberian and the American *encomienda*, i.e. tribute extraction, population and labor administration, military organization and religious indoctrination, are indicative of continuity with the traditions of the Reconquista. The *encomienda* stands out in the process of transplantation of the Iberian civilization in the New World, because it facilitated the shift from governments of military occupation to governments of Hapsburg bureaucracy; the *encomienda* developed the labor and resources of the native populations into the wealth of the Spanish Empire and brought order and structure to the Spanish evangelical effort. In sum, because the *encomienda* was the only legally defined space where natives and Spaniards could interact, it turned into the primary institution of the conquest era (Lemon 2000: 25, 38-39, 51-52).

2.3 The *encomienda* in New Spain

In his overview of the *encomienda*, Simpson introduced the notion of transplantation of institutions and social habits into the New World (Simpson 1950: vii-viii). Known as acculturation, this process consisted in bringing the Christian faith to non-Christian natives. Spain had been accustomed to having contact with various peoples such as the Moors, who invaded them and attempted to convert them to the faith of Islam. For all the above reasons, Spanish people learned to live in a social system that was erected upon the privileges of conquest. This feudal system was based on a relationship of control and subjugation whereby the conqueror would levy a tribute or a feudal due on his vassals. This scheme would make the conqueror the sole protector of the ones which he conquered and would also make those he conquered serve him. In the Mesoamerican scenario peoples had already developed a stable economy based on corn and had learned to adjust their lifestyles around the production and harvesting of the crop. Indians at first were also supposed to be paid and supplied with the sustenance to live on. There was even a time period when the Crown of Spain encouraged the Indians and the Spanish to intermarry so they could help to promote this assimilation process (Simpson 1950: 10). The history and juridical basis of the *encomienda* is found in Zavala (1935: 104 and 1971), who sees a close relationship between maintaining this system and the survival of Spaniards in Mesoamerica, which was also equivalent to maintaining the Catholic faith. Services in mines were needed as tribute due to the silver boom in New Spain. The Spanish settlers founded dozens of towns where they also received tribute in form of corn and wheat. The *encomienda* gradually disappeared and became extinct in the early 1700's (Zavala 1935: 310, 339).

The underlying goals contributed to the establishment of a large and cheap labor supply for Spanish settlers. Not only did the Crown try to prevent the mistreatment of the Indians but others came into the forefront and protested against the abuse. Bishop Bartolomé de las Casas (1474-1566) was one of the main advocates for the suppression of the *encomiendas*, a tenacious humanist who sought the Indians' relief and liberation. In Cuba, las Casas had had an *encomienda* of his own and knew from direct experience that such system succeeded in exploitation more than in acculturation, given that a large number of Indians were dying as a result of the arduous conditions imposed on them. He witnessed the abuses of the *encomenderos* against the native peoples in diverse areas of the New World and fought zealously as an advocate of indigenous rights. His strengths and weaknesses were seen in his inability to change his opinions on issues such as the sins of the *encomienda*. Las Casas was so determined to show the abuses of the *encomenderos* that even after the *encomienda* had been reduced from a thin disguise for slavery into something like a social system, he was still attacking it as if nothing had changed (Simpson 1950: 37). The Spanish Crown was opportunely informed of the new environmental conditions brought about to the natives of the islands and the clashes between explorers and natives. By the time new expeditions were launched to Mexico, it was well known that the Caribbean experiment had been an ecological and human disaster. Cortés was convinced that what had happened on the islands could be prevented in the newly discovered areas of Mesoamerica. What is known today about the explorations of the Caribbean and Mesoamerica derives from the reports that Hernán Cortés himself wrote to the kings of Spain in his *Cartas de Relación* (cf. Cortés 1520/2007).

2.4 The new system of social stratification

The most influential settlers became *encomenderos* and were the principal miners and commercial agriculturalists. Labor, mines, supply and all other activities related to the *encomienda* were headquartered in the nearest Spanish city. Active participants in the conquest of Mexico were rewarded with *encomiendas*, a grant to a Spaniard of the Indians of an indigenous polity, who were to provide the *encomendero* tribute in the form of commodities and service in return for protection and religious instruction, which was normally neglected. Land was not a formal component but the grantee often acquired separate grants of land. Hernán Cortés made the initial assignment and was succeeded by various governors, the *Real Audiencia* (Royal Tribunal), and the viceroy. The municipality in New Spain reflected urban-centered modes of organization where each city dominated a surrounding area while serving as the center for all economic, social, political and ecclesiastical activities. The political body representing the new Spanish city was the *cabildo* (municipal council) administered in the early years by *encomendero* families; the cabildo had jurisdiction over the reassignment of *solares* (urban house lots), *huertas* (suburban tracts for orchards, vineyards, and vegetable gardens), *estancias* and *caballerías* (rural tracts for raising horses, cattle, sheep, pigs, or the cultivation of cereal crops). In turn, the *cabildo* licensed all business and artisan activities, and let contracts for municipal services: *cabildo* officials included *regidores* (councilmen), *alcaldes* (magistrates), *alguaciles* (constables), the *alcaide* (jail warden), *procuradores* (legal representatives), the *escribano* (city clerk), the *pregonero* (town crier), and the *portero* (doorman). The *encomenderos* of New Spain and the officials who granted *encomiendas* paid great attention to distinctions based on time of arrival in New Spain. The basic division between "conqueror" and "settler" distinguished between those who arrived before or after the establishment of the first Audiencia in Mexico City in 1528, a year that marks the end of the conquest period. Conquerors were present at the fall of Tenochtitlan in 1521 or had arrived shortly after the siege and took part in subsequent actions before 1528. In contrast, those arriving after the first Audiencia were merely *pobladores* (settlers), even though many of them earned a claim to an *encomienda* through *entrada* (entrance into a city) service in Oaxaca, Michoacan, and Jalisco (Himmerich 1991: 4-6).

Four rankings have been identified according to the merits of the Spanish protagonists in the conquest and colonization of Mexico: (a) First conquerors were members of the original Cortés *entrada* that passed muster at Cozumel and again at the founding of Veracruz. Almost 400 are identified as such with some degree of authenticity; one-half of those might have survived, and only 133 became *encomenderos*. (b) Conquerors were members of subsequent *entradas* and individual shiploads of reinforcements who arrived in New Spain in time to take part in the siege and capture of Tenochtitlan. The largest group sailed from Cuba under Pánfilo de Narváez; the survivors probably ranged from 400 to 600; of these some 300 have been correctly identified, and of this number, 178 became *encomenderos*. (c) *Poblador antiguo* (old settler) was a resident of the Indies prior to the capture of Tenochtitlan who moved to New Spain thereafter but within the first decade after 1521. Thirty-two of them must have received *encomiendas*. (d) *Poblador* (settler) was the person who arrived in New Spain after the capture of Tenochtitlan, but who had no previous residence in the Indies. Of the thousands who arrived in the second quarter of the century, only 158 became *encomenderos*; some by entrada service; others by purchase, still others by virtue of social status, but the majority by marrying an *encomendera* or lady trustee (Himmerich 1991: 6-7).

2.5 Origins of the first Spanish speakers

The *encomenderos* were mostly Spanish speakers who perpetuated themselves ten years after they took over Mexico City, where they itemized their wealth consisting of mineral deposits, agricultural products, and Indian tribute. The consolidation of the New Empire was possible thanks to arranged marriages and family representation in the local government (Himmerich 1991: 71, 73). Some of the most celebrated *encomenderos* were: Jerónimo de Aguilar (Cortés' loyal interpreter); Pedro de Alvarado (his lieutenant); Alonso García Bravo (the architect planner of Mexico City); Bernal Díaz del Castillo (Cortes' loyal soldier and author of the *Verdadera historia de la conquista de la Nueva España*); Juan Jaramillo de Salvatierra (prominent soldier married to Doña Marina or Malinche); Francisco de Montejo (founder of Merida, Yucatan); Juan de Villaseñor y Orozco (sixth great-grandfather of Miguel Hidalgo y Costilla, leader of Mexican Independence); Francisco

Vázquez de Coronado (the explorer who trekked nearly 5000 miles through Northwestern Mexico and the U.S. Southwest); Cristóbal Pérez de Oñate (founder of the mining town of Zacatecas and brother of Juan de Oñate). The latter led the entry to New Mexico in 1598; Hernán Cortés himself, among many others. Two women descending from emperor Moctezuma were also granted *encomiendas*, Doña Isabel and Doña Leonor, his daughters. Many young males working with Cortés were members of the same family, for example, the three brothers, Gonzalo, Jorge and Pedro de Alvarado had been together in Cuba and Santo Domingo. Some of the well-known family names that made history in the *encomienda* system were the Ávila brothers (Alonso, Francisco, Gaspar, Juan and Luis) and the Gallegos brothers (Álvaro, Gonzalo and Juan). The Gómez family came with Gonzalo Gómez, who was only 12 years old. The López, Maldonado, Ruiz, de la Torre, Villanueva, and many other brothers arrived together to explore the islands. They were indeed from different social strata, but the *encomenderos* had something in common: they had been with Hernán Cortés at the bloody battles of the conquest of Mexico or had arrived from Spain shortly after because of their privileged status. Many of them knew how to read and write, as attested in their own chronicles.

The total number of *encomenderos* amounts to 506; of those, almost 300 had been living in or exploring the Caribbean islands before they embarked themselves in the adventure that led to the discovery of Mexico (Himmerich 1991: 71, 73, passim). Their regional origin reflects the provenance of Spanish immigrants in the 16th century with those from Andalusia, Extremadura, New Castile and Old Castile representing slightly more than one-half of the total and the rest coming from other regions. The four groups of *encomenderos* (Columns 3, 4, 5 and 6) coming from the abovementioned regions comprise more than one-half of the total or 311 (see Table 2.1).

Table 2.1: Origins and numbers of the encomenderos of New Spain

Provinces	Indians	First conqueror	Conqueror	Old settler	Settler	Total
Andalusia		39	42	9	38	128
Extremadura		24	20	8	27	79
New Castile		6	9	4	15	34
Old Castile		16	30	8	16	70
Leon		13	11	--	17	41
Biscay		6	6	--	2	14
Other Spain		8	14	--	12	34
Foreign countries		6	9	2	2	19
Unknown origin		17	37	1	29	87
Totals	3	135	178	32	158	506

Source: Himmerich (1991: 21)

The *encomienda* was for a time a master institution, the source of great wealth and power, the centerpiece of Spanish urban life, and the only military force in New Spain. Its basic nature in any given area was determined by the needs, numbers, the expectations of local Spaniards and the profile of indigenous groups. With the exception of the *pobladores* coming directly from Spain, the *encomenderos* of New Spain were familiar with the Antillean *encomienda*. Those who took part in the Conquest of New Spain were fully aware of the prolonged deliberations concerning the institution, with their own struggle to retain it and the Crown's desire to abolish it. Other colonists conceived it as an opportunity to obtain upward mobility. Hernán Cortés' (re)assignment of *encomiendas* provoked reactions and charges of favoritism; the assignees were delighted to receive tribute in kind (which was a well-established indigenous tradition) and various goods and commodities. In the lands of Mexico, severe population losses ensued and almost destroyed the availability of units sustaining the *encomiendas* (Himmerich 1991: 11-13). Between 1524 and 1526, Hernán Cortés assigned *encomiendas* to his allies while he struggled to maintain his own. He nearly lost Texcoco to royal officials, and in 1528, his enemies proceeded rapidly to usurp his holdings. In 1529 Cortés received title to a large number of towns with 23,000 Indian vassals while other royal orders made him a Marquis and granted him jurisdiction in his *marquesado* (Gibson 1964: 60).

The occupations and professions of the *encomenderos* were varied: Men of arms (*hidalgos*), notaries, medical practitioners, accountants, artisans, mariners, miners, interpreters and merchants made up one-third of the *encomenderos* representing a broad selection ranging from the middle and upper echelons to semi-skilled, unskilled and unspecified occupations but sufficiently diverse to mirror their original societal organization. With respect to residence, the pattern of the newcomers was to prefer to live in or around the Great Tenochtitlan (or Mexico City), which became the initial focus of all Spanish activity. The *encomiendas* were normally concentrated within 75 miles of Spanish settlements. The proximity of about one-half of the *encomiendas* to Mexico City reinforced the city's position as the hub of all Spanish activity. The *encomiendas* were often retained by the family—whether in Spain or in New Spain, although more than half were inherited by a son and more than a quarter by widows. The first and second generation of *encomenderos* arranged marriages for their daughters, widows, and nieces, who were the preferred brides-to-be of the region. At times, the *encomiendas* could also be reverted to the Spanish Crown (Himmerich 1991: 34, 75, 102). A total of 46 *encomiendas* with the corresponding number of Indian towns were recorded in the Valley of Mexico between 1531 and 1702. The largest *encomiendas* ca.1560 were located in Texcoco with a total of tributaries at 16,015; Chalco with 14,842; Tenochtitlan with 12,971; and Xochimilco with 10,583. The remaining 32 *encomiendas'* tributaries ranged from 220 to 8,665 whereas the total number of tributaries for those years was 109,980 (Gibson 1964: 64).

The *encomienda* system used different methods to collect tribute. The first one made the tribute payable directly to local recipients, and the second to the imperial *calpixque* or tax collector. The first generation of *encomenderos* maintained a good relationship with cooperative caciques (chieftain or lord) but the latter protested when the survivors of Indian nobility engaged in legal disputes with the former. Indigenous leaders who wanted to defend portions of their *encomienda* had to learn the ropes of the new legal system. Each *encomendero* negotiated with the cacique of the town of his *encomienda* the amount of payable tribute causing in turn the native upper class to make excessive demands on tributaries while delivering only a portion of the yield to the recipient, who added money, wheat and other goods to the native materials. The pressures imposed on the caciques eventually reduced this class, and by the mid-16th century, each tributary was required to pay only with maize, turkey, firewood and some other products. After 1550, the Spanish class in control of New Spain included the legal escheatment of the encomienda to the Crown. Tribute exaction affected the most vulnerable members of the surviving indigenous society and their municipal finances; from the 1550's to 1575 they abandoned the native agriculture. Free blacks and mulattoes became tributaries in 1580 while mestizos remained exempt from tribute payment. While Indian officials were in charge of collecting tribute arrears, new governors were appointed to ensure the payments. After the late 16th century, community tribute debts were personal debts of the governors and members of the *cabildo*. Indian officials unable to pay were jailed and their properties were seized and sold while the proceeds were taken as payment of (inheritable) debts. The annual tribute and the Indians' position as intermediaries and responsible parties in cases of default eventually impoverished Indian officials. Two major developments of the 16th century were the decay of the *encomienda* system tribute and the intensification of Hispanicization of the procedures on liability and payment (Gibson 1964: 195-196; 202-206; 217-219).

2.6 The New Laws of 1542

A major adjustment to the *encomienda* system was triggered by charges of anti-*encomenderos* who had pressured the Spanish Crown to pass the *Leyes Nuevas de 1542* (New Laws of 1542) making a big impact on the Spanish colonies. The New Laws allowed Indians to own property and stipulated that the Catholic Church merely had dominion over the Christians and held no power over the Indians; they also promoted trade with the Indians as long as the Indians were not harmed.

The removal of the Indians from the service of the *encomenderos* aggravated economic problems, and eventually the *encomienda* system was reshaped to make the conditions less harsh on them (Simpson 1950: 135, 152.). The New Laws were the result of conscientious and responsible research and counsel on the part of theologians, jurists and philosophers who advised Emperor Charles V on the inconveniences of Indian slavery (cf. García Añoveros 2000). Indian slavery was legally abolished at a time when the diminution of the indigenous population was glaring. In view of the booming silver economy, Spanish colonists resorted to African slaves so they could work on the mines and sugar plantations. By 1550 slaves were no longer found among the Nahuas; instead there were *tlacotli* or black slaves owned by Spaniards with sufficient resources; the former turned into objects of trade in the colonization process, and permission was given for their import albeit cautiously and in small numbers (Blackburn 1997: 135).

In the early period Friar Bartolomé de las Casas, the author of *Historia de las Indias* (1547/1875/1951) found the enslavement of Africans acceptable. In his famous three-volume masterpiece, las Casas narrates the negotiations taking place in Hispaniola where there were only about a dozen black slaves who belonged to the king of Spain; presumably the sale of those slaves would have freed the Indians from slavery (las Casas 1547/1875/1951, vol. 3: 274). Las Casas could not have imagined that his recommendations would encourage colonists to massively introduce Africans in hard labor. He expressed his disapproval and antipathy over the destructive impact of such practice for their lives were precarious after a year or two of forced labor, and consequently, they were unable to care for their families. Las Casas regretted having being *"inadvertente"* (archaic Spanish for 'inadvertent') because later on he found out that the captivity of blacks was just as bad as the captivity of Indians. His rejection of Indian slavery was inspired by the sermon delivered in 1511 by Friar Antón de Montesinos, who reprimanded the colonists of Hispaniola over the unkind treatment given to the indigenous (cf. Montesinos 1511/1982). The text from *Ecclesiasticus* (chapter 34, vss. 21-22) or the *vox clamantis in deserto* preached against those who used cruelty or tyranny against innocent human beings (las Casas 1547/1875/1951, vol. 2: 441-444). He recalled having warned the *encomenderos* with the following words: "God condemns the goods taken away from the neighbor's living, and he who defrauds the laborer of his hire" (las Casas 1547/1875/1951, vol. 1: 130). Unfortunately, his sermons did little or nothing to discourage the colonists from obtaining permission after permission to import more and more slaves from the mainland simply to provide a labor force. In the early 1500's there were 30,000 African slaves in Hispaniola and about 100,000 in the Indies; to his dismay, the gross amount of black slaves was ineffective in liberating the Indians from the same backbreaking work conditions that victimized Africans slaves (las Casas 1547/1875/1951, vol. 3: 275-276).

Las Casas' hostility towards the colonists was motivated by his viewpoints on egalitarianism though the rate of importation of Africans increased because Indians were unavailable and the colonists had the resources to pay for the former. His advocacy for the indigenous suit well with the royal powers but his retraction on African slavery had no impact on policy (Blackburn 1997: 136). "At the end of his life Las Casas wrote that he bitterly regretted ever having recommended the introduction of more African slaves, and was unsure whether God would forgive him for this" (Blackburn 1997: 136). His renewed perspectives came about after the discovery of Mexico and Peru and were indeed influential during the discussion of the New Laws of 1542. Unfortunately, by then other nations had joined Spain and Portugal in the practice of human contraband due to "economic" needs. In agreement with popular Aristotelian principles, it was accepted that Africans were the only available slaves, and that their fate was inescapable, since they had been born to be enslaved.[3] According to Hanke (1949/2002: 9), throughout the course of the 16th century, Spaniards did not fight as hard or as consistently against black slavery, although Jesuits did work on behalf of the African slaves in the following century.[4]

In Mexico, the Jesuits were in charge of educating and alleviating to an extent the living conditions of the African slaves. In Veracruz, they established orientation classes in Spanish and Catechism for those who were going to be taken to Mexico City. In the capital city and mining sites throughout New Spain there were established confraternities for blacks; two of these are documented in 1569 and 1582. By 1570, Mexico had a black population of 25,000 (including those who were mixed); by 1650, the estimate increased to 30,000 but mulattoes are counted separately at 20,000. When compared to the Antilles as a whole with 400,000 and Brazil with 100,000, these figures are rather low. The blood-mixing phenomenon, occurring after the discovery and colonization of the Spanish/Portuguese New World, has not repeated itself too many times in the history of humanity. With a three-tier ethnic base (indigenous, black and white), the new major groups were formed rather fast and rendered two more groups: white-indigenous, white-black or indigenous black, in addition to all other possible mixtures (Martínez

---

[3] For discussions on the arguments advanced by Bartolomé de las Casas see André Saint-Lu (1968) and (1982).
[4] A partial English version of the New Laws is found in Simpson (1950: 129-132). For historiography and the climate of opinion in Spain at the time, see Hanke (1949/2002) and (Hanke 1959). Discussions on the New Laws of 1542 can be found in Zavala (1984).

1983/1999: 193, 195, 209-211, 213). The clan of founders of Spanish Mexico was nonetheless effective in maintaining unions with surviving members of the indigenous groups who had access to land and other commodities.

2.7 Spanish speakers in the 16th century: numbers and regions

Scholars have been raising questions about the quantity and provenance of the Spanish speakers settled in the New World in general and the Mesoamerican area, in particular. When compared to the Amerindian population of the early 16th century, Europeans living in Mesoamerica constituted an insignificant minority. Demographic reconstructions provide data extracted from various sources. By 1529, ten years after the arrival of Hernán Cortés in Veracruz, Bishop Juan de Zumárraga estimated a population of 8,000 Spaniards, although many of them were temporarily in the area. Other estimates indicate that by 1570 the European population was only between 6,644 and 7,067 (Velasco 1993). To learn about its territories in the New World, Spain commissioned a survey to cosmographers and historians. In 1574, one of the royal mapmakers, Juan López de Velasco, reported that there were 17,711 people of European descent in New Spain, which included children of mixed legitimate marriages (López de Velasco 1894). Scholars assume, however, that in the 16th century the total number of Spanish immigrants to the entire New World might have been between 200,000 and 250,000, but certainly no more than one-quarter of a million Spanish speakers (Martínez Shaw 1994: 15).

2.8 The new environment

The reconstruction of Mexico took place over the ruins of the Aztec Empire and other Mesoamerican landmarks where the joyful Spanish troopers celebrated their victory over the Aztecs and the fall of Tenochtitlan which took place on Tuesday August 13, 1521. Hernán Cortés himself registered his glory in his *Tercera Carta de Relación* delivered to Charles V on May 15, 1522 (Cortés 1523: 51; also in Cortés 1520/2007: 205). Year after year, on *La fiesta del Pendón* (The Procession of the Flag), a parade from the municipal council to the temple outside of the walls of the city, Spanish speakers commemorated their new identity through their participation in animated spectacles, festivities, and games (cf. García Icazbalceta 1898). While every participant had its own role, all of them ended up having a banquet at the home of the *alférez* (standard bearer). Spanish speakers were building a new nation for themselves; this seems to have been the beginning of

Spanish Mexico (cf. Simpson 1950) or the life of the first (Spanish-speaking) Mexicans (cf. Benítez 1953/1985). The Procession of the Flag was institutionalized by Spanish authorities and went on for almost three hundred years (Garrido Asperó 1998: 190; see also Garrido Asperó 2006).

By the mid-16th century the new landscape inspired Francisco Cervantes de Salazar, the author of *Tres Diálogos Latinos* (1554), to describe the new city: the viceroy was occupying the house that had belonged to Moctezuma's father. Along the sidewalk leading to the Plaza Mayor, there could be found many imported craftsmen such as carpenters, locksmiths, barbers, bakers, painters, stonecutters, tailors, chandlers, sword makers, pastry cooks, grocers, leather cutters, cord makers, shoemakers, weavers, hatters, and many others. The first colonial authority had its litigants, business agents, procurement officers, an attorney general, the chief constable, counsels, clerks and soldiers awaiting a contract, or immigrants looking for work. On the city mall, there was the Plaza Mayor, the only group of buildings that had retained its antique character. There they sold Spanish brocades and Flemish damasks, Chinese silk, laces, velvets, plumes for hats, jewelry, ornament, weapons, and furniture, all goods consumed by the new mercantile aristocracy that was building a solid urban tradition with merchants and bureaucrats committed to working for a new system of social stratification. The protagonists of the story were many Spanish speakers who worked in the *Real Audiencia*, hospitals, convents, shops, and markets. The magnificent residences of the *encomenderos* were lined along the *Calle del Reloj* (Clock Street), where Luis de Castilla, the sensational miner, and the Ávilas, Ávalos, Alvarados, Benavides, Estradas, Mendozas, Saavedras and Villafáñezes, the oldest dynasties of *encomenderos*, occupied the aristocratic sector of the city (Benítez 1953/1985: 15, 16, 18, 28).

2.9 The process of socialization and diffusion

The process of socialization began on the ships that transported Spanish immigrants to the New World and continued unabated during three centuries of contact and (re)contact. Moreover, such process enabled Spanish speakers to acquire the skills and habits necessary for participating within their new society, which was formed with shared norms, attitudes, values, motives, social roles, religious beliefs and even knowledge of language(s). Socialization was not only the means by which social and cultural continuity were attained but an important process by which individual views on certain issues, such as race or religion turned out to be perceived as normal within the emerging society. A speech community of Spanish speakers was formed in a few decades, and socialization occurred at many different levels, domains and spheres of interaction where the new protagonists played the roles they chose or those available to them at certain societal junctures. The informal process of socialization among Spaniards, who were like today naturally gregarious, contributed significantly to the dissemination of oral Spanish not only among Spanish speakers but among those who knew little or none. The residents of the most important cities were regularly exposed to public announcement made by criers.

The crier or *pregonero* was an old position assigned to a man in charge of reading the most important news. *Pregoneros* served the Spanish authorities in all the Spanish colonies. Their voices must have been recognized by Spanish and non-Spanish speakers; the *pregoneros'* broadcasts delivered the official news to the crowds at the same time that the Spanish speakers in charge made statements of public power. The following announcement made by Hernán Cortés after his two-year trip to Honduras on June 10, 1526 was extracted from the *Archivo General de Indias, Justicia* 113, 02 (in Lemon 2000: 84-85). A crier read it aloud in the plazas of Mexico:

> Hago saber, asi a todos los moradores de esta ciudad de Mexico, como los de afuera, que el que tuviese indios encomendados o repartimiento por cédulas obtenidas en mi ausencia y expedidas por mis tenientes el tesorero Juan Alonso de Estrada y el contador Rodrigo de Albornoz, los pierda; declarando las dichas cédulas por nulas; y mando (que) posean otra vez los dueños que anteriormente las gosaban en virtud de sus puestos títulos.

> [I make known, to all those who dwell in Mexico City, as well as those outside it, that those who received encomiendas or repartimientos through certificates obtained in my absence from my lieutenants Juan Alonso de Estrada and the accountant Rodrigo de Albornoz, shall lose them. I declare omit the said certificates null, and command that those who held and enjoyed the encomiendas by virtue of their proper titles possess them again.]

Another announcement was made when Hernán Cortés was disputing the local power with one of his fellow *encomenderos*, Marcos de Aguilar. After Cortés commanded the proclamation read publicly, there was a great commotion in the city and everyone thought that Cortés wanted to arrest Marcos de Aguilar and take over the governorship (in Lemon 2000: 92-93).

> Un domingo en la tarde a dos de Setiempre del año de mill e quinientos e veynte e seys, el dicho D. Fernando Cortes como estava con aquella ansya de governar y aun corrido entre los naturales de la tierra por que veyan que sabia que no hera governador fizo pregonar en la plaza desta dicha cibdad unas hordenanzas sobre el buen tratamiento de los yndios y en la cabeza dellas dezia yo D. Fernando Cortes governador y capitan general desta Nueva España por su Majestad y el primer capitulo de lo que en ellas se contenia hera que mandaba que ninguna persona fuese osada de salir desta dicha ciudad syn su licencia o de su lugar teniente–, y este testigo tiene en su poder el original de la dicha información

sobre este pregón que el dicho Fernando Cortes mandó dar ... (Sumario de la Residencia, v. 1 pp. 294-295).

[One Sunday afternoon, 2 September 1526, don Fernando Cortés, yearning to govern and embarrassed because the natives of the land saw and knew that he was no longer governor, had proclaimed from the plaza of this city some ordinances concerning the good treatment of the Indians; and on the head of the proclamation was written, 'I, don Fernando Cortés, governor and captain general of New Spain for his Majesty.' The first thing contained in the ordinances was the command that no one should dare to leave from this city without his license or that of his deputy—and this witness has in his possession [Cortés'] original proclamation].

The early criers who settled in New Spain were from Spain or from the Caribbean area. The municipal councils issued permission to those who applied for the position. In turn the crier was an appointed professional who had to be loyal and maintain confidentiality. Between 1533 and 1560 in Puebla de los Angeles, the second most important city of New Spain, there were 37 criers working in designated spots of the city. The crier was accompanied by two witnesses and a notary who recorded the agreements that were announced and approved. The announcements can be classified in two major groups: those stemming from the local council and those coming from the Mexican capital and from Spain. The content of the announcements can be further subdivided in social and urban organization, municipal administration, trade, supplies and prices, labor organization, festivities, and public ceremonies. The crier was responsible for providing all kinds of details about the location and logistics of the announced events (Illades 2008).

2.10 The center

Following the instructions of Hernán Cortés, Alonso García Bravo laid down the foundation for urban design, which was modeled after 16th century Spanish cities. It is known as the Spanish *traza* (layout or grid plan) which delimited an area of thirteen blocks. García Bravo traced the layout of the new city over the ruins of the Aztec Empire. His sketch turned into a living scheme: cut stone, heavy timber, and thousands of well-trained sculptors, painters, carpenters, masons and gardeners. Hundreds of Indians tore down one spot while the walls of another were being roofed. Between demolition and construction they built the Cathedral, the city hall, the pillory and the gibbet—powerful symbols of the municipal jurisdiction. The city was built for Spanish speakers who were not missing any of the components of a new Westernized civilization: viceroy and archbishop, cathedral, monastery, and in time, a university, a printing press and a theater (Benítez 1953/1985: 17).

The usurpation of Tenochtitlan as a colonial capital demanded the dismantling of an indigenous urban complex and its reassembly in an altered form (Holler 2007: 107). This was a syncretic process in which the assertion of Spanish identity and sovereignty required the memory of the indigenous past. In order to reach this goal the alteration had to include the island of Tenochtitlan. Though impractical "the rationale for Hernán Cortés's unpopular decision to build the Spanish city on the ruins of the Aztec capital" was based on the symbolic power and on the belief that such space "was necessary to maintain the flow of imperial tribute payment" (Holler 2007: 108-109). The indigenous character of the city was used to either anchor or dispute competing claims among largely Spanish interests. Reserved for Spaniards and their families the *traza* was surrounded by canals on three sides (see figure 2.1). This boundary separated the indigenous sectors of the city from that exclusively occupied, at least in theory, by the Spanish colonists (Holler 2007: 109-110). By 1580, the city had not lost its watery beauty, and it still had two great reservoirs supplying sufficient water for gardening in the convents and to grow vegetables on the *chinampas* (aquatic gardens) while all the basic products arrived in canoes. The Valley of Mexico was more gentle and fertile than Castile, and the European fruit trees such as orange, lemon, apples, clingstone, peach and pomegranate flourished in the new land side by side with avocados, berries and marmalade trees (Benítez 1953/1985: 24, 28).

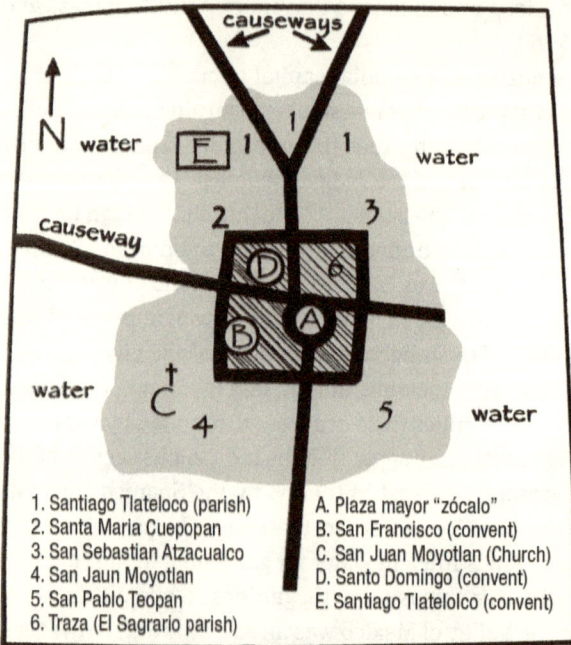

Figure 2.1: Mexico City urban structure, ca. 1520's. Source: Adapted from Holler (2007: 110)

When at the end of the 16th century, the social mobility of the Indian elites was obstructed by the new Spanish rulers, the contradictions of the new society were expressed in social conflict over privileges and land. The differentiation between the contending groups (Spaniards and Indians) was manifested in the opposition between the Spanish city and the Indian countryside. The almost invariable structure of the city was nucleated early in the colonial period with a better-developed center, which grew indefinitely through expansion of the *traza*. While the center maintained a near total stability, where the most powerful of the *encomenderos* dominated the municipal council, the councils favored them in grants of land and mining sites. New residents of the city were usually the conquerors' relatives and fellow townsmen, whereas Indian servants and employees of Spaniards became a major element in the cities and mines. Some lived with their masters, and others, not all steadily employed, lived in the irregular periphery. The *encomienda* was part of the center and was a restricted and well-defined institution in which the holder performed certain governmental duties and in turn received tribute, which residually belonged to the Crown (Lockhart and Schwartz 1983: 67-68, 91-92).

Ceremonies and main events were regimented by a protocol of distinguished groups: those belonging to the religious hierarchy and groups of artisans, students, and college Lecturers. Throughout the chivalry period, ballet spectacles and other performances were seen daily on the streets of Mexico City but there were also funerals and celebrations of the mighty, which were truly solemn, sumptuous, lengthy and costly, and thus requiring special attire. Two of the most garlanded events were the funerals of Charles V in 1559 and Viceroy Luis de Velasco in 1564. Spanish speakers and other groups enjoyed these events together, which contributed to enhance the process of socialization. Some of the prominent Spanish speakers were fond of hunting. Viceroy Velasco kept falcons, geese, and cranes. Where there were cattle, the viceroy and his men used to bait the bulls with dogs; fans of bullfights and horses were always quick and ready to animate the games. The feudal events entertained those who were closer to the royals. In the new colonial society the horse was extremely important since it was only necessary for transportation but also a symbol of luxury and pride. The travels and adventurous spirit of the Renaissance inspired the first Mexicans to engage in expeditions to other regions such as Guatemala, Honduras (then known as Las Hibueras), Florida, Chihuahua, and even the Philippines. At the end of the 16th century Mexico had become the center of exchange that affected a good part of the New World, Europe and the Orient; and despite the fact that the Inquisition was normally monitoring the entrance of proven Catholics, a good number of Jews, Flemish and Protestant Germans were able to enter in New Spain. Mexico also became the center of trade and immigration, activities in the piers and ports, caravans to Acapulco, and the like (Benítez 1953/1985: 49-50, 55-57, 62-65).

2.11 The Inquisition

When the Inquisition was established in 1571, the new Spanish-speaking Mexicans and many others lost their *joie de vivre* since they were exposed to regular monitoring of their beliefs and behavior, primarily in the religious realm but also in their private lives and agendas. The Inquisition was a bureaucratic apparatus administered by members of religious orders known as *comisarios* (commissaries), who occasionally collaborated with the Holy Office, which in turn counted on specialized functionaries with different roles. The *familiares* were lay and permanent collaborators; there was also a *fiscal* or prosecutor, a secretary, and two *notarios del secreto* (notaries of the secret) in charge of endorsing the depositions of witnesses. The notaries in every tribunal had the responsibility of maintaining the *cámara del secreto* (secret chamber) in conjunction with the prosecutor. The inquisitors relied on the judgment of six *consultores* (councilors appointed to give legal advice), eight *calificadores* (evaluators who were doctors in theology or canon and civil law), twelve *alguaciles* (constables), *alcaides* (guards at *cárcel secreta* or secret jail), and a few more responsible for a penitence jail and a perpetual jail. During the colonial period, there were plenty of trials consisting of hearings, where both the denouncer(s) and the defendant submitted their testimony. The *notarios* transcribed verbatim both the interrogatories and the replies of the defendants, who normally had a chance to present favorable proof. The procedure began with *un edicto de fe* (edict of faith), an inventory of heretic actions and beliefs which encouraged the defendants' denunciation of crimes against the faith; those who willingly denounced themselves and showed contrition often received lighter sentences. In contrast, those pronounced guilty were given sentences of reconciliation, including the wearing of *sambenitos* (garment of sackcloth) during the event known as *auto de fe*. Guilty prisoners could be sentenced to death (*sentencia ordinaria*) and punished at the *auto de fe* (cf. Chuchiak 2012: 51 and ff). *Autos de fe* were public spectacles attended by major functionaries of the ecclesiastical and civil governments of New Spain and by the Spanish-speaking and non-Spanish-speaking crowds. During the ceremonies sentences were read upon those brought before the Inquisition and executed by the secular authorities. The functions staged by the Inquisition were meant to divulge the ideological underpinnings of the Spanish (Christian) Empire.

2.11.1 Matters of routine in and around the Holy Office

The sumptuous ceremonies were normally staged in the city plaza in the presence of royalty comprising a lengthy procession, a solemn mass, an oath of obedience to the Inquisition, a sermon, and the reading of the sentences. The victims were normally apostate former Jews and former Muslims, then *alumbrados* (followers of a condemned mystical movement), and Protestants; occasionally also those who had been accused of such crimes as bigamy and sorcery. Life imprisonment was the extreme penalty that the inquisitors could impose whereas the death sentence was imposed and executed by the civil authorities. Major struggles to establish purity-of-blood policies can be traced to the practices of the Old Christian population of Toledo in the mid-15th century, which aimed at protecting the city and the Catholic faith by ensuring that only people with blameless Christian lineages were in positions of power and authority. This was the beginning of anti-Jewish and anti-*converso* rhetoric which spread from Toledo to other Spanish cities. The establishment of the Inquisition in Castile was the result of the hard work of members of religious orders who established an institution with the authority to try *conversos* suspected of heresy (Martínez 2008: 33).

The Spanish Crown was extremely concerned about the Jewish population that had been expelled from Spain after the defeat of the Muslim invaders in 1492.

Of the 200,000 Jews expelled from Spain, one-half had sought refuge in Portugal while the others had fled to France, Italy and the regions controlled by Turkey in the eastern Mediterranean. Those who remained in Spain were presumably persuaded to convert themselves to Catholicism (Hordes 2007: 220). The estimate of voluntary immigrants from Spain is approximate due to last-minute conversions and changes of heart. The figure then "wavers between fifty and one hundred thousand, that is, fewer than half the Jews in Spain" (Pérez 2005: 35-36). Various decrees were issued across Spain in the late 1500's compelling non-Christians to leave the Iberian Peninsula unless they converted in four months. Those unwilling to convert were either executed or burned in effigy.

The focus was on the public shaming of religious deviants and on their reconciliation with the church. The principles upheld by the Inquisition led to the establishment of *probanzas* (certificates of purity of blood) or *limpieza de sangre* which required reliable and iterating testimonies on legitimate genealogy. Factors such as parental identification, social rank, initial demographic imbalances, and level of acculturation could play a role in the patterns of classification of ancestry. Children of Spaniards and indigenous people were considered of privileged status but the need to absorb them into the Spanish group became less common as pre-Hispanic lineages declined, which meant that the mestizo population was also more distant from noble blood (Martínez 2008: 29-37; 146-147). All groups resulting from mixed ancestry were known as *castas* (castes), a notion which was distinct and more neutral than race, the latter term associated with peoples of Muslim and Jewish descent. The caste system was more inclusive because it allowed the different groups to claim genealogical or symbolic connections. In contrast, as early as the 17th century or before, the notion of race was used against persons of African descent and the distinction was attributed to slavery, a condition clearly linked to negation of nobility and religious infidelity (Martínez 2006: 27-30).

A good number of heretics tried by the Inquisition were the Portuguese of Spanish descent whose ancestors had fled Spain in 1492. Before the establishment of the Inquisition in New Spain, Judaism was practiced with great freedom for a short period between 1541 and 1571. However, as a result of the union of the Crowns (1580-1640) they returned to Spain and began to think of the New World like any of their contemporaries who dreamed of an opportunity of obtaining easy fortune and practicing Judaism. Towards the end of the 16th century and the decade 1640-1650 the harassment due to religious beliefs was exacerbated due to internal conflicts amongst the Spanish authorities in New Spain (Alberro 1988: chapter 34). Approximately 34 to 37 of them received death sentences while 97 to 107 were burned in effigy; many others died of illness, old age, desperation, or suicide until their communities were finally annihilated (Alberro 1988: 172, 380).

In appearance, New Spain served as a haven for crypto-Jews who wished to observe their rituals in an atmosphere of relative security, but active periods of persecution have been recorded for posterity. Various dynamic communities had emerged in Mexico City since the early 1500's; some of its members were involved in trade across the Atlantic importing goods from Spain and slaves from Angola, or exporting silver, dyestuffs, and the like. Others worked out of Acapulco and had businesses in the Philippines while certain others maintained ties with Peru, Maracaibo or Caracas. In New Spain there were about 2,000 crypto-Jews (Hordes 2007: 224). Towards the late 16th century, the slave trade in the New World increased considerably inasmuch as Spain and Portugal had agreed with Holland to protect the ships loaded with slaves during the voyage between Africa and the New World. The Jews established themselves in the Caribbean where they were in charge of the slave and sugar trade; they bought slaves in Angola and sold them in Spain, Peru and the Caribbean islands; finally they extended their activities to Guatemala and Honduras and were able to build pretty good networks in South America (Liebman 1971: 158, 159, 267).

Their assimilation to the emerging New Spanish mainstream culture resulted from the pressures imposed on them during critical periods. Some of the Jews living in New Spain were multilingual. Others knew some Latin and Hebrew although there is no evidence that they had studied the latter formally. They were most likely Spanish / Portuguese bilinguals and some of them showed what these days is known as inter-language features in their Spanish writings (Liebman 1971: 186, 182). The changes they made in New Spain gradually eroded the traits of the ethno-culture. For instance, women were in charge of educating children but their Judaic practices were mostly domestic rituals rather than religious teachings. Their diet was slowly modified and adopted the most common foods available in the New World. Although they were inclined to endogamy, the process of socialization did include the intermingling with other groups, e.g. wealthy merchants attracted ladies of Old Christian lineage and ended up in solid engagements. Wealthy men were more distant from true religion while poor women did not have sufficient resources and received payment in exchange of fasting for rich men. The poor began to denounce the rich if the former refused to pay a bribe. At times they married blacks and Indians because these groups could easily convert to Judaism. Lack of religious leaders and religious instruction contributed to discontinuity, and in the end, the attitudes of solidarity collapsed. When the harassment period was over, the far northern frontier served as a haven for converts with Zacatecas as the preferred center for practicing Judaism in New Spain (Alberro 1988: 417-454).

In 1632, the decadence of Portugal was attributed to the influence of the Jews, and an amnesty was negotiated several times if there was conversion in different ways (e.g. exchange of money). From Holland to Madrid, Spanish and Portuguese Jews used their languages and other cultural traits, although they were not loyal to Iberian ways. From Holland, they helped the Iberian Jews and were active in negotiations or bribes offered to the inquisitors in order to get others off the hook, since the bails were not commonly used to free prisoners from the jails. The connections between Holland and New Spain can be reconstructed via the biographies of the Portuguese Spanish Jews, who extended their commercial activities to Guatemala and Honduras and also had networks in South America. In the early decades of the 17th century, the Inquisition extended its tentacles to the northern and southern provinces of New Spain; it is assumed that by 1642 Portuguese Jews were conspiring against the Holy Office and against Spain in order to take over the colonies of Mexico and Central America. On the other hand, the inquisitors wanted to seize the properties that the Portuguese Spanish Jews had in New Spain and were successful doing so in the late 1640's (Liebman 1971: 228, 230, 235, 254-256, 267-268, 271, 272).

The reading and interpretation of Inquisitorial archives may be traced to several decades after the Holy Office was abolished. In his *Bibliografía Mexicana del Siglo XVI*, the 19th century historian Joaquín García Icazbalceta (1886) published important documents describing the foundation of the Spanish Inquisition in Mexico, the miscellaneous roles of its inquisitors, and the routine practices mounted on a yearly basis with the celebration of the *autos de fe*. The first ones took place in Mexico City in 1574 and 1575; between 1575 and 1596 there were eight more functions in which more than 130 penitents were present. The infamous *auto de fe* of 1596 added a new meaning to the word Portuguese, which was almost synonymous with Jew, since the vast majority came from Portugual (Liebman 1971: 223-226). According to García Icazbalceta the function staged on December 8, 1596 was truly solemn. Some of the members of the legendary Carvajal (or Carbajal) family were sentenced to death in person (García Icazbalceta 1886: 370-389).

> Fue cosa maravillosa la gente que concurrió a este Auto famoso, y la que estaba en las ventanas y plazas, hasta la puerta de las casas del Santo Oficio para ver este singular acompañamiento y procesión de los relajados, penitenciados, que salieron con sogas y corozas de llamas de fuego, llevando cada uno de estos un religioso a su lado para que lo exhortase a bien morir, y un familiar de guarda. Los reconciliados judaizantes con sambenitos y familiares a sus lados; los casados dos veces con corozas pintadas significadoras de sus delitos; las hechiceras con corozas blancas, y velas y sogas; otros por blasfemos con mordazas en las lenguas, en cuerpo descubiertas las cabezas, y velas en las manos; todos en orden siguiendo unos a otros. Los de menores delitos delante, y por este orden los demás, quedando los relajados atrás y los dogmatistas y enseñadores de la Ley de Moisés como capitanes y caudillos, últimamente con sus caudas sobre las corozas, retorcidas y enroscadas, siguiendo las falsas proposiciones de sus magisterio y enseñanza; con que fueron

procediendo hasta su Tablado que hacia frente con el asiento del Tribunal a cuyos pies había gradas donde se sentaron los oficiales y ministros del Santo Oficio por su antigüedad (1886: 370).

[It was something glittering the large crowd attending this notorious function, and those standing by the windows and plazas, and all the way to the door of the houses of the Holy Office to see this infamous procession of the sentenced convicts who came out with ropes and white cone-shaped caps with flames, each of them accompanied by a monk who would exhort him to die in peace, and a guarding lay volunteer (familiar). The Judaizers [were] reconciled with sack clothes and guarding lay volunteers by the side; the bigamous [were] wearing white hooded straw caps with paintings of their crimes; the sorcerers with white hooded straw caps and candles and ropes; the blasphemous with gags in their tongues, their heads uncovered and candles in their hands; all of them orderly following the others. Those convicted for minor crimes were ahead with all others following this order, while the accused were at the end, and the dogmatists and teachers of the Law of Moses marching like captains and caciques, last with their trains over the twisted and entangled cone-shaped caps following the false propositions of their teachings; all were proceeding toward their own Forum which was right across from the Tribunal seat where there were more Holy Office functionaries seated according to seniority]. (My translation).

From the original inquisitorial manuscript, García Icazbalceta (1886: 372) transcribed the names of the 67 penitents present at the infamous function the vast majority being Portuguese of Spanish descent. The following members of the Carvajal family were sentenced to death in person for observing the Mosaic Law: Manuel Díaz, Beatriz Enríquez, Manuel de Lucena, Doña Beatriz de Carvajal, Doña Francisca Núñez de Carvajal and her three children (Doña Isabel Rodríguez de Andrada, Doña Catalina de León y de la Cueva, and Luis de Carvajal, single (alias José Alumbroso). The same day ten Portuguese crypto-Jews (9 men and 1 woman) were burned in effigy, while twenty-four of them (18 men and 6 women) were reconciled with the Catholic Church. Twenty-four more crypto-Jews were accused of bigamy, sorcery, or blasphemy; some were persecuted just for claiming that fornication was not a sin; among them there was a woman, Ana Vaes, who was merely a suspect of observing Judaism. *Autos de fe* were read by inquisitors or criers before crowds of curious spectators. According to Alfonso Toro (1944, vol. 2: 255-256), the procession of 1596 was truly memorable for it was presided by 14 *familiares* and 60 friars followed by no less than 800 monks carrying lighted torches while at least 50,000 solemnly silent spectators representing all ethnic groups thronged the streets, the windows, and the rooftops near the offices of the Inquisition.

Although the Inquisition began to operate in New Spain in 1571, Spanish authorities had collected sufficient information on individuals who were suspicious of heresy, blasphemy, bigamy, sorcery and sins of the flesh since 1525. The authorities waited almost five decades to process each case. The cases tried by the first bishop and archbishops from 1525 to 1571 shed light on the tribulations that Spanish speakers and the castes had to endure and also on their lifestyles. The roster prepared by the Santo Officio on November 4, 1571 registered the names, dates, and miscellaneous activities of the accused. This inventory of suspects is known as *El Abecedario de relaxados, reconciliados y penitenciados en la Nueva España*, 1571. A reconstruction of archives on the Spanish Inquisition in Mexico and the analysis of the societal forces, the dynamics of socialization, prevailing moral values, interpersonal relationships and conflicts can be found in Liebman (1963, 1970, 1971, 1974) and Alberro (1988). The Inquisition was not an impartial tribunal; its administration of justice was sometimes based on personal, political or economic interests. The most famous case tried by the Holy Office in 1590 was that of Luis de Carvajal y de la Cueva, known as *el viejo* ("the old man") who is to be distinguished from his own nephew, Luis de Carvajal *el mozo* ("the younger"), known for being irreverent. Luis de Carvajal *el viejo* was a convert of Portuguese descent who led the journey to the New World with about one hundred people who were exempt from *probanzas*; his sister, Francisca Núñez de Carvajal, his brother-in-law, Francisco Rodríguez de Matos and their nine children traveled to the New World under pretension of being Catholic. When Luis de Carvajal *el viejo* arrived in New Spain he explored the northern lands and not only founded the kingdom of Nuevo Leon but also became its governor. His aggressive entrepreneurial spirit was tarnished by the invasion of the territories that belonged to the king of Spain. Falling out of grace with the Spanish authorities, he was persecuted for political rather than religious motives and arrested at the Port of Tampico in 1582 from where he was taken to Mexico City only to be confronted with the inquisitors, who had collected information about his dubious ancestry and also about the new converts who happened to be his relatives (Toro 1944, vol. 1: 225-226). He was sentenced in the *auto de fe* of 1590 and was reconciled with the Catholic church. His full-length trial case in modern Spanish appears in *Los judíos en la Nueva España* (Toro 1932: 207-372).

The fate of his nephew Luis de Carvajal *el mozo*, the son of Francisca Núñez de Carvajal, was memorable because he was tried twice, once in 1590 and again in 1596, when he was sentenced to death in person along with his mother, his two sisters, and some other relatives and friends. He was a single young man who was given a chance to repent from his religious beliefs in the first trial of 1590. He even had a Franciscan mentor and tutor protecting his mother and sisters who were living at the time near the well-known *Colegio de Santa Cruz de Tlatelolco*, where he taught Latin to the children of the Indian nobility. The young Carvajal knew Hebrew, Latin, Portuguese, Spanish, and indigenous languages. His writings include his biography, religious guides to practice Judaism, and poems and songs in either Hebrew or Spanish interspersed with Portuguese glosses. Despite the privileges afforded to him and his family by the inquisitors, his inner struggle must have been so intense that he was unwilling to live a monotonous Catholic life; instead he assumed the consequences of having an audacious existence since he was denounced twice by nosy neighbors, so-called friends, imprisoned spies, and even relatives. Luis de Carvajal, *el mozo*, was the sacrificial victim who died as he had lived, painfully and zealously (Toro 1944, vol. 2 and Liebman 1967). He is considered the first Jewish writer of the New World.

2.12 Spanish and the Holy Office

The Holy Office in New Spain was not organized in the early decades; it was in addition lenient with the rich and powerful, negligent with the poor and powerless, and otherwise replete with irregularities. Because not all functionaries were salaried on a regular basis, inquisitors depended on the funds they confiscated from the accused. They were prone to go after the wealthy colonists since their property, personal belongings, and even their slaves could be legally seized. Black and mulatto slaves were imprisoned with their heretic masters and obliged to serve them in different ways. Slaves had better communication with the outside world, moved around more freely, established various connections with other convicts, and were charged with doing different errands such as bringing the daily meals, select menus, or useful objects such as ink and woolen balls, which were used to write messages. In jail, some Spanish speakers improvised their own secret codes (e.g. telegraph-like wall beats, use of languages other than Spanish). Portuguese, Nahuatl and African languages learned by merchants or Spanish ladies nursed by nannies were used for "secret" communication. Despite the imaginative use of additional codes, the convicts could not succumb to the temptation of chiming in all kinds of conversations in Spanish. Their indiscretions were revealing of personal, financial and family anecdotes or full stories that were conveniently logged in by the more cautious inquisitorial personnel who used the information gathered via chirpy chats against other suspects (Alberro 1988: 236-247).

The higher ranks amongst all functionaries were designated mostly to Spanish speakers born, educated, or with previous inquisitorial experience in Spain. Some of the *familiares* were descendants of the *encomenderos* or established merchants of silver or cacao, while still others were related to the inquisitors. By the beginning of the 17th century, members of the traditional aristocracy were marrying Spanish immigrants belonging to merchant, mining, and manufacturing groups, a pattern emerging between members of the *encomendero* class and the new bourgeoisie in Mexico City, Puebla and Morelia. As opposed to the early colonizers who had married noble indigenous women, this new class was highly endogamous, and their estates and surnames survived through at least the 18th century while their children and grandchildren born in New Spain eventually gained positions within the Inquisition (Martínez 2008: 193). According to Alberro (1988: 60, 67-68), having a post with the Inquisition was prestigious because the functionaries' background was associated with the legacy of Old Christians who formed a stable and compact group maintaining stability in their new land, where their wealth derived from agriculture, commerce, mining, and civil, ecclesiastical, or inquisitorial duties. Some of them were colluded with new Christians because they had the same social class interests. In addition to the personnel needed to triple-check the lineage of new Christians and other suspicious individuals, the Inquisition maintained an active pool of interpreters of indigenous languages, German, English, Flemish, French, and other aides of minor ranks (see Table 2.2).

Table 2.2: Functionaries of the Holy Office in New Spain (1571-1700)

Years	Positions	Origin / Title / Other information
1571-1679	Inquisitors and fiscals 30	12 doctors, 11 licentiates, 7 without title, mostly from Spain
1571-1696	Commissaries 222	17 born in Spain, 2 born in Portugal, 203 born in New Spain (including Guatemala and New Mexico)
1571-1700	Familiares 154	57 born in Spain, 30 born in New Spain, 57 not specified
1571-1696	Evaluators 211	211 priests ordained in regular orders: Franciscan (63), Dominican (47), Augustinian (25), Jesuit (25), Mercedarian (7) and 44 in the secular clergy
1571-1696	Consultants 55	Of a total of 55, fourteen had had previous experience in Spain.

Source: Alberro (1988: 82-136)

Spanish speakers, speakers of other European languages and speakers of indigenous languages living in the capital of New Spain regularly listened to the proclamations of the powerful Spanish inquisitors. Over almost three centuries, the Holy Office had the capacity to disseminate at least the Spanish spoken by empowered speakers, who were not solely those identified as Spain-born but who also were born in New Spain and raised in the Spanish-speaking households. The exposure of *criollos* to Spanish within the family and to the networks they had with recent Spanish immigrants might have reinforced the norms of the mother country for a few generations. Simultaneously learners of Spanish as a second language who attended the ceremonies of the Holy Office on a regular basis might have had more than sufficient passive knowledge of the same norms. The rosters and trials are the best sample of careless writing based on spontaneous speech, which had to be literally registered. The documents prepared by the Holy Office are extremely useful in the reconstruction of the Spanish spoken in New Spain.

2.13 The sins recorded by the Holy Office

In spite of its pitfalls, the Spanish Inquisition provided abundant files in which the crimes of the accused, guilty or innocent, were recorded for posterity. Table 2.3 shows the variety of accusations from two sources: the Archivo General de la Nación or AGN (Columns 2 and 3) and the *Abecedario de Relaxados y Penitenciados* or *APR* (Columns 4 and 5). Individuals accused of heresy are about 500 in both sources. Minor religious offenses are about 30 percent in the AGN sample and 27.3 percent in the *ARP* sample, followed by sexual transgressions and solicitation of sexual favors (more than 20 percent in both archives). Sorcery and civil crimes are not too frequent, whereas heterodoxy and idolatry are virtually non-existent because the Holy Office did not persecute the indigenous peoples. Columns 2 and 4 in Table 2.3 yield 3,369 cases reported for the period 1571-1700. In over a century of persecution one percent of death sentences were recorded (Alberro 1988: 207).

Table 2.3: Distribution of trials according to crimes (1571-1700)

Crimes	AGN	%	ARP	%
Heresy	525	27.5	497	34.1
Idolatry	0	0	1	0.1
Heterodoxy	11	0.6	8	0.5
Minor religious offenses	568	29.7	391	27.3
Solicitation of sexual favors	157	8.2	90	6.2
Sexual transgression	462	24.1	300	20.6
Sorcery	138	7.2	121	8.3
Civil crimes	52	2.7	42	2.9
Total	1,913	100	1,456	100

Source: Alberro (1988: 205, 207)

After the establishment of the Inquisition, religious diversity was not tolerated. The expulsion of non-Christian groups after the unification of the Christian kingdoms involved a great deal of mental and physical exertion; consequently the Spanish Crown expanded its policy to the newly acquired dominions in other parts of the world. The most significant non-Christian groups in the New World were the indigenous peoples, known for being polytheists, idolatrous and inclined to practice human sacrifice, but as the Spaniards became more familiar with them, they realized that they were also flexible and that they could be converted by peaceful means. In contrast, the Spanish Crown was not willing to withstand groups with roots in Lutheranism, Islamism, Judaism, or in any of the African religions encompassing a wide variety of beliefs. For almost three hundred years, the inquisitors were charged with identifying heterodox individuals who could be easily distinguished from Spanish speakers or indigenous groups. The Holy Office not only induced fear, anxiety, and hatred against the crypto-Jews but false piety on the part of those who were Catholic. It built a powerful officialdom with brawny tentacles in various cities and towns of New Spain. It contributed to the dissemination of Spanish as spoken and written by the ecclesiastic and civil authorities in charge of collecting testimonies, keeping files, and reading sentences aloud, but the most effective form of dissemination was the intimidating public functions regularly staged before large crowds. Despite the terrifying experiences reported over centuries, the records of the Inquisition of New Spain show that the rate of death sentences was low. The summary published by García Icazbalceta (1886: 389) indicates that the total of sentenced heretics in person was 41 while 99 were sentenced in effigy. Between 1574 and 1795 there were 11 *autos de fe* where the authority in charge of executing the sentences was the New Spanish Inquisition. Liebman (1964) assumes, however, that there were more *autos de fe* and more individuals sentenced to death.

2.14 Spanish speakers and ethnic groups in the *Abecedario*

In the *Abecedario*, the notaries logged in the name, occupation, origin, and other data related to individuals accused of different transgressions. This bound manuscript has been examined by scholars interested in the fate of Jews and crypto-Jews living in New Spain (Liebman 1964). The roster identifies subjects very briefly, though occasionally it elaborates on the familiar and religious background of the accused as well as on the sentences imposed on the deponents. The names, short biographies, and accusations of subjects appear in Liebman (1971). The *Abecedario* tends to follow the alphabetical and chronological order as of 1525, a few decades before the Inquisition was officially established, but the entries do not appear in strict order. This section sheds light on the diverse origin of both Spanish and non-Spanish speakers registered in the *Abecedario*, a rare manuscript retrieved from the Henry A. Huntington Library. A subsample of 883 subjects classified in Table 2.4 shows the diversity of geographic and ethnic backgrounds. Spanish speakers of Groups 1, 2, and 3 make up 61.4 percent of all subjects. Group 1 includes those born in diverse regions within Spain; Group 2 refers to their offspring born in New Spain; Group 3 consists of those whose origin is unspecified but who were residing in New Spain or other territories belonging to Spain. Group 4 comprises the bilingual Portuguese-Spanish speakers, most likely Jewish or crypto-Jews fluent in Spanish, and Catholics reconverted to Judaism. Speakers of African languages appear in Group 5 while speakers of European languages other than Spanish and Portuguese are put together in Group 6. Finally, since the Inquisition did not regularly persecute the indigenous groups, subjects in Group 7 changed their "mestizo" ethnicity to an "Indian" ethnicity in order to get off the inquisitorial hook. Two subjects in Group 8 appear in this rare category; one of them was born in the kingdom of Granada, the last redoubt of Muslim resistance. Asian Subjects appear in Group 9.

Table 2.4: Groups by origin, language, religion, and ethnicity

Subj.	Ethnic group	Number	%
1.	Spanish speakers born in Spain coming from different regions, cities and villages; most likely monolingual in Spanish and heterodox Catholics	337	38.16
2.	Spanish speakers born in New Spain (including Guatemala, San Salvador and Nicaragua) and other colonies (e.g., Puerto Rico and Peru), most likely belonging to the second or third generation of criollos and mestizos; heterodox Catholics	106	12.0
3.	Origin unspecified, most likely Spanish speakers of first, second, and subsequent generations residing in New Spain, crypto-Jews from Spain or Catholic but uncertain about dogma (including priests)	99	11.21
4.	Portuguese / Spanish speakers from Portugal and Spain, most likely Jewish or crypto-Jews fluent in Spanish, and Catholics reconverted to Judaism.	164	18.57
5.	Speakers of African languages most likely familiar with Portuguese and/or acquiring Spanish; originally non-Christian but converted to Catholicism; their descendants could have been free or of mixed ancestry, fluent in Spanish.	92	10.41
6.	Speakers of other European languages, e.g. English, Flemish, French, Irish, German, Greek, and various Italian dialects, sometimes accused of being Lutheran or Calvinist; most likely learned Spanish.	76	8.60

2.14 Spanish speakers and ethnic groups in the Abecedario — 99

Table 2.4 (continued)

Subj.	Ethnic group	Number	%
7.	Spanish-speaking Indians passing as Indians, or Indian working as *naguatlatos* [interpreters] most likely learned Spanish.	1 + 3	0.45
8.	Spanish-speaking Muslims most likely born in Muslim nations or regions.	3	0.34
9.	Non-Spanish speakers of Asian origin (Chinese or Filipino), enslaved or free.	2	0.22
	Total subjects of all ethnic groups	883	100 %

Though irregularly, the Inquisition logged in the origin, occupation, marital status, and the current residence of the accused subjects. Spanish speakers born in Spain (Group 1) came from different places, large and small, from northern, central, southern regions, and from the Canary Islands or the Philippines. Their occupations were diverse: priests, muleteers, sword makers, silver crafters, book sellers, carpenters, bakers, mariners, servants, merchants, singer-dancers, architects, foremen, iron workers, knife makers, soldiers, captains, hatters, barbers, harpists, scribes, shoe makers, weavers, *encomenderos* or conquistadors, physicians, lawyers, tavern owners, miners, tailors, store owners, socks makers, laborers, slave traders, and the like. They were speakers of the various Spanish peninsular dialects coming from various social strata and had settled in a city or villa in New Spain. Those classified in Group 2 were born in the cities of Mexico, Guadalajara, Antequera or Puebla de los Angeles. There are also subjects born in Indian towns such as Tecamachalco or mining towns such as Taxco and Tulancingo. In this group there are Spanish speakers and mestizos of diverse occupations and backgrounds. Group 3 refers to Spanish-speaking subjects whose origin is uncertain. Spanish speakers are identified as *"natural de"* ('native from') and *"vezino de"* ('resident of') which literally means 'neighbor' in modern Spanish but used to mean 'homeowner' or 'parcel owner'. Groups 1, 2 and 3 make up the growing class of Spanish speakers who were settled on a permanent basis in New Spain. Over the generations, the Groups 4-8 most likely accommodated to the three former Groups.

A select subsample of 221 Subjects retrieved from the *Abecedario* is listed in the Appendix. Ethnic groups are subsumed in six classifications: Group 1 (Ss. 1-100) comprises those born in Spain; it is followed by Group 2 (Ss. 101-125) made up of those born in New Spain, and Group 3 (Ss. 126-145) residents in New Spain. After the three Spanish-speaking groups, Portuguese-Spanish bilinguals appear in Group 4 (Ss. 146-177) and African and Afro-Hispanic (Ss. 178-200) are listed in

Group 5. Speakers of European languages other than Spanish and Portuguese (Group 6) are presented at the end of the Appendix (Ss. 201-221). When the Subject is a native of a town or city within Spain, it is considered a Spanish speaker born in Spain or "first generation"; when the name of the Subject is followed by the indication "native of Mexico", or "native of Guaxaca", it is considered a Spanish speaker belonging to the second or third generation. The basic data of each Subject was not logged in consistently, and many Subjects appear only with name, surname, and the major accusation. Assuming that all Subjects appearing before the Inquisition were adults, all the Spanish speakers who appeared in 1555 or before are considered natives from Spain. At times, the Inquisition only recorded the names of Subjects who belonged to secular or regular orders without specifying their provenance. Many priests were not identified by origin but they were most likely Spanish speakers born in Spain.

Group 4 represents the Subjects who were Portuguese-Spanish bilinguals practicing Judaism secretly while publicly feigning their beliefs in Catholicism. Portuguese and Spanish Jews used their languages and other cultural traits, but they were not loyal to Iberian ways. It is known they transliterated and recited prayers in Hebew (Liebman 1971: 235-6, 254). Their life stories have been well-researched by 20th century scholars (Toro 1932 and 1944; Liebman 1963; 1967 and 1974; Alberro 1988). For decades, the Carvajal family has attracted the attention of scholars for their story begins with the voyage of Luis de Carvajal, his sister Francisca Núñez de Carvajal, his brother-in-law Francisco Rodríguez Matos, their nine children, and about one hundred people of Spanish-Portuguese origin. Most of them were apprehended by agents of the Inquisition a few times. In the *auto de fe* of 1596 Doña Francisca Núñez de Carvajal (S. 161), the matriarch of the family, was sentenced to death with her children, Doña Catalina de León y de la Cueva (S. 163), Doña Leonor de Carvajal, and Luis de Carvajal *el mozo*. The Inquisition awaited a few years to convict Doña Mariana de Carvajal (S. 166), a single young lady who had a nervous breakdown when her mother and siblings were being arrested. The youngest daughter, Anica (S. 167) was a minor when she was also accused of being Judaizer; the Inquisition waited almost five decades to sentence her to death in 1649 for having had Judaizer tendencies. Baltasar and Miguel were able to flee Mexico City before their mother and sisters were arrested; they resettled in Rome, where they continued to practice Judaism but were relaxed in effigy in 1596. Friar Gaspar de Caravajal was the only member of the family who was ordained in the Dominican Order but later reconverted to Judaism.

Finally, Luis de Carvajal, the ex-Governor, appears once in 1590 whereas his nephew Luis de Carvajal *el mozo* appears twice, once in 1590 and relapsing in 1596. Other Subjects include Beatriz Enríquez, who was also executed in the *auto de fe* of 1596. Her role as the female dogmatist and leader of Judaism in her community was noticeable. The case of Blas de Magallanes was dismissed because he committed suicide, while Bernardo de Luna and Constança Rodríguez (S. 157) were reconciled with the Church. Catalina Enríquez, Clara Enríquez, daughter of Manuel de Lucona and Catalina Enríquez, were also reconciled with the Church. Manuel de Lucerna was relaxed in person in 1596. Andrés Núñez, Antonio Machado, Antonio Gómez, Antonio Díaz de Cáceres, Antonio Méndez, Alvaro Rodríguez, Antonio Díaz Márquez, and Leonor Díaz were accused of being Judaizers. The rest of the Portuguese subjects, accused of minor crimes, were relaxed in effigy, or were reconciled with the Church (see Ss. 146-177 in the Appendix).

Group 5 refers to Subjects of African descent, those who were still enslaved at the time they appeared before the Inquisition and those who had been freed. It includes those of mixed ancestry and fluent Spanish-speaking Subjects born in New Spain. The earliest case recorded in the *Abecedario* was as female slave known as Francisca (1537) whose master was Luis Marín. Those who were born in the New World are classified as *mulatos* (Ss. 178, 180, 184, 189) or *negros criollos* (Ss. 181, 183) and free slaves (Ss. 179, 190). The vast majority are however slaves who were classified as *negros* or *mulatos esclavos* (S. 188). When they were *mulatos libres* or *negros libres criollos* it was specified (Ss. 190, 193, 196, 197, 199). Additional information is given about the slaves' masters, who were mostly Spanish-speaking males (S. 194), and with rare exceptions, Spanish-speaking females born in either Spain or New Spain. Another distinction is made about language and ethnicity because *negros ladinos* (e.g. S. 200) were fluent in Spanish. The first generation of African slaves was not fluent in Spanish but might have been familiar with Portuguese just like the Sephardic Jews. The diversity of Subjects is also shown in Group 6, made up of Europeans speaking languages other than Spanish or Portuguese commonly accused of being Lutheran Calvinists. They were speakers of English, French, German, Greek, Irish, or Italian dialects. They were merchants, separators of gold and silver, or adventurers who had relatives or acquaintances in the New World (see Ss. 201-221 in the Appendix).

2.15 Spanish speakers of African descent

The New Laws of 1542 did not apply to Africans who were slaves, whether they were born in Africa or in the New World. Therefore, the slave trade continued unabated in the New World colonies. The origin of African slaves taken to Mexico dates back to the time of the Conquest since many Spanish captains e.g. Hernán Cortés, Pedro de Alvarado, Pánfilo Narváez, Francisco de Montejo, and others transported a few slaves who had been living previously in the Caribbean islands. As compared to Brazil, Cuba, and the United States, Mexico was not a significant recipient of black slaves insofar as it had agreed to take about one-eighth to one-tenth of all of those delivered to Spanish-speaking colonies. The origin of black slaves destined to Mexico was diverse. They were from Zafi-Lisboa, Cape Verde, Bantu ethnic provinces, and São Thome (Aguirre Beltrán 1972: 19, 217).

From Church records it is known that the Spanish colonists encouraged legal unions among slaves so they could secure reproduction of younger slaves at the same time that slave owners were discouraged to sell members of the same family (husband and wife) in faraway regions; in this way, they again protected the labor of adult slaves and their offspring. In 1570 the African population was calculated at 20,569 while the mixed population was less than one-tenth or 2,435 (0.6 %) of the total population of New Spain. Between 1595 and 1650 the highest estimate for Mexico reached 38,974 almost equally divided between males and females. The average for those years decreased to 35,089, and was distributed in the following provinces: Mexico (19,441), Tlaxcala (5,534), Nueva Galicia (5,180), Michoacan (3,295), Oaxaca (898), Yucatan (497), and Chiapas (244). The growth of the Afro-Mexican population was not related to the slave trade but to mixed unions, to the extent that by 1646, there was a larger group of Afro-mestizos distributed as follows: Mexico (95,544), Tlaxcala (17,381), Oaxaca (4,712), Michoacan (20,185), Nueva Galicia (13,778), Yucatan (15,770), and Chiapas (1,330). This makes a total of 116,520 people or 6.8 percent of all groups, a proportion contrasting with the minuscule percentages of previous decades. At the end of the colonial period, Mexico had one of the largest populations of African descent most of them freemen (Aguirre Beltrán 1972: 214-218; 222-230). They were highly dispersed throughout the major urban centers, coastal zones, rural areas, and in selected portions of the northern frontier (Vinson 2000: 269). While in Mexico slavery diminished considerably in the mid-18th century only to disappear at the end, countries such as Brazil, Cuba, and the United States continued slave trading until the 19th century.

The Afro-Mexican population was present, too, in the central valleys of Puebla, Guanajuato, Campeche, Tabasco, Veracruz, Nuevo Leon, Colima, and Tamaulipas. In all these regions, they worked in the mines, agriculture, cattle-raising and the like (cf. Martínez Montiel 1994). Since ca. 1550 Afro-Mexicans were needed in the mining sites. Between 1556 and 1562, miners from Zacualpan, Taxco, Sultepec, Tlalpujahua, Temascaltepec, Pachuca, and Guanajuato owned 867 slaves increasing to more than a thousand in 1579-1582. The textile industry also employed Afro-Mexicans as early as 1594 and continued to do so through 1750. In addition, as of the second half of the 16th century the sugar haciendas introduced enslaved agricultural workers of African descent. In the mining and agricultural centers, Afro-Mexicans (slaved and freed) intermingled with Indians and mestizos. This encouraged the unions of different ethnic groups. Descendants of slaves had an incentive to marry free individuals because their offspring would be free. This policy was encouraged by miners and agriculturalists who found it convenient having a larger and cheap labor force at their service but working under more flexible conditions. At the end of the colonial period, it was common to hire free workers of African descent (von Mentz 2005: 259-276).

2.15.1 Afro-Mexicans and the process of acculturation

The struggles to preserve African cultural patterns, lifestyle, activities in different enclaves and even religious practices have been explored in various colonial contexts. However, researchers find more information on assimilation or acculturation. In Puebla, for example, the registration was implemented in 1540. The slaves' origins and data on their owners were logged in for a fee. The data found cover a very small proportion of slaves, their age, price and general physical condition. In the second largest city of New Spain, Puebla de los Angeles, individuals of African descent worked as cowboys, shepherds, foremen and muleteers. They were also in charge of transporting wares and goods along the colonial roads and worked as cloth shearers and fullers. At the end of the 16th century there is evidence of paperwork done over civil and judicial cases by free slaves and their descendants, a fact that corroborates that they participated in common transactions and in the incipient colonial economy. Their integration in the Puebla society was consolidated in various domains such as trade, paternity suits, and the like. In 1582, cases of social mobility were registered inasmuch as former slaves had the right to inherit other slaves. Some others were even given credit to open small businesses (e.g. grocery shops). The case of Isabel de Limpias, a free slave, is interesting since she was a *"ladina en lengua castellana"* (proficient in the Spanish language); she was born and raised in Puebla and married a Spanish-speaking man who was both a tailor and a merchant. The most effective form of integration was manumission since slave owners were able to grant a certificate of freedom to their slaves and their children (Lara Tenorio 2005: 285-297).

African and Afro-mestizos were introduced in Cholula, an Indian town near Puebla, at the end of the 16th century and the beginning of the 17th century, a period corresponding roughly to drastic losses of the Amerindian population. In Cholula, other trends were recorded such as the disproportion between male and female slaves; the intermingling of African slaves, mulattoes, Indians, apprentices and professional weavers both mestizos and Spaniards, i.e. diverse ethnic groups who shared the same space inside the *obrajes* or wool workshops. This enhanced the contact between those of African descent and other groups while fostering mixed unions. The offspring of mixed unions provoked changes along the semantic categories established by the racial policy and were registered under a different ethnicity; this practice was favorable in obtaining a fee exemption because wool loom owners only paid taxes for possessing Indian workers. Many cases of exogamy were recorded since the early stages of colonial society (Castillo 2005: 299-325).

In Mexico City, women of African descent worked as nannies and nurses and were active in raising Spanish-speaking children. The proportion of Afro-Mexican women working as nannies in New Spain is higher than the proportion of Spanish-speaking or Indian women. Researchers thus assumed that this mere fact endorses the notion of acculturation or integration of Spanish-speaking members of the colonial society with those of Afro-Mexican descent. In addition, they served as cooks and domestics in the households of Spanish and *criollo* families, were employed in the convents, churches, and even in the viceregal palace. Finally, they also acted as sales persons in the distribution of goods produced by their owners or employers. Sometimes free slaves lived with their former owners and even took care of them when the latter could no longer work. All these activities led to building socio-affective relationships that consolidated the practices of manumission (Velázquez Gutiérrez 2005: 335-356). For information on slave labor, identity and manumission, see (Proctor 2003a, 2003b, and 2006).

2.15.2 Afro-Mexican enclaves

An Afro-Mexican enclave was identified in the past century along the coast of the states of Guerrero and Oaxaca on the Pacific Rim. It is known as La Costa Chica (Small Coast) which begins to the southeast of Acapulco (state of Guerrero) and extends for about 120 miles as far as the border with Oaxaca, where the Small Coast of Oaxaca begins. As of the late 16th century, African slaves were assigned to work in sugar mills in the sub-region known as La Cañada. The *bozales* (Africa-born slaves who spoke little or no Spanish) were from Bantu provinces particularly Congo and Angola. This was facilitated by Portuguese slave traders who had the license to deliver slaves to New Spain where the proportion of Bantus was normally 60 percent. The massive arrival of Bantu slaves was conducive to obtaining permission to establish sugar mills. Some of the toponyms of this area are reflective of the Bantu traces: Matamba (also in Zaire, Angola and Tanzania); Amapa, a town founded by *cimarrones* (fleeing slaves from the sugar mills). In Bantu Kikongo, *Mbamba* refers to a large snake that bites rapidly. This is the origin of the dance known as *la bamba* (Motta Sánchez 2005: 357-410). These enclaves have been recently studied by Althoff (1998) and Rosas Mayen (2007). Both studies offer insightful ethnographic analysis of Afro-Mexican communities of the region and sufficient language data showing the popular residual variants of this dialect zone.

The other region of Afro-Mexican presence is Veracruz on the Gulf of Mexico. As early as 1529, Hernán Cortés had obtained a sugar plantation in southern Veracruz. Once Spaniards discovered that Central Veracruz and other parts of Mexico offered ideal climate and soil conditions for the crop, they encouraged its cultivation but were unable to use Indian labor consistently because the New Laws of 1542 had abolished Indian slavery. When colonists began to seek an additional pool of workers, Africans presented a good choice because of their track record in the Iberian Peninsula. In Veracruz, Africans worked in mines and on large livestock-raising estates that supplied mining areas with meat and hides. These coerced laborers proved as multiple and complex as the settings in which they arrived. In major cities such as Mexico, Puebla, Valladolid, and Antequera (or Oaxaca City), they built roads, bridges and buildings; they also transported goods and people within and between these population centers; they hawked wares in the streets, cut and sold firewood, tended gardens and livestock, kept house and waited on their masters. African slave labor was also utilized in the production of sugar. Because it lay on the mainland and encompassed highland and lowland areas, Central Veracruz provided a regional variant of the overall Caribbean black experience in sugar culture. The region lay in the heartland of New Spain's sugar industry until nearly the end of the 17th century. During this time Mexico became a strong market for slaves, and as many as 2,000 Africans arrived annually at the port of Veracruz between 1580 and 1620. In this setting, blacks integrated into variegated labor systems instead of a single slave-dominated system (Carroll 1991: 15-19). Two cities of Veracruz are identified as centers of slave trade and labor, Jalapa and Cordoba. Jalapa's peak period of African slave purchase falls between 1597 and 1610 during which planters purchased two or three *bozales* yearly. In Jalapa, 430 slaves were registered although Jalapa represented one of the many New World markets where trade was not increasing rapidly; in fact, it declined after 1610 and from 1670 onward it virtually ceased. The origins of the slaves sold in Jalapa in the periods of 1578-1610, 1611-1640 and 1641-1670 was extremely diverse, and the total registered was 797. Of all the slaves sold in Jalapa, 219 were identified as coming from Angola in the first period (Carroll 1991: Table 3).

Hernán Cortés integrated slaves into the Veracruz labor force before 1530; by 1534, he had already imported one group of Africans for his mill at San Andrés Tuxtla. Veracruz emerged as a center for the early industry. The royal accountant Rodrigo de Albornoz founded a plantation near Cempoala in 1535 and purchased 150 slaves to work it. During the next decade Spaniards built five more estates in the Orizaba region including a huge plantation belonging to Viceroy Antonio de Mendoza, known as the *Ingenio de Orizaba* or Orizaba Mill, where over 100

African slaves worked. Some urban slaves held skilled occupations in which they had received training from Spanish carpenters, shoemakers, masons, and blacksmiths, while a few held positions as household and body servants. In these capacities, slaves lived and worked in the same surroundings as their owners, and probably enjoyed better accommodations than many of the poorer class of any race. Occasionally, these servants enjoyed near-kin status with their masters; the affective bond was manumission for "the love and loyalty". Slaves of less wealthy masters usually led less secure lives because they were rented to others and lived off the fees of the rent. Renting sometimes gave slaves the opportunity to acquire some capital and property of their own (Carroll 1991: 66).

Little is known about patterns of language maintenance and language shift, bilingualism in African languages and Spanish, and the hypothetical processes of pidginization and creolization. The major question posed by researchers pertains to the formation of pidgins and / or creoles resulting from contact between African languages and Spanish or Portuguese. The enclaves of African *bozales* in Mexico were too small and not efficiently interconnected to produce new forms of speech. The sub-regions of La Costa Chica and Central Veracruz could have been the sites in which Spanish-based creoles might have emerged, but the conditions of isolation and marginalization were not sufficiently strenuous to maintain the social distance between masters and slaves. Daily and face-to-face interaction with the Spanish-speaking families among those who remained in-and-around the Spanish households fostered at least acculturation and later assimilation to colonial life; in turn this seems to have contributed to the acquisition of the popular version of Mexican Spanish and its residual variants. This suggests that Afro-Mexicans most likely skipped one whole stage of language evolution known as creolization, the second-generation process that originated a new speech in those milieux that maintained the social distance between Europeans and Africans (e.g. Haiti, Jamaica, Trinidad, etc.). The absence of full-fledged Afro-Hispanic creoles remains a question in creoles studies. This underlying assumption reads that as of the second generation, speakers of African languages were inclined to acquire or learn the local or regional vernacular of Mexican Colonial Spanish, and that in turn they were the agents of inter-generatioal retransmission of popular residual variants.

How do we know now that Afro-Mexicans were proficient in Spanish? The trials of the Inquisition aid in the reconstruction of the slaves' profile and their personal depositions before the Holy Office. Spanish speakers of African descent were present in New Spain since the 1520's. Those who were born in New Spain were *negros ladinos* (proficient in Spanish), and as such they were able to deliver their own testimonies in Spanish. More than one hundred cases of Afro-Mexicans accused of blasphemy were recorded between 1596 and 1669. Afro-Mexicans commonly used blasphemous speech as a strategy of resistance under unbearable working and living conditions. In most cases the defendant was a young acculturated male from urban settings and a few from rural areas. In both cases blasphemy was the result of excessive physical punishment inflicted by their angry masters. In attempting to stop the abusive punishment, the slaves blurted out expressions of blasphemy against God, an act that warranted the prompt intervention of the Inquisition, where their cases were heard (Villa-Flores 2002).

2.16 Conclusions

(1) Indigenous Spanish. This chapter highlights some of the most important components of the emerging Spanish-speaking society in which Spanish speakers used Spanish. Clearly dominating the life of the Spanish colonies throughout the 16th century, the *encomienda* had manifold functions. It strengthened the position of the newcomers in Mesoamerica, solidified the Spanish alliances despite their own internal conflicts, empowered the clan of Spanish speakers in the new land, and imported slaves from African nations, adding another group to an already multilingual / multicultural scenario. The humanists who tenaciously opposed the *encomenderos* obstructed the legal and permanent enslavement of the native population. If the enslavement of the indigenous peoples had been solidly established during three centuries of colonial life, the process of gradual assimilation would have been delayed. If the process of assimilation had been delayed, the acquisition of Spanish by the indigenous would have rendered a socio-ethnic vernacular variety with features derived from deeper language contact coupled with social distance (e.g. massive Nahuatl-accented Spanish or semi-creolized Spanish with features of indigenous languages). External factors were not propitious to the emergence of a socio-ethnic variety of 'indigenous Spanish' during the first century of colonial life.

(2) Saliency and repression. In the most prosperous Spanish colony, the role of the Inquisition was two-fold: on the one hand, it had the power to repress divergent attitudes, behavior and 'inappropiate' discourse; on the other, it had the ability to record basic statistics referring to the subjects under its control. The Inquisition's files reveal interesting aspects of the daily life in New Spain and narrate ordinary stories about common individuals of diverse origin and religious orientation (cf. Mott 2001). Furthermore, they aid in the reconstruction of the initial ethno-linguistic diversity existing in New Spain and the strategies to eliminate it. Given the saliency of the crypto-Jews, one more hypothesis may be advanced for the reconstruction of New World Spanish. If Spanish-speaking Jews living in New Spain had maintained some of the original traits of late medieval

Spanish (assuming that most were bilingual or recessive Portuguese-Spanish), they might have given continuity to the distinction between voiced and voiceless fricatives (just like in the other communities of Sephardic Jews). Voicing was the pertinent feature that might have made them even more salient, because at the time all the voiced sibilants had been devoiced. In combination, language, ethnicity, and religion led to the extinction of the Spanish-speaking Jews. The writings that have been rescued reveal two major strains: one is the adherence to the prevailing variety of Mexican Colonial Spanish, e.g. the autobiography of Luis de Carvajal (cf. Toro 1944 Vol. 2: 315-350), and the letters delivered to his mother and sisters while in prison (cf. Silverstein 2015). The other is the innovative contribution in the poetry of Leonor de Carvajal (cf. Hamilton 2000), which shows the use of both traditional Sephardic and current skills in Mexican Colonial Spanish. Finally, the evidence gathered thus far points to the multilingual and multi-dialectal resources of a community that contributed to the diversification of ritualized domains of language use (e.g. the home of the religious leaders, the synagogues, and various congregations).

(3) Speech accommodation. Notwithstanding the quantitative disadvantages of Spanish speakers, they were able to settle in a major city where they began the process of language diffusion via acts of identity such as *La fiesta del Pendón*, carefree public spectacles, regular public announcements, and inexcusable functions that gathered thousands of people for about three centuries. The urban space was re-organized to convey images of Christianization. The presence and miscellaneous activities of Spanish speakers during the 16th century were determining in the formation of a new dialect that is known as proto-Mexican Spanish, discussed in the next chapter. Appendix I shows the diverse origins of Spanish speakers: they were from all regions and from tiny places and big cities. They had more than one reason to accommodate or show solidarity with one another. Accommodation took place in face-to-face interaction in the domains of family, work, education, religion or simply in the animated social life they had despite the disadvantages of being a quantitative minority.

(4) Koineization. The process of dialect mixing was accelerated in the highlands of New Spain as a result of the inter-dialectal experience that Spanish speakers had had in the Caribbean area, where the primitive koine had been shaped. The Inquisition files aid in the reconstruction of speakers' regional origins and various backgrounds, their transatlantic experiences, and the experience in exploration.

(5) Absence of creolization. The Inquisition's files complement other sources related to the population of the Spanish-speaking New World. Thirty percent of the cases tried by the Holy Office in the 17th century refer to descendants of Africans. This tends to decrease while the cases of mulattoes increase during the

same century, a trend reflecting a solid pattern towards mestizaje. The total of both groups makes up about one-half of all subjects, and there is no doubt that the individual's ethnic origin was logged in with precision. Their sins were normally blasphemy, curse, sorcery, bigamy, or aggression. The archives also shed light on their lives marked by the disgrace of being uprooted from their families and native lands; finally, despite the fact that the vast majority were victims of excessive corporal punishment, some of them enjoyed surprising freedom and some others were even able to read and write (Alberro 1988: 457-461, 467). The presence of Afro-Mexicans corroborates the multiple regional, socio-economic, and religious origins of the immigrants; they are included in the category of the "first speakers", inasmuch as no enclave or community favored the evolution of an Afro-Hispanic pidgin or creole.

By the second half of the 16th century and the first half of the 17th century, the Spanish-speaking Jews had become the scapegoats of the Spanish-speaking officialdom. As compared to all the other groups, Sephardic Jews had ascended rapidly in the political and economic colonial power. Their involvement in the slave trade had a dual effect: they became wealthy but were doomed by their role as brokers in legal commerce. The Spanish crown was not inclined to empower the *encomenderos* and the non-Christian groups in adventurous enterprises such as the slave trade. According to Hordes (2007: 222, 224), after the scandalous case of the Carvajals, the Holy Office returned to its policy of relative toleration, and from this point on until its demise in 1821, it was not too interested in persecuting converts. In fact, many of them progressively assimilated to mainstream Catholic society, whereas others retained residuals of Jewish practices.

Chapter 3
The Spanish language and its variations in New Spain

3.1 The earliest Spanish documents written in Mexico

This chapter deals with the features that were transferred from peninsular Spanish to the Mesoamerican area in the 16th century. The point of departure is the Spanish written by Hernán Cortés, author of the *Cartas de Relación* that he delivered to the kings of Spain between 1520 and 1526, and some other lesser known documents. The letters were printed in Spain, France, and Mexico in several editions (1520/1522/1866/2007). The *First Letter*, found in modern editions, is still useful to reconstruct language data, particularly lexicon and morpho-syntactic features. The *Second Letter*, handwritten by Cortés in 1520, was printed in Seville in 1522. From this edition it is possible to reconstruct select phonetic, morpho-syntactic and lexical features that in turn serve as a starting line of reasoning to show, on the basis of the available evidence, the earliest version of Mexican Spanish, some of the features that were transmitted to New World Spanish, and those that remained in the Mesoamerican area. The first speaker and writer of Mexican Spanish was Hernán Cortés himself. While it is difficult to look into all the aspects of Cortés' speech, it is possible to analyze interesting traits of his prose. This analysis is conducive to study the chronological development of the same features in subsequent writers of Mexican Spanish.

An ambitious and overly self-confident young man, Hernán Cortés had nothing to lose when he embarked himself on the adventure to the Indies; instead he had a sneaking suspicion that he could gain fame and fortune that would sell well in the Old World. A victorious war was all he needed to climb the socio-political ladder in the Iberian Peninsula. Cortés was not a representative of the officialdom but was determined to secure sufficient merit and riches to become one. He was born in Medellín (Extremadura) in 1485 to parents of Old Christian lineage and limited financial resources; at the age of 14, he was sent to Salamanca to study Law and Latin at the University or with private tutors, but returned to his hometown after only two years. His Spanish did not reach the levels of sophistication prevailing among the men trained within the cloisters of religious orders or that of scholars who had learned Latin well enough to write treatises on specialized subjects. What he learned in Salamanca was however beneficial in the understanding of his own enterprise. Cortés wrote directly to the Spanish monarch asking for acknowledgement of his successes instead of punishment for insubordination. He reported the outcomes of his skirmishes and his intentions to establish a new system in the Mesoamerican lands that became New Spain. Those who knew him believed that Cortés was outgoing, nervy and obstinate; as a young man he was enrolled in the Spanish militia, spent a few years in Italy, and participated in the exploration of Algiers. When he returned to Spain he was ready to join Nicolás de Ovando, the Governor of Hispaniola and distant relative, who was in Seville preparing his next trip to the Indies. Córtés' plans were jeopardized by an accident, and for about a year, he was wandering the ports of Cadiz, Palos, Sanlucar and Seville, and learning in addition about the voyages to the Indies. At the age of 19, he joined the ship of Alonso Quintero and in 1504 he left for Hispaniola, where he became a colonist.

As soon as he arrived in Hispaniola he introduced himself to Governor Ovando and made sufficient merits to receive a *repartimiento* (distribution of property, Indians, services, and the like) in Deaguas along with the notary office in the Ville of Azua. In 1511, he accompanied Diego Velázquez in his exploration of Cuba. There he was awarded another *repartimiento* in Manicarao and later moved to Santiago de Barucoa, where he became Diego Velázquez' secretary, the Governor of Cuba. When he began to explore the Mexican territories, he had had the trans-Castilian, trans-frontier, and transatlantic experience. He had been in northern Africa and had lived in Extremadura, Old Castile, Italy, Andalusia, Hispaniola, and Cuba. Before he arrived in Mexico he had been acquainted with various languages and cultures although he might have been a monolingual Spanish speaker. The scholarly writings of his contemporaries contrast with his improvised but ingenious reports to the Spanish monarchs. While the documents delivered by the friars of the late 15th and early 16th centuries exhibited Latinate syntax, the prose of Cortés is clear, straight-forward, and similar to pre-modern Spanish. He used few Latin phrases, and as of the *Second Letter* (1522), he turned into a master of narration, description, reflection and persuasion. In the *First* and *Second Letter*, he introduced fresh borrowings from Taino and Nahuatl, and continued to use them with only brief definitions or no definitions at all until they sounded natural. The information about his life derives directly from the *Cartas de Relación* (1520/1866/2007), from the *Second Letter* (1522), from *La conquista de México* (1552) by Francisco López de Gómara, and from the *Historia verdadera de la conquista de la Nueva España* (1571) by the *encomendero* Bernal Díaz del Castillo, one of his loyal soldiers.

3.2 The *First Letter* by Hernán Cortés

The original first letter written by Hernán Cortés has been lost, and it is assumed that a copy derived from the original must have been transcribed by a professional copyist who referred to Hernán Cortés in the third person instead of using the first person, as in the rest of the letters. The *First Letter* (1520) narrates the explorations of Juan de Grijalva, the nephew of Cuba's Governor, Diego Velázquez. Juan de Grijalva had experience in the journeying of Cuba and the founding of Trinidad, and was therefore, a veritable rival in the new exploration of the Mexican coasts. Grijalva sailed around Yucatan to the shores of the Bay of Campeche, discovered the Cozumel Island, and mapped the river that bears his name. Despite his endeavors, Grijalva was not able to collect the amount of riches that his uncle was expecting after having subsidized part of the expedition. In Cuba or the Fernandina Island, some Spanish settlers were dissatisfied with Governor Velázquez's arbitrary practices and thought that the young Hernán Cortés was capable of confronting the adverse situation. They asked Cortés to return to Hispaniola to submit the complaints they all had about Governor Velázquez, whose reaction was to ignore them; from that point on, however, the Governor had serious doubts about the adventurous expeditionary.

At that time other explorers had been reconnoitering the coasts of Yucatan. Hernán Cortés was one of the potential appointees to continue surveying the unknown lands, but Governor Velázquez recalled the expedition and reassigned the task to another captain. When Cortés found out that the Governor had dismissed him from the early exploration of Mexico, he issued orders to weigh anchor and set out to the coasts of Yucatan. Accompanied by about 10 ships, 400 men, 16 horses and a small number of cannons, he landed in the Yucatan Peninsula in Mayan territory. He disembarked at Cozumel, where he met the natives of the island. Cortés knew of Spanish captives who were lost on the different islands. At Cozumel he found Gerónimo de Aguilar, a Spaniard who had survived from a shipwreck and who willingly joined the Spanish troops. Aguilar had learned Maya during his captivity and could thus translate for Cortés. Cortés and his men struggled to survive from day to day and somehow managed to gather information from the natives and their caciques. He continued to Campeche then marched to Tabasco and the Grijalva River (see the route of Hernán Cortés in Map 3.1). The *First Letter* also describes the topography, the plants and animals, and diverse customs of the people, housing and religious practices (including human sacrifices) that he observed in both Cozumel and Yucatan. The comparisons with Moorish Spain are glaring; for Cortés, the natives lived *amoriscados* (like the Moors) and were fond of going to *mezquitas* (temples) where they worshipped their idols. Cortés took full advantage of this opportunity to persuade the Spanish monarchs that the natives needed instruction in the Catholic faith. In closing, he warned them of the risks associated with Governor Velázquez, who was selfish and greedy. The letter ends with an itemized inventory of the presents that his envoys should deliver to the monarchs. This is in short the content of his *First Letter* addressed to Queen Doña Juana and Emperor Charles V, dated on 10 July 1519, and dispatched from Villa Rica de la Vera Cruz. The envoys assigned by Cortés and his men to deliver the missive along with some presents were Alonso Fernández Portocarrero and Francisco de Montejo (cf. Cortés 1520/2007: 7-34).

3.3 The *Second Letter* by Hernán Cortés

Dated on 30 October 1520 in Segura de la Frontera (on the coast of Oaxaca), the *Second Letter* offers a flamboyant narration of the battles Cortés fought on his route to the capital of the Aztec Empire and a flashy painting of an empire solidly established in the Great Tenochtitlan. In November 1522, Jacobo Cromberger published the *Second Letter* in Seville. It also appeared in Zaragoza in January 1523. The narration of the *Second Letter* begins 16 August 1519, when Cortés marched to Cempoala with 15 horsemen and 30 troopers; Cempoala was a prosperous Aztec village near the Villa Rica de la Vera Cruz (modern Veracruz), where he left two horsemen and 50 of his best troopers. Thinking that his men would be tempted to desert him in this adventure, Cortés scuttled his ships on the coast but saved one in which his loyal soldiers returned to Spain. In addition, he reported to the Spanish Emperor his concerns about the independent expeditions of Francisco de Garay, Governor of Jamaica, who was working on the premises with a few ships and allies. Cortés' main goal at this point was to meet the lord of the Aztecs, Muteeçuma (modern Spanish Moctezuma) and sent him messages through his *lenguas* ('interpreters').

As he was marching along the coasts of Veracruz, he was welcomed by the natives, who quickly learned of his desires to meet the Aztecs' ruler; some of them even gave him provisions. On his way to the Aztec capital he described the villages and the peoples he met. Taking full advantage of these encounters Cortés inquired about the lord Moctezuma and collected valuable pieces of gold. The towns described in detail as they appear in the *Second Letter* are the following: Tascaltecal (modern Tlaxcala), Churultecal (modern Cholula), Guasucingo (modern Huejotzingo), Temixtitan (old Tenochtitlan), Iztapalapa (modern Iztapalapa), Tezcuco (modern Texcoco), Ocupatuyo (variable names), and Izzucan (variable names). When Cortés reached Tascaltecal, he realized that in that province Moctezuma had numerous enemies. To his surprise, the natives of the province offered him an unholy alliance in order to trounce the feared Aztec Emperor.

Before he finally entered the Great Tenochtitlan, Cortés and his men had imaginative battles once with 100,000 Indians and another time with more than 149,000. The attacks on small towns at dawn forced the negotiations with the native caciques who ultimately pledged allegiance to him and to the unknown Spanish monarchs. The leaders of those towns advised him to leave the countryside and continue on to the great city. Some of them attempted to intervene in arranging a meeting with the Aztec Emperor but he repeatedly turned them down.

The first featured city was Tascaltecal, which he compared to Granada but actually larger and stronger with very good constructions and better supplies. About 30,000 people visited the daily market to trade produce and all kinds of goods. Cortés continued to describe the fertile valley and the beautiful fields. One day he was in his own camp when six caciques and 200 men who were Moctezuma's vassals informed him that they all wanted to become the subjects of His Majesty, Emperor Charles V. At the same time they asked Cortés to specify the kind of tribute that he wanted from them in exchange for suspending his plans to enter Moctezuma's territory. Some other people told him that he should not trust those vassals. From Tascaltecal Cortés wanted to march to Tenochtitlan but he was warned of the perils of this design because the Aztec lord was presumably preparing an ambuscade. On his way to the splendorous capital he made more allies who received him as a guest. Upon learning that some of his men were furtively talking on the premises to some of the Moctezuma's allies, he was so puzzled that he had to resort to the multilingual Aztec woman who was in captivity in order to find out that the Aztec ruler was close to his camp; all the people there got ready to flee the area because they were terrified of Moctezuma's troops. As Cortés became leery of the situation, he positioned himself on the offensive and decided to use his air gun killing about 3,000 people. The surviving native leaders were jolted awake by the fire and conceded defeat not without making a pact of loyalty with Cortés.

His report on Churultecal reads that this town had about 20,000 houses and many slums. This city was independent and people were well-dressed. The land was fertile and had a good irrigation system. Outside of Spain, this was the most impressive city, beautified with 430 towers built on temples. Because the people were presumably loyal vassals of Charles V, Cortés claimed that he wanted to make peace with Moctezuma who most likely had intentions to harm him. Before waging war on Moctezuma, one of the vassals went to see him and returned six days later with 10 gold dishes, 1,500 pieces of garments, and plenty of foodstuffs. Cortés was intent on meeting Moctezuma personally and nothing was going to stop him. At Churultecal his men explored the mountains and the surroundings of the volcanoes. When he departed from Churultecal he continued to Guasucingo, where he was welcomed by the natives. Very soon he gained the sympathy of about 4,000 Indians from the provinces of Tascaltecal, Guasucingo, Churultecal and Cempoala. On his way through the province of Chalco, he reached Amecameca, where he had good hostesses. There some people told him that Moctezuma had asked them to wait for him to give him plenty of provisions. On behalf of Moctezuma, a young 25-year-old cacique delivered apologies to Cortés because he was not able to show up personally. Moctezuma's envoys told Cortés that they were in charge of guiding him in person. Cortés followed a convoy and found a city of 2,000 people, where he was invited to stay overnight; members of his entourage persuaded him to continue to Iztapalapa, which was the territory of Moctezuma's brother. Iztapalapa had about 12,000-15,000 neighbors while the city's lord had new large houses with many rooms and fresh gardens, trees, lakes, and very good stone floors.

The next day Cortés went through an aquatic thoroughfare that led him to Tenochtitlan, which was founded in the middle of the lake along with three small cities. When he finally arrived there, he was received ceremoniously by about 100 men. Then he crossed a wood bridge and Moctezuma finally appeared with 200 men, all of them barefoot and very well dressed. Moctezuma talked to Cortés and exchanged embellished ribbons with him, and then he took him by the hand and led him to a large room. Once all the members of the entourage were seated, the Aztec lord approached Cortés with jewels of gold and silver. Moctezuma gave an enlightening speech but Cortés does not mention who interpreted it for him. After six days of staying at Moctezuma's palace, Cortés determined that the Aztec leader should be imprisoned in the very same room where he himself was staying as a guest. His decision was based on the news delivered to him by a Spanish captain who named Qualpopoca (or Quetzalpopoca) as being responsible for having captured and killed a number of Spanish soldiers in a battle close to Nauhtla after a dispute over tribute. Apparently, Qualpopoca had claimed loyalty to Charles V but had apologized for not being able to come to Cortés and offer his services to His Majesty; his excuse was that he could not cross the territory of his enemies. For that reason he requested the accompaniment of four Spaniards, who were sent to him to his house. Qualpopoca was deceptive and actually wanted to kill them and succeeded killing two while the other two escaped alive.

Intrigued by the incident Moctezuma and Cortés called a few witnesses to tell their side of the story. Cortés wanted to know if Qualpopoca had killed the Spaniards following the orders of the Aztec lord. Qualpopoca's allies first denied Moctezuma's involvement, but under pressure all those implicated finally changed the previous version; furthermore, they stated that there was no other mastermind in charge of the whole operation but Moctezuma, who was held in captivity. In a very weak position, the former Aztec ruler was compelled by Cortés to order Qualpopoca's arrest, to bring him back to Tenochtitlan, and to burn him alive in front of what is assumed to be the *Templo Mayor* (Great Temple). In retaliation, he then made him watch when Qualpopoca, his sons, and some other prisoners were tied to stakes while they were being burned to death before a speechless crowd. Once the prisoners were dead, Cortés told Moctezuma he was free to go, but Moctezuma declined the offer and decided to stay in his own palace where he was comfortable and had everything he needed.

This confrontation was not only the turning point in the Aztec-Spanish affairs but the perfect excuse to justify the arrest of Moctezuma and to cause the downfall the Aztec Empire. Once Cortés had subdued Moctezuma, he began to inquire about the places where he could find gold; debilitated by his mistakes, Moctezuma gave him all the information Cortés wanted without suspecting that the newcomers would be more than thrilled to take away large amounts of gold. The unpopular Aztec leader even provided guides to the rivers and sites where the precious metals could be found. Cortés was open when he said that Charles V needed gold, silver, and other metals, and Moctezuma gracefully agreed to smelt abundant and exquisite objects that would be delivered to the Spanish monarch.

The narration of the marches and exploratory trips of Cortés ended when the description of Tenochtitlan began. This is the first big Western picture of the Mexican capital, its markets, plazas, temples, Moctezuma's houses and his fearful vassals. The episodes of the first part of 1520 made Cortés the virtual ruler of the Great Tenochtitlan while Moctezuma became more and more detested by the different Mesoamerican groups. As Cortés was strengthening his position vis-à-vis Moctezuma, the enemies he had made in Cuba were determined to hunt him. One of them was Diego Velázquez, who was sending another expedition led by his nephew, Pánfilo de Narváez, who arrived in Mexico in April with more than 1,000 men. The large expedition had instructions to bring Cortés back dead or alive. Narváez disembarked at Vera Cruz, where Cortés had left a few of his troops. Planning the counterattack, Hernán Cortés departed from Tenochtitlan in May leaving 200 men there while the rest accompanied him to the coast. When Cortés learned that Narváez was close to the premises, he gathered his troops and defeated the latter. Upon his return to the Aztec capital in June, Cortés tried to regain his former position but his people were in great trouble as a result of another massacre deliberately perpetrated by his lieutenant Pedro de Alvarado. From Cortés' perspective, Spaniards were in the mood of imploring peaceful arrangements or else fighting for control of the causeways; nonetheless, for every Aztec they killed, many more appeared. At a time during the bloody battles, the indigenous combatants were so numerous that they themselves lost track of the identity of their allies serving in the battlefields. In desperation, the final strategy of the Aztecs was to destroy the bridges to prevent the Spaniards' escape.

Taking advantage of Moctezuma's decayed image, Cortés proposed the cessation of hostilities with the native enemies, but by then Moctezuma had provoked the wrath of his own subjects. On July 1, when Moctezuma was attempting to placate his people by delivering a harangue to a crowd, he was stoned to death. That night Cortés decided to flee for Tlaxcala, where he still had confederates. The Spaniards managed a narrow escape from Tenochtitlan across the causeway, while their back guard was being slaughtered. Much of the treasure looted by Cortés and his artillery was lost during this panic-stricken escape from Tenochtitlán. This episode is known as *La Noche Triste* (Sad Night). After another battle in Otumba, the Spaniards and his allies managed to reach Tlaxcala, not without having lost 870 men. In Tlaxcala Cortés plotted the siege of Tenochtitlan and the destruction of the Aztec Empire.

With the assistance of their allies, Cortés's men finally prevailed with reinforcements arriving from Cuba. Cortés planned the retreat of his men towards the city island of Tenochtitlan cutting off supplies and crushing the Aztecs' allied cities, a maneuver that changed the preparation of the siege of Tenochtitlan. In January 1521, Cortés repudiated a conspiracy headed by Antonio de Villafaña, who was hanged for his offense. Finally, with the capture of Cuauhtémoc, the younger *tlatoani* (ruler) of Tenochtitlan, on 13 August 1521, the Aztec Empire disappeared, and Cortés was able to claim it for Spain, thus renaming the city Mexico City. In closing, he solicited authorization to name the new territories as Nueva España (New Spain) due to the similarity of weather with the Iberian Peninsula. The envoy of the *Second Letter* was Alonso de Mendoza. The Aztec empire collapsed when the capital, Tenochtitlan, fell to the Spanish in August. Several months later, on November 25, 1521, Francisco de Oruzco arrived in the Valley of Oaxaca to claim it in the name of Cortés, who had been granted Oaxaca as his prize for conquering New Spain to the Spanish crown, and who was thereafter named *Marqués del Valle de Oaxaca*.

In 1521, the victorious Spanish soldiers settled in a community known as Segura de la Frontera, located in the central part of the Valley of Oaxaca and approximately six miles east of Monte Alban (modern state of Oaxaca). Later known as Nueva Antequera, it was officially raised to the category of a "royal" city in 1532 by decree of Emperor Charles V (Carlos I) with the name of Antequera de Guaxaca. Today it is known as Oaxaca or Oaxaca City. Following the initial settlement of this community, the Spanish quickly introduced new agricultural crops and methods of cultivation into the Valley of Oaxaca. King Charles I of Spain, who had become Holy Roman Emperor Charles V in 1519, appointed Cortés as governor, captain general and chief justice of the newly conquered territory. From 1521 to 1524, Cortés personally governed Mexico. Simultaneously, four royal officials were appointed to assist him in his governing; in effect, however, they submitted him to rigorous scrutiny, criticism, and even defamation. In the face of internal conflicts and political turmoil, the boundaries of New Spain were established and renamed (see Maps 3.2 and 3.3 at the end of this chapter).

3.3.1 Salient features in Hernán Cortés' *Cartas de Relación*

The Spanish spoken and written at the time still belongs to a late medieval period representing the transition to pre-modern Spanish, when it was trendy to maintain the orthography and etymology of Old Spanish; the role of the printing press in addition was to respect the old norms such as the distinction of single -s- and double -ss-. Hernán Cortés falls in the category of writers with average education but plenty of worldly experiences. His writings follow the norms of the northern-central Spanish writers and scribes. By the time he reached the coasts of Mexico, his Spanish had been in contact with Taino, as the *First Letter* shows. When he wrote the *Second Letter*, his use of lexical items from both Taino and Nahuatl was both natural and convenient. The morpho-syntactic features, however, reveal the transitional and inter-dialectal patterns he used. The language data from the *First Letter* (1520/2007: 7-34) referring to morphology, syntax and lexicon are useful to reconstruct the Spanish used by Cortés, whereas the *Second Letter* published in Seville in November 1522 offers leads to reconstruct the pronunciation, morpho-syntactic patterns and lexical innovations. The *Second Letter* (1522) is a rare text of 54 unnumbered pages, which is available in a few libraries. I have numbered each page of my personal facsimilar copy, which was retrieved from the Henry E. Huntington Library.

The *Second Letter* aids in the reconstruction of the earliest stage of Mexican Spanish or proto-Mexican Spanish, a variety which is distinguished by the pronunciation and spelling norms of late medieval Spanish. Phonetic features appear in sub-sections 3.3.1-3.3.8; the adaptation of Amerindian languages is discussed in 3.4; various morpho-syntactic variants are exemplified in 3.5 and 3.6; and all the other variants are listed in 3.7-3.13.

3.3.1. High close vowels of modern Spanish replaced mid open vowels. In the *Second Letter* (1522), Cortés uses both *mesmo* and modern *mismo* as in "la *mesma* voluntad". He preferred the mid vowel in *descobrir* (modern *descubrir*); *sotiles* (modern *sutiles*); *sofrían* (modern *sufrían*) and *cobrían* (modern *cubrían*).

3.3.2. Late medieval Spanish verbs ending in –ÇAR –ÇER and –ÇIR (modern –ZAR, –CER, and –CIR) were spelled with the consonant sequence -sç- as in *favorescí-*

dos, paresçió, resçebido. Cortés omitted the grapheme <ç> or *ç con cedilla principal* and *encima* but he preserved in other words, e.g. *alçar* and *cabeça*.

3.3.3. In the *Second Letter* Hernán Cortés used both F- and H- in initial position, as in *fablar* and *hablar* ('to speak'); *fallé* and *hallé* ('I found'); *fasta* and *hasta* ('until' or 'up to'); *fizieron* and *hizieron* ('they made' or 'they did'). Other duplicate forms also appeared as *fermoso* and *hermoso* ('beautiful'); *fallar* and *hallar* ('to find'), *folgar* and *holgar* ('to enjoy'). The adjective *harto/a* appears with either H or F as in *harta tristeza* (40) *farto trabajo* (42). Phrases such as *filado de algodon* ('cotton thread') (27) and *aquel fumo* ('that smoke') (50) reveal the old medieval spelling. According to Lapesa (1985: 368), in the first half of the 16th century the archaic F- in *fijo, fincar, fecho* was still tolerated.

3.3.4. Modern Spanish has only two contractions, AL and DEL. In medieval Spanish, the prepositions A and DE coalesced with definite articles and demonstrative pronouns as in *alos, dela, della, destos, dellos, dela*. Hernán Cortés preferred the contracted forms.

3.3.5. Cortés used the modern synthetic future and conditional tenses as in: *guiaría, sabría, saltaría, socorrería*, but with other verbs such as *venir* and *tener*, he preferred the medieval forms *vernía, ternía*.

3.3.6. The spelling of the modern verb HABER was restored according to the Latin etymology of the verb HABEO. In medieval Spanish, present tense conjugations omitted the initial H- as in *yo e dicho* (*yo he dicho*) and *loan determinado* (*lo han determinado*). The modern spelling in the pluperfect tense follows, too, the Latin etymology as in *había, habías, habíamos, habían*; however, in the *Second Letter* Hernán Cortés used the norm established by Antonio de Nebrija's grammar (*avia, avias, aviamos, avian*).

3.3.7. In modern Spanish, direct, indirect and reflexive objects can go before or attached to the verbs in the infinitive, *quiero verlo, lo quiero ver*. In medieval Spanish the object was attached to an infinitive form assimilated to the object, as in *velle* or *respondelle* (modern *verle* and *responderle*).

3.3.8. The modern Spanish gender of MAR ('sea') and PUENTE ('bridge'), CALOR and CANAL are masculine. In late medieval Spanish, these nouns were feminine, although occasionally MAR could be masculine. The examples (a) and (b) are from the *First Letter* (1520/2007) while the sentencess (c) through (f) come from the *Second Letter* (1522).

(a) supo de tres indios que se tomaron en una canoa en *la mar* (13)
(b) Los que se quedaron en la barca se hicieron a *la mar* (41)
(c) Passada *esta puente* nos salio a resçibir aquel señor Muteeçuma (17)
(d) murio en *las puentes* el hijo de Muteeçuma (52)
(e) llegan las canoas debajo de *las puentes* por do están *las canales* (29)
(f) cayeron muchos dellos muertos y ahogados de *la calor* (50)

3.4 Adaptation of Amerindian languages

When Spanish speakers had contact with Mesoamerican languages they made adaptations to the Spanish spoken in the region, some of which have remained with high vitality. Select pronunciation traits of Cortés' speech can be reconstructed on the basis of two major sources: the use of Amerindian toponyms and an original handwritten letter found in the Archivo de Indias in Seville (cf. Lope Blanch 1995-1996). One of the first tasks of the Spanish explorers was the recording of the places they found in the Mesoamerican area. Such process entailed the addition of the voiceless affricate Nahuatl phoneme /tɬ which was unknown to Spanish speakers. This phoneme lost the lateral segment and became de-lateralized in the east and southeast of the territory occupied by the Aztecs at the time of the Spanish conquest, resulting in the adoption of –*t*. Spanish speakers wrote the toponyms with the three variants: Chinan*tl*a, Matalçingo and Tascalteca*l*. The Nahuatl diphthong /wa/, which appeared in the Nahuatl Huaxyacac was velarized following the Spanish model in toponyms such as Guadalquivir, Guadalcanal, Guadalajara coming from the Arabic *wad* with the meaning of "river". In his testament, Cortés dictates Teguantepequ*e*, Chapultepequ*e*, Jilotepequ*e*, Ocotepqu*e*, adding the paragogic –*e* or final vowel that is more common in Spanish. Finally, he also wrote Guaxocingo representing the prepalatal voiceless fricative sound /ʃ/, which by chance was similar to Old Spanish /x/ in words such as *dixo*, *baxo*. Once /x/ was inserted in the Spanish inventory of sounds it was easier to pronounce Mexico [meʃiko], Juchitán [ʃotʃitan.

3.5 Morphology and syntax

Primary morpho-syntactic traits listed below are general to Spanish and have evolved from the late 15th century on; they are better identified as the necessary transition from late medieval to modern Spanish.

3.5.1. Use of the coordinator *como* with the function of the relative *que*; such construction became frequent among the Golden Age authors. Example (a) from the *First Letter* and examples (b) to (d) from the *Second Letter* illustrate the use.
(a) [nosotros] vimos *como* venía en ella uno de los españoles cautivos que se llama Gerónimo de Aguilar (15)
(b) el dicho capitan les auia dicho *como* yo en nombre de vra. alteza tenia poblada toda esta tierra (2)
(c) yrse a la isla Fernandia a hazer saber a Diego Velasquez *como* yo embiava la nao que a vra alteza embie (1)
(d) me hizieron saber *como* por la costa della andauan quatro nauios (2)

3.5.2. In modern Spanish, double negatives are almost non-existent, whereas in medieval Spanish it was possible to use sentences (a) through (c) retrieved from the *Second Letter*.
(a) y que *ninguno no* auia saltado en tierra (2)
(b) tardaron aquel dia y otro que *no vinieron* con *ninguna* comida (18)
(c) tenemos noticia que yo *ni* todos los que en esta tierra abitamos *no* somos naturales della sino estrangeros (18)

3.5.3. Use of past participle with an adverbial function to express completion of an action. Medieval Spanish used past participles as adjectives in adverbial clauses. Sentences (a) through (d) appear in the *First Letter*; sentences (e) and (f) are from the *Second Letter*.
(a) *Acabada* de hacer la dicha armada, se partió de la dicha isla Fernando Cortés (12)
(b) *Partidos* de esta isla, fuimos a Yucatán, y por la banda del norte corrimos la tierra adelante hasta llegar al río (16)
(c) *Después* de idos determinó el dicho capitán de ir allá (17)
(d) *Oído* esto por los indios, respondiéronle que hablase desde ahí lo que quisiese (17)
(e) Y *llegados* a me fablar cada vno por si fazia a mi una cerimonia que entre ellos se via mucho (17)
(f) *asi recogidos* y *curados* los heridos nos boluimos al real y traximos con nosotros dos indios (19)

3.5.4. Modern Spanish uses an infinitive preceded by the preposition A + article EL (*al amanecer, al decir, al soltar*). In contrast, 16th century authors used a prepositional gerund with a transitive or an intransitive verb in order to indicate that an event occurred immediately before another. The items below appear in the *Second Letter*.

(a) Otro día *en amanesciendo* dan sobre nuestro real mas de ciento quarenta y nueue mill hombres que cobrian toda la tierra (6)
(b) *en llegando* a un petril que salia fuera de la fortaleza, queriendo hablar ala gente que por alli combatia le dieron una pedrada los suyos en la cabeça (40)
(c) sali *en amanesciendo* por aquella calle donde el dia antes nos auian desbaratado (42)
(d) *en entrando* por tierra dela dicha prouincia salio mucha gente de los naturales (47)

3.5.5. The preposition PARA and its reduced form PA appear in different contexts: (1) to indicate direction in space, as in items (a) and (b); (2) with a noun or noun phrase to indicate intention, purpose or goal, as in (c)-(h); (3) before an infinitive when it is preceded by an object clitic or without the object clitic as in examples (i)-(p); (4) with sentences in which the subjunctive mood is preceded by the relative coordinator *que*, as in (q)-(u). In the *Second Letter* the use of PA prevails, and there seems to be no stylistic distinction between formal and informal discourse, since Cortés, who was an expert in reverential formulae, used *PA* before His Majesty, as in (d) and (e).

(a) el dicho capitán me fizo saber a la hora me partí *pa la dicha villa* (2)
(b) siendo yo salido de la Vera Cruz hasta la ciudad de Cempoal que esta a quatro leguas della *pa de alli* seguir mi camino (2)
(c) *Para mas seguridad* de los que en la villa quedaban traxe comigo algunas personas principales (1)
(d) de las quales todas me dio *pa vra. alteza* (25)
(e) *pa un gran príncipe y señor* (29)
(f) Esteras de muchas maneras *pa camas*, y otras mas delgadas *pa asiento* y *pa esteras* (27)
(g) Colores *pa pintores* quantos se pueden hallar en España (27)
(h) Y *para las aues* que se crian en la mar eran los estanques (30)
(i) *Pa hazer* estancias y *pa sacar* oro (22)
(j) Les pidio canoas *pa mirar* el rio (22)
(k) y con tantos generos de armas *para* nos *ofender* salimos tan libres (6)
(l) auia en esta casa aposentamientos *pa* se aposentar (30)
(m) de allí me fui por la costa por alguna gente *pa saber* lengua (2)
(n) tomaua sus hijos *para* los *matar y sacrificar* a sus ydolos (1)
(o) tuue manera como so color que los dichos nauios no estaban *pa nauegar* (1)
(p) Venden conejos, liebres, venados y perros pequeños *pa comer* castrados (27)
(q) *pa que* el dicho Diego Velazquez *pusiesse* nauios en guarda *pa que* la *tomassen* (1)
(r) Por descubrir la tierra *para que* si algo *ouuiesse* yo lo *supiesse* (5)

(s) hecho otro nueuo de muchos hojos y palos agudos hincados y encubiertos *para que* los caballos *cayessen* y se *mancassen* (10)
(t) tenia muchas de las calles tapiadas y por las açoteas de las casas muchas piedras: *para que* despues que *entrassemos* en la ciudad tomar nos seguramente y aprovecharse de nos otros (10)

3.6 Common verbs in transition

Common verbs such as DECIR, HABER, HACER, TRAER, VER, etc. can have one or more forms in the same tense or in different tenses; they reveal the polymorphism of late medieval Spanish.

3.6.1. Modern Spanish DECIR derives from medieval DEZIR. It was commonly spelled with <z> in various tenses (e.g. *dizes, dezia*, and with <x> in the preterit indicative (e.g., *dixeron*).

3.6.2. Modern Spanish HACER follows closely the etymological criterion while late medieval Spanish varies according to tense and finite forms, thus in the *Second Letter* both HAZER and FAZER are found as in *fize, fizo, fiziesse, faria, hazía, hezimos*, etc. The past participle *fecho* alternates with *hecho*.

3.6.3. In modern Spanish, the verb TRAER and its derivatives in the preterit (*contraer, retraer*) follow the etymological criterion, thus rendering *yo traje, tú trajiste, él trajo, nosotros trajimos, ellos trajeron*. In late medieval Spanish authors hesitated between *traxe* and *truxe* in the same sentence or in the same paragraph. The variation in spelling appears consistently in the *Second Letter*.
(a) *traxe* conmigo algunas personas principales (1)
(b) *truxe* cerca de quatrocientas personas entre hombres y mugeres (6)
(c) si alguna necessidad *traxessen* se podia reparar della (2)
(d) y *traxe*les a la memoria (8)
(e) *traxeron*me diez platos de oro (13)
(f) parecia que toda la tierra se caya abaxo: assí se baxaron y *truxeron* mucha nieve (14)
(g) *traxeron* al dicho Qualpopoca (20)
(h) otro dia me *truxeron* figurada en un paño toda la costa (22)
(i) me *traxo* una carta de un español (32)
(j) les dixe que me *traxessen* una canoa (38)
(k) de cansados nos *retruximos* a la fortaleza (40)

(l) me *traxo* una cama de madera (46)
(m) que se viniessen a sus casas y *traxessen* a sus mugeres (51)

3.6.4. Modern Spanish verb VER was VEDERE in late medieval. The conjugations were *yo vide*, *él vido* in the preterit indicative, and *yo via*, *ellos vían* in imperfect indicative. The examples below are from the *Second Letter*.
(a) donde no me *vian* (7)
(b) que bien *vian* que ellos tenian la culpa (7)
(c) Y que *vian* claro (8)
(d) por las señales que pa ello *via* (9)
(e) ya *vido* que mi determinada voluntad (13)
(f) una cerimonia que entre ellos se *via* mucho (17)

3.6.5. In modern Spanish the verb HABER is used exclusively as auxiliary + past participle or with the special impersonal HAY (for both singular and plural), whereas in Cortesian texts HABER is used with the meaning of TENER as in (a) to (e) and alternates with the verb TENER to indicate possession, as in sentence (f). Examples (a) to (f) are from the *Second Letter*, whereas an expression of time appearing in example (g) is from the *First Letter*.
(a) Vista la discordia y la desconformidad delos vnos y delos otros, no *oue* poco plazer (10)
(b) antes que *ouiessen* lugar de se juntar les queme cinco o seys lugares (6)
(c) y como dexaua aquellos pueblos de paz, *ouieron* mucho plazer (7)
(d) La qual lo dixo a aquel Jeronymo de Aguilar lengua que yo *oue* en Yucatan (11)
(e) E por aquella noche nos dexaron avn que casi al alua *ovo* çierto rebato (44)
(f) E me rogaua que le *tuuiesse* por amigo con tal condicion que los de Culua no entrassen en su tierra (22)
(g) Gerónimo de Aguilar contonos la manera como se había perdido y el tiempo que *había* que estaba en aquel cautiverio (15)

3.7 Verbal clitics

In modern Spanish, direct, indirect, and reflexive object pronouns are attached to the infinitive form of the verb, as in *para defenderlos*, *comenzó a decirles*. In the *First Letter* the same verbal clitics go before infinitives as in (a) to (h), only occasionally attached to them, as in (i).
(a) como el capitán tuviese necesidad de agua, hízose a la vela para *la ir* a tomar a otra parte (9)

(b) comenzó a tomar su agua y a *les decir* con el dicho faraute que les dieran oro (10)
(c) no tenía mucha razón de *se quejar* el dicho Diego Velásquez (11)
(d) teniendo deseo de haber más acordó sin *lo decir* ni hacer saber a los padres gobernadores (12)
(e) tenían necesidad para *se proveer* de cosas (...) para el viaje (12)
(f) El dicho cacique le respondió que él era contento de *lo hacer* así (14)
(g) Y luego quisiera ir con toda la flota con su persona a *los redimir* (14)
(h) Gerónimo de Aguilar les hizo entender como él no venía a *les hacer* mal ni daño alguno, sino a *les hablar* de parte de vuestras majestades (17)
(i) Fernando Cortés hablándoles por medio de una lengua o faraute, les dijo que *no iban a hacerles* mal ni daño alguno (13)

3.7.1. In modern Spanish, reflexive, direct and indirect object pronouns consistently appear before the conjugated verb. Examples: *se hizo, se acordó, se acercaron, le dijeron*. In the *First Letter* the same objects are attached to the conjugated verb as in (a) to (f). The stylistic variations (g) through (i) anticipate the change to modern Spanish since verbal clitics always go before the conjugated verb.

(a) [los indios] vinieron muy recatados y *acercáronse* a los navios (10)
(b) hizo salir a la gente de los navíos y *aposentáronse* en aquel pueblo (13)
(c) *parecióle* que se había rescatado poco (11)
(d) envió dos capitanes con hasta ciento hombres y *mandóles* que el uno fuese a la punta de la dicha isla y el otro a la otra (13)
(e) y yendo su viaje, *acordóse* de volver al dicho puerto o isla Santa Cruz (9)
(f) Echaron a tierra los tres indios, y *enviáronlos* a buscar a los españoles y *estuviéronlos* esperando (15)
(g) Acabada de hacer la dicha armada, *se partió* de la dicha isla (12)
(h) y él *les rogó les dejasen* tomar agua y que luego *se irían* (10)
(i) Gerónimo de Aguilar *nos contó* la manera como *se había perdido* (15)

3.8 Stylistic and dialect variations

The letters by Hernán Cortés reveal not only the transitions from medieval to modern Spanish, but some of the regional, stylistic and dialect variations in both peninsular and New World Spanish that persist until the present. First, the use of direct object pronoun LE referring to [+ masculine + animate] objects represents a major departure from the etymological variant LO, which is older than LE, the pronoun clitic that replaced LO because LO also refers to [+ singular masculine − animate] objects. The trajectory of both pronouns has been examined under the frameworks of historical linguistics, dialectology, and sociolinguistics. The Romance etymological system derived directly from Latin precedes the use of LE as direct [+ masculine singular animate] objects, a divergence emerging in Castile that has remained a distinctive trait of Castilian. The use of this Castilian variant is known as *leísmo*. Modern Latin American Spanish prefers the ancestral etymological distinction between feminine and masculine direct objects for both animate and inanimate objects as in LOS / LOS *encontré* ('I found him' or 'I found it' / 'I found them') and LA / LAS *encontré* ('I found her' / 'I found them'). In contrast, Castilian uses LE and LES for [+ masculine + animate] objects, including animals, as in item (i). Following these norms in the *Second Letter*, Cortés preferred the Castilian variant but occasionally he also used the variant LO, as in examples (a) and the first part of (d). In both cases LO is used with the verb *ver* ('to see').

(a) E viendo*lo* todos le dieron con vnas porras en la cabeça hasta que *lo* mataron (9)
(b) les dixo que no yuan a hazerles mal ni daño alguno, sino para **les amonestar y atraer** (13)
(c) Por no **escandalizarles** ni dar algun desman a mi proposito y camino (43)
(d) hize tomar uno de ellos desimuladamente, que los otros no *lo* vieron, y aparteme con el y con dos lenguas y **amendrentele** para que dixesse la verdad (46)
(e) Cuando salia fuera el dicho Muteeçuma todos los que yuan con el (...) le boluían el rostro y en ninguna manera **le mirauan** (31)
(f) aquellos dos señores que con el yvan me detuuieron con las manos para que no **le tocasse** (17)
(g) [Muteeçuma] boluia siempre muy alegre y contento al aposento donde yo **le tenía** (21)
(h) E me rogaua que **le tuuiesse** por amigo (22)
(i) nos mataron un cauallo, que aunque Dios sabe quanta falta nos hizo y quanta pena rescebimos con **auer** nos **le muerto** (42)

3.9 Indicative and subjunctive

In modern Spanish the imperfect subjunctive forms ending in –RA (–*ara* for the first conjugation and –*iera* for the second and third) are interchangeable with Spanish endings in –SE (-*ase* for the first conjugation and -*iese* for the second and the third). Hernán Cortés preferred the form ending in –SE as in *hablasse, quisiesse, sirviessen, dexasse, partiesse*. In the *Second Letter*, the use of indicative and subjunctive appears like in modern Spanish. The former is used for narration or vivid description of the places, things and peoples that Cortés discovered on his excursions. Subjunctive is used to express command, opinion, wish, need, petition, softened request, doubt, fear, etc. in the subordinate clauses that are normally preceded by a verb in indicative in the main clause (*decir, hacer, mandar, ordenar, rogar, temer, pedir*) that spontaneously generates the subjunctive. Because Cortés was consistently reporting in the past what were presumably the objective events, he overused imperfect subjunctive ending in –SE, the traditional forms of subjunctive with the meaning of [+ subjectivity] or [+ reservation] found in the Latin grammars. The redundancy of the forms in –SE is typical of the prose of the 16th century.

(a) me *dixeron* que yo lo *hiziesse* castigar (9)
(b) en tanto *fize* que la gente de los nuestros *estuuiessen* apersçebidos (12)
(c) me *rogaua* que le *perdonasse* porque no salia su persona a verme (15)
(d) me *rogaua* que si *fuesse* posible no *fuesse* alla (16)
(e) nos partimos con harto *temor* de que aquellos *quisiessen* perseverar en nos hazer alguna burla (14)
(f) Le *rogué* que me *mostrasse* las minas de donde se sacaua el oro (69)
(g) me *dixeron* que no *parasse* sino que me *fuesse* a otra ciudad (16)
(h) *pidiome* que le *diesse* españoles que *fuessen* con ellos pa que lo *viessen* sacar [oro] (21)
(i) les *dixe* que me *traxessen* una canoa (38)
(j) el dicho Muteeçuma les *auia mandado* que *matassen* a aquellos españoles (20)
(k) Yo *dixe* que *uiniesse* su capitan y que se *fuesse* con los nauios (2)
(l) para que *tuuiesse* por bien de le mandar rescebir a su real servicio, que le *rogava* me *diesse* algun oro que yo *embiasse* a vra. majestad (4)
(m) yo *hize* que los *llamassen* y que *uiniessen* y no *ouiessen* miedo (5)

3.9.1 Imperfect subjunctive in adverbial clauses

Imperfect subjunctive forms in –SE prevail in adverbial clauses describing the sequence of events. Several connectors may be used to express anteriority, co-existence, or cause-and-effect subsequence, for instance, *antes que, de manera que, después que, hasta que, para que, sin que,* and unknown antecedent, as in (i). The sentences below from the *Second Letter* illustrate the use.

(a) los auia embiado a ella *para que viessen* nuestro real (6)
(b) auiamos fecho lugar *para que* en nuestro real no nos *ofendiessen* (6)
(c) que de ninguna manera me *partiesse sin que* los señores de la ciudad *viniessen* aqui (10)

(d) *antes que ouiesse* lugar de se juntar, les quemé cinco o seis lugares pequeños (6)
(e) Muteeçuma su señor *les auia embiado pa que me esperasen* allí y me *fiziessen* proueer de todas las cosas necessarias (15)
(f) *pa que* el dicho Diego Velasquez *pusiesse* nauios *pa que* la *tomassen* (1)
(g) me rogauan que *antes de que me determinasse* de perder su amistad y hazerle la guerra que dezia que me *informasse* bien de la verdad (13)
(h) *antes que amanesciesse* di sobre dos pueblos en que mate mucha gente (7)
(i) que *dondequiera* que yo *estuuiesse* le *embiasse* a pedir lo que yo *quisiesse* (13)

3.9.2 Imperfect subjunctive in translation

When he used the form ending in –SE derived from Latin pluperfect subjunctive AMAVISSEM, Hernán Cortés followed the patterns of late medieval Spanish; at the time –SE was the most common and frequent in the subordinate clauses preceded by a verb in the preterit or imperfect indicative, as in (a) through (e). Nonetheless, the main verb can be implicit as in sentence (f), where Hernán Cortés advised his men not to get into trouble.

(a) Y ellos de Cempoal vinieron a mi y *dixeron* me que *mirasse* que aquellos eran malos (6)
[the people from Cempoal came up to me and *told me to be wary* of the bad guys]
(b) *amedrente*le para que me *dixesse* la verdad (6)
[*I intimidated* him so *he would tell* me the truth]
(c) Yo les *satisfize* diziendo que *cognosciessen* como ellos tenian la culpa del daño que auian rescebido (8)
[*I placated* them by saying that *they should acknowledge* their own responsibility for the damages they received]
(d) [Moctezuma] me *dixo* que alli le *esperasse* (17)
[Moctezuma *asked* me to *wait for* him over there]
(e) que todavia me *rogaua* que no *curasse* de yr a su tierra porque era esteril (13)
[he even *begged* me not *to bother* to go to his land because it was sterile]
(f) que si yo era loco y me metia donde nunca podria salir, que no lo *fuessen* ellos sino que se *boluiessen* a la mar (7)
[that if I was crazy and I had gotten into a rut, that *they should not do* the same but instead *they should return* to sea]

3.9.3 Conditional sentences with –SE in translation

In conditional sentences made up of protasis and apodosis, the imperfect subjunctive is used in the former and the conditional indicative in the latter. In imperfect subjunctive the ending –SE appears in combination with the synthetic conditional as in (a) through (e), identical to modern Spanish. Variations to this pattern appear in both peninsular and Latin American social dialects, where the conditional is replaced by imperfect subjunctive ending in –RA in the SI-clause or protasis. All the examples derive from the *Second Letter*.

(a) creyendo que si alli los nauíos *dexasse*, se me *alçarian* con ellos (1)
[believing that if I *were to leave* the ships, *they would* riot against me]
(b) si sus nauios y gente *traxessen* alguna necessidad, les *socorrería* con lo que yo *pudiesse* (2)
[if their ships and people needed anything, I *would help* them with whatever means I could]
(c) si no *viniessen yria* sobre ellos y los *destruyria* (10)
[If *they did not come* I *would go* after them and *destroy* them]
(d) si assi no lo *fiziessen yria* contra ellos con todo el poder que yo *tuuiesse* (32)
[if they *did not do* it in this manner, I *would go* after them with all the power I had]
(e) si no se *fiziesse* grande y cruel castigo en ellos nunca se *remediaría* jamas (47)
[if *they were not* severely *punished* things *would* never *be remedied*]

3.9.4 Conditional sentences with –RA in translation

Forms ending in –RA are not too frequent in late medieval Spanish; they derive from pluperfect indicative AMAVERAM which gradually acquired subjunctive meaning and began to compete with the form –SE derived from AMAVISSEN. In conditional sentences –RA can appear in both the protasis and the apodosis, but the meaning in the apodosis remains indicative and is equivalent to modern conditional forms ending in –RÍA. It is assumed that the combination of –RA and –RA in conditional sentences, although scarce, spread to other contexts and gradually replaced the –SE form in Mexican Spanish (Acevedo 1997: 108). Also, in the *Second Letter* the ending in –RA appears occasionally with the contrary-to-fact phrase *como si fuera* ('as if it had been') or *si no fuera* ('if it had not been'), as in (e) and (f). While the form –SE clearly prevails in the *Second Letter*, the form in –RA is also used anticipating the modern preference of Mexican Spanish for frequent use of –RA in the protasis as in (a) through (d). The semantic convergence of AMAVERAM and AMAVISSEM in Spanish occurred after the 16th century.

Grammarians have assumed that in modern Spanish the two forms are equivalent and interchangeable as long as they maintain subjunctive meaning, but this distinction may be related to regional and social factors. After three centuries of colonial life and two of independent speech habits, speakers of Mexican Spanish are strongly inclined to use the ending –RA though occasionally they do use the forms in –SE.

(a) si en mi mano *fuera* boluerme, yo lo *hiziera* por fazer plazer a Muteeçuma (15)
 [if *I could* return, *I would do* it just to please Moctezuma]
(b) Y temi que me *pusieran* fuego. Lo qual si *acaesciera fuera* tanto daño que ninguno ninguno de nos otros *escapara* (7)
 [And *I was afraid they would set fire* on me. If *it happened, it would cause* so much damage that *none of us would escape*]
(c) se auian visto en mucho trabajo y peligro, y todauia los *mataran* si el dicho Muteeçuma no *mandara* cessar la guerra (38)
 [they had been in a lot of trouble and danger, and *they would have killed* them if said Moctezuma *had not ordered* to stop the war]
(d) *si no ouiera hallado* alli socorro *se muriera* de sed y hambre (53)
 [if *he had not found* help right there, *he would have died* of hunger]
(e) *como si fueramos* los unos infieles y los otros cristianos (35)
 [*as though some of us were* infidels and others were Christian]
(f) nos rescibieron con tanta alegría *como si* nueuamente les *dieramos* las vidas (39)
 [we were received with so much joy that it seemed *as though we had revived* them]

3.10 Extinct and current lexical items and discourse markers

Late medieval lexical items and a discourse marker appear in the letters written by Hernán Cortés. One adverb, *aína* ('rapidly' or 'fast') is no longer used in Mexico but has been documented in regions of the New World (e.g. Paraguay), where it may be considered archaic. In contrast, *asaz* ('sufficient') is almost extinct in Latin American varieties. Examples (a) through (d) derive from the *Second Letter*.

(a) me dixeron que deuia de ser lexos y que no podian venir tan *ayna* (3)
(b) era la mezquita mayor de aquella ciudad *asaz* fuerte (37)
(c) no acauaria tan *ayna* (29)
(d) podia tener manera de mas *ayna* sojuzgarlos (51)

3.10.1. The discourse marker, *dizque*, typical of medieval Spanish appears in the *Second Letter* rather infrequently. *Dis que* or *dizque* (< *dicen que*) is initially equiv-

alent to an impersonal report ("they said that") with the added subjective dubitative meaning. *Dizque* has high vitality in informal Latin American Spanish speech but may be making inroads into more formal domains such as newspapers and magazines. Examples are not abundant in the *Second Letter* (1522) but are identical to modern Spanish.
(a) los dos traya segun me dixo pa que fuessen testigos de cierta notificacion que *dis que* el capitan le auia mandado (2)
(b) *dizque* dixeron a los españoles que los naturales desta prouincia estauan confederados con los de Guacachula (49)
(c) el hijo de Muteeçuma que eredaba el señorio y otros dos hijos suyos quedaron biuos el uno *dizque* es loco y el otro perlatico (52)
(d) que *dizque* venia en busca dela gente que Francisco de Garay auia embiado a esta tierra (53)

Finally, the *Second Letter* offers examples of lexical items that are current in Mexican Spanish: the verb *platicar* 'to chat', instead of *charlar*, which is more frequent in Spain today, the diminutive of the adverb *cerca* ('near), and the noun *alberca* ('pond') instead of the widespread modern *piscina* ('swimming pool').
(a) acerca desto passamos muchas *platicas* y razones (20)
(b) *platicamos* muchas vezes la orden que se deuia de tener en la seguridad desta prouincia (48)
(c) muy *cerquita* de alli estaua mucha gente de Muteeçuma (11)
(d) alli mesmo *albercas* de agua dulce (16)
(e) Sobre cada *alberca* y estanques destas aues auia sus corredores y miradores (30)

3.11 Use of Taino borrowings

Taino borrowings appear in the Mesoamerican area in the *First Letter* (1520/2007). Cortés and other explorers had already appropriated the semantics of the objects, persons and foodstuffs that they encountered in the islands: *ají, cacique, canoa, jagüey, maíz, maizal* were familiar nouns that appeared without a definition (see Table 3.1), or with common Spanish modifiers. The most frequent Taino noun in the *First Letter* is the word *cacique* followed by the word *canoa* while the most common neologism is the word *indio(s)* with the meaning of native or "*natural de la tierra*".
(a) Entraron veinte *indios* en una *canoa* (10)
(b) Se fue con ellos hasta un *jagüey* de agua (10)
(c) Fernando Cortes había hablado a aquel *cacique* (14)

(d) que hablasen a los *caciques* que topasen (13)
(e) les dijo que fueran a llamar a los otros *caciques* (13-14)
(f) y el dicho *cacique* respondió que era contento de lo hacer así (14)
(g) proveyó luego con enviar con ciertos *indios* en una *canoa* (14)
(h) sabían quién era el *cacique* (14)
(i) Se partió con su carta para los otros *caciques* (14)
(j) les rogaba que trabajasen de se soltar y huir en algunas *canoas* (14-5)
(k) vieron venir una *canoa* a la vela hacia la dicha isla (15)
(l) como el capitán reprendiese a los *caciques* de la dicha isla (16)
(m) vinieron ciertos *indios* en una *canoa* y trujeron ciertas gallinas y un poco de *maíz* (17)
(n) envió con ellos sus cartas a los *caciques* (19)
(o) aquellos *caciques* les rogaban que les perdonasen (20)
(p) la tierra es muy buena y muy abundosa de comida, así de *maíz* como de fruta (20)
(q) les dio para los *caciques* dos camisas (21)
(r) vino el dicho *cacique* como había quedado (21)
(s) Los mantenimientos que tienen es *maíz* y algunos *ajis* como los de las otras islas y *patata yuca*, así como las que comen en la isla de Cuba (25)
(t) sesenta hanegas de *maíz*, y diez de frijoles, y dos mill pies de *cacao* (22)
(u) *maíz* y algunos *ajis* (25)

3.11.1 Documentation of Taino borrowings in New Spain

Other Taino borrowings documented in the Mexican sources are the following: *barbacoa, batea, cazabe, guacamaya, guayaba, hamaca, hicotea, huracán, iguana, macana, piragua, tabaco, tiburón, tuna,* etc. These loans were not only vital and far-reaching in the 16th century but persist in contemporary Spanish and other European languages. Their vitality in the primitive lexical system explains their spread against other native forms, inasmuch as the explorers of the 16th century took them to other regions of the New World and used them to express the new realities they encountered (Lope Blanch 1979). The early appropiation of Taino and Carib by Spanish speakers before the discovery of Mexico was conducive to their integration into proto-Mexican Spanish or the earliest version of the Mexican Spanish koine. In the *Second Letter*, Cortés continued to use integrated and Hispanicized Tainismos without definitions and with the noun modifiers that are common in Spanish, e.g. *jagüey de agua* (10), *canoa a la vela* (15), *un poco de maíz* (17), *algunos ajis* (25), *maizales* (47), *cañas de maiz* (77), etc. Moreover, before 1555 Alonso de Molina had gathered the lexical entries for his *Vocabulario*,

Taino borrowings must have sounded just like Spanish to him inasmuch as they had been documented in other sources between 1493 and 1549. Table 3.1 is a short list of common words that were disseminated from the Antilles to Mexico in the early decades of the 16th century and later to the present territories of Central and South America (see Map 3.4).

Table 3.1: Tainismos in Molina's *Vocabulario de la lengua mexicana y castellana y castellana y mexicana* (1555 and 1571)

Item No.	Modern Spanish	First documented	English meaning	Assimilated loan
1	Ají*	1493	Hot pepper	Yes
2	Areito	Before Molina	Dance	No
3	Aura	1549	Bird of prey, vulture	Yes
4	Batata	1516-20	Yam, sweet potato	Yes
5	Batea*	1510	Track pan used to wash gold	Not completely
6	Batey	1535	Ball game played with hips and legs	Yes
7	Bohío*	1493	Hut	Not completely
8	Cacique	1492	Chieftain, nobleman	Yes
9	Canoa*	1492	Canoe	Yes
10	Caribe	1520	Very hot (pepper)	No
11	Coa*	1516	Sharp wooden rod used to till the soil	Yes
12	Cutara	1531	Sandal, sandal for noblemen	Yes
13	Embijar	1532	To dye someone or something	Yes
14	Enagua	1495	Female skirt	No
15	Hamaca	1492-3	Hammock	Not sure
16	Huracán	Unknown	Hurricane, storm	Not sure
17	Jagüey	1518	Cistern	Yes
18	Maguey	1515	Plant of the agave family	Yes
19	Maíz*	1493-1500	Corn	Yes
20	Maizal	1512	Corn field	Yes
21	Sabana	1515	Meadowland	Yes
22	Tuna	1514-16	Prickly fruit of the cactus	Yes

Source: E. Hernández Hernández (1996), *It appears in the edition of 1555

3.12 Pronouns of address

The pronouns of address in New World Spanish were significantly reduced due to the disappearance of the pronouns VOS (singular) and VOSOTROS (plural). Pronouns of address such as *Vuestra Majestad* or *Vuestra Señoría* [+ reverence] can be retrieved from literary and non-literary texts, official documents and the like. In the *Second Letter* (1522), Hernán Cortés frequently used these formulaic pronouns in 3rd person singular to address the king of Spain. In contrast, the fictitious speeches given by Moctezuma to Cortés show the use of VOS (singular formal between men of equal rank) as in (a) through (c), while VOSOTROS (plural informal) is used between Moctezuma and his own vassals, as in (d) through (h).

(a) Y segun la parte que *vos dezis* que *venis* que es do sale el sol y las cosas que *dezis* dese gran señor o rey que aca *os* embio (18)
(b) E por tanto *vos sed* ciertos que *os* obedesceremos y ternemos por señor (18)
(c) Y todo lo que nosotros tenemos es pa lo que *vos* dello *quisieredes* disponer (18)
(d) *veys*me aqui que so de carne y huesso como *vos* y como cada vno: y que soy mortal (18)
(e) todo lo que yo tuuiere *teneys* cada vez que *vos* lo *quisieredes* (18)
(f) de mucho tiempo aca *vosotros* y *vuestros* padres y abuelos *aueys* sido y *sois* subditos y vasallos de mis antecessores y mios (24)
(g) E *vosotros* assi mismo *aveys* hecho lo que buenos y leales vasallos son obligados a sus señores (24)
(h) Y mucho *os* ruego pues a todos *os* es notorio que assi como hasta aqui a mi me *aueys* tenido y obedesçido por señor *vro*. (24)

3.13 General features of 16th century Spanish pronunciation

The period of conquest and colonization of the Spanish-speaking New World coincided with many ongoing internal changes. This fact may explain why there are residual variants in different areas of the Latin American sub-continent, to wit:

(1) Aspiration of initial /f/ represented by writing [h] was ongoing. Writers from northern Spain began to drop the [h] in speaking, which became silent while the same feature was still used in the south. Aspiration is still used with relative frequency in areas of Latin American such as the coastal regions. It has remained in Mexican Spanish at less frequent rates.
(2) The merger of affricates and fricatives was ongoing, but the contrast was resolved in favor of the fricatives, since the affricates lost one distinctive feature [+ occlusive]. In addition, the affricate phoneme from Nahuatl /tɬ/ was incorporated to Mexican Spanish via the use of toponyms, as in T*l*alpan, Ix*tl*accíhuat*l*, etc. In modern Mexican Spanish turned into an allophonic variation [tɬ] with no distinctive meaning.
(3) The merger of the fricatives and affricates from medieval Spanish was completed in peninsular Spanish, and no traces of affrication are found in Latin

American Spanish, except in Mexico, where affrication of /s/ [ts] may be attributed to contact with Nahuatl. The merger of apico-alveolar fricatives and dorso-dental fricatives was completed in New World Spanish, but apical pronunciation of /s/ distinguishes central areas of Colombia. Residuals of *ceceo* reappear in different regions of Mexico and other countries (e.g. Venezuela, Nicaragua).
(4) Loss of voiced sibilants or devoicing was ongoing until voiceless sibilants became the norm. Except as allophones [mizmo], [dezde], there are no traces of voiced sibilants in any of the varieties of the Spanish-speaking world.
(5) Aspiration and/or deletion of final /s/ were advanced in Andalusia and remains along coastal and non-coastal areas of Central and South America but this trait is non-existent in the Mexican Central Highlands where the koine originated, though it may reappear along the coasts of the Atlantic and the Pacific.
(6) By the same token, the merger of voiced and voiceless palatals or de-palatalization was ongoing, and the contrast was resolved in favor of the voiceless, which lost the feature [+ palatal] and became velar represented by the letter *jota*. Common examples are modern Spanish *bajo* and *dijo* (< medieval Spanish *baxo* and *dixo*).

3.13.1 General features of 16th century Spanish: morpho-syntax

It is assumed that some of the most significant features of 16th century Spanish are present in all the areas of the Spanish-speaking world while some others are peculiar to New World Spanish. The primary traits that are general to Spanish and have evolved in the transition from late medieval to modern Spanish are the following: (1) The gender of MAR, PUENTE, CANAL and CALOR are no longer feminine. (2) The combination of indirect and direct object GELO has become SE LO in modern Spanish. (3) Reflexive, direct and indirect object pronouns have two positions: they go either before the conjugated verb or are attached to infinitives or gerunds. (4) Inter-dialectal use of 3rd person atonic pronouns was unstable; Castilian speakers used LE mostly for direct object masculine [+ animate] and another group used LO for the same category. At present, Latin American Spanish is mostly pro-etymological. (5) The pronoun of address *vos* was used for singular and plural [+ familiar] with identical verb conjugations. The New World innovation is known as *voseo*, a combination of forms of *vos* and *tú* for the extreme non-deference domain. (6) Use of *vuestra merced* (singular) and *vuestras mercedes* (plural) for second person was stable; there are however residuals of *su merced* in Mexican rural areas and also in South America. (7) Replacement of *vuestra merced* with *Usted* and *vuestras mercedes* with *Ustedes* has been distributed along different domains; in modern Castilian the plural *Ustedes* indicates [+ deference], but it is ambivalent in the rest of the Spanish speaking Latin America since it can be used as plural for both formal and informal domains.

3.14 Conclusions

The origins of Mexican Spanish can be traced to the prose written by Hernán Cortés, a man of Old Christian lineage, active in military enterprises, and average education. His whereabouts in both the Old and the New World attest to the diversity of his regional contacts. His writings exhibit the features of late medieval Spanish, transitional choices, and lexical items from both Taino and Nahuatl. The contemporary scribes also exhibit mixed traits, similar to the Cortés' prose. Based on the data available in the *First* and the *Second Letter* this chapter has discussed features that belong to the general evolution of the Spanish language, changes in regional dialects and standard models, variations in 16th century Spanish, and variants that continued to be used in Latin America. The documentary evidence points to the existence of an earliest variety of Mexican Spanish or proto-Mexican Spanish that exhibited a combination of features derived from late medieval Spanish, Taino borrowings and Nahuatl loans (see chapter 4).

Features that were retained in Mexican Spanish and became components of the Mexican Spanish koine originated in the Central Highlands, particularly within the capital city, which was the Mecca of all social, commercial, and political activities since the early 1500's when Mexico City had more Spanish speakers involved in all kinds of pursuits. The magnificent capital turned into the centripetal force that attracted more immigrants from Spain and simultaneously the centrifugal force that propelled the dispersion of tendencies in the small surrounding cities and towns of New Spain. The spread of Spanish through koineization occurred before diversification via two simultaneous processes: (a) social stratification, and (b) vernacularization. Social stratification was first based on the caste system that was later transformed into a class system. The class system contributed to the distinction of hierarchical strata, which in turn established speech indicators that were reallocated along mostly rural or isolated spots when the normative style(s) finally took shape. The origin of residual variants that are herein considered popular (i.e. 'archaic') can be traced to the first part of the 16th century (e.g, *truje < truxe, vide < vide*), as exemplified in the *Second Letter* (1522).

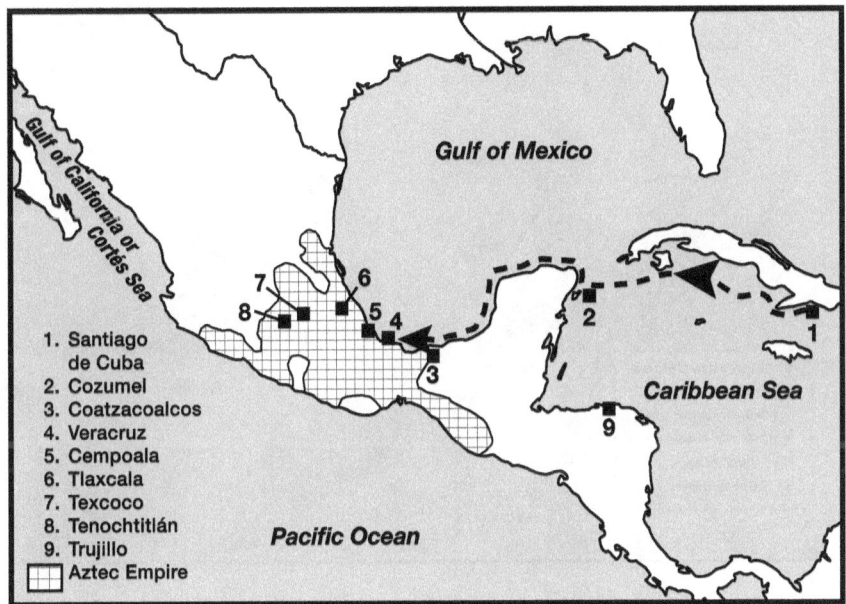

Map 3.1: The Route of Hernán Cortés from Cuba to Mexico

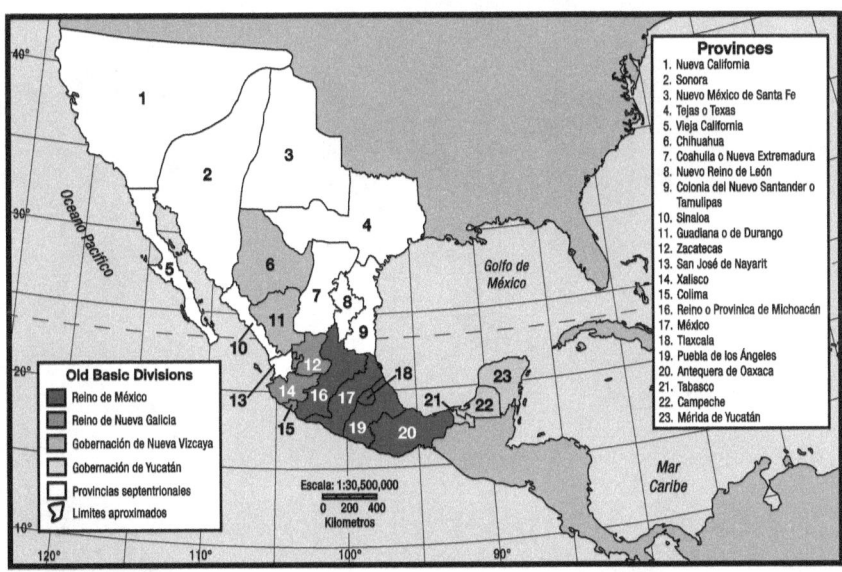

Map 3.2: Old Division (Provinces and Kingdoms): 1550-1776. Source: *Nuevo Atlas Nacional de México* (2007). Universidad Nacional Autónoma de México (Lámina H III 1A)

138 — Chapter 3 The Spanish language and its variations in New Spain

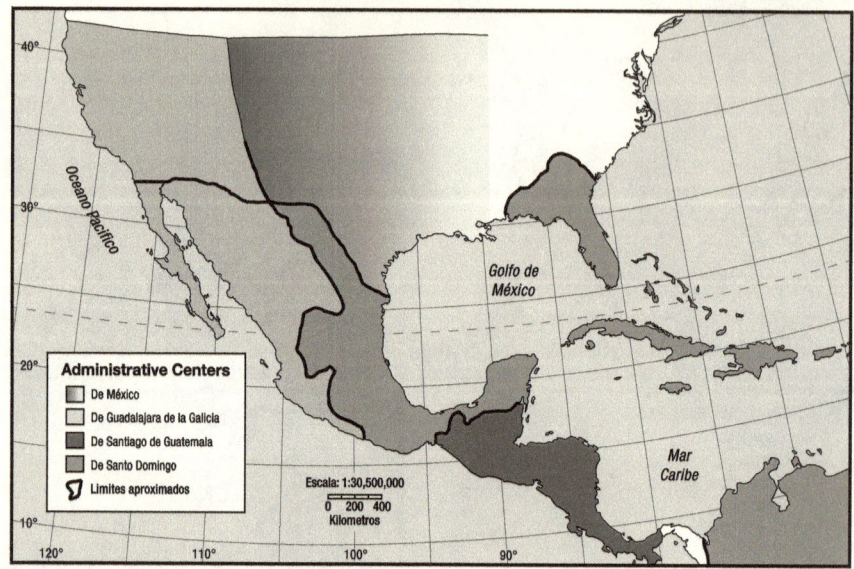

Map 3.3: Division in administrative centers, 16th-17th centuries. Source: *Nuevo Atlas Nacional de México* (2007). Universidad Nacional Autónoma de México (Lámina H III 1B)

3.14 Conclusions — 139

Map 3.4: The spread of *Tainismos* in the 17th Century. Source: Adapted from Mejías (1980: 156)

Chapter 4
Koineization and the first generation of Spanish speakers

4.1 The first generation

This chapter is concerned with the emergence of the earliest variety of Mexican Spanish spoken and written in the capital city and surrounding areas, where Spanish speakers of diverse peninsular regions and social strata not only settled but became protagonists of major political, ecclesiastic and social activities. It is assumed that Castilian, Andalusian and some other regional dialects were used in New Spain in the 16th century: the oldest peninsular variety, *toledano* was prestigious in the New World, and for this reason it was superposed over other varieties in formal domains (Granda 1994) and used and among men of letters (Perissinotto 1994). The earliest colonists (1520-1539) coming originally from Seville, Toledo, Badajoz, and Valladolid, and secondarily from Caceres, Salamanca, Cordoba, Burgos and other provinces (Boyd-Bowman 1968: 592) made up nonetheless a compact group of settlers residing with relative stability in New Spanish soil, where they used various peninsular varieties and/or mixed dialect features in the emerging spheres of interaction. The linguistic evidence appears mostly in the letters that they delivered to officials in Spain while they were in New Spain, when they replied to personal missives while in Mexico or in personal missives they wrote to their relatives in Mexico when they were in Spain. Scholars have retrieved numerous documents from various archives including those of the Spanish Inquisition in both Spain and Mexico. This chapter examines language subsamples from representative sources of the Central Highlands, to wit: *Documentos Lingüísticos de la Nueva España: Altiplano Central* (Company Company 1994) and *El habla de Diego de Ordaz* (Lope Blanch 1985). Language data from the earliest contact zone in the Gulf of Mexico are retrieved from *Documentos Lingüísticos de la Nueva España: Golfo de México* (Melis et al. 2008). Select variants belonging to the first part of the 16th century are analyzed from these three sets of colonial texts.

The koine may be considered the informal variety that evolved with vernacular features and co-existed with a more formal variety used by privileged members of the New Spanish society. It is the result of the mixture of features of diverse peninsular varieties, whose speakers intermingled in Hispaniola and Cuba before they discovered Mexico. Koneization began to take place on the islands, and by the time Spanish speakers reached the Mexican coasts, they were already acquainted with one another's dialects. Koineization was accelerated in New Spain due to the inter-dialectal experience of explorers, *encomenderos*, and other Spanish speakers who had been in the Caribbean. In New Spain it may be traced from the early 1520's to the mid 1550's and may be extended through the end of the 16th century, the decades in which the first generation of Spanish-speaking adults explored and founded numerous towns and cities. One of the most intriguing questions about the origin of any emerging variety has to do with the external processes and mechanisms that serve as catalysts of development and change. In the case of New World Spanish the external stimulus is clear insofar as the dynamic transplant was possible due to a wide diversity of speakers from peninsular regions and social strata. The first generation Spanish speakers settled in or around the capital city have been identified as belonging to the *encomenderos*, their families, and some others who arrived from Spain shortly after. *Encomenderos* were mostly adult males who had compelling incentives to claim legal rights in the new lands, and for this very reason, they established dense social and political networks that would keep them in the position they had gained at least for a few decades. The *encomenderos*' regional diversity was not a strong motivational force to keep them apart; on the contrary, their most pressing need was to remain solidary against the indigenous groups, which were still a menace despite the fact that they had been fragmented.

4.1.1 Spanish space and Spanish institutions

First-generation Spanish speakers resided mostly in the capital of New Spain, where they built Spanish institutions that kept them in power for at least three centuries. The layout of the city, known as the *traza*, was a large square in the center, a grid-work of straight streets extending from there in all directions with the cathedral on one side of the square, the municipal council building on the other, and the residence of the governor on yet another. The residences of the most prominent citizens, usually the *encomenderos*, were located facing the square. Spanish settlers of lesser ranks had their homes in an outer ring of lots, and beyond these, whole blocks were given over to gardens. Beyond the *traza* the streets were open-ended as a bordering edge, where temporary huts or ranchos—mainly for Indians serving Spaniards—were built. The initial structure grew indefinitely through the expansion of the *traza*. In and around the center the largest of the *encomenderos* dominated the municipal council while the councils favored them in grants of land and mining sites. New residents of the city were usually the conquerors' relatives and newcomers from the same towns, whereas Indian servants and employees of Spaniards began to reside in the cities and around the mining sites. Some lived with their masters, and others, not all steadily employed, lived in the irregular periphery. The *encomienda* was a major part of the center where the holder performed certain governmental duties and in turn received tribute that belonged to the Crown (Lockhart and Schwartz 1983: 66-68; 91-92). The viceroy and the *audiencias* (administrative centers and courts of appeal) became significant social and professional nuclei, where the new officialdom concentrated both wealth and power. The viceroys were authentic high nobles, close relatives of counts, dukes, and marquises, or they themselves holders of such titles. They brought dependents and other people from their own circle of friends and acquaintances. In addition, an administrative bureaucracy accompanied the core of New Spanish high society with all kinds of officials such as notaries, lettered men, lawyers, and other officials in charge as sub-governors and judges acting in areas of dense population (Lockhart and Schwartz 1983: 104-106).

Built over the ruins of the Great Tenochtitlan, the vice-royal capital soon became the most important urban center comprising both the city and the suburban fringe or densely settled territory lying outside of its boundaries but adjacent to them. The urban space was not identical with the locality but an additional geographical unit which included more than one locality with more than sufficient commuters going back and forth on a daily basis. The emergence of areas as urban or rural is bound up to historical, political, cultural and administrative considerations mostly referring to different forms of labor. Since the beginning of colonization the urban-rural dichotomy had an important role to play in the initial patterns of social stratification and turned into one of the determining factors in the formation of new lifestyles and attitudes. After this layout was established, a mass of indigenous natives turned into commuters who created a vital urban-rural pattern of sociolinguistic interaction, where Spanish and Nahuatl found their compartmentalized loci once sufficient Nahuatl speakers became bilingual and began to recognize the functions of both languages.

Spanish speakers of all regions and social strata resided and interacted in various domains playing all the roles that were needed to perform their institutional, familiar, social or personal activities and errands. The close-knit circle of Spanish speakers and the recreation of the new institutions inspired in the metropolitan model fostered the use of Spanish, which at the institutional level followed approximately the model of *toledano-castellano*, the result of convergence of the two oldest dialects inasmuch as *toledano* accepted the phonetic innovations of Castilian during the second half of the 16th century and the beginning of the 17th century (Lapesa 1985: 370-381). It is assumed that a formal variety, which in Granda's model is only *toledano*, was superposed over the *español koiné* (Granda 1994a: 47). The semi-formal variety had less vernacular features than the Spanish koine. Both were used simultaneously, but the semi-formal standard was associated with the upper strata and higher functions and the koine with the lower strata and informal functions. Notwithstanding, the most common language heard and spoken in the Mesoamerican area was Nahuatl. In the newly stratified society, the languages and language varieties were functionally allocated to serve distinct purposes in different domains. Social stratification enhanced the prestige and compartmentalized use of a semi-formal variety of Spanish exhibiting some of the Castilian features. This was most likely consolidated at the end of the 16th century, when at least one generation of Spanish speakers coming from Spain and one generation of New Spain-born adults had had the opportunity to fully develop different genres and styles in Spanish. The role of Spanish as a language of power and prestige was firmly ensconced by the end of the 16th century when a small but politically significant speech community sharing the same values and attitudes towards the transplanted language was established. This small Spanish-speaking community had a proclivity for literary endeavors and made New Spain a productive colony, where a trend towards standardization was favored at least in the capital city and amongst select groups of Spanish speakers. A minority of Spanish speakers moved to the rural areas that began to emerge as of the second half of the 16th century. The gaps in forms and functions between a standard variety and a koine led to diglossia, on the one hand, and role compartmentalization, on the other.

A comparative study by Perissinotto (1994) provides samples of adult emigrants from Spain who used the variety from Toledo. Fernán González de Eslava, born in Spain in 1534, reached the New World in 1558, became one of the early writers of Mexican literature, and followed the normative speech of Toledo. For example, he paired *pieça* with *cabeça* and *promessa* with *confiessa*, and did not confuse voiced <z> with voiceless <ç>, but maintained all the oppositions of medieval Spanish including aspiration of initial *h* (< Latin F). The speech of Toledo was still perceived as being the normative speech model by a considerable number of Spaniards and native-born Mexicans who were compelled to use the orthography of *toledano*, though their speech might have followed Andalusian patterns. Another representative of traditional norms was Diego de Ordaz. Born in 1480 in Castroverde de Campos (current province of Zamora), Ordaz migrated to the New World in his twenties and reached Mexico at age forty. Ordaz used the ideal sibilant model since he maintained the voiced/voiceless and fricative/affricate distinction of educated Spaniards from Castile and distinguished apical and dental points of articulation. The letters he delivered from Spain to his nephew living in Mexico have been thoroughly examined in the realms of phonetics, morpho-syntax and lexicon (Lope Blanch 1985)

4.2 The formation of the Mexican Spanish koine

New Spain proved ideal for koineization to take place because it was not depopulated like other New World regions, and because many indigenous towns were not completely destroyed by the war and ensuing epidemics. Spanish speakers engaged in agricultural activities and cattle-raising, and did not have any objections to settle in or around small towns, where they built haciendas and ranchos surrounded by masses of Indians needy of work and basic goods. The various peninsular varieties must have been spoken in the new Great Tenochtitlan as early as 1525, when the city had about 150 houses of Europeans. By the 1550's they numbered between 1,500 and 2,000 and were firmly settled in the central area, whereas 80,000 Indians lived in four of the major native barrios. Historians indicate that by the mid-16th century a compact top layer of Spaniards and mestizos governed a nation-to-be and vented a social exclusivity based on the moral values of conquest and caste (Liss 1975: 135ff, 154). On the basis of the available evidence it may be claimed that the Spanish koine originated in Mexico City amongst the speakers of diverse peninsular dialects residing there; from there the koine was spread to villages and towns founded by Spanish speakers throughout the 16th century and was disseminated to smaller towns and spots in both rural and semi-urban areas where there were still enclaves of Mesoamerican descent, which had at least partial exposure to the informal registers of Spanish. In sum, Spanish in New Spain evolved from three strains: (1) works of literature that followed, to an extent, the metropolitan trends and genres that were cultivated by the elite of Spanish speakers entrenched in positions of power and prestige. (2) Non-literary documents of educated Spanish speakers who paved the way for writing and speaking in the emerging institutions. (3) The informal variety or Spanish koine spoken by educated Spanish speakers who also used it as a colloquial register, Spanish speakers with less than average education, speakers of indigenous languages, speakers of ancestral African languages, and speakers of European languages other than Spanish.

4.3 The Spanish spoken and written in the 16th century

The New World Spanish archives of the 16th century differ very little or are identical to those kept in Spain because the Spaniards born or raised in Spain prevailed in the main court clerkships. The origin of the scribes aids in understanding the colonial period, inasmuch as in any given area of the New World, both Andalusians and non-Andalusians recorded and spread their own habits of pronunciation. From this competition and synthesis, a new Atlantic variety emerged, not necessarily homogeneous but marked by the southern pronunciation that eventually prevailed, particularly in reference to the spatial and social extension of *seseo* (Frago Gracia 1987: 73-74).

Two documents analyzed by Frago Gracia (1987: 80-82) reveal the writing habits of Spanish speakers of miscellaneous origins. Document 1 was written in 1544 by Alonso de Herrera, a native from Seville, who aspirated initial /f/ as in *[h]aze, [h]ará, [h]iziere, [h]azienda, des[h]azer* showing both the original etymology and the hyper-correct tendencies which prompted the aspiration in words in which etymological /f/ did not exist, as in *[h]elado, [h]era, [h]orden*. Following medieval scribes Herrera omitted the letter H in derivatives from the verb HABERE, e.g., *ay, aya, e, an* + past participle. Despite his Andalusian origin, the learning of norms aided in maintaining the distinction between <ç> and <z> as in *çibdad, çient, nesçesidad, pareçe, proçedido, relaçión, azeite, hazer, hazienda, sazón* but he did not make the difference between <-s-> and <-ss->, and therefore wrote *asi, boluiese, diese, fuese, pasar, resultase*. The author of document 2, García de Escalante Alvarado, was either born in New Spain or arrived in New Spain at a very young age and might have been from Asturias (Ribadeyeva). He was trained in traditional orthography and became the Mayor of Veracruz. His letter of 1553 reveals the consistent use of H to represent an etymological /f/ as in *hato, hazer, deshacer, hasta, huracán*, but the H also had an orthographic and etymologizing role in *humedad, he visto*, etc. He used simple <-s-> as in *mudase, pasado, vasallo, viniese*, words that do not contrast with *casa, cosa, costosa, poderosa*. The graphemes <ç> and <z> are distinguished without errors as in *Audiençia, braças, çiertos, çiudad, março, pareçido* while he writes *diez, dizen, hazer*. A modern trait is the omission of <-b-> as in *çiudad*, which could have been *çibdad*.

It was customary that a master scribe would transmit his knowledge to young pupils but this did not mean that academic training was required; it was merely a skill. Scribes had average education and very few attended universities. In both Spain and the New World colonies, spelling was the result of individual personality and skill. The periodization of Spanish documental history in Santo Domingo proposed by Carrera de la Red (1998: 28) is useful to identify the features of pronunciation of three periods: In Period 1 (1509-1550) documents reflect the continuity with peninsular Spanish showing the vacillation of vocalic timbre and the differentiation of two types of sibilants. In Period 2 (1551-1610), documents show phonological innovations such as abundant *seseo*, neutralization of /ʃ/ and /ʒ/ with the gradual shift to a laryngeal aspiration, and interchange of /r/ and /l/. Period 3 (1611-late 17th century) shows all the aforementioned traits in addition to *yeísmo* and interchangeable use of /r/ and /l/. It has been assumed that there exists an almost perfect correspondence between the sound and the graphemes because the relationship between the two is in constant evolution. Those scribes trained in the writing of the medieval standards do not necessarily reflect the typical or vernacular pronunciation or morpho-syntactic patterns of their places of origin but the norms that were acceptable at the time. According to Frago Gracia (1993: 234-235 and ff.) in the 16th and 17th centuries there was a trend to maintain the orthography and etymology of Old Spanish, and the printing press attempted to respect the old norms such as the distinction of <s> and <ss>, although many scribes rejected the latter and overwhelmingly preferred the former.

4.3.1 Evidence of dialect contact and dialect change

There is no doubt that at the end of the 16th century, Spanish was regionally differentiated. The survey of speakers of the several peninsular dialects who immigrated to the New World confirms the linguistic heterogeneity of the early settlers (see Map 1.5). Additional evidence derives from texts from the various regions such as Old Castile and Leon, New Castile, Navarre and Aragon, Andalusia, etc. For instance, the settlers from Old Castile tended to be *leístas*; in contrast, those from Leon distinguished LE/LES from LO/LOS. Speakers from both regions, however, normally distinguished the sibilants by point of articulation. The regional evidence is highlighted by Frago Gracia (1999: 17, 19). Some of the writers who had lived in the New World for a long time were inclined to mix some salient features of the dialects. Those belonging to the first generation like Friar Toribio de Benavente (from Benavente in the north of the province of Zamora) exclusively used <s> and confused <ç> with <z>. A distinguished Leonese, Fray Bernardino de Sahagún, had been in New Spain for about fifty years when he wrote the well-known *Historia General de las cosas de la Nueva España*, an original work revealing his proclivity for Andalusian pronunciation: -s deletion, indistinct use of <s>, <ç>, and <z>, etc. (Frago Gracia 1994).

Immigrants from northern Spain show that they were able to adapt to the New World writing norms. The case of Antonio Aguayo illustrates this pattern, since he was originally from Valladolid but settled in Cuba as early as 1525; his writings show both pre-modern and archaic features, that is, *seseo* and the conjunction *e* (< Latin *et*). On the other hand, immigrants from Old Castile and Leon comprised about one-fourth of the total population in two periods (1509-1515) and (1530-1539). They maintained this demographic weight throughout the 1630's, though after this date the population descended. Another interesting case is Alonso de Estrada (from Toledo), who headed for the New World in 1516; ten years later he wrote a letter to the Emperor in which he used modern <s> distinguished <ç> and <z>, and used etymological H, as in *hazia, hicieron, hecho*). Also, Diego de Ocaña (born in 1466 and from Toledo) was gone to the New World in 1512, where he wrote two *denuncias* in 1526. Ocaña adhered to the norms of medieval Spanish, as in the following cases: use of the past participle with the verb SER (*hera venido*) and preference for the subjunctive form ending in *-ra*, as in *[pero si Dios no lo remediara, no lo pudiera escusar, y si se hiziera, Dios sabe quién mandara la Nueva España]*). While his *leísmo* is infrequent, he aspirated initial F as in *[h]ablar, [h] allé, [h]asta*. Finally, Nuño de Guzmán (from Guadalajara) immigrated to the New World in 1514. He preferred to use the ending –RA in pluperfect subjunctive or as conditional perfect, aspirated F in initial position as in *ahorcar, hallar*, but he was not *leísta*, and did not distinguish the sibilants (Frago Gracia 1999: 20, 39, 40). In sum, some of the settlers to the New World preserved the basic traits of their regional pronunciation, while others followed to varying degrees the patterns of southern Spain. In the opinion of Frago Gracia (1999: 30), the impact of colonization is not necessarily and always related to the influence of a majority group. As a case in point, the missionaries were truly effective in spreading speech forms in the areas of which they were in charge; the *capuchinos* (monks from Aragon) disseminated forms in the vast territory of Cumaná (presently Colombia). Catalans from the past were *seseantes*, but as opposed to those from southern Spain, they preferred the apical pronunciation [ś]. For the notion of Castilianization, see Frago Gracia (1999: 27).

4.4 Other documents related to Hernán Cortés

The ideal use of the sibilants is found in the letters by Diego de Ordaz, born in Castroverde de Campos in 1480, an explorer, conquistador, and *encomendero* who lived in Santo Domingo, Tierra Firme and Cuba before joining Hernán Cortés in 1518. While in Mexico, he made sufficient merits both in the militia and exploration, and consequently gained a respectable position. In 1526 he returned to Spain from where he wrote six letters to his nephew who had stayed in New Spain taking care of his uncle's properties (Lope Blanch 1985: 9-16). In Ordaz's letters the old opposition between the voiced fricative apico-alveolar /ż/ (spelled as intervocalic -*s*-) and the corresponding voiceless /ś/ (spelled -*ss*-) had disappeared. However, Ordaz preserved the graphic difference between <s> and <ç> or <z> as in *pesos, casa, tesorero, vasallos, preso* as opposed to *negoçiar, conoçer, petiçión, pedaço, reçelo, reçibir* or *dezir, hazer, vezes, razón, hazienda*, etc. By the same token he preserved the distinction between the voiceless affricate dental /ŝ/ (in spelling *c* or *ç*) and the corresponding voiced /ẑ/ (in spelling *z*), as in *pieça, moços, encareçer, ofreçiere, çiento, çédula* vis-à-vis *pazes, vezinos, doze, goze, López, Rodríguez*, etc. Identical distribution appears in consonant clusters as in *calça, alço, dolençia, fianças, março, mudança* as opposed to *parezca, ofrezca, quinze,* etc. (Lope Blanch 1985: 41-43). In conclusion, the pronunciation of Diego de Ordaz is similar to that of Castilian speakers and to those from Seville who were conservative and who preserved the difference between <s>, <ç> and <z>. Ordaz used one single voiceless apico-alveolar /ś/, was not *ceceante*, and distinguished the affricate from the fricative dentals, respectively (Lope Blanch 1985: 46), even though the preservation of the affricates is still a debatable issue.

While Hernán Cortés was ascending in the new political order of the Spanish colonies, other Spaniards attempted to curb the almost instantaneous power he had gained as a result of his victorious raids against the Aztecs and his clever alliances with other Mesoamerican groups. Charles V received miscellaneous reports on the ethnic cleansing policies that had been presumably implemented by Cortés in the recently established and somewhat disorganized communities of New Spain. These reports and some other documents (e.g. personal letters, notes and bills) are useful to reconstruct some of the most important traits of New World Spanish in general and those that distinguish Mexican Spanish in particular. The manuscripts compiled in *Documentos Lingüísticos de la Nueva España. Altiplano Central* (henceforth DLNE-AC 1994) were handwritten by some of the most distinguished protagonists of the Mexican colony, e.g. Rodrigo de Albornoz, a native from Salamanca who was the king's secretary and royal accountant. He arrived in New Spain in 1521, returned to Spain in 1526, and went back to Mexico City in 1529. As an *encomendero*, he received tribute from a number of towns but his income from this source ended in 1544 under the provisions of the New Laws. The author of Document 2, Alonso de Estrada, became co-lieutenant governor during the period in which Cortés was on leave (1524-1526). Estrada arrived in New Spain from Ciudad Real with his wife and six children. After his death in 1530, his widow arranged the marriages of her daughters with the dynasty of settlers who also owned *encomiendas* (Alvarado, Ávalos, Sosa and Vázquez de Coronado). The consorts were from Cordoba, Seville, Badajoz and Salamanca. The Estradas also lost their *encomiendas* after the enactment of the New Laws. The *encomenderos* were interrelated by blood and marriage and solidly entrenched in the new institutions governing Mexico City (Himmerich 1991: 68-74, 116). An entirely different character playing the role of the antagonist was Nuño de Guzmán appearing in Document 5. Guzmán, founder of the city of Guadalajara in Nueva Galicia, was the envoy of the king of Spain and native of Guadalajara, Spain. He arrived in New Spain in 1527 and became a colonial administrator and Cortés' most infamous enemy because he attempted to use ruthless practices to (re)sell and enslave the native population. For information on this topic, see Zavala (1952) and Martín-Tamayo (1956).

The DLNE-AC (1994) also include reports delivered by Spanish speakers belonging to the ecclesiastic hierarchy: Friar Juan de Zumárraga, the first archbishop of Mexico City, opposed the practices of the Spanish auditors and reported to the king of Spain the turmoil of the new colony. Friars Luis de Fuensalida, Toribio de Benavente, Francisco de Mayorga, Francisco del Toral, and Nicolás de Witte gained important posts within the ecclesiastic hierarchy. While the king's secretary and the Franciscan friars had superior education, the rest seemed to have been, like Cortés, individuals of average education. Together they can be considered the forerunners of the newer Mexican society and amongst the first speakers and writers of proto-Mexican Spanish. The documents from the Altiplano Central (henceforth Central Highlands) render more than sufficient examples of diverse pronunciation traits. The use of the grapheme <ç> is glaring in this collection not only because of its high frequency in nouns and verbs but also because most writers almost never neglect the use of the *cedilla*. Document 1 is the letter by Rodrigo de Albornoz (1525), who followed Diego de Ordaz's system except for the preservation of <ss> as in m*andasse, enbiasse, sacasse,* a prevailing practice in his lengthy letter to Charles V, although occasionally he did use single <s>. In the official epistle genre there are about two dozen letters addressed to either Charles V or the Council of Indies by the protagonists of the colonization of New Spain.

The first 27 documents appearing in DLNE-AC (pp. 23-139) cover exactly three decades (1525-1555), and may be considered Cortesian texts since they highlight the linguistic and thematic trends established by Cortés. The missives written by prominent authors such as Alonso de Estrada (1526), Diego de Ocaña (1526), Jerónimo López (1532, 1534, 1543), Lope de Samaniego (1537), friars Juan de Zumárraga (1529), Luis de Fuensalida (1531), Toribio de Benavente (1550), Francisco del Toral (1554) and Nicolás de Witte (1555) preferred to use single <s> in imperfect subjunctive as in *abriesen, diese, proveyese*. This fact supports the theory proposing that the devoicing of the voiced sibilants had been completed amongst the speakers and writers belonging to the upper socio-cultural level. In Documents 1-27 the medieval sibilant <ç> continues to appear in *alcançar* (65), *çibdad* (159), *començaron* (127), *condiçiones* (50), *coraçon* (102), *conçiençia* (65), in the integrated Amerindian loans to the Spanish lexicon, e.g. *caçiques* (31), *çapotecas* (48), *caçonzi* (63) or *casulçin* (32), *maçeguales* (131); and in the toponyms *Cuçalmeco* (25) and *Çacatula* (38). Simultaneously some authors preserved the grapheme <z> in *azul* (87), *borzeguies* (87), *donzellas* (83), *juezes* (96), *hazienda* (99), *hazemos* (101), *merezco* (96), *paz* (144), *razón* (103), *plazer* (157), *vezes* (103). There are in addition sporadic cases of *seseo* as in Doc. 7 by Juan de Zumárraga (*ofresco* 82), in Doc. 15 by Friar Francisco de Mayorga (*faser* 102), *desir* and *compadesiesen* (103), and in Doc. 17 by Friar Nicolás de Witte (*notisia* 138). The first case of *ceceo* appears in 1533 in Doc. 15 (*çubçedido* 103), whereas some of the authors begin to replace the grapheme <ç> with the grapheme <z> indicating *zezeo* as in *azertase* (127), *reduzido* (100), *regozijaba* (90), *zeloso* (134). Also, the grapheme <ss> reappears in *permitiesse* (113) *supiesssen, mjrasse* and *truxesse* (138), a grapheme that spread to other items that did not have it, as in *desseamos* (116). In sum, in this period authors tend to maintain the *toledano-castellano* sibilant system (see Table 4.5A at the end of this chapter). Isolated cases of other variants are anticipated, as in Doc. 6, the letter of Antonio de Godoy, servant of Nuño de Guzmán, in which he used *faboresca* (seseo), *quizieren* and *prezidente* (zezeo), and *preçona* (ceceo) (64). Showing his preference for the grapheme <z>, Nuño de Guzmán (Doc. 17) wrote *favorezidos, conozer, amanezen, alcanze, cazique, zufrir* and *acreziente* (109-110).

4.4.1 The features of Cortesian texts

The letter delivered by Rodrigo de Albornoz to the king of Spain (Doc. 1, 1525) contains several Taino loans that are used without definitions and with common Spanish modifiers: *mahiz* or *mays, agi, canoa, hanegas de maiz, maçorcas de maiz, piraguas*. In addition to lexical items derived from Taino and Nahuatl, the innovations of the koine include the introduction of two affricate Nahuatl phonemes /tɬ/ and /ts/ primarily in toponyms and nouns that have vitality even at present. From the 27 documents of the first period (DLNE-AC 1994), it is inferred that the features of late medieval Spanish alternated with those of pre-modern Spanish. The spelling of words with initial F- alternated with the spelling of initial H (e.g. *hasta* and *hallar, fasta* and *hasta, fijo* and *hijo*). The past participle of the verb HACER was both *hecho* and *fecho*. Some of the old traits remained for the entire colonial period while others were replaced by those representing the transition to pre-modern Spanish: (1) The close vowels of modern Spanish (*i* and *u*) replaced mid open vowels (*e* and *o*). The words *and*o*vo* (51), *b*o*lliçios* (68), *çertefico* (77), *m*e*smo* (41), *p*o*diendo* (45), *rreç*e*bido* (54) changed to modern Spanish into *and*u*vo, b*u*llicios, certifico, m*i*smo, p*u*diendo, rec*i*bido*, etc. (2) The grapheme <x> represented the voiceless pre-palatal fricative /x/, which was widely used by the first generation of Spanish speakers, as in *dixoles, quexosos, vexaciones*. (3) Direct and indirect objects remain assimilated to the infinitive verb forms as in *buscalles* (75), *castigalle* (75), *encargallo*, though the modern infinitive and the object *encargarlo* also appears. (4) Authors were fond of adding a palatal between vowels in verbs like SER and VER, as in "*beyendo esto, hablé al presidente*" (82) or "*beyendo yo su disolución*" (82), and "*seyendo ellos los acusadores*" (85). (5) There are rare cases of *seseo*, as in *conoscan, resiben, faser, faserme*, interchange of liquids /r/ and /l/ as in *flayles* and *flayres*, and substitution of –r– by –l–, as in *ultramalinos*.

4.4.2 Spellings of common verbs

Spellings of common verbs such as DECIR, HABER, TENER, TRAER, and VER had variable spellings. Modern Spanish DECIR was spelled with both <ç> and <z> *dezia* (imperfect indicative) *diziendo* (gerund), but *dixe* and *dixeron* in the preterit indicative. Late medieval Spanish shows considerable variation in spelling according to verb tense. The spelling of the verb HABER shows the addition of the initial H- in the present tense, as for example, *ha acontecido, he sabido, he sido, se ha hecho, ha avido, huviesse, huviera, havia* etc., but forms without H- in other tenses are also common: *ay, aya, avia, avrá, avrán, aviendo, obieron, oviérame*. The verb HABER is used with the meaning of TENER and alternating with it. The verb HABER is also used in time expressions with the meaning of modern HACER. The conjugations of the verb VER were (*yo*) *vide*, „él *vido*" in present indicative but (*ellos*) *vían* in imperfect indicative. The 3rd person singular of the verb VER can be the medieval *vido* and the modern *vio*, while the present participle appears as *viendo* and *beyendo* (a) "*como vido esto antes que el factor supiese del, fuese al monasterio*" (71).

Throughout the 16th century writers from both sides of the Atlantic hesitated between two forms of the preterit of the verb TRAER. Whereas some followed the etymological form *traxe*, others preferred *truxe*. The spelling with modern <j> begins to be used as well as the form *trahen*, the latter suggesting that there was aspiration in intervocalic position.

(a) a quien los *trahe* el cacique (32)
(b) entre si los usan y *traen* (32)
(c) podrian venir los navios que *traxessen* la especieria (35)
(d) y que *traxesse* cada uno su adereço de labrança (36)
(e) como se *trahen* de lexos, vale todo en subido precio (44)
(f) y afirmó que hera muerto y *traxo* ciertos yndios que lo dezian (51)
(g) los otros se *retraxeron* por los monasterios (70)
(h) don Hernando *retraxose* al monasterio de san Francisco (71)
(i) seria bien que todo nabio *traxere* algunas plantas (94)
(j) recogio hasta çincuenta jndios y los *truxo* cargados de mayz (109)
(k) que mandase vuestra magestad que los *trujesen* en recua (130)
(l) la carta dize que los que no *trujeren* frutos nj cria de que den dos diezmos (131)
(m) y treynta *truxe* a esta Nueva España. Y si *truxera* mil, fuera harto menester (133)
(n) que me *truxesse* aquj al monesterio al dicho don Joan Xancal (138)

4.4.3 Morpho-syntactic features of Cortesian texts

Cortesian texts maintained some of the key traits of late medieval Spanish and anticipated those of modern Spanish. The question raised at this juncture is whether or not some of those traits have remained in Latin American Spanish, and more importantly, if they have evolved with newer social meanings. Some features changed in all varieties of the Spanish-speaking world while others disappeared in Spain but have been retained in colloquial regional or rural Latin American varieties.

4.4.3.1. The gender of the noun MAR ('sea') remained feminine, as in (b) through (e) but began to appear in masculine as in (g) through (h), which is the modern use. When the name of the 'sea' is explicit, the noun 'mar' is masculine but when 'mar' is general appears as a bear noun, as in (a).
(a) enviamos por *mar* (25)
(b) cuando *la mar* andava brava (34)
(c) por *la mar* del norte (67)
(d) *aquellas mares* (57)
(e) en *la mar* del sur (57)
(f) lo llevó Nuestro Señor en *el mar* (134)
(g) por *el mar Adriático* (35)
(h) Entraban por el seno y estrecho *del mar Rubro*, y por muchas yslas que venian a la punta *del dicho mar* (35)

4.4.3.2. Examples (a) through (g) show the addition of the preposition A before [+ animate] objects, which is considered a pre-modern trait and appears consistently in New Spain.
(a) y con el fuego desbarataron los indios *a los christianos* (25)
(b) dizque dieron sobre los que quedan y prendieron *al capitan* (25)
(c) que los esclavos que los caciques y señores dieren y ayan dado *a los christianos*, se hierren aquellos que fueron esclavos (31)
(d) hizieron tenientes de Medellin y Villa Rica *a Alvaro* de Saavedra (52)
(e) yban acompañar de noche y de dia *al dicho licenciado* (61)
(f) çiertos perros lebreles (...) los hechavan *a los jndios* pa que los mordiesen (84)
(g) me dixo y certificó que él mesmo encontro *al hermano* de Delgadillo (84)

4.4.3.3. Modern Spanish uses an infinitive preceded by the preposition A + article EL (*al amanecer, al decir, al soltar*) with the meaning of progressive action. In contrast, authors of Cortesian texts used the prepositional gerund.
(a) Y luego otro dia lunes *en amaneciendo* el licenciado dio mandamiento (60)

(b) los otros se retraxeron por los manasterios *en publicando* esta nueva de la muerte de don Hernando (70)
(c) *en pidiendoles* diezmos dejarian de criar y hazer granjerias (128)

4.4.4 Position of verbal clitics

The use of verbal clitics aids in tracing the evolution directly from Latin to emerging medieval varieties of Romance to modern Spanish and other languages. The movement of Spanish clitics can be reconstructed from the Spanish texts belonging to the first generation of colonists, which exhibit the in-transition trends from medieval to pre-modern to modern Spanish.

4.4.4.1. The use of GELO represents the oldest medieval contracted form. It is actually rare in the emerging variety of Mexican Colonial Spanish, as in (b) and (d), and alternates with the modern SE LO/LOS as in (a), (c) and (e).
(a) que cada uno ternia otro cuydado y manera en el tratamjento de los indios, que no tiene al presente con pensar que mañana *se los* han de quitar (42)
(b) Y enbiando tal persona de gobernador o oydores e pesquisador, quales conviene al serviçio de vuestra majestad, *gelas* mande todas dar para que la traya aca (46)
(c) que su persona sola de cada compañero bastaria a *se lo* traer preso (71)
(d) y holgamos mucho de ver*gelos* llevar (93)
(e) y agora azen*selos* dar tan grandes (126)

4.4.4.2. Indirect and reflexive pronouns continue to be placed before infinitives as in sentences (a) through (h). As in modern Spanish, they are attached to the infinitive, as in (i).
(a) nasçimos para *le servir* (32)
(b) tenjendo los christianos tiempo para *se armar* y ponerse a cavallo (43)
(c) el tesorero tenja mucha gente armada en su casa para *se juntar* con él (50)
(d) Fue el veedor a *los pacificar* y a poblar una villa (51)
(e) sy Hernando Cortés diese de noche en alguna parte, como hizo a Narvaez, los otros se hallasen fuertes pa *le socorrer* (61)
(f) porque so color de *lo buscar*, los spañoles lo robavan (67)
(g) jnformado de la riqueza de la tierra donde yba, acordo de *se alçar* contra él (67)
(h) Y no asosegado con esto, acordo yr en persona a *le prender* (67)
(i) para autorizar*la* y traer*le* mas a su propósito (75)

4.4.4.3. In the 16th century, the objects are attached to the conjugated verb as in *satisfízole, parescióle*. The stylistic variations in (i) and (j), when the object goes before the conjugated verb, anticipates the change to modern Spanish.
(a) *bolvjeronla* a Hernando Cortés y *tomaronla* ellos en su nombre (52)
(b) *pusieronlos* presos en dos camaras (52)
(c) Despues de esto *juntaronse* procuradores (57)
(d) y a las bozes que dava *fueronle* a socorrer, y *quitaronsele*, y acordaron por aquellos de poner fuego a la casa y a ellos *quemaronlos* (109)
(e) y por todos los cercos *danles* grita (110)
(f) *desanparanla* y *vienense* a la çibdad de Compostela (110)
(g) *ponenlos* en peligro de hazer muchas ofensas (129)
(h) *murieronsenos* tres rreligiosos (133)
(i) *le entregó* todas las varas de justicia (72)
(j) *los tenia* por enemigos y *les hazia* tales obras (73)

4.4.5 Pro-etymological and anti-etymological verbal clitics

Verbal pronouns referring to [+ / – animate] objects stem from two systems: one based on Latin etymologies marked by case (accusative vs. dative) and the other one originating in the Castilian provinces. In the traditional system, the Latin demonstrative pronouns ILLE and ILLA rendered definite articles and object pronouns in each of the Romance languages. Spanish object pronouns LO / LOS (masculine) and LA / LAS (feminine) derive from the ancestral pro-etymological accusative case singular and plural system (Column 3). They have functioned as direct objects [+ / – animate], while LE and LES (derived from the dative) refer to indirect object pronouns (Column 2).

Table 4.1: Latin demonstrative pronouns and Spanish object pronouns

Number and Gender	Latin		Spanish	Latin		Spanish
Singular + Masculine	*illī*	>	le	*illum*	>	lo
Plural + Masculine	*illīs*	>	les	*illōs*	>	los
Singular + Feminine	*illī*	>	le	*illam*	>	la
Plural + Feminine	*illīs*	>	les	*illās*	>	las

The Castilian innovation known as *personal leísmo* can be traced to the 12th century. Occurrences in the Poem of Mio Cid undermined the case distinction introducing the dative LE for accusative [+ masculine + animate], and by the first half of the 16th century, LE prevailed among writers coming from Old Castile, Alcala and Madrid (e.g. Cervantes, Lope de Vega, Tirso de Molina, Calderón de la Barca, etc.). The point of departure of this innovation was the regimen of certain Latin verbs that were originally intransitive and were used with the dative case (*servire* 'to serve', *minari* 'to threaten', *oboedire* 'to obey'). However, the respective Spanish-derived verbs (*servir, amenazar, obedecer*) functioned as transitive but continued to use the dative pronoun LE referring to [+ masculine + animate] objects. In this way a new personal domain emerged (Lapesa 1985: 405-406). Also, some of the internal changes intervening in the adjustment from the LO system to the LE system may have to do with the fact that the direct object pronouns ME and TE (identical to those that are indirect) have a resemblance to third person singular LE, thus creating the series, ME, TE, LE (Urrutia Cárdenas 2003: 520-521). Another internal change may be associated with the apocopation of objects pronouns (LO and LE) that in medieval texts were represented by the use of ambiguous –L'. The koineizing contexts might have been ideal for extending an innovation like *leísmo* provided sufficient numbers of speakers were likely to produce it and accept it. The early apocopation of object pronouns was conducive to structural ambiguity (Tuten 2003: 194).

The rise of *leísmo* generated additional changes in the pronominal system to the extent that other phenomena known as *loísmo* and *laísmo* replaced the dative LE(S) with the intention of focusing on gender, inasmuch as LE appears to be neutral. For instance, *le doy el libro a él* ('I give the book to him') could be transformed into *lo doy el libro* ('I give him the book'). The same change occurs with the feminine object as in *le hablé a ella*, which could render *la hablé* ('I talked to her'). According to Flores (2002) these innovations have the same underlying motivation associated with the degree of transitivity of the event and a process by which new pragmatic values have been added to the meaning of the clitic pronouns. In order to test this hypothesis, the use of direct and indirect object pronouns as clitics was analyzed in a very large sample from 15th and 16th centuries texts. The use of LO(S) and LE(S) for [+ masculine + animate] objects seems to be determined by verb transitivity, which is gradual. The dative case marks [+ animate] entities tangentially affected by the event while the accusative is strongly affected by it suggesting that to a higher degree of transitivity there is a greater possibility that the select object pronoun will be accusative LO (44-49). Because the semantic nature of actions varies from speaker to speaker, the same verb can be cliticized with either LES or LOS. At present, this tends to occur among speakers and writers of *leísmo* or those who are transitional, but rarely amongst speakers using a clearly pro-etymological system (i.e. modern Latin American Spanish).

When the external causes of *leísmo* have to be reckoned with, Basque contact with Castilian Spanish is considered to be a factor intervening in the suppression of accusative pronouns and the exclusive appearance of use of LE(S) for dative cases (Tuten 2003: 178). Research on *leísmo* is prolific, and in addition to the two basic systems, scholars find subsystems stemming from the divergence to a non-etymological system, which vary according to region, social stratum and formal education. Proponents of language contact assume that the change from the pro-etymological to the non-etymological system occurred in the Castilian regions in ancestral contact with Basque. Finally, data from current Basque-dominant and Basque recessive bilinguals sheds light on the net effect that ancestral contact of Basque with Spanish may have on Spanish speakers of northern peninsular regions. Basque contact is observed as a cause in the change to *leísmo*, the suppression and duplication of the accusative pronoun, and the addition of other object pronouns (Urrutia Cárdenas 2003: 527-528).

First generation writers from New Spain used both LO(S) and LE(S) with a strong preference for the latter. Variation can be explained by internal changes [+ / − transitive] and by inter-dialect contact in the new colonial environment where variants LE and LES were vital. First generation writers had strong tendencies towards *leísmo* but they did not discard the contending variants LO and LOS (see Hidalgo 2013). For instance, the letter delivered in 1529 to Charles V by Friar Juan de Zumárraga clearly reveals his preference for LE. Zumárraga was from Durango in the historical territory and province of Biscay. The author of Doc. 7 narrates the skirmishes in which Hernán Cortés was engaged when he arrived in Mexico under the initiative of Governor Velázquez, whose intention was to search for the other captain, Juan de Grijalva. Upon finding Grijalva, Cortés was supposed to return with him because the governor did not have permission to initiate the colonization of this territory; however in case he could not find him, he should have recovered as much gold as possible. In the passage below, Juan de Zumárraga, the first Bishop of Mexico, consistently used the clitic LE, a trait that still distinguishes the northern-central provinces from the southern region.

> Hernando Cortés vino a esta tierra, al prinçipio por mandado de Diego Velazquez, governador de la ysla de Cuba, que **le embió** por capitan de çierta armada a buscar a Juan de Grijalva, otro capitan que el primero havia embiado a descobrir, y **hallandole** se volviesen ambos juntos porque diz que Diego Velazquez, no tenia liçençia de vuestra majestad para poblar; y que si no **le hallase** en la costa desta Nueva España, rescatase todo el más oro que pudiese (66).

In the subsamples below there are 13 cases of LE, 11 cases of LES, and only 7 cases of LO, indicating the preference for *leísmo*. There are however 16 cases of LOS which can be [+ plural masculine or ambivalent]. The alternations between LE and LO indicate that the preference for the former may be motivated by the interpretation [+ / − transitivity] assigned to the verb e.g. *engañar* ('to deceive'), *prender* ('to apprehend'), *castigar* ('to punish'), *echar* ('to throw out'), *ahorcar* ('to hang'), *mentar* ('to mention'), and *destruir* ('to destroy'). The use of LE may be also related to sentences that have two verbs as in (a) *poder engañar* ('to be able to deceive') or a verb and a predicate as in *tener ganado* ('to have subdued someone'), or *haber preso* ('to have someone in jail'), as in items (k) and (n). Juan de Zumárraga continued narrating the state of affairs in the recently discovered land that was in turmoil as a result of the conflicts between Hernán Cortés and other colonists who wanted to debunk him, as in items (a) through (r). He also expressed his concerns for the indigenous, whose situation was uncertain before the New Laws of 1542, as in examples (s) through (u).

(a) el Juez que ha de juzgar con equidad, que nadie **le podra engañar** (65)
(b) por muchas vezes y diversas vias procuraron de *lo* matar (66)
(c) porque so color de *lo* buscar, los spañoles *lo* robavan (67)
(d) fueron muy bien rescibidos y ospedados de don Fernando, el qual en nombre de vuestra majestad *los* admitio a sus ofiçios (67)
(e) Y no asosegado con esto acordo yr en persona a **le prender** (67)
(f) el factor y veedor le prometieron de **le castigar** por lo pasado (68)
(g) porque le acudian los amigos de don Hernando para que *lo* favoresçiese (68)
(h) pidiendole la mandase paresçer y **les admitiese** al dicho cargo (68)
(i) so çierta color que para ello buscaron, y **le hecharon** de la tierra (69)
(j) despues de preso, hizieron su pesquisa (...) y en poco espacio **le ahorcaron** (69)
(k) Y **teniendole ganado** y seguro dio tras el thesorero y qontador que *los* tuvo presos (68-9)
(l) a fin que si viniese don Hernando, que por defender sus repartimjentos **les defenderian y seguirian** (70)
(m) antes que el factor supiese dél, fuese al monasterio de san Francisco de miedo que no **le ahorcase** (71)
(n) muchos días antes **le avia preso** el fator y embiado a Castilla (71)
(o) si don Hernando fuese vibo, que su persona sola de cada compañero bastaría a se *lo* traer preso o darle de lançadas (71)
(p) a unos afrentó publicamente **haziendoles açotar** (...) por otros entró en los termjnos e jurisdicçion desta çibdat y *los* prendio e ahorcó (...) metiend*olos* en su governaçion, prendiendo los señores dellos e haziendoles vexaçiones, y molestánd*olos* con capitanias de spañoles (...) para **hazelles** que sirviesen en su governaçion (73)
(q) Nuño de Guzmán (...) venia enponçoñado contra don Hernando y con quantos en su boca **le mentasen y toviesen** sus cosas por buenas (75)
(r) le hazian aquel favor a cautela y para dar después en él rezio y **castigalle** (75)

(s) han sido de acuerdo y paresçer muy claro y notorio a quantos en esta tierra viben, de ser muy dorrotabatido contra don Hernando para **le destruyr** totalmente (76)
(t) y todavia andan en la labor jnumerables yndios que *los* hazen trabajar como sclavos, (...) **haziendoles** traer todos los materiales a cuestas (84)
(u) çiertos perros lebreles que los yndios llevaban a cuestas (...) *los* hechavan a los jndios pa que *los* mordiesen (84)
(v) *los* aprisionavan y buscavan causas para mollesta*los* y destruy*los* (85)

Another distinguished colonist and encomendero was Rodrigo de Albornoz, His Majesty's direct envoy. Albornoz was in charge of reporting the conditions observed in New Spain. In Doc. 1 (1525) he used LES with the verbs *tomar* ('to take'), *tener* ('to have'), *capturar* ('to capture'), *matar* ('to kill'), and *maltratar* ('to abuse').
(a) encontro con siete o ocho mercaderes indios que venian en una canoa y juntósse a ellos y **tomóles** (25)
(b) prendieron al capitán (...) y llevaron*lo* en señal de victoria a un templo (...) y alli *lo* sacrificaron a sus ydolos (25)
(c) no *los* tiene seguros, sino que oy **les tiene** uno y de aquj a un mes *los* dan a otro, y cada uno procura de *los* despojar aquel tiempo que *los* tiene (27)
(d) que si no lo quisjeren hacer, **les capturen y tomen** como esclavos (29)
(e) su amo, el christiano, atemoríza*los* a que digan que son esclavos aunque no lo sean. Que aunque **les maten** no quieren dezir sino que son esclavos (30)
(f) algunas vezes *los* hierran como a los esclavos (31)
(g) a otro **le hacen esclavo** porque hurtó diez maçorcas de maiz (31)
(h) Destos esclavos (...) que los christianos sacan de sus caciques, pues se *los* dan en lugar del oro que antes les solian dar (33)
(i) no aviendo qué les sacar, es pues fuerça que **les han de maltratar** (36)

Finally, Friar Francisco del Toral, author of Doc. 25 (1554), also wrote to the king of Spain and described the disadventageous circumstances imposed on the natives, as in (a) through (c). Friar del Toral was from Jaen (Andalusia) and attended the convent in this locality.
(a) Quel pobre del yndio, como no tiene esos parientes poderosos ni sabios ni rricos, siempre **le olvidan, dilatan y amedrentan** (134)
(b) En otras cosas de serviçios personales andan los yndios vexados, porque se a puesto una ynposiçion que **les mandan** a los pueblos (134)
(c) asi son vexados, y en **les hazer yr** de los pueblos comarcanos a servir por fuerça (134)

For a few years when Hernán Cortés was on leave, Nuño de Guzmán, a native from Guadalajara, became his antagonist. Guzmán, the author of Doc. 17 (1535), tells his version of the story to the Council of Indies. In the passage below, he narrates how the person in charge of capturing Indians actually picked up about fifty of them and brought them loaded with maize to a place called Piastla, where the Indians were locked up in a house until the marquis had time to see them the following day. When they were trapped and unable to escape, a Spanish official went to check them out. As the Indians saw only one of them, they grabbed him, beat him up, and as he was yelling, others rushed to rescue him, but in revenge the other allies set the house on fire and burned all those who were inside. In the intense fragment Guzmán used LE for the most pressing and harsh actions of the narration.

> [el encargado] recogio hasta çincuenta jndios y *los* truxo cargados de mayz al dicho Piastla; y acordaron aquella noche de encerra*llos* en una casa pa vernirse al marqués otro dia; y teniendo*los* alli, entró uno de ellos a requerir*los*. Y como los jndios **le vieron** solo, asen dél, y **comienzanle** a mal tratar, y a las bozes que dava *fueronle* a socorrer, y **quitaronsele**, y acordaron por aquello de poner fuego a la casa y a ellos, y quemaron*los* a los más dentro (109)

4.4.6 Variable use of PARA and PA

The first generation of writers from the Central Highlands show three basic patterns of PARA and PA usage in the contexts discussed in 3.5.5. In contrast with Hernán Cortés, who alternated between the two prepositions, the Spanish speakers representing the protagonists of the colonization of Mexico can be divided into three groups: the first one used mostly PARA; the second group used both the full and the reduced form; and the last group only used the reduced form. These three patterns may not be explained by socio-educational or regional differences because all the writers had similar backgrounds. The full form may have been perceived by some writers as the most appropriate to address the Emperor. Nevertheless, a distinguished colonist close to the Spanish nobility, Rodrigo de Albornoz, was not concerned with this stylistic variation. The author of Doc. 1 used abundantly the abbreviated form PA. The variation in colonial documents may have to do with the same pragmatic alternatives that speakers have at present. If they are in a hurry to complete a fragment of their discourse, they use PA; otherwise they use PARA. The subsample below derived from the lengthy letter delivered to Charles V. The reduced form PA appears partially in italics, whereas the full form appears complete as *para*. In all subsamples where the alternation needs to be shown, I make the difference between *pa* and *para*.

(a) *para que* los venda (34)
(b) *pa que* de alli los enviasen (34)
(c) *pa ayuda* a sus grandes gastos (34)
(d) porque es la tierra más aparejada *pa* servir a Dios (38)
(e) *pa que* los hijos de los caciques y señores (…) se instruyan en la fee (38)
(f) *para que* ninguno exceda ni tome más de lo que fuere (41)
(g) *para poder* ser aprovechados (81)

4.4.7 The use of imperfect subjunctive

The verb tense system in the indicative and subjunctive moods was considerably and gradually reduced from Latin to modern Spanish. Like Hernán Cortés, first generation speakers / writers clearly preferred the subjunctive form ending in –SE in the subordinate clauses as in examples (a) through (g). The use of –SE is preferred over the use of –RA even in sentences in which such ending appears five or more times, as in (f) and (g).

(a) lo qual fue descubierto antes que se *pusiese* en efeto (53)
(b) en toda mj residencia no ubo persona que demanda me *pusiese* nj de mj se *quexase* (97)
(c) Que vuestra señoria y esos señores (…) se *compadesiesen* déstos y *oviesen* dellos misericordia y los *desagraviasen* y *quitasen* algun pedaço siquiera de sus cargos (103)
(d) que *mjrasen* bjen lo que sentençiavan porque si de otra manera lo *hiziesen*, (…) él avja de apelar de la cabsa (123)
(e) Sería gran piedad que pues que Dios a multiplicado aca muchos caballos, que *mandase* vuestra magestad que los *trujesen* en recua (130)
(f) Y que a cada uno dellos se le *repartiessen* en la provinçia donde a*ssentase* çiento o duzientos yndios para que *tuviesse* en administraçion, o se les *diessen* por suyos pa que se *sirviesse* dellos e le *ayudasen* en sus labranças e grangerias; e los *impusiesse* en sus lavores (36)
(g) Yo le respondj que *mjrase* bien lo que hazía, y que luego que la sentencja *fuese* dada, la *apelase* antes que *ovjese* lugar de rogar o mandar, por que yo le avjsava que avja de ynformar a vuestra magestad lo que *pasase* (123)

In conditional sentences, the SI-clause appears with both the ending –SE and the ending –RA. The alternation is justified because the –SE form is slightly more intense expressing the [+ reservation] and [+ subjectivity] intention of hypothetical situations ranging from those that are interpreted as possible to those that are uncertain (in imperfect subjunctive). Sentences with forms ending in –RA in both

the protasis and the apodosis follow one of the structures of medieval Spanish and appear in Cortesian texts as in (a) through (d).
(a) si Dios no lo *rremediara* no se *pudiera* escusar, y sy se *hiziera*, Dios sabe qujén *mandara* la Nueva España (53)
(b) si mucho se *tardara* la venjda de Hernando Cortés, sabe Dios sy *parara* aquj (53)
(c) si él *muriera* nunca la tierra se *ganara* (66)
(d) si no se *oviera* ydo a Hibueras que ya él lo *oviera* preso (70)

The other structure used in the 16th century is similar to modern Spanish conditional sentences made up of the protasis and apodosis with subjunctive in the former and indicative in the latter. The examples (a) through (c) show sentences in imperfect subjunctive with the ending –SE in combination with the synthetic conditional ending in –RÍA as in modern Spanish. The contrastive structures are explained by the process of attrition of –RA with a function of pluperfect which was changing to simple conditional (Acevedo 1997: 98).
(a) si no *tovjese* judicatura, le *aseguraria* diez mjll pesos de oro (54)
(b) porque sy hazer se *pudiese*, yo *daria* fe de todo esto como escrjbano público (56)
(c) sy *huviessen* de conprar las cassas donde agora está ell Audiencia, *serian* menester para ello cinquenta mill pesos (115)

4.4.8 Pronouns of address: from Cortés' letters to 1555

The first generation of Spanish speakers settled in New Spain was not made up of professional writers interested in creative writing; they were rather pragmatic representatives of the epistolary prose of the times. Colonial documents are useful to retrieve the data on the patterns of address between the different actors, and to an extent. they reflect the schemes of social stratification existing in both Spain and the New World colonies. The pronouns of address used today in Latin American Spanish are the result of a long process of simplification, which not only eliminated the opposition between VOS and VOSOTROS but the two pronouns altogether, on the one hand, and VUESTRA MERCED and VUESTRAS MERCEDES, on the other. Through evolution of intermediate forms, the second dyad turned into the modern USTED and USTEDES prevailing in all varieties. The difference at present lies in the ambivalence of USTEDES, which indicates both [+ / – deference] in Latin American Spanish, whereas in Castilian Spanish indicates only [+ deference]. The DLNE-AC (1994) also show the forms of address that are [+ deference / reverence], since the major protagonists in charge of the New

World colonies regularly reported to the authorities in Spain the state of affairs across the Atlantic. Common forms of address used exclusively with the king, the president of the Council or the members of the Council are the following: *Vuestra catholica cesarea magestad*, *Vuestra sacra majestad*, *Vuestra magestad*, *Vuestra señoria*, *Vuestra reverencia*; these forms were often abbreviated and conjugated with verbs in the 3rd person singular masculine and feminine. Occasionally, the members of the Council were addressed as *Vuestras mercedes*, abbreviated as *vs. ms.*, which appears 6 times in the letter by Diego de Ocaña (Doc. 3, 1526).

Other patterns of address appear in the brief correspondence between Nuño de Guzmán and his servant (Doc. 5, 1529). When Nuño de Guzmán headed to Mexico to scrutinize the new government, he had the full support of the Spanish Crown. His servant, Antonio de Godoy, was addressed with *vos* 17 times making *vos* agree with its corresponding verb forms, possessive adjectives and object pronouns as in (a) through (c); in contrast, in Doc. 6 Nuño de Guzmán received *vuestra merced* 15 times from his servant as in (d). *Vuestra merced* (abbreviated *v.m.*) appears many more times in short informal business notes between buyers and sellers. In sum, at this stage the singular pronouns between interlocutors are only *vos* and *vuestra merced*.

(a) resçebi una carta *vuestra*. Y en lo que *decis* del caçonzi y su hermano, pareçeme que en algo *teneys* razón (63)
(b) que acudan a su tiempo a donde les *hordenaredes* (63)
(c) yo no querria que *vos os apartasedes* dello, sino que *enbiasedes* el oro que ay y que p*rocureys* de que en ese rio que se ha hallado se hechen mjs quadrillas (63)
(d) Aqui me escrive *vuestra merced* (...) Suplico a *vuestra merced* le haga bolver (64)

4.4.9 Diffusion of Spanish, discourse markers, and lexical items

It has been proposed from the onset that the most significant agents of diffusion and change of Mexican Spanish were the Spanish speakers residing in the different regions of New Spain, but particularly those who lived and worked in the Central Highlands. Some of the features that appeared in 16th century colonial sources disappeared when the colonial period ended. Others have survived through the 21st century and are vital today in colloquial Mexican Spanish. This section highlights three items that have relevance today: (1) the verb *platicar* meaning 'to chat', but which had the meaning of a more formal talk. (2) The use of the verb *pregonar* ('to announce publicly' or 'to proclaim'), because it is directly related to the diffusion of Spanish. (3) The discourse marker *dizque*, which is obsolete in Spain, but still common in Latin American Spanish.

4.4.9.1. The verbs *platicar* and *charlar* mean 'to chat', but first generation Spanish speakers clearly preferred the former in [+ formal] domains and registers. In Spain the verb *charlar* is preferred over *platicar*, but in Mexican Spanish *platicar* descended to a colloquial register.
(a) he *platicado* con muchos esta materja (31)
(b) que se *platycava* entrellos que hera pa prender al fator y veedor (50)
(c) que su jntinçion hera qual con ellos habia *platicado* (83)
(d) Hanme jnformado, y en esta çibdat asi se *platica* entre quien lo sabe (85)

4.4.9.2. The role of the *pregonero* in the diffusion of Spanish cannot be underestimated. The crier was an official representative of the local governments and was supposed to maintain confidentiality except when it was the right time and place to make public announcements. The expressions '*dar pregones*', '*pregonarse*', '*voz de pregonero*' and '*hacer pregonar*' were common in colonial texts.
(a) Fueron alla el fator y veedor con mucha gente y *dieronse pregones* (50)
(b) y *dieronse pregones* (…) pa deriballe la puerta y hecho otro requerimjento por *boz de pregonero*, abrieron con çiertas condiçiones (50)
(c) Hernando Cortés (…) hazía rrepartimyento de yndios a muy gran priesa y *hizo pregonar* conqujstas y armadas (54)
(d) Este mjsmo día en la tarde *se pregonó* en la plaça desta çibdad, *por pregonero* y ante escrjbano, çiertas ordenanças que Hernando Cortés hizo (…) y otras muchas otras ordenanças que *se pregonaron* (59)
(e) los servjdores de su magestad dixeron que este *pregon* era crimen magistatis (59)
(f) El liçenciado salio a la plaça y hizo llamar a Hernando Cortes y *hizo ciertos pregones* en que dixo que a su notycia hera venjdo (60)
(g) Lo que suçedera Dios lo sabe. Lo mejor seria asegurallo todo con *prender* media dozena de *pregones* que se puede hazer muy bjen aquj (62)
(h) mandó el factor *pregonar* publicamente que ninguna persona fuse osado de dezir que don Hernando era vibo so pena de çient açotes (69)

4.4.9.3. The discourse marker *dizque* or *diz que*, derived from the impersonal 3rd person plural, *dicen que* ('they say that'), appears frequently in DLNE-AC (1994) where most of the documents deal with narrations of hypothetical situations.
(a) y ya que amanecio *diz que* dieron sobre los que quedaban y prendieron al capitan (25)

(b) y a los indios que de aca yban con los christianos *dizque* guardaron para comer, y a los christianos hechaban en la laguna porque *diz que* los han provado y son duros y amarga la carne de ellos (25
(c) aunque el estrecho no se halle, como no *dizque* le ay, podrian venir los navios (35)
(d) venian a la ysla Scoyra donde *diz que* habitan christianos, (...) y ahi *dizque* la tomavan en camellos (35)
(e) y assi *diz que* sería muy provechoso que vuestra majestad mandasse venir tres o quatro mill labradores (36)
(f) Hernando Cortés (...) *diz que* escrivjo al dicho Proaño pa que le rrevocase el poder y lo diese a otro, y *diz que* enbjó a Geronjmo Lopes escrjbano del rrey (61)
(g) porque *diz que* Diego Velasquez no tenia liçençia de vuestra majestad (66)
(h) Y para vuestra majestad *diz que* señaló algunas cibdades y provjncias bien principales (67)
(i) hera cosa admiraçion las quexas que *diz que* le yvan a dar (72)
(j) que *diz que* fue cosa mucho admirable (72)
(k) y por esto *diz que* han querido ahorcar un señor destos (82)

4.4.10 Loans from Taino and Nahuatl

In describing the economic and political situation that the envoys of Carlos V found in New Spain, authors used the most frequent Tainismos that the Spanish-speaking men had brought from the islands. Most of them sounded natural and adjusted to Spanish, the most frequent being *cacique*, which was spelled both *caçique* and *cazique*, followed by *maiz* (also spelled *mays, mahiz, mayz*), which by then was preceded by common phrases as noun modifiers: "*mazorcas de maiz*" (31), "*alhondigas de maiz*" (78), "*puño de mahiz*", (84) "*hanegas de mayz*" (94), "*cargas de maiz*" (134). Some others are not too frequent in the Mexican colonial sources (*areytos* and *piragua*). On the other hand, the Nahuatl loans include the equivalent of the Taino loan *cacique*, which was *caçonçi* with variable spellings (*cazonzi, calsulsin*). First generation speakers introduced toponyms such as *Çacatula* (28), *Piastla* (109), and *Tlaçhinolticpac* (137), and a few patronymics representative of the peoples they slowly discovered such as *çapotecas* (48) and *chichimecas* (110). The loans also show the incipient knowledge they had about the societal roles and social stratification of the Mesoamerican culture and their objects: *maçeguales* ('laborers'), *caconzi* ('chief leader'), *tequilatos* ('tax collectors'), *tianguez* ('markets'), *calpisques* ('majordomos'). During the first three decades after the conquest of Mexico, the noun *caçonçi* was in open competition

with *cacique*, but the former did not survive in the modern lexicon of Mexican Spanish, except in discourse referring to Mesoamerican culture, as in item (i).
(a) encontro con siete o ocho mercaderes indios que venian en una *canoa* (25)
(b) yo procuré con el *caçique* de Çacatula (28)
(c) que diese de cuatro en cuatro meses (...) y *maiz* y *cacao*, que son unas almendras que ellos usan por moneda (28)
(d) demandar a su *caçique* oro (30)
(e) un dia que ellos estaban en sus *areytos*, que es su fiesta (31)
(f) avian bendido tres o quatro vezes en sus *tianguez*, o mercados que tienen cada dia (31)
(g) venian en una grandes *piraguas* (34)
(h) por el *cacao* se da oro (38)
(i) por temor del *caçonçi* (40)
(j) aunque viniessen en diez mill *canoas* no pararian (44)
(k) haze hahorcar al *cazique* y al otro (110)
(l) los *maçeguales* no tienen tierras propias (130)
(m) a todos los azen pecheros y tributarios: a los señores principales, *tequjlatos* (130)
(n) tortillas y *chile* y un poco de *atule* (130)

4.5 The speech of Diego de Ordaz

El habla de Diego de Ordaz is a major contribution to the history of New World Spanish (Lope Blanch 1985). Diego de Ordaz represents the educated Castilian man of arms and letters with clear ambitions to climb the social ladder via his own merits as explorer and soldier. His letters (1529-1530) belong to the documents of the first generation of Spanish speakers living in the Central Highlands who were Cortés' contemporaries. Ordaz' traits correspond to the Castilian norms prevailing during the first half of the 16th century.

The pronunciation of vowels was one of the features defining the transition from late medieval to modern Spanish. The vacillation of strong mid vowels (*o, e*) and weak high vowels (*i, u*) identify writers of this era. Diego de Ordaz confused the following pairs: *espicial / especial, escrevire / escrivire, perjoizio / perjuizio, encorporado / incorporado, recebir / recibio, recibieron / recebido*. He also used strong vowels as in the following variants: *venieredes, envierno, posieron, podieron, morio, tovieron, conplio, ovieran, morio, acochillar, mesmo, doplicada, delegencia, sofrir, fondir*; and occasionally he also used the modern Spanish variants with weak vowels, as in *invierno, descubierto*.

The pronunciation of consonants reflects the norms of educated individuals of this period. Ordaz distinguished between (a) the palatal lateral /λ/ (in writing <ll>, <li>, <ly> or simply <l>) as in *hallo, lleve, allá, vasallo, caballero, valle, Castilla, lyeva, lieva, levar*, and (b) the central palatal /y/ (in writing < y> or <i>) as in *aya, mayo, huyendo, sayo, yegua, suyas, joyas*. He also maintained the distinction between the voiceless palatal fricative /ʃ/ (in writing <x>) and its corresponding voiced counterpart /ʒ/ (in writing <j> and <g>) as in *dexar, caxa, dixo, baxas, taxo*, as opposed to *conejo, mujer, ajeno, mejor, viejos, espejos, trabajo* and *ovejas*. This distinction corresponds to both *toledano* and Castilian. With respect to voiced labials Ordaz differentiated between occlusive /b/ and fricative /β/, the former appearing in intervocalic position as in *abierta, cabo, abrir, cabeçera, saber*, and the latter in *aver, dever, cavallo, provecho, ovejas, llevar*. Although the confusion between these two phonemes had started in earlier times, he shows systematic correction according to medieval standards. Also, the aspiration of initial H- derived from Latin F- appears to be the norm; he writes *hanbre, hazer, hablar, holgar, hasta, harto, harina, hallar, hijos, enhilado*; and there are no anti-etymological aspirations since he writes *aver, ay, ahora, eredad, abito, oy, os, onrra*. Diego de Ordaz spoke and wrote like the educated Castilians of his time: he did not distinguish the voiced apico-alveolar fricative /ż/ from the voiceless /ṡ/, but he did distinguish the affricate dentals /ẑ/ and /ŝ/. Finally, he was neither *ceceante* nor *yeísta*, and aspirated initial H due to either the preservation of an articulatory habit or a good knowledge of orthography.

4.5.1 Morpho-syntactic features of Diego de Ordaz

The analysis of the morpho-syntactic features that appear in Diego de Ordaz' letters aids in the reconstruction of the different variants used since the early decades of the 16th century. The evolution of atonic pronouns, use of imperfect subjunctive, and the combination of tenses with the SI-clause can be traced from first generation writers to modern times.

4.5.1.1. In Diego de Ordaz' letters the position of the atonic pronouns varies according to the verb tense. In modern Spanish, the atonic pronoun is placed before the conjugated verb, as in "*se había* hecho". With verbal phrases, the atonic pronouns can have various positions: before the auxiliary verb: "*lo he* de hacer", before or after the infinitive, "*helo* de hacer" or "he de hacer*lo*". The second variant is infrequent in modern Spanish. With non-conjugated forms, verbal clitics can go either before the infinitive, as in (a) "hazeme escritura de *me volver*"; (b) "para *vos dar* parte"; (c) "Vase a Sevilla para *se embarcar*", or after infinitives, as in (d) "trabaje *por enviarla* mas firme" (Lope Blanch 1985: 64, 67-68).

4.5.1.2. In Diego de Ordaz' letters, there are 156 sentences where 79 SI-clauses appear in the protasis, and where the –SE form is used in both the protasis and the apodosis, as in (a)-(c). In temporal clauses expressing anteriority or posteriority with the connectors *antes de que* or *quando*, the subjunctive form in –SE was commonly used as in (d) and (e). When the result was hypothetical, as in (f), the imperfect subjunctive form in –SE was also preferred (Lope Blanch 1985: 97-98).
(a) Si *hallaseis* a quien vender la casa, la *vendieseis* (107)
(b) Si quando el *fuese*, vos las *ovieseis* vendido, la venta vuestra valga y la mia no (110)
(c) Si *viniese* algun navio i me *enviaseis* dineros (112)
(d) Antes que me *partiese* a Madrid (...) *os* escrevy (115)
(e) quando yo *volviese* a la tierra a vsar el regimiento, le bolvere sus dineros (115)
(f) les dexo vna carta o dos para que os las *diesen* con el oro (115)

4.5.1.3. Forms ending in –RA appear in main, concessive or adversative clauses and refer to events in the past when the events are uncertain or impossible. In cases (b) through (d) writers of modern standard Spanish would have preferred the indicative conditional form ending in –RÍA. The concurrence of the forms ending in –RA and in –RÍA was not a remarkable trait in the Spanish of the 16th century, but it is today in varieties of both peninsular and Latin American Spanish.
(a) por esto no pude aca aver el perdon, aunque *dieran* diez mil ducados (113)
(b) las cartas de favor para los oidores bien *podieran* ir antes (113)
(c) a el mejor le *fuera* esperar (113)
(d) se esperaba su residencia (...) pensando que la *hizieran* como juezes sin pasion (113)

Like other writers of his time, Diego de Ordaz gradually replaced the simple form in –RA with the compound form *hubiera* + past participle. As the typical construction for past contrary-to-fact invaded the space of the present contrary-to-fact, it was necessary to select a structure that would be unambiguously past. The perfect tenses were available in different combinations. All in all Diego de Ordaz reveals his superior education in the epistolary genre and appears to be the most versatile user of verb tenses and verb modes. Other letter writers who did not reach that level of education were not able to maneuver the stylistic variations of medieval and pre-modern Spanish (cf. Lope Blanch 1985).

4.5.1.4. In Castilian Spanish the pronoun *vos* was the most common subject pronoun used to address those in a subordinate position (master to servants, servants and servants) but it was also used as an object pronoun. Lope Blanch (1985: 17) documents a fragment of the 1530 letter that the Queen of Spain delivered to Diego de Ordaz, who was addressed with the subject pronoun *vos* as in sentence (a). In items (b) and (c), *vos* is used as object pronoun alternating with *os* in sentence (d).

(a) Por quanto *vos* el capitan Diego de Ordaz, vezino de la Nueva España me heziste rrelacion que por, por la mucha voluntad que *teneys* al servicio del Emperador y Rrey mi señor y mio.
(b) Primeramente *vos* doy licencia e facultad para que por nos y en nuestro nombre y de la Corona Real de Castilla *podays* conquistar y poblar dichas tierras.
(c) por honrrar vuestra persona e por *vos* hazer merced prometemos de *vos* hazer nuestro governador e Capitan General.
(d) Otrosy *os* hazemos merced del titulo e nuestro Adelantado.

4.5.2 The origins of *voseo*

The letters that Diego de Ordaz wrote to his nephew reveal the trends on the use of *tú* and *vos*, pronouns that at the time belonged to the same semantic domain. Because Ordaz was worried about his properties in New Spain, he delivered many recommendations to his nephew. Diego de Ordaz did not use mixed forms (e.g., *tú pedís* or *vos dices*), but he did omit the final –*d* of the affirmative command of the pronoun *vos*. In addition, he also inverted the order of consonants in those commands ending in –*d*. Table 4.2 shows the normative forms of the three conjugations (–AR, –ER, –IR) of the verbs *tomar, tener, pedir*. The pronoun *tú* appears in Column 1 and the pronoun *vos* in Column 5 with their corresponding conjugations in the present tense (Columns 2 and 6), preterit indicative (3 and 7), and affirmative commands (Columns 4 and 8). These paradigms are helpful to understand the internal changes that originated the New World Spanish innovation known as *voseo*.

4.5 The speech of Diego de Ordaz

Table 4.2: *Tú* and *vos* in three conjugations and three tenses

1	2	3	4	5	6	7	8
TÚ	Present	Preterit	Command	VOS	Present	Preterit	Command
Tomar	Tomas	Tomaste	Toma	Tomar	Tomáis	Tomasteis	Tomad
Tener	Haces	Hiciste	Haz	Tener	Tenéis	Tuvisteis	Tened
Pedir	Pides	Pediste	Pide	Pedir	Pedís	Pedisteis	Pedid

New World Spanish *voseo* may have its origins in an internal change originating in final –*d* dropping of affirmative commands corresponding to the pronoun *vos* (see Column 8). Examples (a) through (g) illustrate the forms that were normative at the time (Lope Blanch 1985: 206-209). A verbal clitic appearing before the affirmative command was also used, as in (h).

(a) *dad* a esos señores esas cartas
(b) *tened* mucha vijilancia
(c) *hazed* todo lo que podierdes
(d) *echad* conejos y venados
(e) *enviad* todo lo que buenamente podierdes
(f) I *criad* en Guaçoçingo muchos puercos
(g) *mirad* si podéis dar un corte
(h) I luego *le poned* la demanda

Although the normative use prevails in Diego de Ordaz' correspondence, occasionally he dropped the final –*d*, as in (a) *tomáØ* posesión; (b) *PasáØ* a Guaçoçingo algunos naranjos; (c) I *tenéØ* quenta con esos señores (Lope Blanch 1985: 206, 214, 219). More interesting examples of affirmative commands appear when the verbal clitic goes after the affirmative command, since via metathesis, the final –*d* takes the place of the initial –*l* of the verbal clitic. This use appeared consistently 37 times (Lope Blanch 1985: 209, 212, 213, 219).

(a) *Daldes* de comer
(b) *hazeldos* que entiendan
(c) i *traeldo* bien tratado
(d) *quitalde* la india Isabel
(e) i *sabeldo* pedir a su tiempo

The tendency to drop the final –*d* in words other than commands is common in both Castilian and Andalusian. In addition, alveolar consonants L + D do not appear in clusters but in syllable-coda position (e.g., *al-da*-ba, al-*cal-de*, *bal-de*) thus increasing the probabilities of deleting final –*d* in other positions. Diego de Ordaz and other speakers might have pronounced their commands in coda position: *dal-des, hazel-dos*. Final *–d* dropping in affirmative commands and the semantic overlap of the 2nd person singular pronouns *tú* and *vos* may have been conducive to the emergence of *voseo*. One more internal change dealing with reduction of diphthongs complements the explanation of *voseo*. The present tense (as in Column 6 in Table 4.2) eventually rendered monopthongized forms in verbs of the 1st and 2nd second conjugations: *vos tomás, vos tenés, vos llamás, vos querés* in those sub-regions in which *voseo* survived (most Central and South American countries).

4.6 Nahuatl loans in the *Vocabulario de la lengua castellana y mexicana*

The opposite of Hernán Cortés was the young Alonso de Molina, who immigrated to New Spain with his parents and a younger brother when he was in his mid-teens. Molina learned Nahuatl for preaching and teaching the Christian doctrine, was educated within the cloisters of the Franciscan Order, and never returned to Spain. He is the author of two major works of philology: the Nahuatl grammar and the *Vocabulario de la lengua castellana y mexicana y mexicana y castellana* (henceforth *Vocabulario*, 1555/1570) which has been used mostly as a source of Nahuatl lexicography but rarely as a source to investigate the origins of Mexican Spanish. In the prologue Molina claims that faith should be taught in the language of the native people; those who preach and teach should know the propriety of the words they use, for the language and phrases of the natives are very different from Latin, Greek and Castilian. The *Vocabulario* not only contains Tainismos and Nahuatlismos, but it gathered the most vital Spanish items at the time and those that were conveniently translated into Nahuatl. Molina was fluently bilingual and bi-literate but he claimed he did not know the Nahuatl language like a native speaker. Nahuatl lexical items were selected by Spanish speakers who had been in contact with Nahuatl from the 1520's on. Proto-Mexican Spanish was enriched with borrowings recorded in the Spanish section of the *Vocabulario* (see Table 4.3). The Spanish / Nahuatl section of the *Vocabulario* integrated the loans from Nahuatl that were being used in the New Spanish society before 1555. Spanish speakers had a good ear and transcribed the loans following closely their original pronunciation. The Mexican Spanish koine differs from other regional koines in that in addition to incorporating lexical items from Taino, it integrated those from Nahuatl. Appearing in the first edition of the *Vocabulario*, Nahuatl borrowings were adapted by Spanish speakers in the following manner.

First, the grapheme <x> represented the Nahuatl sibilant that appeared as voiceless pre-palatal fricative in initial position; this coincided with the same medieval Castilian phoneme that went through regular evolution and ended as modern *jota*, as in items 19-23 in Table 4.3. Second, voiceless dental fricative /s/ appears before consonants as in items 6, 17, 25, 39; and in intervocalic position as in items 42 and 45. Third, the affricate phoneme /tɬ/ is distinctively Nahuatl. It appears in items 1, 5-10, 15, 17, 20, 22, 23, 25, 27, 31, 40-44 and 46-47. In contact with Spanish, such pronunciation, however, resulted in at least two variants: the first one retained the affricate quality and the second one added the paragogic letter –*e* as in *aguacate* (1), *cacahuate* (5), and *camote* (9). The second variant omitted the affricate as in *jícama* (20) and *tequio* (41). The frequency of nouns ending in /tɬ/ and the numerous toponyms with the same phoneme contributed to the retention of the affricate in modern times. Such persistence is associated to the prestige of Nahuatl. Some Spanish speakers used [tɬ], which they heard from other Spanish speakers who were highly educated such as Alonso de Molina and Bernardino de Sahagún. Yet some others preferred -*te*, which was the Hispanicized variant of informal speech. The geminate lateral /l:/ in final position was reduced to a Spanish liquid –*l*, or endings –*le* or –*ra* (see items 11, 12, 14, 16, 18, 19, 21, 24, 26, 34, 36, 37, 39, 42 and 47). These variations show the prominence of Spanish speakers as agents of diffusion and change because most of the Nahuatlismos are vital at present.

Table 4.3: Nahuatlismos in Molina's *Vocabulario de lengua castellana y mexicana* (1555)

No.	Modern Spanish	Original Nahuatl	Dated	English equivalent	Assimilated
1	Aguacate	AVACATL	1535	Avocado	Yes
2	Aguachil	Spanish 'agua' + CHILLI	Molina	Water of hot pepper	No
3	Aje	AXIN	Before Molina	Unguent	No
4	Atole	ATULLI	Before Molina	Thick drink made of corn	Yes
5	Cacao	CACAHUATL	1525 or earlier	Cocoa drink	Yes
6	Cacastle	CACAXTLI	Molina	Pannier	No
7	Cacle	CACTLI	1532	Sandal	Not completely

Table 4.3 (continued)

No.	Modern Spanish	Original Nahuatl	Dated	English equivalent	Assimilated
8	Camalote	AMALACOTL	Molina	Water plant of rounded leaves	No
9	Camote	CAMOTLI	1551	Yam, sweet potato	Yes
10	Cimate	CIMATL	Molina	Root of plant used as a condiment	No
11	Comal	COMALLI	1532	Clay utensil used to cook *tortillas*	Yes
12	Copal	COPALLI	1532	White or colorless incense	No
13	Chía	CHIA, CHIAN, (CHIANTLI)	1544	Seed of the salvia columbariae	Yes
14	Chile	CHILLI	1521	Hot pepper	Yes
15	Chiquigüite	CHIQUIUITL	1521	Basket	Yes
16	Guacal	VACALLI	Molina	Pannier or box	Yes
17	Huistle	VICTLI	Molina	Shovel	No
18	Hule	OLLI, VLLI	1532	Rubber	No
19	Jacal	XACALLI	1532	Adobe house or hut	Yes
20	Jícama	XICAMATL	1532	Edible tubercle	Yes
21	Jícara	XICALLI	1532	Recipient made of one-half pumpkin	Yes
22	Jilote	XILOTL	1532	Ear of the corn	Yes
23	Jitomate	XITOMATL		Tomato	No
24	Macegual	MACEUALLI	1532	Vassal, laborer	Yes
25	Mastel, mastate	MAXTATL	1532	Underwear	?
26	Mecapal*	MECAPALLI	Molina	Wide and flat string	Yes
27	Metate	METATL	1532	Stone to grind the grains	No
28	Milpa	MILPAN: MILLI + PA(N)	1540	Corn field	Yes
29	Mitote	MITOTL	1545	Vociferous dance	Yes
30	Nahua	NAHUATL, NAHUA		Speaker of Nahuatl	No
31	Nahuatl	NAHUATL		Adjective referring to language	No

Table 4.3 (continued)

No.	Modern Spanish	Original Nahuatl	Dated	English equivalent	Assimilated
32	Nahuatlato	NAHUATLATO	1530-1	Translator, interpreter	Not completely
33	Oyamel	OYAMEL	Molina	Oil-producing tree	Not completely
34	Petaca	PETACALLI	1530-5	Box made of wood rods	Yes
35	Piles	PILLI	Molina	Aztec noblemen	No
36	Pinole	PINOLLI	1532	Drink of toasted corn and chia	Yes
37	Tamal	TAMALLI	1552	Corn bread	Yes
38	Tameme	TLAMAMA, TLAMEME	1540	Cargo carrier	Yes
39	Temascal	TEMAZCALLI	1532	Small steam bathroom	No
40	Teponaztli	TEPONAZTLI	1532	Wood drum	Not completely
41	Tequio	TEQUIOTL	ca. 1539	Labor imposed as tribute	Not completely
42	Tezontlale	TEÇONTLALLI	Molina	Porous sand used in construction	No
43	Tomate	TOMATL	1532	Tomato	Not completely
44	Tlaxcalmimilli	TLAXCALMIMILLI	Molina	Long corn bread	No
45	Tuza	TOÇAN, TUÇAN	Molina	Gofer	Not completely
46	Yelosóchil	YELOXUCHITL	Molina	Aromatic flower	No
47	Zoalli	TZOALLI	Molina	Roll bread of seeds	No

Source: E. Hernández (1996: passim) period *It appears in the edition of 1555

4.7 The explicative model of proto-Mexican Spanish

Spanish language contact with indigenous languages, particularly Nahuatl, has to be reckoned with in the explicative model of proto-Mexican Spanish. The fact that Mexican /s/ ended up with a [+ tense] quality may be explained by the direct contact of Spanish speakers with Nahuatl during the decades in which it was the most widely heard and spoken in Mexico City and its surroundings. It was also a language that was first codified in the Romanized tradition and implemented to fulfill certain functions in religious domains. The transliteration of Nahuatl and other indigenous languages began in the early decades of the 16th century. Therefore, its prestige was beyond doubt. Nahuatl borrowings were added to the Spanish spoken in New Spain after the addition of Tainismos had taken place. It can even be argued that the sibilants coming in from *toledano-castellano* merged with those of Nahuatl rendering a new (proto-Mexican Spanish) sibilant slightly more tense than the one used in most Spanish varieties. Tenseness of /s/ occurred after Spanish speakers selected and incorporated sufficient Nahuatlismos to the Spanish spoken in New Spain.

A corpus consisting of 94 documents (1524-1578) shows the patters of transliteration of Nahuatl sibilants into Spanish consonants (Arias Alvarez and Báez 1996). Table 4.4 shows Nahuatl voiceless dentals in initial and implosive position (1 and 2); also, voiceless palatal fricative 3 appears in initial position in names of places or persons such as Xilotepec and Xochitl, while Nahuatl voiceless affricate 4, identical to Castilian, appears in words such as Michuacan or Mechuacan, Opochtli, Tenochtitlan, Tlacochcalcatl, etc. When sounds are identical, researchers do not find variations of graphemes, but when sounds between the two languages differ, researchers found two systems: one utilized by the missionaries, which is closer to the Spanish grammar described by Elio Antonio de Nebrija, and the second one used by all the other Spanish writers who adapted indigenous sounds to their own speech and writing systems, and for this reason, there is more variation in graphemes.

Table 4.4: Transliteration of Nahuatl borrowings

No.	Description	Symbol	Grapheme	Examples
1.	Voiceless dental fricative	/ŝ/	<c>, <ç> or <z> in initial position; <z> or <s> in implosive position	Zacatl > çacate [initial]. Tepoztli > tepuzque or tipusque or cocoliztli > cocolistle
2.	Voiceless dental affricate	/ŝ/	<tç>,<ts>, <tz> in initial position; <ts> and <tz> in implosive position	Caltzoltzin > caçonçi, caçonzi [initial]. Quetzalcoatl > Quetsalcoatl
3.	Voiceless palatal fricative	/ʃ/	<x> or <s> in initial position; <s> or <z> in implosive position; or is lost.	Oaxaca > Guaxaca; Xicalli > xicalas; Mexico > Mexico [initial]. Calpixqui > calipisques

Table 4.4 (continued)

No.	Description	Symbol	Grapheme	Examples
4.	Voiceless palatal affricate	/tʃ/	<ch> in initial position; <s> in implosive position.	Chalco > Chalco; Cholula > Cholula [initial]. Tenochtitlan > Tenozttitlan, Tenoxtitlan, Tenostitlan

The analysis of Nahuatl sibilants is conducive to propose that voiceless dentals 1 and 2 merged with de-affricated Castilian dental sibilants, and added the extra-articulatory tension present in Nahuatl. With respect to voiceless palatal fricative 3, it must be clarified that it remained as such until the process of de-palatalization was completed in Spanish in the 17th century. However, numerous Nahuatl toponyms have retained the palatal fricative 3 and are still used in the area of Nahuatl influence, for example, Santiago *Xalitzintla* (a small town near the Popocatepetl volcano), *ixtle* (string or lancet made of fiber), *paxtle* (hanging plant). Finally, voiceless palatal affricate 4 is identical to Spanish <ch> and has remained as such in both Nahuatl and Spanish. This completes the preliminary formula of the explicative model of proto-Mexican Spanish both in the realm of non-Spanish lexicon and pronunciation of the sibilants. Nahuatlismos appearing in DLNE-AC (1994) complement the invaluable data published in 1555 by Alonso de Molina.

4.8 The Gulf of Mexico

Twenty-three manuscripts belonging to the Cortesian period (1520-1555) appear in *Documentos Lingüísticos de la Nueva España: Golfo de México* (DLNE-EG 2008). Document 1 is a letter by Hernán Cortés, in which he informed the king of Spain of the arrest of Moctezuma. It was handwritten by Cortés himself in Segura de la Frontera at Tepeaca (present day state of Puebla). The rest of the documents were issued at Cempoala, Veracruz, Antequera, Panuco, Tehuantepec, Xalapa, towns spawning along the coasts of the present states of Tamaulipas, Veracruz, Tabasco, Campeche, Quintana Roo, and Yucatan proper, a region that was explored before or at the same time that the Central Highlands, but which was neglected by the New Spanish officials. These manuscripts reveal the preoccupation of the writers with the precarious conditions of the area, which was teeming with a diversity of problems. One of them was the absence of authorities such as mayors, judges, and military personnel. According to the missionaries who were able to visit the region in this period, the few Spanish speakers in charge of this region were oblivious of the regulations on the treatment of slaves and Indians, who were at the personal services of the *encomenderos*. Despite the severe conditions, there was trade and reports on trade and other activities. All of the documents were prepared by the personnel of the Inquisition, friars and scribes, that is, all of them deal with the topics discussed in Cortesian texts and show the features of the early period, although Tainismos and Nahuatlismos are not abundant.

The close vowels of modern Spanish (*i* and *u*) replaced mid open vowels (*e* and *o*) in words such as in *escrevir* and *escreví* (71) *oregynales* (85), *recebir* (74, 77), *remetirme* (79) in the first group and *estoviese* (42) and *sotilezas* (57) in the second. (2) The grapheme <x> representing the voiceless palatal fricative was used by the first generation of Spanish speakers as in *dixo* (49) *truxeron* (61). (3) The spelling of words with initial F- alternates with the spelling of initial H: *faria* (31), *fazen* (28), *fecho* (28), *hazerme* (30), *hizo* (80), and *hiziese* (41). At the same time anti-etymological aspiration can be found in *harriero* (47), *hedad* (50), *henemigo* (45), *hera* (35) *henojo*, *hevidente* (37) *hordena* (59), *hebrero*, *hechar*, etc. (4) Addition of a palatal between vowels in verbs like SER and VER appears in "*beyendo esto, hablé al presidente*" (82), "*porque beyendo yo su disolución*" (82) and "*Seyendo ellos los acusadores*" (85).

The variations of pronunciation are glaring in *crus* (43), *desía* and *desían* (44), *Veracrús* (45), *disiendo* (49), *hiso* (47), *vesino* (45), *fise* (67), and <z> in *paresze* (55), *avizo* (83), *dezasosiego* (83). Although there is no aspiration or deletion of /s/ in implosive or final position, the opposite trait occurs in rare occasions, that is, there is an additional –*s* in implosive position as in the *ornasmientos* [ornamientos] (81), perhaps representing a tendency towards hypercorrection.

Spellings of the verbs TRAER and VER were variable. Like the authors from the Central Highlands, those from the Gulf hesitated between *truxe* and *traxo*, as in (a), (b), (d), (e) and (f), even in the same manuscript, while the medieval spelling of preterit tense of the 3rd person singular of the verb VEDERE was *vido*, as in (c) and (g).

(a) Se me avian perdido los que *truxe* (40)
(b) *traxo* uno de los officios de la Casa de la Contrataçión (45)
(c) estaba muy mala quando este testigo la *vido*, con la candela en la mano (51)
(d) se [ha] de hazer consçiençia de aver cargado los yndios que lo *truxeron* (61)
(e) las cartas que *truxo* el primillo (68)
(f) la plata que *traxo* de la costa de la Florida (85)
(g) una vez *bido* cubrir parte de la dicha iglesia a los dichos yndios (82)

4.8.1 The sibilants in the Gulf

The documents from the Gulf belonging to the first part of the 16th century (1-23) are useful to illustrate the traits of the first generation of writers, who with few exceptions were representatives of the Spanish Crown or local functionaries occupying diverse positions. There are letters to the king, testimonies, interrogatories, inventories, business letters, statements, petitions and a few personal missives. In Doc. 1 (pp. 27-31) Hernán Cortés did not use <ss> in imperfect subjuctive (e.g. *hiçiese, estuviese, dixesen, declarasen, supiesen, fuesen,* but preserved the use of <ç> as in *obedeçían, alçado, relaçión, apelaçiones, notiçia,* etc. He preferred the sequence -sç- in verbs with this combination in the stem (*paresçió, conosçer*) and used the grapheme <z> in *paz, fazen, hizo, perjuyzio, dezia, dozientos*; only in one occasion did he alternate between *hiçiese* and *hiziese*. In Doc. 2 (pp. 32-38), Cristóbal de Tapia, used single <s> in *pusyesen, consentiesen,* preserved the grapheme <ç> (*alteraçión, bolliçio, poleçía*), and preferred the sequence -sç- in *paresçe, resçiban, reconosçen,* but once he used *mereçió*. He also used *dézimo, juezes, gozaba* and anticipated the *seseante* tendency in *hisyese, rasón*. Doc. 3 (pp. 39-42) is the letter addressed to Carlos V by Francisco de Montejo, who wrote *hize, reçebir, nesçesidad, esperança, mudança*. Documents 4 and 5 (pp. 43-47), drafted by the notary of the Inquisition in Antequera, narrate Melchior Romero's testimony against Ruy Díaz; in both documents he used single -s- in *supiese, hiziese, viniese, fuese,* but there is a case of -ss- in *tress*. The notary used the grapheme <ç> in *conoçe, provinçias, liçençia, governaçión, perteneçe,* and the grapheme <z> in *hazen, hizo, dize,* etc. He also included samples of *seseo* in *crus, desían, disiendo, hiso, relasión, hasía, vesino,* etc. The remaining documents 6-23 cover almost two decades from 1537 to 1555. The authors tend to preserve the grapheme <ç> according to the etymological use as in *sentençia, çien, començó*; at the same time, the grapheme <ss> in imperfect subjunctive is rare or almost obsolete, while single <ç> alternates with -sç- in *conosçe* (51), *paresçe* (52), *resçibido* (54), *nasçimiento* (66). The alternate use of <z> and <ç> also appears in *dezia* and *deçía,* and the grapheme <z> began to appear in anti-etymological position as in *azero, prozeso* (54, 55), *paresze* (56), *rezio* (66), *azeyte* (68), *avizadme, avizo* (83). Although in the Gulf the grapheme <z> did not prevail, it was the most frequent practice. As the century goes on <ss> reappears in words that did not have it as in *quissiese* (74) and alternated with single <s>, as in *pesos* (70) and *pessos* (71). Finally, the cases of *seseo* are extremely rare, *fise* (67).

4.8.2 *Leísmo* in the Gulf

The language data from the Gulf reveal patterns that are similar to those found in the Central Highlands. Cortesian documents confirm the tendency towards the use of *leísmo*. In the sub-sample below, there are 28 cases of clitics referring to [+ masculine accusative]. Singular LE appears 18 times while there are 12 cases of LO. In sentences (a) through (l) the author of Doc. 1 (pp. 27-38), Hernán Cortés refers to Moctezuma using both LE and LO, which means that Cortés was at times *leísta* and at times pro-etymologist. The rest of the authors are also inclined to use both pronouns. (For discussion of plurals LES and LOS, see Hidalgo, 2013).

(a) se a dado notiçia del dicho Moteçcuma después que *lo* tuvo preso (27)
(b) *lo* syguró fasta que *lo* prendió pa del todo saber los sujetos desta tierra (27)
(c) E los naturales destas partes *lo* tienen por gran señor (28)
(d) asý a él en nombre de sus Altezas **le an tenido e obedeçido** (28)
(e) algunos de los naturales destas partes que **le yvan a ver** (30)
(f) quel era el dicho Moteçcuma y se *lo* hiziese soltar (30)
(g) en prendiéndo*lo* o soltando al dicho Moteçcuma, luego se avía de yr (30)
(h) **viéndole** a él salir de la dicha çibdad (...) y que *lo* sacasen de la presyón (30)
(i) Muteçcuma tenía conçertado, aviendo muerto a los españoles que **le aguardaban** (30)
(j) **le avía enviado** con ciertos navíos y gentes a descubrir y a poblar esta tierra (31)
(k) siempre **le ha visto** ser arriero de esta tierra [a Ruy Diaz] (44)
(l) Fue preguntado que sy al dicho Ruy Diaz **le ha oýdo** blasfemar o dezir mal (44)
(m) Fuele preguntado sy es pariente del dicho Ruy Dias este testigo, o sy es su henemigo o **le quiere mal** (45)
(n) ni **le quiere mal** más de a las malas obras que **le a visto** hacer [a Ruy Diaz] (45)
(o) lo que sabía del dicho Ruy Dias a la justicia lu[e]go que *lo* conoció en estas partes (45)
(p) que **le vee facer** obras de buen cristiano [a Viçençio] (52)
(q) **le oyó** decir este testigo sobre cierta deferençia [al acusado] (54)
(r) "Dios no tuvo padre, y se llamó Josepe, y **le llamavan** hijo de un carpintero" (55)
(s) Fuele preguntado sy conoçe a Gonzalo Bernal o de qué tiempo a esta parte *lo conoçe* (57)
(t) Dixo que *lo* conoce avrá quatro o çinco años [a Bernal] (57)
(u) Ni él (el Padre Alonso Ruyz) *lo* a confesado ni menos sabe quién *lo* a confesado (57)

(v) porque sy se desmandava, **le castigaran** como merecía [al autor de las calumnias] (68)
(w) se ha apartado este testigo de **velle** jugar [al acusado] (72)
(x) y se fue por no **oýrle** decir más (73)
(y) "más **le he oýdo dezir** que eso, que ha dicho:..." [el acusado] (73)
(z) no e podido **favorecelle** como quisiera [al yerno Gerónimo] (83)

4.8.3 Use of subject pronouns: *vos, vosotros, vuestra merced*

The missives of this period are addressed to the king or to other civil and ecclesiastic authorities in Spain; for this reason personal pronouns are not too frequent, but appear as null subjects as in *vosotros* (a) and *vos* as in (f). The most frequent form of address was *vuestra merced*, normally abbreviated *v.m.* All of them agreed with the same possessives *Vuestra Real Corona, vuestros vasallos, vuestros servidores*, etc.

(a) *avizadme* si sallió buena (83)
(b) y prohoverá *v.m.* pa quando sea neçesario (63)
(c) la pipa de vino habrá *v. m.* recibido (83)
(d) suplico a *vuestra merced* enbíe a mucho recabdo a Martin de Alberruçia (68)
(e) las dos calderas que *v. m.* enbió pata Tustla (83)
(f) hallaron al dicho Gonzalo Bernal comiendo una gallina un viernes, y que le dijo el dicho Andrés de Valladolid: ¿por qué *coméys* oy viernes carne? (58)

4.8.4 Imperfect subjunctive: variations in –SE and –RA

Spanish speakers belonging to the first generation exhibit the miscellaneous uses of –SE and –RA in imperfect subjunctive in the different contexts in which it commonly appeared. Hernán Cortés is the author of Doc. 1, 1520, a letter delivered to the king narrating the capture of Moctezuma in Tenochtitlan. Cortés clearly preferred the ending in –SE, items (a) and (b), but he switched to –RA and –RA in the SI-conditional sentence (c). The subsamples in imperfect subjunctive are grouped under three categories: (1) all the –SE forms in nominal, adjectival and adverbial clauses; (2) –RA forms in the protasis, because this context was the first one in which –RA appeared with subjunctive meaning; and (3) other –RA forms with subjunctive meaning (see Table 4.8A).

(a) E porquel dicho Moteçcuma (...) no *hiçiese* ayuntamiento de gentes y *alborotase* la tierra contra él (27)
(b) que no *estuviesen* en esta tierra e que *saliesen* della (28)

(c) Lo qual no *oviera* sy el dicho Narváez no *dixera* lo que dicho es (30)
(d) si lo tal se *pudiera* fazer, diríamos que sy *salieran* al camino e me *tomaran* en Castilla (33)
(e) E sy se proyvió que no *viniesen* otras personas fue porque acá no se *supiese* (35)
(f) convenía que *viesen* e *supiesen* que se cunplían los mandos de Su Magestad (37)
(g) si *conosçieran* que quería oro *pusiéranse* en hazerme alguna trayción por no dallo (39)
(h) lo que Vuestra Magestad me hizo merçed *viniese* a conquistar y poblar en su nombre (41)
(i) si *estoviese* dividido de la del norte, no tendría por dónde se poder proveer (42)
(j) estava con grandísima calentura, como sy *estuviera* en un horno metida (50)
(k) no se casaría con esta muger que al presente tiene si de çierto no *supiera* que era muerta su muger en los reynos de Castilla (52-53)
(l) *Pudiera* escrevir a Guaxaca, pues estava tan çerca como de aquí, y *fuera* luego proveýdo (64)
(m) *Quisiera* saber las vaziedades que me escrive que dezía, porque sy se desmandava, le *castigaran* como merecía (68)

4.8.5 Lexicon

Lexical items can be identified along different semantic categories: (1) Words that refer to indigenous objects are not as abundant as in the Central Highlands, where Tainismos and Nahuatlismos were common, for instance, *calpisques* (76), *naguatato* (68), *tameme* (68, 77), *tyangues* (62), *petacas* and *petaquilla* (71), and *caçonci* (40). (2) There are terms referring to currency and objects made of metal, as in *castellanos* (monetary unit or gold peso with fractions in *reales* and *maravedíes*) (41); *pesos en tostones* (coins of lesser value) (59); *typuzque* (monetary unit made of copper) (59); *pesos de minas* (currency valued at 450 maravedíes) (62, 64), *pesos y tomines* ('pesos and small silver coins') (85); *reales de plata quintada* (coins of sterling silver) (66); *petacas de plata rrefina* ('big boxes of refined silver') (70); *planchas de plata* ('slabs of silver') (70); *rreales de plata* ('silver coins') (85). (3) There is also a semantic category that refers to work, ethnicity, and slavery as in (a) through (g).
(a) tenemos *gente de yndios y negros* carpinteros (60)
(b) Hellos quedan contentos, *y los esclavos muy buenos y bien tratados* (61)
(c) conviene meter un *oficial calafate con los negros* (64)
(d) Mi *moço* lleva cinco *tamemes* o seis suyos (68)
(e) careçen de *calpixques y negros y mestizos* que tienen ordinariamente los encomenderos en sus pueblos (76)

(f) hecha la tasa y mandado que no uviese *tameme ni esclavo* (77)
(g) Y ansí les sacan la sangre a los míseros *yndios en los tributos y serviçio personal* (77)

4.9 Conclusions

The first generation of Spanish speakers, protagonists of the conquest and colonization of Mexico, were the speakers of proto-Mexican Spanish. Simultaneously a smaller group of Spanish speakers settled in the Gulf of Mexico; consequently, Spanish speakers from both regions welcomed the arrival of more Spanish speakers with whom they interacted in the newer domains. In the Central Highlands, they created various permanent institutions: the vice-royal Court, the courts of appeal, the churches and monasteries, and a few schools that stimulated the use of the Spanish variety that was perceived as being formal or semi-formal. Despite their regional differences Spanish speakers remained solidary. Evidence from a variety of documents provides useful information on the variants and variations of the formative period in which various genres generally followed the norms of Castilian Spanish. First generation speakers from Castile and from other regions counted on a model based on late medieval Spanish and at the same time exhibited inclinations towards koineization (1520-1555), a period distinguished by the adoption of Amerindian loans from both Taino and Nahuatl, documented in the most reliable source, the first part of the *Vocabulario* by Alonso de Molina. The external circumstances enhancing this process was first the exploration of the Caribbean islands where Spanish speakers picked up the native lexicon, and later the conquest and colonization of Mexico, where Nahuatl was since pre-Hispanic times the most widespread lingua franca used for intra- and inter-group communication.

The phonetic traits analyzed in this chapter must have presented more variation in the colloquial registers used for daily communication, though in the earliest period none of the features that later defined New World Spanish emerged clearly. For instance, in the realm of the written language, *seseo* is moderate amongst first generation writers. *Seseo* is most reliable evidence of koineization, but is not represented in the early decades of the 16th century for the writers followed mostly Castilian(ized) norms (see Tables 4.5A and 4.5B). In the second half of the 16th century there are more cases of *seseo* (see 6.2.1.). Other traits such as aspiration of –s in implosive position, neutralization of -r and -l, weakening of -d- and -d are conspicuously absent in this subsample. There is more evidence on the aspiration of initial H (< Latin F) which alternated with the full pronunciation of initial F.

Table 4.5A: Traditional graphemes in the Central Highlands

Period	<s>	<ss>	<ç>	<z>	Total
1525-1555	225 (15.85%)	93 (6.55%)	835 (58.84%)	266 (18.74%)	= 1419 (100%)

Table 4.5B Traditional graphemes in the Gulf

Period	<s>	<ss>	<ç>	<z>	Total
1520-1555	78 (16.01%)	2 (0.41%)	307 (63.03%)	100 (20.53%)	= 487 (100%)

With respect to morpho-syntactic variants, proto-Mexican Spanish had the same assortment of forms transmitted from Spain. Spanish speakers used both the ancestral proto-etymologist system and the innovative *leísta* system. The samples from the Central Highlands (or Altiplano C.) and the Gulf (or El Golfo) reveal the preference of LE over LO. The inclination for *leísmo* is reflective of the patterns of prestige and formal education, since the speakers were either from northern-central Spain or educated in Castilianized regions. *Leísmo* indicates the divergence from Andalusian drifts (see Table 4.6).

Table 4.6: LE and LO in the first half of the 16th century

Region	LE	LO
Altiplano C.	37 / 52	15 / 52
El Golfo	22 / 37	15 / 37
Total = 89	59 (66.29%)	30 (33.70%)

In the realm of pronouns of address, New Spain counted with a tripartite system of singular forms: (a) *vos* [+ / − solidarity]; (b) *tú* [+ solidarity] and (c) *vuestra merced* [+ deference], the latter eventually resulting in the neologism Usted. The pronoun *vos* prevailed in the intra-familiar domain, as revealed in Diego de Ordaz's letters to his nephew. *Vos* was common in the informal registers and was used to address those speakers perceived as being subalterns. At the same time, mixing *vos* with the verbal paradigm of *tú* fostered the New World *voseo*. Whereas *tú* and *vos* derive from Latin, *vuestra merced* stemmed from the possessive adjective *vuestro/s*. During the colonial period, *vuestra merced* was the most frequent pronoun of address in the two regions, followed by *vos* while *tú* and *su merced* do not appear in the first half of the 16th century, primarily because the missives of the first generation writers are addressed directly to the king of Spain or other authorities (see Table 4.7). In this subsample, the form *vosotros*, the plural of *vos* and *tú*, is absent, whereas the plural formal *vuestras mercedes* and *sus mercedes* appear only three and two times, respectively.

Table 4.7: Singular pronouns in the first half of the 16th century

Region	Vos	Tú	V. Md.	S. Md.
Altiplano C.	15	0	11	0
El Golfo	3	0	129	0
Total = 158	18 (11.39%)	0 (0%)	140 (88.6%)	0 (0%)

Finally, Table 4.8A shows the alternating variants –SE and –RA, which have been examined in the Central Highlands by Acevedo (1997: 100-101). Acevedo's methodology is useful to subsume the varied uses of two variants in three main environments (see 4.8.4). This methodology aids in the comparison of the data between regions, as shown in Tables 4.8A and 4.8B.

Table 4.8A: Uses of –SE and –RA in the Central Highlands

Period	–SE forms	–RA forms in protasis	Other uses of –RA	Total tokens
1525-1549	92% / 252	5.5% / 16	2.5% / 7	275

Acevedo (1997: 99, 108)

Table 4.8B: Uses of –SE and –RA in the Gulf

Period	–SE forms	–RA forms in protasis	Other uses of –RA	Total tokens
1520-1555	78 / 90 (86.66%)	9 / 90 (10.0%)	3 / 90 (3.33%)	90

Chapter 5
How Spanish diversified

5.1 Occupational activities and social networks

This chapter aims at describing the different occupational activities and social networks derived from the presence of Spanish speakers in Mesoamerica, particularly those that are relevant to the diffusion and diversification of Spanish in the vast region. Mining, agriculture, construction, textiles, and services were the main loci of activities of Spanish and non-Spanish speakers during the 16th century, activities that in combination were sufficiently motivating to build a new society. Mining sites nurtured the immediate productive activity of the area, where Spanish explorers founded cities or sites, which became the centripetal centers generating other pursuits such as trade of mining equipment and retail sales among those working in or around the sites; mining sites attracted Spanish speakers, Afro-Hispanic workers, and missions and missionaries to take care of religious needs. If precious metals had not been found, Spanish explorers would have abandoned the area, or the area had not been infused with mercantile, cultural and educational enterprises, which developed rapidly via labor. Investments in the mining sector acted as the propeller of a series of economic activities that made the miners the most important members of the new national bourgeoisie.

It is proposed that labor practices fostered language contact between Spanish and non-Spanish speakers. In the beginning, labor was dependent on the *encomienda* tributary system, which was normally securing a cheap and massive supply of Indians. In theory, the *encomienda* system was beneficial for the indigenous since the Spanish grantee was required to protect the Indians living in his land. At this stage, language contact must have been basic given the disproportionate quantitative gap between Spanish speakers and Indians. Spanish speakers had control over the indigenous population, which were required to pay tribute from their own lands, and in addition, were involved in personal services. Then labor was controlled by the draft or *repartimiento*, which required distribution of laborers, goods, and services. After the draft was found too harsh, Spanish entrepreneurs opened small plants known as *obrajes* or *obrages* (cotton or woolen mills) where individuals were sequestered for long periods. Labor brought individuals of Spanish and non-Spanish descent in contact in different domains. When everything else in agriculture failed, the movement for the hacienda made a niche for the indigenous peoples who were freer to move around, and the process of Hispanization rendered productive results. The New Laws mandated the reduction of the *encomiendas* and the return of the Indians to the crown. This reform was enhanced by the ideal of free work and the intention to eliminate involuntary work (Zavala 1984). Between 1521 and 1576 there were plenty of workers but they diminished significantly at the end of the century due to the shrinking of the indigenous population triggering at the same time a reduction of the economy. In order to augment the direct revenues of the hacienda, the mining sector became the focus of the renovated economy (Assadourian 1989).

Other activities contributing to diversification are closely interrelated: religion, education and literary projects advanced by the introduction of the printing press in New Spain. In the early stage, religion per se did not have a major impact on Spanish diffusion because the missions resorted to both Latin and indigenous languages to promote Christianity, but when the zealous advocacy for the latter came to an end, Spanish had a more influential role in and around religious activities. Religion is bound to formal education of the Spanish-speaking elites who were exposed to Latin for classroom assignments and many other focused tasks. Spanish was used for everything else until instructors of Latin became unavailable. Formal education of the Spanish-speaking elites is a major factor contributing to the cultivation, preservation and further development of Spanish in miscellaneous domains.

5.2 Mining and metallurgy

The development of the mining sector in New Spain was defined by the discovery of mining resources in the arid regions of the North (with scarce indigenous populations), an event that triggered a process of territorial expansion of the mining frontier which was almost simultaneous with an agrarian frontier. Silver became the economic axis of the colony. At this stage both the private and the public sector supported various means to protect the new frontier, the technological innovations, and the migration of indigenous workers towards the northern mining sites. By the mid-16th century, Spanish officials were inclined to enforce the New Laws, an act that would prevent the delivery of Indians to *encomenderos*. Although there were strategies to enforce mandatory labor in some areas, in New Spain mining was exempt from forced labor (Assadourian 1989: 428-432).

In the western region of Mexico (especially among the Tarascans), metallurgy and metal working developed later than in the Andean highlands. These activities were based on copper and its alloys, although most metal objects were considered to be sacred, to be used for ornamentation in religious ceremonies, and to enhance the sociopolitical status of select groups. Spaniards began exploitation of precious metals in New Spain immediately after the conquest of the Aztec and Tarascan states, first by looting native gold and silver artifacts followed by mining of gold and silver ores. The artifacts were obtained from palaces, temples, graves and other sacred places, where the Aztec and Tarascan nobility had collected them for generations. The surfaces of such artifacts resembled pure silver or gold and were not used as symbols of wealth but by the native priests in ritual and status functions (West 1997a: 45-46 and 1997b: 58).

Map 5.1 shows the location of the major Spanish mining activities to about the mid-16th century. Silver mining on a commercial scale began in the early 1530's. The Tamazula area was quickly claimed by Cortés as his own and as a main source of silver (West 1997b:59). "During the early 1530's natives of Tamazula and neighboring towns continued to supply small amounts of low-grade silver as tribute to *encomenderos*" (West 1997b: 60). Simultaneously royal officials in Mexico requested the presence of experts in ore reduction because Spanish settlers were not knowledgeable of metallurgy. Once the mines were opened, numerous high officials were eager to purchase them and registered claims in the hope of quick returns. Hernán Cortés owned all or parts of twenty mines in Sultepec (or Zultepec). From the 1530's through the 1540's, the main labor force in the mines of Sultepec, Taxco and neighboring *asientos de minas* (mining sites) consisted of numerous Indian slaves captured in the just wars, many of whom were distributed among the high ranking officers (65). Cortés owned several hundred, used mainly in gold placers. Despite the abolition promulgated by the New Laws slavery persisted until 1550, and after the mid-century blacks from Africa and native freemen gradually replaced native slaves in the mines; by 1569, over 800 black slaves worked in the Taxco mines (66). Indians living in villages under an *encomienda* in the vicinity of the mines also contributed with significant source of labor for the early silver industry. *Encomenderos* were allowed to commute tribute of their subjects, who performed lighter tasks such as cutting wood, building huts, or carrying food and other necessities (66-67). The discovery of silver deposits in Sultepec and Taxco in the early 1530's soon led to a rush of potential Spanish miners of many social classes seeking quick wealth, but also of merchants and traders interested in a lucrative market for food, clothing, and mining equipment. Many of the miners from Mexico City were *encomenderos* controlling Indian villages near Toluca or in Cuernavaca. "As an *encomendero*, Hernán Cortés exacted tribute of food and cloth from his villages in both areas in order to supply slaves in his mines in Sultepec and Taxco, and to sell to other miners" (West 1997b: 68).

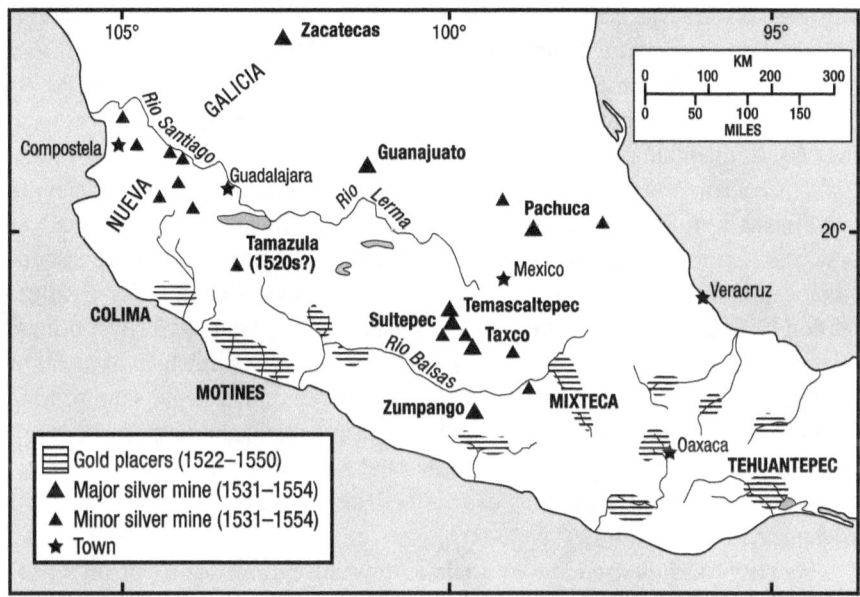

Map 5.1: Spanish Mining Activity in New Spain, 1522–1554. Source: West (1997b: 58)

In general, the lifestyle, diet and varied activities at the mining sites were accommodated to the Spanish speakers' taste and needs and to the advantage of the Mexico City merchants who were selling luxury foods for Spaniards (e.g. olive oil, wine, vinegar), mining tools (e.g. iron picks, crowbars, sledge hammers, and bellows) equipped with copper or bronze nozzles (68). The newer activities attracted not only merchants and traders but also thieves, vagabonds, and other drifters loitering around in Taxco. The reaction in Mexico City was to issue special ordinances to control commerce in the mining centers. Commercial transactions dealing with the sale of food and equipment were permitted only outside a radius of four leagues from the mining town. These ordinances reflect the hectic manner of life in the early mining communities. Between 1534 and 1548, the increasing cost of mining activities led to financial difficulties. In spite of this, the more affluent miners (Hernán Cortés, Juan de Burgos, and others) continued to produce substantial amounts of silver. The abolition of personal services in *encomiendas* caused a shortage of labor resulting from the policy of freeing Indian slaves, who were being paid in money for agricultural products. In 1555, the short-lived difficulties ended with the introduction of the amalgamation process perfected by leading miners (West 1997b: 68-69).

As early as 1530, vast silver deposits were found at Zumpango, Sultepec, Taxco, and Tlalpujahua in central Mexico, within 150 kilometers of the capital.

The silver wealth was made known by the mid-1540's, when the Spanish exploration reached the first ore deposits of the northern plateau at Zacatecas and from there to other northern discoveries at Santa Barbara in 1567 and San Luis Potosi in 1592. At the border between central Mexico and the arid north, silver ores were found at Guanajuato ca. 1550, a site made public about two centuries later; eventually it became the model of the empire, outstripping any other silver centers of New Spain or South America by a wide margin. The amalgamation of silver ores was a refining process that radically transformed production in the Spanish-speaking New World. Known in the Old World since Roman times, amalgamation had been used on a small scale in the recovery of gold and silver filings. Mercury was found in the remains of the first New World Spanish town in Santo Domingo, from where gold may have been extracted from alluvial sand or rock amalgamation. The Romans were familiar with the amalgamating properties of mercury but their application on an industrial scale was a Mexican innovation of the mid-1550's. This is perhaps Latin America's most significant technological advancement (Bakewell 1997a: 175-177).

Mercury was first used in New Spain to draw silver from its ores on an industrial scale, and by the 1550's the abundant ores smelted for a profit were not available, while large quantities of lower grade ore were brought up from increasing depths causing yields to drop as their cost rose. The miners resorted to amalgamation with its capacity to refine great volumes of poor ores in an effective manner. By 1555 there were over 120 refiners spreading in the following years to nearly all Mexican silver centers. Crushing ore into a fine powder was part of the amalgamation process, and when the mercury was added it could come into close contact with as much of the mineral as possible. In the Andes the amalgamation plant was known as *ingenio* and as *hacienda de minas* in New Spain. This business required a mill and its own paraphernalia, living quarters for workers and supervisors, and even enough space for a small chapel. The large investment needed in the processing of metals turned into an almost exclusive activity of Spaniards. In New Spain, where the native rule of the silver production was limited to laboring, the technical innovations did not have a positive impact on the indigenous (Bakewell 1997a: 179).

Investors were able to exploit the mines as long as they paid taxes at the rate of *un quinto* ('one-fifth') of the metal produced, but the Spanish law stipulated that subsoil rights remained with the Crown. Tax reductions were granted from the mid-century onward in order to stimulate mining. Spanish-American silver output from its start until 1600-1610 was at 375-400 million pesos. After 1550 the Andean region of Potosi and the northern Mexican mines produced at an annual rate of 2.3 %. Ore quality began to fall in the 17th century whereas the cost of extraction rose with the increasing depths of the mines. While the South American sites at Potosi were still the largest silver production in the New World, in Mexico it continued to rise until the 1620's before dropping slightly for about 40 years. As compared to silver production gold output was growing slowly. The total amount of gold gathered by the Spanish in New Granada, New Spain and Peru from 1521 to 1610 has been estimated at more than 48 million pesos, representing about 12 % of the projected c.400-million silver extracted in the Spanish-speaking New World to 1610. When amalgamation became the normal method of refining silver ores, mercury was distributed through the royal treasury system and sold at fixed prices, a method ensuring supply, partly to force silver miners to pay the royalty due on silver because the treasury office would not sell mercury until the fifth or the tenth they owed on previous refineries had been paid. By the end of the 16th century, silver mining was the most significant activity in Spanish America. The entire colony counted on 372 active *haciendas de minas* in which 399 animal-driven stamp mills and 205 powered by water were installed (see Table 5.1). It was clear that the value of silver mined was superior to gold. If the enticement of gold was the initial motive driving Spain and Spaniards to the new continent, it was the actual exploitation of silver that kept them there (Bakewell 1997a: 180-181).

Amalgamation was widely adopted in the 1570's because it required the processing of great volumes of low-grade ore, thus the manual labor for smelting was provided by the skilled Indians working under Spanish management. There is no evidence, however, that mining was responsible for mass deaths among the native populations. Its effect was not as substantial as the destructive effects of epidemics. Indians were not forced to work involuntarily but became wage laborers. The arrangements for draft labor or *repartimiento* set up in the 16th century continued to send Indians to mining centers for most of colonial times. In the smelting industry, labor disputes were reported over the high prices for African slaves, a situation that caused miners to constantly complain to the Crown, and to apply for tax reductions and lower costs of slave labor. In order to placate the agitated miners, thousands of Indians held on deceptive pretexts were released to the mining sites where they were supposed to work at day's pay on the rotating system. These conditions were aggravated due to the predisposition of indigenous workers to lead poisoning from smelter smoke. In order to reduce mortality, African slaves were introduced under stipulations requiring rigorous training. While rich deposits were hard to find, as predicted by employers, the enforcement of the New Laws of 1542 was having detrimental effects. This crisis was aggravated by the demands of the Spanish kings, who required more bullion shipment each year (Probert 1997: 102). Despite the difficulties, the New World's Spanish-speaking region became the world's leading supplier of silver. From the middle of the 16th century to the end of the colonial era, it produced about 100,000 tons of silver, a substantial part of which was exported to Europe causing inflation during the second half of the 16th century and the early 17th century (Garner 1997: 225).

5.2.1 Mining centers and ethnic groups

New Spain was dominant in silver production with the central mines of Pachuca and Taxco yielding two-thirds of the total in the 1590's. The northern plateau flourished in the early decades of the 17th century with the great boom at Zacatecas, San Luis Potosi and Parral. The twelve largest refining centers of Mexico in 1597 by numbers of *haciendas de minas* appear in Table 5.1 (Bakewell 1997c: 188-189). The labor force employed in the mining industry can be divided in slaves most likely African blacks, *naborías* (free Indian laborers) hired for a wage by miners, and *repartimiento* Indians (drafted into tasks of general public utility). To experts in the colonial mining industry, this is a very small labor work force since there were fewer than 10,000 workers in the whole of the silver industry producing two-thirds of the of New Spain's exports to Europe. At the end of the 16th century, free-wage workers comprised 70 % of all laborers (Bakewell 1997c: 184-185).

Table 5.1: Refining centers: regions and *haciendas de minas*

Refining centers in 1597	Regions	Haciendas
Pachuca	New Spain	82
Taxco	New Spain	81
Zacatecas + Pánuco	Zacatecas	65
Guanajuato	New Spain	46
Sultepec	New Spain	40
Zacualpan	New Spain	26
Cuautla	New Spain	26
Fresnillo + San Demetrio	Zacatecas	25
Tlalpujahua	New Spain	19
Sombrerete	Zacatecas	18
Temaxcaltepec	New Spain	17
San Martín	Zacatecas	15

Source: Bakewell (1997c: 189)

A mining district consisting of a settlement of medium size and the mines dependent upon it was however sufficient to attract population of diverse ethnicity, religious leaders in charge of missions, and miscellaneous activities such as agriculture, trade, road and building construction, to name a few. The most significant piece of information at this point refers to the Spanish-speaking people working in the mining centers. Reports from the last quarter of the 16th century focus on the number of Spaniards living in the silver mines in the *Audiencias* of Mexico, Guadalajara and Zacatecas. The totals of Spanish-speaking males amounts to 16,637; of these 1,912 were working in the silver mining districts with a total of workers ranging from 16,000 to 18,000 (Zavala 1987: 301-302). This report is complemented with the information appearing in Table 5.2, pointing out the distribution by ethnic groups (Zavala 1987). This information is useful to make inferences about the diffusion of Spanish and the agents of diffusion.

Table 5.2: Labor force in mining sites (1597)

District	Total Slaves	%	Total Free Indians	%	Total Draft Indians	%	Total Labor Force
New Spain	892	14.6	3,582	58.8	1,619	26.6	6,093
Zacatecas	200	9.3	1,956	90.7	0	0	2,156
Guadalajara	110	16.4	559	83.6	0	0	669
Guadiana	61	27.1	164	72.9	0	0	225
TOTALS	1,263	13.8	6,261	68.5	1,619	17.7	9,143

In addition, Table 5.3 shows the different ethnic groups working in smaller mining centers. Spaniards made up a small but active minority playing a key role through the end of the colonial period. Slaves in this industry were normally of African descent; their number contrasts with Indians in *encomienda* and free laborers, who were a majority. This distribution reveals two faces of language contact. Contact must have been limited to interactions between a few Spanish speakers and the rest, but must have been continuous because mining centers were functional and dynamic. The growth of the Spanish-speaking population depended on the effectiveness of the mining industry to the extent that some towns were large enough to be considered *ciudades de españoles* (Spanish cities), as opposed to the *pueblos de indios* (Indian towns) populated by Indians (Tanck de Estrada 2005). The former were multilingual at the beginning and later became mostly Spanish-speaking while the latter were either monolingual or bilingual in indigenous languages and gradually added the Spanish language to their linguistic repertoire. Mining centers stimulated the establishment of private schools for Spanish speakers, missions, and religious and cultural activities. The dichotomy between Spanish cities and Indian towns is derived from the observed pattern of settlements in urban centers and rural areas.

Table 5.3: Mining districts and workers. Guerrero, Mexico and Michoacan: 1579–1582

Districts	Mines	Spaniards	Slaves	Encomienda Indians	*Naborías*
Tlalpujahua	5	20	50	200	----
Temascaltepec	30	50	250	100	150
Sultepec	10	50	50	250	----
Taxco	30	150	600	200	----
Zacualpan	5	50	150	----	2,300
Espíritu Santo	1	2	----	50	150
TOTALS	81	322	1,100	800	2,600

Source: Zavala (1987: 300)

Despite the fact that they were small for modern standards, the cities populated by Spanish speakers were opposed to the Indian towns in terms of their cultural components. All of them were founded by Spanish speakers in the 16th century and continually recreated the Spanish-like institutions that defined them through the end of the colony. An example of urban development is New Spain, which illustrates the functions of Spanish cities, de facto administrative centers acting as models of orthogonal structures that simultaneously built a network of control of its own territory at all the right angles. In the beginning these urban centers were exclusive to Spaniards. Cities founded before 1545 (Antequera or Oaxaca City in Oaxaca, Valladolid, presently Morelia in Michoacan, and Puebla de los Angeles in Puebla) support the configuration of the urban theory that had conceived cities for Spaniards, although they were mixed societies since in the marginal neighborhoods indigenous workers lived and were gradually integrated to the urbanized environs. These small cities were actually the largest centers of the period and formed a network of contacts and connections that were effectively superposed over the bay work of Mesoamerican peoples (López Guzmán 2005). Mining sites and Spanish cities built their own infrastructure over similar material and human components.

5.2.2 Taxco

Tin deposits were found in Taxco or Tasco (presently in the state of Guerrero) in 1524. The fluctuations of the mining population are reflected in the tributary data. There were 4,570 native tributaries in 1570, decreasing to 4,050 in 1581, and to 1,012 in 1643. In 1688 there were 765 tributaries while the 1743 census logged in 1,047 Indian families. Exploitation of silver ores started in the early 1530's. The mines which were in full production in 1552 attracted a considerable number of Spaniards, castes and Indians. Toward 1570 there were 100 Spanish *vecinos* ('house or lot owners'), 900 Indian miners, and 700 black slaves living at the various *reales de minas* ('mining districts'). In 1743, about 260 non-Indian families are reported; by 1794, when the mines were again in a state of decline, there were 892 free black and mulatto tributaries (Gerhard 1993: 252-253).

5.2.3 Pachuca

The mines of Pachuca (presently the capital of the state of Hidalgo) opened in 1531. Silver deposits were discovered early in 1552. Franciscans and Augustinians founded a mission at San Pedro Tezontepec ca.1554, and additional secular parishes were established at the mines of Asunción Pachuca ca.1560. Other parishes followed: in 1569 there were only 70 married Spaniards, 48 unmarried Spaniards, and 6,233 Indian families. In 1597 Pachuca was the largest mining center in New Spain with more than 1,600 laborers; by 1643 there were only 136 tributaries in seven Indian communities. On a reduced scale much of the labor was carried out by black slaves. The bonanza of the late 17th century caused a great influx of people, with about 12,000 mestizos and Indians while the census of 1791 registered 2,755 Spaniards, 3,821 mestizos and 3,039 mulattoes (Gerhard 1993: 210-211).

5.2.4 Sultepec

In Sultepec or Zultepec (in the southwest corner of the state of Mexico) deposits of silver were discovered before 1532. Sultepec and Temazcaltepec were combined under a single magistrate. In 1569 there were 211 Spaniards (probably *vecinos*) and 692 blacks. The mining zone in general is referred to in colonial documents as Provincia de la Plata. During the mining slump of the 17th century some miners left while others acquired cattle and sugar haciendas. In 1743 there were 695 families of Spaniards, 404 of mestizos and 206 of mulattoes. The number of slaves is not recorded while the census of 1801 shows 386 black and mulatto tributaries in the jurisdiction. The various *reales de minas* moved about as the old deposits were exhausted and new ones were discovered ca.1580 in San Andres, Los Rios and Real Viejo. By 1743 the Temazcaltepec miners were dispersed in three settlements within half a league of other reales (Gerhard 1993: 267-269).

5.2.5 Puebla

The city of Puebla (presently the capital of the state of Puebla) was established with the founding of a Spanish settlement in 1531. There were monasteries of mendicant orders and other parishes. The jurisdiction had 3,760 tributaries in 1588 decreasing to 3,275 in 1600, to 2,622 in 1626, and 4,387 in 1696. In 1746 there were 3,200 Indian families. Puebla de los Ángeles was organized to accommodate Spaniards who had arrived in Mexico after the Conquest, but too late to participate in the *encomienda* system. In 1531 Puebla had 50 vecinos and 81 in 1534. The total population in 1681 was 14,500 Indians, 19,170 Spaniards, and 34,095 persons of mixed blood. Within the city, the total population in 1681 was over 63,000 persons; 88,000 in 1740, and 70,000 in 1800 (Gerhard 1993: 221-223). According to Tanck de Estrada (2005: 267-268), it was considered a *ciudad de españoles* (city of Spaniards or Spanish speakers). In 1790 it had a population of 81,046.

5.2.6 Queretaro

Queretaro (presently the capital of the state of Queretaro) was considered to form part of the encomienda of Xilotepec, which had a magistrate by the late 1540s. It became a Franciscan mission by 1567. In 1582 there were only 50 Spanish-speaking families; they increased to 200 in 1605; to 1000 in 1662 and 1,430 by 1743. In this year there were also 2,236 families of mestizos, mulattoes and blacks, many of them living on haciendas (Gerhard 1993: 224-225). With a population of 35,000 people it was also considered a *ciudad de españoles* in 1790 (Tanck de Estrada 2005: 267-8)

5.2.7 San Luis Potosi

San Luis Potosí (presently the capital of the state of San Luis Potosi) was settled as *real de minas* and had its first contact with Spanish speakers in 1542. Sedentary Indians (e.g., Tlaxcalans, Otomis, Tarascans) immigrated from the south to work in mines and haciendas and gradually replaced the nomadic Chichimecs, although the latter continued to raid Spanish settlements into the 18th century. With the establishment of Franciscan missions and the opening of Guadalcazar mines, the eastern and northern parts of the jurisdiction came under Spanish control in 1616-17. Franciscan monasteries opened in 1591 followed by secular parishes. Beginning in the 1590s, Spaniards, mestizos, mulattoes and blacks formed a large proportion of the total in mining camps and haciendas but the population fell off during the mining depression of the mid-1600s and recovered toward the end of that century. In 1743-44 the census reported 4,560 families of Spaniards, mestizos and mulattoes. In 1800 there were 4,817 free black and mulatto tributaries. The city of San Luis Potosí was founded in 1592; the mines at Cerro de San Pedro discovered in 1592, and those of Guadalcazar in 1615 (Gerhard 1993: 234-235). In 1803 with a population of 12,000 it was considered a *ciudad de españoles* (Tanck de Estrada 2005: 267-8).

5.2.8 Guanajuato

Founded in 1553-54, Guanajuato (presently the capital of the state of Guanajuato) was also a *real de minas*. By 1570 it was reported to have 600 Spanish miners in two camps. Silver production fell drastically in the 17th century, and with it, the Spanish population. Only 85 vecinos are reported in 1639 and 150 in 1649. Despite high rates of mortality from starvation and disease in 1785-86, the 1791 census registered 39,529 Indians. Over 5,000 families of Spaniards and castes lived in the *reales* of Santa Fe, Santa Ana and Marfil. The total non-Indian population of Guanajuato-Marfil-Santa Ana in 1791 was 43,198 (Gerhard 1993: 121-23). With a population of 32,098 in 1790 it was considered a *ciudad de españoles* (Tanck de Estrada 2005: 267-268).

5.2.9 Zacatecas

Zacatecas (presently the capital of the state of Zacatecas) was founded by Juan de Tolosa, Diego de Ibarra, Temiño de Bañuelos and Cristóbal de Oñate in 1548. Oñate was an *encomendero* from New Biscay who had worked in New Spain as assistant of Rodrigo de Albornoz (the king's secretary). The rise of Zacatecas meant a shift in economic balance in New Galicia from west to east. Religious orders established houses over the 60 years following the foundation, starting with the Franciscans who never left during the colonial period. By 1569 the townspeople had settled in the city and had established a monastery and a church. The Franciscans noted the continued wealth of the mines and the lack of ministers to care for the host of Spaniards, Indians and blacks, and as a result they built a mission in 1572 or later; this elevated Zacatecas to the rank of *cabecera* (municipal head). Augustinians, Jesuits, Dominicans and regular orders established themselves between 1590 and 1609. At this time, it had a permanent population of 1,500 Spaniards, 300 Indians, in addition to blacks and mestizos, all of whom managed to survive in surroundings useless for cultivation. For this reason a flow of goods from the south was continuously arriving via different roads. The mine owners invested in the construction of their *haciendas de minas* and attracted all kinds of traders in every direction. More silver was extracted in Zacatecas than in all other mines in New Spain, and both Zacatecas and New Spain were sustained by the Zacatecas mines. Maize was one of the most important foodstuffs imported into Zacatecas. In Jerez, people were growing maize for the mines of Sombrerete and Fresnillo. Spaniards preference for wheat stimulated the import of wheat over maize. The competition of the two grains suggests there were changes in the size of the Indian vs. mestizo labor force or otherwise periods of depression in the local mining sites, which had to reduce the number of Indians working for them. In times of mining prosperity, the number of Spaniards increased considerably while that of Indians and mestizo workers, who were the maize eaters, was multiplied. In sum, Zacatecas became a focal point for the whole to the north. It was the richest city in New Galicia, New Biscay and New Leon (Bakewell 1971: passim). With a population of 25,495 in 1790 it was considered a *ciudad de españoles* (Tanck de Estrada 2005: 267-8).

5.3 Forms of labor and language contact

As compared to the total population, the quantity of Spanish-speaking Europeans was always a minuscule minority. Quantity was not as important as the empowerment of the first-generation of Spanish-speaking Mexicans who, in a few decades, became aristocrats by means of importation, (re)creation and construction of some of the most significant institutions already existent in Spain. Wage labor appears to have been the most significant activity conducive to diffusion of Spanish, directly or indirectly, from Spanish speakers to speakers of indigenous languages, who had no other option but to work in newer activities related to the (re)construction of a very complex society, where the process of socialization and the building of social networks resulted in stronger ties among Spanish speakers and the loosening of ties among the indigenous, who were already devastated by the losses of the conquest period. Close-knit ties among Spanish speakers consolidated their position in New Spain with all the economic and political advantages derived from being in relative control of the means of local production. Their mere presence in the mining sites, towns and small cities seemed to have been more than sufficient to spread Spanish and to foster language contact. In contrast, the disempowering conditions of the indigenous peoples facilitated loose-knit ties that in the end fostered language and culture shift, at least partially.

Drastic changes to the rules of labor had a dual effect on language maintenance. On the one hand, the different forms of labor kept large groups of Indian together working under one cacique. On the other, the same Indian groups were disenfranchised and uprooted. According to Gibson (1964: 220-221), in Aztec society workers performed communal tasks with minimal individual assignments because they were accustomed to providing their own sustenance to both local and distant service without pay, a source of satisfaction, though some occupations were monotonous or degrading in European eyes. Indians' disposition to work on a voluntary basis made them vulnerable to demands for labor, because in Europe unskilled mass labor was equivalent to coercion or enslavement. Indian peoples lost the feeling of joyous participation in work for it was moved from the social, moral, and spiritual categories into the economic or physical spheres of interaction. After the enactment of the New Laws, Spaniards did not need any mass enslavement insofar as their expeditions introduced Indian captives from outside the Valley, who were sold in the capital in the early years. *Encomienda* more than slavery controlled native forms of mass labor but both systems were selling or hiring employees for various services. In Tenochtitlan and Tlatelolco, the first Spanish tribute exaction demanded services to the viceroy (construction, repair and filling of canals) and other tasks contributing to the maintenance of the capital, which caused the decentralization of natives' organization while Spanish recipients of Indian labor profited from the authority of each community's *tlatoani*.

For the early Spanish construction labors in Mexico City, the drafts were subdivided by barrios and by specializations. Those in charge of supervising labor such as *encomenderos*, ecclesiastics, and employers of all sorts had to rely on *tamemes* (Indian carriers) for the provision of goods and for transport. New working conditions based on wages altered the relationship between employers and workers during the mid-16th century and were regulated by royal orders, which banned the use of *tamemes*. By mid-century tribute was considerably reduced causing a shortage of Indian laborers during the critical period that followed the plague of 1545-1548. Orders of the late 1540's also prohibited unrecompensed labor, which was replaced by rationed, rotational labor, presumably in the public interest of a larger employer class; this scheme however did not fulfill the royal demands for moderate work conditions and all procedures were scrutinized for the first time. The principles of compulsion and rotation had precedents in both pre-conquest and early colonial labor antedating 1549. After the draft was separated from *encomienda*, the two systems competed for labor services. The major advantage of the former lied in the perceived convenience of public benefit (e.g. in floods, urban construction or agriculture), the perfect excuse to convoke a huge labor force of thousands of Indian workers repairing for months major damages due to floods. In times of crisis, urban labor was forbidden in order to massively recruit agricultural workers (Gibson 1964: 222-224).

As the Spanish-speaking population was growing, agricultural drafts for the cultivation of wheat plantations were deemed necessary. The draft was responsible for the administration of the Indian workers and their distribution to administrators who were assisted by various employees, including interpreters. Indians were supplied from the towns in weekly shifts at fixed quotas and delivered to those Spanish employers who had properties in the same jurisdiction. The Indian governments of the towns were provided with records listing the names, sujeto affiliations and *tequitlatos* (town officers or tax collectors) of all laborers. Every Monday morning the Indians from the selected towns assembled at a given distribution point from where they were dispatched by the community officials and taken to the draft center by local *alguaciles* (constables). Inside a corral the *juez repartidor* (distributing agent) turned in the assigned workers according to the amount of wheat each had under cultivation. With this procedure, no single individual was held liable to the draft more often than three or four times annually. When the demand for urban construction was high, Indians were drafted from nearby towns such as Chalco, Xochimilco, Texcoco, Tacuba, and other jurisdictions to work in public spots, monasteries, the Cathedral, the streets, or the city's water supply. At times thousands of laborers were leased to private local employers and to the local government, a practice more or less intermediate between labor and tribute. From the earliest days of the colony, designated towns had to bring to the city daily canoe loads of eatables and materials for the royal officials and other citizens. Other Indian towns (e.g. Coyoacan, Tacuba, Tenayuca, Culhuacan, Coyotepec, Tacubaya) were affected by demands for services. Until the end of the century, when another plague hit the Indian population in 1576, there was a good supply of laborers. As in tribute, Indian communities abandoned tradition and their governments and were held responsible for the supply of quotas. When Indians workers were in high demand, the competition between Spaniards for the former led to aggressive strategies such as the sequestering of laborers in less than human conditions (Gibson 1964: 226, 231). This organization of labor had a dual effect: it maintained workers of the same group together for a long time and likewise exposed them to indirect language contact with Spanish speakers. At the same time, it acted as a conduit of incomplete Spanish acquisition and/or Hispanization.

As a result of the epidemics of 1545-48 and 1576-81 which caused a shrinking supply of able workers, employers had no other option but to make adjustments in hiring. In agriculture there were more laborers for private hire (*gañanes*). By the late 1580's in the wheat farms of the Valley, the *gañanes* were working for hacienda owners from Teoloyuca, Tepoztlan, Huehuetoca, and Coyotepec but they were not considered reliable for extra community tasks. By the late 16th and early 17th centuries, the agricultural employers were making large strides in the direction of full *gañán* labor; however, when they were needed in *repartimiento*, they had to serve other employers (Gibson 1964: 247-248). The hiring of *gañanes* for other than private labor was the cause of debate and concern because at times the Spanish business owners and *hacendados* (landowners) would harass them to leave their houses to work for them. Authorities had to intervene to prevent abuse, and at times they were successful because these workers were excluded from massive compulsory labor (Zavala 1987: 186-187, 236, 239-240). For all the abovementioned reasons, these laborers had more frequent and more direct interaction with their Spanish-speaking employers. In sum, all the strategies of forced, wage or voluntary labor along the different domains of interaction were conducive to socialization via Spanish and acquisition of Spanish whether it occurred face-to face with Spanish-speaking supervisors, or indirectly with speakers of Spanish as a second or additional language, that is, co-workers.

5.3.1 Losing the ties to the land

Regardless of the notorious rigors of the hacienda, this system did not imprison the workers and offered positive advantages to Indian workers. Labor hired in the 1530's and shortly after was recompensed at different rates according to skills. Agricultural labor, labor services for *corregidores* (chief magistrates), and those working in *obrajes* (workshops for cotton and wool) received a monthly salary. Commuters received extra benefits, such as food and additional pay for travel but maize-producing haciendas raised a supply for their own workers. In all these occupations however it was common to incur in debt. Indian laborers might be forced to accept money payable in work, or they might be required to purchase with a loan the equipment to be used in the *obraje*. Debt peonage affected fewer than half the workers on haciendas. The hacienda offered solutions to economic conditions not to be found elsewhere and to those who had lost their lands (largely to haciendas) and provided a dwelling and a means of acceptable livelihood. In the Valley of Mexico, Indian labor for Spanish employers became progressively less severe (Gibson 1964: 243-245). The presence of wage laborers in this period suggests that the Indians played a more active role in the formation of the hacienda system of production that is generally acknowledged. Together with textile manufacturing and mining, the hacienda adds variety to the colonial systems of production, which after *encomienda* and *repartimiento* depended on various incentives. Wage laborers resided on the units of production; some were described as servants who were coming from mixed-blood groups and were Hispanicized (Melville 1994). Daily and face-to-face interaction with Spanish speakers might have contributed to Spanish language (re)acquisition in an environment that appeared to be less alienating than the *encomienda* and the draft.

In contrast to the flexible conditions that favored different Indian laborers, the epidemics of the mid-and late 16th century contributed to major losses in Indian communities, weakened by a newer compact society of Spanish speakers who had sufficient resources to make transitions in an advantageous legal manner. The loss of native land augmented the disadvantages of the indigenous populations, a major event that might have had the net effect of accelerating language shift. The shortcomings are explained by Gibson (1964: 281-282), for the native survivors had to readjust themselves to new patterns of coexistence once the land was sold and converted into genuine money. Such alterations only benefited Spaniards who acquired new tracts of land via direct land alienation. In the face of Indian's protest against land usurpation, some of the Nahuatl-speaking towns were surrounded by Spanish properties, and eventually the greater part of the land passed from Indian control to Spanish-speaking owners. In the 1530's, laws required that all Indian land sales be made voluntarily and be transacted before Spanish judges. The vice-regal government promoted the use of vacated lands and ordered offending individuals to pay for damages. In spite of the attempts to protect the Indians from incursions of cattle owners, regulations against dispossession were difficult to enforce. At first, the Mexico City Council (controlled by Spanish speakers) ordered the revocation of grants and the abandonment of herding areas that interfered with Indian properties. Lands without Indian inhabitants were up for grabs thus available to Spanish intrusion without injury. Actual transfers were accomplished by sales, forced scales or formal grants executed by Indian officials. These transactions benefited Spanish landowners, and in the end Indian lands in the communities of the city's environs were taken for the Spanish-speaking population, the Indian occupants being compensated with lands elsewhere. Once the lands were unoccupied, they were registered as abandoned.

5.3.2 Labor and agriculture: indigenous vs. Spanish crops

A major issue of contention in agriculture was the harvesting of maize vis-à-vis the harvesting of wheat, the former being the preferred form of sustenance of the Mesoamerican peoples. During the first decades efforts were made to introduce wheat into the agricultural repertoire of the Indians with the intention, among various officials and priests, of converting them into the main producers of this grain for the European population, but they may have been reluctant to switch from maize to wheat (Assadourian 2006: 295). Cultivating wheat might have been seen as an imposition when Spaniards appropriated the land and applied irrigation mainly to wheat. Following the harvest, maize was stored for the unproductive winter, while its price made the cost of all other products (lard, wheat, beans, and other foodstuffs) fluctuate in both Indian and Spanish markets, a fact also indicative of the Indian population decline (Gibson 1964: 308-311). The 16th century Spanish farms provided Indians with their earliest experience in Spanish cultivation of wheat, but on their own land they preferred maize. Occasionally Indians planted wheat for sale to Spaniards and established mills and ovens for the Spanish bread market. For the most part Indian wheat appeared to be directly associated with Spanish intrusion. The wheat farms marked the beginning of a Spanish institution that was controlling agricultural supply and eventually intruded upon Indian production. After the large-scale wheat production taking place between 1563 and 1602, Spanish enterprises were engaged in maize production on a large scale and impacted Indian maize cultivation. Between harvest and consumption of maize, supplies fell under the control of *encomenderos*, *corregidores*, purchasers of royal tribute maize, and private dealers. Since the mid- and late 16th century Indian maize lands came into Spanish hands, a factor that diverted Indian labor to a variety of new activities (Gibson 1964: 322-323, 326). Information on land unappropriation and cultivation of European vegetables in both the Andean and Mesoamerican regions can be found in Assadourian (2006).

5.3.3 The *obrajes*

Another productive activity was the textile industry, a natural development of the sheepherding industry, which started at small scale in the mid-decades. The workshops for the manufacture of woolen cloth, known as *obrages* or *obrajes*, were introduced by Spanish artisans. Woolen looms worked by Indians under Spanish direction were first established in Texcoco as early as the 1530's or before. It was a branch of labor promoting private employment of Indians who learned to card, spin and weave, while blacks and mulattoes were used as guards.

Work was hard, food and living conditions were deplorable and physical abuse all too common. Indians convicts frequently worked as slaves or were trained for long-term specialization. Such scheme ensured the control of a working force which was cheaper than black slavery. Furthermore, in the 16th and 17th centuries, Indians were offered private contracts normally favoring the employer who forced the contracted employees to work behind locked doors (Gibson 1964: 243-245, 247). *Tlacotines* or Indians originally enslaved in pre-Hispanic societies were hired by the proprietors of the *obrajes*. *Tlacotines* were also employed in bakeries, haciendas, mining sites and other centers where Indians went to work on a voluntary basis. They were in essence free salaried laborers protected to an extent by the legislation of the Crown, which in theory was concerned about labor conditions (Viqueira 1985).

The industry of *obrajes* flourished over a small area in the Central Highlands, the Yucatan peninsula, and the Panuco region. In the early phase of the textile industry cotton was the most important raw material with very successful centers operating in the latter regions, where Indians were paying their tribute in *mantas* (coarse cotton cloth), a product that was distributed in New Spain, Honduras-Higueras and the Antilles (Miño Grijalva 1993: 26-27). Indians were employed in the vegetable gardens, the shops, and even the houses owned by Spaniards where the former learned spinning and weaving (Zavala 1985: 227-228). In addition to the manufacture of cotton, the textile industry added wool and silk; the three products were growing so rapidly that by 1562 New Spain was exporting textiles to Peru (Viqueira and Urquiola 1990: 45).

The industry offered such a good supply of products that artisans from Spain established in New Spain became entrepreneurs and trained their employees in order to guarantee quality control. In Tlaxcala, Cholula and Puebla the shops operated with a small number of *obrajeros* (*obraje* owners). In Puebla, some 40 *obrajes* employed up to 2,500 Indians, some of whom were highly specialized. When the contracts of workers were examined closely it was found that almost three-fourths of the total fall within the type of voluntary work, and the rest were engaged in varied forms of forced labor. The most common situation affecting voluntary work appeared to be partial advance of the salary, which in turn originated debt (Viqueira and Urquiola 1990: 61-63, 132-133, 195).

The evidence derived from the labor conditions aids in making inferences about language contact and language acquisition. As opposed to the draft and *encomienda* labor that generated the hiring, the moving, and the performance of a large mass or masses of Indian laborers, the textile industry was more selective and counted on small groups of workers who were in direct contact with Spanish-speaking employers. The conditions of both voluntary and forced labor were not enviable; the *peonaje* (a system of voluntary service based on indebtedness to the creditor) was prevalent throughout the colonial period. Like mining, the textile industry became a permanent economic activity, which might have enhanced the opportunities for acquisition or (re)acquisition of Spanish in a milieu that was less alienating than the *encomienda* and the *repartimiento*.

5.4 Formal education

Higher education was available in 1551 via royal decrees; it was open to Spanish speakers and *naturales de la tierra* (indigenous people) and offering classes started in 1553. The offspring of Spaniards *hacendados*, miners, and merchants found in the university the endorsement of their social rank while for all the others it only meant an opportunity for upward mobility. The mission of the university was to divulge Christian orthodoxy and forge both civil and ecclesiastical functionaries. The first class ever taught was Theology whereas the focus of the curriculum was on Liberal Arts of classic tradition offered at the five colleges of medieval origin (Theology, Canonical Law, Civil Law, Medicine and Arts). The university issued Bachelor's, Master's, and doctoral degrees. All classes and lectures on arts, philosophy, grammar, and rhetoric were taught in Latin. Although the studies of Latin classics decreased in popularity, grammar was privileged and adherence to the curriculum was closely supervised. Students who were not reading in Latin were reprimanded. The use of Romance (i.e. Spanish) was allowed in informal events, which were sometimes attended to by the viceroy. Some of the most ostentatious events taking place at the University included the graduation ceremony, councilmen meetings, inauguration of rectors, and the like. The Jesuits continued the tradition of teaching Latin according to Renaissance ideals because it was mandated by the *Ratio Studiorum*, a manual of procedures reconciling the commitment between the medieval tradition and modernity. Latin was mandatory in regular courses and public acts; but in drama and tournaments such recommendation was lenient; Spanish was used instead with exceptions such as the *égloga latina* or *discurso latino* (Gonzalbo 1990: 65-69, 96-97, 109-110).

Teaching of Latin grammar continued throughout this century, when schools were opened in Oaxaca, Zacatecas and Durango. Even after the Jesuits were expelled their influence was preserved in the many institutions they founded. Moreover, their activities were versatile. The Jesuit preachers delivered hundreds of sermons annually in addition to organizing all kinds of events; they were responsible for the initiation, management and charitable organization of both academic and religious activities. In the late 16th century, the viceroy Luis de Velasco sent his children to study with the Jesuits and he himself attended the academic events; in this way he endorsed the prestige of the Jesuit schools and consolidated their identification with the new class of native *criollos*. It was reiterated that education was a commodity for the children of well-to-do *criollos* who were functionaries, merchants or artisans. Sometimes Spanish speakers hired their own private tutors. Those who resided in the *zona centro* (center square) represented the social elite and well-to-do families of the New Spanish society. Because they were attracted by the many social, civic and intellectual activities, merchants, miners and landowners lived in the capital city although they had their businesses in distant places. Jesuit educators also turned into writers of poetry in Latin and Spanish; after being teachers for many years they turned into preachers preaching in schools and student residences of the Jesuit province. Religious activities included poetic tournaments and festivals whereby they showed off the stylistic resources, symbolism, and games of intellectual prowess (e.g. Christmas celebrations) (Gonzalbo 1990: 228-229, 234-237, 244-245).

Heavily influenced by Erasmus and the novelties of the Renaissance, the formal education of Spanish speakers was initiated by the Jesuits in 1572. By then, the *criollos* (offspring of Spaniards) were firmly entrenched in the New Spanish society and had become the preferred candidates of the educational mission of the Jesuits, who since the beginning, worked closely with the well-to-do families and adopted the defense of the *criollos* because their emerging culture was taking shape as a colonial baroque Counter-Reformist enterprise. The initial work of the Jesuits in New Spain coincided with the establishment of the Spanish Inquisition (1571). The Jesuits founded elementary schools in almost all the colleges of New Spain. What is known today as elementary education was then known as "first letters" and was offered via religious institutions oriented towards the teaching of Latin. Spanish families with sufficient resources opted for private education for their children while the newcomers of Spanish-speaking descent with relatively adequate preparation assumed the role of teachers of "first letters". Reading, writing and basic arithmetic were the most important components of the basic curriculum. Those aspiring to a teaching post were required to go through the testing procedures designed by the *Real Consejo de Castilla* and to show *probanzas* (Gonzalbo 1990: 3, 27-38, 136-146, 159-60).

Schools were opened in Patzcuaro (Michoacan) serving 300 pupils–inclusive of Indians, Spaniards, blacks and mulattoes, who were taught the Christian doctrine and reading and writing in Spanish; here Spanish and Indian boys studied together although Latin classes could easily be suspended. At times, extra-curricular activities were bilingual (Tarascan / Spanish). In Valladolid (currently Morelia, Michoacan), the schools were teaching Latin to boys of different ages. The city of Puebla de los Angeles was one of the most active places since the late 16th century while in Guadalajara there were 500 Spanish families. Educators from the different orders extended their activities to towns and small cities already considered *capitales mineras* (mining capital cities) where Spanish families had been settled or relocated as a result of activities around silver mines. Between 1546 and 1588 schools of first letters were opened in Veracruz (Veracruz), Zacatecas (Zacatecas), Guanajuato (Guanajuato), and Durango (Durango). In sum, during the 16th century, the Jesuits founded a total of 50 elementary schools, colleges, and seminars where boys studied Humanities (Gonzalbo 1990: 169-173, 178-9).

Children of Spanish-speaking families were exposed to the formal study of Latin since 1572. In order to enhance the learning and the use of Latin, the Jesuits encouraged the composition of two types of short plays: the first one was performed for the indigenous and had a Christian theme; it was preferred during religious holidays and used to edifice and entertain Spanish speakers living in the vicinity of Mexico City. The second type, known as *festejo* ('feast'), was performed to commemorate social events related to New Spain or to Spain. The short catechizing dramas for the indigenous were staged since 1533 and continued through 1545. Celebrating peninsular topics, the second type was initiated with the *Conquista de Rodas* (1539). The performances in this genre continued through the 16th century showing affection for the viceroys, archbishops, birthdays of the princes, etc. Some of them are titled and dated (1566, 1572 and 1574), although they might have been represented more frequently than the dates can show. The performances were staged at the end of the courses or during the festivities to honor the patron saint. The didactic short plays were also prepared for entertainment and at times the authors inserted farce(s), games and jokes, but the comic scenes were considered profane, and civil authorities eventually suppressed them (Quiñones Melgoza 1982).

Following the procedures of the Spanish universities, the Jesuits in charge of the different schools of the *Colegio de San Pedro y San Pablo* represented drama in Latin once or twice a year. In the beginning the compositions and dialogues were partly in Latin and partly in Spanish. The first work in Latin was staged in 1575, and more works were performed through 1583; about three-fourths of them had content in Spanish and one-fourth in Latin. The first one completely in Latin was represented in 1585, and a few more followed through the end of the century. All the compositions were influential in shaping the national drama, although most had an eclectic content. Students enrolled in these colleges did learn Latin with instructors who had been trained in Spain. At the end of the century the dramatic plays were drafted almost always in Latin, which was a component of the pedagogical method (Quiñones Melgoza 1982: xv-xlv).

The education of the surviving Mesoamerican elites in the classics preceded the education of the Spanish speakers. Since the early 1520's basic Latin was taught to children of the Indian elites living in the convents, and what they learned was sufficient for the roles they had to play in the Catholic liturgy. In almost all the monasteries the friars integrated chapels and choruses of great quality and even trained the Indians in music. Singing in Latin was a preliminary practice to learn formal Latin. In the early decades of the colony several schools were founded with an enriched curriculum. The formality of the schooling established a solid foundation for the education of the indigenous but ended with the century. Samples of Latin documents written by the indigenous students and the indigenous clergy can be found in Osorio Romero (1990: 1-58).

5.4.1 Education for women

Coming from all social strata, the vast majority of women emigrated from Spain after the conquest. Their education was more selective than the education afforded to males but there were some opportunities for three groups: (1) women coming from Spain became educators of Indian, mestizo, and *criollo* children; (2) women who were married and had free time; (3) women who chose to live in the convent. Towards the end of the 16th century, some women of independent means donated their inheritance in order to build the *Convento de San Jerónimo*, where many *criollo* women lived and died. Spanish-speaking women acquired culture according to their social position. They were inclined to study reading, writing, basic mathematics, music, religion and domestic chores in schools for girls, convents and nunneries. Some were even able to pay for lessons of Latin and Spanish. They were exposed to books on all subjects, from the ancient classics to chivalry novels, history and historical novels, in addition to poetry and philosophy. Women found solace in the writing of their biographies or became the chroniclers of the convents in which they lived. Most of them were born in the late 16th century and became actively involved in literary pursuits in the following century (Muriel 1982).

5.5 Additional activities promoting the use of Spanish

Juan Cromberger, the son of printer Jacob Cromberger, secured the rights to publish and sell books and other materials in Mexico. At the initiative of Viceroy Antonio de Mendoza and Bishop Juan de Zumárraga, the printing press arrived in Mexico from Seville in 1538. In the beginning the cost of production was lower than in Seville and the paper was available on a regular basis. Juan Pablos was the first printer who worked directly for Cromberger, and the first manuscript published in the House of Juan Pablos was the Latin devotional manual known as the *Escala Espiritual* (ca. 1535 or 1537) by San Juan de Calimaco, translated by Friar Juan de la Magdalena. Until 1554 Juan Pablos was the exclusive printer. Five years later Antonio de Espinosa and his partners traveled to Spain to obtain a printing license, and paved the way for other printers. Because there was sufficient demand for religious manuals, other printers found plenty of business: Antonio Álvarez, Sebastián Gutiérrez, Juan Rodríguez, Pedro Ocharte, Pedro Balli and Antonio Ricardo were engaged in the publication of miscellaneous books in Latin, Spanish and indigenous languages. Until 1554 the preferred typography was gothic, and after that year Roman and cursive types prevailed. Printers catered to the most pressing needs of the pedagogical and ecclesiastic activities, although philosophic and scientific publications were not absent in the collection of published works (García Icazbalceta 1858-1866: ix-xxiii).

One of the most active domains contributing to the elevation of language(s) in the public life of New Spain was the University, whose personnel were selected among the local scholars. In 1551, Philip II issued a royal decree, and the university established on January 25, 1553 with the attendance of both the viceroy and the members of the *Audiencia* present at the first class of every course. Faculty members in charge of the new curriculum were known for their merits, and many young and eager students were enrolled to be trained in the Humanities program, which was equivalent to the Salamanca program. Students and faculty were regularly engaged in all sorts of activities and inclined to initiate intense debates on substantial issues. One of them was grammar, also known as language sciences, a subject that attracted talented faculty. The University set the precedent for solid and independent teaching. Francisco Cervantes de Salazar was twice the University's rector and described its mission in México in Tres *diálogos latinos* (1554/1988). Other fields such as Medicine encountered an auspicious environment in New Spain. The physicians trained in Western medicine founded hospitals, pharmacies and a shelter for the disabled. During the 16th century, several medical doctors wrote treatises of medicine and taught at the university (García Icazbalceta 1858-1866: 159-179).

5.6 Spanish literature in Spain and in New Spain

The most significant professional activity contributing to the status and prestige of Spanish was literature, which in New Spain evolved in a different direction. Spanish literature in the metropolis had a good start after Spain was reunited by the marriage of Isabel de Castilla and Fernando de Aragon, the Catholic kings who promoted Castilian as the most common written language (via Nebrija's grammar). Spanish literature had the potential to attract Europeans readers due to the printing boom of the early 16th century, which made books increasingly available to a wide audience. Readers were interested in chivalric and pastoral novels, narratives that paved the way for the picaresque novel and also for the poetry of the Golden Age. The most popular chivalric novel was *Amadís de Gaula* (1508), but this genre was displaced by the pastoral novel (e.g. *La Galatea* 1585) by Miguel de Cervantes Saavedra. The most meaningful innovation of the Golden Age was the picaresque novel that focused on the adventures of the mischievous characters working for a deceitful master. The anonymous *Lazarillo de Tormes* (1554) and *Guzmán de Alfarache* (1599-1605) established a trend reflecting the realities of Spanish society. In addition, after the expulsion of the Moors and the Counter-Reformation movement, the Catholic zeal inspired a group of authors best known for their mysticism: Fray Luis de León, San Juan de la Cruz, and Santa Teresa de Jesús were searching for a path to God when they were living under duress. Finally, lyric poetry is represented by two major names: Juan Boscán and Garcilaso de la Vega, who found inspiration in the poets of the Italian Renaissance, a gracious trend derived from Francesco Petrarca. The Spanish poets are known for having adapted the eleven-syllable verse to the Spanish language allowing for greater flexibility, a technique that aids in maintaining a basic rhythm for a longer period of time.

The abovementioned trends contrast with those that unfolded in Mexico. According to historians of Mexican literature, the first professional writers in the Spanish language credited for introducing innovating themes in the 16th century are Hernán Cortés and Bernal Díaz del Castillo. The letters of the former inaugurated a new genre in historical chronicles, while the latter is the author of *La verdadera historia de la conquista de la Nueva España* [The True History of the Conquest of New Spain] (1568). Díaz del Castillo was a soldier and an eyewitness of the conquest of Mexico. His history is a vivid account of the military skirmishes of Cortés and his men, a narrative intended to redeem the actions of the Spanish troops who were instrumental in planning the battles against the Aztecs. Born out of the realities of the New World, the historical chronicle contrasts with the works of the friars who narrated and described in Spanish and / or Nahuatl the civilization of the Aztecs. *Historia de las cosas de la Nueva España* (1540-1585/1950/1982) by Bernardino de Sahagún; *Historia general de Indias* (1561) by Bartolomé de las Casas; *Historia de los indios de la Nueva España* (1542) by Toribio de Benavente; and *Historia Eclesiástica Indiana* (1597) by Gerónimo de Mendieta, among other monumental volumes, were drafted in the 16th century and published later. The prose of the chronicle is original, controversial, and succeeds in establishing a solid precedent of writing in a genre that differs significantly from the narrative of the 16th century in Spain (i.e. the picaresque novel).

Another genre in Spanish is the poetry ensuing from the various ecclesiastic celebrations in honor of Charles V. The best known was the *Túmulo imperial de la gran ciudad de México* [Imperial Sepulcher of the Great City of Mexico] by Francisco Cervantes de Salazar, who in a few years had become the official chronicler of Mexico City. The introduction in prose announces the grandiosity of the topic, the death of the Emperor; it offers not only a minute description of the posthumous ceremonies but of the decorations and structures raised for the occasion. The Doric style catafalque was built on two levels with the funeral urn lying over the first, which was covered with a black cloth and a cushion where the crown rested. The funeral procession was led by the Indian rulers of Mexico City: Tacuba, Texcoco and Tlaxcala. Published in 1560 in the well-established House of Antonio de Espinosa, the versified section glorifies the king of Spain and Emperor of the Holy Roman Empire, who is confronted with Death but is at the same time immortal. Charles V deserved a funeral, lavish and splendorous, similar to that of Caesar or Alexander the Great (in García Icazbalceta 1886: 95-121).

Whereas the first generation of Spanish speakers set the precedent for writings in prose, the second generation contributed with the Italian-influenced genre of lyric poetry. The Spanish speakers arriving after 1550 were mostly bureaucrats or royal attendants who knew first-hand the in vogue literary styles circulating in Spain. Poetry was a practice of those with courtly experience who wanted to be à la par with professional poets from Madrid and Seville. Because its repertoire excludes ballads, proverbs and legends, the poetry is known as *poesía culta* (cultured poetry). The authors found inspiration in topics referring to love, lack of love, ingenious games, dreams, and female beauty. The main players were Gutierre de Cetina (born in Seville in 1520) and Juan de la Cueva (born in Seville in 1547) while Francsico de Terrazas was the first poet born (1525) in New Spain. Fernán González de Eslava (born in Toledo ca. 1534) resided in Mexico, where he wrote the *Coloquios espirituales y sacramentales y coloquios divinos* [Spiritual and Sacramental Colloquia and Divine Colloquia] appearing early in the next century. The distinguished poets almost never published their works while they were alive, but their poetry was divulged in manuscripts and memorized via recitation (Blanco 1989: 132).

5.7 Conclusions

The economy of New Spain was based on the utilization and efficient management of the indigenous labor, which was cheaper than and less aggravating than slavery. Ensuring an effective workforce for the mining, agricultural, textile activities and services became the priority of the new officials in charge. Though a good portion of the revenue was delivered to the metropolis, there were periods of sustainable growth that were instrumental in supporting the education, entertainment and cultural endeavors of the local elite. Spanish speakers belonging to the upper crust of the colonial hierarchy had sufficient resources to cultivate their proclivity for the Spanish letters. The economic boom was noticeable in the larger towns and cities where the grand central plazas played a significant role in the commercial, civic, and religious distribution of space, opportunity, and wealth. The printing press was an additional project that promoted publications in indigenous languages, Latin and Spanish. By the end of the 16th century, Spanish was in good standing and ready to be implemented in solid, original, and diversified domains. The literary genres that unfolded were not a mirror image of the peninsular literary trends, since at least the initial prose is quite distinct from the narrative cultivated in Spain. The only genre that was not stimulated or emulated in the New World was the *novella* presumably because the content was susceptible to periodic evaluation on the part of the Inquisition. All in all the activities of the Spanish speakers contributed to the persisting course of action of diversification. The Spanish language positioned itself in newer and permanent domains of interaction (i.e. labor, education, church, monasteries, nunneries, urban commerce, medicine, entertainment, bureaucracy, and literature, among others). Interaction in the different realms of labor counted on Spanish speakers, speakers of other European languages, a good number of speakers of indigenous languages, and not too many speakers of African languages. In most cases, the diffusion of Spanish amongst non-Spanish speaking groups was indirect and not too intense but it must have been continuous. The linguistic niches built in and around the work domain enhanced the stability of Spanish as a common language for multiple forms of communication.

Chapter 6
Continuity and change: The second generation

6.1 The innovations of the second generation

The second generation of Spanish speakers living in New Spain can be dated from 1555 to the end of the 16th century. Those who were born in New Spain during the long colonial period resisted the dispositions of the Crown, which did not allow the children of Spaniards to maintain the *encomiendas* inherited from their parents more than once. The second generation of Spanish speakers enjoyed the benefits and educational opportunities offered by those who founded the University and schools for the Spanish-speaking youth. Their cohesiveness is exemplified in the connection between Brihuega, a small town in New Castile, and Puebla de los Angeles, the second largest city in New Spain, where about one thousand people or one-fourth of the population of Brihuega settled in the mid-1500's. Puebla evolved as a rich agricultural zone and as a locus for textile production where skilled immigrants were able to work and succeed in the colonial market. The immigrants were sufficiently numerous, and created a niche for themselves in many ways resembling their native hometown, in turn a major factor contributing to identity maintenance (Altman 2000). The socio-cultural and linguistic connections established by Spanish speakers on both sides of the Atlantic in the 17th century attest to the continuity of focused variants in the Mexican Colonial Spanish corpora available at present.

In order to extrapolate the features that might differentiate second generation from first-generation speakers, three sets of documents are examined in this chapter: (1) DLNE-AC (1994) and (2) the *Tratado del descubrimiento de las Yndias* (1589) by Juan Suárez de Peralta represent the Central Highlands, whereas (3) DLNE-EG (2008) represent the Gulf region. The analysis of select variants sheds light on the innovations of the second generation, which are indicative of unstable variability stemming from the contact with both the New World and the mother country. The process of unstable variability may not be glaring because it is not controlled, while the result of the process is unpredictable. The output poses new challenges to researchers, who may want to utilize multiple instruments of scrutiny though the outcomes may still be uncertain. Second-generation speakers were the leaders of change in the new environment because they had exteriorized a type of social conduct that was reacting in opposition to values of the first-generation community. Spanish speakers of the first generation took all the risks, were more adventurous and attempted to become acclimatized to the new soil, though they did not always succeed. Notwithstanding, the two generations had in common their participation in dense social networks built in the new land. The second generation began to perceive the New World under a different perspective, partially accepted the values of the first, and struggled to assume those of their native land.

6.2 Linguistic documents: the Central Highlands

The published documents covering more than two decades (1562-1585) include personal letters, applications to travel to New Spain, denunciations, testimonies on various matters, and inquisitorial trials. The authors are diverse and overlap with those of the first generation. A few letters from illustrious protagonists are excluded from this analysis: one by Friar Pedro de Ayala, the Second Bishop of Guadalajara; another by Pedro de Gante, the Flemish monk who arrived before the twelve Franciscan friars; yet another authored by Friar Miguel Navarro, an active member of the Seraphic Order who was a longtime protector of Bernardino de Sahagún (see Chapter 7). The rest of the documents were written by ordinary Spanish speakers who were extremely concerned about staying in New Spain and doing all the paperwork necessary to help their relatives in the process of relocation to a different environment. Many of the documents are appropriate to examine the regional pronunciation traits, primarily the sibilants, the evolution of verbal clitics, the use of pronouns of address *tú*, *vos* and *vuestra merced*, their corresponding direct objects and objects of preposition, alternation of –SE and –RA in different contexts, and select lexical items.

6.2.1 Pronunciation traits

The departure from the system of medieval Spanish is more noticeable amongst speakers / writers who were not as active as colonial leaders. Documents 32-78 (pp. 150-239) include applications and personal letters between relatives who share things in common. The use of dental sibilants continues to appear according to the norms of the times: *reçebido* and *bendiçión* (152), *ausençia* (153), *paçiençia* (154), *encareçer* (154), *cabeça* (154), *desgraçiada* (163), *liçençia* (192), *soliçitan* (214), *negoçios* (214), *denunçiaba* (215); and also *plazera* (152), *agradezca* (153) and *agradezco* (154), *plazer* (157), *dezimos* (160), *lazos* (161). Considering that neither *seseo* nor çeçeo-zezeo was the general rule amongst educated speakers / writers, it may be inferred that these Spanish speakers distinguished the traditional spallings. From the graphemic variations, it is obvious that the cases of *seseo* supersede those of *çeçeo-zezeo*. Authors who were inclined to use *seseo* wrote *acontesido* and *acontesca* (170), *beses* and *besino* (170), *consertase* (186), *juysio* (187), *Rodriges* (191), *onse* (209), *resibi* and *resibire* (213), *veses* (220), *parese* (222), *espesial* and *espesialmente* (238). At the same time *limpiesa* was alternating with *limpieza* (238). Examples of lexical items with the grapheme <z> in intervocalic position are the following: *capazidad* (146), *escandalize* (162) *parezido* (144), *suzias* (199), *lizenzia* (238), *afizionado* (238). Occasionally the grapheme <z> appears after consonant, as in *desparzieron* (209). In contrast with the abundance of cases of normative pronunciation, the examples of *çeçeo* are just a few: *mençajero* (172), *miceria* (198), *demacjados* (221), *aviço* (222). There is also double interchange of sibilants in *neseçjdad* (220). The variations observed in the second generation of writers contrast with the adherence to general rules of medieval Spanish shown by speakers / writers belonging to the first generation.

6.2.2 Other pronunciation features

Language data from the abovementioned sources show some of the features of the prevailing dialects spoken and written in New Spain in the second half of the 16th century. With the exception of the letters delivered by Extremaduran Alonso Ortiz to his wife (see 6.2.6), all the other documents reveal the general inclination to preserve the consonants /d/ and /s/ in absolute final and implosive position. While in the first generation the practice of *seseo* was incipient, in the second generation *seseo* occurred more frequently. Also, the pronunciation of /d/ in final and intervocalic position is preserved in common nouns such as *salud, claridad, brevedad, voluntad, lodo, descansadas, dignidad, fidelidad, salido, marido, servido, querido, acometido*, etc. Occasionally however the omission of /d/ can occur, as in (a), (b) and (c), but such omission is sporadic and clearly contrasts with its preservation as in (d) and (e).
(a) he *biviØo* en Mexico (167)
(b) en *amistaØ* y concordia (186)
(c) *hermandaØ* y *qujetud* (187)
(d) tanto trabajo y *soledad* (157)
(e) limpieza y *rectitud* (230)

In this subsample the aspiration of initial H includes cases that are clearly anti-etymological: *horden* (155), *hera* (164), *husamos* (164), *henero* (165), *henojado* (167), *hedad* (194), *huna* (233), and one infrequent case of aspiration extended to *hebrero* (152), which contrasts with *febrero* (177). A difference between the first and the second generation is the variety of sibilants used, the most frequent being the use of <s> for etymological <z> and <ç> as in *acontesido* (169), *acontesca* (170), *beses* (171), *besino* (171), *haselle* (171), *veses* (220), *ves, resibo* (221), *alguasiles* (222), *conosco* (238), *sien* (212), *vejes* (220). *Seseo* is not entirely regular but alternates with other spellings as in *hasienda* (172) and *hazienda* (173) *resebi* (169) and *recibi* (175), *parese* (201) and *parece* (200). Etymological spellings are consistent in some lexical items such as *liçencia* (175). Finally, *çeçeo* is less frequent but also appears as in *mençajero* (172) and *desasoçiego* (166).

Preservation of final /s/ in noun phrases consistently marks number agreement and is clearly redundant, even when there is no need for disambiguation as in *dos o tres meses* (213). In the noun phrases below, all noun and their corresponding modifiers (articles, adjectives and nouns) preserve both final /s/ and /s/ in implosive position.

(a) las mujeres cuerdas (156)
(b) sus humildes vasallos de aquellas partes (160)
(c) yndios principales y naturales (173)
(d) delitos tan orrendos (166)
(e) mis sobrinos y deudos (184)
(f) a todos los demás parientes y amigos (191)
(g) las causas de sus deudos (214)
(h) los leales vasallos (214)
(i) los cojos y los mancos (222)
(j) los dichos tres pesos (201)
(k) sus espadas desnudas (201)
(l) sus torpezas y deshonestidades (229)
(m) dos sclavos negros e dos sclavas chichimecas (236)

By the same token, the redundancy principle operates in all the sentences with a verb or a clitic marked by the desinence -s, where /s/ in implosive position is preserved, except in item (f).

(a) Dios les pague las buenas obras que siempre nos hacen (156)
(b) qualquiera dellas os dara lo que ubierdes menester (176)
(c) Todos nos pondremos (157)
(d) besamos las reales manos (160)
(e) dezimos que nosotros venjmos astos rreynos dEspaña a negoçios e de algunos no hemos despachado (160)
(f) leØ diese a los dichos mis hermanos o a sus herederos, los pesos de oro que se concertase entre ellos (186)
(g) no dexeis de hacer lo que os pido, pues sabeys cierto que lo que yo tengo lo quiero para vos y para vuestros hijos (189)
(h) os envio trecientos pesos de a ocho reales (189)
(i) esos mochachos que los queria tener conmigo (193)

(j) los días y las noches no los ocupa en otra cosa (225)
(k) les faltara todo a sus criados (226)

6.2.3 Morpho-syntactic features

This subsample shows mixed morpho-syntactic traits: those belonging to pre-modern Spanish and others that adhere to late medieval standards. Late medieval Spanish features appear in verbal clitics, which are attached to the infinitive, as in: *negociallo* (157), *despachalla* (158), *vestillo, dolelles, regalallo* (183), *dexallos* (192), *ponella* (195). In contrast, verbal clitics used with infinitive forms can also end in a thematic vowel + R as in *enbiarles* (192). Finally, clitics are stll used before verbs in the infinitive, as in *para me poder quitar de dicho ofiçio* (235) and *le prometio de le hazer bien* (236). The use of cliticized object pronouns LE and LO with accusative function appearing in a subsample of documents (56-63) is equally varied. They deal with the testimonies of witnesses who appeared before the Holy Office as a result of a violent incident.

The story begins in Doc. 56, when Melchior de Valladolid sent an Indian woman to buy some bread and candles. She went back home saying that when she was taking out the money to pay for the groceries, Juan Maldonado, a trooper, took it away from her. An old man whose name was unknown saw the incident as it happened. The old man had to run away from Maldonado, while yet another witness intervened with his sword in order to settle the fight. After that three or four troopers attacked the old man and stabbed him repeatedly while some other witnesses attempted to defend him. The doorman of the Inquisition, Pedro de Fonseca, came out and tried to bring order in the plaza where the brawl had started, but he was also stabbed in the head from behind. The narration of this incident, from the witnesses' perspectives focuses on the most significant events for which verbs of movement and perception were used: *alcanzar* ('to reach someone'), *prender* ('to apprehend'), *conocer* ('to know someone'), *defender* ('to defend'), *herir* ('to wound'), *maltratar* ('to abuse'), *matar* ('to kill'), *traer* ('to bring') and *ver* ('to see').

The occurrence of LE as direct object pronoun [+ singular masculine] may be explained under different perspectives. When the internal factors are highlighted, the verbs of perception become truly relevant since they are preferred in passages of vivid narrations. But if the focus shifts to external factors, then variation may be attributed to the regional provenance of the protagonists and to dialect contact. In point of fact, the regional origin of the notaries and secretaries of the Holy Office, their level of education and the network of connections that they had across the Atlantic may be considered factors associated with their speech habits. Many speakers were raised and educated in the northern-central region of Spain or were coming from regions that were Castilianized; others were raised and educated in southern Spain under the speech models of the northern-central regions. An additional element that has to be factored in is the speakers' variable exposure to other dialects because some had had more inter-dialect contact than others. In the sentences shown below there are 20 cases of LE and 8 cases of LO, where LE is used mostly with verbs of perception and movement.

(a) *viendole* sacar el dinero, se lo avia tomado (200)
(b) porque no *le conoçia* de vista (200)
(c) El que puesto caso que *le trataron* mal (201)
(d) de otra manera *le alcançara* y cree que *le matara* (201)
(e) Y somo este testigo estava reparandose, no vio quién *le hirio* (202)
(f) que no *le matase* sin que *lo* sintiese la tira (203)
(g) ¿pues cómo al official del Sancto Officio *tratale* de esa manera? (203)
(h) Y los dichos soldados *lo* dexaron (203)
(i) Y entiende que *lo* mataran sino fuera por las bozes de la ventana (204)
(j) *le conoçera viendole* questá herido (205)
(k) Y viendo cómo *le venia maltratando*, se pusieron (...) a poner paz (205)
(l) que no *le mal tratasen* más de lo que *le avian maltratado* (205)
(m) Y vio este testigo cómo el dicho mestizo o mulato que *le hirio* (205)
(n) viendo cómo *le avia herido*, huyeron de él (206)
(o) unos querian arremeter a él, yotros *lo* defendían (207
(p) que *lo* conocera mostrandose*lo* (207)
(q) vio la capa del viejo, (...) *le alcançaron* en ella (207)
(r) que *lo* dexasen que hera viejo (207)
(s) no save quién *le hirio* (207)
(t) no sabe de qué manera porque no *lo* vio (207)
(u) le pareçe que con mostrar se*lo le conoçera* (209)
(v) tras el viejo *alcançandole* algunos golpes (211)
(w) no *le ttraxeron* preso a la Jnquisicion (211)

Two external factors may explain the alternating use of LO and LE: (a) peninsular origin and (b) level of formal education. Those from the northern-central region and with higher education tended to be *leístas*, while speakers from southern Spain and less formal education were pro-etymologists. In most subsamples, *leístas* prevailed because they had more access to positions in which they used their writing skills. It must be underscored that pro-etymological variants LO / LOS were not stigmatized. Finally, because *leísmo* represents the divergence from the ancestral system, other usages ensued such as *laísmo*, *loísmo* and inanimate *leísmo*. These changes may be considered irregular variations that did not survive in New World Spanish (see Chapter 10).

6.2.4 Imperfect subjunctive

Writers belonging to the second generation preferred imperfect subjunctive –SE forms in subordinate clauses, but –RA forms appear in the protasis and the apodosis of conditional sentences and concessive clauses as in (a)-(f). This combination, which derives from late medieval Spanish, is still found among speakers residing in rural and marginal urban areas of the New World.

(a) si *fuera* posible luego dexar los negoçios y yrme, lo *hiciera* (154)
(b) si su marido *tuviera* gana de venirse aca, el *fuera* con Antonio Lopez a la corte y *truxera* licencia con que se *vinieran* (175)
(c) aunque yo *fuera* no le *igualara* (183)
(d) si *ubiera* de vender los bienes quél dexó, no *bastara* para cunplir sus mandos (187)
(e) si yo *estuvjera* bueno, le *escriviera* (190)
(f) si *ubiera querido* casalla con alguno (...) ya la *ubiera casado* (222)

6.2.5 Pronouns of address

The pronouns of address found in the personal missives delivered in this period are: *Vos*, which appears a total of 9 times in letters from father to son, 5 times in letters from husband to wife, and only once from uncle to nephew and sister to brother. *Vuestra merced* appears a total of 7 times in missives from brother to brother, twice in letters from sister to sister, and only once between brothers-in-law, son to mother, and also from a male friend to female friend. The plurals *vosotros* (1) and *vuestras mercedes* (2) are infrequent. *Vuestra merced* appears consistently a as subject, with 3rd person singular verb forms, which are not mixed with any other pronoun. In addition, the series of possessive adjectives *vuestro(s)* and *vuestra(s)* agree with the personal pronouns *vos* and *vuestra(s) merced(es)*, creating ambiguity in most sentences with a null subject. Documents 56-62 narrating the testimonies of witnesses who rendered different versions of the violent dispute abovementioned show the use of *vos*. While the testimonies were redacted in the standard style of inquisitorial documents, *vos* prevailed in reported speech indicating the colloquial quality of this pronoun and its use with verb forms corresponding paradigmatically to the pronoun *tú*, as in (a), which is

a rare case of *voseo*. Sentences (b) and (d) use *vos* to indicate plurality with the corresponding verb forms while sentence (c) refers to singular *vos*.
(a) ¡*calla[d]*, viejo!, y *ten[ed]* por bien de perdonar los tres pesos porque si no *os* juro que *os* an de matar ¡y *calla[d]* la boca! (200)
(b) este testigo acudio con su espada (...) y diziendo ¡*teneos*, aya paz! (202)
(c) que *vos* mi dinero me *aveis* de pagar pues me lo *deveis* (203)
(d) Pedro salio diciendo: ¡*teneos*, hombres de bien, *teneos* (207)

6.2.6 Original letters by Alonso Ortiz

Two original letters delivered by Alonso Ortiz to his wife, Docs. 44 and 45 reveal the use of *vos* as subject and the mixture with verb paradigms corresponding to *tú*. *Voseo* stemmed from a combination of internal changes such as the following: (1) Reduction of diphthongized forms (AI to A and EI to E) corresponding to *vos*, as in examples (a)-(d). (2) Omission of final -*d* in the affirmative command, as in *entendeØ*, item (c). (3) Use of the paradigm corresponding to the pronoun *tú* as in *determinas* and *dexes* with the object corresponding to *vos*, as in item (d). (4) Preservation of *vos* as an object of preposition, as in (e) and (f).
(a) La presente para por ella *os* rogar que *hagas* [hagás] por mi, *bos* y *buestros* ermanos los solteros (177)
(b) Y si acaso fuere, *podes* [podés] dalle a este poder para que *os* lo negoçe en Sebilla (177)
(c) Lo quél *os* ruega por ella *entendeØ* ques para probecho de *vuestros* (sic) hijas (178)
(d) si no *determinas* [determinás] de venir que no se *os* dé el dinero, si no *determinas* [determinás] de benir, no por eso *dexes* [dejés] de proqurar el dinero (178)
(e) porquestoy ganando de comer *para bos* y para mis hijos (181)
(f) que estas cartas ban *para bos* las puedes tener por tuyas (178)

Three features of southern peninsular Spanish can be found in the same documents: (1) omission of –*s* and -*d* as in items (a)-(l); (2) interchange of intervocalic –*r*- and –*l* as in (m)-(t); and (3) rhotacism as in (t) and (u).
(a) recebire muy gran *merceØ* (177)
(b) si fuere *necesidaØ* de yr a la corte, él lo negoçará (177)
(c) se acabe mas ayna mi *soledaØ* y pena (178)
(d) onde quedo bueno de *saluØ* (179)
(e) Le *deziØ* que rueguen a Dios por mi *saluØ* (181)

(f) no quero trabaxar más de la *solicituØ* porque no me dé alguna enfermedaØ (180)
(g) que pueda estar en esta *ciudaØ* de Mexico (181)
(h) *podes* [podés] aca determinar, y con *brebedaØ*, de benir de esta misma *frota* (182)
(i) a Melchor Goncales y a Alonso Goncalez *leØ deziØ* que quando de aca no se *leØ* enbiara nada (181)
(j) si no *benis* [venís] *entendeØ* que no nos podemos ver tan ayna (178)
(k) De lo que determinardes de hazer, me lo *esqribiØ* en el nabio (178)
(l) A vuestro padre y madre *leØ podes* [podés] decir que por amor de Dios que me perdonen (178)
(m) para los *fretes* [fletes], ay enbio yo mi poder a *bos* (177)
(n) para que me *podas* [podás] *obrigar* [obligar] por los *fretes* [fletes] (177)
(o) desta Nueba España, ba un hombre por su muger en esa *frota* [flota] (178)
(p) Que *cumpra* [cumpla] con *bos* la palabra (182)
(q) y mira que *habra* [habla] mucho (180)
(r) estoy *obrigado* [obligado] (181)
(s) yo estoy puesto y *entabrado* [entablado] para ganar de comer (182)
(t) no sabe acabar de *habrar* [hablar] (180)
(u) Es grande mi deseo de os *borber* [volver] a ver (180)

In some other cases, Alonso de Ortiz uses final –*s* in the present indicative. Third conjugation verbs retained final –*s* as in (a), while the diphthong reduction in the verbs belonging to the 1st and 2nd conjugations does trigger the reduction of final –*s*: *podés* < *podéis*, *hallarés* < *hallaréis*, *podás* < *podáis*), except in the monosyllabic verb *dar* as in (i). Finally, final –*d* in affirmative commands may be lost as in the second part of (h), or goes through metathesis as in (g) and (j).

(a) si *benis* [venís] quiza estaré yo en el puerto (178)
(b) a buestro padre y madre le *podes* [podés] decir que me perdonen (178)
(c) este dinero lo *hallares* [hallarés] en Sebilla en poder de un jurado (181)
(d) *podes* [podés] aca determinaros (182)
(e) les *podes* [podés] decir que en estotra lenbio [le envío] cien queros (181)
(f) Yo os enviaré mi poder a bos para que lo *podas* [podás] sostiuyr en quin bos *quisierdes* (181)
(g) si acaso lo *bierdes* [vieres], *miralde* [miradle] las manos (181)
(h) si *acordades* de no venir, *enbiame* [enviaØme] a Francisco (181)
(i) y le *da[is]* mis encomiendas (178)
(j) *encomendaldo* [encomendadlo] todo siempre a Dios (179)

6.2.7 Mixing *tú*, *vos* and *vuestra merced*

The documents from this period offer valuable data on the use of *vos* in New World Spanish and may explain the origin of *voseo*, which seems to have originated in the intra-familiar domain, from where it extended to other informal domains (friends and acquaintances). Such innovation might have reached additional public spheres of interaction during the colonial period. *Voseo* derived from the overlapping use of two common subject pronouns, *tú* and *vos*, and the mixture of paradigms. The most striking change is the use of the subject pronoun *vos* with the object pronoun *te*, which corresponds paradigmatically to the subject pronoun *tú*. The second change appeared in the present indicative since the verb forms of the New World Spanish *voseo* derive from older forms corresponding to the old plural *vos* and the neologism *vosotros* (< *vos* + *otros*). In this respect, the second generation of New World Spanish speakers shows unstable language patterns, resulting from their having weakened contact with Spain. A constant topic in the letters delivered to relatives is the preoccupation with moneys sent in cash and the acknowledgement of receipt, which was normally uncertain. In Doc. 64, a letter addressed by Alonso de Alcoçer to his brother, the opening salutation appears with the indirect object *te* as in sentence (a), but the author continues with the corresponding reflexive pronoun *vos* as in (b). The use of *vos* with the corresponding verb form of *tú* appears in example (c). In sentence (d), there is triphthong reduction and omission of final –*d*.

(a) esta sera para *hazerte* saber (212)
(b) yo sierto quisiera que *os binieredes* a esta tierra (212)
(c) yo *os* lo embiaré algun dia porque en esta tierra no *podras* medrar nada (212)
(d) Y las cartas qu*escrivier[e]is, enbiaØlas* a Sevilla, a mi cuñado (213)

The New World Spanish innovation known as *voseo* may be explained by at least four internal changes: (1) Diphthong reduction in indirect affirmative and direct negative commands. (2) Use of object pronouns that belong paradigmatically to the subject pronoun *te*; diphthongized standard forms *miréis* (< MIRAR), *tenéis* (< TENER), *hagáis* (< HACER) in sentences (a) and (b) were reduced to *mirés*, *tenés*, *hagás* later becoming the most frequent verb forms in entire regions and countries where the personal pronoun *tú* was rather infrequent or obsolete. (3) The reduction of the standard triphthong –IAI– as in *espantaríais*, which in rapid speech is acoustically similar to the form of the pronoun *tú* (*espantarías*) as in (c) with the use of *tú* appearing again with the verb form corresponding to *tú* as in the first part of sentence (d). (4) Finally, when *voseo* omitted the final –*d* corresponding to affirmative commands, a subtle stress shift occurred, too, changing from *enviad* → *enviá* + clitic pronoun, as in the second part of sentence (d). (See also 6.2.6).

(a) Lo que *os* ruego es que por amor de Dios que *mireis* que no *teneis* padre ni madre (212)
(b) que *mireis* por *bos* y que *hagais* como hombre de bien (212)
(c) si bien lo *supiesedes* os *espantariaØs* [espantaríais] y *abriais* [habríais] lástima de mí (213)
(d) Y tanbien mi cuñado *te* ayudará para que *puedas* benir. Y las cartas qu*escrivier[e]is*, *enbiaØlas* a Sevilla (213)

Alonso de Alcoçer closed the letter addressed to his brother using the glaring features of *voseo*, which mix the subject pronoun *vos* with the object pronoun *te* and the possessive *tú*:

> Mas si ser pudiera, *seais bos* el mensajero. Y con esto ni tengo mas que dezir sino que plega Dios Nuestro Señor me dexe *berte* en esta corte. *Tu* hermano que mas deseo tiene de *verte* qu*escrivirte* (213).
>
> [If at all possible please do be the messenger. And with this I have nothing else to add but to pray to God Our Holy Father to let me see you in this land. Your brother, who really wants to see you; more than he wants to write you].

Finally, in Doc. 43 (1574) Juana Bautista invited her sister to join her in New Spain. This writer shows the use of possessive adjectives (*su*, *suya*) corresponding to the 3rd person singular *vuestra merced* as in (a) and (b). The same writer used *vos* (+ *otros*) in direct speech. This abrupt change seems to indicate that the writer opened the letter with a softened salutation but continued with harsh criticism when she addressed her sister's husband behavior.
(a) Una *suya* recibi abra dos dias, que truxo Antonio Lopez (175)
(b) si *su* marido tubiera gana de benirse aca, el fuera con Antonio Lopez (175)

The use of *vos* with the corresponding diphthongized paradigm in the 1st conjugation, i.e. *pensasteis* < PENSAR ('to think') and *malbaratasteis* < MALBARATAR ('to philander'), appears with the reduced diphthong in the passage below. On the other hand, the forms of the verb TENER (*teníades* and *tuvierades*) are used according to old medieval patterns. In contrast, the verb PODER is similar to PENSAR and MALBARATAR, appearing with the reduced diphthong:

> ¿Qué *pensastes*: que *teníades* otros dos pares de casas que trespasar? Pues tan presto lo *malbaratastes*. ¡Qué me hiziera si *tuvierades* media dozena de hijos a quien sustentar! Quando siendo *vos* y *vuestro marido*, ni con eso ni con esotro nos [no *os*] *pudistes* abiar. Yo creo que aunque *os* enbíe munchos dineros no *os podreis* abiar porque me dicen que *vuestro* marido es amigo de traer galas y trabajar poco (175).

[Did you think you had two more houses to transfer? You sold them really fast. What would I do if you had one-half dozen children to support? Because you and your husband are the way you are, you did not have enough to pay for the trip. I think that even if I send you money you won't be able to get ready for the trip, because I'm told that he likes to show off a lot and work a little].

6.3 Suárez de Peralta's *Tratado del descubrimiento de las Yndias y su conquista*

Juan Suárez de Peralta was born in Mexico City in 1537 of Spanish parents from northern Spain who settled in the Caribbean area during the first years following the discovery of the New World. He was a true *criollo*, representative of the second generation of Spanish speakers, and author of the *Tratado del descubrimiento de las Yndias y su conquista* [Treatise on the Discovery of the Indies and its Conquest (1589/1990). In his writings there is no trace of the opposition between the sounds corresponding to medieval Spanish by <ss> and <s>, between /ʃ/ and /ʒ/ spelled with <x> on the one hand, and <j> and <g>, on the other, because all sibilants had been devoiced and de-affricated. It is assumed that the voiced / voiceless opposition was resolved during this period, if not entirely gone. Suárez de Peralta also represents the coalescence of /ṡ/ and /ż/ into a single voiceless /s/ and the apical-alveolar articulation which was absorbed by the dorso-dental variety pronunciation of the old /ŝ/. The evidence leads to believe that by 1579, when Suárez de Peralta left Mexico City, his *seseo* was firmly established (Perissinotto 1994). There is no evidence of /s/ aspiration or deletion in implosive position or interchange of –r– and –l–, but there are a few cases of final –d omission, as in *berse en mucha neçesidáØ*. There are also a few cases of *çeçeo*: *reçuçitada* (104), *Çoliçita* (132), *çuçedió* (144), *suçeda* (235). Thus, while pronunciation features reflect more regular patterns, morphology, syntax and lexicon display greater and more irregular variation that can be considered evidence of polymorphism. His *Tratado* may be considered illustrative of the second generation of Spanish speakers, who spent a good part of their lives in the New World without losing the ties with the mother country (see also Perissinotto 1992).

6.3.1 Relevant features in Suárez de Peralta's *Tratado*

The *Tratado* is a lengthy essay dealing primarily with the memories and vision that the author had about New Spain. It is not a strictly historical account of the conquest and colonization of Mexico but an imaginative report about the desires of the *encomenderos* to become perpetual lords of vassals in the face of the implementation of the New Laws. Narrated in the third person the author utilizes other literary resources such as definitions, descriptions and dialogue (in direct and indirect speech). Dialogues between well-known protagonists and common people aid in the reconstruction of forms of address prevailing in the 16th century. The author sounds even more innovative because of the abundance of borrowings, calques and phrases derived from the contact of Spanish with Amerindian languages. It is relevant that Suárez de Peralta was using a variety of traits derived from late medieval Spanish: (1) omission of the preposition *a* before [+ animate] object with the function of direct object, as in *vio los cristianos*; (2) use of verbal clitics before infinitives, for example, *ydos a los ver*; (3) coalescence of infinitive –*r* and verbal clitics, for instance, *sacrificallos*; and (4) the preposition EN with a gerund, as *en saliendo*. Like other speakers and writers born in the New World, he was exposed to various peninsular dialects: the use of LE(S) for direct object pronouns singular and plural prevailed in the *Tratado*, but he also used the modern etymological system of direct object pronouns LO(S). Anti-etymological features are perceived as being an "ism", and for this reason, the use of LE(S) is known as *leísmo*.

The inclusion of definitions of lexical items derived from Amerindian language is noteworthy, inasmuch as the author conveys his desire to explain with brevity and clarity some of native things, peoples, and customs. His definitions incorporate Tainismos: (a) *ají* ('pepper') and (k) *maíz* ('corn'). The rest are Nahuatlismos: (b) *chalchihuites* ('jade stone'); (c) *xuchiles*, ('flowers'); (d) *iepales* ('seats'); (e) *petates* ('woven blanket from palm fibers'); (f) *piçietl* ('cane' or 'reed'); (g) *jochiococot* ('liquidambar' or 'sweet gum tree'); (h) *poquietl* ('hollowed cane filled with perfume'); (i) *mecapal* ('leather strap with two cords attached'); (j) *tianguez* ('market'); (l) *tiçatl* ('white powder like gypsum'); (m) *cenalco* ('cave'); (n) *suchiles* ('flowers for the wrist'); (o) *cocoliztli* ('disease'), (p, q, r) *jícara* ('round recipient'). Suárez de Peralta thought of the speakers of Amerindian languages as the "Others" when he consistently refers to 'they' as in *ellos llaman* ('they name something').

(a) Exemplifican en el *ají*, que son los pimientos de las Yndias (40)
(b) otras que llaman *chalchihuites*, ques una piedra verde, (…), y no transparente (41)
(c) Flores hechos ramilletes quellos llaman *xuchiles* (42)
(d) pieça y çercada de asientos, que llaman *iepales* (42)
(e) unas esteras hechas de lo mismo que los asientos que aquí llaman *petates* (42)
(f) llenos los canutos de tabaco, que llaman *piçietl* (45)
(g) otras rayzes y liquidámbar, que allá llaman *jochiococot* (45)

(h) Hazen de todo esto una masa y della ynchen los canutos de la caña, la qual llaman *poquietl* (45)
(i) Se ponen unas çinchas que llaman *mecapales* (47)
(j) Negocian ellas en los mercados que llaman *tianguez* (48)
(k) el *maíz* ques el pan que comen (54)
(l) tienen un terrón de tierra muy blanca (...) que llaman los yndios *tiçatl* y con esta tierra se untan los dedos (60)
(m) en una cueua, quellos llamauan *çenalco*, donde dizen que abía grandes secretos (103)
(n) otras [flores] para las manos quellos llaman *suchiles* (121)
(o) abía algunas enfermedades y peste, quellos llaman *cocolitzli* (254)
(p) tomábanle la sangre con una *jícara*, ques um baso hecho de calabaças (254)
(q) no hacen fiesta sin aquel brebaje, que llaman *jícaras de cacao* (168)
(r) flores en *jícaras* que son unos basos como porçelanas (121)

The author born in New Spain was concerned about the meaning of some lexical items referring to cultural objects needing an identifying code. For instance, in sentence (a), the meaning of the word 'drum' (*teponaztl*) can be guesstimated by the referent 'drum sticks' (*maçuelos*) or the 'to the tune of the drum' (*al son del tenopaztle*). In item (b), the author uses a synonym to refer to the *cañas* or *poquietls* ('canes or reeds'). In sentence (c), he included a full definition ('*tortillas* are the pieces of bread made of corn'), and in example (d), there is a description ('big canoes are tiny ships'). Typical Spanish diminutives *–illo*, *–illa* are suffixed to the integrated Taino-derived noun '*canoyllas*', as in example (e). There is also the semantic extension of *cacao* (originally meaning 'cocoa bean'), an item so valuable that also meant currency or coin as in sentences (f) and (g).

(a) con estos maçuelos dan en el *teponaztl* (42) or al son del *teponaztle* (255)
(b) No hacen fiesta ni presente que falten estas *cañas* o *poquietls* (45)
(c) Llevaba algunas *tortillas*, que som *los panecillos* quellos usauan, hechos del *maíz* (54)
(d) *canoas grandes*, que son a manera de *chiquitos barquillos* (95)
(e) El marqués y los que con él yban sescaparon en unas *canoyllas* (140)
(f) corre una moneda que llaman *cacao* la qual es una fruta (166)
(g) en los mercados se ponía tendido en una estera que llaman *petate*, a bender el *cacao* por menudo, contándolo (167)

As opposed to the Spaniards or *los españoles*, Suárez de Peralta refers to ethnic groups that are perceived as being nations or sub-nations. The patronymic Mexican, which had a double spelling *mexicanos* (100, 116) and *mejicanos* (115, 116), is constantly highlighted when he intends to stress the difference between

Mexicans and Spaniards. He also refers to the beginning of the war between *españoles* and *mejicanos* (128). Other groups are merely mentioned by the patronymic: *mistecas* (116), *otomites* (117), *tarascos* (119), and *chichimecas* (171). The ethnic groups of the Mesoamerican area are identified by a defining trait, a reference to history, or their regional / national origin, as in examples (a) through (d).
(a) los *tlaxcaltecas* binieron de paz (126)
(b) llegó a Acámbaro, donde halló los *tarascos*, que son los de Mechuacán (119)
(c) Para poblar y señorear y conquistar a los naturales, queran los que llaman *otomíes*, *chochones*, *mistecas*, *çapotecas* y otras naciones (48)
(d) los *çempoalas*, que eran mucha gente, sujeta a los *mejicanos* (116)

Suárez de Peralta also knew of the places (towns, mountains, woods, and sierras), prominent people, and even divinities associated with the Mesoamerican culture. For this reason, toponyms are abundant and sound natural: Chapultepec (114), Huaxaca (115), Escapuçalco (116), Suchimilco (117), Tezcuco (120, 136) Tlatelulco (120) Acámbaro (119), Huajoçingo (117) Amecameca (117), Chalco, Chinampa, Mezquique (117), Estapalapa and Mezquique (136). Suárez de Peralta knew the protagonists of Aztec history: Ahuitzontzin (109), Ajayacatzin (120), Acamapuchtli (115), Cacamatzin and Huauhtimutzin (136). The famous name of the Aztec Emperor was spelled in two ways: Moçeçuma (122) and Monteçuma (128).
(a) Del primer señor de la ciudad de México se tiene noticia que se llamó *Acamapichtl* (48)
(b) Vn ydolo de los suyos que llamauan *Çihuacoatl* andaua llorando de noche (105)
(c) era de dios *Huitzilopuchtli*, que se llamaba tlacalteca (109)
(d) llegó la fiesta de un ydolo que llamaban *Huitzilibuchcatl* (127)

His knowledge of Nahuatl must have been limited to toponyms, common objects of the Mesoamerican culture, and the like. It seems that he was monolingual or a receptive bilingual since he was familiar with a few phrases such as (a) *Ypaltzinco Dios* ('God's faith'); (b) *Qui mo, ma chitia* ('God may know'); and (c) *Matla cateçolotl nech, huica* ('May the Devil take me away!') (63). Phrases with Amerindian integrated loans and Spanish phrases are common and sound natural: 'media hanega de *maíz*' (54), 'día de *tianguez*' (120), 'miel de *magueyes*' (164). Other lexical items derived from Taino and Nahuatl are: *macanas* ('wooden weapon or truncheon') (55), *tanate* (< tanatli) ('backpack'), (59) *malacate* (< malacatl) ('hard spindle') (59), *quilontlontli* ('homosexual') (115). With the meaning of 'blouse' or 'woman's shirt', he offered three variants: *hueypil* (115), *hueypili* (120), and the modern *huipil*.

6.3.2 Object pronouns LES and LOS in the second-generation

Suárez de Peralta was an inter-dialect speaker and writer since in his *Tratado* there can be found more linguistic variations than those observed in first generation of Spanish speakers. The author's father was from Avila and the mother from Navarra. It can thus be assumed that his first dialect, northern Castilian, was the one acquired from his parents, and that other dialect traits were learned in New Spain's multidialectal environment and from his trips to the mother country. In the *Tratado*, the use of LE(S) or the anti-etymological system [+ animate masculine] prevails over the pro-etymological system for a margin of 15 percent. This author used singular LE as in (a) through (e) and the modern etymological system LO(S) as in (f) through (i).

An interesting variation occurs when the direct object LE (*le hazían pedaços*) alternated with LO in the same sentence (*lo repartían*) in example (j).

(a) era bueno su padre después que *le açotó* (52)
(b) al cautibo por guerra jamás *le reduzen* a esclavo (77)
(c) que creyó, çierto, Cortés que *le yba a matar* (85)
(d) Como *le adorauan* [al demonio] y le tenían debución (...) encomendábanse a él (63)
(e) los yndios *le temían* [a Moctezuma] en estremo y (...) enojado no *le osauan* mirar (111)
(f) se siruen destos negros y *los* tienem por esclauos (77)
(g) Y los unos y los otros tienen costumbre uenderse o que *los* bendan (77)
(h) Y *los* meten en el pueblo con muncho contento y *los* sirven y regalan dándoles de comer (64)
(i) açota*los* públicamente y tresquila*los* las caueças a panderetes (52)
(j) si alguno deuía a munchos y no tenía de que pagar *le hazían* pedaços, y lo repartían entre sí los acreedores (52)

The narrations and description of the conquest of Mexico refer to victories or defeats of both groups (Aztecs and Spaniards). Therefore, the verbs *matar* ('to kill') and *sacrificar* ('to sacrifice') are not only abundant but the author used both pronouns LE(S) and LO(S) with these verbs, though the etymological LO(S) system prevailed in the plural form.

(a) *los matan* y hazen del menudo y sangre (75)
(b) allí les dieron de lançadas y *los mataron* (127)
(c) aunque fuesen criados de Montecuma y pribados, *los matavan* (128)
(d) estando todos los yndios y señores prinçipales baylando, *los* acometió en el patio, acorralados, y *los mató* (128)
(e) porque a sauello no se lo consintieran, sino antes *le mataran* (94)

6.3 Suárez de Peralta's *Tratado del descubrimiento de las Yndias y su conquista* — **227**

(f) volviesen contra él como cuando **le mataron** (113)
(g) ya enpeçaban a sentir el çerco y los que **les mataban** (128)
(h) que si no yba **le matarían** quando más descuydado estubiese (213)
(i) **le abían de sacrificar** (110)
(j) **le sacrificaron** en un cu questaba en México (110)
(k) mandó engredar çiertos yndios para luego *los* sacrificar y untar con sangre a los mensajeros (102)
(l) les mandó que (...) les lleuasen algunos cautivos para *sacrificarlos* (102)

With verbs of perception such as *conocer* ('to know someone'), *oír* ('to hear'), *sentir*, ('to feel'), and *ver* ('to see'), speakers may be more consistent and may use LE(S) more regularly, although exceptions can be found. Presumably the *leísta* speaker focuses on the activity or event 'to know someone' as in sentences (a)-(c), or 'to hear someone' as in sentence (d); or 'to see someone or something', as in sentences (e)-(g).

(a) Yo **le conoçí** caçador mayor que tenía más de dos mil ducados (171)
(b) echauan menos al birrey don Antonio, al qual tenían por padre y **le conoçían** munchos años abía y **le querían** en estremo (171)
(c) **le conocí** antes de ser sacristán, harto desbenturado (197)
(d) le mandaron que fuese al marqués y **le oyese** y supiese del punto en questaua el negoçio (199)
(e) le hablé y **le uí** con sus lacayos y tantos pajes (209)
(f) ¡**belle** de aquella manera oy! (209)
(g) y como **le uio** así, hincóse de rodillas, y tornó a reconciliarse (211)

Although the use of LE with [– animate masculine] objects is considered rare, in the *Tratado* the following examples referring to inanimate objects can be found: in (a) *el cubilete* ('copper baking mold'), in (b) *el sacramento* ('the sacrament'), in (c) a *un trapillo* ('small rag'), in (d) *mando* ('command'), (e) *el volcán* ('the volcano'), and (g) *remedio* ('remedy'), etc.

(a) Como **le vio** [*el cubilete*] la Marina dijo que de aquella color y suerte tenía muncha plata (94)
(b) El dia que **le reçiben** [*el sacramento*] se uisten de nuebo (62)
(c) sacó *un trapillo* que traya en el carcaje de las flechas, **le desemboluió** (91)
(d) Si Hernando Cortés tubiera *mando*, que no **le tenía**... (97)
(e) dio en subir a **belle** [*el volcán*], él y unos frayles (106)
(f) si en España su magestad **le tubiera** [el bosque de Chapulteque], fuera de muncho regalo y contento (114)
(g) Y quando quisieron procurar *remedio*, ya no **le tenía** [el dolor] (141)

(h) no se aprobechan luego del [*el cacao*] en sacándolo de la maçorca, sino *cúranle* primero a sol (168)
(i) quando se benefiçiaba el metal por fundiçión (...), no tenían la ley que bastaua para *fundirle* [*el metal*] (176)
(j) "Bendéme *aquel desechadero* que tenéis, que *le quiero* para çierto negoçio". El otro, que no *le tenía* en nada, *bendiósele* por çien pesos (177
(k) ¡Y tenía el otro *el tesoro* en casa, lo bía por momentos y no *le conocía*! (177)
(l) [*el corazón*] *le echaban* a rodar las escaleras abajo del cu (254)
(m) bajarom por *el coraçón* y quando *le subieron* hallaron la yndia en pie (255)
(n) Toman *el coraçón* después de *abelle* subido y al son del teponaztle (...) cantándole lo tornan a meter en el cuerpo (255)

In sum, in the *Tratado* there is total of 457 cases of [+ masculine human] direct objects and a few that refer to [+ masculine animals]; therefore, the entire category can be considered [+ animate]. Less than 15 percent of the total refer to [– animate] objects. In all cases, LE is more frequent with singular than with plural objects and it almost never refers to feminine. Table 6.1 subsumes singular and plural masculine LE(S) and LO(S) and discards feminine gender. The results show that Suárez de Peralta does not betray his northern origins inasmuch as he used Castilian LE(S) in more than one-half of the tokens counted, while in the remaining 35 percent he preferred the pro-etymological system. He was clearly *leísta* when referring to singular and plural [+ animate] objects; when he was referring to [– animate singular masculine] objects, he was strongly *leísta*; of a total of 73 clitics, he used LO only 10 times whereas in the remaining 63 tokens, he used LE.

Table 6.1: Number and percent of LE(S) and LO(S)

LE(S) + Animate + Masculine	270	(50.94 %)
LO(S) + Animate + Masculine	187	(35.28 %)
LE(S) – Animate + / – Masculine	73	(13.77 %)
Total cases = 530		(100 %)

6.3.3 Other object pronouns

Pronouns LE / LES and LO have been cliticized in verbs that refer to the subject thus creating a duplication, as in (a); the subject becomes a dative after an infinitive as in (b), and a neutral unknown antecedent as in (c). An additional clitic LE appears with intransitive and transitive verbs SER and DAR, as in (d) and (e); the

6.3 Suárez de Peralta's Tratado del descubrimiento de las Yndias y su conquista — 229

verb HACER with the clitic LE in sentence (f) has become an idiomatic expression with the meaning of manner or means ('to do things in a certain way'). Finally, the redundancy of direct and indirect objects is obvious in (h).

(a) **Le tenía** muy severo *el rostro* (121) or **Le tenía** muy lindo *el rostro* (206)
(b) les pedía pareçer primero en las cosas que se **le ofreçian tomarle** (99)
(c) y Dios *lo* permitió que el tubiese miedo (103)
(d) el que *lo* era bueno **le ennobleçía** con dalle preminençias (115)
(e) los tenían apretados y çercados hasta que fueron los españoles y se **les dieron** de paz (116)
(f) Así **le hizo** por todo el camino hasta llegar a México (147)
(h) **Le** mandaron que fuese al marqués y **le oyese** y supiese del punto en que estaua el negoçio y que **le concediese** todo lo que **le pidiese prometiéndole** de **le ayudar** (199)

When two clitics appear before a verb, one of them is a reflexive and the other one the indirect object pronoun LE(S). This type of construction focuses on the idiosyncratic involvement of the subject (expressed by the indirect object) with the action of the cliticized verb, as in (a)-(e). These are innovative examples with a reflexive SE and the clitic object LE. With LE, the verb ANDAR acquired a different meaning in modern Mexican Spanish and at present is used as the interjection "¡ándale!" with the meaning ('It's all right'!).

(a) temía que la jente **se le quería** bolber y le pareçia no andaban con gusto (97)
(b) Las malas voluntades (...) **se le descubrieron** al capitán (98)
(c) **Se les yban quedando** yndios muertos del frío (106)
(d) Acordaron de bolberse, **auiéndoseles muerto** más de quinze personas de frío (107)
(e) Así mismo **se le pasaron** los de Huajoçingo (117)
(f) no le llamaron, de lo qual él se sintió y se corrió muncho, y *lo* andava en estremo corrido (151)
(g) Francisco Bázquez, después de aber visto el engaño de la tierra procuró bolberse con harto trauajo. Auiendo rodeado el mundo y **andádole**, llegó a México y luego fue a besar las manos al birrey (158-9)

A case of feminine singular indirect object pronoun LA appears in the *Tratado* only with the verbs *avisar* ('to warn') and *hablar* ('to talk'), although in other documents *laísmo* is also used with *rogar* ('to beg') and *preguntar* ('to ask'). *Laísmo* is vital in modern peninsular varieties with the verbs *avisar, exigir, creer, hablar, pegar*; such innovation can spontaneously generate sentences such as *la aviso, la creo, la hablo, la pego*, which are rare in Latin American Spanish. With the verb *gritar* ('to yell'), Colombians may use LA, as in '*no la grite*' ('don't yell at her')

(a) Hernán Cortés dio en que nayde *la* hablase [a la Malinche]. Malas lenguas dijeron que de çelos (96-97)
(b) se ponían algunos a las bentanas con sus mujeres, y las madres con sus hijas porque no *las* hablasen libertades. Y visto que no podían hablar*las* (190)

6.3.4 Verb forms

Verb forms derived from frequent verbs such as TRAER ('to bring') and VER ('to see') appear in different spelling variants, but the non-etymological form *trujo*, *trujeron* prevailed over *trajo*. Likewise, the form *vía* is mostly used in lieu of the modern *veía*.
(a) eran en piedra, de las quales yo *truje* a España (41)
(b) Y este nauio *trujo* nueba de alguna tierra (57)
(c) *trujeron* la comida, que fue toda de carne (75)
(d) luego hallaron ahua y la *trujeron* a los nauíos (90)
(e) que *trujese* una señal para que fuese conoçido (115)
(f) los *retrujese* a su casa y allí los ospedase (120)
(g) *trujo* muy buena casa de criados y criadas (140)
(h) y *trajo* esta nueba un fraile (149)
(i) bí cueros de los que *trujeron* estos soldados (154)
(j) Los ingleses que auían preso en la isla, mandó se *trujesen* a Mexico (249)
(k) ya no *bía* la ora de verse rebuelto en aquella riqueza (94)
(l) mostraba tan gran señorío que muy pocas bezes le *uían* reyr (115)
(m) lo que el mundo auía mostrado en aquello que *bía* presente (209)

6.3.5 Pronoun of address in the *Tratado*

The use of direct speech in some of the *Tratado*'s passages facilitates the identification of the pronouns of address and the corresponding verb forms. The narratives, descriptions and dialogues available show a variety of pronouns, to wit: *tú*, *vos*, *vosotros* and *vuestra(s) merced(es)* and related forms such as *vuesa(s) merced(es)*. The uses of the informal pronouns of address are defined as *tuteo* (where *tú* agrees with its paradigmatic verb forms, possessive adjectives, etc.) and *voseo* (where *vos* may be used as a subject pronoun and as an object of preposition with verb forms corresponding to the pronoun *tú* in select tenses). *Tuteo* is used with both feminine and masculine, and prevails in informal domains between those of equal rank. *Tú* is directly derived from the second person singular Latin pronoun TU. In both medieval and modern Spanish, the personal pronoun *tú* may

be a null subject and the possessive adjective *tu* agrees in number with the possessed object as in item (a).
(a) *Calla*, bellaco (…) que por ser cobarde y por miedo *as* bendido *tu* reyno (…) Pues *tú* con ellos, *as* de morir (129)

The pronoun VOS is also directly derived from Latin. In peninsular varieties, the subject pronoun normally agrees with its verb forms, possessive adjectives, and direct and indirect objects. The passages below show the use of singular *vos* in a laconic, exhortative and fictitious welcome speech delivered by Moctezuma to the Spanish speakers who had just arrived in the Emperor's territory. At the time Suárez de Peralta wrote his essay, the memories about the conquest of Mexico were alive and intense. He consistently used the traditional diphthongized forms of the verbs *ser*, *haber*, *querer*, *meter* and *poner* but they also show the omission of final –*d*.
(a) "Señor mío, *seáis* muy bienbenido. *Abéis* llegado a *vuestra* tierra y pueblo, México, y a *vuestra* casa, ques la mía, que *os* ofrezco para *vuestro* seruiçio. *Abeis* benido para sentar*os* en *vuestro* trono y señorío, el qual yo en *buestro* nombre e poseydo" (121)
(b) Un caballero de los criados del birrey, bístole tan metido con Cortés, le dijo un día: "Señor, ¿qué *queréis* hazer con este hombre? ¿Gastar *vuestro* dinero y enbia[d]lle…? (150)
(c) "Nos [no *os*] *metáis* con el sino *tomáØ* otro medio y *seguíØ vuestra* bentura. *Hazed* por *bos* solo esta jornada" (150-151)
(d) "con *bos* armado, *os* diera que hazer" (152)
(e) "Pues señor, *dezíØselo*, quel lo hará" (199)
(f) "Sí, señor; y lo que combiene es que *os pongáis* bien con Dios y le *supliquéis* perdone *vuestros pecados*" (206)
(g) Le dijo su hermano Alonso de Abila: "*Andad* acá, hermana al monesterio de las monjas, que quiero y nos combiene que *seáis* monja y *abéislo* de hazer, donde *seréis* de mí y de todos *vuestros* parientes muy regalada y seruida" (214)

Vosotros is the neologism arising from the addition of *otros* to *vos*, which is used as plural of *tú*. In the fictitious speeches delivered by Moctezuma to his vassals and others in the crowd, *vosotros* appears as a subject pronoun, *os* as an object pronoun, and *vuestros /as* as possessive adjectives. All parts of speech are unambigoulsy plural.
(a) "¿Para qué *tornáis bosotros* otra uez a benir acá? ¿Ques lo que *queréis*?" (108)
(b) ¿Por demás es *vuestra* venida. Ya no haré más cuenta de México y para siempre *os* dejo. No terné más cargo de *vosotros* ni de *vuestro* rey Monteçuma. *Apar-*

taos de mí, que no quiero hazer lo que me *pedís* ni el que me pide. *Bolbeos* y *mirad* a México" (108)

(c) Yo *os* beo con mis ojos (...) beo *vuestra* cara y cuerpo y jente que con *bos* viene (122)

(c) ¿De dónde *abéis* benido? (...) Ellas *os* trujeron (122)

(d) Qué *abíades* de bolber a reynar en estos reynos y *os auyades* de sentar en *vuestra* silla y trono (122)

(e) Se subió al terrado y les hizo esta plática: "Hijos míos y mis queridos basallos (...), a quien los españoles mataron en la fiesta y sacrifiçio que se hazía a *vuestro* deboto ydolo Huitzilibuchcatl. La qual mortandad no fue por orden del gran señor y capitán como *auéis* bisto. CreØ del [de él que él] que *os* bengará y hará justicia. Y io en *vuestro* nombre se la pediré. *Doléos* de mí, questoy preso, y de los que por *vosotros* mueren en esta guerra; y de nuestros biejos y niños, que todos hemos de morir si *vuestra* yra no se aplaca" (129)

6.3.6 *Vuesa(s) merced(es)*

Vuestra merced and *vuesa merced* agree with the verb in the 3rd person singular as in (a), (b) and the second part of (c). Both pronouns function as an object of preposition, can be masculine or feminine, and can take a direct object in LE, as in item (h). Similarly, *vuesas mercedes* can appear as an overt pronoun as in (d) through (f) or as a null subject as in (h). It can also function as an object of preposition as in the first part of (c), second part of (d), and first part of (i).

(a) "Esta no *puede vuesa merçed* llevar (201)
(b) "No es tiempo este, señor que *haga vuesa merced* eso, sino que mire por su ánima" (211)
(c) Aquellos señores llaman a *vuesa merced*. Y el luego pidió la capa y la espada y se la trujeron. Y le dijo: "No *puede vuesa merced* llevar, porque ba preso" (201)
(d) "señores dom Pedro y dom Baltasar, *oyan vuesas mercedes*: estos señores an sentenciado a *vuesas merçedes* y es ésta la sentencia" (226-7)
(e) *Vuesas mercedes se aprovechen* desta poca de vida que les queda (227)
(f) "ténganle *uuesas mercedes* y hagan sus dilijencias" (227)
(g) Aquellos señores llaman a *vuesa merced*. Y el luego pidió la capa y la espada y se la trujeron. Y le dijo: "No *puede vuesa merced* llevar, porque ba preso" (201)
(h) "¡Señores, *encomienden* a Dios a estos caballeros, que ellos dizen que mueren justamente! (211)
(i) "Me mandaron llevase *a vuesa merçed preso* y como a tal *le* llevaré" (201)

6.3.7 Use of imperfect subjunctive

One of the remarkable traits of medieval Spanish was the use of <ss> representing the voiceless apico-alveolar fricative, a spelling that was irregularly preserved in the imperfect subjunctive beyond the second generation. Suárez de Peralta used consistently single <s> in all cases.
(a) para que los *encaminase* a la buena tierra y les *siruiese* de lengua (95)
(b) que le *escondiesen* [a Monteçuma] en el ymfierno, y en el paraíso terrenal o en la casa del sol (103)
(c) que (...) *suplicasen* a Nuestra Señorar los *fauoresçiese* y que ellos (...) se *animasen* (97)
(e) enbió (...) echizeros y agoreros para que *hiziesen* todo el mal que *pudiesen a* los españoles y les *enechizasen* de manera que *emfermasen* y *muriesen* todos (102)
(f) les mandó *trujesen* biem en la memoria y no se les *olbidase* nada que ellos *biesen* y su dios les *dijese* y les *mandase* (101)

6.3.8 Conditional sentences ending with –RA

Like the letter writers mentioned in the previous section, Suárez de Peralta still uses the imperfect subjunctive ending in –RA in conditional sentences with protasis (conditional clause) and apodosis (main clause), as in items (a), (b), and (c).
(a) si *durara* gobernando lo que biuió, *fuera* de muncha ymportançia para la tierra (137)
(b) Si dom Martín Cortés, segundo Masqués del Balle, *permaneçiera* en la Nueba España, que della no *saliera* ni le *sucediera* el negocio que le sucedió de tanta desgracia, *fuera* de los más ricos señores d'España (138)
(c) Si él *procediera* diferente de lo que proçedió, el *permançiera* en la tierra y *fuera* el más rico de España (185)

6.3.9 Discourse markers, idiomatic expressions and other features

Suárez de Peralta used discourse markers, idiomatic expressions and features that at present are considered popular or colloquial. The marker *dizque* is not too frequent but it is identical to that used by the first generation and by today's speakers, as in sentences (a) through (c).
(a) le dijo el gouernador negro al cauallero que le quería mostrar su casa, la cual *diz que* era como de negros (76)

(b) Y destas cosas *diz que* dezía munchas (236)
(c) fuese con Hernando Cortés hasta el aposento del adelantado, el qual estaua muy descuydado y aun *dizque* dormido (84)

While the discourse marker *dizque* has spread all over the continent, other variants remained in certain regions. This is the case of the definite article added to first names and surnames, which is unusual in the Central Highlands, but common in the Mexican northern region and Central America.
(a) *El Baltasar de Aguilar* aún no estaba siguro hasta que bió salir al secretario (227)
(b) Preso *el Baltasar de Sotelo*, dierom abiso a los juezes (230)
(c) *El Sotelo* sacó un perdóm destos (230)

Some other idiomatic expressions were spread across New Spain and across social strata, for example, *cuantimás* ('and there's more') as in (a), and *de veras* ('really', 'honestly') as in (b) through (d).
(a) *Quantimás* que dizen estauan baylando y cantando (133)
(b) Que muy *deberas* suplicasen a Nuestra Señora los fauoresçiese (97)
(c) Ellos pagaron las burlas muy *de beras* (163)
(d) Para quel no se declarara tan *deberas* contra ellos (195)

Finally, the adjective *lindo* ('nice', 'pretty') is at present associated mostly with feminine discourse, but for Suárez de Peralta it was a modifier associated with pleasantness, legitimacy and masculinity (see Cuervo 1902/1954).
(a) *Lindísimo* gobernador, sin jénero ninguno de yntereses (170)
(b) El era muy *lindo ombre* (171)
(c) Hizo donde se corriese un toril *muy lindo* (172)
(d) que le virrey le viese correr y tener sus adereços *muy limdos* (172)
(e) Era un hombre de *muy lindo talle* (245)
(f) El rostro le tenía *muy lindo* (206)

6.3.10 References to ethnicity

Because Suárez de Peralta belonged to the second generation of Spanish speakers, he was able to observe the ethnic changes resulting from contact experienced by Indians and Spaniards; from his viewpoint, the former had acquired traits that distinguished them from the latter. The author referred to culture and language contact, as in (a) and (b).
(a) está ya tan *españolada* [la gente] que en munchas cosas nos semejan (58)

(b) están ya *tan españolados* y admitidos en los tratos y contratos con los cristianos, que en ellos se hallan munchos oficios mecánicos y otros de aprovechamiento (122)

6.4 Linguistic documents: the Gulf

The documents 24-48 (pp. 88-155) belonging to the second part of the 16th century (1558-1598) and representing the Gulf region (DLNE-EG, 2008) shed light on the different trends, which are similar to those of the Central Highlands and also similar to those of the first part of the 16th century. The medieval sibilant <ç> continues to appear according to etymological norms, as in *ençima, serviçio, ofiçio, Gonçalez, provinçial, oçeano, exerçiçio, negoçio* (93-94), spelling that is used through the end of the century: *veneraçion, açertado,* (97), *espeçial, oraçiones* (103), *conçiençia* (105), *naçer* (107), *purificacion* (108), *çiudad, alguaçil* (123). By the same token, the old grapheme <z> is preserved in *juez, vezino* (91), *fortaleza, dezir* (110), *paz, hizo* (121), *izquierda* (128), etc. Also, following medieval spelling standards, the sequence –sc– appears in *padesçen* (111), *caresçiendo* (152). Finally, the grapheme <z> alternates with <ç> in *dezia* and *deçía*, while <z> begins to appear where it does not correspond etymologically, as in *azero, prozeso* (54-55) *paresze* (56) *rezio* (66) *zelo* (97), *avizadme,* (83), *rezelo* (121), *cozina* (121), *regozijo* (129), *zielo* (133), *favorezido* (133), *suzeda* (134), *setezientos* (133), *suzzeso* (142), *rezebido* (145), *conozerá* (151), *zercan* (146), *cárzel* (145), etc. Although in the Gulf the grapheme <z> does not prevail, it is a frequent practice. As the century goes on, -ss- reappears in words that normally do not have it as in *quissiese* (74), while <-ss->alternates with single <-s-> as in *pasó* and *passó* (106), *confesado* and *confessaba* (108), *comisario* and *comissario* (123), *cassa* (142), *ssabe* (143). Finally, the cases of *seseo* are very few: *nesesario* (101), *veses* (121), *agradesco* (146); there are also rare cases of *ceceo* as in *çufria* (91), *ençuçiar* (149), and one truly rare item revealing aspiration of sibilant in intervocalic position as in *favoreherá* (147). Tables 6.2A and 6.2B show the total number of sibilant graphemes and their distribution in percentages.

In sum, with respect to the use of the sibilants, 16th century texts point to varied trends rather than to one single trend. The paucity of -ss- indicates that the voiceless apical sibilant had converged with its corresponding voiced -s-. From the variants of the graphemes it can be inferred that there were variants of pronunciation: (1) Spanish speakers of northern and central regions might have distinguished the two points of articulation, that is, apical versus dental; (2) the frequent use of <z> in intervocalic position could indicate vestiges of voicing; (3) some other Spanish speakers exchanged <ç> and <z>, and might have been inclined to use moderate *ceceo-zezeo* with the different sub-variants (*siseante or ciceante*) that preceded *seseo*, though this type of pronunciation was not consolidated among educated speakers of any region because since early in the 16th century it was identified with marginal groups like the gypsies (Catalán 1956-57, 1957). Some other speakers preferred to use full-fledge *seseo* and fused the four sibilants. Finally, it is possible to speculate that some Spanish speakers did distinguish the sibilants in writing according to their educational profile, but their speech differed from the writing perhaps because they empathize–consciously or unconsciously–with the speakers already acclimatized in New Spain.

6.4.1 Miscellaneous traits in the Gulf

Like the writers from the Central Highlands, those from the Gulf exhibit some of the traits that in this study are considered popular residual variants; they are not optimal because they may been relegated to use in rural, "rurban" or marginal communities that have been distant from mainstream education and modern socio-economic development The most frequent variants from this sub-sample appear in (1) while the rest may (re)appear in isolated coastal communities.

(1) Writers hesitate between open and close vowels as in the following words: *avezados* (88) modern *avisados*; *seguiente* (88) modern *siguiente*; *dizía* (91) modern *decía*; *escrebí* (88) modern *escribí*; *besitar* (151) modern *visitar*; *obidiente* (153), modern *obediente*; *reszebí* (110) and *rezebí* (135) modern *recibí*. The conjunction *o* ('or') as in *tres o cuatro*, is reinterpreted as a close vowel *u* as in "*han de venir Moreno hu otra persona*" (103) and "*ttres hu quatro pares de botillas*" (103).

(2) They also aspirate non-etymological H as in *heran* (89), *hordinario* (93, 123), *hacá* (101), *horden* (92), *hante* (105), *hera* (119), *harriero* (118), *hedad* (139), *husurpar* (124), *honzas* (126),), *hordénelo* (143).

(3) Aspiration of initial F- as in *hebrero* (125) (< *febrero*) is not too common but seems to be an extension of aspiration in initial position. It also appears in intervocalic position, as in *caher, trahernos* (96), *mahiz* (113), and in the phrases such as *hera huidor* (119). Etymological H is present in the following words: *huidores, hacienda* (115), *hozicos* (127), *honor* (129), *hallo* (133), *hijo* (143), *hanegas* (116), and in the adjective *harto*, which is normally placed before a noun as in *hartos bienes* (146), *hartas cosas* (96), and functions as an intensifier.

(4) The interchange of liquid consonants, which is common along coastal areas, is rare in New Spain. In EG 37, 1585 (Veracruz), the scribe interchanged liquids /r/ and /l/ in *çelebro* (127) [cerebro] and *calcañales* [carcañales] (128). The tendency to substitute a consonant with /-l-/ appears in *colodrillo* (128) [cocodrilo].

(5) The verb TRAER ('to bring') appears with both old and modern spellings, as in (a) through (c). The medieval Spanish form of the verb VER ('to see') *vido* was used when the speaker happened to be an eyewitness of a revelant event or was staring at someone, as in (d) and (e). Finally, with the verb REÍR, some writers used the epenthetic palatal <y>, as in (f).

(a) *truxo* a esta villa otra esclava (94)
(b) lo *traxeron* a Mexico (118)
(c) me *trajo* la respuesta (142)
(d) el dicho Gonzalo d'Avila miró a él, y *vido* estar una cruz encima (106)
(e) *vido* después cómo la metió en el aposento (138)
(f) se *riyeron* de ver que salía descolorido (130).

6.4.2 The system of pronouns of address: *tú, vos, vosotros, vuestra merced, su merced*

At the end of the 16th century, the system of pronouns of address was sufficiently diversified so as to render three sets of dyads. The first one consisted of the two traditional pronouns, *tú* and *vos*, which were allocated along the [+ intimate informal] domains with a plural which was a neologism made up of *vos + otros*. The second set is also a neologism derived from the possessive adjective of *vos*, which rendered *vuestra merced* in singular and *vuestras mercedes* in plural. The third dyad, not too frequently used in these documents, was *su merced* and *sus mercedes*.

Singular informal: The examples in singular informal appear with the null subject *vos* and the corresponding diphthongized conjugations in (a), (b), (c), (e) and (g). The null subject *tú* appears with its corresponding paradigmatic forms in (d). Another example appears in the last part of example (e), which mixes the reduced form *hicistes* with the indirect object pronoun *os*.

(a) "señor, *no digáys* eso, que Nuestro Señor es misericordioso y *os* puede perdonar a *vos* y a todo el mundo, por mucho pecados que *ayáis* fecho" (105)
(b) el dicho Gonzalo dÁvila miró a él, y vido estar una cruz ençima, y alçó la mano señalando la cruz y dixo dos veces: "aý *estáys*, aý *estáys*" (106)
(c) "¿no me *queréys* dar tamemes?, que me quiero yr" (88)
(d) "señor, no hay agora indios, mañana *te yrás*, no *tengas* tanta priesa" (88)
(e) asiéndole de la manga de un capotillo que traía cubierto le dixo: "¿negro, y no *os* e mandado que *hagáis* de hozicos todo lo que *os* mandaren los españoles questán en mi casa?" y el respondió que ansí era, y este confessante rreffirió:

"pues ¿cómo no *hiçistes* [or hicisteis] lo que esta mañana *os* mandó Luis?" (128)
(f) Martín Ochoa (...) dixo al dicho negro: "*anda, vete, quítate* de aý" (128)
(g) "¡*callad!*, señora, no *lloréys* ni *tengáys* pena que yo *os* trataré mejor que don Pero Leño" (130)

Singular formal: The innovative pronouns *vuestra merced* (abbreviated *v.m.* or *v.md.*) and *su merced* are used as a subject as in items (a) through (d). Th common usage appears in letters between young and older adults, i.e. children to parents, nephews and nieces to uncles, and other family members. Both pronouns function as an object preposition as in (e) through (k). They agree with all verb forms corresponding to 3rd singular pronouns *él* and *ella* as in (a) through (d); semantically they correspond to the 2nd person, whereas the possessive adjective also corresponds to the 3rd person singular and plural (*su* and *sus*) as in (g) and (k).
(a) dixo *su merçed* estar informado (90)
(b) ansí *su merçed* no puede ni deve proçeder (126)
(c) *V.m.* dé horden como se hagan un par de varriles descabeche (143)
(d) "bien sabe *vuestra merced* que yo fuy alcalde" (124)
(e) avía benido en casa *de su merced* a entregarle al negro (125)
(f) Señor padre. Pena rezibo en ver que se pasen los años (...) y no vea *de v. md.* letra ninguna (132)
(g) *De v. md. su* humilde hijo, Francisco [in the closing] (136)
(h) De lo que toca al negocio de mi hermano yo no trataré *a v.m.* cosa ninguna (103)
(i) "señor, yo vengo acá a tomar consejo *con vuestra merced*" (124)
(j) ninguna cossa me tiene tan afligida como no saber de la salud *de v.m.* y carezer de *su* vista (143)
(k) Ubediente hija *de v.md.* que *sus* manos vessa (143-144)

Plural informal and formal: In peninsular Spanish the corresponding plural pronoun of *tú* is *vosotros*, exemplified in (a) and (b). In Doc. 24, 1558, *vosotros* appears with its paradigmatic verb forms and the corresponding object *os*. The informal context and domains of *vosotros* contrasts with the formality of *vuestras mercedes*, a pronoun that agrees with the conjugated forms of the 3rd person plural pronouns, *ellos* and *ellas*. In contrast, in Doc. 33, 1589, the letter of Francisco Olivares de Collazos to his father, he addressed his father and mother with *vuestras mercedes* as in (c) and (d). The corresponding object pronouns of *vuestras mercedes* is [+ plural masculine] *los*, which covers both genders as in (c). Doc 42, 1594 is the letter drafted by a scribe of a mulatto woman who requested support from her parents as in (e) and (f).

(a) "*Vosotros estáys* abezados de los frayles que son unos hombres mentirosos y no *oyáis* lo que *os* dizen, que *os* mienten en lo que *os* dizen e predican" (88)
(b) "Sí, quiero yrme luego, que a *vosotros os* deven de aver mandado los frayles que no *déys* tamemes (88)
(c) mi desinio es el año que viene que vaia por *vuestras mercedes* y *los* traiga donde yo estoi (132)
(d) no me falta (...) sino ver en esta casa a *vuestras mercedes* en la qual tengo ya trazado la vivienda de *vuestras mercedes* y mía (134)
(e) Una de *vuestras mercedes* rezebí con el correo el viernes a medio dia (145)
(f) aunque *vuestras mercedes* no se aquerdan en sus cartas ymbiarme a deçir cómo están (146)

Mixed forms: The conjugations corresponding to *vuestras mercedes* were occasionally mixed with the object pronoun that corresponds to *vos*. This rare case appears in Doc. 32, 1572 which is a sermon delivered by Friar Melchor as in (a). Singular *voseo* occurred in (b) when the priest was scolding the young male belonging to the ethnic group known as *criollos* (children of Spaniards born in New Spain).
(a) "Hermanos, *procuren* de poner *vuestros* coraçones con Dios, que esto del açotaros poco inporta" (108)
(b) el padre vicario se levantó y dixo [al joven criollo]: ¡*calla!*, [or *callad*] que *soys* muy desvergonçado, y que el fraile dixo en presençia de los yndios y españoles que allí estaban: "*mentís* como ruin hombre", y que entonces le asió el padre vicario y dijo: "*sé* [or *sed*] preso, *andad* a la cárcel de un mal fraile, que *vos* no *andáis* para menos" (138)

Reverence: The honorifics *vuestro* and *vuestra* (possessive adjectives derived from *vos*) were used to address individuals occupying positions of power and prestige, as in (a) through (c).
(a) "Aquí se vino a confesar conmigo un seglar que *vuestra reverencia* avia confesado..." (109)
(b) Conbendría muncho a *vuestro real servicio* que desta tierra obiese más cantidad de gente (110)
(c) sin liçençia de *vuestra real justiçia* (111)

The variety of forms of address used during the 16th century reveals the miscellaneous situations in which Spanish speakers were involved and intermingled with other Spanish speakers and with the castes, who also acquired or learned the pronouns of address. In some cases the speakers' roles were symmetrical, while in others a wide social distance was marked by the use of honorifics, which were also extremely diverse. The epistolary genre is the most convenient to examine the patterns of pronouns of address from generation to generation and in general throughout the colonial period.

6.4.3 Clitic pronouns as direct objects

The use of LE as a direct [+ animate singular masculine] object pronoun does not differ from the trends of the first half of 16th century or from those of the Central Highlands. The subsample below lists 22 cases of LE and only 9 cases of LO. With the verb TRAER, the authors use both LO and LE, as in items (g) and (l), while the verb ESCAPAR is used as transitive in item (j).

(a) quando ven los yndios algún conquistador, *lo* salen a reçebir con flores (89)
(b) le dio una puñalada en los pechos, de que *lo* mató [a Juan] (93)
(c) El señor Dios *lo* encamine [a Vuestra Majestad] como él sea servido (98)
(d) ablarán a Pedro de Murga para que **le reçiban** en la nao (102)
(e) Juan Gomez escribe a v. m. sobre ello y el buen deseo que tiene de trabajar para **librarle** [al hermano del autor de la carta] (103)
(f) vino a mí pensando que yo [fray Melchor] **le avía de absolver** [a un seglar] (108)
(g) **le traxo** tan enfermo de allá que dentro de un día que llegó murió (114)
(h) murió en Xalapa, camino de la Beracruz, que **le enbiaron** [a Antón Golofe] a sus negoçios fuera del yngenyo (118)
(i) hera negro ageno y *teníalo* Gerónimo Pérez (118)
(j) bendió su negro al padre Juan de la Cruz, y *lo* escapó y traspusyeron (118)
(k) prestó a Juanillo, criollo (...) a Francisco Bravo para que **le sirviese**, y **le mandaron** domar un potro, el qual potro le dio una coz que *lo* mató [a Juanillo] (118)
(l) quando Françisco Brabo pasó por allí y *lo* halló tan malo, *lo* traxo a la hazienda (119)
(m) le mandó echar los grillos al sobre dicho guardián, y **prenderle** y quitar la comida (121)
(n) Que me yniba del conoçimiento del dicho negro y *lo* entregue a vuestra señoría (123)
(o) el dicho negro nunca más se levantó, de ahí **le llevaron** a una cama, y hizo llamar este conffesante al doctor Bravo y a Mendoza, çirujano, para que **le biesen** y **le bieron** (128)
(p) pusieron en un palo al dicho Pedro Leño para que **le viniesen a encontrar** (130)

(q) **le rezebí** [a un conocido] en mi gracia con aditamento que lo pasado, pasado (135)
(r) nunca **le a visto** *traer* ábito negro sino blanco, y que tenía sospecha que no era fraile porque **le veya andar** muy liviano, escandalizando a la gente natural y española que **le vía y trataba** (137)
(s) como él era sabio **le avian aborreçido** [al fraile] (...) y que así hazían a todos (138)
(t) el bachiller Bartolomé Barriga (...), **le llevó** con mucha gente a la yglesia y **le metió** en la sacristía [al fraile] (138-9)
(u) **le tuvo** arrinconado, hasta que otro llegó y **le asió** [al fraile]. Y luego el bachiller Barriga **le llevó** a la cárcel (139)

6.4.4 Imperfect subjunctive: variations of –SE and –RA

The second generation of Spanish speakers residing in the Gulf region follow the syntactic patterns used by Hernán Cortés and other representatives of the first generation (see 4.4.7). The ending in –SE prevails in the second half of the 16th century in subordinate clauses preceded by a verb in indicative and in conditional SI- clauses, but it also alternated with the form in –RA.

(a) dería verdad de lo que *supiesen* e les *fuese* preguntado (87)
(b) Francisco Hernandes (...) fue a casa de este testigo y le dixo que le *diesen* tamemes (87)
(c) se dió provisión real para que libremente *pudiesen* usar dellos (96)
(d) está avisado de hacá que se les *diese* todo recaudo (101)
(e) todos allí le dixeron que *mirase* lo que dezía (105)
(f) que si el diablo *viniese*, que poco aprovecharía estar allí la cruz (106)
(g) como si *dijera*: "no nos aprovecha que *encarnara* ni que *naciera*..." (109)
(h) [Rodrigo de Escalona] hizo pregonar que no *diesen* a los religiosos servicio sin su mandado ni menos *acudiesen* a reparar la iglesia, aunque se *estuviese* cayendo (121)
(i) podría correr rriesgo mi vida si no se *rremediasse* con el mandamiento (152)
(j) ynoçentemente la llamó y le dixo que se *fuera* (138)

6.4.5 Lexical items referring to ethnicity

Throughout the second half of the 16th century the issue of indigenous slavery was still debated but there were no deliberations about the slavery of blacks. In a few decades the discourse about African descendants unfolded in two main strains. A reference to blacks was simply a form of precise identification though most individuals were categorized by age, regional origin, ethnicity, marital status, slave master, and physical defects. On occasion, they were also distinguished by their perceived proficiency in Spanish for which the word *ladino* was used in phrases like "*negro ladino*", which meant Spanish-speaking black in item (n) or "*indio ladino*" (Spanish-speaking Indian). The ethnic label *ladino* assigned to Sephardic Jews was extended to the castes emerging in New Spain.

(a) riñó e obo paçión a Juan, *negro esclavo* de su Majestad Real (93)
(b) Van con los novillos quantos ay *negros y mulatos, indios y españoles* (99)
(c) Y ansí quedan a la muerte *un negro y dos mulatos y una negra* (99)
(d) Más ha de pagar *los más negros* que murieron por sacallos fuera de las haziendas (117)
(e) lo que se aberiguare *questos negros* valían (117)
(f) hizo dejarretear *un negro* de los de su señoría (119)
(g) ansy queda *el negro manco* y syn ser de provecho (119)
(h) Juanillo, *criollo*, de hedad de quinze años y *los otros negros* (118)
(j) que me yniba del conocimiento del *dicho negro* y lo entregue a vuestra señoría (123)
(k) Y hera *negro ageno* y teníalo Gerónimo Péres (118)
(l) *quatro negros y una negra* que andaban echos cimarromes (123)
(m) procedí contra *los negros culpados* y los castigué (124)
(n) y por su esclavo a Juan, *negro ladino*, llamado Juan de Tierra Congo, casado con una *negra llamada* Leonor ansimismo *esclava* deste confesante (127)

6.5 More examples from the second generation

The analysis of Friar Juan de Córdoba's documents (1578) highlights the contrast between Castile and Toledo in the south, which had maintained the voicing and voiceless opposition in an era in which Castile and the north had lost it. Juan de Córdoba, who spent all his life in New Spain, was either from Toledo or from Córdoba but distinguished <c> and <z>, as in ynformaçión, merçed, neçesidad, obligaçion, provança as opposed to hiziesen, maíz, parezco. Córdoba also aspirated initial F- as in hago, hará, hizo, hanega. Another writer was Friar Diego de Carvajal, whose document (1577) includes the following words: marvedí, las casa reales, esterelidad, Generar instead of maravedí, las casas reales, esterilidad, and General. His traits reveal the Andalusian or New World neutralization of /-l/ and /-r/ and the simplification of the old pairs of sibilants as in fiansas (< fianzas), nescecidades (< necesidades), and zasón (< sazón). The relevance of the pair of graphemes <s> and <ss> lies in the process of readjustment of the two resulting in its simplification, as in *castigase, esos, llevasen, obedieçiese*, etc. Finally, the aspiration is marked by the use of the grapheme H as in *hazer, contrahecho, hambre, hasta* (Frago Gracia 1987).

6.6 Conclusions

Although eventually it was accepted by a significant majority of speakers, *seseo* was moderate in 16th century documents. In the initial stages of Castilian / Andalusian development *seseo* appeared to be irregularly spread throughout the New World until it became the norm in spoken Spanish. The grapheme <s> representing *seseo* was scarce in the 16th century and competed with other graphemes, a fact that is conducive to put forward alternate theories of sibilant pronunciation. The features defining New World Spanish can be examined along a continuum of residual distribution.

(1) Those that have remained in vast zones of Spanish-speaking Latin America, i.e. *seseo* and /-s/ deletion and aspiration in implosive and final position may be considered optimal, though in Mexican Colonial Spanish /s/ weakening is rare. This means that its preservation in all positions must have been the norm amongst the vast majority of writers who immigrated to New Spain. The convergence of the sibilants prevailed in the entire continent, whereas weakening of [s] survived in many regions in variation with the full pronunciation. In the modern varieties of Latin American Spanish, aspiration of final *-s* is not stigmatized in formal domains as long as it occurs in the prescribed environment and speakers do not incur in hypercorrection.

(2) *Leísmo* prevailed in the 16th century at the rate of two-thirds versus one-third. The alternate use of clitics LO and LE validates the theories of koineization since the pro-etymological forms and the *leísta* forms co-occurred in the emerging colonial society. The formality that defined the topics and styles of the first generation gradually deteriorated and paved the way for innovations of the clitic LE and its introduction in newer colloquial registers, where LE may appear as a dangling object, e.g. ("*le* tenía muy lindo el rostro"). When all the tokens of LE and LO are added, it is clear that the *leístas* from northern-central Spain prevailed in bureaucratic, governmental and ecclesiastic positions.

(3) *Voseo* was rare in New Spain, and for this reason, it did not have continuity in the following centuries, though it was present in other regions of the New World and remained vital for the following centuries. *Tú* emerged timidly in New Spain but *vuestra merced* superseded all forms of address in the family domain and interpersonal relationships.

(4) The choice of imperfect subjunctive endings representing peninsular Spanish prevailed in the Central Highlands and the Gulf of Mexico; the use of –RA in the protasis of conditional sentences and in other contexts where subjunctive is categorical was advancing slowly.

(5) Aspiration of initial F- and deletion of –d– and –d appear at low frequencies in both the Central Highlands and the Gulf. The first generation of speakers and writers replicated the features of their original dialects at varying degrees, while variation was gradually intensified not without going over an intermediate stage of instability represented by the second generation, which shows signs of vacillating standards in writing.

Tables 6.2A and 6.2B show the distribution of medieval Spanish graphemes in both regions, where the Romance grapheme <ç> appears correctly written in the vast majority of documents; it is followed by <z> and <s>, whereas the use of <ss> lags far behind in all the cells. The items in which *seseo* and *ceceo* appeared comprised a fraction of all possible spellings and are not computed in these subsamples. When the tokens of Tables 6.2A and 62B are added, the patterns of the sibilants model those of the first generation, except for the use of <z>, which advances because writers began to identify the sibilants <ç> and <z> as though they were equivalent. Table 6.2C shows the summary of the two periods in both regions. When the subtotals in Tables 4.5A and 4.5B are added to the subtotals in Tables 6.2A and 6.3B, the final total for the 16th century amounts to 3,374 tokens, the vast majority of which correspond to the grapheme <ç>.

Table 6.2A: Traditional graphemes: Second half of the 16th century: Central Highlands

Period	<s>	<ss>	<ç>	<z>	Total
1562-1585	112 (12.19 %)	31 (3.37 %)	562 (61.15 %)	214 (23.29 %)	= 919 (100 %)

Table 6.2B: Traditional graphemes: Second half of the 16th century: The Gulf

Period	<s>	<ss>	<ç>	<z>	Total
1558-1598	79 (14.39%)	26 (4.73%)	286 (52.09%)	158 (28.78%)	= 549 (100%)

Table 6.2C: Summary: Traditional graphemes in the 16th century (the two regions)

Period	<s>	<ss>	<ç>	<z>	Total
1520-1598	494 (14.64%)	152 (4.50%)	1990 (58.98%)	738 (21.87%)	= 3374 (100%)

During the second part of the 16th century the distribution of verbal clitics LE and LO is similar to the distribution of the first three decades, when the anti-etymological pronoun LE had an advantage over the alternate LO, the former representing speakers from northern-central regions and those from other regions who were educated under Castilian standards. The use of these two variants in the emerging environment is an indicator of the inter-dialect contact that preceded the process of accommodation. The use of the clitics in the second half of the 16th century is identical to the rates observed in the first half (see Tables 4.6 and 6.3A). When all the tokens of the 16th century are examined in the summary of Table 6.3B, it is clear there is no difference between the first and the second generation.

Table 6.3A: LE and LO: Second half of the 16th century

Region	LE	LO
Altiplano C.	23 / 38	15 / 38
El Golfo	38 / 54	16 / 54
Total = 92	61 (66.30%)	31 (33.69%)

Table 6.3B: Summary: LE and LO in the 16th century

Region	LE	LO
Altiplano C.	60 / 90	30 / 90
El Golfo	60 / 91	31 / 91
Total = 181	120 (66.29%)	61 (33.70%)

The calculation of pronouns of address includes the subjects, corresponding verb forms, possessive adjectives agreeing with the subject, the direct objects, and the objects of preposition. This aids in distinguishing the use of mixed forms, which in the Mexican colonial subsamples are rare. *Vos* and the derived innovation *vuestra merced* clearly prevailed in this century, while *tú* and *su merced* were incipient. *Vosotros* appears 5 times as singular and 16 times as plural, while *vuestras mercedes* and *sus mercedes* are used at low rates in the Gulf region. Tables 6.4A and 6.4B show a similar distribution of singular pronouns, where more than one-half correspond to *vuestra merced*. In addition, Table 6.4C shows that *vuestras mercedes* was ahead of the other plural forms. In colloquial registers, however, *vos* was preferred over *tú* in the Central Highlands due perhaps to the length and the quantity of the documents examined. When the tokens of the two regions are added, *vos* prevails over *tú* by a large margin. In both singular and plural, personal pronouns are implicit with no need for disambiguation, provided the context is unanmbiguos. In Doc. EG 30 (1568), *sus mercedes* is an overt subject 3 times; it is however implicit in verb paradigms, and it is therefore omitted 21 times because the author of the letter was consistently addressing her parents and other relatives as a collective entity (see Table 6.4C).

Table 6.4A: Singular pronouns in the second half of 16th century

Region	Vos	Tú	V. Md.	S. Md.
Altiplano C.	313	12	287	2
El Golfo	43	7	140	11
Total = 815	356 (43.68%)	19 (2.33%)	427 (52.39%)	13 (1.59%)

Table 6.4B: Summary: Singular pronouns in the 16th century

Region	Vos	Tú	V. Md.	S. Md.
Altiplano C.	328	12	298	2
El Golfo	46	7	269	11
Total = 973	374 (38.43%)	19 (1.95%)	567 (58.27%)	13 (1.33%)

Table 6.4C: Plural pronouns in the second half of 16th century

Region	Vosotros	Vs. Ms.	Ss. Mds.
Altiplano C.	0	18	0
El Golfo	16	18	3 + 21
Total = 76	16	36	24
	(21.05%)	(47.36%)	(31.57%)

Finally, the imperfect subjunctive variant–SE had a robust beginning in the 16th century, while the variant –RA was used in a minority of cases. Tables 6.5A and 6.5B show the attrition rates of –SE in the Central Highlands and in the Gulf, respectively. In addition, Table 6.5C shows the comparative summary of the two regions, where the –SE form prevailed in traditional contexts where imperfect subjunctive is categorical. At the same time the –RA form was struggling to find its own functions as a contender of the –SE form. This alternation may represent the most radical type of morpho-syntactic attrition, which eventually augmented the differentiation between peninsular and New World Spanish. The difference between the Central Highlands and the Gulf lies in the overwhelming use of –SE in the first half of the 16th century (at 92%), a period stamped by the contributions of prominent scholars shaping the destiny of New Spain. In the second half of the 16th century –SE declined to 70 percent, while in the Gulf the ending in –SE remained under 90 percent in both periods (see Table 6.5A).

Table 6.5A: Use of –SE and –RA in the Central Highlands in percentages

Period	–SE forms	–RA forms in protasis	Other uses of –RA	Total tokens
1525-1549	92% / 252	5.5% / 16	2.5% / 7	275
1550-1599	70% / 98	13.5% / 19	16.5% / 23	140

Source: Acevedo (1997: 99, 108)

Table 6.5B: Use of –SE and –RA in the Gulf in percentages

Period	–SE forms	–RA forms in protasis	Other uses of –RA	Total tokens
1520-1555	78 / 90 (86.66 %)	9 / 90 (10.0 %)	3 / 90 (3.33 %)	90
1558-1598	89 / 103 (86.4 %)	3 / 103 (2.91 %)	11 / 103 (10.67 %)	103

Table 6.5C: Summary: Uses of –SE and –RA in the two regions

Region	–SE forms	–RA forms in protasis	Other uses of –RA	Total tokens
Altiplano C.	350 / 415 (84.33 %)	35 / 415 (8.43 %)	30 / 415 (7.22 %)	415
El Golfo	167 / 193 (86.52 %)	12 / 193 (5.21 %)	14 / 193 (7.5 %)	193
Totals =	517 / 608 (85.3 %)	47 / 608 (7.73 %)	44 / 608 (7.23 %)	608 (100 %)

Chapter 7
Religion, bilingualism and acculturation

7.1 Religion as a driving force

This chapter deals with the numerous interrelationships between religion, language and ethnicity, the first one considered herein an external factor impinging on the development of indigenous languages, on elite bilingualism amongst speakers of indigenous languages, and on the creation of ethnicity within a framework of categorical adscription. Religion was the driving force in the Iberian Peninsula for Christian resistance has a steady record first during the invasion of the Visigoths and immediately after with the prolonged incursions of the Muslims in Spain. In the history of Spanish, Christian confrontation and the rise of Castilian are inseparable inasmuch as Castilians led the movement of expulsion of non-Christian groups during the *Reconquista*. Spanish speakers were accustomed to fighting the infidels; those who were not engaged in real battles were used to hearing about religious wars; still some others knew first hand of the conversion process that consequently affected the life of many individuals. The religious endeavors of the mendicant orders assigned to New Spain illustrate, too, the accomplishments in the areas of language learning and teaching, translation of sacred texts, lexicography, and descriptive grammars, all these endeavors oriented towards the major challenge posed by conversion. There is agreement in that all these scholarly pursuits flourished in a new environment following the initial catastrophe, which entailed the defeat of the Aztecs and the destruction of the Aztec Empire. The Mexican Renaissance in the realms of history, linguistics and religion began in 1524 and ended ca. 1580 (cf. Hidalgo 2006a).

This chapter also explores the language contact situation that ensued as a result of the intermingling of Spanish speakers and speakers of indigenous languages. The most significant group acquiring or learning Spanish as a second language were the Nahuas inhabiting the Valley of Mexico. Speakers of indigenous languages were first exposed to Spanish via informal encounters with Spanish speakers who settled in the area of Nahuatl influence and with those who were in charge of emergent institutions such as the *encomienda*, the *repartimiento*, and other forms of labor and free employment. Exposure to Spanish did not occur swiftly or massively but slowly and selectively first in religious domains and almost simultaneously in the work domain. Bilingualism amongst members of the indigenous elites was the result of education in the new Christian faith within the cloisters of the mendicant orders. Second, native leaders who were not affiliated with mendicant orders found ways to accommodate themselves to the conditions imposed in the new environs of New Spain, where Spanish speakers built new institutions protected by legislation enacted in both Spain and New Spain. The caciques, *principales* or *señores*, and some other Indian officers were in direct contact with some Spanish speakers from whom they must have learned at least basic Spanish, which was useful to maintain important posts in local governments. Third, the mass of speakers of indigenous languages nonetheless retained their language and forms of organization for about one hundred years. Massive bilingualism was more likely initiated in the 17th century, while vestiges of language contact features are found until the 18th century.

Contact between and among ethnic groups was conducive to miscegenation, which in turn led to the emergence of different socio-ethnic categories: *españoles*, *criollos*, *mestizos*, blacks and mulattoes, among others. The mass of indigenous speakers can be distinguished by their reactions toward the newer multicultural / multilingual situation: some of them were acculturated Indians or *indios ladinos*, and many others were merely resistant to the Spanish language and the institutions and domains in which it was used. Early bilingualism among the elites of Nahua origin has been consistently reported in diverse sources; this contrasts with another type of bilingualism facilitated by the advent of the hacienda as another form of socialization between and among the different ethnic groups. An economic transformation of the colonial period unfolded in the 17th century.

7.2 Population losses and language shift

The reduction of Indian tributaries can be used as a criterion to estimate the losses of speakers of indigenous languages. Language shift was aided by epidemics responsible for large-scale population decline. The most serious epidemics have not been clinically identified (smallpox, typhus, typhoid or measles) because pre-conquest analogues have not been found. Spanish methods of treatment added anemia to the other debilitating consequences of disease. In the Valley of Mexico, the Nahua population declined from a high of 117,270 in 1570 to a low of 22,659 in 1644; about five decades later, in 1692 only 24,566 tributaries were recorded; and in 1742 there were only 37,854. The final estimate before the end of the colony ranges between 47,080 in 1787-1794 and 64,485 in 1797-1804, which represented ten per cent or more of the total tributaries of New Spain (Gibson 1964: 137, 142). The reconstructed data are useful to show the dimensions and directions of language shift. External factors contributing to language shift—other than the losses resulting from disease amongst the speakers of indigenous languages in Mesoamerica—are distinguished as junctures that either accelerated it or delayed it. The glaring reason of language shift was the massive loss of speakers, which in turn caused the realignment of survivors to conditions restructured by the Spanish-speaking newcomers, who found numerous strategies to disenfranchise the non-Hispanic groups from their own cultural traditions and material possessions. Changes to Nahua organization proceeded in strides, going back and forth until the different communities reached high ratios of bilingualism and sufficient Spanish monolinguals to the point that they were no longer considered ethnically Nahuas.

7.3 Factors contributing to maintenance: new political organization

Indians retained memories and their own culture during the first four generations after the conquest. In the 1550's they still knew in detail of the original forms of organization and were able to react accordingly. However, one hundred years later models of organization displaced the aboriginal concepts. By the late 16th century, knowledge of tribal divisions was drawn mainly from legend and historical records. Nine basic ethnic divisions at the time of the Spanish conquest have been identified along with the hierarchy of status in 1519: Mexica, Acolhuaque, Tepaneca, Chalca, Xochimilco, Cuitlahuaca, Mixquica, Culhuaque and Otomi, groups that maintained separate identities, the latter being the only major group of non-Nahuatl origin. In pre-conquest times, miscegenation was not too relevant because ethnic groups preserved separate ethnic affiliations. Migrations, refugee movements, and some systematic inclusion of one group in the area of another resulted in enclaves, not mixtures of populations. Some of the new forms of organization maintained the indigenous together, while others fragmented their communities. After the conquest the surviving groups realigned themselves with their own and initiated a slow process of exogamy with non-Mesoamerican groups leading to boundary delineation and continuity, though the colonial administration altered the original ethnic divisions. Spanish speakers prevailed over ethnic areas because they were in control of conquest, church, *encomienda*, political jurisdictions, and draft labor. The strongest native units were weakened by new relations of power and reinforced at the same time the positions of intermediate groups; the *encomienda* system took advantage of various communities and provinces while the church selected those with a dense population. Also, new jurisdictions created the dependency of a capital town on a surrounding province and vice-versa whereas the labor draft maintained pre-conquest organization where Indian workers were assigned to work according to pre-Hispanic criteria: Mexica, Acolhuaque, Tepaneca and Chalco. Finally, separation continued despite the fact that the Spanish policies favored programs of Indian *congregación* (resettlement), which occasionally resulted in new associations of peoples (Gibson 1964: 22-23, 27).

More recent proposals suggest that the presence of Nahuatl-speaking peoples is crucial to explain how Mesoamerica was organized from the innovations of the Nahuas, whose world vision was fused with the components of other cultures. The end-result was a multiethnic society with different enclaves sharing many of the features of the Nahuas. Throughout centuries of co-existence, cultural continuity prevailed despite the fact that each group maintained its own identity and preserved the same codes that helped them build a temple or perform their rituals. In this context, language was more vulnerable to change than culture. The first *mestizaje* (blood-mixing phenomenon) is the byproduct of this fusion. The second mestizaje occurred when the Spaniards arrived in the region and gave continuity to the process of blood mixing (cf. Duverger 2007). Nahuatl expansion and diffusion go hand in hand insofar as a number of attributes shared by languages of the culture region known as Mesoamerica have been used to categorize a linguistic area. Distribution of shared features suggests that Mesoamerica's development as a linguistic area at least involved the partial diffusion of Nahuatl traits, given its role as a lingua franca, to other languages of the region. This phenomenon might have occurred either at post-contact times or immediately preceding the Nahuatl Post-Classic or the pre-Hispanic era (Brown 2011)

It has been proposed that after the losses of the Aztec Empire, all groups were exposed to changes related to the organization of space according to Spaniards' views, who were more concerned with urban rankings and designated four Valley sites as cities, i.e. Tenochtitlan and Texcoco in 1543, Xochimilco in 1559, and Tacuba in 1564. Smaller entities such as Coyoacan and Tacuba were considered *villas* (villages) while all remaining populations of moderate or large size were considered *pueblos* (towns). This taxonomy derived from Castile, where cities such as Guadalajara or Toledo occupied a rank above villas such as Madrid or Alcala, which outranked the more numerous pueblos. Lesser entities were known as *aldeas* (very small villages) or *lugares* (places). Other institutions such as *cabeceras* referred to the seats or capitals of Indian governments while *sujetos* meant very small villages or places. Subdivisions of towns were called barrios when they were connected to their seats; *estancias* if they were located some distance away in a cluster of Indian dwellings. Larger communities were the seats of Indian government around which a group of nearby villages was nucleated. The Indian *sujeto* became the Spanish village and was subordinate to the seat where the *tlatoani* (native ruler) resided. In post-conquest times, the *tlatoani* principle served as the basis for the colonial seat organization, the center of tribute collection, and the point for the recruitment of labor. When the native system was finally abandoned Spanish institutions gained more control, the Indian nobility lost its authority, and Spaniards reorganized the procedures for tribute collection and labor recruitment (Gibson 1964: 32-34).

The structure of Indian society was reflected in the *encomienda*, a single seat or several seats with villages possessing *tlatoani* or a new seat with one village possessing a discontinuous *tlatoani* tradition or none at all. The number of tributaries in *encomienda* ranged from six to some 20,000. The *encomienda* maintained one group of Indians and their respective *tlatoani* in close contact. The total number of *encomiendas* in the Valley as of the mid-1530's stood at thirty, with an estimated 180,000 tributaries. Indians built the *encomenderos'* houses in Mexico City, where they deposited all goods collected as tribute; they also worked in farming and mining. The *calpixque* logged in tributes in precious metals, grains, textiles, and many other valuable items, which made the *encomenderos* even wealthier. The *encomienda* compressed the Indian social classes, reduced the authority of Indian leaders, and drained the local economy, but it did not annihilate the Indian society. After the 1550's, no new instances of Indian exploitation were found and new *encomiendas* were granted in the 16th and 17th centuries to noble families in Spain or in the colony with all profits remaining in royal hands. Although the New Laws of 1542 were repealed by the *encomenderos* in 1545, the restrictions imposed on the *encomienda* tribute became effective in the 1550's, and in 1570, the *encomenderos* lost the battle to the crown, which finally eliminated the most lucrative grants (Gibson 1964: 58-61, 62-65, 70). The fact that the *encomenderos* did not succeed in making the indigenous permanent or semi-permanent slaves had a dual effect. On the one hand, the Indians were (more or less) free to seek employment on their own; on the other hand, the new freedom fragmented the most disintegrated communities contributing to language shift. Despite disruptions to the native organization, the *encomienda* was effective in maintaining large groups of Indians working together even after slavery of the indigenous was abolished, a fact that would have a positive effect on language and culture maintenance at least for a few decades after the Conquest.

While the *encomienda* was declining the civil government was appointing its own representatives: the viceroy, the members of the *Audiencia* (court and governing body under the viceroy, or the area of its jurisdiction), and the local *corregidores* (magistrates). Established in the late 1520's, the civil government remained effective until the end of the colonial period. An important branch was the *corregimiento*, a jurisdiction of a Spanish officer in charge of a district, responsible for collecting tribute. The magistrates' salaries depended upon tribute and the daily goods and services provided to them and to their assistants. Each jurisdiction had a deputy, a constable, a secretary, and an interpreter. Magistrates were appointed from Spain, and some of them appointed their own subordinates. By the 1550's the *corregimiento* was overseeing the *encomiendas*, and in 1570, most jurisdictions lay within the Valley and the intendancy of Mexico. These units were organized around the original Indian seats, which in turn regulated the relations and contacts between magistrates and Indians officials, although the Indian communities had infrequent contact with magistrates, except in confrontations related to petty squabbles over land, debts, thefts, and women (Gibson 1964: 81-85). The empowerment of Spanish speakers in key civil positions also hindered the chances of the indigenous speakers to maintain their communities and the corresponding cultural components.

7.4 New religion and language maintenance and shift

At the beginning religion played a major role in the maintenance of Indian language(s) and culture(s). Much to their dismay, the missionaries assigned to Mexico found a multilingual/multicultural society engaged in complex rituals and unknown deities. Tenochtitlan, Tlatelolco, Texcoco, Tlalmanalco, and Xochimilco, the foremost Indian towns were occupied by Franciscans, where the young upper class Indians were trained to occupy high places in their own society. As in *encomienda* and *corregimiento*, Indian society itself furnished structured jurisdictions for ecclesiastical purposes. Integral seat-village units were transformed into parishes, with the Indian seats becoming seats of *doctrina* (missions) and the villages becoming *visitas* (inspections). By 1570, a total of 86 parochial foundations had been established by the mendicant orders, as follows: Franciscan, 38; Dominican, 30; Augustinian, 9; and Secular, 9 (Gibson 1964: 99-101, 106). At this juncture, religious endeavors are intertwined with the works on translation and linguistics, the language policy of the Spanish Crown launched for the New World before the arrival of Spanish speakers to the Mexican coasts, and with other aspects of re-structuring which were necessary for the settling of a new society of Spanish speakers.

A rescue mission had been initiated by Hernán Cortés himself immediately after the conquest of Mexico; the history of conversion was narrated by Gerónimo de Mendieta, who completed his commissioned chronicle known as *Historia Eclesiástica Indiana* in 1595-96 (published in 1870 by Joaquín García Icazbalceta). Divided into five parts, the second and third give a thorough account of the pre-Hispanic religious practices and the emergence of the Catholic Church in Mexico through the endeavors of the Franciscans and the subsequent decline of this Order. In 1522, Charles V authorized the journey of three Flemish friars to Mexico. Juan de Tecto, Juan de Aora and Pedro de Gante reached the Mexican coasts before the arrival of the Twelve Franciscans friars; of the three, only Pedro de Gante lived long enough in New Spain to pursue his religious endeavors

(Mendieta 1596/1870: part 2, chapter 4). The twelve Franciscan friars authorized to sail to Mexico in 1523 were the following: Martín de Valencia, Francisco de Soto, Martín de la Coruña, José de la Coruña, Juan Juárez, Antonio de Ciudad Rodrigo, Toribio de Benavente, García de Cisneros, Luis de Fuensalida, Andrés de Córdoba, Bernardino de la Torre, and Francisco de los Angeles (Mendieta 1596/1870: part 3, chapter 10). Their presence in New Spain had major consequences for the language and religious policy enacted in the new soil, inasmuch as the friars believed that their mission was to facilitate the simultaneous conversion of thousands of souls; this would presumably compensate for the adepts lost to other religions, particularly Lutheranism. Gerónimo de Mendieta was convinced that once Aztec rulers admitted baptism, its massive reception among the Indians would follow smoothly. The friars had to be actively engaged in understanding and even participating in pre-Hispanic socio-political structures; only by being participant observers could they devise an original Nahua Christian subjectivity. Conversion was in appearance a swift process, while teaching Spanish to thousands of individuals was a gigantic project that motivated the friars to initiate their tasks by learning the native languages themselves. This had a positive effect on indigenous language maintenance for at least five decades.

During the 16th and 17th centuries, many other members of the mendicant orders were devoted to describing, using, promoting, and translating the indigenous languages they gradually encountered in the field. Understanding the indigenous population of Mexico and recording their languages was a unique endeavor undertaken by the Franciscans and their aides, who produced one work of philology after another. Between the late 1540's and the late 1570's, the Franciscans wrote two grammars, one Spanish-Nahuatl and Nahuatl-Spanish dictionary, and an encyclopedic corpus covering every aspect of pre-conquest Nahua life in Nahuatl texts drafted by the indigenous aides (Lockhart 1992: 6). The scientific studies conducted by those engaged in missionary linguistics emphasized the exhaustive description of Nahuatl language, history, cosmogony and all aspects related to Nahua culture. Nahuatl was the most frequently and widely spoken language in the Mesoamerican area. In spite of the shattering experiences of the conquest, Nahuatl speakers were still the quantitative majority while the functions of their language were being reallocated to different domains, primarily to the arena of Christianization. Those in charge of this mission confronted the resistance of indigenous peoples and the different strategies they utilized to feign that they were indeed accepting the values of the new ethno-culture.

On the surface all works of grammar, translation and linguistics were favorable for language maintenance but as the study of Mesoamerican ethno-cultures advanced, Spanish-speaking clerics took over the tasks of Christianization. Some of the scholarly endeavors of the 16th century rearranged notions of Christianity and brought them together in a fused scheme that is not easily understood. The lives and works of Alonso de Molina and Bernardino de Sahagún offer clues to look into the most creative aspects of religion, language and ethnicity. Alonso de Molina was probably born in Extremadura ca. 1513 and arrived in New Spain with his parents and a younger brother when he was nine or ten years old. The friars belonging to the Seraphic Order asked his mother to allow the oldest child, Alonsito, to live with them in the convent. Alonsito, who had learned Nahuatl with childhood playmates, moved in with the friars, lived in his cell and followed their steps throughout his life. He professed in the Convent of St. Francis in 1528, was ordained in 1535 or 1536, and worked as a preacher for several decades. In this way he became the interpreter of the friars and the teacher of the preachers of the Gospel. In the face of opposition of newcomers from Spain with different attitudes and ambitions, his abilities as an interpreter were subsidized by the Franciscan Order (León Portilla 1970: xx-xxvi).

The transliteration of Nahuatl and other languages into Romanized writing was not the result of frivolous undertakings but the outcome of meticulous scholarship. Alonso de Molina is the author of the *Doctrina Christiana* (1546), *Vocabulario en lengua castellana y mexicana y mexicana y castellana* (1555 and 1571) published in Mexico City by the local printer (House of Antonio de Espinosa), and *Arte de la lengua mexicana y castellana* printed in the House of Pedro Ocharte in 1571. He is also the author of the *Confesionario Mayor* (Confession Manual) published in 1565, 1569 and 1578 in both Spanish and Nahuatl. In the prologue to his *Vocabulario* (1571), he underscored the need to learn the indigenous languages, since he himself had had some difficulties: Nahuatl was not his mother tongue, thus it was not natural to him. He had to practice and use it and learn in addition "the variety and diversity of its words". He also explained that he had followed the Grammar's model presenting the Castilian part first and the Nahuatl part next.

In the *Confesionario Mayor*, Spanish words appear as independent lexical items (e.g., *ciudad, faraón, hostia, jubileo,* and *leyes*). Some other times they appear with Nahuatl prefixes or suffixes as in **mo**compadre, **t**anima, eregesme, sabado**tica**, sancto**huan**, cruz**titech**. A total of 195 *hispanismos* of varying frequency were inserted in the Nahuatl part of the manual, e.g. *Dios* (143), ánima (58), *Santa Iglesia* (55), *sacerdote* (54), *sacramento* (52), *confirmación* (37). Allusions to God appear in the two languages as in *Dios, toetl, totecuijo Dios, incelteotl Dios, teolt Dios, tlatocatzin Dios*. Seventy borrowings from Spanish (known as *hispanismos*) refer to topics of the Catholic religion and are divided in eight semantic categories: divinity and enlightened beings, dignitaries and ecclesiastical / governmental offices, feasts and calendars, sacraments, objects and sacred places, teachings and Christian moral, social and religious relationships, and objects.

Forty of the 70 *hispanismos* had appeared in the Spanish section of Molina's *Vocabulario* with the corresponding translation, for instance, *santo – tlayectilli, profetas – tlaachtoplaitoani, confesión – teyolmelahualiztli*. Scholars have questioned Molina's decision to insert Spanish words that had already been translated in his *Vocabulario*. The most plausible explanation has to do with religious dogma. Original concepts such as *Trinidad, Espíritu Santo*, or *Redención* were not easily decanted into Spanish; thus, the presentation of new Christian notions would prevent deviations from orthodoxy. The comparison of the *Confesionario Mayor* with the *Confesionario Menor* (an unpublished synthesis) confirms that the most frequent *hispanismos* refer to basic notions of Christianity: *Anima* (58 and 7); *Santa Iglesia* (55 and 10); *Sacramento* (52 and 1); *sacerdote* (54 and 6); and *testamento* (19 and 1). Those referring to the Sacraments (absolution, penitence, baptism, confession, confirmation, and ex-communion) appeared in the two languages presumably because Molina wanted to clarify that their equivalents were separated from the indigenous religion (Máynez 1998, 1999; and 2002).

Alonso de Molina was resourceful not only because he was bilingual and bicultural but because he knew the two religions very well and was aware that they could not be easily reconciled in their most fundamental tenets. The *Sumario de las indulgencias concedidas a los cofrades del Santíssimo Sacramento traduzido en lengua Mexicana por el muy Reuerendo Padre Fray Alonso de Molina de la orden de los menores por mando del muy Ilustre y Reverediissimo señor Don Alonso de Montúfar, Arçobispo meritíssimo de México* [Summary of indulgences granted to the members of the Sacred Sacrament translated into Nahuatl by the Reverend Father Friar Alonso de Molina of the Order of the Minors as per instructions of His Illustrious and Reverend Alonso de Montúfar, Archbishop of Mexico] (1568-1572), was redacted in reverential Nahuatl according to the rules of *tecpillatolli* (learned style). This manuscript expressed in Nahuatl those concepts of Christian thought without equivalents in this language. In order to prevent the invasion of Spanish terms referring to spiritual Christian notions, Molina became an expert in the creation of neologisms. For example, in the native language *mictlan* referred to "the place of the dead" or Hell, frequent in the pre-Hispanic tradition. *Temictiani tlatacolli* referred to "painful killer" or mortal sin. *Titotoyolomelahua* literally means "we straighten our hearts"; for Molina and Sahagún it meant "we go through confession". *Temaquixticatzi* ('Savior') meant "the one who frees people". This unpublished manuscript also uses Spanish loans (Hernández de León-Portilla 1999).

The fusion of the members of the mendicant orders with the indigenous individual could be accomplished through Franciscan principles of piety, poverty, and humility. The Franciscan project was oriented towards the reactivation of the native languages and their protagonist role in the task of conversion. As preachers, they knew of the potential distortions of interpreters so they decided to learn the language of the potential converts. Getting close to the speakers meant getting close to their minds and souls. When Molina elaborated his *Vocabulario*, he was thinking of an instrument that would serve to initiate a dialogue with the speakers of the languages for the purposes of evangelization but with a transcendental aim: to create a common space between two different cultures with a projected future in both the divine and human dimensions. The language-culture equation was instrumental in understanding the way of thinking of the Nahua people, and at the same time, it paved the way for an indigenous-oriented Church. This method is known today as "linguistic immersion" (Hernández de León Portilla 2007). Linguistic immersion fostered bilingualism among the members of the indigenous elite who were seriously engaged in studying the works on Christian religion.

7.5 Rescuing the past for the future

The ethnographic work of Friar Bernardino Ribeira de Sahagún stands out in the 16th century due to the depth and breadth of knowledge on the history and cosmic vision of the Nahuas and his clear intention to rescue for posterity what was left after the destruction of the Aztec Empire. With his disciple Alonso de Molina, Sahagún was engaged in the recovery mission of the past. They belong to the first generation of humanists who were committed to learning the language and culture of their adoptive land. The work of Molina in the realm of language and linguistics was complemented by Sahagún in the area of history and ethnography. The *Historia General de las cosas de la Nueva España* is an encyclopedia of the Nahua people before the Conquest. The endeavors of humanists of the stature of Molina and Sahagún attest to the significance of the initial fusion of Christian and indigenous practices. Their bilingualism and biculturalism was the key in searching for the cultural patterns that were superficially compatible, but such vast knowledge was baffling to those who had no sympathy for the Mesoamerican peoples. The first generation of the clergy had the inspiration, the endurance and the knowledge to appreciate and adapt to the New World under extremely adverse conditions. The magnitude of the works of the Mexican mission and the cumulative effects during the 16th century had positive effects in the dimension of language maintenance (see Hidalgo 2006a and 2006b). Sahagún's *Historia General* was no doubt ambitious. It sounded like the *Grand e General Estoria* conceived as of 1272 by the Spanish King Alfonso X, drafted with the assistance of his collaborators from the *Escuela de Traductores de Toledo*, the multilingual and multicultural scholars who contributed with diverse perspectives to making the world history a truly encyclopedic (but incomplete) enterprise.

7.5.1 The second generation and the good memories about Tlatelolco

An interesting manuscript transcribed and published by García Icazbalceta (1886: 360-366) is the prologue to a *Sermonario* (collection of sermons) written in Nahuatl by Friar Juan Bautista, born in New Spain in 1555. Juan Bautista belongs to the second generation of friars ordained in the Convent of San Francsico, where he taught philosophy and theology; he also lived in Tlatelolco, Tacuba and Texcoco. Like other *criollos*, when he was a child, he was not fond of learning Nahuatl, but his fellow Franciscan Francisco Gómez taught him the grammar, and when he mastered it, he finally admitted that it was necessary to teach it to the Indians. While he was a student in the *Colegio de Santa Cruz de Tlaltelolco*, he took full advantage of the bilingualism of Nahuatl-speaking students who translated for him anything he found convenient. His prologue to the *Sermonario* in Spanish was printed in 1606, more than two decades after the prohibition to publish materials in vernacular languages had been issued. The prologue sheds light on many aspects of his life and that of his fellow priests. Friar Juan Bautista claimed that with the assistance of colleagues and students he had been studying Nahuatl for 28 years. Some of them were *ladinos y hábiles* ('skillful translators'), and since he was so fond of them he proceeded to offer a short biography to honor their memory.

The first one mentioned by Juan Bautista is his colleague Hernando de Ribas, a native Indian from Texcoco, a religious man and great translator of "Latin and Romance to Mexicano" (Latin and Spanish to Nahuatl). Hernando de Ribas assisted Friar Alonso de Molina when the latter was writing his *Vocabulario* and *Arte* (Nahuatl grammar). He died on September 11, 1597. Friar Juan Bautista was also assisted by Friar Juan Bernardo from Huexozinco, who used to write in plain Latin; he died in 1594. Diego Adriano, a native from Tlatelolco, was so good in Latin (*"buen latino"*) that he was able to translate just anything from Latin to Nahuatl with great precision. Francisco Bautista de Contreras, governor of Xochimilco, was a great writer of Castilian and helped Bautista in the writing of *Contemptus Mundi*. Esteban Bravo, a native of Texcoco educated in *Santa Cruz* was so skillful (*"muy buen latino"*) that he used to translate just about anything from Latin, and Romance to Nahuatl, and had an admirable lexicon. Next, Don Antonio Valeriano, a native of Azcapotzalco, governed the Mexican Indians for about thirty years. He was one of the best *"latinos y retóricos"* and so proper and elegant that sounded like Cicero or Quintilian. Valeriano was fond of writing letters in Latin to Friar Juan Bautista, who lamented the scarcity of Indians who knew the ancient language at the time he was writing his prologue. Those who knew Latin used "corrupted words" just like Spanish speakers. Bautista claims that "nowadays one has to be cautious in consulting with Indians about the mysteries of the faith because most likely they will confuse basic notions". He knew from personal experience that Indians had made mistakes, for example: *Dios itlaneltoquitzin* ('the faith in which God believes') instead of saying *Dios ineltococatzin* ('the faith with which one believes in God'), and many more instances like this. The case of Agustín de la Fuente is an exception, for he was an Indian who did help him for about ten years, for he had been trained as a scribe by Friar Bernadrino de Sahagún and had worked with both Sahagún and Pedro de Oroz. He had such ample expertise in language matters that all published materials went through his eyes and his hands before they went to the printer. He died in 1594.

Some of the friars belonging to the first generation (born in Spain) are mentioned by Juan Bautista. Pedro de Gante was Bautista's mentor with whom he consulted for about eight years while they were both at the *Colegio de Santa Cruz*. Juan Bautista claimed that he also learned from the illustrious work carried out by Bernardino de Sahagún, who had the hallo of a saint because he preached, baptized and wrote in Nahuatl for about 60 years. Another friar born in Europe was Arnaldo de Basacio, who wrote many sermons in Nahuatl adjusting the language to the needs of newly converted Indians. In his roster of sermon writers, Bautista included others such as Alonso de Trujillo, a preacher for more than 26 years; and Pedro Oroz, who spent more than 45 years preaching in Nahuatl and Otomi. For the true knowledge of God they had, he could not forget Juan de Ribas, Andrés de Olmos, and Juan de Romanones.

Friar Juan Bautista highlights the information he knew about Alonso de Molina, born in Spain, but arriving in New Spain when he was a child. Bautista knew all the works published by Molina. In closing, Bautista thanks his mentor Friar Francisco Gómez, who was still alive at the time he wrote his prologue; Gómez persuaded him to learn Nahuatl just like Bautista himself was persuading others who did not want to learn. Juan Bautista was also a disciple of Friar Miguel de Zárate and Gerónimo de Mendieta, who arrived in New Spain in 1554 and also learned Nahuatl. According to Bautista, Mendieta was better known for his Spanish skills in the pulpit. In Spanish he wrote the *Historia Eclesiástica Indiana*. Finally, Bautista extols the virtues of the *lengua mexicana* (Nahuatl), for it is truly elegant and rich, and one cannot write only a brief line in it because Nahuatl is more expressive than Latin and Castilian. The young men who were trained in religion and humanities belonged to the trilingual elite protected by the first generation of Spanish clerics, who were in turn fervent believers in their own projects of language and ethno-cultural maintenance.

One of the documented manifestations of a cultural transition to Hispanization was learning writing skills among select children of the Aztec nobility. With the arrival of the Franciscans friars in New Spain began the practice of teaching language(s) in Romanized or alphabetized Nahuatl and the exposure to engravings and illustrations of the Christian icons. In the Amerindian pre-conquest tradition, however, pictographic and ideographic writing was the usual form of expression with the transition to alphabetic writing occurring ca. 1540 and sharing for a few decades the space of pictographic writing. The latter, nevertheless, had to be accompanied by glosses and interpretations in either Romanized Nahuatl or Spanish. Writing was the subtle instrument of acculturation to the demands of the colonial society, since the bureaucracy of the new viceroyalty needed able writers and interpreters to file all kinds of records; the newly trained scribes learned the different writing styles. Despite the prohibitions of the Church and the *Concilios Provinciales*, in the 16th century writing began to replace the oral forms of expression; nonetheless some groups continued to maintain the oral traditions particularly in revival rituals although they did not regain the significance they had had among members of the pre-conquest nobility. They gradually declined and became associated with the reminiscence of the past and with the indigenous masses. At the same time writing in Romanized Nahuatl enabled the indigenous to advance to important posts such as those of *alcaldes* (mayors), *regidores* (councilmen), *escribanos* (scribes), and even governors. In this way, some plebeians gradually invaded the echelons of the colonial order in diverse regions such as the Altiplano, Michoacan, and Oaxaca. The writing practices among the indigenous groups and the social mobility they attained were sabotaged by the Inquisition (as of 1571), as a result of the new censorship that had curbed the publication and circulation of books, but in particular those in Amerindian languages (Gruzinski 1988/1991: 55, 61-64, 68-69, 71-73). These policies reversed the relentless labor of the Franciscans while the political weight of other ethnic groups, i.e. Spaniards, mestizos, blacks and mulattoes, increased in direct proportion to the decrease of the native population. All these changes eventually contributed to indigenous acculturation, tarnished the indigenous Renaissance, and stimulated a more pronounced language shift.

7.6 Strategies of Hispanization

Another effective strategy of Hispanization was the manipulation of indigenous leaders known as majordomos, who were responsible for properties, the sheep herd, the jail, or any other communal possessions that required maintenance or yielded an income. In the 16th century, many towns supported majordomos with subordinates for special tasks; the former held their positions for long periods of time or were appointed by governors or municipal councils. At the lowest levels of community government a less deliberate process of Hispanicization was taking place. Despite significant losses, the *calpultin* (native town) survived as barrios or estancias or subdivisions of these. Members of the surviving *calpulli* (basic organizational units) recognized the position of their leader, a member of the in-group, while in some cases the barrio and estancia officers adopted ranks that were equivalent to Spanish posts. Lower-rank Indian officers enforced attendance, summoned congregations, or inflicted punishment due to absence or to eliminate pagan survivals. Indians were reminded of their obligations by town sectors, each with its banner honoring its barrio saint. Many towns of the 16th century maintained separate religious *alguaciles*, one for each barrio, and posts for Indians ensued as a result of town activities (e.g. *topil de la iglesia* or fiscal). In the interests of Hispanization, salaries were established as incentives to seek and hold town offices (Gibson 1964: 182-185).

7.6.1 Religion and the indigenous masses

Since at least the mid-1550's, the indigenous masses were disaffected with the tenets of Christian religion. Various reports pointed that men were less concerned with church attendance than women; that only a third of the native population of Mexico City were receiving the sacraments; and that even in the most Christianized areas, only about one-fifth of the population attended church. Poor attendance was the result of hostility generated in and around the *encomienda* and the gradual disruption of social order. In a few towns such as Tizayuca, Tequixquiac, Tepozotlan, Hueypoxtla, Zumpango, Huitzilpochco, and Huehuetoca there were insufficient ministers to perform all the tasks. On the main festival days, the curates preached and heard confessions, and Indians who failed to confess were punished. Priests were in charge of counseling betrothed couples, keeping marriage and baptismal books, confessing the sick, and administering the Eucharist. They adhered to the Christian doctrine according to the text of Alonso de Molina or equivalent via an Indian spokesmen working in the courtyards of the churches. In some parishes instruction was given in Nahuatl, Otomi and Latin. Distance from the Church was the end-result of the clerics' excessive work (including punishment). When punishment was no longer recommended, the clerics failed to amend their relations with the Indians. Church jails, forbidden by royal order in the 16th century, were still functioning in some missions in the late 17th century. Through the whole colonial period, Indians served the ecclesiastical institutions as gardeners, janitors, cooks, sacristans, carriers, acolytes, and musicians, services that exempted them from tribute liabilities (Gibson 1964: 111-121).

Indian associations facilitated the transition from native practices to institutionalized Catholicism. Known as *cofradías* (guilds) parishioner's associations became a part of indigenous life in the 16th century and several hundred operated in the following century. In some towns, almost all members of the community belonged to *cofradías*, where they experienced the feeling of collective identity normally missing in colonial life. *Cofradías* had been designed to protect native craftsmen, who could be audited by inspectors from Mexico City, and who normally looked down on the Nahuatl-keeping records. The funds collected were used to finance the various expenses of annual masses, shrouds, coffins, vigils, Indian-only burials, and the like. The *cofradías* ensured a steady income, payments to the clergy, provisions for church ceremonies, etc. Around these associations the indigenous celebrated services, fiestas, public Christian rituals, processions, dances, floral decorations, fireworks, costumes, and music. The observance of the various ceremonies helped the Indians reconcile the Christian and the native pagan worlds. Communal festivities embodied self-protection or the propitiation of supernatural forces. The most popular cult was that of the Virgin of Guadalupe at Tepeyac, an act of faith dating to the early 1530's. Its fiesta in the 17th and 18th centuries, as in modern times, was the greatest indigenous event in all Mexico. An alternative to other forms of Spanish colonialism, the Catholic Church did contribute to preserve native manifestations of life among Indians (Gibson 1964: 127-135).

The information at hand about religion between the 1520's to the 1580's is conducive to endorse a proposal stating that religious conversion might have been more effective in maintaining indigenous cultures and languages had the religious leaders been supported by the Spanish Crown and the Catholic Church. The early colonial project was fostering language maintenance in the domain of religion, and only among members of the native elite and some Spanish-speaking *criollos* who had sufficient contact with the indigenous elites. The Church did not support the training of a native clergy committed to giving continuity to the original mission as it had been expressed by the first generation of preachers and teachers. The Spanish speakers born in Spain became bilingual and bicultural in New Spain, in many cases never returned to Spain, devoted their whole lives to rescue the traditions of the native peoples via religious dogma, but their heritage was not wholly appreciated beyond the second generation of the clergy. Religious endeavors were passed on to the Spanish-speaking *criollos*, who were more concerned with maintaining their own positions than with maintaining the indigenous languages. Spanish-speaking *criollos* were in charge of the parishes and maintained for a long time a hierarchical relationship with their potential clients. Some of them learned the indigenous languages only to keep a leash on the indigenous masses; unlike their homologues of the early generations of the mendicant orders, they were uninterested in teaching indigenous literacy. In this way the Spanish-speaking members of the clergy empowered themselves while at the same time disempowered the indigenous communities.

7.6.2 Hispanicization of the indigenous

During the conquest period, lower class Indians known as *maceguales* (commoners), occupied vacancies left by local leaders. *Maceguales* engaged in commerce, gained wealth and local influence, served in a monastery and skipped tribute and labor duties. In order to retain their status and pass as *principales*, surviving caciques and other upwardly mobile individuals became thoroughly Hispanicized in their material culture. Some of them even gained the favor of *encomenderos*, who elevated them to positions of gubernatorial power through the creation of Indian governments or *gobernadoryotl*, which were assigned to existing *tlatoani*. Some others even preserved their lands and paid servants through the 17th century. Indian candidates to these positions were persuaded to Hispanicize their speech. Caciques' powers were further reduced after the mid-16th century, when elected Indian officers occupied town offices similar to those in Spain's municipal government. In municipal councils all seats were staffed with Indian mayors and councilmen. Elected officers traveled to Mexico City to consolidate their duties and vice-regal confirmation, well-orchestrated strategies that protected their own against land usurpation. The judges appointed to Indian government were either Spaniards or Indians. Below the governor and council members, the Hispanicized offices required all kinds of tasks such as copying documents for the archives. By the late 16th century, small communities had one or two specialized scribes and larger communities more. Scribes were in charge of eliminating the large pictorial content of pre-conquest records thereby Hispanicizing their own functions. After about 1590, the pictorial forms were abandoned in Indian records, and the services of the Indian scribes were no longer needed in most community businesses (Gibson 1964: 167-168, 177-181). The Hispanicization of Indians in the different domains of the new colonial society (religion, government, and labor) seems to have occurred before full linguistic assimilation took place.

Hispanicized Indians played the role of critical intermediaries and mediators between the indigenous society and the Spanish speakers living in the New World colonies. These acculturated persons were normally of mixed Spanish and Amerindian parentage (mestizos). The label *ladino* was invented by Spanish speakers who wished to pass judgment on the Spanish proficiency of the members of the out-group but was extended to other forms of acculturation. Even before the conquest of Mexico, "*ladino*" referred to a person possessing variable knowledge of Spanish and certain personality traits such as prudence and sagacity. At the end of the spectrum, those personality traits included, too, slyness and craftiness. *Ladino* Indians were known for their works as petitioners and plaintiffs in colonial litigations over land. They appeared as Messianic leaders rejecting Christianity and adhering to ancestral rituals; paradoxically they also played the opposite role as *fiscales* (prosecutors) or *mandones* (bossy bosses) who gathered people of their barrios and took them to the teaching of the Catechism and the mass. They had all sorts of functions in the church and in the municipal governments. They were artists, mapmakers, chroniclers and ethnographers, and represented a broad range of relationships between the Amerindian traditions and the Spanish Christian culture. For *ladino* historians the reevaluation of the past had relevance in the present because they encoded the practices of the ancient culture into formulas appropriated for the advocacy of their own rights and privileges (Aguilar Moreno 2002).

7.7 Transculturation and miscegenation

Another view on the issue of Hispanization is offered by Mörner (1970: 21-37), who proposed that Christianization was in theory conducive to miscegenation even before the discovery of Mexico and before Indians were living close to Spaniards. The Spanish Crown was in favor of founding racially integrated populations presumably because Spanish speakers would set good examples. The theory of the 'good (or bad) example' can be traced to 1535. It was promoted by Vasco de Quiroga, Bishop of Michoacan, on the grounds that the behavior of Spanish speakers was reprehensible because the *encomenderos* were not acting as protectors of the Indians. To make things worse, some mestizos were also setting bad examples. Mestizos and mulattoes were marginal individuals and were abusing the Indians until they succeeded in their extermination. After major losses, it was questioned if Christianization was equivalent to Hispanicization. Religious leaders blamed abusive Spanish speakers for the epidemics of 1545. About 90 percent of the Indian population had been decimated in communities that were in contact with Spanish speakers. Throughout the 16th century non-exemplary models of behavior were not only abundant but easily contagious. All agreed in the necessity to separate the pristine souls of the natives from contact with Spaniards. Such policies were challenged and contrasting proposals were advanced in order to justify both language contact and social intermingling with the hopes that natives might learn Spanish by emulating good habits. Hispanization was reiterated more formally in instructions delivered to the Viceroy of New Spain and Peru on June 7, 1550. The means of effective Hispanization was the teaching and learning of Spanish. Others proposed to encourage the emigration and settlement of good Spanish-speaking people to the New World.

In some other instances religious leaders argued that for Christianization to take place it was necessary to eliminate the contact with Spanish speakers. If Indians were maintained in isolation, they could express their desire to be converted provided Spaniards did not get too close to their territory, at least temporarily. Christianization could be achieved without the presence of Spanish speakers, an idea more influential in peripheral areas. This experiment was characteristic of Central America. The policy of Indian segregation was enforced in rural settings but was flexible in Spanish settlements and in mining and factory towns. It was less effective as the pressures of landless mestizos and Spaniards on Indian lands increased. In the urban sectors it was validated on the grounds that Muslims and Jews had been segregated in the Iberian Peninsula. Despite the strategies invoked to separate Indians from Spaniards, the flow of a large number of the former to all the Spanish cities was unrelenting due to the demand of a workforce needed in construction and services. Indian workers began commuting from rural areas to the cities eventually settling in indigenous barrios in the periphery of the Spanish-speaking cities, except when they served as domestics. In the urban setting, the case of Mexico City illustrates the separation of Indians from Spaniards, first in the famous *traza*, from which they were removed and relocated in four boroughs of Tlatelolco and Tenochtitlan. In 1574 the Indians living in these districts complained to the king about the abuses they had suffered because they were living too close to Spaniards, their servants and their slaves. This problem was aggravated as a result of the flood of 1628-29, which resulted in the exodus of the Tlatelolco Indians, a vacuum filled by Spaniards, mestizos and mulattoes. The revolts of 1624 and 1692 put in bold relief the deleterious conditions of the indigenous masses and castes which in the end led to dangerous insurrections. An investigation revealed that Indians were still living among Spaniards and castes both in the central area and in the different districts. In order to evade both the tribute and the spiritual monitoring of the *doctrineros* (priests in charge of missions), many Indians imitated Spaniards looking more like mestizos (Mörner 1970: 38-39, 41, 53-55).

In the big city, it was very difficult to separate ethnic groups, and as they were learning Spanish, Indians were learning evil things. Presumably the contact with Spanish speakers converted them into *ladinos* (proficient in Spanish and relatively acculturated). In contrast, in Puebla de los Angeles, Spaniards welcomed all those who were scattered among Indians. In 1555 the Magistrate of Puebla attempted to remove them; and again in 1569 and 1607 there were unsuccessful attempts to take them away. Similar practices were enforced in other colonies. Segregation was normally incomplete because in some spaces (e.g. hospitals), it was impossible to maintain all the boundaries effectively. As of 1570 mestizos, mulattoes, and blacks were officially excluded from Indian towns, while the *encomenderos* themselves posed a major problem because they spent more than sufficient time collecting tribute in the Indian towns and setting bad example to the natives. In turn the *encomenderos* would invoke their right to live in their own houses surrounded by servants. In the semi-populated and poor areas such as Guadalajara and Campeche, there was not a problem, but the intermediaries were not interested in protecting their own Indians. Their apathy was advantageous to the Spanish Crown because it helped diminish their influential status in the New World (Mörner 1970: 57, 83, 85, 87).

Justified on moral and religious grounds, the policy on the separation of the Indians was extended to black slaves supposedly because their relations were irregular and irritating. Although the church did not give up its policy to prevent free unions, its success was limited. Black slaves were also setting bad examples and even threatened their own integrity. There were other strong reasons that prevented the contact between Indians and blacks. Slaves married to a free Indian would be legally free and the offspring would also be free. In addition, the absence of Spaniards and castes in Indian towns facilitated the collection of tribute. Finally, Spanish authorities feared an unholy alliance of Indians and blacks against the Spanish power. The earliest attempt to separate the groups by race dates back to the decree issued in Peru and another in 1565 by which Indians were banned from having slaves. In 1551 another decree was issued prohibiting *encomenderos* from having black slaves living in the indigenous communities. Many Spaniards freed their black slaves, and once freed, they themselves re-settled in *palenques* or *cumbes* (their newer communities) though many were roaming around Indian towns and presumably looking for trouble. In the 1570's, about 2,000 individuals or one-tenth of the total Afro-Mexican population (freed or slaved) was hanging out in New Spain's interior (Mörner 1970: 95-99).

The most forceful decree of 1578 ordered to punish blacks and mulattoes if they were living among Indians. In northern New Spain it was reported that blacks were working for their masters in the mines, and for this reason they were already separated from the natives. Mestizos had been excluded, too, from Indian towns because they would set a bad example to Indians; moreover, this group was the fastest-growing and also the most pugnacious and quarrelsome, a real 'pain in the neck' or a 'plague in the local courts'. There was also a mestizo elite, offspring of distinguished Spaniards who had been raised among Spanish speakers but were bilingual in the indigenous language(s). Mestizos had restrictions of different types, and by 1549, they were not allowed to inherit *encomiendas*. They were excluded from engaging in select occupations such as those of notaries, caciques of Indians, or priests. By the 17th century the position for Indian governor required the knowledge of Spanish and proof of pure indigenous background. This would prevent Spaniards from influencing mestizos who would in turn exploit the Indian masses. Despite the obstacles that prevented black and mulattoes from living in Indian towns, the increase of Spaniards and mestizos residing there and the number of native mestizos continued to grow steadily (Mörner 1970: 99-107; 109-110).

According to the ecclesiastical authorities, Spaniards caused more ambiguities in policy making than any other group. On the one hand, the Spanish Crown had been warned about the abusive manner in which some Spaniards treated Indians. On the other, Indians needed to learn the Christian doctrine from virtuous Spanish speakers. The presence or absence of Spaniards was also related to land property because many had purchased land in Indian towns. The Crown had to pay compensation for the losses and also for the exclusion in Indian towns, which would affect both agriculture and transculturation of Indians. The arguments were not strong enough to permit the residence of Spaniards in Indian towns. The case of Spanish magistrates in Indian towns was worse because they could hire subordinates known as *jueces de comisión* (commissioned judges) who abused their power just like the scribes working under the supervision of magistrates. Many local positions were abolished in New Spain, Guatemala and Yucatan, or were reduced to those deemed to be indispensable. The disintegration of indigenous institutions, the shock of the conquest, the demands of the new Spanish landowners and all other forms of slavery and servitude led to a process of transculturation giving rise to marginal individuals. *Ladino* or acculturated Indians were Spanish-speaking but some of them were marginal. The presence of *ladinos* in the Indian towns was, too, a constant source of apprehension among civil and ecclesiastical authorities. Since 1555 abuses of *ladinos* were glaring for they were acting as though they were merchants and were wandering through the towns and markets. The regulations dictating residential separation were issued between 1536 and 1646, and simply reiterated the 'leave-the-Indians alone' notion. Despite the fact that the regulations were to be effective in all the colonies, some were specific for a certain region. In New Spain vagabonds should not live among Indians and Indians should not offer services to *encomenderos*. Indians should be taught Spanish and should be informed about the liberating content of the New Laws of 1542 (Mörner 1970: 117-119, 123, 125, 130-131).

The presence of other-than Indians in Indian towns was a complex issue for the church since the same priest was assigned to serve all ethnic groups. The growth of "other groups" exacerbated the process of transculturation of the natives, and at the same time, many *doctrinas* (newer missions) were transformed, in turn affecting the residential separation in the non-religious realm. Separation was based on religious criteria: when a mission was stabilized, it was to be transformed into a *doctrina* in charge of a priest. Its place of residence was the seat of the *doctrina*. Other communities under the jurisdiction of a *doctrina* were considered *visitas*. It was more practical to assign the parishes for Spaniards and mixed population to Spanish-speaking priests. The dilemma of the Church stemmed from the language problem and the natives' cultural background, a dualism comparable to that experienced by the Church, which was split in regular and secular. Parishioners organized their *cofradías* and saint cults in a separate form. Regular clerics prevailed in the New World missions. The division established in the ecclesiastical sphere between the priests of souls for the Indians and the priests of souls for Spaniards was challenged by the intrusion of non-Indians in the *doctrinas*. Finally, it was admitted that the *de facto* separation in the civil society was not possible in the ecclesiastical domain. The missionaries in charge of Indians were also in charge of administering the sacraments to Spaniards residing in their missions, which could turn into parishes in order to serve a large number of Spanish speakers living in Tlaxcala, Tepeaca, Cholula, Tecamachalco and others (Mörner 1970: 142-144).

As the process of transculturation was accelerated in the mid-17th century, new problems were passed on to the ecclesiastical administration. According to Manuel Pérez, author of a manual for priests of Indians published in Mexico in 1713, the priests were not able to distinguish natives from non-natives because the former had changed their attire, hair, and general appearance. The newer mestizos were turned to the priests in charge of Spaniards but did not receive the special treatment for the soul. The change from Indian to mestizo identity entailed the exemption from tribute. In 1684 in the provinces of New Spain (Guadalajara and Monterrey) the missions were suppressed. The administrative hierarchy was complex and included so many functionaries that the status of the Indian vis-à-vis this system was similar to that of a minor who was under the protection of religious and civil authorities and had at the same time limited rights. In the early period there were no special courts for Indians. The Indian towns distributed in *encomiendas* to the residents of a city were normally registered in the same city. Thus the mayors or magistrates were responsible for the administration of justice in their own district. In cities of Spaniards there was an overabundance of judges of Indians, but Indians did not have authority to apply the law against Spaniards. It was deemed sufficient to separate Indians in Indian towns to prevent abuses. But the caveat was clear in that the Spanish city or villa close to the closest Indian town belonged in the same jurisdiction. It was common to find depopulated Indian towns because the dwellers had fled massively to work in the mining sites or in the nearby haciendas. At the same time Spaniards could leave their villas and occupy Indian towns. Out-migration of Indian towns became more common during the 17th and 18th centuries. For Spanish authorities the policy of segregation and the protection of Indian land were not a source of conflict (Mörner 1970: 145, 148-149, 150, 161, 170).

Initiated since the early 1520's and continuing in the 17th century among the Coyoacan *cacicas* (women leaders) who married Spaniards and born mestizo children, Hispanization was also the result of miscegenation. The 17th and early 18th centuries caciques enjoyed their privileges and displayed their arms on the church tower beside the royal arms. With an intrusion in the succession in the last quarter of the 18th century, the traditional privileges were lost, the family members came to be treated as *maceguales*, and the cacique heir was placed on the tribute lists. On the eve of the Independence from Spain, the caciques were hardly distinguishable from the mass of the Indian population in their economic circumstances and lifestyle. Nothing restored the decayed prestige of the Indian nobility. The word 'cacique' lost its hereditary significance and acquired the meaning of political boss or local tyrant (Gibson 1964: 156-157; 162-166).

The policy on the separation of the Indians from other groups was expressed in varying practices that rendered different outcomes. The fusion of units from the *calpultin* was moved to *cabeceras* (centers with temples, markets and dwellings) where they turned into streets or barrios or *visitas* sharing the parish or the market. The *congregaciones* or the sites of relocation or resettlement occupied the oldest territories of the *calpultin*, although the Indians did not necessarily stay in the newer locations, and some of the native towns were reduced to smaller *congregaciones*. Relocation was supposed to occur on a voluntary basis but at times Indians were congregated against their will. Some other times the Indians ended up running away from an unpopular place, and about a decade later were dispersed in many estancias. Reports to Viceroy Velasco estimated population losses of about 150,000 families during the relocation period. The *congregaciones* occurred in two periods (1550-1564) and (1593-1605), and were carried out after a series of epidemics that decimated the native communities. The underlying motive was not the notion that it was bad for the indigenous to be dispersed, but the fact that conversion, tax collection and administration could be accomplished more effectively if the indigenous were living in accessible places in an orderly fashion near or around a parochial center. The oldest *congregaciones* prevailed with the settlements of central and southern Mexico being essentially the Indian pueblos founded between 1550 and 1564 (Gerhard 1977). These findings lead to surmise two opposite trends, one for language maintenance when the indigenous were rearranged in the original regions, and one for language shift when they were reshuffled unwillingly or ended up in locations that were hostile.

Another interpretation on the policy of *congregaciones* reads that these resettlements resulted from the synthesis of urban centers (*altepetl*) and the rural townships that were scattered on the hillsides. The *altepeme* (plural of *altepetl*) were communities organized in groups and made up related families known as *calputin*. The spot of the *congregación* or urban nucleus in which the Indian dwellers were territorially concentrated was the *pueblo de indios* (Indian town). The newer communities were conceived as a series of dwellings built over a flat surface close to a river to get water, restricted by a semi-circle, and defined by a straight line, which became the center; the layout of the center was like a chessboard from where parallel and perpendicular streets grew indefinitely. The newer Indian towns were detached from their original sacred landscape, but were permanently rebuilt with components of the original culture and the indigenous toponymy, which preceded the name of the patron saint (Fernández Christlieb and Urquijo Torres 2006). This syncretism is equivalent to continuous mestizaje, while mestizaje can act both as a deterrent and a stimulus to language shift.

7.8 Language contact, bilingualism, and socio-ethnic groups

Available records on religious practices and language contact show that there was elite bilingualism or trilingualism in Spanish, the native language of the priests, Nahuatl the native language of the students, and Latin, the language of the Catholic liturgy. Latin was compartmentalized by a small group of religious and political leaders born in Spain and another small group of Nahuatl-speaking indigenous trainees. In spite of the fact that some second-generation Indians were not fond of learning Nahuatl, some of them eventually did (re)learn the language of their ancestors, but this project was discontinued after the mid-17th century. As compared to the effectiveness and swift spread of elite bilingualism, massive bilingualism must have started at the end of the 16th century and was authenticated by the mid-17th century. Since then it has been gradual and continuous. The Catholic Church did endorse the indigenous languages for internal ecclesiastical use but had no intention of promoting them among the speakers of native communities beyond the common practice of evangelization. Some of the activities around the church domain, however, enhanced the use of Indian languages. In addition, language maintenance was facilitated by the policy of segregation, on the one hand, and the need to hire indigenous workers in different economic activities, on the other. Segregation was operational in fostering language maintenance in Indian towns that were not overrun by outsiders; at the same time, select groups of indigenous became bilingual when they had to commute to work. In the work domain they were in contact with Hispanicized caciques or *indios ladinos* who had had personal or work experiences with Spanish speakers. Indians working as domestics in Spanish-speaking households had a more direct contact with all-Spanish sites and domains. Finally, Indians who were raised in a Spanish-speaking family were more likely prone to acquire and / or assimilate to Hispanic cultural values and language norms. Elite bilingualism clearly preceded massive bilingualism, and the latter has had continuity over the centuries (Lockhart 1991). From the information available about indigenous labor it is also inferred that the indigenous became bilingual while performing the different activities in the many occupations that unfolded during the colonial period. The indigenous were not only bilingual but diglossic since they learned to use Spanish in the interaction with Spanish speakers in select domains.

7.8.1 Bilingual individuals and bilingual groups

The effects of language contact were multiple. Nahuatl incorporated hundreds of nouns belonging to several semantic domains: flora and fauna head this list, but loans of a high degree of abstraction can be found in the realms of religion, law, economics, measurement, and calendars. This period represented a cultural and linguistic revolution consisting of substitution of Nahuatl sounds with Spanish sounds; and because words lacked any universal spelling they followed the writer's actual speech, conforming to the Nahuatl phonetic system. Since the attitude towards Spanish loans was pragmatic, they were assimilated phonologically, morphologically, and semantically (Lockhart 1992: 285, 294-297; and 1991: 13-14). The inferences about monolingualism and bilingualism are neither abundant nor precise. It is assumed that both Nahuatl and Spanish speakers became bilingual to a degree, although many more Nahuas attempted to speak Spanish than Spaniards Nahuatl. By the second and third generation, the bilingual groups might have been comprised by the majority of the professional translators acting as intermediaries between the two languages, mostly speakers of Nahuatl, Spanish ecclesiastics, and some lower-level labor supervisors who habitually tried to converse in Nahuatl. Members of the clergy had powerful reasons to learn indigenous languages since the Spanish Crown had mandated it since around 1599 and had offered rewards with positions in churches. Finally, Spaniards born in Mexico could speak some Nahuatl in case of necessity, relying on what they must have learned from childhood playmates or servants. The originators of equivalents for Spanish expressions may have been a small proportion of all speakers, especially Nahuas in direct contact with Spanish (Lockhart 1992: 302).

Researchers also propose that in the 17th century there were reciprocal influences amongst bilingual individuals of all ethnic groups, but that the Spanish-speaking monolinguals were responsible for phonetic adaptations and substitutions. Derivatives of words like *cacahuate > cacahuatería* and *atole > atolero* are *nahuatlismos* that consistently appeared in the documentation of the Spanish monolingual population (Mejías 1980: 40-41, 53). Words ending in the suffix *–tl* (voiceless affricate) were adapted to the Spanish ending *–ate* or *–ote* and the respective plurals *–ates* and *–otes*, as in items 1-14 in Table 7.1, though *xicamatl* omitted the ending affricate. The cluster *–lli* was introduced with common Spanish variants: *–le* and final *–l*, as in items 15-23. Common nouns related to edibles such as *aguacate, atole, camote, chile, chocolate, tomate, tamal, zapote*, domestic tools such as *jacal, comal, metate, molcajete, petate, petaca*, and derivatives that emerged in different stages of diversification were borrowed by Spanish speakers and have been preserved with considerable vitality in the 20th century (Lope Blanch 1979). It is assumed that the knowledge of Nahuatl and the use of *Nahuatlismos* in the Spanish spoken in the New Spanish society was a feature that distinguished *criollos* from *peninsulares* with the former having an identity based on the mixed sociocultural values of the two groups. The frequent use of *Nahuatlismos* in various domains has given Mexican Spanish the regional zest that persists until today. The majority of the Nahuatl borrowings adapted in the 17th century have survived in modern Mexican Spanish with the same suffixes that the Spanish speakers assigned them in the past. Furthermore, some of them have been preserved in the United States Southwestern states with different degrees of vitality.

Table 7.1: Nahuatl borrowings and Spanish suffixes

No.	Nahuatl	Spanish	English
1	Ahuacatl	Aguacate	Avocado
2	Cacahuatl	Cacahuate	Peanut
3	Camotli	Camote	Sweet potato
4	Chocolatl	Chocolate	Chocolate
5	Coyotl	Coyote	Coyote
6	Mecatl	Mecate	String, rope
7	Metatl	Metate	Ground stone
8	Mitotl	Mitote	Uproar, brawl
9	Papalotl	Papalote	Kite
10	Petatl	Petate	Woven bedroll
11	Tomatl	Tomate	Tomato
12	Tzapotl	Zapote	Sapote
13	Tzopolotl	Zopilote	Black vulture
14	Xitomatl	Jitomate	Small tomato
15	Xicamatl	Jícama	Jicama

Table 7.1 (continued)

No.	Nahuatl	Spanish	English
16	Atulli	Atole	Hot corn beverage
17	Comalli	Comal	Utensil to cook tortillas
18	Huacalli	Huacal	Wooden crate
19	Mezcalli	Mezcal	Beverage from agave
20	Nopalli	Nopal	Prickley pear
21	Pinolli	Pinol	Drink of toasted corn
22	Tamalli	Tamal	Tamal
23	Xacalli	Jacal	Adobe house or hut
24	Cactli	Cacle	Rustic leather sandal
25	Tzictli	Chicle / chiclete	Chewing gum

7.9 Ethnicity and socio-ethnic labels

When the leadership in religious activities was reassigned to the Spanish Inquisition, the Inquisition prescribed the religious, societal and educational norms of Spanish- and non-Spanish speaking groups. Based on the system of *probanzas*, the Inquisition was effective in selecting groups and individuals according to kinship, ethnic background, or Catholic (un)orthodoxy. The inquisitorial activities stressed the values of the preferred Old Christian population over those who were New Christians or recently converted individuals of Muslim or Jewish descent. Categorization based on religious, linguistic or ethnic traits was bound to socio-cultural status, inasmuch as individuals of Old Christian descent had more and better opportunities in the appointment to prestigious positions or distribution of property in the New World colonies, where a discourse of marked ethnicities unfolded since the early decades of the 16th century. The new discourse pointed to the separateness of non-Christian and/or non-Hispanicized individuals who might have become salient in the emergent colonial societies. The profile of ethnic groups is useful to reconstruct some of the values and the roles of language(s) in a multilingual and multicultural society that was coming to grips with its own unsuspected diversity. Ethnic labels such as *negro ladino* (Spanish-proficient black), *indio ladino*, (Spanish-proficient Indian), *mestizo* (individual of Indian and Spanish background), *cripto-judío* (secretive Jew practicing Catholicism in public), or *judaizante* (individual of Judaizing tendencies) were conveniently exploited to maintain non-Spanish, non-Christian groups in disadvantageous positions. Even the word *criollo* (Spanish speaker born in New

Spain) must have had a derogatory meaning as compared to *español* (Spaniard) or *cristiano viejo* (Old Christian).

At the end of the 16th century, patterns of classification were based on ancestry; for this reason children of Spaniards and indigenous people were considered of privileged status. However, the need to absorb offspring of mixed unions into the Spanish group became less common as pre-Hispanic lineages declined— which meant that the mestizo population was also more distant from the expressed criterion of nobility (Martínez 2008: 147). The participation of African descendants in civil and ecclesiastical tribunals was restricted because their Old Christian status could not be confirmed with all the details needed to issue a *probanza*. Descendants of Africans from the Kongo and Angola had accepted Christianity and were acknowledged for being sincere Christians. In addition, a significant number served in colonial militias, which were avenues to honor and social advancement; in central New Spain, they provided military services as early as the 16th century and in subsequent centuries, they played an important role in the Spanish defense of the circum-Caribbean. Furthermore, they participated in various rural and urban economic activities and had a visible presence in Spanish households (Martínez 2008: 160).

7.10 Hispanization of the Afro-Mexican population

Slave experiences in northern New Spain were not limited to the role of passive companions to Spanish explorers. Early in the 16th century they used slaves in central Mexico to replace the Indians in the mines, sugar mills, and haciendas. Although the promoters of slave trade would have preferred to isolate the black population from the other groups—to prevent revolts and interbreeding—they did not succeed because in many instances African blacks sought women from other castes because they were free subjects and their offspring would be free, too, regardless of the status of the father. Slaves also became free by fleeing and hiding in the mountainous areas occasionally preying upon travelers. The mining centers in the north led to the establishment of communities which expanded towards the north via *el camino real* (the royal road), an artery that connected most places back to Mexico City. The mining industry facilitated the construction of presidios throughout Nueva Galicia (present-day Aguascalientes, Colima, Jalisco, Nayarit and Zacatecas) and Nueva Vizcaya (modern states of Chihuahua and Durango). The black population was introduced in New Spain in these presidios and communities. From Nueva Galicia, miners and companions migrated northward into Nueva Vizcaya, where small towns sprang up and attracted in turn the military presence. Some free black and mulattoes became militiamen while many of those were sent to the northern outposts remaining there after service. The mining centers became *asientos de minas*, i.e. localities with mixed features of a town and city or a ranch-mine structure protected by military garrisons. These were the locales where African slaves lived and worked, and as their numbers declined, miners requested more slaves (Franco 2004).

7.11 Conclusions

In spite of the endeavors of civil and ecclesiastic authorities to separate the various ethnic groups, mestizaje became the predominant trend in 16th century New Spain. The earliest strategy was the learning the indigenous languages by those in charge of conversion because it was a more practical than teaching Spanish to a large mass of individuals. The result was a hefty production in Nahuatl-Spanish philology imbued with religious pursuits. Such practice was extended to other Mesoamerican languages. A unique type of trilingualism emerged amongst select members of the Spanish and Nahuatl-speaking elites. Such scholarly endeavor ended with the century.

The second strategy to separate ethnic groups was the dissemination of a discourse on the damaging effect that Spanish speakers and Afro-Hispanics were having on the indigenous. After having observed the decimation of the indigenous populations, the strategies of Hispanization ranged from separation to integration. The former strategy was effective, because it aided in the relocation of the indigenous to compact communities where they were closer to their own culture. At the same time, some individuals of indigenous origin experienced a transformation of ethnic and linguistic values to the extent that they looked and sounded like Spanish speakers. This was conducive to the creation of ethnic labels such as *ladino*, a term used to describe and exacerbate the conflictive realities of newer socio-ethnic groups. The indigenous who could not escape having contact with Spanish speakers turned out to be bilingual, and the bilinguals struggled in the process of Hispanization for their survival depended on acclimatization to the environment. In the realm of language, the indigenous began adapting features of colloquial Spanish varieties to Nahuatl, and Nahuatl-accented Spanish emerged as a contact variety used exclusively in some of the indigenous communities. On the other hand, the early wave of Nahuatlization reaching Spanish speakers continued throughout the century and consolidated the integration of loans into Spanish, primarily in the lexical realm. Nonetheless, the elite bilingualism promoted by the clergy had the net effect of compartmentalizing the use of Nahuatl for linguistic and religious pursuits, an endeavor that restricted the scholarly activities in this language to a small group of natives and Spanish speakers. At the end of the 16th century, Spanish had gained speakers who were initially indigenous or descendants of Africans. Adding speakers of non-European languages contributed to both dissemination of Spanish and diversification.

Chapter 8
Diversification and stability: 17th century

8.1 Spanish speakers in the 17th century

Research on emigration from Spain to the New World has focused primarily on the 16th century. The socio-demographic reports are not only abundant by region and by period, but also provide precise information on the personal activities and whereabouts of the colonists (cf. Bermúdez Plata 1940-1986; Boyd-Bowman 1976). Emigration from Spain has continuity in the mid-colonial period, although in contrast with the previous century, the figures on this phenomenon are neither precise nor readily available. Calculations for the first half of the 17th century yield results varying from 100,000 to 200,000 new emigrants, the latter figure based on a yearly average of 3,896 emigrants between 1601 and 1650. Optimal population density figures appear in Rosenblat (1954: 59). In addition, a fortuitous sample of 1,172 Spaniards living in Mexico City in 1689 reveals their diverse regional origins: 30.2% from Andalusia, 28% from Old Castile, 14.5% from Biscay; 6.8% from Galicia; 5% from Navarre; 2.9% from Extremadura, and the rest from other regions such as Murcia, Valencia, Catalonia, the Balearic Islands, and the Canaries (Mörner 1976: 741, 743, 767). As compared to the scarcity of information on population, data available on commerce is abundant for the years 1650-1699, when New Spain was the preferred market for perishable goods and the number of fleets of merchant ships making a round trip to Indies amounted to 1,851. The transatlantic traffic of this period was dominated by the merchants from Seville and Cadiz (García Fuentes 1980: 417-425 and chapter 1), a factor that may explain the theory on the quantitative and qualitative weight of southern Spain in the consolidation of Spanish ties with the New World.

Socio-demographic data bring up to light reinterpretations on the population growth of the mid-17th century when the total was 1,712,615 people in provinces densely populated by Indians (Table 8.1). The majority or 74 percent (Column 3) was still of indigenous origin, while other groups were on the rise. Table 8.1 shows the division by ethnic group and the small proportions of Spanish speakers from Europe and first-generation Africans at 0.8 and 2 percent, respectively (Columns 1 and 2). In contrast, mixed groups (Euro*mestizos*, Afro*mestizos* and Indo*mestizos*) account for a significant minority (23%). As compared to the 1570 report (Table 1.5), the information available for the mid-17th century shows the three mixed groups in the hundreds of thousands. Euro*mestizos* at 9.8 percent were directly related to the miniscule proportion of Spanish speakers born in Spain.

Table 8.1: Population by caste in 1646

Bishopric	Europeans	Africans	Indians	Euro-mestizos	Afro-mestizos	Indo-mestizos
Mexico	8,000	19,441	600,000	94,544	43,373	43,190
Tlaxcala	2,700	5,534	250,000	17,404	17,381	16,841
Oaxaca	600	898	150,000	3,952	4,712	4,005
Michoacan	250	3,295	35,858	24,396	20,185	21,067
Nueva Galicia	1,450	5,180	41,378	19,456	13,778	13,854
Yucatan	700	497	150,053	7,676	15,770	8,603
Chiapas	80	244	42,318	1,140	1,330	1,482
Totals	13,780	35,089	1,269,607	168,568	116,529	109,042

Source: Aguirre Beltrán (1972: 219)

By the end of the 16th century, Spanish-speaking people had settled in different places in New Spain. The period from 1590 to 1660 was the heart of the middle colony, during which the transformation of the New Spanish society from an Indian to a blood-mixed population continued to evolve. These years are defined by the impressive growth of silver and gold production reaching its highest point of 42 million pesos in 1591-1600, an amount that rose to more than 53 million from 1611 to 1620, a decade of trans-Atlantic trade. Domestic and international trade was an important source of income across the social spectrum of professional merchants, who enjoyed a favorable position and were regarded as members of a prominent group. Merchants were divided into two categories: wholesalers and retailers with silver dealing as the common denominator of the Mexico City traders; wholesalers were allowed to join the guilds and conducted their businesses as independent traders, possessed an estate, a warehouse, and a shop managed by an employee. Finally a diversified economy contributed to open routes of commerce in all directions. The trend toward urbanization that had defined the end of the 16th century was pronounced between 1580 and 1630 with the largest concentration of householders in Mexico City, where hospitals, schools, religious institutions, public works and architectural monuments multiplied accordingly. Urbanization was linked to a new market and a specific group of suppliers. In this way, merchants made possible the material basis for a higher social status for all groups. Despite the advances in material wellbeing, social changes from 1590 to 1660 were not actively promoted because the newer caste society fostered the status quo and discouraged mobility (Schell Hoberman 1991: 7, 9-17). By the mid-17th century, it was clear the difference between urban and rural life. The cities were just propitious for the growth of the Spanish-speaking and mestizo groups (Gonzalbo 1990: 27, 320).

8.2 Education of Spanish speakers

The history of education for the children of Spaniards illustrates the long-term goals, curricula and general mission of the different institutions founded for this group. During the 17th century the *Colegio de San Ildefonso* consolidated its prestige and was accredited as the breeding ground of secular and ecclesiastical functionaries not only due to the students' preparation but to the frequency and brilliance of the public acts. Application for admissions was accompanied with the necessary documentation needed for *probanzas*. The *Colegio de San Pedro y San Pablo* later merged with the *Colegio de San Ildefonso*, when it was boasting the coat of arms of Castile and Leon. Literacy acts were normally conducted in Latin and were well-attended. Students were also engaged in oral drills in order to demonstrate their knowledge before a tribunal. When they desired to participate in private and public tournaments, applicants were compelled to show that they were children of Old Christians, and that it was fruitful to compete in lively debates of logic and rhetoric. The graduates from the various colleges occupied in turn high positions in both ecclesiastic and lay institutions. Children of Spaniards admitted to schools had to be legitimate, while some schools balanced the staff members between Spaniards and *criollos*. Dominicans and Franciscans were also active in University activities. Indigenous students remained in the rural areas, whereas the cities became the propitious environment of the Spanish-speaking society (Gonzalbo 1990: 236, 246, 251, 261-264-266, 273, 278, 295, 298, 311).

In the early 17th century, the principles of purity of blood were still applied in the selection of students and teachers, and for this reason, blacks, Indians and mulattoes were not allowed to become instructors. Schools were founded throughout the colony first in central Mexico (e.g. Mexico City, Queretaro, Puebla) where young girls were educated in the *escuelas de amigas* (schools for girls) or simply "*amigas*". Since the early 17th century, the Jesuits founded schools in Merida (with 70 students), in San Luis Potosi (with 200 students) and in Queretaro, which was a village in 1606 but became a city in 1656. A few years later in 1671, Queretaro had turned into the third city of the viceroyalty because of the economic prosperity in the areas of agriculture and cattle raising; it also became a trade center strategically located at the crossroads of the mining sites to the north. Throughout the 17th century the Jesuits continued opening schools to the northwest. The *criollo* population increased gradually in and around the schools; one of the most important schools was that of San Nicolás in Valladolid. The Jesuit schools became the centers of cultural and intellectual life. In Zacatecas (1617–1620), Spanish speakers requested courses and the schools received donations from the mine owners. In this city there were 1000 Spanish families who had priority to take Latin grammar courses. By the mid-17th century, some schools were still requiring a certificate of purity of blood or *probanzas* (Gonzalbo 1990: 205, 211, 213 and passim).

Like their homologous Franciscans and Dominicans, the Jesuits were knowledgeable of those indigenous languages that were advantageous to establish missions in the northwest or colleges in the central area. The Jesuits' curriculum was not very different from the Calvinists centers founded in Strassburg or Heidelberg. The mastery of languages was a prerequisite for studies of Theology for it provided the basis to proceed in Latin. Boys started as young as 7, and between the ages of 12 and 14 they had completed their course of studies in the Humanities. Between 16 and 18, they began studies of Theology, which lasted four years. Classes started with the reading of a Latin text followed by corresponding explanations or clarifications. In lower-division courses, discussions were conducted in the mother tongue but from the third year onwards, the use of Latin was exclusive. Their insistence on the classic curriculum gave the Jesuits the reputation of being elitists. The average number of years needed for a member to graduate was 14. As the *Compañía de Loyola* spread over the vast expansion of the New Spanish territory, local Jesuit congregations gained relative autonomy at the same time that the requirements for admission turned looser. Towards the end of the 17th century, the academic standards on the Humanities had declined considerably, and consequently the Jesuits attempted to search for strategies that could make the study of Latin attractive. Because it was impractical to adhere to the all-Latin rule, extra-curricular activities were oriented towards colloquia and dramas in Romance (i.e. Spanish); as expected, when tradition was altered, the academic standards were no longer upheld. Written assignments for advanced students were required in Latin but Spanish was just fine in basic courses. The long-term goal was to have 12-14 year-old students writing Latin prose and verse (Gonzalbo: 217, 221 and passim).

8.3 Uprooting and integration of the castes

In contrast with the quality of life that Spanish speakers enjoyed, other groups struggled in the process of integration to colonial society which was constantly challenging their loyalties and expectations. The study of the caste system in New Spain probes into the many contradictions posed to the different ethnic groups (Martínez 2008: 196-198). As the decades of the colonial period went by, the exigencies of the caste system were more difficult to meet. In order to introduce a coherent design, as of the late 17th century Spanish speakers produced sufficient memorials extolling the alliances of the early colonial times which stressed the notion of nobility by adding the ancestry from elite Amerindians. Spanish-speaking *criollos* constructed a native identity separate from Castile claiming kinship to historical narratives related to the imperial pre-Hispanic past. In this way, scholars gave literary expression to the growing hybrid cult of the Virgin of Guadalupe. The transformation of the pre-Hispanic past into New Spain's classical antiquity enabled Spanish speakers to create deeper roots in the New World; this was the beginning of the rupture with Spain. Indigenous ancestry, if only symbolic, was not an impediment to issue a *probanza*. Due to changes in marriage patterns and legitimacy rates, the caste system in central Mexico was not intact. In Puebla, for example, marriages between Spaniards and women of partial African descent experienced modest increases at the end of the 17th century. By then, the Church had intensified its campaign to compel couples in informal unions to marry. Because the Church was upholding the principle of free will in the choice of marriage partners, families had no legal mechanism to impede such unions. Legitimacy rates among castes were also rising. The growing instability of the caste system was due to the greater complexity of the colonial society, which had a dramatic surge in the population of mixed ancestry; the beginnings of a working class culture (especially in the northern mining towns, Mexico City and Puebla) and increasing social mobility was simultaneous to the expansion of mercantile capitalism (Martínez 2008: 238-239).

Many colonial officials used their slaves as public symbols of the economic, social and military power because there were no separate plantations for black slaves (Martínez 2008: 146-147; 159-160). "By the early 17th century both Mexico City and Puebla had rising numbers of free and enslaved Africans who were relatively integrated into Spanish colonial society. Many lived in close proximity to Spanish residents and tended to be relatively acculturated, especially those who had been raised in the Americas and worked in Spanish households" (Martínez 2008: 160). Acculturated blacks and mulattoes were Spanish proficient or so well assimilated that they were indistinguishable from authentic Spaniards. Mobility went in both directions but economic trends were not uniform. Improvements in mining and agricultural production and greater integration into the Atlantic economy gave Mexico modest but steady economic growth rates. Some regions experienced more decline in out-migration growth, e.g. Puebla, where many Spaniards became impoverished while the city itself lost its charm. During these decades of economic fluctuations, colonial officials believed that the craft guilds were models of order, and a good portion of the working population played a role in reproducing social hierarchies. In Mexico City, a good number of working males participated in artisan crafts, which despite the growing numbers of non-Spaniards who owned their own shops, was structured according to racial lines. Even if master artisans were no longer all Spaniards and *criollos*, and even if workers were by no means people of indigenous and black ancestry, the most important trades and small workshops were still controlled by people of European descent. In the Puebla-Tlaxcala basin, Michoacan, Jalisco, Guanajuato and the Mexico City area, almost all owned by Spaniards, the workforce was made up exclusively of people of mixed ancestry and black slaves (Martinez 2008: 161, 240).

In this century more than 350 slaves were brought to Parral (presently Chihuahua) mostly from Angola, Mozambique, Biafra, Portugal and Calabar. In Parral, slaves, free blacks and mulattoes worked in the mines and as servants of the local people; they intermingled with one another, became part of the community, got married and had children. Some turned into cowboys and looked after cattle. Finally, in the early 1700's in other mining locations, blacks and mulattoes played a significant role in the economy and furthered their assimilation into mainstream Mexican culture. They resided in the towns of El Real de San Francisco de Cuéllar (present day Chihuahua City) and Santa Eulalia (Chihuahua), where they worked as domestic servants, miners, muleteers, and blacksmiths. By the early 18th century blacks had become an integral part of colonial society, and by the end of the colonial period they had adopted all aspects of their European counterparts' culture including religion, language, food and general lifestyle (Franco 2004: 47-54)

Regarding the hacienda in the state of Morelos, Wobeser (1986) offers a good example of the activities of black slaves, who made up the nucleus of labor force because of their specialized skills; they were in charge of sugar manufacturing and worked together with Indians, mestizos and Spaniards where they acted as supervisors, administrators, accountants, artisans, and the like. However, Indian and mestizos made up the largest group in the vast majority of haciendas where they served as shepherds, raised cattle or worked in agriculture. Some lived permanently in the haciendas while others were temporary employees. The number of black slaves was variable, since its availability depended on the law of supply and demand. Most haciendas purchased slaves in the early 1600's but after 1730 they decreased, only to disappear at the end of the 18th century. Slavery was normally dwindling, and there is no information on any hacienda maintaining or augmenting its original numbers. Overexploitation, low fertility rates, high mortality rates (including suicide) were the main reasons of population loss. Women worked in the sugar mills, but they were also in charge of other duties such as cooking, baby-sitting for working women, teaching catechism, or midwifery. Some of the male slaves worked as supervisors, and as such they served as a bridge between the administrators and the black community, whose members often lived in huts inside the hacienda. There was one supervisor for males and another for females, and many problems were resolved by the oldest and most judicious ones. Aside from working in the sugar mills they were supposed to go to church and learn the Christian doctrine. While the *hacendados* imposed many restrictions on them and were constantly watching them, some managed to escape and never returned to the haciendas. With few exceptions, during the first half of the 17th century almost all the adult slaves had been born in West Africa, e.g. Senegambia, coasts of Kongo and Angola, and the Ghana region. The offspring of this first generation were known as *negros criollos* (native blacks), a group that outstripped those born in Africa. As a consequence of interbreeding with Europeans, Indians and castes, members of the second generation were not necessarily 'racially pure'. Overall, they held different attitudes towards slavery: many adjusted themselves to exploitation while others sought to overcome their condition and fought for their freedom via confrontation, evasion, or integration into the free society.

About thirty percent of the cases tried by the Holy Office in the 17th century refer to descendants of Africans. This proportion tends to decrease while the cases of mulattoes increased during the same century, a fact that reflects the new trends of mestizaje. Due to the emphasis on castes the total of both groups makes up about one-half in which the individual's ethnic origin is logged in with precision. Their sins were normally blasphemy, curse, sorcery, bigamy, and aggression. The archives shed light on their lives marked by the disgrace of being uprooted, not only from their families but from their lands, and whereas the vast majority were victims of excessive corporal punishment, some enjoyed surprising freedom. Diego de la Cruz, for example, was sold by his master because he was disobedient and was going out on a spree having a lot of fun (Alberro 1988: 457, 461).

It is assumed that there was complicity between African slaves and crypto-Jews, who were communicating in African languages. Some of the merchants and children of Portuguese descent Jews were raised by African nannies who taught them their languages. In addition, some of the wealthy merchants, who lived surrounded by slaves, used African languages for different periods of time. This disconcerting alliance stems from a common experience in the repressive circumstances of the New World. For instance, Gaspar Rivero de Vasconcelos, born in Tanger of Portuguese parents, lived as a free literate subject and conspired with a Portuguese Jew. He was accused of bigamy and was rebellious and maladjusted (Alberro 1988: 469-471).

8.4 Colonial Spanish in the oldest Spanish-speaking regions

In the multilingual / multicultural scenario of New Spain, the Spanish language unfolded in varying domains and spread in different directions. This section examines 17th century language data and compares the emerging trends with those of the previous century. The variants selected are retrieved from DLNE-AC (Docs. 79-176) and from DLNE-EG (Docs. 49-105). The analysis of the 16th century language data reveals that the Spanish used in the Gulf region does not differ substantially from the Spanish written in the Central Highlands. Thus, the occasional dissimilarities are not suitable to probe into differing models that might explain minor disparities. The variants analyzed in the following sections and the interpretations advanced therein derive from the examination of language data in both regions.

8.4.1 The spelling of the sibilants in Castilian

The *Documentos Lingüísticos de España* collected by Menéndez Pidal (1919) offer numerous clues and examples of lexicon and verb forms that are representative of the different regions and sub-regions where Castilian or medieval Spanish was spoken, particularly the 13th century, when the spelling of medieval sibilants was relatively consistent. Based on the etymological criterion, many of the spellings of words with <c>, <ç>, <z>, <s> and <ss> did have continuity beyond the 13th century. In the New World nonetheless the departure from the etymological principle was glaring until the 17th century. The examples in Table 8.2 show the Castilian pattern matching the spelling with the dental pronunciation: <c>, <ç> and <z>, graphemes that were later modernized and finally became the norm. When the connections with Spain weakened, New World Spanish speakers lost awareness of the metropolitan norms. The distinction of the sibilants was one of the affected areas to the point that scribes and other writers preserved mostly items ending in Latin –*tiō*, spelled –*cion* in Castilian.

Table 8.2: Words and verb forms: 13th century

Year	Document	Item	Normative
1227	86, p. 125	acaezen	acaecen
1228	87, p. 126	fazer	hacer
1228	87, p. 126	cielo	cielo
1237	91, p. 131	decima	décima
1241	93, p. 134	precioso	precioso
1241	93, p. 134	establecido	establecido
1242	94, p. 135	pedaço	pedazo
1242	94, p. 135	cerca	cerca
1247	97, p. 138	sazon	sazón
1254	100, p. 140	palaçio	palacio
1262	102, p. 143	Lucifer	Lucifer
1279	105, p. 146	deuocion	devoción

Source: Menéndez Pidal (1919)

Another group of words with sibilants also appear in the *Documentos Lingüísticos de España*; they represent the apico-alveolar pronunciation of the graphemes <s> and <ss>. A complete divergence from this pattern was also multi-secular, and eventually double <ss> was dissolved in favor of the single <s> grapheme. Table 8.3 shows the difference between the 13th century spelling and the modern spelling.

Table 8.3: Words and verb forms: 13th century

Year	Document	Item	Normative
1237	189, p. 241	cosa	cosa
1239	190, p. 245	esa	esa
1255	196, p. 252	confirmasse	confirmase
1261	197, p. 253	podiessemos	pudiésemos
1262	102, p. 142	remission	remisión
1262	103, p. 143	condessa	condesa
1279	105, p. 146	ffiziessemos	hiciésemos
1279	105, p. 146	missas	misas
1285	107, p. 149	vassallo	vasallo
1285	108, p. 150	presentes	presentes
1304	143, p. 188	successores	sucesores
1325	145, p. 190	possession	posesión

Source: Menéndez Pidal (1919)

8.4.2 The spelling of the sibilants in the Central Highlands

The confusion of sibilant graphemes permeated the documents issued in the New World Spanish colonies, where the spelling of words with <c>, <ç> and <z> was replaced with <s>. The spelling of the sibilants in the New World shows alterations and vacillations of different sorts. The most common practice was the spelling of <c> and <z> words with consonant <s>, particularly in items of high frequency. As seen in Table 8.4, in the Central Highlands there is sufficient evidence of anti-etymological spelling trends (Docs. 79-132).

Table 8.4: Words and verb forms: first half of 17th century

Year	Document	Item	Normative
1621	83, p. 251	conosia	conocía
1621	83, p. 251	hechisera	hechicera
1621	84, p. 252	hasian	hacían
1625	89, p. 265	vesino	vecino
1625	89, p. 265	asotasen	azotasen
1625	89, p. 265	obligasion	obligación
1625	89, p. 265	consiensia	conciencia
1628	91, p. 268	prensipio	principio
1628	91, p. 268	lus	luz
1629	93, p. 272	cavesa	cabeza
1629	93, p. 273	empesaron	empezaron
1629	94, p. 275	escandalisado	escandalizado
1629	94, p. 277	espasio	espacio
1629	94, p. 278	paresia	parecía
1629	94, p. 279	calsadilla	calzadilla
1630	103, p. 295	resevi	recibí
1632	120, p. 325	desir	decir
1634	121, p. 336	alcansar	alcanzar
1634	121, p. 336	obligasion	obligación
1634	122, p. 336	acresentamientos	acrecentamientos

Source: Company Company (1994)

Writers of the colonial period are divided in two major groups: (1) those who tend to follow the etymological patterns derived from late medieval Spanish, and (2) those who deviating from the norm incurred in the replacement of <c>, <ç> and <z> by single <s>, a practice that initiated the trend known as *seseo*. In the computation of the sibilants, the following items were excluded: words that are abbreviated or reconstructed, numbers, months of the year, first names, surnames, and toponyms. Items spelled with <c>, <ç>, and <z> exemplify traditional trends: *gracia* (240), *reverencia, braços, voces, diciendo* (241), *contradiciendolo, conocia, noticia, cabeça* (242), *cruzada, cobranza* (341), whereas items spelled with <s>, which could have been spelled with any of the other sibilants, represent the *seseante* trends: *hiso* (244), *averiguasion, pareser, desia* (245), *conosieron* (246) *anochesió, senaron* (246), *serrojo* (247), *asul, plasa* (272). The analysis of documents of the 17th century reveals that there are minor differences between the Central Highlands and the Gulf, and that other spelling practices were present in documents drafted by notaries, paid scribes, and common letter writers.

8.4.3 Sibilants in the Gulf

Subsamples retrieved from DLNE-EG (Docs. 49-105) reveal a minor difference between regions, since the sibilant graphemes used in the Gulf are more diverse; although all the variants appear in both regions, alternate graphemes are more abundant in the Gulf. This may be due to the personnel assigned to the Gulf, who might have been closer to Spain but not well trained in the Castilian norms of the times. In this century, anti-etymological spelling practices may be interpreted in different ways:

(1) Use of <z> in inter-vocalic position, as in *dezir* (164), *hazen* (167), *regozijos* (168), *azerca* (189), *alguazil* (193), *cruzes* (177), *hazienda* (225), *dozenas* (226), *calzetas* (243), *raízes* (244), *nezesario, lizenzia, rezivia* (257) might have been associated with voicing in intervocalic position, or at least with vestiges of such pronunciation. The same principle was probably applied to the use of <z> in the Latin suffix –*ciō*, as in *presenttazion* (256), *determinazion* (289), and to the use of <z> in initial position as in *zedro, zerradura* (244), *ziudad* (189), *zepo* (289). After a voiced nasal consonant, the same abovementioned criterion might have been applied, as in for example, *marzo* (256), *ofenza* (276), *amanzevamientos* (303), etc.

(2) Use of false <z> before a voiceless consonant as in *ajuzte* (226) or *berberizca* (230) might have been merely a performance error.

(3) Spelling with <ss> imperfect subjunctive verb forms represent traditional trends, as in *descubriesse* (186), *hiziesse, vissitasse* (189), *informasse, pagassen, perturbasse* (221), *ubiesse* (222) *reduxesse* (223), *declarasse* (268), *llegasse, opusiesse* (282), but alternated with single <s>.

(4) Use of <ss> in false *seseo*, as in *conossidos* (188), *favoressido* (189), *hasse* (218), *confirmassion* (221), *partissipan, gosso* (223), *mossa* (268), *alcanssó, caballerissa* (289) might have been a passing trend that imitated the model of late medieval Spanish.

(5) Use of <ss> in false etymology, as in *perssonas* (188), *franzesses* (188), *descanssa* (223), *casso* (188), *pressente* (218), *pressume* (268), *usso* (278); and use of <ss> in correct etymology as in *passión* (160), *comissario* (166), *sucesso* (211), *missa* (218).

(6) Finally, the tendency to use medieval Spanish <ç> to represent a *ceceante* pronunciation in lieu of etymological <s> reappears in the 17th century documents of the Gulf, as in *descanço* (161), *peços, graça* (161), *paça* (162), *ygleçia* (206), *aviça* (163) *omiçión, viçita* (246), and *puçieron* (279).

8.4.4 "Regular" *seseo*

Most of the miscellaneous graphemes used in the colonial period show divergence from the etymological norms but the variety of graphemes did not establish an unusual tradition. The only spelling practice perpetuated by writers was the "regular" *seseo*, primarily in frequent words. Spelling words with <s> when the etymological rule (<c> or <z>) must apply is now a peculiar routine amongst Latin American Spanish speakers who have not had opportunities to attain a solid tertiary education. Table 8.5 shows a subsample of common words that can be misspelled in both colonial and modern documents. In combination with other features (e.g. archaic verb forms such as *vido* and *truje*), commonly misspelled words point to the existence of popular or vernacular varieties that are still used in rural or marginal areas of the American continent.

Table 8.5: Examples of "regular" seseo in the 17th century

Year	Document	Seseo	Normative
1603	50, p. 161	sielo	cielo
1621	59, p. 191	asen	hacen
1621	59, p. 193	publisidad	publicidad
1625	62, p. 199	corason	corazón
1626	62, p. 200	isquierdo	izquierdo
1631	64, p, 205	capás	capaz
1646	71, p. 225	acsident	accidente
1668	83, p. 259	relasion	relación
1668	83, p. 260	consiensia	conciencia
1668	84, p. 263	amenasas	amenazas
1681	93, p. 287	obligasiones	obligaciones
1689	97, p. 293	asotara	azotara

Source: Melis et al. (2008)

Despite the divergences of spelling trends in this century, the difference between traditional graphemes and *seseo* points to a preference for the Castilian norms. Table 8.6 shows the spellings representing *seseo* in two periods and two regions. In Period I, normative graphemes prevail with two full thirds (67.78 %) in the Central Highlands and almost three-fourths (74.62 %) in the Gulf. The decline of normative graphemes occurs in the second half of the 17th century when slightly more than one half (52.18 %) of the spellings in the Central Highlands and 41.32 percent in the Gulf, respectively, represent *seseo*. In Period II, *seseo* increased from about one-third to slightly more than one-half in the Central Highlands, and such increase was slightly more moderate in the Gulf. The total for both periods in both regions reached 3,325 tokens. A majority of tokens represents traditional norms with 60 percent of all the tokens tallied; in comparison, sibilants representing *seseo* amount to roughly 40 percent in this century. *Seseo* was still moderate in both regions in Period I taking an upward swing in Period II (20 % in the Central Highlands and 16 % in the Gulf). Local writers indulge in the exclusive use of *seseo* and total disregard for the traditional variants (see AC Doc. 162, 1692). Notwithstanding, *seseo* did not prevail because some writers were following metropolitan norms. Other trends are exemplified by the graphemes <ss>, <zz>, <cs>, which may have represented various allophones, misspellings, or simply performance errors.

Table 8.6: Summary: Anti-etymological and traditional sibilants in the 17th century

Region	Period	Seseo	<c>, <ç>, <z>
Altiplano C.	I. 1609–1640	306 / 950 (32.21 %)	644 / 950 (67.78 %)
Altiplano C.	II. 1681–1697	598 / 1146 (52.18 %)	548 / 1146 (47.81 %)
El Golfo	I. 1602–1647	159 / 609 (26.10 %)	450 / 609 (73.89 %)
El Golfo	II. 1651–1699	258 / 620 (41.61 %)	362 / 620 (58.38 %)
Tokens	Total = 3,325	1,321 (39.72 %)	2,004 (60.27 %)

8.4.5 Residual verb forms

The forms of the verbs TRAER and VER frequently appear in the preterit of the indicative tense in both the Central Highlands and in the Gulf region. The verb TRAER derives from Latin TRAHERE; the medieval spelling in the preterit was both *traxe* and *truxe*, while the alternate spelling appeared after the 16th century: *yo truje* (modern *traje*), *tú trujiste* (modern *trajiste*), *él / ella trujo* (modern *trajo*) and *ellos / ellas trujeron* (modern *trajeron*). The verb VER derives from Latin VEDERE, and the preterit forms in medieval Spanish were *yo vide* (modern *vi*), *él / ella vido* (modern *vio*), *nosotros videmos* (modern *vimos*). In the 17th century two forms of the same verb may appear in the same sentence, as in (b) and (k). More interestingly, some of these forms are still used in rural and marginal regions and communities of the Spanish-speaking New World, and may reappear in the United States Southwest in both rural and urban communities.

(a) Y que de allí a quatro semanas *trujeron* a esta testigo a este pueblo (EG 54, 1609)

(b) aviendo descargado las mercaderías que *truxo*, (...) la gente llegó a este puerto, donde asimismo echó algunas mercaderías, y dél se *retrujo* al puerto de Campeche (EG 58, 1620)
(c) De do *vido* esta testigo (EG 55, 1610)
(d) Sólo *vide* salir de un aposento de la dicha negra Ursula a un español llamado Juan Gallegos (...), y *vide* que estaba detrás de la puerta arrimado a la pared (EG 55, 1610)
(e) hize a los indios serrar las puertas de la sala y les mandé *trugesen* cordeles para maniatarlo (EG 55, 1610)
(f) pedía que *truxesen* brasas (EG 55, 1610)
(g) Y despues que *truxeron* luz le conosio mas bien (AC 81, 1618)
(h) Donde *bido* este testigo al dicho capitan (AC 82, 1618)
(i) Este testigo dio bozes a los indios y los mandó llamar para que le *truxesen* caballo; y se lo *truxeron* como al amanezer (AC 82, 1618)
(j) Y descubriéndole *bido* como estaba desnudo (AC 82, 1618)
(k) Entre la gente que *truxo, traxo* seis o siete franzesses (EG 58, 1620)
(l) Y *bide* en este tiempo la dispusisión de todo (EG 64, 1631)
(m) Aunque lo *vide*, no me atrevo a dezirlo por no parezer encareçedor (EG 66, 1636)
(n) *trujeron* a esta villa a la justicia hordinaria (EG 73, 1647)
(o) este declarante *vido* lo referido (EG 104, 1696)

8.4.6 *Leísmo* in the Central Highlands and in the Gulf

The items of the subsamples below refer to events that were relevant for the subjects who had to deal with stressful events in which immediate attention or involvement was needed. The narrators were normally the Spanish speakers who appeared before the Inquisition or the civil authorities where there was an office in charge of registering the testimony of a party or witness in civil or criminal proceedings taken before a trial. Because the verbatim transcriptions were unaltered, they most likely reflect the spontaneous speech habits of those who were deposed in public.

Items (a) through (j) retrieved from AC 80 (1618) relate the denunciation of Marianna's sister against an Indian doctor who was called to see Marianna's baby boy. The narrator is the baby's aunt, who was dissatisfied with the presence of the Indian doctor; in the end the doctor cured the baby, and the mother was grateful because he had a healthy life for many years. Marianna's sister may have been identified exclusively with Spanish speakers, and thus in her testimony the use of LE prevailed, but at the end of the drama the baby's mother used a categorical LO in item (j).

(a) **trayendole** en braços de un parte a otra dava voces diciendo: "¡Ha, que se me muere mi hijo!"
(b) se despidio para yr a ver a su hijo, que tambien **le tenia** enfermo en su casa
(c) Y andando a buscar a quién **le curasse** [al bebé]
(d) no conoçia al médico (...) ni en su vida **le avia visto**
(e) y para effecto de **curarle** pidio un tepalcate con brasas, copal y algodon
(f) el yndio Alonso, criado que *lo conocia* y les acabava de dar noticia dél. Y luego a la tarde volvio y *lo traxo*
(g) el yndio **le estava saumando** con copal y haziendo cruzes sobre él y hechandole bendiciones
(h) assi mismo **le vio vaxar** el rostro sobre la cabeça del niño
(i) lo qual no oyo esta declarante ni **le vio mover** los labios
(j) dixo la doña Marianna que *lo avia curado* muy bien

The sentences below from AC 81-82 (1618) deal with another unexpected incident narrated by the witness of a murder where the victim was Diego de Quesada, the Mayor of Pinotepa (Oaxaca), who was having an affair with Gregorio Basques' wife. The case of marital infidelity, items (a) and (b), caused a lot of commotion in the nearby towns. The perpetrator of the crime, Gregorio Basques, had a few buddies who heard the story, and rushed to his place where they found the Mayor's body. The narrator stumbled over words and repetitively described the place and the manner in which the corpse had been found, items (f) through (h). According to the witness, the protagonists were involved in the shrouding of the dead for burial, items (c) and (f). The author alternates the clitics LO and LE particularly with the most intense verbs *hallar* ('to find'), *matar* ('to kill'), and *amortajar* ('to shroud'). For the witness, 'to shroud' was probably more intense in (c) than in (e).

(a) despues que truxeron la luz **le conosio** mas bien, y sabe **le mató** el dicho Gregorio Basques porque **le halló** con su muger en su aposento
(b) **le halló** desnudo enserrado
(c) este testigo *lo hizo sacar* a la sala para **amortajarle**
(d) El dicho Santoyo abló con él **saludandole**
(e) [el testigo] bido antes de *amortajarlo* cómo tenia en las espaldas dos agujeros
(f) por aver visto la sangre rrepresentada donde **le mataron** y el rrastro de ella, que yba donde este testigo **le halló**
(g) y tambien *lo mataron* en la dicha sala y arrastraron a la recamara
(h) este testigo *lo halló* [al capitán], porque en la dicha sala fue donde el dicho Gregorio Bazquez **le mató** y el dicho Francisco de Sosa *lo dexó* alli muerto
(i) preguntandole este testigo si savía quién *lo avia arrastrado*, pues *lo avian muerto* en la sala

8.4 Colonial Spanish in the oldest Spanish-speaking regions — 293

Document EG 52 (1606) is the letter that Francisco Torralva wrote to Friar Rodrigo Ortiz with news about the conflicts between the Governor and the Bishop of Yucatan. Items (a) through (d) refer to the unsettling issues related to caciques, Indians, some other subjects, and the reprimands recommended for the subalterns.

(a) El día que *lo reçibieran* en cavildo [al teniente Paniagua]
(b) requirió el padre provincial que **le castigase** al Padre Cuevas
(c) al otro fraile (...) también **le mandó castigar**
(d) también lo ha quitado porque no **le salio** a reçebir

Document EG 55 (1616) is the letter delivered by Hernando de Valdés to the Holy Office in which he informs about the crimes committed by Juan de la Peña, assistant to the Mayor. Again, the narrators seem agitated over the episodes and the protagonists involved.

(a) fui a casa del dicho Fabián de la Peña donde vivía el dicho su sobrino, y **le hallé** vestido y recostado sobre su cama
(b) Yo di vozes a un indesuelo niño que llamase dos indios que *lo cargasen* [a Juan]
(c) yendo a serrar la puerta de donde **le saqué**, él se salió corriendo
(d) busqué al dicho Juan de la Peña por la casa y no **le hallé**
(e) El dicho teniente quiso salir, haziendo campo con la espada, y yo **le detuve** con la mía
(f) Yo dige que *lo avía* de llevar preso
(h) yo **le absolvería** de la excomunión
(i) en la yglesia **le aguardaba** y que en las puertas della **le absolvería**
(j) **le embi**é a llamar para **absolverle**, y **le aguardé** buen rato

Document EG 65 (1632) is to the biography of Father Alonso Guillén, a virtuous young man who was sent to Salamanca to study law; he was constantly teased by his colleagues and was unable to prevent them from playing the deceitful games that got him in trouble, items (a) through (e).

(a) *lo enbiaron* a Salamanca para que estudiase el derecho canónico y çivil, lo que hazía con ventaja entre los de su edad, quando el señor **le llamó**
(b) Un hombre grave y público estuvo determinado de poner en él las manos y aun de *hazerlo* matar
(c) encarecidamente le rogó que no **le alavase**, sino que **le tuviese** por pecador
(d) Una persona (...) *viéndolo* tan zeloso de la pureza y castidad, se determinó de vuscar medios y valerse de mugeres perdidas para *lo enechizar* a fin de **hazerle** caer en el sucio deleyte
(e) entre el padre y los juezes que **le traýan** engañado

Documents in which spontaneous speech appears contrast with biographies, because in the latter there seems to be no urgency to narrate unexpected events, and the emphasis lies on the life of the subject. In EG 84 (1668), a witness gave a detailed account of Joseph de Reynoso's whereabouts. The verb *conocer* ('to know someone') is consistently used with the clitic LE, as in (a) and (b). The witness however makes a difference between *vido* and *vio* (alternating preterits of the verb *ver* ('to see'), where the difference might have been the intention of observing or meeting a person, as in the second part of (b), and just seeing him / her, as in items (c) and (d).

(a) dixo que este testigo conoçe a don Joseph de Reynoso, y **le conoció** en el reyno de la Nueba España
(b) después assimismo **le conoció** en esta ciudad (...) donde **le vido** muchas veçes
(c) este declarante **le vio** con una capa blanca larga (...) así mismo **le vio** por más tiempo
(d) asimismo **le a visto** andar (...) a cauallo

Documents EG 94 (1681) and 96 (1689) tell stories about the ethnic groups who had been living under extremely disadvantageous conditions. The theory on inter-ethnic relations may apply in these contexts. Using LE might have served to enhance the Spanish identity of the narrators; for this reason, the clitic LO alternates with the use of LE. Document 94 deals with the strategies of Francisco Marcos de Velasco and his cellmates to escape from jail, items (a) through (f).

(a) entraron las perssonas que cuidavan su prissión y le metieron los pies en el sepo donde donde **le dejaron** asegurado
(b) trajeron presso a dicha su prissión a un yndio ladino llamado Juan, y que al *meterlo* en el sepo donde él estaba ...
(c) dio voses a Juan Chiquito, mulato, esclavo del dicho señor alcalde mayor, para que *lo cuidase*
(d) el dicho alguasil mayor **le cojió y aprendió** (...) hasta que con orden de dicho señor alcalde mayor **le an traído** a la deste pueblo
(e) todo a sido caminar de noche hasta que **le cojieran**
(f) Y que al indio que salió con él no **le vido** más

Finally, EG 96 is the denunciation of Cristóbal de Frías against a black slave accused of blasphemy, items (a) and (b), while EG 99-101 (1691) deal with charges of sexual harassment filed by an Indian against a mulatto, items (c) through (e), and the mulatto's defense from the accusations, items (f) through (j).

(a) aviéndole echado unas esposas para **traerle** [al esclavo] con seguridad renegó de Dios i de los santos

(b) [el negro] desía que le echassen de ahí unos perros que **le atormentavan**
(c) llegó un mulato, que no **le conoce ni le avía visto** nunca
(d) diciéndole *lo llevaría* a Campeche (...). Y entonces *lo empezó a pellizcar*
(e) [el mulato] **le vio venir** hablando con un yndezuelo (...) **le empezó** a llamar
(f) la primera vez que **le vio y conoció** [a Juan Ramírez] fue en casa del cappitan (...) y que no **le vio** después
(g) antes de la festividad de la Concepción de Nuestra Señora, **le volvió** a veer esta declarante en la puerta de su solar
(h) aviéndose despedido de esta declarante, no **le vio** más
(i) no **le volvía a ver** hasta el día siguiente [al mulato]
(j) que *lo mataría* [a quien mirase hacia un cuarto de la casa]

The [+ animate] *leísta* patterns of the 17th century are not very different from those reported in the 16th century, although attrition might have been expected. In junctures like this, the researcher may resort to an explanatory model that puts in bold relief the inter-ethnic relations of the 17th century when Spanish speakers might have desired to be distinguished from the castes. In situations of stress and before civil or ecclesiastic authorities, Spanish speakers might have enhanced their allegiances with the colonial system that was favorably working for them. In like manner, LE might have been used to show a prudent distance from the "ethnics" who were not original native Spanish speakers. A summary of the verbs and clitics appears in Table 8.7. This random subsample includes both independent verbs and some that are used with auxiliaries. The most frequent verbs used with LE are *absolver* ('to absolver'), *coger* ('to grab'), *conocer* ('to know someone'), *hallar* ('to find'), *tener* ('to have'), *traer* ('to bring') and *ver* ('to see someone'). The results are similar to those of the 16th century (in Table 6.3A), where the use of LE stands out with two full-thirds of the tokens.

Table 8.7: Subsample of verbs with LE and LO

	Verb	LE	LO
1	Verb	LE	LO
2	Absolver	3	
3	Aguardar	2	
4	Alabar	1	
5	Amortajar	1	1
6	Aprehender	1	
7	Atormentar	1	
8	Cargar		1
9	Castigar	1	1
10	Coger	3	1
11	Conocer	5	1
12	Cuidar		1
13	Curar	2	1
14	Dejar	1	1
15	Detener	1	
16	Enhechizar		1
17	Enviar		1
18	Enviar + Aux. V	1	
19	Hacer + Aux. V	1	2
20	Hallar	4	1
21	Llamar	1	1
22	Llevar		1
23	Mandar	1	1
24	Mandar + Aux. V	1	1
25	Matar	2	2
26	Meter	1	1
27	Morir		1
28	Pellizcar	1	1
29	Poner	1	
30	Recibir		1
31	Sacar	1	
32	Saludar	1	
33	Reprender		1
34	Sahumar	1	
35	Tener	3	1
36	Traer	4	1
37	Velar	1	
38	Ver	12	
39	Ver + Aux. V	2	
40	Volver	2	
	Total = 89	63 / 89 (70.78 %)	26 / 89 (29.21 %)

8.4.7 Inanimate objects and *leísmo*

The rise of *leísmo* in northern-central Spain triggered other innovations which were extended to [– animate] objects, as in sentences (a) through (c), which refer to a book with a certain mysterious content.
(a) el qual libro le mostró (...) diçiendo que **le leyese** y que vería en el una cosa muy superior (EG 60, 1624)
(b) "lea v. md. adelante". Este declarante le respondió: "ora es ya de comer", después **le leería**, y que le rogó le dexase aquel libro para **leerle** más despacio (EG 60, 1624)
(c) el manuscripto **le rasgó** porque no conoçiessen las personas que **le viessen** que lo que éste havía predicado era de sermón ageno (EG 91, 1680)

Another and more complex innovation stemming from the departure to a non-etymological system is *laísmo* or the use of the pronoun LA as indirect object, which replaces a LE as in (d), in which a female subject is to be warned of something evil.
(d) abía de llamar a la justicia para *abisarla* de las maldades y echiserías que hasía (EG 97, 1689)

The total number of tokens referring to [+ animate masculine] singular objects appears in Table 8.8 showing an overwhelming majority of *leístas* with a difference of almost one-fifth between the Central Highlands and the Gulf. While it is difficult to ascertain that there are significant regional variations explaining the contrast, other variables such as situational context, topic, emphasis, intention, and the inter-ethnic attitudes of the subjects involved in the selected subsamples may be factored in the examination of variation, which on the surface appears to be random. The cases of [– animate] LE enhance the *leísta* pattern but are not computed in Table 8.8.

Table 8.8: LE and LO in the 17th century

Region	LE	LO
Altiplano C.	135 / 220 (61.36 %)	85 / 220 (38.63 %)
El Golfo	69 / 86 (80.23 %)	17 / 86 (19.76 %)
Total = 306	204 (66.66 %)	102 (33.33 %)

8.4.8 Pronouns of address: *tú, vuestra merced, su merced, Usted*

Between the 16th and the 17th century a major shift occurred when *vos* was replaced by *tú*, the trend known as *tuteo*, which was coming from Madrid. *Tú* was invoked by those who worshipped God and the saints, as in (a) and (b), whereas all the priests commonly addressed their parishioners with *tú* regardless of sex, age and sociocultural status, as in (c).

(a) "corte del çielo, *mírame*", ... "corte del cielo, *óyeme*", ... "corte del çielo, *respóndeme*" (EG 56, 1616)
(b) "San Juan de Dios, *duélete* de mi alma, que la tengo muy negra" (EG 88, 1675)
(c) el dicho padre le dixo: "no *digas* 'Dios', sólo *as* de dezir 'compañero' (EG 54, 1609)

In addition to the routines described above, *tú* was used in asymmetrical relations between master and servant, where the latter received *tú* and the former *vuestra merced*, as in items (a) and (b). In husband and wife relationships, the use of *tú* was reciprocal as in (c) and (d).

(a) don Lucas de Dosal llamó a un criado suyo, mestiço, y le dijo: "*tráeme* mi reliquia que está en la petaca" (EG 74, 1651)
(b) don Lucas, llamó a voçes a su criado diciendo: "*anda, tráeme* mi reliquia" y (...) le preguntó: "qué reliquia es la que *v.md.* tiene para los rayos y estas tempestades?" (EG 74, 1651)
(c) don Lucas del Dosal dixo a su muger (...) "¡*quítame* de aquí esta cara de diablo (...) ya *te* e dicho muchas veçes que lo *quites* de aquí (...) y lo *eches* en la cocina, yo *te* juro (...) que si no lo *quitas* de aquí y lo *echas* en la cosina, ¡que me la *as* de pagar!" (EG 74, 1651)
(d) "con la patatiña *te* quiero untar porque de mí no *te puedes* apartar (EG 62, 1629)

Tuteo was quite common in the interaction between Spanish speakers and the castes, who were addressed with *tú* by Spanish speakers, as in items (a) and (b); they in turn received *vuestra merced* from the castes, as in the first part of item (a). The castes belonging to the same ethnic group addressed one another with *tú*, as in items (c) through (f), while the young normally received *tú* from older interlocutors, as in (e). Speakers belonging to different non-Spanish ethnic groups (a mulatto boy and an Indian) also addressed one another with *tú* as in item (f), where the speakers used *tú* 4 times with the corresponding paradigmatic forms in the 2nd person singular. Likewise, Spanish-speaking friends of the same sex as in (g) or different sex as in (h) used reciprocal *tú*. Occasionally, an officer in a high-ranking position re-asserted his power using *vos*, as in (j), where the commissary of the Inquisition clearly invokes his right to use *vos* as the subject pronoun that was becoming obsolete in New Spain.

(a) "*míreme* qué tengo, que dicen tengo la voca tuerta y el ojo isquierdo tuerto", y la denunciante le dijo: "veamos", y vídola y le dijo: "no *tienes* nada" (EG 63, 1628)
(b) Juana de Saavedra dijo a la dicha negrita: "no *baias* porque se lo [h]e de desir a *tu* amo" (EG 102, 1691)
(c) "¿qué *tienes* que estás tam flaca?", y le respondió la negra Gracia: "qué tengo que hacer si ando mala?" y le dijo la otra (...): "qué me *darás*? Yo *te* daré sana (EG 63, 1628)
(d) "el diablo se *te* a metydo en la boca (EG 63, 1628)
(e) "no *sabes* lo que me susedió ayer", y que le respondió: "¿qué *te* susedió?" Y que le dijo: "*As* de saber que oy salió un clérigo de mi cassa (...), y le dije a mi negra: '*as* bien de comer y temprano' (EG 89, 1675)
(f) "¿de dónde *eres*?", y, diciéndole que era de Santa Lucia, le dixo: "*mientes* que no *eres* de Santa Lucia, y entonces este declarante le preguntó: "¿de dónde *eres tú*?" (EG 99, 1691)
(g) "*aprende* niña lo que *t[e]* digo para que *te* quiera *tu* hombre" (EG 88, 1675)
(h) Yo *te* quiero mucho, si es por aquello que *te* digo ¿por qué no *quieres* ser mis amores? (AC 86, 1621)
(i) "*calla*, que burlando *te* lo devio de decir" (AC 86, 1621)
(j) llamo de *vos* a las personas que parescen ante mí (EG 51, 1603)

8.4.9 *Vuestra merced*, *Usted* and *vosotros*

By the 17th century the pronouns *vos* and *tú* had become so frequent and popular in Spain that there was hardly any difference in symmetrical / asymmetrical relationships. *Vos* and *tú* were used between interlocutors of equal social standing until *vos* was replaced by *tú*. In order to make the difference along the axis of [+ / − deference], *vuestra merced* (derived from the possessive adjective of the pronoun *vos*) was used more frequently and normally alternated with the pronoun *tú*. *Vuestra merced* (< Latin *misericors* 'mercifulness') was a treatment of courtesy which invoked the mercy of the interlocutor, who was perceived as an honorable person (Nebrija 1492/1984: 181). *Vuestra merced* (abbreviated v.m.), *su merced* (abbreviated s. m.), and *Usted* (abbreviated U or V) appeared in the 17th century colonial documents (3rd person singular) in opposition to *tú* (see Table 8.9). *Vuestra merced* was overused in the 16th and 17th centuries in both formal and informal domains but particularly in business affairs and the family (Acevedo 1997: 70). In this subsample, *vuestra merced*, *su merced* and *Usted* account for two-thirds of all the singular pronouns, whereas *tú* accounts for the rest. Table 8.9 excludes the pronouns found in the 'love' letters of one writer (Table 8.10). The modern personal pronoun *Usted* appears for the first time at the end of the 17th century in both regions, where it contended disadvantageously with *vuestra merced*, and occasionally with *vuesa merced* (see Doc. AC 169, 1694).

(a) la verdad desto *v.md.* la *save* (EG 50, 1603)
(b) que *vuestra merced* le *mande* llamar y reprehenda (EG 51, 1603)
(c) *Lea vuestra merced* esta conclución y verá cosa grandiosa (EG 60, 1624)
(d) Díxome: "*sea v.m.* muy bien venido, señor liçençiado" (EG 55, 1610)
(g) "*uste deber* ser laurin, que todo lo que *dixo* salio berdad" (AC 166, 1694)
(h) le dixo dicho alcalde mayor al sussodicho: "¿*es usted* el señor don Sebastian de Guzman?" (AC 169, 1694)
(h) Juana de Saavedra, su suegra, le dijo a este testigo (…): "*tiene usted* razón" (EG 102, 1691)
(i) fue a la cassa dste testigo Melchiora, negra libre (…) y le dixo a este testigo: "¿qué *le* paresse *a usted* de la vellaquería y maldad de Laureano Núñez…?" (EG 86, 1673)

The plural of *tú* that unfolded in Spain was *vosotros*, which appears as a null subject in item (a), whereas the plural of *vuestra merced* and *su merced* was *vuestras mercedes* and *sus mercedes*, respectively, which is also used as a null subject in item (b). Plural pronouns are rare in the colonial documents examined in the subsamples of both regions.

(a) "¿cómo *os tardasteis* tanto, que yo prestito me confessé? (AC 86, 1621)
(b) "christianos, *favorescanme*, que me matan" (EG 101, 1691)

The most relevant change in this century is the replacement of *vos* by *tú* presumably because *vos* was overused and had lost its quality of deference between interlocutors of high rank (see Table 8.9). *Vos* was originally plural but intruded in the domain of *tú*, a change that originated the neologism *vosotros* (*vos* + *otros*), which was used with the same paradigm belonging to singular *vos*. The overlap in meaning and forms triggered another alteration, conducive to the disappearance of *vosotros* in New World Spanish in general (Acevedo 1997: 68). The few cases of *vos* and *vosotros* point to the fragmentation of the peninsular pronominal system in the New World. The items available in the Central Highlands refer to female Spaniards who addressed their female friends (a) and a mother who addressed her daughters (b) with *vos*.

(a) ¿cómo *os tardasteis* tanto? (AC 86, 1621)
(b) "*callad* locas, no *andéis* diziendo esso (AC 86, 1621)

The same object pronouns used for plural *vosotros* were used for singular *vos*, an additional structure that contributed to ambiguity particularly when the subject pronoun is not overt, as in (c). With the elimination of *vos* and *vosotros*, the entire verbal paradigm in all tenses and moods disappeared in New World Spanish leading to a drastic simplification that at present distinguishes New World from peninsular Spanish (see Company Company 1997).

(c) Y que de ahí a pocos días, estando en la puerta de la Merced, le dixo a este testigo, Andrés de Vega, pardo libre, (...) "¿qué *os* parece, cómo el secretario Barrios, le a pedido a María Roteta para su sobrino?" (EG 101, 1691)

Table 8.9: Pronouns of address in the 17th century

Region	Vos	Tú	V. Md.	S. Md.	Ud.
Altiplano C.	0	76	198	7	7
El Golfo	0	73	91	16	4
Total = 472	0	149	289	23	11
	(0.00 %)	(31.56 %)	(61.22 %)	(4.87 %)	(2.33 %)

8.4.10 Change of pronouns in the personal domain

The seven 'love' letters written in 1689 by a young man who wants to elope with his sweetheart illustrate the change of pronouns in the personal discourse (DLNE-AC Docs. 144-150). The suitor is a baker delivering missives to his girlfriend, who was living in a convent. He starts with confidence addressing her with *tú* and thinking that he is going to persuade her to escape at night with the help of some of his buddies. In the third letter, he is still using *tú*, but in the fourth one which serves as a transition, he becomes frustrated and begins to use *Usted* and *vuestra merced* in order to show personal distance. In the fourth letter he actually used the three pronouns *tú*, *Usted* and *vuestra merced*, but in the fifth and sixth he reiterated the use of *tú*. In the seventh and last letter he used *tú* 31 times while *vuestra merced* appeared 23 times. The latter pronoun of address expresses his resignation, since he did not get a single reply from the girl. The pronoun *tú* agrees with its verb forms, direct objects and possessive adjectives about three-fourths of the time; its redundancy serves a major purpose, which is to assert the young male identity and his intentions to succeed in the romantic adventure (Table 8.10). The use of *vostra mercede* in Courly love and despair for the soul belongs to the medieval Romance tradition of troubadors and singers. Francesco Petrarca (1303-

1374) is one of the representative poets inspired by Laura, a young lady of unusual sweetness, who is present in his vast production (Petrarca 1962: 97).

Table 8.10: Seven 'love' letters (1689)

Letter	Document	Tú	Ud.	V. Md.
1	144	23	0	0
2	145	16	0	0
3	146	23	0	0
4	147	15	28	4
5	148	18	0	0
6	149	21	0	0
7	150	31	0	23
Total = 202		147 (72.77%)	28 (13.36%)	27 (13.86%)

8.4.11 Imperfect subjunctive with –SE and –RA

The analysis of the forms in –SE and –RA is divided in two periods. In the first period in the Central Highlands, the traditional form in –SE recovered its frequency reaching 80 percent but decreased to 58 percent in the second period (Table 8.11). In contrast, in the Gulf region the –SE form declined to 73 percent in the first period and to 68 percent in the second (see Table 8.12). The –SE form continued falling in the Central Highlands, where the mixed population (Euro*mestizos*, Afro*mestizos* and Indo*mestizos*) was growing faster, and where those born in New Spain had consolidated positions of relative prestige. When the tokens of all the periods in the two regions are added, the –SE and –RA variants resulted in a two-thirds and one-third dispersal, respectively. This distribution is similar to the distribution reported for the variants LE and LO; in combination, they show the modeling patterns of central-northern peninsular norms in the first half of the 17th century (Tables 8.8 and 8.13). The –SE form in sentences (a) through (d) illustrate the use of imperfect subjunctive with subjunctive meaning, while the items (e) through (h) show the variation of –RA (originally indicative) to the newer subjunctive meaning in New World Spanish.

(a) me rogó no *tuviese* disgusto con el dicho su teniente (EG 55, 1610)
(b) El padre Cuevas en Oxcutzcab *mandava* al caçique que *castigase* a los indios (EG 52, 1606)

(c) don Lucas de Dosal *dixo* a su muger que *quitase* una ymagen de San Antonio (EG 74, 1651)
(d) le *dixo* que *cojiese* un pedasito de gueso de difunto y en polvos se lo *diese* en el vino a su marido (EG 78, 1655)
(e) la dicha indisuela les *dijo* que no *dijeran* a nadie (EG 97, 1689)
(f) *esperando* a que vuestra magestad le *hiciera* alguna merced (AC 118, 1630)
(g) *le dio limosna* al dicho confesor para que le *dixera* las misas de san Agustin (AC 121, 1634)
(h) para proceder contra la mulata *era menester* que *dieran* pruebas (AC 132, 1682)

The medieval Spanish patterns of conditional sentences with the form –RA in both the protasis and the apodosis are still used in the 17th century as in (a) through (e). In modern normative Spanish present conditional is preferred in the apodosis.

(a) si no *fuera* Juan de Alarcón que me prestó sien peços para gastos de marineros y cassa, no sé qué *fuera* [sería] de mí (EG 50, 1603)
(b) si *estubiera* aquí el patache, ya le *ubiera* [habría] *dado* carena (EG 50, 1603)
(c) si yo lo *uviera sabido* y v.m. me lo *uviera dicho*, ya lo *uviera* [habría] *hecho* (EG 55, 1610)
(d) Si (...) estas palabras *fueran* verdad, no *tubiéramos* [tendríamos] los ombres que desear más (EG 60, 1624)
(e) desde que entré en esta siudad no e poseído ni poseo balor de quatro reales para comprar unos çapatos, i si no me los *dieran, andubiera* [andaría] descalso (EG 83, 1668)

Table 8.11: Summary: Uses of –SE and –RA in the Central Highlands

Period	–SE forms	–RA forms in Protasis	Other uses of –RA	Total tokens
1600-1649	80 % / 67	4.7 % / 4	15.3 % / 13	84
1650-1699	58 % / 151	3.5 % / 9	38.5 % / 98	258

Source: Acevedo (1997: 99 and 108)

Table 8.12: Summary: Uses of –SE and –RA in the Gulf

Period	–SE forms	–RA forms in protasis	Other uses of –RA	Total tokens
1602-1647	110 / 150 (73.33 %)	7 / 150 (4.66 %)	33 / 150 (22.0 %)	150
1651-1699	61 / 89 (68.53 %)	6 / 89 (6.74 %)	22 / 89 (24.72 %)	89

Table 8.13: Summary: Uses of –SE and –RA in the two regions

Region	–SE forms	–RA forms in protasis	Other uses of –RA	Total tokens
Altiplano C.	218 / 342 (63.74 %)	13 / 342 (3.80 %)	111 / 342 (32.45 %)	342
El Golfo	171 / 239 (71.54 %)	13 / 239 (5.43 %)	55 / 239 (23.01 %)	239
Totals	389 / 581 (66.95 %)	26 / 581 (4.47 %)	166 / 581 (28.57 %)	581 (100 %)

8.4.12 Ethnic groups

The terms related to ethnicity reveal the preoccupation with diversity and the distinguishing traits referring to regional origin as in (a), which designates the individual who looks or speaks like someone from the Basque region (*'avyzcaynado'*), or someone else who looks or speaks like people from Andalusia (*'andaluzado'*), as in (a). The differentiation by ethnic group was not necessarily used to profile individuals but to describe casualties, as in (b). Ranking in the new social hierarchy is also revealed in (c), while affection or disaffection may be expressed with a diminutive as in (d).

(a) Miguel de Olabarría, que es muy *avyzcaynado*, y el Murguía, muy *andaluzado* (EG 51, 1603)
(b) En la rrefriega murieron de los nuestros catorçe *españoles*, y algunos heridos, más de veinte *yndios*, algunos *negros* y *mestisos* (EG 64, 1630)
(c) Y los *nauatlatos* escriven a los *caçiques* que no castigen a los *yndios* (EG 52, 1606)
(d) este testigo se quedó dentro del patio, y oyó que el dicho alférez Ximenez abló con *su negrita* (EG 102, 1691)

8.5 Literature in Spanish

The consolidation of the Spanish language is beyond doubt because in this century creative literature was abundant and of high quality; the major players were born in New Spain and belonged most of the time to privileged individuals working close to the viceroys. Their inspiration derived from the works of peninsular writers, which in the 17th century were splendid due to the excellence and quantity, diverse genres, and the immediate impact it had in the Spanish society of the time. Miguel de Cervantes' masterpiece *El ingenioso hidalgo Don Quijote de la Mancha* also known as *Don Quixote* (1605) is not only considered the first modern European novel, but inaugurates the second century of the Spanish Golden Age. Cervantes (1547-1616) was a master of narration, and like many men of letters of his time he was immersed in the literary trends, art and architecture of the Italian Renaissance. He is also the author of short novels, plays, and poetry. One of the best dramatists of European literature, Lope de Vega (1562-1635) was second only to Cervantes; he was devoted to refurbishing the Spanish theatre when it was turning into a massive spectacle. Due to the matchless volume of his plays, he was nicknamed 'The Phoenix of Wits' and 'The Monster of Nature'. Along with Pedro Calderón de la Barca and Tirso de Molina he adapted the Spanish drama to models based on the social realities of his times. When Lope de Vega passed away, Pedro Calderón de la Barca (1600-1681) initiated the next phase of the Spanish Golden Age with about 200 plays known for having perfected the structure, the exquisiteness, and existential view of the Spanish drama. His best-known play is *La vida es sueño* [Life is a Dream], where the central theme is the conflict between free will and fate. Tirso de Molina (1579-1648) was also a prolific author but only a small fraction of the 300 pieces that he authored survived. His best-known play is *El burlador de Sevilla y convidado de piedra* [The Trickster of Seville and the Stone Guest] whose content focuses on divine justice, repentance, and predestination. The vast production in the dramatic style is complemented by the poetry of Francisco de Quevedo (1580-1645) and Luis de Góngora (1561-1627), representatives of the schools known as *conceptismo* and *culteranismo*, respectively, which belong to the Baroque period, the former emphasizing the ideas in order to impress the intelligence and the latter focusing on the beauty of the pompous forms.

As the world of the Renaissance worries acquiesced to complex ideas of the Baroque era, the grounds of literature bore new fruit, especially in the New Spanish poetry and drama. The Spanish *conceptismo* of Luis de Góngora and the *culteranismo* of Francisco de Quevedo found sustainable growth in Mexico. Writers embracing the Baroque sensibility include those born in Spain and those whose works were written in the new soil. Carlos Sigüenza y Góngora (1645-1700) and Juan de Palafox y Mendoza (1600-1569), among others, were known for their erudition in different subjects. One of the shining stars of New Spain was Juan Ruiz de Alarcón y Mendoza (1581-1639) capable of competing with the famous Spanish playwrights (Lope, Calderón and Tirso). Alarcón's most famous plays remain *Las paredes oyen* [The Walls have Ears] and *La verdad sospechosa o el mentiroso* [The Truth Suspect or the Liar] which was condensed in Cornielle's *Le Menteur* (Cortés 1992: xxx-xxxi). The most outstanding poet, playwright and essayist was Juana de Asbaje (1651-1695) also known as Sor Juana Inés de la Cruz ('The Tenth Muse'), the most sensitive writer from Spain during the Golden Age. For generations her works have inspired countless other authors and literary critics. She found inspiration in the classics and explored the topics of ethnicity that distinguished the dynamic *criollo* society of New Spain. She inserted *tocotines* (dramatized dance in either Spanish or Nahuatl) in the religious plays known as *autos sacramentales*. In addition, she also indulged in the composition of *villancicos* (carrols) that exhibit the traits of the Afro-Mexican speech of the times (cf. Megenny 1985). The versatile literary creativity of this century epitomizes the pinnacle of the Spanish language in New Spain and the continuity of diversification in all genres, except the novel.

8.6 Conclusion

The major change observed in this century is the growth of the mixed population which gained sufficient speakers for the Spanish language to maintain all the domains of interaction incepted in the 16th century. In this period the quality of literary production is equivalent to major poetic and dramatic trends in Spain. Additionally, language data for this century corroborate the gradual attrition of some of the variants that are considered typical of peninsular Spanish, though the triumphant variants corresponding to New World Spanish do not yet prevail. (1) *Seseo* ascended to 40 percent while the traditional graphemes persisted with 60 percent of the tokens. (2) *Leísmo* remains in its former 16th century position with two-thirds of the cases tallied in both regions. (3) In considering the –SE vs. –RA opposition, the –SE form still had the leading role with more than two-thirds of all the tokens counted in the two collections of documents. (4) Finally, *tú* and *vuestra merced* made strong inroads in the personal and business relationships, while the subject pronouns *vos* and *vosotros* were not used in this century; *tú* and *vuestra merced* gained the slots and functions that *vos* had lost. In the selection of personal pronouns, direct objects, possessive adjectives, and objects of preposition, Mexico and the Caribbean region adhered to the unfolding trends in peninsular Spanish, which stabilized the singular dyad *tú / vuestra merced*, presumably because these colonies had been politically closer to Spain than all the other regions.

Representing opposite trends, *seseo* (New World) and *leísmo* (Spain) co-existed with glaring vitality in the 17th century. Whereas the pairs of sibilant variants followed their own path of erosion, towards the end of the century, some local writers may have overused "regular" incorrect *seseo*, but simultaneously preserved the features that are identified with peninsular Spanish (see Doc. AC 162, 1692). Finally, the external factors that were shaping the patterns of attrition of normative sibilants, *leísmo* and the –RA / –SE opposition may be related to the wave of acclimatization of native Spanish speakers and the subtle integration of the castes into the diversified economy of the viceroyalty. Spanish gained new speakers progressively, not abruptly. Those speakers who lost contact or who never had contact with Spain may have accelerated language change because they lost track of the polymorphic assortment of variants coming directly from the metropolis. Non-Spanish speaking groups acquiring and / or learning Spanish had sufficient exposure to face-to-face interaction with Spanish speakers in the different domains: the households of the Spanish speakers where they worked, the church, the hacienda, the shop, the construction site, or even the schools. This was possible because the physical dividers and the social pressures and regulations turned looser in the process of separation or segregation of the castes from Spanish speakers. An additional variable that must be factored in the diversification of Spanish is the fact that it gained both speakers and prestige, and that New World Spanish literature made original and significant contributions in the age of its own apogee.

Chapter 9
The end of the colonial period: 18th century

9.1 Attrition of peninsular Spanish variants

The analysis of variants selected from *Documentos Lingüísticos de la Nueva España. Altiplano Central* (1994) and *Documentos Lingüísticos de la Nueva España. Golfo de México* (2008) shows that the gradual erosion of variants of peninsular Spanish in the New World continued through the end of the colony with no projections of recovery or newer trends shaping the features that define modern Latin American Spanish. While it is assumed that *seseo* was widespread at the level of pronunciation, noteworthy variations of graphemes still appeared in 18th century. The variations indicate that a minority of writers did follow all the rules of peninsular Spanish (distinguishing the three sibilants), whereas others mixed the sibilants <c>, <z> and <s>, and yet some others never distinguished the rules and opted for one single <s> that replaced both <c> or <z>. Also, the alternation of the clitics LE and LO was resolved in favor of the latter, although *leísmo* was not replaced *in toto* by the variant LO. In addition, in this century *vos* disappeared altogether, whereas *vuestra merced* prevailed over *tú*, and the use of *Usted* alternated incipiently with the use of both *vuestra merced* and *su merced*; in the end the use of *Usted* and its plural *Ustedes* triumphed in modern Spanish. Finally, the examination of the variants –SE and –RA from the abovementioned collections is complemented with a set of manuscripts related to mercantile activities in New Spain. *Comerciantes mexicanos en el siglo XVIII* [Mexican Merchants in the 18th century] (Yuste 1991) presents the correspondence between the officials in Spain who were in charge of regulating commerce in New Spain, and the homologous in the Mexican consulate. The variant –SE distinguishing peninsular Spanish is more frequent when these documents are added into the final quantification of –SE versus –RA. Stemming from the dramatic divide between Spaniards and *criollos* that characterized the dreadful wars of Independence, the variant –SE was the last one to decline in colonial Spanish. The shift to the almost exclusive use of the contending variant –RA is indicative of the radical polarization between Spanish speakers born in Spain and those already rooted in New Spain.

The demographic data available for the 18th century are useful to verify the ascending patterns of mestizaje and the growth of the population that was using Spanish. Subsamples from the most densely populated provinces aid in the extrapolation of data by the well-defined ethnic groups that emerged in the 16th century. Also, in light of new interpretations on language and ethnicity, this chapter reviews the results of the famous Revillagigedo Census (1790). The last colonial period is truly appealing to study major societal changes from a dependent nation-to-be to an autonomous entity that had no other option but to become distant in values, attitudes, and lifestyle from those prevailing in the metropolis.

At the end of the colony the Mesoamerican languages had lost sufficient speakers to natural disasters and disease but also to miscegenation. It is assumed that massive bilingualism was noticeable in this period, but there is no reliable quantitative information to substantiate this claim. The data on the outcome of Nahuatl/Spanish language contact in the Central Highlands refer to the elite bilingualism originated in the 16th century, which failed to have the desired continuity over the rest of the colonial period. This was due in part to the separateness built around indigenous speaking and Spanish-speaking communities and the lack of support for the education of Indian leaders. While Nahuatl evolved throughout the post-conquest period making its own adjustments independently of Spanish, or adapting selective Spanish components, Spanish-speaking Nahuas did not experience much growth at the societal level. It seems that Nahuas began to write in Spanish a few decades before the beginning of the 19th century (cf. Lockart 1991). Their mastery of Spanish, albeit limited, progressively augmented the number of Spanish speakers.

9.2 The growth and decline of the colony

Charles II, the last of the Spanish Hapsburgs, designated his grandson Philip of France and Duke of Anjou as his heir. The potential unification of Spain with France incited the Spanish War of Succession (1701-14), facilitated in turn by the British and Austrian armies that invaded Spain with the intention of removing Philip V, also grandson of Bourbon King Louis XIV of France. In the end, Philip V was victorious and his administration initiated long-term reforms known for their modernizing strategies. A French cultural movement emphasizing reason rather than tradition and the reorganization of government is known as the Age of Enlightenment, truly influential in Spain, where the monarchs created intendancies headed by a regional intendant. The main goal was to collect larger revenues and to have more control of each region. For this reason, there is more information on the population of New Spain and its varied activities.

The type of Spanish emigration and the unfolding occupations might have had an impact on the consolidation of the diversifying roles of Spanish. In the newer economy of the 18th century, merchants had a significant role to play in the growing cities of New Spain. The thought-provoking data derived from the 18th century reveal the similarities of this period with the modern age in showing the concentration of commercial and educational enterprises in various cities. It seems that while the capital attracted all kinds of residents, other cities began to compete with the capital at a smaller scale. Merchants enjoyed a prestige in society equal to landowners whose recognition was enhanced by titles of nobility normally granted by the Spanish Crown to those who had acquired significant wealth. The appreciation of Spaniards went further, since all of them were respectable citizens. Upward mobility was not always fluid, and Spanish speakers born in New Spain (i.e. *criollos* and mestizos) could not strive to those positions held by Spaniards (Brading 1971: 21-22). The significance of mining was increased as a result of the exclusivity Spaniards had in this enterprise and the exclusion of those born in New Spain who were not too interested in exploiting the resources of their native land; instead they preferred to dedicate their lives to literature, the professions, and public service (Brading 1971: 209-211). During the 18th century the Crown granted some 50 new titles of nobility to residents of New Spain. In most cases the criterion of selection was the possession of great riches. The Mexican aristocracy was recruited from the financial elite. A model of labor and ethnic distribution is Guanajuato, where the gainfully employed population was clearly adult, male, local, and multi-ethnic. This stability was derived primarily from mining where workers were engaged in related activities, e.g. dealers, cashiers, apprentices, managers, etc. (Brading 1971: chapter 6).

9.3 Spanish emigrants to New Spain

Emigration from Spain to New Spain was high during the 16th and 17th centuries, and the quotas increased in the 18th century due to the spectacular economic reactivation of the silver mining industry and to the trade growth in both the domestic and international spheres. As a result of the solid silver production, Mexico had a high purchasing power, and more candidates to emigration selected New Spain as the final destiny. Three groups of Spanish emigrants to the New World have been distinguished in this century: (1) *provistos* or individuals with designated administrative positions; (2) merchants; and (3) *llamados* (migrants petitioned by relatives). All of them had the privilege of traveling legally with their servants, who are included in the final log. Data from the first half of the 18th century revealed that they were mostly young adult males: the *provistos* amounted to 4,414 in addition to 3,456 merchants and 333 *llamados*. The total of this subsample was 8,203; of these, about one-half or 3,999 were established in an urban center in New Spain because in the cities the Spanish colonists preserved their cultural identity and maintained the economic and administrative activities that would eventually help them realized their dreams. If in the 16th century the dream was to obtain land and *encomiendas*, the aspiration of the newcomer two centuries later was the facile integration into the vice-royal society. The Mexican capital attracted 30 percent of all migrants, followed by the most populated cities: Puebla de los Angeles, Merida, Veracruz, Guadalajara, Antequera, Valladolid, Campeche, San Luis Potosi and Zacatecas, where 34 percent of the Spanish speakers were concentrated. As in previous centuries, migrants to the New World in general and to Mexico in particular were coming from diverse peninsular regions, though New Spain was normally preferred by migrants from all regions within Spain (Macías Domínguez 1999: 45, 175, 177-179).

A subsample of illegal immigration is also available for the second half of the 17th century. The emphasis lies on the regional provenance of 1,361 Spanish speakers coming from diverse provinces with Andalusia prevailing at 28.9 percent of the total and followed by northern and central regions; only a few immigrants from Leon, Valencia, and the Canary and the Balearic Islands are represented in this subsample. The migrants from Andalusia were coming mostly from Seville and Cadiz (Macías Domínguez 1999: 95). Table 9.1 shows the diversity of origins and the fact that more than half of all illegal immigrants or 52.51 percent were from northern-central provinces: Basque-Navarre, Old Castile, New Castile, Asturias, Leon, and Aragon. Spanish speakers from these regions continued to intermingle with Spanish speakers from the southern provinces of Andalusia, Extremadura and the Canary Islands.

Table 9.1: Regional origins of illegal migrants

Regions	Total	Percent
Andalusia	395	28.90
Basque-Navarre	271	19.82
Old Castile	257	18.80
New Castile	100	7.31
Galicia	95	6.95
Asturias	61	4.46
Extremadura	43	3.14
Leon Kingdom	24	1.75
Canary Islands	22	1.62
Valencia Kingdom	8	0.59
Aragon	5	0.37
Balearic Islands	4	0.29
Unknown origin	76	5.56

Source: Macías Domínguez (1999: 94)

9.4 Population of New Spain

Two continuous and opposite trends are observed by the mid-18th century: one is the decrease of the indigenous population and the other is the growth of the Spanish-speaking population, primarily by miscegenation. Table 9.2 shows the evolution of the six ethnic groups in the 18th century in seven provinces with dense indigenous population. The total of all groups amounts to 2,477,277 with the largest at more than 1.5 million or 62 percent (Column 3), which decreased by 10 percent from the previous century. The second largest at 391,512 or 15.8 percent was the group of Euro*mestizos* (Column 4), individuals of mixed ancestry raised in Spanish-speaking households, followed by Afro*mestizos* (Column 5) and Indo-*mestizos* (Column 6) at 266,196 and 249,368, respectively. These two groups made up one-fifth or 20.8 percent of the total. More interestingly, however, is the combined growth of groups from Columns 1, 4, 5 and 6. When they are summed, a sizeable percentage of the population of these provinces emerges with a total of 916,890 or 37 percent of the Spanish-oriented people.

Table 9.2: Population by caste in 1742

Bishopric	Europeans	Africans	Indians	Euro-mestizos	Afro-mestizos	Indo-mestizos
Mexico	5,716	7,200	551,488	222,648	100,156	99,756
Tlaxcala	1,928	8,872	350,604	40,348	39,444	38,228
Oaxaca	416	240	231,892	9,220	10,716	9,120
Michoacan	171	492	147,808	55,508	45,896	47,884
Nueva Galicia	1,028	2,913	36,252	44,568	31,256	31,420
Yucatan	498	274	190,032	17,660	35,712	19,588
Chiapas	57	140	32,180	1,524	3,016	3,372
Totals	9,814	20,131	1,540,256	391,512	266,196	249,368

Source: Aguirre Beltrán (1972: 219)

9.4.1 The Revillagigedo Census

In contrast with the paucity of information about population trends in the 17th century, the 1790 Census offers substantial descriptions of New Spain. It was administered by the Count of Revillagigedo, who not only had experience in surveying the population in Spain but was at the time viceroy of New Spain. According to Castro Aranda (2010) the Revillagigedo Census is the most complete report of a long-forgotten account with data gathered in 1770 at the initiative of the new Bourbon administration (see Table 9.3).

Table 9.3: New Spain: Total population by sex and jurisdiction in 1790

Jurisdictions	Males and females	Males	Females
NEW SPAIN	4 636 074	2 302 600	2 333 474
Alta California	8 540	4 472	4 068
Baja California	4 076	2 258	1 818
Durango	125 918	62 844	63 074
Guadalajara	513 366	235 075	278 291
Guanajuato	454 873	227 483	227 390
Mérida	364 022	180 579	183 443
México	1 147 973	574 786	573 187
Nuevo México	30 953	16 039	14 914
Oaxaca	419 309	207 187	212 122
Puebla	542 288	271 769	270 519
San Luis Potosí	242 280	124 944	117 336
Sinaloa	55 062	27 772	27 290
Sonora	38 305	20 473	17 832
Tlaxcala	59 148	29 997	29 151
Valladolid	322 951	159 638	163 313
Veracruz	163 539	85 694	77 845
Zacatecas	143 471	71 590	71 881

Source: Castro Aranda (2010: 164)

According to the Revillagigedo Census, the total population of the kingdom was more than 4.5 million people living in jurisdictions or intendancies (i.e. large regional districts) that approximate the present political division of the Mexican Republic: the intendancy of Mexico followed by Puebla, Guadalajara, Guanajuato, and Oaxaca. The northern regions were depopulated at the time, while there were intermediate intendancies of medium-size population (e.g. Merida, San Luis Potosi and Valladolid). At the end of the 18th century, the urban population of 17 select intendancies was less than 10 percent of the total. The intendancies with high population density were Mexico, Puebla, Guanajuato, Merida and Guadalajara; of these, the intendancies with low percentages of urban population were Guadalajara, Oaxaca and Valladolid (Table 9.4). Zacatecas, a privileged mining center, stands out with a high urban population of 19.57 percent. The data confirm that the rural-urban dichotomy emerging in the 16th century was still characteristic of the late colonial period.

Table 9.4: New Spain: Urban population by intendancy in 1790

Jurisdiction	Total	Urban	Percent
NEW SPAIN	3 982 869	323 066	8.11
Guadalajara	505 428	24 249	4.80
Mexico	1 162 856	112 926	9.71
Puebla	566 443	52 717	9.31
Oaxaca	411 336	19 069	4.64
Valladolid	289 314	17 093	5.91
Guanajuato	430 127	32 098	7.46
Zacatecas	130 273	25 495	19.57
Durango	123 070	11 027	8.96
Mérida	364 022	28 392	7.80

Source: Castro Aranda (2010: 165)

The division by caste includes five groups with a majority of Spaniards and a tiny minority of "other Europeans" who must have been non-Spanish speakers. At the end of the 18th century Indians still represented a sizeable proportion of the population while mulattoes were the second largest minority. It is remarkable that the terms 'criollo' and 'mestizo' are conspicuously absent in this survey, which may be indicative of a late-colonial trend that refused to distinguish Spaniards from their own offspring, that is, *criollos* and mestizos. It may be inferred that "Spaniards" was subsuming three groups that had been separated in earlier stages of the colonial period: (a) Spanish speakers born in Spain, (b) children of Spaniards born in Mexico or 'criollos', and (c) 'mestizos' or children of Spanish speakers and Indians. If this interpretation is correct, it means that one-half or more of the total population of Mexico City was Spanish-speaking (see Column 2 in Table 9.5), while the rest of the vice-royalty might have had different groups of Spanish speakers and varying degrees of bilingualism or multilingualism in the Mesoamerican languages. For a discussion on the inconsistencies of the Revillagigedo Census, see Lerner (1968).

Table 9.5: Mexico City: Total population by caste and sex in 1790

Mexico City	Total	Spaniards	Other Europ.	Indians	Mulattoes	Other castes
Males	45 478	21 338	2 118	11 232	2 958	7 832
Females	59 282	29 033	217	14 371	4 136	11 525
Totals	104 760	50 371	2 335	25 603	7 094	19 357

Source: Castro Aranda (2010: 223)

When Mexico City is compared with the rest of the Mexico intendancy, the difference between ethnicity and language stands out. Only a small proportion 134,965 (13%) of the population is included under the category "Spaniards", which might have been conceived as a composite of Spanish speakers born in Spain and Spanish speakers born in the New World (i.e. *criollos*). In contrast, the indigenous groups make up a large majority (71.1%). Table 9.6 shows the total by sex and caste in the intendancy of Mexico, which included about 50 mayoralties and small towns heavily populated by speakers of indigenous languages surrounding the capital city. In the small towns and villages of the different intendancies the mestizo families are logged in with all the other ethnic groups.

Table 9.6: Mexico Intendancy: Total population by caste and sex in 1790

Mexico Intend.	Total	Spaniards	Other Europ.	Indians	Mulattoes	Other castes
Males	529 308	66 795	1 308	378 024	27 070	56 111
Females	513 915	68 170	22	364 162	25 559	56 002
Totals	1 043 223	134 965	1 330	742 186	52 629	112 113

Source: Castro Aranda (2010: 212)

Local data gathered in the city of Queretaro reveal a stricter grouping distinguishing the mestizo caste and other groups. Tables 9.7A and 97B show that in the city and the intendancy, the largest ethnic group was the indigenous with 42 and 67 percent, which is followed by Spaniards with 26 and 16 percent, respectively. The mestizo group, which is absent in the general Revillagigedo Census, reappears with 18 and 10 percent of the total, while *castizos* (offspring of mestizo and Spaniard), *negros* (African descendants), and *lobos* (offspring of a Spaniard father and a Moorish mother) make up small minority groups (Super 1983: 273). More significant than the distinction of the mestizo group is the fact that by the 18th century, mestizos had attained upward mobility, had learned diverse occupations, were able to purchase small parcels, cattle, equipment for their businesses, and were debt-free. In essence, all these advantages gave them the option to marry Spanish-speaking women (Super 1983: 217-218), a factor that may have fostered Spanish language growth.

Table 9.7A: City of Queretaro: Ethnic composition in 1778

Indian	Spaniard	Mestizo	Mulatto	Castizo	Negro	Lobo	Total
11,470	7,080	4,997	2,732	257	34	829	27,399
42%	26%	18%	10%	9%	.01%	3%	100%

Table 9.7B: Intendancy of Queretaro: Ethnic composition in 1778

Indian	Spaniard	Mestizo	Mulatto	Castizo	Negro	Lobo	Total
35,960	8,341	5,867	2,589	64	3	874	53,698
67%	16%	10%	5%	1%	.0005%	2%	100%

An additional component of the basic statistic profile, occupation illustrates the type of activity and the proportion of people working at the time of the 1790 census. Table 9.8 shows the occupations listed in nine intendancies; it sheds light on the type of activity and the rates of gainfully employed individuals. More than 1.5 million workers in different positions as laborers (Column 3), tributaries and peons (Column 4), miners (Column 5), merchants (Column 6), artisans (Column 7), and others (Column 8) were registered in each category. Spanish-speaking merchants and miners were concentrated in the intendancies of Mexico and Guanajuato. By this time, they had reached faraway localities such as Sonora and Sinaloa in the north. The commercial and mining activities explain the quantitative preponderance of laborers, tributaries, artisans, and peons in the intendancies of Mexico and Guanajuato. Artisans learned different European-oriented skills in the silver and loom industry, and were exposed to Spanish for several generations until they became fluent in it. The different occupational activities were expanded to the north with a good representation in New Mexico and Sinaloa, followed by Durango and Sonora. At this time the Californias were virtually depopulated. The data available for northern intendancies reveal that before the independent period, Spanish was making slow but steady progress.

Table 9.8: Occupation in nine intendancies by type of activity (1790)

Intendancies	Total	Labor.	Various	Miners	Merch.	Artis.	Other
Total	568 557	71 567	406 820	10 490	4 759	43 448	31 473
Alta California	502	38	123	5	-	27	309
Baja California	203	1	102	5	-	22	73
Durango	6 177	325	1 181	-	33	966	3 672
Guanajuato	111 270	53 867	17 877	9 369	1 031	16 605	12 521
Mexico	400 349	5 406	359 453	881	3 360	19 589	11 660
New Mexico	9 457	5 862	-	-	-	2 518	1 077
Sinaloa	10 291	4 306	5 172	188	151	288	186
Sonora	4 996	933	2 319	41	64	498	1 141
Tlaxcala	25 312	829	20 593	1	120	2 935	834

Source: Castro Aranda (2010: 205)

9.5 The growth of the cities

It is assumed that miners and merchants were Spanish-speaking entrepreneurs with a great deal of power and prestige. They employed workers in the different occupations and districts of central Mexico and had at the same time good connections in the local and regional governmental offices. According to Kicza (1990: 198-199), the role of migration in the development of urban centers in the 18th century was pivotal because cities such as Guadalajara and Oaxaca experienced dramatic growth after barely growing over much of the colonial period. The population of mining centers such as Zacatecas and Guanajuato varied considerably according to the profits of their lodes. For most of the colonial period there were three conurbations in Mexico: Mexico City, Puebla and Guanajuato, and during the 18th century they were joined by Guadalajara. The cities were the centers of business and government, not just for their immediate regions but for all or a larger part of the colony; residing in them facilitated the completion of all sorts of business and miscellaneous activities. Mexico City was the center of education and intellectual pursuits; it possessed the most sophisticated urban economy with a good number of residents earning wages and participating in both the internal and the international market system. As in the previous century Mexico City merchants belonged to the privileged class, while families from other prominent cities migrated to the capital; although migration was not massive, it was recurrent and aided in the process of revitalization of this lofty sector. Migration of local agrarian and mining-active elites contributed to the consolidation of the colonial elite.

Scholars have distinguished two migration patterns within the merchant community: one was a cyclical movement away from and then back to the cities by young members of commercial firms, and the other, which involved movement to major cities by independent merchants who sought to establish themselves in more lucrative enterprises. Imports of late colonial Mexico City routinely maintained retail branches in provincial towns, especially those in mining and commercial agricultural zones. Throughout the colonial period there was continual movement of commercial agents out of and sometimes back into the main cities, which acted as poles of attraction for professionals who were educated in their youth; and when they began their careers and wanted to further advance, they requested transfers to a city or close to a city. Professionals travelled longer distances than artisans and skilled workers. Doctors and surgeons were also attracted to the cities in two cycles, initially to be educated and later to establish their practice. All physicians were born in New Spain and from families scattered throughout the colony, but for the most part they preferred to work in the capital because they could accommodate both teaching and practice. Continual migration to the cities by various occupational and social groups, including skilled artisans and unskilled construction and service workers, was determined by the waves of the economy which lured all types of migrants seeking employment (Kicza 1990: 201-205).

9.6 Education

At the beginning of the 18th century, schools and residences were conducive to the consolidation of the Jesuits' position in the New Spanish society. They opened 50 more elementary schools, colleges and seminars where boys studied Humanities. The variety of opportunities offered in the north attracted the Hispanic origin population (native and recent arrivals from Spain) where the Jesuits found sufficient interested persons in educational enterprises. In the northern cities such as Monterrey and Chihuahua the Jesuits influenced the New Spanish society and the New Spanish society influenced the Jesuits. At the same time, they turned into entrepreneurs who invested resources in haciendas where Spaniards and *criollos* worked as administrators (Gonzalbo 1990: 217, 221, 224, 228-229). The Jesuits' contributions to prosperity were unquestionable but their influence ended in 1767 when they were expelled from the New World colonies by royal order.

Latin texts such as anthologies of the classics, manuals of rhetoric and notes on Nebrija's grammar were edited in the printing press of the schools. The activities in colleges and student residences were so varied that accounted for 600 annual sermons in addition to publications, conferences and participation in extremely varied public acts. The best known Jesuit school was the *Colegio de San Pedro y San Pablo*, where scholars such as Francisco Javier Alegre (1750-51), Francisco Javier Clavijero (1759-60), and Rafael Landívar (1750-60) delivered their lectures. During the 18th century, hundreds of students were enrolled in the Jesuit schools while non-religious schools of higher education were opened in almost every city of New Spain. Daily activities included lessons on philosophy, theology and moral. With an enrollment of about 150 very young pupils, the *Colegio de San Ildefonso* became the ideal place to celebrate the conquest of Mexico on the day of San Hipólito, which was organized by the students (Gonzalbo 1990: 243, 246, 266).

The rudimentary education afforded to women depended on social rank and available space. Only Spanish and *criollo* women of any position or status, residing or established in the centers of urban life, received some form of education. Some were able to afford governesses and did not attend regular schools. Girls also studied in *escuelas de amigas* where they learned manual labors, catechism, sewing, and the habit of discipline, which consisted in just being quiet. Very few knew how to read and write, and those few were the ones living in convents. This was the situation until the second half of the 18th century when reading and writing were offered in public schools; girls also had to show *probanzas*. The content of education improved gradually and extended offerings of reading, writing, arithmetic, music composition, and music instruments. Convents for young women proliferated in Puebla, Oaxaca, Guadalajara, Valladolid and Patzcuaro. Only occasionally did young women receive education in Latin. Many more girls around the age of 10 attended the girls' schools. All in all, the education of *criollos* resembled to a great extent the education of Spanish speakers in the mother country (Gonzalbo 1990: 320, 324, 327, 332, 337, 339).

9.7 The Bourbon reforms, the economy and ethnicity

The Bourbon reforms of Charles III (1759-1788) promoted free trade, a factor that enhanced the status of the Spanish-speaking *criollo* elites (lawyers, landlords and churchmen), Spain-born officials and merchants. These reforms were a fiscal success for Spain though the effects on New Spain's economy were mixed. While textile manufacturers flourished for a time, they were not at the cutting edge of technology. By the end of the century, the population was being drained with high taxes, and about 40 percent of the revenues were being delivered to Madrid, causing a serious budget deficit that affected mostly rural working people. At the same time Spanish speakers born in New Spain were increasingly joining the lower ranks of respectable people. The sharp stratification consisted of the upper crust made up of almost exclusively Spaniards and *criollos* and the lower one of unskilled indigenous laborers. A new stratum might have emerged since more and more Spanish speakers joined the middle ranks (Martínez 2008: 241-242).

Since the 1730's the Inquisition had noticed that many individuals of obscure genealogy were buying *probanzas*. Others had noticed the rising incidence of mestizaje, and in particular the Spanish lineages mixed with black blood. This preoccupation derived from an increase in marriages between *criollos* and castes, and because those unions were more common, social mobility for the latter became more feasible. Because *criollos* were marked as "impure", the use of the word "criollo" became the subject of debate. Both religious and secular officials discouraged Spanish and native unions with people of African descent. A 1754 pamphlet entitled *Ordenanzas del baratillo de Mexico* [Decrees of the Mexico City market] mocked the endeavors of Spanish authorities to create exclusivity on the basis of purity of blood. Social mobility did not affect owners of large estates and mines, wholesale merchants, high-ranking royal officials and clerics, and large-scale retailers, nor did it apply to the bottom social levels, mainly consisting of unskilled indigenous laborers. On the other hand, fluidity did affect the colonial middle strata which included *criollos* and Spaniards in artisan and rental occupations, people of mixed descent, and acculturated Amerindians (Martínez 2008: 242-244).

In spite of the inconsistencies of the notion of purity of blood, it retained its basic religious tenet. This was true for all Spanish speakers (Spaniards and *criollos*). The purity status of the indigenous population and its religious basis were strengthened in the first half of the 18th century when the church and the state founded new institutions for them, such as convents for women (whose criteria for admission included nobility, legitimacy, and proof of not having idolatrous antecedents). These convents were opened in Mexico City, Valladolid, and Oaxaca, among other cities. Native people did have a theological status, which fostered the rise of a *criollo* vision of a Catholic mestizo kingdom under the protective image of the Virgin of Guadalupe. Prominent *criollos* and Spaniards (mostly members of the clergy) defended unions with the indigenous population but not with blacks. Mexico City's *Audiencia* prompted priests to warn their indigenous flock that if they married persons of African ancestry, their descendants would not have access to important posts. Religious and secular officials were more protective of indigenous noblewomen, who still occupied a special place in the order of signs. The emerging Mexican vision of a Catholic mestizo nation was compatible with the Bourbon administration's social policies. These regulations consecrated the principle of indigenous purity, and mestizos were not only allowed to receive the sacred orders but were exempt from tribute. Other institutions emphasized that *criollos* were just as noble as Spaniards and that natives were apt to hold public posts. The obsession with genealogy gave birth to a new genre known as *casta* painting, which reveals the vision that colonial artists had of the relationship between race and gender and colonial hierarchies. The caste system, which had always been unstable, grew in the latter half of the colonial period because of the ambiguities contained in the notion of purity of blood. In the end it was not clear whether purity was a natural condition or a social construct determined by oral testimonies (Martínez 2008: 249, 252, 258, 267-269).

9.8 Language attrition in the Central Highlands and in the Gulf

Variants transmitted from Spain to New Spain are examined in light of the ongoing structural changes of the pre-modern era when the attrition trends observed in previous centuries were stabilized. A major discrepancy in pronunciation must be reckoned with in the overall analysis of the sibilants retrieved from DLNE-AC (Docs. 177-277) and from DLNE-EG (Docs. 106-181). Table 9.10 shows that in all four periods the traditional graphemes <c> and <z> prevailed; it also indicates that the medieval grapheme <ç> was used sporadically. In both regions writers exhibit mixed traits. In the Central Highlands, they followed normative spelling rules at 68 percent in Period I and about 66 percent in Period II. It is inferred that slightly less than one-third of the writers in Period I and about one-third in Period II made the errors that today are considered to be typical of speakers / writers who have less than tertiary education, i.e. spelling *decir, hacer, veces* with the anti-etymological sibilant <s> as in *desir, haser, veses* (this is *seseo*-W).

Table 9.10: Anti-etymological and traditional sibilants in the 18th century

Region	Period by region	Seseo	<c>, <z>, <ç>
Altiplano C.	I. 1731-1750	316 / 1005 (31.44 %)	689 / 1005 (68.55 %)
Altiplano C.	II. 1751-1799	366 / 1095 (33.42 %)	729 / 1095 (66.57 %)
El Golfo	I. 1702-1748	298 / 691 (43.12 %)	393 / 691 (56.87 %)
El Golfo	II. 1753-1799	138 / 789 (17.49 %)	651 / 789 (82.51 %)
Tokens	Total = 3,580	1,118 (31.23 %)	2,462 (68.77 %)

It must be underscored nonetheless that in the Central Highlands in Period I there are 15 (or 15 % of the total) exceptional documents that consistently follow modern orthographic norms. The rest show mixed trends ranging from incipient *seseo* to intense and total *seseo*. *Sesantes* were most likely educated in New Spain, and for this reason, they may have lost awareness of traditional writing norms. A minority of documents showing norms similar to modern Spanish might have been drafted by newcomers in good positions or well-educated *criollos*. In Period II most documents also show mixed trends and many exhibit the modern rules with just one or two typical errors, which like today can be considered "spelling errors" or performance errors that can be easily corrected. The 75 documents belonging to the Gulf of Mexico can be examined in two periods, Period I (1702-1748) comprising Docs. 106-139 and Period II (1753-1799) including Docs. 140-181. Writers from this region exhibit the same trends observed in the Central Highlands, and a few in each period follow the modern spelling rules with only a few exceptions (see Docs. 114-118 in Period I and Docs. 144, 146, 147, 163, 171, 174 and 175 in Period II). Document 118 is the testimony of an Indian via an interpreter, which was redacted by the secretary of the Inquisition. The author adheres to all modern norms, but he still uses *vido* and *vio*. Other writers follow the modern rules most of the time, though the vast majority of writers exhibit mixed trends, that is, they use both "correct" and "incorrect" spellings (see Table 9.11 for examples). Finally, in this collection the opposite trend can be found, that is, the flagrant violations of the rules using exclusively the grapheme <s> for words that go with either <c> or <z>.

Table 9.11: Incorrect and correct spellings with sibilant graphemes

No.	Doc.	Year	Region	Seseo-W	Normative	English
1.	203	1740	AC	capasidad	capacidad	capacity
2.	204	1740	AC	ensendieron	encendieron	to light up (3rd person plural preterit)
3.	207	1741	AC	benefisio	beneficio	the benefit
4.	207	1741	AC	amenasado	amenazado	threatened (masculine)
5.	221	1745	AC	pertenesiente	perteneciente	belonging to
6.	221	1745	AC	meresco	merezco	to deserve (1st person present)
7.	236	1752	AC	denunsiar	denunciar	to denounce
8.	236	1752	AC	obligasion	obligación	obligation
9.	246	1773	AC	horrorisado	horrorizado	frightened (masculine)
10.	259	1796	AC	isquierdo	izquierdo	left (side)
11.	109	1704	EG	consiensia	conciencia	consciousness
12.	110	1707	EG	prinsipio	principio	principle
13.	119	1721	EG	reconosco	reconozco	to admit (1st person present)
14.	123	1732	EG	bengansa	venganza	revenge
15.	136	1746	EG	solisitaba	solicitaba	to apply (1st and 3rd person singular imperfect)
16.	150	1774	EG	quisá	quizá	perhaps
17.	155	1778	EG	vergonsosa	vergonzosa	ashamed (feminine)
18.	155	1778	EG	mansana	manzana	apple

9.9 Attrition of morpho-syntactic variants

Long-term structural changes in this century were conducive to differentiated activities and a more fluid society that was ready to modify peninsular-oriented attitudes and values. The external factors described in the previous sections contributed to the gradual decline of the morpho-syntactic variants associated with Spain. The variation of the clitic pronouns LE and LO clearly diminished in the New World, but the displaced pronoun LE has survived in some regions in some contexts and with some verbs. However, Mexican Spanish shows at present a more regular preference for LO and less variation than the national dialects and / or regional dialects of other independent countries. Mexican Spanish reduced the pronouns of address *vuestra merced* and *su merced*, although *su merced* is recessive in various New World regions. Finally, the variant –SE survived in Mexican Spanish at extremely low frequency rates, while in other regions it persisted at higher rates, although it has not prevailed in any of the independent nations.

9.9.1 Direct object pronouns LE and LO

In this century the variant LO finally surpassed the variant LE with more than one-half of all the occurrences in most contexts. The Central Highlands was ahead of the Gulf region with a distribution of two-thirds in the former and one-half in the latter. Documents from the middle decades (1731-1771) representing the Central Highlands still show mixed trends. Some documents reveal the consistent use of LO, as in items (a) and (b), while in others a sentence referring to the same subject could start with LE and end with LO as in (c) through (e), where the verbs *poner* ('to place'), *coger* ('to grab'), and *ayudar* ('to help') are used with LE. The clitic pronoun LE was used to refer to animals, as in (d) and (e).
(a) que a no *haverlo* favorecido al testigo [Romero], *lo matan* (AC 182, 1731)
(b) Quel dicho Muñoz es mestizo y siempre *lo ha conocido* mal inclinado (AC 183, 1731)
(c) y mando (…) aprehendan la persona del dicho Francisco Muñoz y con toda guardia y custodia **le pongan** en esta hacienda vien asegurado y me avisen de *haverlo* ejecutado (AC 185, 1731)
(d) aunque el dicho buey se defendia, el referido Diego *lo cogio*, y (…) **cogiendole** por el lado ysquierdo, en el qual le hizo con la llave un araño (…) que ni *lo derribó* (AC 187, 1733)
(e) [el inquisidor] **le coxió** de un brazo y me mandó a mí (…) **le ayudase** a levantar y **le pusiese** en su asiento (AC 197, 1739)

The testimonies of witnesses, occasional bystanders or spectators in civil cases are the sources of vivid narratives visualizing the events that caused commotion or curiosity. Documents AC 222-224 (1746) anticipate the search of a male suspect who was fleeing hastily from the mob that in the end entrapped him, threw him to the ground, and took a machete away from him. All those who chased the subject assisted the authorities in taking him to jail. The scribe used 18 clitic pronouns referring to the male suspect; 16 of those are LO and only twice did the narrator use LE with the verbs *absolver* ('to absolve') and *matar* ('to kill'), as in items (d) and (e).

(a) su compañero, no *hallandolo*, salio propio su merced en persona a *buscarlo* (AC 222, 1746)
(b) *hallandolo* en la puerta de el dicho Pedro Cavallero, platicando con Barbara Cavallero, a el *aprehenderlo* le quitó el dicho que declara un machete rozador (AC 222, 1746)
(c) dandole orden al dicho que declara que *lo prendiera* (AC 222, 1746)
(d) le pidio perdón, pidiendole **le absolviesse** (AC 222, 1746)
(e) casi **le hubieran matado** (AC 222, 1746)

The predominance of LO is obvious in AC Doc. 265 (1797), the testimony before the Holy Office of a young Indian male who narrated his experiences when he went for confession. The notary might have been a Spanish speaker born in New Spain of parents who were also born in New Spain. There are 14 cases of LO and not a single one of LE. Table 9.12 shows the distribution of LE and LO in the two regions, where it is clear that the pro-etymological variant eventually prevailed. The difference in the rate of attrition between regions has to do with the fact that the 16th century writers from the Central Highlands were not only the best-educated protagonists of the colonization of Mexico, but they were from central-northern regions within Spain where *leísmo* originated. With few exceptions, during the previous centuries LE was more frequent than LO; however, by the 18th century, there must have been more scribes, notaries and employees born and raised in New Spain working in the different public posts.

Table 9.12: LE and LO in the 18th century

Region	LE	LO
Altiplano C.	41 / 125	84 / 125
	(32.8 %)	(67.2 %)
El Golfo	45 / 93	48 / 93
	(48.38 %)	(51.61 %)
Total =	86 / 218	132 / 218
	(39.45 %)	(60.55 %)

9.9.2 Pronouns of address

The rare cases of singular *voseo* disappeared in New Spain giving way to generalized *tuteo* and to the use of *vuestra merced*, which in combination with *su merced* and *Usted* account for more than one-half of all the occurrences in this century. *Vuestra merced* (*v. m.*), *su merced* (*s. md.*) and *Usted* (*U* or *V*) appear in the sphere of formal and business relationships mostly among adult males. The final tally of these three pronouns is boosted by the redundant use of objects of preposition corresponding to each pronoun. This pattern contrasts with the use of *tú*, which is reserved for the intra-familiar domain, where such disambiguation or redundancy was not deemed necessary in dialogues between two interlocutors. The use of *vuestra merced* is incremented by the repetition of both pronouns as overt pronominals as in items (a) through (c); as indirect objects in item (d); and as objects of prepositions, as in items (e) through (h). They are redundant particularly in business and personal letters, because they agree with 3rd person singular forms which are identical to those used with 3rd person singular *él* ('he') and *ella* ('she').

(a) Beo cómo *resivio v.m.* de don Thomas de Zerezeda quatrosientos pesos (AC 178, 1731)
(b) Me alegro que *v. md. gose* de cabal salud (AC 186, 1731)
(c) *se serbira v. md.* de dar al portador de éste mi ropa (AC 213, 1743)
(d) si *a v.m. le parece*, imbíe al dicho su marido (AC 196, 1736)
(e) Y quedo para servir *a v.m.* (AC 178, 1731)
(f) Nuestro Señor dé *a v. md.* muchos años (AC 177, 1731)
(g) pido a Dios me guarde *a v.m.* muchos años (AC 195, 1736)
(h) al mismo tiempo apreziaré que la salud *de v.m.* sea mui próspera (AC 209, 1742)

Business letters seem to have originated by the many retailers who were eager to buy, sell and dispatch their products. A business letter was aimed at the reader's needs; its main goal was to communicate clearly the message of the retailer and create a positive impression of the business at hand. For all the above reasons they were extremely courteous. Documents from the Gulf illustrate the format of several pieces of correspondence normally opening with a personalized salutation, followed by a statement justifying the reason for writing, and the necessary background information. Retailers were mindful of the different strategies utilized and the variations involved in the courtesy formulas regardless of the items (e.g. metals, almond, cacao, boxes, mules, etc.) they needed in order to complete the transaction. The use of *vuestra merced* as a subject or as an object of preposition conveyed the impression of concern and wellbeing for the person receiving the letter at the same time that the sender was indulging in softened requests.

(a) Señor don José Palacio Lazarte: *Estimado amigo y señor: por la favorecida de vuestra merced* del 3 del corriente quedó entendido en que recivió los 402 cabos de fierro platina con merma de 7 arrobas (EG 151, 1776)
(b) *Doy a v.m. las gracias* por la venta de la almendra, cuio líquido producto de doscientos ochenta y cinco pesos y seis reales *dexo a v.m.* cargados en nuestra corriente (EG 151, 1776)
(c) *he de estimar a v.m. se sirva mandar solicitar* su venta al menor corto precio que se pueda y verificar su salida sin despreciar marchante (EG 151, 1776)
(d) *quedo en el agradecimiento de la exactitud de v.m.* en agenciar la renta del fierro, y en misma espero no se experimente dilación (EG 152, 1776)
(e) *suplico a v.m.* que si ay en ese pueblo algunos cajones para mí, me avise. *En tanto ruego a Dios guarde a v.m. muchos años* (EG 157, 1781)
(f) Señor don Nicolás Casado. *Muy estimado señor mío*. Ban estos arrieros con tres mulas *para que me haga v.m. el favor* de remitirme los tress cajones (EG 160, 1781)
(g) *v.m. me ha de haser el favor* de que las tres mulas restantes se pasen a Tuxpa (EG 160, 1781).

While the use of *vuestra merced* was increasing in this century, the use of Usted advanced timidly in both regions, where the contexts are identical to modern patterns, as in (a) through (c).

(a) "amigo, tráigole a *usté* una carta de su padre" (...) "¿quién le dio a *usté* esta carta?, y este le dijo: "su padre de *usté*" (EG 108, 1703)
(b) por lo que consulto a *vd.* (...) para que me dictamine lo que deva hazer (AC 246, 1773)
(c) Ya *usted* vee cuál estaría yo, afligidísimo, y sin poder remediarlo (EG 177, 1799

Table 9.13 shows the distribution of the five singular pronouns in the 18th century in the two regions, where *tú* replaced *vos* in all informal domains. On the other hand, the pronouns *vuestra merced*, *su merced* and *Usted* account for 60 percent of all cases, which include subjects, objects of preposition, and verb forms in 3rd person singular. The replacement of *vos* by *tú* in the informal domain was favorable to stabilize the usages of *tú* in non-reciprocal patterns of address such as those maintained between priests and parishioners, but also between interlocutors in symmetrical relationships such as close friends, close colleagues and comrades, and those involved in romantic relationships (see EG, Docs. 136, 1746; 141, 1755; 154-156, 1778). All in all the subsamples examined in this section indicate that, with only one exception, writers were not inclined to use mixed forms. The agreement of overt and null subject pronouns with their corresponding verb forms and objects of preposition was consistent throughout the colonial period, a pattern that explains the rejection of *voseo* in New Spain where there was not a socio-historical foundation supporting the use of mixed pronouns. As a corollary, it can be proposed that the colonies that embraced the *voseo* and *voseante* forms during the colonial period were then, as they are at present, consistenly inclined to use mixed forms in various domains of interaction.

Table 9.13: Singular pronouns of address in the 18th century

Region	Vos	Tú	V. Md.	S. Md.	Ud.
Altiplano C.	0	59	121	34	25
El Golfo	1	212	200	16	15
Total = 683	1	271	321	50	40
	(0 %)	(39.67 %)	(46.99 %)	(7.32 %)	(5.85 %)

Finally, in the Gulf region the use of *vosotros* and *vuestras mercedes* appears a few times but second person plurals are not computed in the total of pronouns of address listed in Table 9.13.
(a) Yo, verídico informante, *os* digo lo mismo que *vosotros sabéis* por el padre Torres (EG 149, 1774)
(b) deseo que Martín acabe describir para enviárselo a *vuestras mercedes* para los estudios (EG 142, 1755)

9.9.3 Use of –SE and –RA in conditional clauses and imperfect subjunctive

In this century the variant in –SE continued declining in both the Central Highlands and in the Gulf giving way to the uses of the –RA variant in subordinate clauses preceded by a verb requiring categorical subjunctive. A document from the former region (1740) is the testimony of a native woman in a trial over witchcraft against four other women who were playing games and unearthing skulls. The narrator uses the form –RA in all cases except in items (c) and (e).

(a) que por la curiosidad les *rogó que* se lo *enseñaran* (AC 204, 1740)
(b) les *mandaron* (...) *que volviesen* a enterrar los dichos huezos (AC 204, 1740)
(c) la citada Maria, loba, le *dixo* que si queria aliviar sus travajos, *que* la *diera* unas velas (...) y *que estubiera* cierta que nada dexava de parezer ensendiendole velas al muerto (AC 204, 1740)
(d) le *mandó* lo *fuese* a denunciar al padre Ramires, y asy lo hizo (AC 204, 1740)

The use of the –RA ending continues to appear in most documents drafted by scribes or notaries born in New Spain. The denunciation of Juan Bruno Eusebio de Palma over issues of sexual harassment against a teacher and presbyter appears in another document from the Central Highlands. The offended young male in turn requests counseling from another minister.

(a) No obstante *resolbimos* en *que comulgara* (AC 208, 1741)
(b) me e*ngargó* no le *dixera* a otra persona y que no *dexara* de verlo (AC 208, 1741)
(c) me *aconsejó denunciara* de lo dicho (AC 208, 1741)
(d) *me puso* de precepto *no bolbiera* a confesarme con él (AC 208, 1741)

Documents from the middle decades of the 18th century show three basic patterns: (1) writers use typical sentences of peninsular Spanish where –SE prevailed, as in (a) through (c); (2) sentences in which –RA prevails, as in (d) and (e); (3) sentences that mix –SE and –RA, as in (f) though (h). The last two sentences deal with the trial of three women who were accused of casting love spells on men.

(a) le dixe que don Lorenço necessariamente procuraria saber de mí lo que avia; que en caso que me *hablase*, si le podia decir sí o no, que con libertad y gusto me *respondiesse* (AC 218, 1744)
(b) por estas rasones *condescendia* la dicha su maestra en que *respondiesse* a las cartas del padre confesor (AC 225, 1747)
(c) [un topile] le dixo con mucho ymperio a don Agustin, su fiscal mayor, que se *revolviesse* y *fuese* a la presencia del gobernador (AC 240, 1768)
(d) llegó la declarante a decirle y suplicarle que la *absolviera* porque estando arrepentida, no *fuera* que *volbiera* despues al pecado (AC 227, 1747)

(e) porque no se *siguiera* el que *supieran* y *leyeran* sus trabajos y *huviera* otras pesadumbres (AC 227, 1747)
(f) llegó a él [Antonio de Errera] un negro nombrado Joseph Colina y le dixo que le *perdonara* por vida suya, que él era la causa de que *hubiese padesido*, por haverle dado el malefissio para que *padesiese* Antonio de Errera, pero que no le *diera* cuidado (EG 120, 1723)
(g) [la Zeybana] les pedía que *dispusiesen* modo o forma de encantarlo [a don Francisco Puig] para que no se *apartara* de su amistad ni se *ausentase* para su tierra (EG 153, 1777)
(h) noticiándoselo a un tal don Josef Victoria (...) amigo de don Francisco, para que, avisándoselo al citado don Francisco, se *cautelara* y *procurase* escusarse de este daño (EG 153, 1777)

In the 18th century writers still were using the medieval Spanish SI-clause construction with the forms in –RA and –RA in both the protasis and the apodosis as in items (a) through (f), which alternated with the modernizing sentences in which the conditional tense ending in –RÍA is used, as in (g) and (h).

(a) le dixo el dicho religioso [a Magdalena]: "si *quisieras* tratar conmigo, yo te *diera* de vestir y de comer" (AC 221, 1745)
(b) de manera que si *estuviera* con el christo ... *hisiera* mayores diligencias (AC 229, 1748)
(c) si *entendiera* ser voluntad divina acer que la *arrojara* al infierno para siempre, halli *estuviera* gustossa (AC 229, 1748)
(d) si la muerte *no huviera cortado* el hilo de la vida (...), sin duda *huviera seguido* las huellas de su antescessor (EG 140, 1752)
(e) y si lo *hic[i]era*, el pobre indio, luego el señor cura *diera* el castigo (EG 150, 1774)
(f) si no te *tubiera* yo a ti que me cuidas, no sé qué *fuera* de mí (EG 156, 1778)
(g) el que si *volviese* a ver [al oficial] *conocería* (EG, 173, 1794)
(h) el dicho padre le dixo entonces que la amaba [a Luisa Antonia de Zárate] y que si *fuera* secular se *casaría* con ella (EG 132, 1745)

The syntactic patterns observed in the subsamples above validate the assumption that writers were coming from different regional and Spanish language acquisition backgrounds. When all the uses of –SE and –RA are added in the three contexts examined since the beginning of the colonial period, it is obvious that there was a drastic change in the second part of the century in the Central Highlands, where –RA reached about 70 percent of all cases, a majority trend that later became a pattern in Mexico (see Table 9.14). The distribution of the same variants in the Gulf, where attrition is slightly less pronounced, can be seen in Table 9.15

Table 9.14: Uses of –SE and –RA in the Central Highlands

Period	–SE forms	–RA forms in Protasis	Other uses of –RA	Total tokens
1700-1749	47 % / 54	8.5 % / 10	44.5 % / 52	116
1750-1799	28 % / 59	1.4 % / 3	70.6 % / 150	212

Source: Acevedo (1997: 106)

Table 9.15: Uses of –SE and –RA in the Gulf

Period	–SE forms	–RA forms in protasis	Other uses of –RA	Total tokens
1702-1748	89 / 124 (71.77 %)	5 / 124 (4.03 %)	30 / 124 (24.19 %)	124
1752-1799	67 / 125 (53.60 %)	15 / 124 (12.09 %)	43 / 125 (34.4 %)	125

When the percentages of the two regions are compared in Table 9.16, it is evident that the attrition of –SE in the Gulf did not reach one-half of all the cases, and that the attrition in the Central Highlands proceeded with more celerity than in the Gulf. The balance of the contending forms is obtained when all the tokens of –SE and –RA are added, and the form in –SE turned out to be more than 46 percent of the times vis-à-vis more than 47 percent of –RA.

Table 9.16: Summary: Uses of –SE and –RA in the two regions

Region	–SE forms	–RA forms in protasis	Other uses of –RA	Total tokens
Altiplano C.	113 / 328 (34.45 %)	13 / 328 (3.96 %)	202 / 342 (61.58 %)	328
El Golfo	156 / 249 (62.65 %)	20 / 249 (8.03 %)	73 / 249 (29.31 %)	249
Totals = 577	269 / 577 (46.62 %)	33 / 577 (5.71 %)	275 / 577 (47.66 %)	577 (100 %)

9.9.4 The use of –SE and –RA in official documentation

The trade system established by Spain in the New World colonies was a restrictive monopoly. In the 16th and 17th centuries Spaniards were able to act as carriers, sailors and merchants; in contrast, in the American continent only Spaniards and their children were allowed to buy products in the trade fairs. Seville and later Cadiz had exclusivity in Spain while Veracruz (in Mexico) and Portobello (in Panama) had permission to receive the fleets. The idea was to promote the continuous demand of the products, which were not offered at retail but at wholesale prices. The merchandise received in Veracruz satisfied the demands in New Spain and Central America while that received via Portobello covered the needs in Caracas, New Granada, Peru, Chile and Rio de la Plata. The products shipped to the New World were wine, olive oil, vinegar and miscellaneous textiles, such as cotton, wool and silk; also species, dry fruits, wheat flour, paper, ceramics, books and furniture; in exchange the Mexican merchants would deliver silver in ingots, dyes, vanilla, and chocolate. Between the mid-16th century and the late 18th century, the trade routes utilized in the exchange and supply of manufactured products were Veracruz on the Atlantic and Acapulco on the Pacific. By royal decree, the latter had become the exclusive port of entry since 1561. Veracruz received vessels from Caracas with loads of cacao; on the other hand, Acapulco was the port of entry for sea traffic coming from El Callao (Peru) and Guayaquil (Ecuador). However, Acapulco rose to prominence because it was the legal port of entry for the Manila galleon (or the China's ship) which sailed from the Philippines to New Spain and anchored yearly at Acapulco (Yuste 1991: 8-9).

The 18th century trade is closely associated with the consolidation of the wholesale Mexico City merchants whose activities contributed to the dynamic economy of New Spain. Associated since 1592 around the Consulate of Mexico, the exporters established the business rules for the silver and dyes trade. These merchants represented the firms from Andalusia and private dealers who normally financed the trips and distributed their products in Mexico, Puebla or Oaxaca. In order to control the internal sale and distribution of their products, those residing in Mexico yearned for autonomy from the European counterparts. To this effect, they created networks with retailers, miners, customs agents, and civil authorities. The network resulted in one dominant, complex and large group within the colony. In this context, the Consulate functioned as an ally, competitor or enemy of the colonial power, which either supported or confronted, whenever necessary, the vice-regal authorities (Yuste 1991: 11-16).

Sixteen out of 17 documents compiled in *Comerciantes mexicanos en el siglo XVIII* (Yuste 1991) show that the –SE forms prevailed in both periods (Table 9.17). The use of –SE is identical in the first and the second part of the century accounting for about 70 percent in both cases, whereas the forms in –RA account for over a little more than one-fifth of the tokens, a trend that appears in documents drafted by individuals whose identity is already firmly rooted in New Spain (see for example, Docs. 5, 11 and 17). Document 16 is omitted from Table 9.17 because by itself it accounts for 374 items divided in the following manner: 346 are –SE forms (92.51%), while the forms in –RA are used 4 times (1.06%) in SI-clauses in the protasis, and 24 (6.41%) in other contexts. Document 16 is lengthy, was drafted by the Cadiz Consulate, and reveals the fractures that the Mexican merchants had had with the Spanish authorities over trade regulations. It is assumed that the rifts between Spaniards and Mexicans were exacerbated in the 18th century, and that these and other conflicts over power, inheritance, and basic rights led to the Wars of Independence in all the New World colonies. Authors agree in that after the War of Independence the rate of change in both variables was rapidly accelerated, leading to the predominance of –RA and the noticeable decline of –SE (cf. Wilson 1983: 152; Acevedo 1997, Martínez 2001). Acevedo overemphasizes the fact that the language change initiated in the 18th century anticipated the major political upheaval of the 19th century (1997: 112).

Table 9.17: Summary: Uses of –SE and –RA in the two periods

Period	–SE forms	–RA forms in Protasis	Other uses of –RA	Total tokens
1701-1745	52 / 74 (70.27%)	11 / 74 (14.86%)	11 / 74 (14.86%)	74
1753-1781	141 / 204 (69.11%)	13 / 204 (6.37%)	50 / 204 (24.50%)	204
Totals = 278	193 / 278 (69.42%)	24 / 278 (8.63%)	61 / 278 (21.94%)	278 (100%)

Source: Extrapolated from Yuste (1991)

9.10 Lexicon

In the new economy of New Spain, the lexicon referring to trade and other mercantile activities can be classified in two major categories. The first one includes items frequently used in previous centuries, when the economy was based on agriculture and labor: for instance, *cargas de cacao* ('cacao loads'), *tamemes* ('Indian carriers'), *naguatato* ('interpreter'), *meceguales* ('commoners'), *tepuzque* ('copper coins'), *hanegas de mayz* ('corn fanegas'), *millpas* ('single corn plant'), *matolaxe* or *matolaje* ('provisions for a trip'), *aviamiento* ('equipment or kit for a trip'), *mercar* ('to purchase'), *fardo de mercadurías* ('bundle of goods', 'parcels'), *pagar la alcabala* ('to pay the sales tax'), *avíos de mercaderías* ('merchandise shipments)', *vara* ('linear measure or yard-stick'), *fojas* ('leaf of legal documents'), *gravamen* ('tax'), *mercaderes* ('merchants'), *naos mercantes* ('trade ships'), *marchantes* ('clients in the market place'); *garitas* ('inspection stations'), among many others. The second category includes items used in the modern economy of services and manufacturing: *comerciante* ('merchant'), *hombres de comercio* ('businessman'), *factura* ('original invoice), *mercancías* ('manufactured products'), *remitir el expediente* ('to send the file'), *ventas por mayor y por menor* ('retail and wholesale'), *superávit* ('surplus'), *tiendas del menudeo* ('retail stores'), *venta al contado* ('cash sale'), *tomar fiado* ('to sign a promissory note'), etc.

When compared to the previous centuries, the use of diminutives increased from 31 percent in the 17th century to 60 percent in the 18th century. Diminutives with the suffixes *–ito* and *–ita* appear not only in nouns such as *bebito* ('baby'), *muertito* ('dead person'), but also in adverbs such as *ahorita* ('now'), *despuesito* ('after'), *lueguito* ('then'), indefinite pronouns such as *alguito* ('something'), *tantito* ('some'), and even gerunds of verbs of movement (*llegandito*). Nouns ending in *–ito* are so abundant that the other Spanish suffixes used to mark diminution (e.g. *–ico*, *–illo*, *–uelo*, *–ecito*) are indeed rare. Colonial texts of this century register diminutives in which the suffix *–ito* is used for different meanings not only size: for instance, *muletita* ('small crutch'), *oregitas* ('pretty ears'), *sacatitos* ('pretty grass'), and *burrita* ('short female donkey'). In addition to the overuse of Spanish patrimonial diminutives, nouns from indigenous languages (re)appeared in three glosses: (1) As an equivalent to a Spanish noun, as in **cocoliztle** or *tabardillo* ('illness'). (2) As a definition in an independent sentence, for example, *la grama, llamada en idioma mexicano* **zacate** ('grass'). (3) As a scientific gloss that describes a specific object, for example, **pilpitzitzintlis**, a mix of herbs and seeds of cannabis (Company Company 2012: 268, 278-279).

Witnesses describing ritualized contexts and retailers requesting miscellaneous products also resorted to borrowings of indigenous origin and used them without definitions or equivalent meanings. The original indigenous word appears with Spanish modifiers and other Spanish nouns belonging to the same semantic domain. The integration of borrowings in the Gulf, items (a)-(k), was completed after the integration of the same loans in the Central Highlands. Sentences (a) and (f) refer to rituals in which *copal* (an aromatic tree resin) is used for curative purposes. In sentence (g) the noun *petaca* (< Nahuatl *petlacalli*), which originally meant 'woven hamper', reappears with the meaning of 'trunk' or 'large suitcase' for travel as in (b) and (g), but the diminutive *petaquilla* was assigned varied meanings in Spain ('flask for liquor', 'small box for letters' or at present 'cigarette case'). The word *chile* (< Nahuatl *chilli*) is used with a series of other edibles as in (k), but also originated the transitive verb *enchilar* ('to season with hot pepper') or the reflexive verb with the meaning of 'feeling the effects of the seasoning'. An additional semantic extension referring to provoked irritation or anger is common today and was used with this meaning, as in item (c).

(a) *jícaras de agua* que hazía componer de cascarilla y miel, con *copal* enzendido (EG 121, 1724)
(b) los géneros los puse en mi quarto en *petacas*, y el paño sobre una mesa (EG 128, 1734)
(c) *enchilándola* en presencia de esta testiga, le impusieron graves penas (EG 129, 1735)
(d) que no tiene oficio alguno, que se exercita en vender *zacate y leñas* (EG 139, 1748)
(e) hizo su viaje en una *piragua* (EG 140, 1752)
(f) el que declara cogió un *poco de copal* y le saumó las piernas (EG 139, 1748)
(g) Parece que perdieron mis *petacas*, con todos mis papeles y ajuar, ni quedó en el navío otra cosa más que mi *petaquilla* con las cartas (EG 146, 1766)
(h) Me resta v.m. *un petate*, y real y medio (EG 165, 1785)
(i) v.m. propio me ofresió el *tequesquite* a 3 reales y medio (EG 165, 1785)
(j) Llega la Pasqua, y aquí no hay más dulces que *zapotes* (...); y *quatro reales de cacahuates* (EG 166, 1785)
(k) muchos se an atracado de *chile, aguacate,* naranjas tiernas y aguardiente (EG 179, 1799)

In the realm of ethnicity, the designations for different groups are used as in previous centuries. They are merely a component of the basic statistics of the subjects that are mentioned in the various documents: *negro, mulata, moro, española, ladino, mestizo* and *pardo* were used in the colonial nomenclature. One more identifier, *gachupín*, designates pejoratively the Spanish speaker born in Spain as in item (g). The use and frequency of the modifier *gachupín* to refer to Spaniards was intensified in the decades preceding and following the War of Independence and points acrimoniously to the conflicts between Spanish speakers born in Spain and those born in the new soil.

(a) [Francisco Limón] tubo unas boses y pleito con otro *negro*, esclavo de Su Magestad (EG 120, 1723)
(b) llegó a él un *negro* llamado Joseph Colina y le dijo que le perdonara (EG 120, 1723)
(c) susedió delante de un *moreno*, esclavo, cuyo nombre no save (EG 120, 1723)
(d) le llamaron [al curandero] para que curase a una *mulata* (...) que tenía un pie baldado (EG 121, 1724)

(e) el denunsiado (...) es el capitán Agustín Barranco (...) tenido por *desendiente de moro* por aver sido (...) su abuela *mora*, esclava en Cadis (EG 124, 1732)
(f) pareció (...) Anna Francisca de Ibanes, *española*, natural y vezina de Xalapa (EG 136, 1746)
(g) fray Francisco, que no save su apellido, sí ques *gachupín* (EG 136, 1746)
(h) dirá verdad una india que dixo llamarse María Covoh (...) muger de Felis Tus, *yndio*, baquero (EG 137, 1746)
(i) juró en forma que dirá verdad una muger de color *pardo* (...) vecina del varrio de Guadalupe (...), casada con Juan de Salazar, *mulato*, aunque se tiene por *mestizo* (EG 141, 1755)
(j) otro *indio* que dixo ser natural del mismo pueblo de Papantla (...) *ladino* que entendía y hablaba bien en lengua castellana (EG 148, 1767)
(k) que de los soldados que lo llebaban sólo conoce a dos (...) y que eran milicianos *pardos* (EG 148, 1767)

9.11 Language reforms, journalism and literature

Protected by the Spanish state, the Real Academia Española [Spanish Royal Academy] was founded in 1713. Its role was to establish norms for the use of lexicon, orthography and grammar. It published the *Diccionario de Autoridades* (1726-1739), an *Orthographia* (1741) and the *Gramática de la lengua castellana* (1771). The attention to language was also reflected in the monumental *Orígenes de la lengua castellana* (1737) by the royal librarian Gregorio Mayans y Siscar. The 18th century philologists and linguists were successful in completing the restoration of the Latin spelling in consonant clusters in words such as *concepto, efecto, digno, solemne*; the system of graphemes used in previous centuries (derived from medieval Spanish) was streamlined in order to deter the confusion of duplicate forms. In the end, the rules for spelling the sibilants <c>, <z>, and <s> were clearly explained, and the modern orthography was fixed in the eighth edition of the Real Academia Española 1815 (Lapesa: 1985: 419-423).

One of the most prolific writing fields was journalism, distinguished by the apparition of *El Diario de los Literatos de España* (1737-1750), *Diario de Madrid* (1750-1770), *El Mercurio Histórico y Político* (1738-1784), and the *Correo de Madrid* (1787), which published José Cadalso's famous epistolary novel *Cartas marruecas* [Moroccan Letters]. Though all these papers had a minority of readers, they circulated in large and small cities within Spain. Some of the prominent men of letters of this century were also devoted to journalism (Saiz 1983). Journalists found inspiration in the Illustration, and were inquisitive, versatile, innovative and broad (cf. Cebrián 2003). In intention and content the papers published in Spain contrast with those published in New Spain, which were constrained by the local administration. In peninsular literature, the dominant trend was neoclassicism, the cultural movement oriented towards a new expression of criticism, didactics and moralization inspired in the Illustration, which in turn attempted to curb the excesses of the Baroque and to privilege the gust for philosophy and science. The essayists of the 18th century are known for addressing diverse topics germane to the spirit of the Illustration. Benito Jerónimo Feijóo (1676-1764) believed in the renovation of society and the aperture of Spain to new ideas, experimental science and freedom. Reason gave him direction to understand the perspective of modern science and philosophy. He also advanced a reflection on the origin of language, which is not possible without a speech community. His essays have encyclopedic scope and value. In literary theory, Ignacio de Luzán (1702-1754) contributed with the criticism of national drama in his *Poética*, which according to him has the same purpose of moral philosophy. José Francisco de Isla (1703-1781) wrote the satire of sacred oratory, whereas the studies on the location and origin of world languages were advanced by the Jesuit Lorenzo Hervás y Panduro (1735-1809), author of the *Catálogo de las lenguas de las naciones conocidas* [Guide to Languages of Known Nations], a work on comparative philology (Valbuena Prat 1937: 506-559).

The similarities between the playwrights of the French Illustration, such as Molière and Racine and Spanish authors, have been highlighted by literature historians. The dramaturges included are, for instance, Leandro Fernández de Moratín (1760-1828), the most influential neoclassicist and author of *El sí de las niñas* [When the Girls Say Yes], *El viejo y la niña* [The Old Man and the Girl], and *La comedia nueva o el café* [The New Comedy or the Café], among other plays. Juan Ramón de la Cruz (1731-1794) introduced new genres such as the *sainetes* (short interludes) and *zarzuelas* (musical comedies) in which the author satirically depicts all the popular characters living in Madrid at the time. The outstanding lyric poet was Juan Meléndez Valdés (1754-1817). In the second part of the century, Manuel Josef Quintana (1772-1857), a prose writer and an enemy of absolutism reignited the theme of freedom and change. Some of the authors were chastised for expressing independent opinions while many of the men of letters affiliated with the Company of Jesus were exiled in Italy (Valbuena Prat 1937: 566-612).

In contrast to the beginning of journalism in Spain, journalism in New Spain was not extremely varied. A series of monthly gazettes appeared in the 17th century, but all of them were replaced by the *Gaceta de México y Noticias de la Nueva España* [Gazette of Mexico and News from New Spain] in 1722. The pamphlets were periodicals of at least eight pages and served not only to inform the local audience but to galvanize the social conscience. They reported on public events, civil and religious festivities, travel, battles, literary contests, natural disasters and the like (Reed Torres and Ruiz Castañeda 1995: 40). The editor-in-chief of the *Gaceta* was Juan Ignacio de Castorena y Urzúa; he was followed by other editors who changed the title of the main gazette to *Mercurio de México* [Mercury of Mexico]. The content of these papers reveals the preoccupation and restlessness of the times with an emerging distinction made between *criollos* (Spanish speakers born in Mexico) and Spaniards. All the editors of the gazettes were *criollos*, a term that gradually acquired political, economic, and in general, cultural undertones referring to an ethnic group and social class (Reed Torres and Ruiz Castañeda 1995: 64-65).

In the 18th century the *criollos americanos* (Spanish speakers born in the New World) were the major leaders in the publication business. The famous editor of the *Gaceta de Literatura de México* (1788-1795), José Antonio de Alzate y Ramírez, was knowledgeable of the scientific developments implemented in the viceroyalty and also a major contender in the public affairs of the colony dominated by the Bourbons. His disagreements with the Count Revillagigedo over the 1790 Census turned into an object of censorship, and consequently, the *Gaceta de Literatura* was suspended eight years after its foundation (Aureliano et al. 1996: 32-33). The content of the issues of the *Gaceta de Literatura* covered a wide range of themes leading to the investigation of methods that would increase the resources of the land as a territory separated from the Spanish Empire. The readers were exposed to the language standards of the times and were being informed about mining and metallurgy, flora and fauna, medicine and public health, meteorology, astrology for amateurs, classical literature, and many other topics which can be found in the synthesis of Aureliano et al. (1996).

With respect to the Spanish literature produced in New Spain, literature historians call attention to the first work of Mexican historiography known as *Biblioteca Mexicana* by Juan José de Eguiara y Eguren (1735-1755), the byproduct of a reaction against the disregard for New World literature. His goal was to defend the values prevailing in New Spain and to highlight those of the indigenous cultures. Another author, José Beristáin de Souza initiated similar research in 1790 logging in 3,687 authors (including handwritten manuscripts). Beristáin exacerbated his inclination for all things coming from Spain (Garza Cuarón and Baudot 1996: 14-16). A group of Jesuits is recognized for their contributions to the emergent nationalist spirit. The first Mexican historian who used a scientific method to describe the Aztec civilization and the accomplishments of the Spanish conquistadors was the Abbot Francisco Javier Clavijero, author of *Storia Antica del Messico* [Ancient History of Mexico] (1780). Also, Diego José Abad published various works of scientific character and Francisco Javier Alegre furthered Latin translation. Finally, Rafael Landívar is the author of *Rusticatio Mexicana*, a poem in Latin hexameters which depicts the nature and country life in the New World (González Peña 1968: 125-136).

Expelled from New Spain in the late 18th century the Jesuits sought refuge in Italy, where they revived the nostalgia for their native land. In the dramatic genre, they followed to an extent the peninsular cannons by staging some of the plays of the Golden Age or the works in vogue in 18th century Spain. Following the rules of the Bourbon reforms they composed plays and comedies that were supposed to be both didactic and entertaining. A good number of works, however, were censored by the Inquisition due to political commentary. The best known playwright is Eusebio Vela, author of *Apostolado en las Indias* [Apostolate in the Indies], a comedy inspired in the chronicles of the 16th century which recreated the endeavors of the missionaries to convert the indigenous to Catholicism and the epic of Hernán Cortés. Another play *Si el amor excede al arte* [If Love Surpasses Art] was one of the viceroy's favorites and the scenario was not the New World but ancient Greece. The third comedy is *La pérdida de España* [The Loss of Spain] which narrated the legend of king Rodrigo's defeat and the triumph of the Moors. Finally, a heroic comedy composed by Fermín del Rey was *Hernán Cortés en Cholula* (1782) whose goal was to resuscitate the old topic of conflicts between Christians and Moors (Peña 2006).

9.12 Spanish-accented Nahuatl

By the time Spanish speakers were consolidating the features of Mexican Colonial Spanish, 18th century Spanish texts written by Nahuas show their mastery of Spanish pronunciation and lexicon; the differences between Spanish and Nahuatl speakers had to do mainly with morpho-syntax and idiomatic expressions, the result of transfers from Nahuatl to Spanish. Most Nahuatl speakers appeared to know basic principles of Spanish word order, number and gender agreement, and verb subjects. The Spanish object-of-verb system was, nonetheless, more complex than the Nahuatl equivalent, so Nahuatl speakers tended to simplify verb objects by using *lo* to cover all cases. Too, they omitted the preposition *a*, when personal *a* functions as an object (as in *veo a Juan*), and overused progressive constructions but handled Spanish tenses and subjunctive mood with relative accuracy (Lockhart 1991:113). In essence, a Nahuatl substratum appeared on the surface in various sub-regions (Toluca and Mexico City) yielding a Nahuatl-accented Spanish that was used for intra- and inter-group communication (Lockhart 1991).

Four texts written by bilinguals show a continuum of styles. Text 1 (land grant, 1750) is a sample of Nahuatl / Spanish code-switching. Text 2, a bill of sale of 1733, lacks gender and number agreement, verb inflections, idiomatic expressions, and the like. Text 3 (obligation of the Council, 1781) shows mastery of lexicon, inflection, agreement and overall syntax and idiom, but contains typical contact features such as vowel raising, N intrusion, $r - l$ interchange, and confusion of voiced and voiceless stops. Text 4 (land grant, 1783) is cast in a Spanish that follows general conventions but retains contact features such as auxiliaries with a progressive meaning (e.g. *fue dexando, mas que se ofrece lo esta dando*) (cf. Lockhart 1991: 105-121). This accented–Nahuatl Spanish "was a transitional phenomenon on the way to a broader acquisition of the more standard variety spoken by most bilingual Nahuas today" (Lockhart 1992: 323). It can be identified as a socio-ethnic variety still spoken in the area of Nahuatl substratum. It is similar in many ways to Quechua-accented or Mayan-accented Spanish of the Andean region or the Yucatan peninsula, respectively. Indian Spanish (or *español indígena*) seems to be characterized by inter-language features encountered in a continuum of varieties ranging from colloquial/vernacular to creolized versions of Spanish. Its emergence in the late 18th century is one more piece of evidence of sociolinguistic stratification and dialect diversification.

By the 18th century, speakers of Nahuatl were beginning to show their writing skills in different documents. In previous centuries, the communication modes between Nahuas and Spaniards did not generate a pidgin-like or 'barbaric' Nahuatl though Spaniards played an important role in Hispanicizing innovations (Lockhart 1992: 571-572). In the beginning Spanish conversations by Nahuatl speakers occurred between individual Spaniards outside the context of the indigenous world. Some Nahuatl speakers, including interpreters, employees and traders in cross-cultural relations habitually spoke Spanish. In the 16th and early 17th centuries Nahuas testified through an interpreter, despite the fact that many of them were fluent in Spanish. However, from the late 17th century forward, an interpreter continued to be used not only because of the potential legal challenges of statements made in Spanish by indigenous speakers but also because the interpreters were eager to maintain their positions in the courts. In the last decades of the 18th century Nahuatl speakers began to testify directly in Spanish or even to translate for others. Data available from the texts examined indicate that Nahuas were "reasonable masters of Spanish pronunciation and had few vocabulary problems". Outstanding features have to do with syntax, particularly with distinguishing direct from indirect objects, masculine from feminine, and singular from plural objects in terms of individual words. After 1760-1770, the development of a critical mass of Spanish competence is observed but not until the end of the second half of the 18th century did Spanish-speaking Nahuas produce a substantial amount of written texts in Spanish (Lockhart 1992: 319-320).

Indian towns were able to retain both their language and many indigenous practices because a sizeable proportion of Spaniards were residing in a few large cities and somewhat removed from a largest part of indigenous speakers. During the 17th and 18th centuries, significant nuclei of Spanish speakers living in the countryside created new Spanish-style settlements until the whole area was honeycombed with them. Spanish entrepreneurs hired a large number of Indian workers, and in the regional markets Spanish speakers with connection to the cities were predominant. Spanish-speaking administrative officials positioned themselves near the Indian towns, where the presence of Spanish speakers fostered Nahuatl / Spanish bilingualism amongst the leaders of the communities due mostly to the fact that the testimonies of Indians in the courts were to be rendered in Spanish directly or via interpreters. Also, the bilingualism that was unfolding amongst indigenous leaders can be examined in the texts they were producing, i.e. normally prepared under the Spanish models, where the legal terminology eventually dominated (Lockhart 1992: 106-107).

Nahuatl writers were able to distinguish Spanish structures including verb tenses. The most interesting features of the Spanish texts composed by Nahuas have to do with the use of some prepositions, which sometimes are omitted (e.g. preposition *a*) and sometimes were integrated (e.g. prepositions *hasta* and *para*). The use of progressive tenses was transferred from Nahuatl to Spanish in expressions like *fue dejando* ('he went leaving'), "an attempt to reproduce a Nahuatl model construction meaning 'left something or someone on departure or death'"(Lockhart 1992: 322). All in all there seems to be a socio-ethnic dialect showing variants that are typical of common non-professional Spanish speakers and other features that are only produced by Nahuatl writers (Lockhart 1991: 111-112, 117-118). The first group includes variants of non-standard Spanish dialects: use of strong open vowel /o/ instead of weak close vowel /u/ as in *comonidad* ('comunidad'); velarization of the diphthong /ue/ as in *güérfanos* ('huérfanos'); interpretation of the grapheme <c> as <s>, as in *ofisiales* ('oficiales'), *obligasion* ('obligación'), *pedaso* ('pedazo'), *mais* ('maíz'), *besino* ('vecino'), *asotes* ('azotes'); the use of velar /x/ or *jota* before initial /f/, as in *jue* ('jue'), and the use of late medieval *onde* in lieu of modern *donde*. All of them are typical of Mexican Colonial Spanish, whereas the variants distinguishing Nahuatl speakers writing in Spanish were the following: intrusive –N, mostly at the end of a noun, as in *pedason de tierras* ('pedazo de tierra'), *testigon* ('testigo'), *republican* ('república'), *perjuision* ('perjuicio') *hijon* ('hijo'), *justisian* ('justicia'). The use of progressive tense to express completion of actions, as in *se lo fue dexando* ('se lo dejó'), *todo lo esta pagando* ('todo lo pagó'), *y mas que se ofrece lo esta dando* ('y ha dado más de lo que se necesita') derives from Nahuatlized Spanish.

9.13 Conclusions

This century simultaneously represents the end of the colony, the transition to Independence, and the beginning of a modern era. Introduced by the Spanish Crown under several monarchs, the Bourbon Reforms were modern since they promoted manufacturing, technological, commercial and fiscal development in both Spain and the New World colonies. These reforms opened opportunities for trade, though their main goal was to consolidate the Spanish power, collect higher taxes, and diminish the influence of the Society of Jesuits. In the strictly political realm, this set of regulations was counterproductive because the economy of the colonies was strangled, and as a result, the reforms accelerated the movements of Independence masterminded by the surviving Jesuits, who had been the intellectual leaders of those born in New Spain. The rift between Spaniards and those born in the colony was not only exacerbated at the end of the century but was conducive to an intestine war that was prolonged through 1821.

Journalists and men of letters residing in New Spain were not granted the same privileges enjoyed by intellectuals working in Spain; on the contrary, they were censored and repressed by the pro-Bourbon local authorities. Showing their concern for their native land, journalists clearly catered to the audience of literate *criollos* and mestizos. In contrast, literature in Spain followed neoclassical models, whereas the literary production in New Spain turned to ancient themes or the themes of the Conquest. The journalists, writers, merchants, and artists of New Spain had their own agenda, which was not intersecting at any juncture with the agenda of their homologues in Spain. For all the abovementioned reasons, both historians and lay people believe that no other former colony experienced a more dramatic rupture with Spain than her favorite possession, New Spain. This theory has been put forward by Spanish linguists who have repeatedly asserted that the alternation between –SE and –RA is reflective of such rupture, therefore explaining the almost exclusive use of –RA in modern Mexican Spanish.

The attrition-focused variants examined in this book reveal the consolidation of the trends initiated in the previous century. (1) Though it is assumed that *seseo* was general in the pronunciation habits of all Spanish speakers living in the New World, it did not prevail in writing. (2) The clitic pronoun LO ascended 60 percent over the contending pronoun LE. (3) The pronouns of address *tú* and *vuestra merced* prevailed over all the other pronouns of address, while (4) the use of –RA at almost 50 percent indicates that the changes were not regressing but progressing towards the Latin American Spanish patterns observed at present. The sibilants <c>, <z>, and <s> followed most of the time (more than 60%) normative standards, albeit significant residuals of errors in discrete units appear at high rates. At the end of the colonial period, *seseo* was general in pronunciation, which can be identified as Seseo-P. From everyday pronunciation habits, it spread to writing, which can be considered Seseo-W, a socio-educational variety that regularly violates the normative standards. The ability to spell the sibilants according to prescribed rules turned into a habit of only a few Spanish speakers who were exposed to normative Spanish through formal education, literary activities, and the like. The rates of Seseo-W have not changed significantly since the beginning of the transitional period.

Other notorious modifications observed in the 18th century can be considered the breakthrough experienced in New Spain from the linguistic patterns prevailing in the metropolis (Company Company 2012). It has been proposed that the series of languages changes were ahead of a major political cataclysm, the War of Independence, which was preceded by a series of fractures at all levels. The question raised is whether language change exemplified in attrition-focused variants can anticipate major societal changes. This hypothesis is advanced in the context of New Spain, a multilingual society in which values and attitudes unfolded in opposite directions that eventually resulted in a major divergence. The set of features and variants distinguishing Mexican Colonial Spanish from peninsular Spanish were supported by the resistance to ways-of-speaking like Spaniards, and the cumulative changes that over the centuries have marked the differentiation between the two varieties. While language is not strictly regulated in a setting of resistance, select variants can be eroded by the speakers in subtle, overt or vacillating ways, and social movements can proceed at a slower pace than language change. In fact, social movements (social, cultural, and political) can be more distressing to newer communities of speakers who may be unaware of the drifts that they themselves provoke. Ultimately, social movements shape the direction of society and give voice to newer concerns and attitudes. Internal language changes per se may be contrastingly insufficient to foster actions in broad social and cultural terms; though they normally stand as the dependent variable, when their social significance is enhanced or exacerbated, language drifts can prefigure major social changes at particular junctures. By reaffirming their preference for those variants that were instrumental in shaping their identity, Spanish speakers born and raised in the New World acted as the catalysts of change. Their collective attitudes can be considered the major external factor promoting simultaneously attrition, variation and diversification.

Chapter 10
Diversification, attrition and residual variants

10.1 Attrition-focused variants

The diversification of New World Spanish is the result of a successful transplantion of peninsular Spanish into the American continent. Not all transplants survive the conditions of new soil and weather, and some trees may die due to improper removal of the roots and installation. This is not the case of New World Spanish for the shock of the transplant did not destroy the deep roots of the language tree that grew and blossomed in the new ground. The peninsular variety transplanted into the New World was already in transition from medieval polymorphism to pre-modern Spanish, and for this reason the inventory of available variants was lavish. The attrition of contending variants in the milieu of diversification reflects the decline of those that acquired a social meaning identified with peninsular-oriented attitudes. The coexistence of miscellaneous forms for identical functions within the same community of speakers is not cost-effective; in the New World environment the various contending variants were reduced to one in most cases, or to a dyad. In order to examine the rates of attrition, four focused variants were selected from Mexican colonial documents (see 1 through 4 below). The transplanted variants from Spain were altered by means of erosion, simplification, and elimination. The processes of change were successful in reducing the assortment of sibilant variants, the pronominal system, the pronouns of address, and the endings with subjunctive meaning in the following manner:

(1) The four sibilants represented by the graphemes <s>, <ss>, <ç> and <z> gradually merged into one in the general pronunciation of New World Spanish. After the language reforms of the 19th century, the one-single sibilant pronunciation or Seseo-P has been accepted in all speech styles and registers in all domains of interaction. There is no evidence of emulation of northern-central peninsular Spanish distinguishing in speech the subtle acoustic difference between /s/ and /θ/. This merger caused nonetheless a major crisis in the writing practices of speakers of all ages who for diverse reasons did not complete tertiary education. Sibilant distinction in writing may be restricted to individuals with solid and continuous formal training in colleges and universities.

The analysis of *Documentos Lingüísticos de la Nueva España. Altiplano Central* (1994) and *Documentos Lingüísticos de la Nueva España. Golfo de México* (2008) shows that in the 16th century the four sibilants were used like in the northern-central peninsular varieties, and that the trends of Seseo-W were rather moderate. Moreover, from the documents examined it is gleaned that Seseo-W did not become a regular pattern until the following century. Graphs 10.1 and 10.2 show the rates of Seseo-W vis-à-vis traditional variants in the 17th and 18th centuries when writers used more frequently the grapheme <s> instead of the graphemes <c>, <ç> and <z>. High rates of spelling errors are found in the second half of the 17th century in both regions and also in the first half of the 18th century in the Gulf region. This means that a good proportion of all writers in both centuries had lost awareness of traditional norms, most likely because there were fewer first-generation speakers in bureaucratic positions, and at the same time, a good number of Spanish speakers who were born and raised in New Spain had not yet learned the writing rules *in toto*. This explains why other variants were used, e.g. <c> in lieu of <s>, as in for instance *precensia* (in lieu of *presencia*). Notwithstanding, when all the tokens of Seseo-W and all the items of traditional spelling are calculated and comparisons drawn for the 17th and 18th century documents, the latter practice prevailed in all periods, except in the last two decades of the 17th century in the Central Highlands (see Graph 10.1).

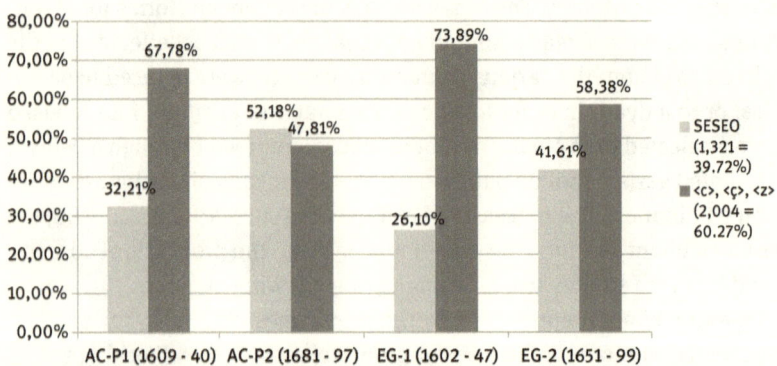

Graph 10.1: Summary of sibilant graphemes: 17th century

In the 18th century, traditional graphemes prevailed in all four periods in the two regions. This may have to do with the socio-cultural background of the writers working in key positions within the bureaucracy of New Spain. A major difference stands out in the Gulf between Period I and Period II when irregular or "incorrect" *seseo* or Seseo-W appeared at 43.12 percent in the former and 17.5 percent in the latter. The highest rate of traditional graphemes <c> and <z> appears in the second part of the 18th century, a trend strikingly similar to that observed in the first two decades of the 19th century. The second part of the 18th century and the first two decades of the 19th century may be considered the pre-independent period when Spanish speakers born in New Spain were thinking of severing themselves from

Spanish speakers residing in the metropolis. These results lead to believe that there was a cadre of highly educated individuals who was not enjoying the privileges afforded to their stratum.

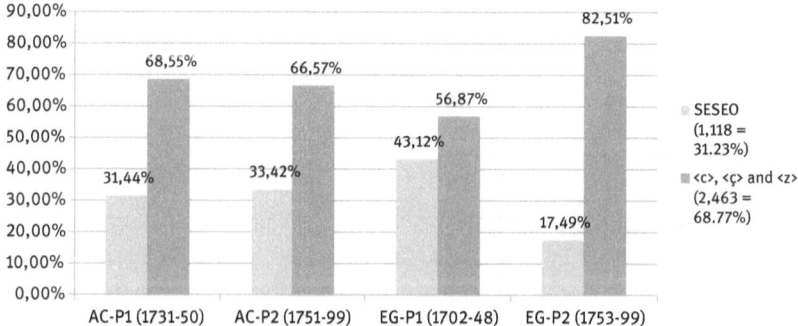

Graph 10.2: Summary of sibilant graphemes: 18th century

Furthermore, Table 10.1 shows the rates of *seseo* in the first two decades of the 19th century. By then, the grapheme <ç> had disappeared altogether, and the writers followed for the most part the rules of modern Spanish with a small percent of "spelling errors". The most common spelling error was then, like today, the use of <s> where the graphemes <c> and <z> are supposed to be used, for instance, *alcansaron, comensó, conosco, paresco, hiso, afiansar* in lieu of *alcanzaron, comenzó, conozco, parezco, hizo, afianzar*. Occasionally, the opposite practice can occur, when the grapheme <c> is used instead of the grapheme <s>, as in *demaciado* (in lieu of *demasiado*). In these decades, the sibilant system was complete and stabilized, and no changes in spelling rules have been made after the movement of Independence (1810-1821). In the short period of the 19th century for which data have been gathered, writers show an exceptional rate of correct spellings most likely because they had a solid foundation in normative Spanish. Nevertheless, the spelling errors observed in the colonial period have been perpetuated for two centuries in all the independent nations of the Spanish-speaking world, and are in turn related to the illiteracy rates prevailing in each country. In the middle decades of the 20th century, for example, they ranged from a low of 8-9 percent in Argentina and Uruguay to a high 51 and 62 percent in Honduras and Guatemala, respectively (Padua 1979: 6).

Table 10.1: Summary of sibilant graphemes: 19th century

Region	Seseo-W	‹c›, ‹z›
Altiplano C.	126 / 819	693 / 819
1800-1816	(15.38 %)	(93.63 %)
El Golfo	68 / 399	331 / 399
1802-1821	(17.04 %)	(82.95 %)
Totals =	194	1,024
1,218	(15.92 %)	(84.07 %)

(2) Towards the end of the colony, the use of the clitic pronouns LE and LO was also mature and complete in New Spain. Graphs 10.3 through 10.6 show the distribution of the two variants in the 16th century, when the clitic pronoun LE, representative of northern-central peninsular varieties, was used in New Spain two-thirds of the time (66.29 %) in both regions, a rate which remained stable in the 17th century. This coincides with the Golden Age period when professional New Spanish writers found inspiration in peninsular models of poetry and drama. A sharp contrast transpired in the following century when the use of LE declined to less than 40 percent, that is, the trend of the 18th century was exactly the opposite of that observed in previous centuries, and became the pattern in the following centuries.

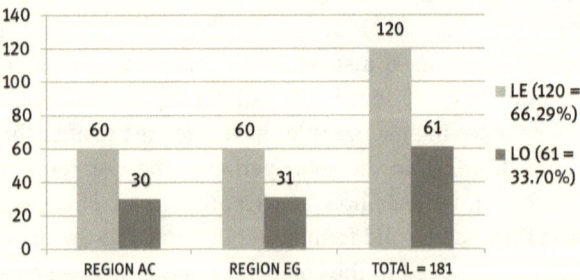

Graph 10.3: LE and LO in the 16th century

10.1 Attrition-focused variants — **347**

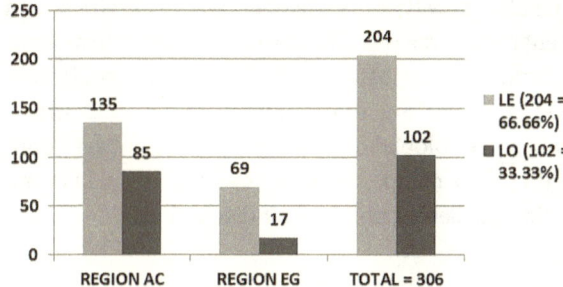

Graph 10.4: LE and LO in the 17th century

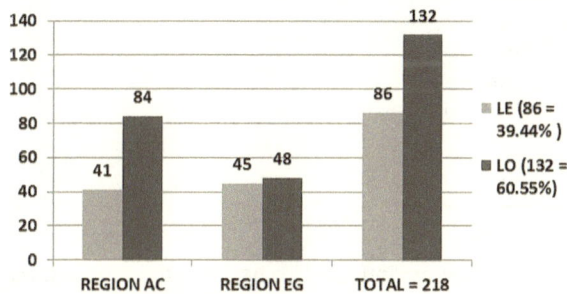

Graph 10.5: LE and LO in the 18th century

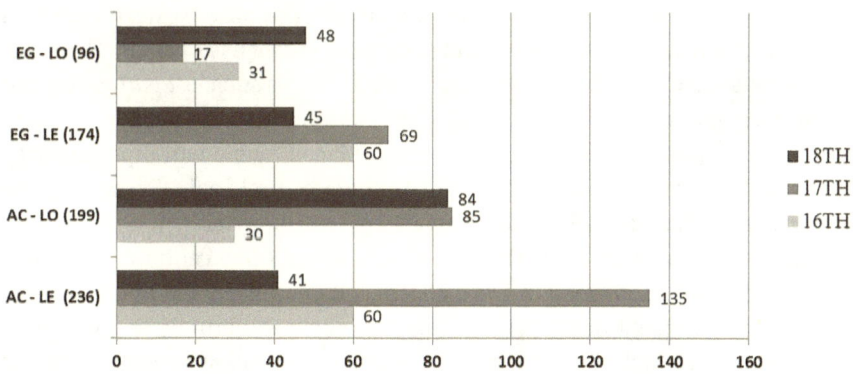

Graph 10.6: LE and LO in the colony: Central Highlands and the Gulf (raw figures)

In the pre-independent period (the first two decades of the 19th century), LE appears only 12 times in the Gulf region (see Table 10.2); three of those are used with the verb *saludar* ('to greet' or 'to say hello'), which is like today interpreted as an intransitive verb. The results show that the use of LO was also settled with an average of almost 80 percent in both regions. The use of LO is stable in modern varieties of Mexican Spanish, and only few instances of LE have survived. Moreover, the variations that ensued in northern-central peninsular Spanish known as *laísmo* and *loísmo* do appear in some colonial documents but did not have continuity in New Spain because they were competing with pro-etymological LO and because their frequency was limited (see section 10.8 for discussion).

Table 10.2: LE and LO in the 19th century

Region	LE	LO
Altiplano C.	16 / 67	51 / 67
	(23.88 %)	(76.11 %)
El Golfo	12 / 66	54 / 66
	(18.18 %)	(81.81 %)
Total = 133	28	105
	(21.05 %)	(78.94 %)

(3) In most Central and South American regions and/or nations, the pronoun *vos* is used with singular meaning as a subject and object of preposition, but was infrequent in the Mexican regions. The *voseo* branch is still growing in various New World regions with different verb paradigms that do not correspond entirely to the old forms derived from medieval Spanish. The only Mexican region in which researchers have reported a bud of the *voseo* branch is Chiapas. The medieval Spanish tree branch in which long verb paradigms such as *apartasedes* and *enviasedes* appeared did not survive at all. These forms were used as in Spain with the pronouns *vos* (singular) and were replaced by modern diphthongized forms such as *apartaseis* and *enviaseis* in northern-central Spain. Eventually, due to semantic ambiguity both forms disappeared in the new soil.

In the Central Highlands, the total tokens in the three centuries examined amounts to 1,167 subdivided in five categories. Representing the informal registers, *vos* was frequent in the 16th century, but declined abruptly to give way to the pronoun *tú*, which showed a modest increase in the following century. In this region, *vuestra merced* appeared in more than 52 percent of all the occurrences, while *su merced* and *Usted* were still incipient (see Graph 10.7). The tokens of the five pronouns totaled 961 in the Gulf region, where the pronouns *vos* and *tú* were uncommon due to the official nature of the documents of the first part of the 16th century. It is clear that the prevailing form of address in the colonial prose was *vuestra merced*, while all the other pronouns competed disadvantageously with it (see Graph 10.8). The difference between regions may be due to the type of document found and the demographic density of the writers representing diverse backgrounds in the early decades of the colonial period. Notwithstanding the differences, the common denominator in both regions is the use of *vuestra merced* (v.md.) and the modest increment of *su merced* (s. md.), which had appeared a few times in the 16th century. In contrast, in the 17th and 18th centuries, *su merced* (s. md.) and *Usted* (U) were used more frequently, but did not compete with the frequencies attained by *vuestra merced* (v. md.). In order to validate the hypothesis that *voseo* was not used in New Spain on a regular basis, all subject pronouns were counted with the corresponding verb forms and objects of prepositions. Data show that the personal pronoun *vos* had virtually disappeared at the onset of the 16th century, and that the instances of mixed pronouns were extremely low (see section 10.8).

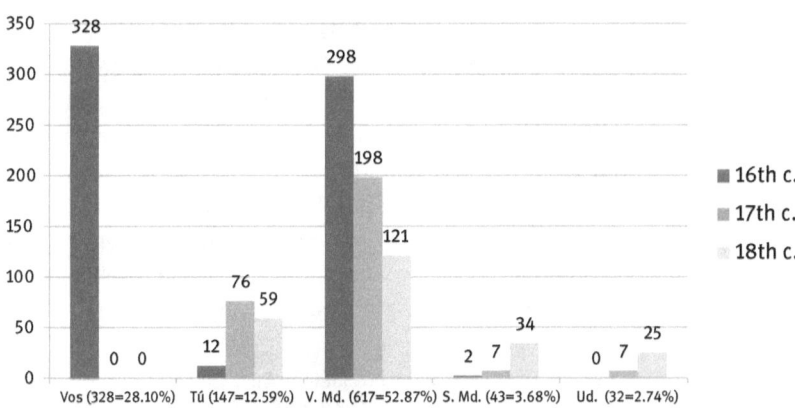

Graph 10.7: Pronouns of address in the Central Highlands by century

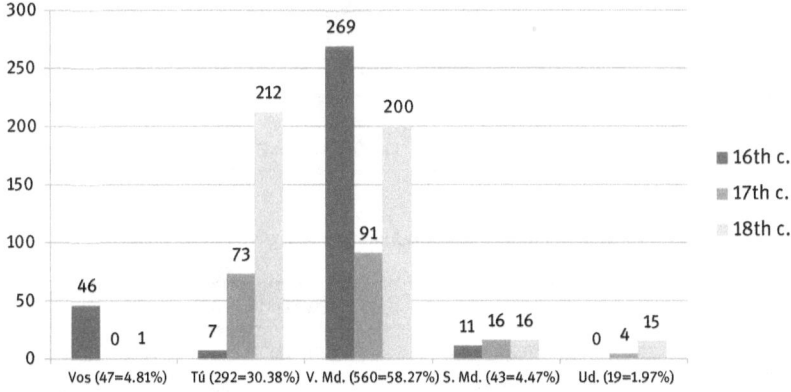

Graph 10.8: Pronouns of address in the Gulf by century

A variety of pronouns of address was still used in the first two decades of the 19th century. Table 10.3 shows *Usted* and *tú* ahead of the other pronouns while *vuestra merced* was still used and occasionally mixed with *Usted*. The other forms of address, *vos* and *su merced*, survived at low rates while the innovation *Usía* (< *Vuestra señoría*) appeared in the Gulf but not in the Central Highlands; in this region, subjects preferred *vuestra señoría* or *Ilustrísima* when they had to address a judge or a higher authority. All subject pronouns correspond to the paradigmatic verb forms. In the Gulf, the personal pronoun *vos* survived in formulaic interrogatories before the tribunals, a trend opposed to the extremely informal use of *vos* in the Central Highlands. The polarized functions of *vos* seemed to have contributed to its disappearance in Mexico. Finally, the most frequent pronouns in the preindependent period were *tú* and *Usted*, a dyad that established the usage patterns for the rest of the 1800's to the present. The alternating forms of address *tú* and *Usted* prevailed in Mexico and other New World regions, mostly along coastal areas, where *voseo* and honorifics such as *su merced* are not too commonly used. The pronominal system of modernizing New World Spanish was simplified, and in the end, it functioned with only two pronouns in singular and the corresponding plural *Ustedes* for all domains (see Table 10.4). In conclusion, in the realm of pronouns of address, the polymorphism of late medieval Spanish was transmitted *in toto* to Spain's favorite colony, but the semantic complexity in different domains was conducive to its own simplification to the extent that at present one slot is duplicated in the Latin American Spanish dyad.

Table 10.3: Pronouns of address in the Central Highlands and the Gulf: 19th century

Region	Vos	Tú	V. Md.	S. Md.	Ud.	Usía	V.S./ I.
Altiplano C.	4	56	14	4	52	0	35
Total = 165	(2.38%)	(33.93%)	(8.48%)	(2.38%)	(31.51%)	(0%)	(21.21%)
El Golfo	12	21	0	0	21	4	0
Total = 58	(20.68%)	(36.20%)	(0%)	(0%)	(36.20%)	(6.89%)	(0%)
Totals = 223	16	77	14	4	73	4	35
	(7.17%)	(34.53%)	(6.27%)	(1.79%)	(32.73%)	(1.79%)	(15.69%)

Table 10.4: Pronouns of address in Spain and Latin America: 21st c.

Region	Northern-Central Spain		New World	
Number	Singular	Plural	Singular	Plural
Informal	Tú	Vosotros /-as	Tú	Ustedes
Formal	Usted	Ustedes	Usted	Ustedes

(4) The contending imperfect subjunctive forms –SE and –RA survived in the New World with an eventual preference for –RA, which was used in colonial documents less frequently, as in (a) and (b). In each case, the –RA form can be replaced with the –SE form and vice versa in (c).
(a) [Ella] le dio limosna al dicho confessor para que le *dixera* las misas (AC 121, 1634: 336)
(b) para proceder contra la mulata era menester que *dieran* pruebas (AC 132, 1682: 352)
(c) El señor liçenciado me embió a mandar que le *dexase* yr sobre Juan Rodrigo (EG 15, 1542: 69)

In SI-clauses, the –RA form in both the protasis (conditional) and the apodosis (resulting clause) appears in modern popular Spanish in the same contexts used in colonial documents, which seems to indicate that –RA has maintained its ancestral indicative meaning. This combination is spontaneously generated in popular varieties of modern Mexican Spanish. The resulting clause in sentences (a), (b) and (c) appears with the conditional –RÍA in normative Spanish.
(a) si *fuera* posible luego dexar los negoçios y yrme, lo *hiciera* (AC 33, 1568: 154)
 [If *I could drop* all the businesses right away and leave, *I would do* it]
(b) Si tú *buscaras* trabajo, luego luego lo *encontraras*
 [If *you looked for* a job, *you would find* it right away]
(c) si no *fuéramos* ayudados del favor y consolación divina, creo nuestro trabajo totalmente se *perdiera* (EG 20, 1559: 79)
 [if *we were not helped* by divine mercy and consolation, our work *would be completely lost*]

The data drawn from colonial documents show that the alternation between –SE and –RA throughout the centuries is extremely variable. In the Central Highlands, the endings in –SE fluctuate from an all-time high (92%) in the first half of the 16th century to a bottom low of 28% in the second half of the 18th century. Graphs 10.9 and 10.10 show the progresssive changes in seven periods and the recuperation of –SE in the first few decades of the pre-independent period (see also Tables 10.5 and 10.6). When all seven colonial periods are seen together in Graphs 10.11 and 10.12, the regression of –SE is glaring in the Central Highlands, while its decrease in the Gulf is not as sharp. However, the two regions are similar in that the –SE form was restored in the two decades preceding the movement of Independence, when the variant –SE regained its frequency. The hypothesis that the variant –SE was the last one to be replaced from the inventory of peninsular variants is corroborated with the 19th language data in both regions. By the end of the independent period, the variant –SE had become a social marker of Spaniardness, and its decline must have been associated with the political upheaval that distinguished Spanish speakers born in Spain from those born in the New World. The wars of Independence resulted in the creation of a number of independent nations identified as Spanish-speaking Latin America.

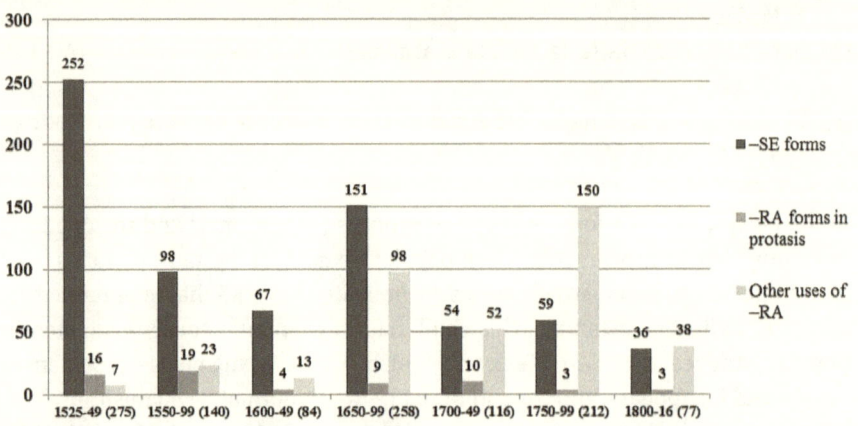

Graph 10.9: Summary: Uses of –SE and –RA in the Central Highlands by period

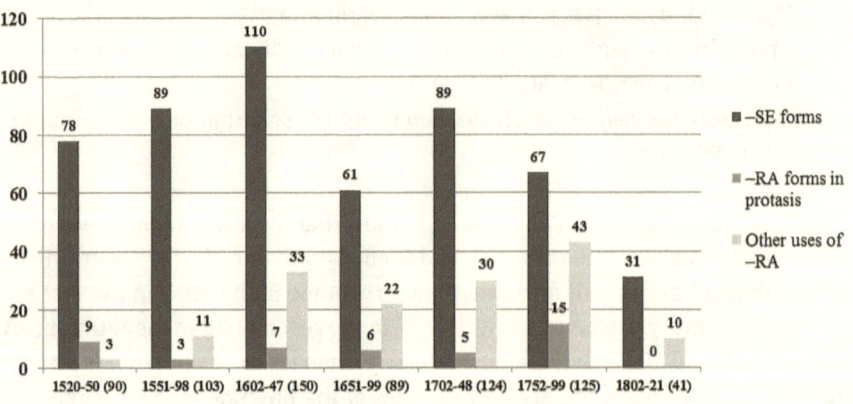

Graph 10.10: Summary: Uses of –SE and –RA in the Gulf by period

Table 10.5: Summary: Uses of –SE and –RA in the Central Highlands by period

Period	–SE forms	–RA forms in protasis	Other uses of –RA	Total tokens
1525-1549	92 % / 252	5.5 % / 16	2.5 % / 7	275
1550-1599	70 % / 98	13.5 % / 19	16.5 % / 23	140
1600-1649	80 % / 67	4.7 % / 4	15.3 % / 13	84
1650-1699	58 % / 151	3.5 % / 9	38.5 % / 98	258
1700-1749	47 % / 54	8.5 % / 10	44.5 % / 52	116
1750-1799	28 % / 59	1.4 % / 3	70.6 % / 150	212
1800-1816	46 % / 36	4.0 % / 3	49.0 % / 38	77

Source: Acevedo (1997: 108)

Table 10.6: Summary: Uses of –SE and –RA in the Gulf by period

Period	–SE forms	–RA forms in protasis	Other uses of –RA	Total tokens
1520-1550	86.66 % / 78	10.00 % / 9	3.33 % / 3	90
1551-1598	86.40 % / 89	2.91 % / 3	10.67 % / 11	103
1602-1647	73.33 % / 110	4.66 % / 7	22.0 % / 33	150
1651-1699	68.53 % / 61	6.74 % / 6	24.71 % / 22	89
1702-1748	71.77 % / 89	4.03 % / 5	24.19 % / 30	124
1752-1799	53.60 % / 67	12.00 % / 15	34.4 % / 43	125
1802-1821	75.60 % / 31	0 % / 0	24.39 % / 10	41

The variations in Graph 10.11 (derived from Table 10.5) show the progressive decline and recovery periods of –SE in the Central Highlands reaching a bottom low in the second half of the 18th century and a sudden upswing in the 19th century. Both forms reached the same frequency during the first half of the 18th century only to show a drastic divergence in the next period. This may have to do with the massive presence of speakers / writers born and raised in New Spain (*criollos* and mestizos). In contrast, the data shown in Graph 10.12 (derived from Table 10.6) indicate that in the Gulf there might have been a more pronounced separation of writers. The –SE writers were probably those with cultural roots in Spain (either by birthplace or because they were raised in all-Spanish speaking families), while the –RA users may have been locals. In this region the decline of –SE occurred in the second half of the 18th century, but it is not as sharp and does not converge in any period with the rise of –RA in other subjunctive contexts. Moreover, the emerging trends of –RA in the protasis and other uses of –RA seem to have grown together.

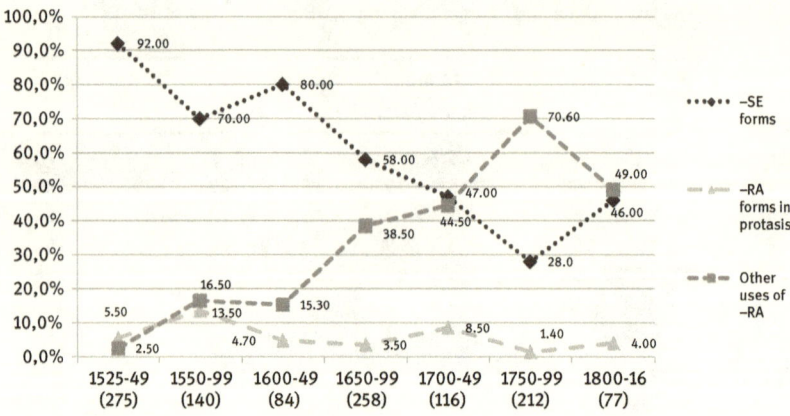

Graph 10.11: Uses of –SE and –RA in the Central Highlands by period in percentages

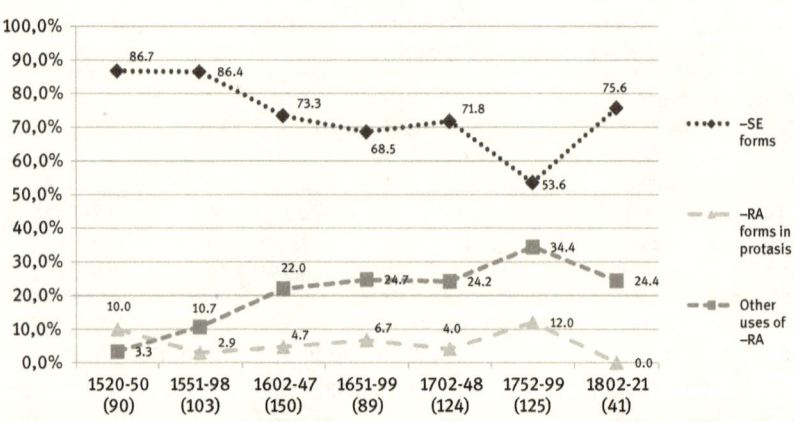

Graph 10.12: Uses of –SE and –RA in the Gulf by period in percentages

10.2 Optimal residual variants

Optimal residual variants are those that appeared in the colonial sources and that are still used by a vast majority of speakers mostly in colloquial registers. The earliest source of residual variants is the *Second Letter* (1522) by Hernán Cortés, where the following items appear: the derivative diminutive of the adverb *cerquita* ('very close'), the noun *alberca* ('pond') instead of the modern *piscina* ('swimming pool'), *maleta* (< Old French *malete*) with the original meaning of 'travel sack' in lieu of the more widespread *valija*. All of them are vital at present across regions and socio-economic strata. Idiomatic expressions, the indirect speech marker *dizque* or *diz que* ('they say that'), common phrases, nouns, adjectives, and verbs belonging to the colloquial register have their roots in the colonial period and have passed the test of time. In the subsample below, items appear with the original source, year, page, and translation.

(a) Sobre cada *alberca* y estanques destas aues auia sus corredores y miradores (*Segunda Carta* 1522: 30)
[In the birds' *ponds* and basins there were navigable waterways and watchtowers]

(b) Hize aquella noche que los heridos y dolientes que lleuauamos a las anchas de los cauallos y acuestas hiziessen *maletas* y otras maneras de ayuda (*Second Letter* 1522: 45)
[That night I ordered that all those who were badly wounded and those that we were taking on our backs be ready to prepare their *travel sacks* and some other useful things]

(c) levantaronse çiertos yndios en la provjnçia de Guaxaca, *diz que* con acuerdo del dicho Pedro de Alvarado (AC 3, 1526: 51)
[*they are saying that* some Indians rioted with the complicity of Pedro de Alvarado]

(d) *diz que* escrivjo al dicho Proaño para que le rrevocase el poder (...) y *diz que* enbjó a Geronjmo Lopes (AC 4, 1526: 61)
[he *presumably* wrote to said Proaño to get the power revoked (...) and *presumably* he sent Geronimo Lopes]

(e) porque el presidente le favoresçiese, le hizo *de balde* muchas obras (AC 8, 1529:.88)
[because he wanted the favors of the President, he did a lot of work *for free*]

(f) *Quien quita* que no tengan deseo de verse como en su prinçipio (AC 16, 1534: 107)
[*Who may say* that they won't have the desire to see one another like in the beginning]

(g) adonde trabajé mucho, por ser las más agras tierras del mundo, y adonde *heché el bofe a pie* (EG 12, 1540: 61)
[where I worked a lot, as they were the most arid lands of the world, and where *I was sweating and walking*]

(h) havjan de ser hombres que aca *havjan hechado el bofe* por estos miserable naturales (AC 26, 1555: 136-7)
[those must have been the men who *were sweating and walking* for the sake of the poor native people]

(i) creo lo hara porques honbre que lo suele haçer y *muy de beras* (AC 33, 1568: 153)

[I think he'll do it because he is the kind of guy who *honestly* does it often on his own]

(j) Luisa de Gallegos, *acuitándose* y llorando, dijo... [Luisa de Gallegos, all *depressed* and crying, said...] (AC 55, 1576: 199)

(k) vuestra magestat (...) mande y encargue muy *de veras* a su vissorrey (AC 68, 1578: 217)
[I wish His majesty will order and *honestly* delegate onto his viceroy]

(l) le dan todo lo que pide *de balde* (EG 59, 1621:192) [He gets everything he wants *for free*]

(m) era un *conchudo* y miserable [he was a *cynic* and mean] (EG 89, 1675: 275)

(n) no vio lo que pasó porque *luego luego* se salió (EG 103, 1691: 306)
[he did not see what had happened because he *immediately* left]

(o) tenia bendido un coche y *conchabado* ya para entregarlo aqui (AC 162, 1691: 423)
[he had sold a carriage and had *arranged* the delivery over here]

(p) con tantos ruegos a todos y asta su padre de vd. y a la *gachupina* (AC 147, 1689: 382)
[I was begging everyone I knew, and even to your father, and to the *Spanish woman*]

(q) un indio ladino en *castilla* (AC 171, 1694: 451) [Indian fluent in *Spanish*]

(r) el Padre Figueroa, religioso de la Compañía de Jesus, que llaman el *gachupin* (AC 176, 1697: 463)
[Father Figueroa, minister of the Company of Jesus, who is known as the *Spaniard*]

(s) como assiendo burla y *chacota* (EG 107, 1703: 319)
[just like making fun of and *mocking someone*]

(t) que *luego luego*, pasados ocho días, se sintió accidentado de dolores (EG 120, 1723: 350)
[and *immediately* after eight days, he felt the torment of pain]

(u) Y *luego luego* se apareció en un cavallo el dicho Juan de Herrera (EG 122, 1724: 358)
[And *immediately* said Juan de Herrera showed up on his horse]

(v) dixo que era para saver de un *gachupin* llamado don Francisco de Soto (AC 215, 1744: 530)
[he said he wanted to hear from a *Spaniard* known as don Francisco de Soto]

(w) yndio, *baquero* de la dicha estancia (EG 137, 1746: 390)
[Indian, *cowboy* working in said small hacienda]

(x) le venía a dar la notizia de una conbenienzia con un *gachupin* (AC 230, 1748: 563-4)
[he was coming to give him the news about a good deal with a *Spaniard*]

(y) y *luego luego* oyo una vos (AC 245, 1772: 595) [and *immediately* he heard a voice]
(z) aier te soñé a la siesta y *luego luego*, ya sabes, me sucedió (EG155, 1778: 441) [yesterday while napping, I dreamt of you and *immediately*, you know, it happened to me]
(aa) a bien tengo con quien *chiquearme* (EG 154, 1778: 438) [I have someone who *spoils me*]
(bb) assí empeña la vergüenza para conmigo, y no *le saques* (EG 155, 1778: 441) [don't feel too bad, and *don't chicken out*]

10.2.1 The prepositions PARA and PA

The preposition PARA and its reduced form PA appear today in the same contexts that appeared since the times of the *Second Letter* (1522) by Hernán Cortés and the correspondence of Rodrigo de Albornoz with the king of Spain (AC 1, 1525). The first bishop of Mexico, Juan de Zumárraga (1468-1548), author of Doc. AC 7 (1529) had a strong preference for the preposition PARA while his contemporaries mixed PARA and PA or used only PA. Zumárraga's usage is considered today the standard practice in the formal written registers, whereas alternating between the full form and the reduced form is common in rapid speech in both Spain and Latin American Spanish varieties regardless of the topic and the socio-educational background of the interlocutors. At present, the contexts in which PARA may be reduced to PA are identical to those found in the colonial sources: (1) with the meaning of direction as in (a) and the second part of (b); (2) with the connector *que*, as in (c), (g), (i), (k) and (m) through (p); and (3) before an infinitive or a noun, as in (d)-(f), (h) and (l).

(a) E visto lo que el dicho capitan me fizo saber, a la hora me parti *pa* la dicha villa (*Second Letter*, 1522: 2)
(b) hacen panes de la dicha sal que venden *pa* los naturales y *pa* fuera de la comarca (*Second Letter*, 1522: 17)
(c) se enbíe a esta Nueva España *pa que* aca los oficiales de vuestra majestad tengan cuidado de lo hazer cunplir (AC 1, 1525: 28)
(d) es la tierra más aparejada *pa servir* a Dios y sacar fructo (AC 1 1525: 37)
(e) ellos ternian mucho lugar y aparejo *para hinchir* su cobdiçia (AC 7, 1529: 76)
(f) no se ha visto que aya tenido descuydo en cosa que les toque *para* su interese y provecho (AC 7, 1529: 77)
(g) dizque han embiado muchas mercaderias del president e oydores a Mechuacan *para que* las venda a los mjneros (AC 7, 1529: 81)

(h) Estando *para partir*me a besar las manos de vuestra magestad (AC 12, 1532: 95)
(i) *pa que* todos los bassallos de vuestra majestad que en estas partes bibimos le ynportunemos (AC 13, 1532: 99)
(j) *pa* la buena orden y serviçio del culto divino (AC 14, 1532: 101)
(k) *para que* a vuestra magestad suplique (AC 14, 1532: 101)
(l) Es tanto su trabajo y tan de doler, que aun *pa adereçar* o remendar sus cosas no tienen tiempo ni *pa hazer* su sementera (AC 15, 1533: 102)
(m) Vuestra majestad me hizo merçed de me dar una çedula *pa que* el presidente e oydores (…) diesen mj repartimjento de yndios (AC 16, 1534: 108)
(n) no tengo *pa qué* nj por qué, mas de hazer sabidor (…) (AC 17, 1535: 110)
(o) *pa que* diesen frayles que fuesen a la provincia de la Nueva España (AC 28, 1562: 141)
(p) *pa que* esto çese, y todo agrabio y daño se escusen a vuestros basallos (AC 65, 1577: 214)

In modern Spanish the reduced form *pa* appears frequently with the adverbs *aquí, allá, arriba, abajo* and with the connector *que*. In examples (a) through (c) the independent lexical items are reduced phonologically and further reanalyzed as a single word.
(a) voy *pa'quí y pa' allá* [I go *from here to there*]
(b) me traen *pa'rriba y pa' bajo* [they make me *go up and down*]
(c) lo digo *pa' que* lo sepas [I say it *so that* you know it]

10.2.2 Dissolution of hiatus

The tendency to dissolve the hiatus of the adverb *ahí* ('there') has created a diphthongized form '*ay*', which is confused with the homophonous *hay* ('there is' or 'there are'), as in sentences (a) and (b), which can be spontaneously generated in modern Spanish with different meanings. At present the dissolution of the hiatus is general in informal registers of Mexican Spanish. The form of the verb *traer* appears too in item (c).
(a) *Ay* [ahí] ba con estas cartas mias [y] una de mi compañero (AC 44, 1574: 177-8)
    [*There* he goes with my letters (and) some that belong to my buddy]
(b) no *ai* [hay] pa qué tratar mas de ello (AC 32, 1567: 154)
    [*there is* no need to deal with this any longer]
(c) Calderon me dio la palabra que *trayria* [traería] a Diagito (AC 71, 1578: 222)
    [Calderon promised me that *he would bring* Diagito]

10.2.3 Addition of –s in the preterit

Residual variants may gravitate from normative to colloquial registers. The addition of –s to the 2nd person preterit indicative is frequent and widespread across varieties of both peninsular and modern Latin American Spanish, and may have originated from an overlap of the verb paradigms corresponding to pronouns *tú* and *vos*, as in items (a) through (e). This occurrence appears in 16th century colonial sources and has been perpetuated all over the Spanish-speaking world, including urban peninsular varieties.

(a) *pensastes* [pensasteis], *malbaratastes* [malbaratasteis], *pudistes* [pudisteis] (AC 43, 1574: 175)
(b) si *recebistes* [recibisteis] cinquenta pesos de Alonso Peres (AC 50, 1575: 191)
(c) ¿cómo no *hicistes* [hicisteis] lo que esta manaña os mandó Luis? (EG 37, 1585: 128)
(d) le dijo esta declarante: "¿qué fue lo que *oýstes* [oísteis]?" (EG 88, 1675: 273)
(e) no me olvido de lo que me *pedistes* [pediste] y te prometí (EG 156, 1778: 443)

10.2.4 Duplicate possessives

Duplicate possessives were transmitted from Spain to New Spain and for centuries have remained mostly in the Central Highlands where these noun phrases have become a distinctive component of the regional koine. This construction can be traced to the origins of Castilian in the 13th century and has been documented since the late 15th century. The possessed entity is mostly [+ human] and in the vast majority of cases it involves a [+ human] possessor (Company Company 1994a). The low frequency of duplicate possessives has limited the area of diffusion to the extent that they are unknown in subregions far away from the Central Highlands, where speakers can even use triple possessives as in (h).

(a) *su hermano de Delgadillo* (AC 7, 1529: 84)
(b) en las fiestas del casamjento de *su hijo del visorrey* (AC 23, 1543: 123)
(c) *Doña Isabel Rodríguez de Andrada su hija de Francisca Nunez de Carbajal* (*El Abecedario*, 1590)
(d) llegó el clerigo de estas minas de esta ciudad con *su carta de v.md.* (AC 98, 1629: 284)
(e) Esto declarará *su madre della* que bibe en casa... (AC 108, 1630: 307)
(f) y por fin de todo responde *su padre de Vd.* (AC 147, 1689: 382)
(g) fue *su mamá de la niña* la que contó la historia (modern Mexico City)
(i) con el sudor de *su frente de uno* (modern Mexico City)
(h) *su amiga suya de usted* (modern Mexico City)

10.2.5 Amerindian loans

Nahuatl loans with different degrees of vitality are herein considered optimal residual variants. Some of them were supplanted by Taino loans, e.g. the noun *caçonçi* (< Nahuatl) was replaced by the more widespread noun *cacique* (< Taino), but most of the oldest Nahuatl borrowings documented in Molina's *Vocabulario* (1555) are still a major component of the daily lexicon of Mexican Spanish: e.g. *aguacate* ('avocado'), *atole* ('corn drink'), *cacao* ('cacao') *camote* ('sweet potato'), *comal* ('cooking grill'), *chía* ('savila seed'), *chile* ('hot pepper'), *jacal* ('adobe hut'), *mecate* ('string'), *metate* ('grinding stone'), *mitote* ('loud dance'), *petaca* ('hamper'), *pinole* ('corn and chia drink'), *tamal* ('corn bread'), *tomate* ('tomato'), etc. As attested in the sources of the following century, a total of 75 loans had vital continuity in the 17th century and on to the extent that they were documented in the 20th century along the 1-to-6 scale, i.e. from generally known to almost unknown (Mejías 1980: Table 2).

10.3 Residual variants belonging to the vernacular realm

Variants derived from colonial Spanish that have remained in popular varieties of Mexican Spanish may be considered residuals forms with varying degrees of vitality. The data from Cortesian texts shed light on features that stand out because they have been redistributed along the wide spectrum of popular use or rural domains of the Spanish-speaking world, and are still used today. Modern standards have replaced the non-standardized forms in normative styles, but residual variants have not disappeared. Features that seemed to be common in both Spain and the New World have been relegated to isolated areas, to use among rural speakers, or speakers residing in areas of high marginality; today they can be identified as features that together make the common denominator of popular varieties spoken across regions and sub-regions of modern Spanish-speaking Latin America. The variants presented in Table 10.7 appear in DLNE-AC (1994) and DLNE-EG (2008), and some other colonial documents. Because they belong to the dialect realm, they are infrequent, though in modern times they alternate with the variants used in normative Spanish. Their significance lies in the centuries-old survival and their redistribution along non-normative styles and registers. For this reason they can be considered the residues of Mexican Colonial Spanish.

(1) Vowel changes. The use of strong vowels commonly alternated with the use of weak vowels in medieval Spanish. Variants involving changes from strong to weak vowels in modern normative Spanish are the most abundant and can

be considered Type A1. In the early 1500's they were used by some of the best educated men in charge of the colony such as Juan de Zumárraga (first bishop of Mexico and author of AC 7, 1529) and Toribio de Benavente, leading colonial scholar and author of AC 24 (1550).

Table 10.7: Strong vowels in residual variants

Item	Colonial Spanish	Normative Spanish	Item	Colonial Spanish	Normative Spanish
1.	apercebida	apercibida	11.	bollicios	bullicios
2.	certefico	certifico	12.	descobrir	descubrir
3.	concebieron	concibieron	13.	encobrir	encubrir
4.	defuntos	difuntos	14.	complida	cumplida
5.	escrebir	escribir	15.	complimiento	cumplimiento
6.	juresdicion	jurisdicción	16.	mochacho	muchacho
7.	mesmo	mismo	17.	soplicar	suplicar
8.	polecia	policía	18.	sostituyas	sustituyas
9.	prençipal	principal	19.	ouiessen	hubiesen
10.	recebir	recibir	20.	posimos	pusimos

Variants in which weak vowels were used in colonial Spanish and were regularized in modern Spanish with strong vowels can be considered Type A2, as in for example: *intincion* > *intención*; *inconviniente* > *inconveniente*. Variants in which diphthongs were eventually dissolved in normative Spanish can be considered Type A3 (e.g. *priesa* > *prisa*).

(a) que es *carpentero* [carpintero] de ribera (AC 7, 1529: 81) Type A1
(b) su *jntincion* [intención] hera qual con ellos habia platicado (AC 7, 1529: 83) Type A2
(c) asi por los bibos como por sus *defuntos* [difuntos] (AC 9, 1529: 94) Type A1
(d) di la mayor *priesa* [prisa] que pude (AC 12, 1532: 97) Type 3
(e) Otros muchos *ynconvinjentes* [inconvenientes] ay (AC 13, 1532: 100) Type A2
(f) que heran la *prençipal* [principal] cosa desta tierra (AC 15, 1534: 105) Type A1
(g) hartos dineros que deven a los *defuntos* [difuntos] (AC 17, 1535: 110) Type A1
(h) Sobre esto yo *escrevi* [escribí] en los navjos pasados (AC 23, 1543: 124) Type A1
(i) vjenen con esto a ser mas más *aflejidos* [afligidos] (AC 24, 1550: 128) Type A1
(j) no sería pequeño provecho para la doctrina y *polecia* [policía] umana (AC 24, 1550: 129) Type A1
(k) "señor, no ay agora indios, mañana te yrás, no tengas tanta *priesa*" [prisa] (EG 24, 1558: 83) Type A3

(l) la *fedelidad* [fidelidad] que devemos a su rreal servjcio (AC 36, 1569: 161) Type A1
(m) como lo hemos visto por *expiriençia* [experiencia] (AC 35, 1569: 163) Type A2
(n) que a esta causa se *desimule* [disimule] con delitos tan orrendos (AC 37, 1570: 166) Type A1
(o) quien no sabe ofiçio, ni leer ni *ecrevir* [escribir], no sé qué puede ser (AC 64, 1577: 212) Type A1

(2) Variants in which consonantal changes have occurred are considered Type B, the most relevant of all in today's Spanish being the aspiration of initial F, which was spelled with the graphemes <h> and <j>. Initially common amongst speakers of average or higher education, aspiration of *h* became silent in the written language and its pronunciation was later relegated to marginal varieties. In this context, regular aspiration has not survived in modern Mexican Spanish, but it is common in other regions of the Spanish-speaking world. The data found in colonial sources indicate that there may have been two types of variants with aspiration: (a) those derived from words that in Latin had initial F; and (b) those with an anti-etymological aspiration. The first group may include the following: *hacienda* (< FACIENDA), *hacer* (< FACĔRE), *herido* (< FĔRĪRE), *herir* (< FĔRĪRE), *hierro* (< FĔRRUM), *hijo* (FILIUS), *herrar* (FĔRRARE), *horadar* (< FORĀTUM), *holgar* (< FŎLLICARE), *harto* (< FARTUS), *ahorcar* (< FŬRCA), etc. In chronological order, items (a) through (n) below exemplify the cases in which aspiration is derived from initial F. The use was extended to aspiration in medial position such as *atraher* and *traher* (< TRAHŌ, –TRAHERE). The following items can be considered Type B residuals.

(a) para los *atraher* a nuestra fee (AC 1, 1525: 30)
(b) se *hierren* aquellos que sus padres fueron esclavos (AC 1, 1525: 31)
(c) ay *hartos* marineros, y que dessean yr el viaje (AC 1, 1525: 34)
(d) en este tiempo la puede *traher* de Castilla (AC 1, 1525: 42)
(e) el mejor de la tierra se *holgaba* de yr a ellas (AC 1, 1525: 45)
(f) va *huyendo* en estos navios (AC 3, 1526: 56)
(g) concluyo con dezir que ellos están bien *ahazendados* (AC 7, 1529: 79)
(h) ni me puedo *hartar* de plazer (AC 11 1531: 93)
(i) *haze hahorcar* al cazique y al otro (AC 17, 1535: 110)
(j) con poco temor del *hierro* que avian hecho (AC 1535: 110)
(k) se empeñan y adeudan para dar a parientes veynte, y más, mill ducados de *hazienda* (AC 25, 1554: 133)
(l) llegué *harto* fatigado (AC 52, 1576: 193)
(m) Unos *hihos* de Martin Hernandez me enviaron un poder (AC 38, 1571: 168)
(n) por no *caher* en descomuníón (EG 36, 1582: 125)

(o) ¿yo no os e mandado que *hagáis* de *hozicos* todo lo que os mandaren...? (EG 37, 1585: 127)

In his *Gramática de la lengua castellana* (1492), Antonio de Nebrija stated that "the *h* is not a letter, but the signal of the spirit, just a breathing sound" (113). Moreover, the letter *h* was used to pronounce the first letter of words such as *hago* and *hecho*, and although in Latin it was insignificant, we pronounce it distressing the throat like the Jews and the Moors, from whom we received it (118). In his *Manual de gramática histórica española*, Menéndez Pidal (1977: 114) confirms that the Spanish of the 15th and 16th centuries counted on an aspirated *h* (in words such as *hazer*, *humo*, *holgar*) that is today entirely silent in the written language. The representation of aspiration with <*h*> or <*j*> was common among writers such as Rodrigo de Albornoz and other protagonists of the colonization of Mexico

The spelling with the grapheme <*h*> is followed chronologically by the representation of the aspiration with the grapheme <*j*>, appearing in documents where the practice of *seseo* is more frequent, as in (a) through (g). Document EG 64 (1631), where the narrator is an eyewitness with sufficient experience in maritime battles tells the story on the siege of Campeche by the Dutch. Item (g) appears in the Gulf region, which is the testimony of an eyewitness living in the mountains among the Indians.

(a) rresivieron los olandeses poco daño, y ellos, con pérdida de más de beinte, sin los *jeridos* (EG 64, 1631: 205)
(b) Bino una bos de la plaça de armas que los *jiso* rretirar (EG 64, 1631: 205)
(c) Tienen más de sinquenta *jeridos*, de los quales se les ban muriendo algunos (EG 64, 1631: 206)
(d) Lo *jisieron* así, enbistiendo la plaça por tres partes (EG 64, 1631: 205)
(e) con la mesma *jumareda*, halló por dónde entrarla [la plaza] (EG 64, 1631: 205)
(f) piesas de bronce y *jierro* (EG 64, 1631: 206)
(g) estando embriagados de dicho balché él y los dos yndios, le *joradaron* las narises (EG 90, 1679: 279)

The second type of *h* in writing is anti-etymological, and appeared in words such as *enero*, *edad*, *orden*, *ordinario*. Aspiration functioned as a hiatus, which prevented the coalescence of two strong vowels, as in most of the sentences below. In the colonial documents at hand, the most frequent words with anti-etymological *h* are *hera* (< Latin ERAT) and *hedad* (< Latin AETAS). Occasionally, aspiration occurs after final –*s*, as in item (g), (h) and (n).

(a) por ser, como *hera*, gran señor, no hiçiese ayuntamiento de gentes (EG 1, 1520: 27)
(b) paresçió que *hera* Pánfilo de Narváez (EG 1, 1520: 28)

(c) aquella tal causa no *hera* final (EG 1, 1520: 34)
(d) cómo *husan* dellos (AC 10, 1529: 91)
(e) la paga *hera* reçibida tan buena (AC 11, 1531: 93)
(f) No queda sino *hecharnos* en presiones (AC 11, 1531: 94)
(g) de los alcaldes *hordinarios* (AC 12, 1532: 96)
(h) por la *deshorden* tan grave que esta tierra tiene (AC 16, 1534: 106)
(i) que *hera* fama que *hera* muerto (AC 3, 1536: 50)
(j) que *heran* amigos (AC 3, 1536: 50)
(k) del mes de *henero* (AC 23, 1543: 125)
(l) Dixo ques de *hedad* de treynta e tres años (EG 21, 1551: 81)
(m) al tiempo que de *hesos* rreynos salieron (AC 29, 1563: 145)
(n) Vuestra muger mescrivjo una carta questavades *henojado* (AC 38, 1571: 167)
(o) Dominguilla, negra que diz que *hera* de Sahagún (EG 34, 1576: 119)
(p) se llama Juan de Villaseca, que es de *hedad* de quarenta y cinco años (EG 37, 1585: 127)
(q) Y ques de *hedad* de veinte años poco más o menos (EG 40, 1590: 139)
(r) la exhaló con el *haliento* algunas vezes (AC 80, 1618: 242)
(s) El día que a v. md. escreví donde Alvarado, me salí de *hahí* (EG 67, 1637: 214)
(t) "no sabía que tenía *habuela*" (EG, 192, 1814: 517)

(3) In sharp contrast with aspiration of F in initial and intervocalic position, aspiration and deletion of /s/ in implosive position has remained in regular variation with the full pronunciation. Aspiration of /s/ in implosive position is not stigmatized in formal domains provided the aspiration occurs in the prescribed environment and speakers do not incur in hypercorrection. These are cases of optimal spread. Considered together, these facts are consistent with what has been observed in situations of dialect contact, where variants that appeared diffuse or stigmatized eventually gain prestige if not widespread acceptance. Aspiration and deletion of /s/ in syllable-final or absolute final position might have occurred in New Spain at different junctures, but neither became the common pronunciation of a large majority of speakers. Aspiration and deletion were probably rejected by speakers and writers who attempted to compensate for the perceived loss; and as a result, they added /s/ in words that had no syllable-final /s/, as in (a) and (b), items that are similar to hyper-correction in modern Caribbean Spanish, as in (c).
(a) [la iglesia] tiene pocos *ornasmientos* [ornamentos] e pobres (EG 21, 1555: 81)
(b) una muger que dixo llamarse María Gerónima, mulata, muger *lesgítima* [legítima] de Francisco de Govea (EG 57, 1607: 170)
(c) Este carro tiene mucha *po[s]tencia* (modern Caribbean Spanish)
[This automobile has a lot of *power*]

10.3.1 The diphthong /we/ in various positions

Other consonantal changes in popular varieties include the velarization of /b/ before the diphthong /we/ preceded by bilabial stop as in *abuelo*, which rendered [*agüelo*], [*agüela*] and [*agüelos*], as in (b), (c), and (f). With the exception of (m), the rest of the items exemplify the velarization of the diphthong /we/ in initial position, which rendered *güérfanos*, *güevos*, *güésped*, *virgüelas*, a feature that remains a residual variant derived from Mexican Colonial Spanish. These can be considered mixed Type A-B variants because they involve both vocalic and consonantal changes. Normative Spanish eliminated the velarized diphthong and added a silent *h*, rendering *huérfanos*, *hueso*, *hueco*, *huevos*, *enhuecaron*, etc. There is also a case of bilabialization in (m).

(a) *guerfanos* [huérfanos] de sobrinos (AC 78, 1585: 238)
(b) Frasquito llora cada día por su *aguelo* [abuelo] (EG 43, 1594: 146)
(c) Frasquito besa a v. m. las manos y a su *aguela* [abuela] (EG 44, 1594: 149)
(d) *guebos* [huevos], ensalada, pescado (EG 49, 1602: 159)
(e) cosa que *guele* [huele] a su ydolatría (EG 52, 1606: 167)
(f) su *aguelo* [abuelo] sirvio a vuestra magestad de alcayde (AC 118, 1630: 321)
(g) un pedasito de *gueso* [hueso] de difunto (EG 78, 1655: 246)
(h) llegando al *gueco* [hueco] de una viga (EG 86, 1673: 265)
(i) para saber de un *guesso* [hueso] que halló (EG 86, 1673: 265)
(j) assimesmo le daba un *guesso* [hueso] de difunto (EG 86, 1678: 266)
(k) *guespeda* [huéspeda] en casa de doña Maria Sausedo (AC 162, 1692: 427)
(l) pan, tortillas, espeseria, *guebos* [huevos] y demas cosas menesterosas (AC 170, 1694: 450)
(m) abriendo un *abujero* [agujero] chico (EG 153, 1777: 435)
(n) un *guesesillo* [huesecillo] o caracol pequeño (EG 112, 1707: 330)
(o) antes de la epidemia de *virguelas* [viruelas] (EG 109, 1704: 322)
(p) *enguecaron* [enhuecaron] más de media arina de trigo (AC 207, 1741: 520)
(q) dandole un palo a Sanches, sonó a *gueco* [hueco] i desaparesio (AC 241, 1771: 585)

10.4 Verb forms

Verb forms preserved in popular varieties can be considered Type C variants. They include the following forms: (1) The preterit of the verb VER ('to see') in the 1st and 3rd person singular *vide* and *vido* and the 3rd person singular of the imperfect indicative *vía*, items (c), (e), (f), (i)-(k), (q) and (t). (2) The preterit of the verb TRAER in the 1st and 3rd person singular, *traje* and *truje* (items (a), (b) and (g). (3) The present subjunctive of the singular pronouns of the verb HABER (*haiga*), when it is used as an auxiliary as in (l) through (p), (r) and (s). (4) The intrusion of palatal /y/ in verbs such as REIR and SER, items (d) and (h) is still heard in rural speech communities. The sentences (a) through (t) presented in chronological order were vital throughout the colonial period. These verb forms were later regularized in normative Spanish, but *vide, vido, vía, truje* and *trujo, seyendo* and *riyendo* are still used in marginal and/or isolated areas, while *haiga* has remained in both rural and urban varieties. The writer of Doc. EG 92 (1681) used both *aiga* and *aia*, which in normative Spanish has reappeared as *haya* (< HABERE), while Doc. EG 93 (1681) is the petition of a farmer. Residual popular variants may be frowned upon by some speakers in some contexts, but this does not mean that they are doomed to disappear.

(a) quatro cientos indios de los que *traxe* de Cempoal (Cortés, *Second Letter* 1520: 6)
(b) E *truxe* cerca de quatrocientas personas (Cortés, *Second Letter* 1520: 6)
(c) *vido* este testigo que quemaron tress honbres y tress estatuas (EG 4, 1532: 44)
(d) después de aver jurado en forma debida de derecho e *seyendo* preguntado (EG 6, 1537: 50)
(e) una vez que [él] *bido* cubrir parte de la dicha yglesia a los dichos yndios (EG 21, 1551: 82)
(f) fueron infinitas las gentes que yo *vide* quemar vivas (las Casas 1552: 87)
(g) si *truxera* mil, *fuera* harto menester para rremediar algo de lo mucho que está perdido (AC 25, 1554: 133)
(h) *riyendose* a manera de hazer burla (AC 54, 1576: 196)
(i) Sólo *vide* salir de un aposento de la dicha negra Ursula a un español (EG 55, 1610: 179)
(j) si de allí en adelante *vía* entrar a alguno en ella (...) que los castigaría (EG 55, 1610: 176)176)
(k) *vide* allí en un clavo colgadas las llaves del convento (Erauso 1652: 94)
(l) Fuele preguntado (...) si sabe o a oído decir que alguna persona *aiga* dicho o fecho alguna cosa que sea o paresca ser contra nuestra santa fee Catholica (EG 92, 1681: 284)
(m) Fuele preguntado si sabe o presume que alguna persona *aia* en conversación tratado de otra con fundamentos o dudas de averse casado dos veses (EG 92, 1681: 284)
(n) Andrés Peres Ortis, besino de La Cañada en esta juridisión y labrador en ella, paresco ante v.md. en la mejor forma que *ayga* lugar en derecho (EG 93, 1681: 287)
(o) Y, por vida tulla, que no *ayga* falta (AC 147, 1689: 378)

(p) en mi linaje no avido ninguno que sea ni *aiga* sido contra la santa fe (AC 175, 1696: 461)
(q) le *vido* bendesir el agua con todas las seremonias del manual y *bido* confesar el día de Todos los Santos algunas personas (EG 110, 1707: 325)
(r) Vien habrá extrañado v.m. que no le *haiga* respondido a tantas cartas (EG 126, 1733: 366)
(s) ¿*haiga* quien tenga esto aqui? (AC 199, 1740: 502)
(t) dixo que los *bido* casar y belar en este pueblo en la capilla (EG 133, 1746: 380-381)

10.4.1 The endings –RA and –RA in protasis and apodosis

The repetition of the ending –RA in Si-clauses and adverbial clauses with a renewed subjunctive meaning is also a residual variant that is heard in isolated, marginal and also in not so isolated or marginal areas. It is actually being disseminated from rural to urban or mixed communities (i.e. 'rurban'), and can be actively used in the southwestern communities of the United States as in (j). However, in the colonial period, –RA and –RA alternated with the modern peninsular construction –SE and –RÍA, as in (a), (c), (e). The author of AC 7 (1529) is Bishop Juan de Zumárraga.

(a) si no *tovjese* judicatura le *aseguraria* diez mill pessos de oro en un año (AC 3, 1526: 54)
(b) si no se *oviera ydo* a Hibueras que ya él lo *oviera preso* (AC 7, 1529: 70)
(c) si don Hernando *fuese* vibo, que su persona sola de cada compañero *bastaria* a se lo traer preso (AC 7, 1529: 71)
(d) si se *hallara* presente me *hechara* el púlpito abaxo (AC 7, 1529: 83)
(e) sy *huviessen* de conprar las cassas donde agora está ell Audiencia, *serian* menester para ello çinquenta mil pessos (AC 19, 1537: 115)
(f) Y entiende que si no *acudiera* tanta gente, *hirieran* al dicho alcaide (AC 58, 1576: 206)
(g) si *ubiera querido* casalla [a mi hermana] con alguno, como la gente que ay en Sant Andres, ya la *ubiera casado* (AC 71, 1578: 222)
(h) aunque yo *fuera* un honbre moço y lego y muy pródjgo de mj onrra, *tuvjera* temor de mostrarme en las cosas de v. m. (AC 76, 1583: 233)
(i) que si no *fuera* por su primera muger, Ysavel de Alcoçer, [él] se *hubiera* ahorcado (EG 73, 1647: 233)
(j) si nos *dieran* un rato libre a todos, *fuera* justo (modern United States Southwestern Spanish) [if *they gave* us all a break, *it would* be just fair]

10.5 Lexical items and idiomatic expressions in popular speech

Lexical items and idiomatic expressions derived from colonial sources can be considered Type D variants. The different versions of the modern adverb *así* ('in this way' or 'in this manner') still alternate with *ansi, ansy* or *ansina*.

(a) lo esconderan lo que *ansy* an avido por maña (AC 10, 1529: 91)
(b) sienpre lo e echo e *ansi* lo continuaré (AC 16, 1534: 105)
(c) se me hazia mucho agravio, *ansi* por no tener aquj de comer (AC 12, 1532: 95)
(d) *ansi* an benjdo abajando hasta agora (AC 16, 1534: 105)
(e) *ansi* en lo spiritual como en lo temporal (AC 24, 1550: 127)
(f) A*nsimesmo* es necesario para el buen tratamjento de estos naturales (AC 24, 1550: 128)

Likewise, the adjective *harto* ('many', 'very' or 'a lot') has survived in today's popular and rural Mexican Spanish as a modifier of a noun. In the *Second Letter* (1522: 14), Hernán Cortés wrote: "nos partimos con *harto* temor" ('we departed with much fright'). The adjective *harto* + noun makes up a phrase of high frequency in the colonial sources, as in examples (a) through (d). It can also function as an adverb as in sentence (e) or as a modifier / internsifier of an adjective as in items (f) and (g). In the documents examined, *harto* appears mostly with initial H indicating aspiration, and remains with aspiration in modern Caribbean Spanish.

(a) ha estado en las yslas ocho o diez años y en esta tierra *hartos* días (AC 1, 1525: 32)
(b) con *harta* ventaja de navegacjon (AC 1, 1525: 35)
(c) con *harta* difficultad le sacamos (AC 1, 1525: 40)
(d) venimos con *hartos* trabajos (AC 25, 1554: 133)
(e) que *harto* lo vozeo aca y no aprovecha (AC 26, 1525: 137)
(f) estaban pueblos de los jndios cristianos *harto* enruynados (AC 28, 1562: 143)
(g) llegué *harto* fatigado (AC 52, 1572: 193)

In combination, the velarization of /ue/ (as in *abuelo* > [agüelo], use of *harto* + noun, *muncho, mesmo, nadie[n], ansina* comprise the features distinguishing today's rural varieties. The origin of *ansina* might be *a + sí* modified with an intrusive –N, the same nasal consonant that modified adjective *mucho > mu[n]-cho*. These variants distinguish modern social varieties used in [– urban formal] domains, though they were components of the linguistic repertoire of the first and subsequent generation of speakers / writers of Mexican Colonial Spanish who had average or above average education. At present, they may be considered 'archaisms'. Residual features appeared in the common speech of the 16th and 17th centuries, but were redistributed along vernacular varieties once the forces of standardization made strong inroads into the habits of Spanish speakers. Belonging to the second generation, Juan Suárez de Peralta, author of the *Tratado del descubrimiento de las Yndias* (1586) was fond of *muncho*, which was used both as an adjective and as an adverb: *Munchas* colores (55), Dende a *munchos* días boluió (56), los yndios los quieren *muncho* (64), *munchos* colgaderos de morçillas y longanizas (76).

(a) de la *mesma* manera fue quando al gobernador Cortés desbarataron (AC 1, 1525: 43)
(b) declara la *muncha* bondad dellos (AC 11, 1531: 93)
(c) olgaría de tractar con Vuestra Majestad *hartas* cosas de que Dios se sirviese (EG 28, 1565: 98)
(d) le besan las manos *munchas* beses (AC 40, 1572: 171)
(e) se ganan los dineros con *muncho* trabajo (AC 43, 1574: 175)
(f) a Merchor Gonçalez se lo ruego más que a *nayde* (AC, 44, 1574: 177)
(g) Y *ansi mesmo* vio a otros dos hombres (AC 63, 1576: 211)
(h) Y *asina* os digo que de ninguna manera bengáis (AC 64, 1577: 213)
(i) E tenido, a Dios graçias, *munchos trabajos* (AC 71, 1578: 222)
(j) Y que assí la dixo que se fuese y que no dixesse a *nayde* nada de lo que con ella avia pasado, y que ella se lo contó después a su *aguela* (EG 48, 1598: 155)
(k) Y no te fies de *nayde* (AC 146, 1689: 381)
(l) si no savía que a su casa no se yba a prender a *naide* (EG 104, 1696: 308)
(m) dijo que, lo primero, *nadien* más que aquellos dos lo presenciaron (EG 187, 1808: 505)

10.6 The common denominator: residual variants

Residual variants embody the basic layer or common denominator to all varieties of New World Spanish transplanted in the 16th and 17th centuries. They exemplify the features of the Spanish koine, and have become a significant part of the inventory of colloquial varieties, better known as popular Spanish, in turn representing all mutually intelligible forms of speech that arrived in the American continent with the first and subsequent generations of Spanish speakers. Because many were common in colloquial registers, they have been (re)transmitted inter-generationally for hundred of years. The agents of (re)transmission have been the Spanish speakers who had little or no competition in the domestic domain, in the extended family, or in the compact Spanish-speaking communities where Spanish prevailed while doing their daily errands or when they were requesting services from major institutions. Simultaneously, a semi-standardized version of Spanish was being used as a superposed variety with wide acceptance in most social and institutional networks. The relationship between the koine L(ow) variety and the quasi-standardized H(igh) variety has given rise to diglossia, as described by Ferguson (1959). The residual variants have been studied by scholars for more than one hundred years in all independent nations and also in the Spanish-speaking communities of the United States Southwestern states, normally in reference to or in comparison with the perceived variety of normative Spanish that progressively unfolded throughout the colony. While it is difficult to evaluate the effects of the Spanish Royal Academy on literacy and writing practices from the mid-18th century on, language standards and the perception of those standards have been disseminated via formal education, literature, and major institutions.

In his *Apuntaciones*, which appeared shortly before the end of the 19th century, Rufino J. Cuervo addressed the use and social significance of residual variants. Other comparative studies on the speech of the different independent nations were published by Henríquez Ureña (1938) in *El español en Méjico, los Estados Unidos y la América Central*, a collection of articles representing major works of dialectology (1896-1919) on the northern region of the American continent. This was volume IV of the series *Biblioteca de Dialectología Hispanoamericana* sponsored by the University of Buenos Aires. It was followed by the most outstanding work on New World Spanish entitled *El español en Santo Domingo* (1940) also by Pedro Henríquez Ureña, who focused on the dialect division of New World Spanish and the persistence of old words and expressions transmitted from peninsular Spanish to the earliest settlement in the New World, Santo Domingo. Henríquez Ureña admitted that the foundation of Caribbean Spanish in general and Dominican Spanish in particular was derived from Andalusian, while the archaic components were mostly of Castilian origin. Some of those "archaisms" appear also in New Spain (e.g. *aína, dizque, dende, creder, veder*, etc.). In addition, he dwelt on the use of *tú* with its corresponding verb form, a usage that did not facilitate the emergence of *voseo*. He also looked into the overuse of diminutives in adverbs such as *ahorita, adiosito, apenitas, afuerita*, a trait that distinguishes New World from peninsular Spanish. The similarities between Caribbean and Mexican Spanish are put in bold relief in the koineization period.

In the United States, Aurelio Espinosa (1911) contributed with the study of Spanish as spoken in New Mexico and southern Colorado, the oldest regions of Spanish settlements. In like manner, the works of Anita Post (1933 and 1934) shed light on the vernacular variety of Spanish spoken in what is today the state of Arizona. Also covering all regions, genres and morpho-syntactic features before the end of World War II is Charles Kany's superb compendium on *American-Spanish Syntax* (1945). After World War II the same author published another seminal book entitled *American-Spanish Semantics* (1960). The contribution of Angel Rosenblat on the speech of Venezuela *Estudios sobre el habla de Venezuela* (1956) confirms the researchers' proclivity for advancing distinctive criteria (normative and popular) of language use. Along the same lines, one hundred years later, Luis Flórez (1973: 8) commented and updated Cuervo's *Apuntaciones* (1872) where the the former scholar still distinguished between popular and normative variants of the Spanish spoken in Bogota and some other places, whenever he found useful data. Following the trend initiated by Pedro Heneíquez Ureña on the identification of archaic components of New World Spanish, Manuel Álvarez Nazario (1982) has offered an exhaustive analysis of language use in Puerto Rico along the normative and popular domains that emerged in the 16th and 17th centuries.

10.7 Infrequent variants in modern Mexican Spanish

Some of the traits that are typical of coastal varieties did not have regular continuity in New Spain. One of them is the substitution of lateral /l/ by /r/ or rhotacism, which can be found routinely in many other varieties of the Spanish-speaking world, as in (a) through (d).
(a) ba un onbre por su mujer en esta *frota* [flota] (AC 44, 1574: 177)
(b) es grande mi deseo de os *borber* [volver] a ber (AC 45, 1574: 180)
(c) se pagarán a los demas a quien yo debo y estoy *obrigado* [obligado] (AC 45, 1574: 181)
(d) estoy puesto y *entabrado* [entablado] para ganar de comer para bos (AC 45, 1754: 182)

In the morpho-syntactic realm, *laísmo* is the use of LA with intransitive verbs such as *decir, demandar, hablar, hacer, preguntar* as in (a), whereas a variant of [+ animate] *leísmo* may use LE with [– animate] objects as in (b) and (c), where the clitic refers to [– animate masculine singular objects] in the accusative. In item (d), the clitic LE is used as a dative to express an attitude, but in (e) it appears as a typical northern-central variant of *leísmo*. In (f) the peninsular idiomatic expression with the verb *pasar* ('to go through a good time or a bad time') is used with the neuter clitic LO, and as such, it is preserved today in Spain. Modern Mexican Spanish diversified the clitic LO to LA, and today (f) reads: "por mal que *la pases*, *la pasarás* mejor".

(a) *dezirla* y *hazerla* creer después, y a sus hixas, que le havía arrojado [el sapo] (EG 121, 1724: 353)
[to tell *her* and later make *her* believe, and her daughters, that he had thrown the toad]

(b) su marido (...) le tomó un rosario en que rezaba y *le ech*ó en la lunbre (AC 1577, 66: 215)
[her husband took a rosary which she used for praying and *threw it* on the fire]

(c) *el qual libro* le mostró (...) a este declarante que *le leyese* y que vería en él una cosa muy superior (EG 60, 1624: 194)
[he showed *said book* to this deponent so that *she could read it* [and] that she would see something really extraordinary]

(d) si a b. m. [vuestra merced] no se *le haze* de mal, me enbje aca a un hermano mjo (AC 70, 1578: 220)
[if it is not *unpleasant to you*, please do send me my brother]

(e) tengo grandisimo deseo de *le ber* (AC 78, 1585:. 238) [I really want *to see him*]

(f) por mal que *lo paseys, lo pasareys* mexor (AC 50, 1575: 191)
[even if you *don't have a good time, things will be better for you*]

10.8 Variants discarded in Mexican Spanish

Voseo did not survive in New Spain or in the Caribbean colonies, an occurrence justified by the political distance from Spain: colonies closer to the mother country followed the metropolitan trends, whereas those that were farther away (politically) did not follow the peninsular model where *vos* had been replaced by *tú*. Many of the variants that identify the second generation of Spanish speakers living in New Spain appear in the personal letters they sent to their relatives in Spain. Most of the time they showed their desires to assist them in the process of relocation by discussing the inconveniences of the trip and related issues. Documents 38 through 52 (1571-1576) and Doc. 64 (1577) reveal the peninsular variants that went through attrition in the New World. In this short period second generation writers normally addressed their loved ones with the pronoun *vos*, the object of preposition *vos*, the corresponding object *os* and the possessive adjective *vuestro/a* with both the long and the reduced paradigmatic verb forms, as in (a) through (e). Affirmative commands appeared with both final /d/ and omitted /Ø/, as in modern times, as in (b) and (c) and with a clitic pronoun in which final /-d/ and initial /l-/ are transposed, as in (f) and (g). Writers were also inclined to mix the pronouns *vos* and *vuestra merced*, as in (h). In direct speech between husband and wife, the use of *vos* was common as in (i).

(a) *os venj*[Ø] lo más presto que *pudieredes* (AC 38, 1571: 167)
(b) Si *determjnares* de *venjros*, vended lo que *tubieredes*, y *venjos* con *vuestros* hijos y muger (AC 38, 1571: 167)
(c) Y en estando en Xalapa *escrevi*[Ø] con el harriero cómo *quedays* ay, que yo yré por *vos* (AC 38, 1571: 167)
(d) si bien lo *supiesedes os espantarias* y *abriais* lástima de mí. Y asina *os* digo que de ninguna manera *bengais* (AC 64, 1577: 213)
(e) *vuestra* madre que hera el abrigo que en esa tierra *teniades* (AC 50, 1575: 191)
(f) Y *encomendaldo* todo siempre a Dios (AC 44, 1574: 179)
(g) Mas antes dixo a los indios: "*anda, dexaldo*, que no bolverá por aquí" (EG 52, 1606: 168)
(h) La pipa de vino habrá *vuestra merced* recibido con Antonillo de Grebe, que es negro de recado, y *avizadme* si sallió buena (EG 22, 1554: 83)
(i) "*mereçiades* ser encoroçada porque *os quereys* yr a confesar" (AC 66, 1577: 215)

Many lexical items referring to the colonial reality in which Spanish speakers lived and interacted are infrequent or have disappeared in Latin American Spanish, as in (a)-(f), or replaced by modern words, examples (b) and (d). Some items became obsolete in Mexico but have survived in other countries (e.g. Paraguay), as in (c). Some others mean more or less the same in the Dominican Republic, as in example (e).

(a) que se les diese ansí para el *matolaxe* de aý a Sevilla (EG 30, 1568: 101) [modern *los víveres* ('foodstuffs for the sea trip')]
(b) estoy nescesytado porque e *mercado* una estançia (AC 38, 1571: 167) [modern *comprar* ('to buy')]
(c) porque se acabe más *ayna* mi soledad y pena (AC 44, 1574: 178) [*más pronto* ('fast, immediately')]
(d) que os determines luego de *aviar* buestro biaxe (AC 44, 1574: 177) [modern *prepararse para el viaje* ('to get ready for the trip')]
(e) mozo de la *tienda pulpería* de don Andrés Budillo (EG 164, 1785: 453) [*pulpería* ('convenience store']
(f) fue el declarante a componer una *calesa* de don Francisco Ortiz (EG 173, 1794: 471) [light low-wheeled *carriage* with a leather top or hood]

10.9 Modern *Usted*

The most common innovation referring to pronouns of address, *Usted* is derived from *vuestra merced*, an overabundant form in the personal and business correspondence of the 18th century. The neologism appears in the Mexican colonial sources since the late 17th century, and has had continuity in the same contexts through the present time. In spoken Spanish, *Usted* may be pronounced with or without the final –*d* as in previous centuries.

(a) ¿qué le paresse a *usted* de la vellaquería y maldad de Laureano Núñez? (EG 86, 1673: 266)
(b) Juana de Saavedra (...) le dijo a este testigo (...): "tiene *usted* razón" (EG 102, 1691: 304)
(c) me [h]a de aser *usté* favor de llevarme a México a mi hijo (EG 108, 1703: 320)
(d) Tráigole a *usté* una carta de su padre (EG 108, 1703: 320)
(e) "¿quién le dio a *usté* esta carta? (...) Su padre de *usté*" (EG 108, 1703: 320)
(f) "*Usté* mire lo que ase, y, luego que llegue, bea a su cura" (EG 108, 1703: 321)
(g) Me alegraré que *usté* esté bueno en companía de mis hijos (EG 182, 1802: 491)

10.10 Conclusions

The select variants examined in this work went through gradual attrition over the centuries. The evolution has to do with the environmental changes and speakers' attitudes and values. The most radical transformation occurred in the realm of pronunciation of the sibilants, which are still posing a major challenge to the educational system of the Spanish-speaking independent nations. The alternation between LE and LO and –SE and –RA was resolved in favor of the latter in the 18th century, though –SE partially recovered its frequency in the 19th century. The most drastic modification occurred in the pronouns of address; the Castilian system gradually eliminated *vos* and *vosotros* with all the corresponding verb paradigms. In the process of diversification, it is important to underline the multiple paths followed by colonial Spanish in general and by its particular components. While optimal residual variants have not changed at all, popular variants have been redistributed to almost exclusive use in isolated or marginal varieties where the effects of higher education and/or standardization have been limited. Some other variants have disappeared altogether as a result of a complex process of simplification (e.g. the verb system) or the technological developments that either slowly or swiftly replaces obsolete objects (e.g. *calesa*). After a century of research in New World Spanish, the definition of diversification as proposed by Cuervo still holds sway today. For Cuervo even a minor change of meaning, recognized today as polysemy, entailed a process of diversification, which is still extremely dynamic given that the newer version of New World Spanish, i.e. modern Latin American Spanish, is constantly re-diversifying itself. As a case in point, at the dawn of the 21st century, a new stage of diversification began with the introduction of terms related to high technology. Today they are making strong inroads in the private and public lexicon, and even morphology, particularly in desinences of verbs such as *tuiteo* (< to tweet), 1st person singular present tense indicative of the neologism *tuitear*. Those belonging to this social network are known as *tuiteros* (< tweeters).

11 Conclusions

11.1 A tridimensional study

A tridimensional study is useful in assessing the reconstruction of sociolinguistic phenomena and also in representing a more realistic account during an important period in the history of Latin America. This view considers the interconnection of the three dimensions (history, society and language) and less ambiguous configurations of the outcomes. The tridimensional approach offers a more complete perspective on the role of history and society and their impact on the concatenation of events affecting directly or indirectly language phenomena.

The variants selected for this study represent the ways of speaking first like newcomers from Spain, then like acclimatized Spaniards, and finally like Spanish speakers born and raised in the New World. The cause of attrition of select variants may be found in the environmental conditions experienced in the new soil. The variants available in late medieval Spanish were transformed via elimination, simplification, and reduction. At the same time, Spanish in the New World followed its own path to diversification via the continual building and maintenance of domains of interaction. In addition to the personal and situational domains that unfolded in all the colonies, in New Spain complementary domains such mining, commerce, journalism, and creative literature generated the use of specialized lexicon and styles unknown in most informal domains. At this juncture, it is useful to bring to mind alternate theories of language evolution and diversification, since the changes occur in languages impacted by sociocultural development, which can be gauged by linguistic traits per se such as vocabulary (Swadesh 1971: 10-11, 44-46). The motivations of language communities are responsible for the unfolding innovations, but internal changes may occur independently of external factors, a theory that leads to a broader question proposed in the introduction. Is language evolution based or justified on purely linguistic grounds or do we have to resort to expound external factors, and if so, to what extent?

11.2 The role of history: direct external factors

Amerindian loans do derive from direct language contact with speakers of indigenous languages. Spanish speakers were active in exploring the new soil and responsible for adopting and adapting to Spanish the lexical items that were more convenient for their needs. Over the centuries, the borrowings sounded natural and were used as though they belonged to the patrimonial inventory of Spanish. Speakers who were going back and forth between continents were the transmitters of Amerindian borrowings. In Spain, they may have acquired a different meaning. One of the common examples of transatlantic diversification is the noun *petaca(s)*, which in Nahuatl meant 'woven hamper', and in today's Mexican Spanish it means 'suitcase' but figuratively it also means 'large hips'. In Spain however it referred to a 'small box to save letters or cigars', while its diminutive *petaquilla* means 'flask for liquor'. Language contact may be seen through the lens of the daily needs of Spanish speakers, who selected the nouns, adjectives, or verbs that were essential for their communicative, pragmatic and survival needs.

The ideological power of the Inquisition in spreading Spanish and the restrictions of its discourse may be considered, too, a direct influence. Spanish speakers empowered by the Spanish Crown were in charge of reading aloud and writing for posterity the biographies, denunciations, and sentences dictated to the suspects. They created a style of reprobation and condemnation against those who were resistant to the dictates of the Holy Office. They utilized their power to curb the spread of divergent ideas, and by doing so, they built solid tentacles of intimidation. The thousands of documents archived by the Inquisition are today more than traces of colonial language. They provide reliable evidence of language use and language attitudes in New Spain showing a wide range of beliefs and practices that had an impact on the public and private lives of ordinary people. The inquisitorial documents illustrate the regularities and irregularities of the spontaneous speech of notaries, scribes, deponents and witnesses that appeared before the tribunals during almost three hundred years. The direct influence can thus be divided in two major categories: (1) the ideological discourse of coercion; and (2) the language variants available for further analysis.

11.2.1 Creole and semi-creole varieties

The paucity of creole or creolized varieties of Spanish is the direct result of a movement of resistance against the slavery of the indigenous, where the roots of the Latin American liberation theology can be found. A major shift in Western thought was initiated by Bartolomé de las Casas, who viewed the indigenous as participating subjects, not simply as objects, in the newer discourse with the peoples of the recently discovered world. In turn, the pro-human rights and anti-colonialism discourse deterred the complacent legality of comprehensive slavery and slave trade, though simultaneously permitted other forms of dispossession and alientation. The critical work of las Casas has been essential in understanding the notions of cultural relativism and multi-culturalism, largely misunderstood by the proponents of the 'black legend', an invention utilized to undermine the principles of Spanish humanism. Finally, according to Forti (1989), the work of las Casas aids in examining the issues of social justice from the perspective of those whose conscience or false conscience has been following the values of the Western civilization over the past four hundred years.

Resulting from the admixture of a European language and African languages, the radical popularization of Spanish might have been epitomized by a continual process of creolization, but the environmental conditions that lead to such syncretism were not deep-seated in most regions of the new soil, where intermixtures and aggregations of language, culture, and music might have taken place. Several external factors explain the non-existence of Africanized creoles. The first one has to do with the quantitative disproportion of African descendants vs. native indigenous; the second is related to the emergent economy where it was more expensive to engage in the slave trade, an enterprise that was both cost-ineffective and politically incorrect. At the end of the colony, there were about 9,000 to 10,000 slaves, who were freed by the Independentist leaders. The abolition of slavery in the New World was proclaimed specifically for the remaining population of African descent.[5]

The economy of the Spanish-speaking New World did not depend only on slavery but on other forms of labor that fostered face-to face interaction and alternate strategies of contact with and within the Spanish-speaking society. This made the difference in the separation of the castes from Spanish speakers who loosened the tight spectrum of rankings in the enterprise of colonialism. Towards the end of the colony, the end-result was a socio-ethnic variety of Nahuatl-accented Spanish with features that are typical of bilingual groups and bilingual individuals exposed to European languages in disadvantageous conditions; it must be emphasized that a full-fledge creole did not emerge in any of the communities in which indigenous languages have been spoken for centuries. The Yucatan peninsula with a high demographic density of bilinguals concentrated in a compact and homogeneous region might have been closer to rendering a Spanish contact vernacular with glaring features of Mayan languages; however, there is only evidence of Mayan-accented Spanish in bilingual groups, which may be considered the result of interference (cf. García Fajardo 1984; Lope Blanch 1987). In addition, research on Afro-Hispanic varieties leads to making inferences

---

[5] A discussion on the abolition of slavery in Mexico and the political motivations leading to its early proclamation by the leader of Independence, theologian and philosppher Miguel Hidalgo y Costilla, both nationwide and in the provinces, can be found in Olveda Legaspi (2013).

about the existence of regional and social dialects that have maintained many of the residual features that are the common denominator of New World Spanish. In some of the enclaves where population of African descent (e.g. Veracruz, Acapulco and the Costa Chica) has been documented, researchers have found merely vestiges associated to the African presence. The recent reports on the Costa Chica point to the acquisition of the Spanish local popular dialect on the part of speakers of African or Afro-Mexican descent.

11.3 From the past to the present: indirect external factors

The emigration of Spanish speakers from Spain and their continual participation in mining, the textile industry, commerce, and other activities were directly responsible for the growth of the Spanish-speaking population. In turn, their mere presence promoted the use of alternate variants derived from the late medieval peninsular tree:

(1) The neutralization of the series of sibilants <s>, <ç>, and <z> can be traced to the latest stage of medieval Spanish and the many internal and external forces that weighed in their transformations over the centuries. The resulting variant known as Seseo-P is one of the outstanding common denominators of the vast Spanish-speaking region accepted as the norm in all domains, registers, and socio-cultural strata. Seseo-P includes the sub-variants of New World *seseo* since the sibilant [s] can be [+ tense] in the Central Highlands or [– tense] in the Gulf region and other areas of the Spanish-speaking world. In addition, this book has introduced the notion of Seseo-W, which is strongly associated with [+ / – literacy] rates that vary widely across regions and nations according to modern criteria of socioeconomic development.

(2) The use of LO and LE points to the co-existence of forms that in the first two centuries of the colony veered in the direction of *leísmo* or the metropolitan norm. The shift to the ancestral pro-etymological form occurred in the 18th century and did not regress, but has remained stable since then. Whereas at present speakers overwhelmingly prefer the pro-etymological clitic LO for [+ animate masculine singular] direct object pronouns, there have been found variations with select verbs, e.g. *ayudar* ('to help') and *entender* ('to understand'), though they do not resemble the typical *leísta* patterns. However, researchers do find a preference for LE with a group of verbs known as 'stative verbs of emotion', when LE is used as a dative. When the same verb is used with the accusative, it may mean something slightly different, e.g. *complacerlo* (pleasing someone by granting that person's wishes or desires), as opposed to *complacerle* (to be pleasing to someone) (DeMello 2002: 276). Table 11.1 shows the capital cities where data

have been collected and the sum of the total tokens of LO = 17 (6. 65 %) and LE = 239 (93.35 %). The use of the clitic LE as a dative rather than accusative discards previous proposals on the existence of *leísta* patterns in modern Latin American Spanish. The few cases in which LE is used, say, with the verb *conocer* ('to know'), as in *le conozco* ('I know him'), refer to an event in which distance or respect is indirectly conveyed, whereas in northern-central peninsular Spanish *le conozco* is the routine structure used in everyday speech.

Table 11.1: *Lo / le* with stative verbs of motion

Capital city	Com-placer lo/le	Encantar lo/le	Interesar lo/le	Molestar lo/le	Pre-ocupar lo/le	Other lo /le	Total lo/le
Bogota	2/1	0/4	0/12	1/1			3/18
Buenos Aires		0/8	0/34	2/1	0/1		2/44
Caracas		0/6	0/20	0/3	1/0	1/0	2/31
Havana		0/1	0/3			0/1	0/5
La Paz		0/4	1/11	1/3			1/18
Lima		0/5	0/11	0/3	1/0		1/19
Mexico	2/0	0/7	0/12	1/1		1/0	4/20
San Jose, C.R.		0/2	0/7		0/2		0/11
San Juan, P.R.			0/16	0/4	0/3	0/1	0/24
Santiago, Chile		0/4	2/39	2/2	0/4		4/49
Total	4/1	0/41	2/165	7/18	2/12	2/2	17/239

Source: DeMello (2002: 276)

Originally a dative, the clitic pronoun LE has been moving to other functional spaces corresponding to a primary object through the weakening of accusative marking. In modern Mexican Spanish LE appears with a [– transitive] verb such as *correr* ('to run'), as in ¡Córrele de ahí! ('Run from there!'), an expression focusing on the pragmatic argument and the positive reaction of the hearer. The other construction is the affixation of LE to non-verbal parts of speech such as interjections used to exhort the interlocutor to react in a certain way: ¡Órale! ('Oh, yeah'), ¡Híjole! ('Wow!', 'Gee whiz'). The dative LE in Mexican Spanish can be reanalyzed in a sequence of concatenated changes that have resulted in the opacity of the verb. The most popular expression is ¡Ándale! ('Go ahead!'), in which the verb *andar* loses its original meaning ('to walk') and is transformed into a de-verbalized expression ('It's just fine!'), where the meaning of the verb no longer has to do with movement and the clitic carries the load of a new pragmatic argument (cf. Company Company 2002a, 2004 and 2008).

(3) In Mexican Colonial Spanish the verbal endings –RA and –SE alternated for more than two centuries until the former prevailed with minor reservations. Again, the comparison of rates in ten capital cities indicates that the ending –RA is ahead of the ending –SE in subordinate clauses where subjunctive meaning is categorical. Summarized in Table 11.2, the subsample includes spoken language data collected in the 1960's showing that Bogota, Lima and Mexico City were ahead of all the other capitals. The only exception to the overwhelming use of –RA was San Juan, Puerto Rico, which appears to be more conservative than Madrid and Seville. All in all speakers of peninsular Spanish are inclined to use –RA in the colloquial registers but not necessarily in formal written codes. It seems that both varieties are slowly converging in colloquial registers, and that other variations in the more formal and written genres need to be closely examined.

Table 11.2: Use of -RA and -SE verbal forms

Capital city	–RA forms	–SE forms
Bogota	408 (98 %)	8 (2 %)
Buenos Aires	393 (94 %)	4 (6 %)
Caracas	511 (94 %)	32 (6 %)
Havana	227 (96 %)	9 (4 %)
Lima	165 (99.4 %)	1 (0.6 %)
Madrid	188 (84 %)	36 (16 %)
Mexico City	362 (98 %)	9 (2 %)
San Juan, P. R.	249 (80 %)	61 (20 %)
Santiago, Chile	299 (86 %)	13 (4 %)
Sevilla	110 (87 %)	16 (13 %)
Total	2912 (93 %)	210 (7 %)

Source: DeMello (1993: 235)

Studies on Latin American capital cities have been mostly descriptive of the features of spoken Spanish and have contributed with insights into the general trends observed primarily in the 20th century. The variationist approach nonetheless can aggregate more internal and extra-linguistic variables that shed light into more specific patterns and can even be predictive. As a case in point, the analysis of the endings –SE and –RA in imperfect subjunctive, which in most grammars are described as being interchangeable, lends itself to further analysis and interpretation. Based on the corpus of 160 native informants divided in four generations and five social strata, a study on the speech of Caracas reveals an overwhelming preference for the –RA ending, 94 vs. only 6 percent for the –SE ending. Data from the late 1980's was examined according to the weight given to both internal and extra-linguistic variables. The minor variation observed in –SE leads to raise questions about the impact that those additional variables had on the traditional variant. The group belonging to the fourth generation (60+ and older) was discarded because not a single case of –SE was tallied, as opposed to the younger generation that reported a tiny proportion of –SE. The most important internal variant explaining the use of –SE is the presence of a compound verb tense followed by the use of negative statements and another subjunctive verb in the preceding clause. The extra-linguistic variable that is significant in this subsample is middle socio-economic status, which accounted for slightly higher rates than the upper stratum, perhaps because –SE is associated with the bookish tradition. Finally, the analysis detected the variable generation (30-45), a group that is considered to be under pressure in their own community. The *GoldVarb* program aids in seeing that there is a curvilinear model that permits to anticipate the beginning of language change (Asratian 2007).

(4) The pronouns of address *vuestra merced*, *vos* and *tú* highlight the complexity of social relationships experienced in the colonies. A mixture of paradigms, *voseo* is the innovative contribution to New World and Latin American Spanish. The analyses of pronominal variants corroborates that while Spanish speakers prevailed in the sociocultural and political scenario of the colony, the variants associated with Spain remained stable. Their decline anticipated the political independence of the nations-to-be that were willing and ready to embrace a modified Spanish code. The connections with Spain are deemed responsible for the preservation of the pronouns of address *tú* and *Usted* in New Spain, as opposed to Central and South American independent nations, where miscellaneous versions of *voseo* seem to have been accepted as the daily norm. On the other hand, reports on the state of Chiapas indicate that *voseo* was common in the 1950's. Forms such as *vos vivís, querés, llorás* (present indicative), *vos vivás* (present subjunctive), and *viví, andate, venite, tené, esperá* (affirmative commands) are similar to typical *voseante* variants vital at present in many of the independent nations where *voseo* has been reported (Francis Soriano 1960: chapter 3). The external factors explaining the survival of *voseo* in Chiapas have to do with its isolation from the rest of Mexico during colonial times.

The difference between most of Mexico and other nations lies in the choices that speakers had in the past. Whereas in New Spain *vos* was replaced by *tú* and normally alternated with *vuestra merced*, in other colonies *vos* became a frequent pronoun of address in [+ symmetrical] relationships, a fact explained by the type-of-role relationship encountered in speech communities where solidarity between Spanish speakers was stronger. On the other hand, the overuse of *vuestra merced* in the colonial period explains the preference for the neologism *Usted* in [– symmetrical] relationships once the movements of Independence were complete. As a corollary to the usage patterns examined in New Spain, it is inferred that where the mix of pronouns was rare or non-existent, the singular dyad *tú / Usted* prevailed, and where pronouns were routinely mixed, *voseo* unfolded in different versions. Updated language data collected in various nations and the multiple intervening variables in the regions, subregions, and / or speech communities (Madrid, Alcala de Henares, Cadiz, Canarias, Mexico, and Central and South America) corroborate the existence of dynamic variations of *voseo* and other pronouns of address over the entire Spanish-speaking world (cf. Hummel et al. 2010). Adittionally, data collected among college students reveal the trends of the youth in Medellin and Cali (Colombia), where *vos*, *tú*, *Usted*, and mixed pronouns were examined in connection with a number of independent variables such as: sex, age, socio-economic status, place of interaction, dialect, topic, and emotional closeness. The results indicate that in Medellin the most frequent given and expected pronoun of address in informal discourse is *Usted*, followed by *vos*, while *tú* and mixed pronouns show very low use rates. When all the other variables are factored in, similar results are displayed except in the home domain where *vos* is the preferred pronoun. Analysis of frequencies in Cali indicates that *Usted* is used at slightly higher rates in informal contexts and mostly when other intervening variables are correlated. Where *voseo* alternates with *tú* and *Usted*, the disciples of New World and modern Latin American Spanish are required to find the desired parameters and semantic features observed in multiple contexts (cf. Millán 2011). The preference for the most modern use of *Usted* in Colombia may have to do with the speakers' desire to circumvent the use of *voseo*, which necessarily derives from the mixing of *vos* and *tú*. This may have occurred at an earlier stage of diversification when *Usted* became popular in the well-established and nascent urban networks of Spanish speakers.

In contrast with the widespread of *voseo* as a diversified but modern form of address, research on *vuesa merced* in the New World, a less common variant, is not abundant. In Cervantes' masterpiece *Don Quijote de la Mancha* (1605), which exploits the effects of colloquial Spanish, *vuesa merced* alternates with *vuestra merced* in the conversations between Don Quijote and Sancho Panza, who addresses his master with the two honorifics. In their glaringly [– symmetrical] relationship, Sancho Panza regularly received *tú*. A residual variant from colonial Spanish, *vuesa merced*, may still be used in Colombia in romantic relationships stirred by Courtly love where the personal protocol dictates a unidirectional male-to-female [+ reverence] turn that may be simulataneously nominative and vocative.

On the other hand, according to Granda (2007), *su merced* is limited to subregions where it remains as a residual variant. *Su merced* or *su mercé* can be traced to the late 15th century and the 16th century with continuity through the 20th century in rural areas within Spain. In the New World, it has been preserved in Santo Domingo, Puira and Arequipa in Peru, northwestern Argentina and southwestern Bolivia, not to mention Colombia. *Su merced* was [+ reverential] in the 16th century haciendas; in the following century it descended to [+ symmetrical] relationships, though it was more prestigious than the neologism *Usted* derived through various stages of internal evolution from *vuestra merced*. Among Colombian privileged groups, *su merced* is still used because it is identified with an ancestral restricted upper-class stratum and social networks, where it is [+ equal] and conveys exclusive and mutual respect. *Su merce(d)* appears too as a residual variant in villages of central Mexico close to a major town (e.g. Chalco), a traditional community where speakers make a distinction of status within the family domain, social networks, and also in the local markets, a locus where the client may be addressed with an honorific of a higher rank. The use of pronouns of address in New World and modern Latin American Spanish has turned into a major challenge in studies of sociolinguistic variation across social classes, societal domains and role relationships (cf. Uber 2011 and Díaz Collazos 2015).

One more piece of evidence supporting the theory of diversification is the distribution of *vos* and *tú*. Map 11.1 illustrates the complexity and approximate distribution in modern Latin American Spanish, where *Usted* does not appear. Because forms of address represent a multiplicity of psychosocial dimensions, they are difficult to predict with precision even when the researcher probes into the sociolinguistic history of the speech community, the subregion, or the independent nation. The object of study can be the domain of interaction, the interactional nature of role relationships, the intentions of the speakers, the patterns and prejudices acquired or learned in the nuclear family, the extended family, the school, and the available social networks. In regions where the dyad *tú / Usted* has prevailed over the past two hundred years, forms of address may be studied exclusively along these two axes. In contrast, where *vos*, *tú*, *Usted*, and mixed pronouns are used, a tripartite system may unravel more complex [+ / – symmetrical] societal connections and interconnections. Where *voseo* prevails, e.g. Argentina, variations of *tú* can be studied in inter-group relations, that is, with speakers from other Latin American nations.

11.4 Peninsular, New World and Latin American Spanish

After almost five hundred years, the mutation of the peninsular tree in the New World has experienced a permanent change that is not reversible. Derived from the peninsular varieties, New World Spanish was diversified in pronunciation, morpho-syntax, and lexicon. After the Wars of Independence, the New World

Spanish tree has evolved in differentiated regional and / or national varieties generally identified as Latin American Spanish. Research on comparative dialectology points out that the Castilian variety is referential and focuses on grammatical categories such as number, gender, tense, etc. while the Mexican variety is relational, and tends to enhance the values that the speaker has about what is said. The split occurred at the end of the 15th century and continued in the 16th century triggering a differentiation between varieties; it is assumed that the differences are semantic and pragmatic, though both varieties share the similar underlying syntactic structures. This proposal considers four syntactic-semantic variables accounting for the differentiation between the Spanish used in Spain and the Spanish used in the Mexican Spanish, to wit: (1) duplicate possessives; (2) diminutives; (3) *leísmo*; and (4) the use of tenses in present perfect. While peninsular Spanish focuses on the observable semantic properties of the entities in question, Mexican Spanish is more sensitive to the reactions that the speaker may have about those entities and the relations of the entities within the discourse (Company Company 2002b).

11.5 Stages of diversification

The study of Mexican Colonial Spanish aids in finding some of the roots in the peninsular tree, which may be deeper than what appears on the surface. In modern Spanish lexical items revive with the same meaning as in (a), where the noun *correo* indicates that there was a sack with news, meesages and letters from the king.

(a) Llegó un *correo* con la nueva y cartas; el *correo* era el pliego del rey (Suárez de Peralta 1585: 201)

Before the advent of wireless communications, *correo* meant 'the means or act of mailing', 'the post office', or the sack where correspondence is saved. When electronic messages became popular, *correo* reacquired the old meaning of 'message', and these days it competes with the English 'e-mail', as in *mándame un correo* or *mándame un mail* ('send me an e-mail message'). The major contributor to the diversification of New World Spanish, transformed into modern Latin American Spanish, still is the daily lexicon of colloquial registers. General or optimal residual variants derived from colonial Spanish persist in modern colloquial varieties, a fact that shows the deep roots of the late medieval Spanish tree. In contrast, popular residual variants derived from the same tree have been redistributed along registers belonging at present to marginal or isolated varieties, in turn impacted by socio-economic marginalization. This dichotomy (optimal vs.

popular variants) may be traced to the colonial period that defined the urban / rural axis of interaction. The different stages of diversification can be paired off with historical periods that are already distinguished by major transformations. The first stage of diversification has been spelled out in this book via the analysis and interpretation of attrition of select colonial variants. The next stage of diversification may be identified in the 19th century during the Independent period, which is known for the work of the intellectuals who accepted a language code representative of the newer Spanish-speaking Mexicans.

Marking the beginning of an era in which the process of "de-ruralization" was intensified in both Mexico and some other independent nations, Independence was followed by the Mexican Revolution of 1910-1921. Since the 1940's the creation of new jobs and the expansion of trade, commerce, and other tertiary activities have stimulated intense domestic migration from rural areas to major Latin American cities. Since then the urban population has increased in direct proportion to the decrease of the rural population. The inversion of the rural / urban dichotomy points to newer forms of diversification emerging under different circumstances; one of them has been identified as a new constellation of 'rurban' dialects (Hidalgo 1990: 58). Defining the non-urban varieties as "archaic" and the urban as "educated", this dichotomy has been highlighted in Puerto Rico by Álvarez Nazario (1982), and is applicable to the rest of Latin America.

In spite of the fact that this notion is commonly accepted, researchers have not explored the allusions to diglossic patterns because they normally associate diglossia with the position of Spanish vs. indigenous languages. Implying that there exist higher and lower registers used in semi-exclusive situations, Spanish has not been considered a diglossic language. Nevertheless, as stated in previous chapters, researchers do distinguish normative from popular Spanish. The former adheres to rules established by grammars, academies, dictionaries, and educational institutions, among other prestigious sources of the 'norm', which is allocated within the speech community that recognizes the linguistic norm as opposed to the popular varieties. Though some may argue that speakers do not acquire the 'norm' in a natural setting (e.g. the home domain), the conditions to learn the idealized variety can be propitious in the home domain and later complemented in formal schooling. The stability of the norm at the societal level enhances its preservation in the contexts and domains in which it is routinely used (higher education, government, media, etc.). As compared to other languages that may have ritualized domains, modern Spanish is not associated with strict religious practices. Nonetheless, since the advent of radio and later television, the perception of the norm is stronger in some independent nations where there may be active censorship on the means, transmission, form, and content of communication. Studies on the perceived linguistic norm have proliferated since the 1960's when a group of researchers was engaged in the *Proyecto Coordinado de la Norma Lingüística Culta de las Principales Ciudades de Iberoamérica y España* [Coordinated Project on the Cultured Linguistic Norms of the Main Cities of Spain and Latin America (1964). The goal of the program was to study the Spanish segmental, supra-segmental, consonantal, and morpho-syntactic system in the capital cities around the Spanish- and Portuguese-speaking world. The partial results of studies in Havana, San Juan (Puerto Rico), Mexico, Caracas, Buenos Aires and Santiago de Chile are available in Lope Blanch (1977).

Acquiring and learning normative Spanish involves a lengthy process that requires reinforcement for at least 12+ consecutive years of solid education. Using this criterion as the basis for judging "normative" vs. non-normative Spanish leads to believe that very few individuals or groups of individuals could be identified as 'normative Spanish speakers'. In modern Spanish, the linguistic norm is recognized by the use of regular morpho-syntactic features, while the lexicon can vary according to topic, context, interlocutor, and some other variables. When speakers of modern Latin American Spanish use the corresponding colloquial register, speakers of the norm do not alter the morphological and syntactic patterns of normative Spanish; instead, they switch to the popular variety of their region or nation by exploiting the lexicon of vernacular Spanish. They may also resort to some other variables associated with informal contexts, such final /s/ aspiration, or deletion of final and intervocalic /d/ at moderate rates. The vernacular, however, is not brought into play in the interaction with servants, fellow workers, friends, and family members; speakers of the norm do not switch up and down between the norm and the popular variety or varieties. Instead, the switches to vernacular variants may be motivated by pragmatic constraints such as topic, place, or phatic communication.

The studies on the linguistic norm of major capital cities began to appear after World War II when a more diversified society was emerging in traditional urban centers, where newer roles were growing in professional, managerial, and manufacturing activities. As the Latin American societies become immerse in the global economy, Spanish and Portuguese speakers also get involved in newer activities. Despite the fact that variation in modern Latin American Spanish has been studied since the 1970's, the shift to studying again sociolinguistic corpora in major cities is more recent. These days it is represented by the project known as *Proyecto para el estudio sociolingüístico del español de España y América* PRESEA [Project for the Sociolinguistic Study of Spanish in Spain and the Latin America], whose goal is to identify both internal and external variables affecting the variation of a cluster of specific variants. Researchers are engaged in studying both conditioning and extra-linguistic factors affecting language variants.

11.6 PARA and PA in Venezuela

Data collected in the last decades of the 20th century in Maracaibo, Caracas and Merida are analyzed on the basis of 72 recordings of subjects stratified by sex, generation (30-45 and 60+) and sociocultural status (SCS); in this subsample the researcher found 2,144 tokens, which were split in 48 percent for *pa* and 52 percent for *para*. The semantic value seems to exert an influence on the selection where the meaning of purpose or finality is present. The next factor is SCS (low, mid, high) with a distribution of 45 percent of the cases of *pa* reported by speakers in the low group, and the rest distributed equally in the mid and high strata. Male subjects showed a slight preference for the reduced variant than females. Finally, speakers from Merida and Caracas were not inclined for any of the variants, but a majorty of those from Maracaibo (60 %) actually used *pa* (Guirado 2007). Also in Caracas, data on the same variants are compared with the contemporary reports available for Spanish. The non-prescribed use in Caracas is larger than in Spanish cities such as Alcala and Murcia. Again, the samples from the Caracas youth are analyzed in 24 recordings, two select groups (20-24, 25-30), mostly college-educated belonging to the upper-middle crust of the Venezuelan capital. The place of residence selected was the central district known as *El Libertador*, the hub of intense commercial, cultural, and tourist-oriented activities, and another district. *Para* seems to be preferred in the context of finality, while the younger group used the variant *pa* at higher rates. Speakers from *El Libertador* were inclined to use *para*, and speakers from other districscts were inclined to use *pa*. The use of *pa* increases if the speaker is a young male (Guirado 2011). Variationist studies are useful to examine usage patterns in time and space and aid in understanding the dynamic nature of some variants across generations. The sophistication of the analysis on the use of *para* and *pa* yields slightly—though not radically—different results. The choices that speakers had during the colonial period are similar to those observed in the present. Speakers of higher SCS seemed to prefer *para* over *pa*, but such preference is not overwhelming.

11.7 Diversification of the New World Spanish tree

The transplantation of the peninsular tree was so successful in the New World that a newer and gigantic tree of modern Latin American Spanish has blossomed with diverse branches that are recognizable in at least three levels:

(1) National 'standardized' dialects for each independent country, which may sound similar, although objectively none is identical to the other. In the Caribbean region, Dominican, Cuban and Puerto Rican Spanish share numerous features

that can be traced to the 16th century. As a result of the intense interminglings occurring from island to island, speakers are differentiated from one another within the area, and such distinctiveness may arise from nationalist attitudes. Those who are not familiar with this regional variety may confuse the national provenance of the speakers. Very close to the Caribbean are Panama and the coasts of Colombia and Venezuela, whose speakers may be confused with those from the islands. Similarly, the Spanish spoken in Mexico may be confused with the Spanish spoken in Guatemala, particularly with Guatemala City, which was an important subregion of New Spain. For the neophyte, the Spanish of Honduras, El Salvador, and Nicaragua may sound identical, but Central Americans are aware of their 'national' distinctiveness. In South America, the Spanish spoken in Colombia and Ecuador may also sound alike to those who have not traveled extensively, though Colombians and Ecuadorians would readily hear or see the differences, large or small, objective or subjective, of their own 'national' dialects. The same principle holds for Peru and Chile, on the one hand, and Argentina and Uruguay, on the other. Finally, Chileans may be confused with Bolivians, but the Spanish of Paraguay seems to be unique in the large constellation of South American dialects.

(2) The second level of dialect distinctiveness is associated with popular 'national' dialects spoken by everyone, and sometimes represented in the national media as part of the Latin American folklore, i.e. dance, music, oral history, proverbs, jokes, popular beliefs, idiomatic expressions, food, and in general, the local customs. The popular national dialect traits may be flaunted in the lyrics of popular songs, while each nation may have its own popular rhythm represented by a few songs that in turn embody the 'national' dialect. The popular national dialect may have a faster tempo and intonational patterns. In the rural space and marginal speech communities, the popular 'national' dialects may still carry some of the features of the 16th and 17th century koine: *ansi, muncho, onde, truje*. In addition, the lexicon may have features or vestiges of indigenous languages, Afro-Hispanic varieties, or diversified meanings whose origins may be found in the history of Spanish literature or the popular history of the local region.

(3) National 'popular' dialects are not identical to regional vernaculars or local dialects spoken within the modern Latin American nations. In the regional vernaculars, the researcher and the common observer may find higher frequencies of 'popular' features, e.g. final –s aspiration and deletion, omission of intervocalic –d– and final –d, and in general, more noticeable consonantal reduction. Spanish-based regional vernaculars have evolved independently in each country, and may (or may not) be associated to language contact features: *pororo* in Santo Domingo, *bozal* in Cuba, *español indígena* in Mexico, or *español motoso* in Peru are vernaculars that unfolded as a result of contact with either indige-

nous languages or with the African presence. Notwithstanding the differences in time and space, all the vernacular dialects are intelligible provided the speakers have a good attitude and predisposition to understand speakers of other vernaculars. Contact vernaculars are derived from transfers initiated by speakers of Amerindian languages who carried overgeneratizations of the native language to Spanish. In turn, structural transfer results from the interaction of social variables related to various types of Amerindian societies impacted by central, intermediate or peripheral Spanish colonization, though occasionally the researcher can find bi-directional transfers from the Amerindian languages to Spanish and vice versa. Transfer occurred mostly in regions in which these variables fostered situations of intersection that promoted changes such as borrowing and language shift. Yucatan, Paraguay, and the Andean region—from northwestern Argentina to northern Ecuador—are areas of considerable transfer, which was originally common amongst Amerindian ethnolinguistic groups but whose features were later (re)transferred to the Spanish-speaking population, who in turn integrated them as part of the common regional dialect (cf. Granda 1999; see also Hidalgo 2002 and 2008).

The abovementioned Spanish-based vernacular dialects are not to be confused with vernaculars originating from contact between Amerindian languages or Afro-Hispanic varieties and Spanish. These may be found in Honduras, Belize, and to a lesser extent in Guatemala and Nicaragua, where *garífuna* (derived from diverse indigenous, African, and European languages) makes the difference in the constellation of Central American languages. Speakers of *yopara* (derived from Guarani in contact with Spanish) contribute to the unique linguistic diversity in Paraguay. Spanish speakers of contact vernaculars may find that these varieties are not readily intelligible. Finally, the Spanish-based creole *palenquero* or *Palenque*, spoken in northern Colombia, stands alone as the living testimony of the extended African roots of the colonial period, and may not be readily understood by Spanish speakers.

11.8 Final conclusions

This study has shown that variation is the key to understanding diversification, which is more encompassing than variation itself. Variation allows the researcher to plow deeply, plow again, and harrow until more work can be done on the surface. Minor variations can stir the conditions of the variants under observation, while the researcher looks into the social and linguistic history of speech communities with more precise insights. The role of historical sociolinguistics is to single out the changes that are considered internal from those that are identified as external. Over the past three decades, historical sociolinguists have contributed to a better understanding of operational definitions needed to explain the reliable and valid assessment of external variables impinging on language change and its variations across time. Because the past is not directly observable, the researcher gathers optimal information from all sources useful for interpretation. This strategy has the advantage of following changes in real time (Nevalainen and Ramoulin-Brunberg 2012).

The examination of the variants selected herein has attracted scholars over many decades, and consequently, some of the internal changes are distinguished from those that are external. In the case of the Spanish sibilants, for example, disciples of Spanish historical linguistics have looked into the route of inherent evolution beginning with the distinction of pertinent features of all phonemes (voiced vs. voiceless, affricate vs. fricative, dental vs. alveolar) and the resulting mergers of the neutralized oppositions. In this respect, new questions point to the historical and social milieu that might have triggered the change. The distinctive Castilian sibilants would not have converged into Seseo-P (one single [s]) had Castilian speakers not moved southward and across the Atlantic in the repopulation and colonizing movements. This tridimensional study considers this framework in the differentiation of the sibilants, which was sustained only in the original Castilian and Castilianized regions amongst speakers who remained in the region where the distinction has prevailed, although at present is also reduced in a significant opposition often invoked by the distinction of /s/ and /θ/. The most-often quoted example is the noun *casa* [kasa] 'house' and its minimal pair *caza* [kaθa] ('hunting'), which have identical pronunciation in the southern Spanish provinces and in the New World, and which are disambiguated only by the context. This makes clear that Seseo-P unfolded in the repopulated areas of southern Spain and later accelerated its course of development in the Spanish-speaking New World, where colonizers had lost contact with the original distinguishing Castilian varieties. This study has also highlighted that Mexican Colonial Spanish did not adopt immediately the *seseo* variants because the presence of Spanish speakers from northern-central regions within Spain made a significant difference in the colonial affairs.

The framework that assigns a role to the historical and social environment (or the social history of language) as proposed by Martinet (1953) is beneficial to explain the use of the contending verbal clitics LE and LO, the former innovation emerging in opposition to the pro-etymological Latin and Vulgar Latin system. Both clitics were transplanted to the New World, where they co-existed during the colonial centuries. Whereas LO was in clear disadvantage with LE, in the end LO prevailed for the same reasons that sustained Seseo-P. Spanish speakers who were progressively acclimatized in the new soil lost track of the variations of *leístas*, who were more irregular than the variations of pro-etymological users; they had at their disposal the pro-etymological system for [+ animate singular masculine] direct objects. The competition of verbal clitics in the New World environs is one of the distinguishing traits of Mexican Colonial Spanish. In like manner, the contending verb endings –SE and –RA in imperfect subjunctive are associated to the sociolinguistic history of the speakers (cf. Thomason and Kauffman 1988) in the colonial milieu, where speakers of diverse origin co-existed for the entire period. The inclination for the use of –RA has to do with the attitudes of a group of Spanish speakers already adjusted and identified with the lifestyle of the New World-born, who in the end rejected the –SE form in order to show their desire to severe themselves from Spain. Finally, the tridimensional framework explains the continuous trend of reduction and simplification of the pronominal system. For this reason, in New World Spanish the pronoun *vosotros* (< *vos* + *otros*) was eliminated with all the verb paradigms. The surviving innovation known as *voseo* is one more example of diversification because this variant has evolved in assorted forms around the regions and speech communities, where different groups and subgroups of speakers assign and reassign socio-semantic values to the surviving singular pronouns, *tú* and *Usted*, that contend with a singular modern Latin American *vos*. The use of singular *vos* has a long and independent history from all the other features of Mexican Colonial Spanish, a variety that did not promote the mixture of personal pronouns.

In sum, ignoring external factors in the search for language evolution, change, innovations, and variation leads to ignoring the transfomations of a certain historical period and meaningful social events that may offer clues to grasp those internal changes that are germane to all languages and dialects, the passing fads, and the more permanent patterns of diversification. Social history and sociolinguistics are not connected in a vacuum but are actually adjoined by the pleasant intermingling of the past and the present. Linking history, society, and language under a coherent "historical sociolinguistic model that may help explain the stages and substages of change across regions, chronological periods and socioeconomic determinants" (Hidalgo 2001: 10) will be the major challenge to students of New World Spanish. Historical sociolinguistics and the (re)interpretative ramifications along postmodern trends that view the multiple dimensions (i.e. classic, popular and modern) of language occurrences is indeed a promising field. I hope this book will inspire diversification studies showing the paths followed by New World Spanish and its transformations in different Latin American regions and/or nations.

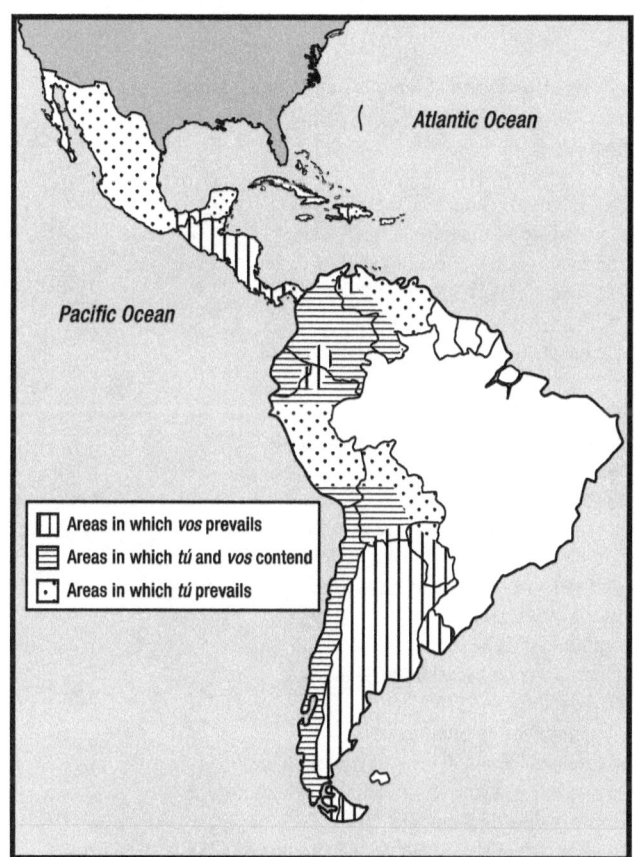

Map 11.1: Distribution of *vos* and *tú*. Source: Adapted from Lapesa (1985: map facing page 575)

Appendix

Subsample of ethnic groups from *El Abecedario* (Henry E. Huntington Library)

Key to identification of subjects by group

Group 1: Subjects 1-100 (Spanish speakers born in Spain)
Group 2: Subjects 101-125 (Spanish speakers born in New Spain)
Group 3: Subjects 126-145 (Spanish speakers residing in New Spain)
Group 4: Subjects 146-177 (Speakers of Portuguese and Spanish)
Group 5: Subjects 178-200 (African or Afro-Hispanic speakers)
Group 6: Subjects 201-221 (Speakers of other European languages)

1. Ana de Segura n de Çaja residente en Mexico 1532
2. Alvaro de Ordaz n de Castro Verde de Campos, stante en Mexico 1537
3. Alvaro Matheos n de Medellin vez de Mexico 1539
4. Alonso Garcia Cordero ortelano n de Sevilla 1551
5. Ana Hernandez la serrana partera n de Toledo vez de Guaxaca 1560
6. Alonso de Castilla librero n de Castilla en el Reyno de Toledo 1563
7. Alonso de Scalante n de Sevilla casado dos vezes, açotes, coroça y destierro 1563
8. Ana de Çayas n de ciudad Rodrigo 1567
9. Anton de Sepulveda carpintero n de Pozo Blanco 1567
10. Antonio de Sosa n de Canaria vez de Xocotlan 1569
11. Antonio Diaz de Pangoa n de Almagro 1570
12. Antonio Garcia n de Salamanca vez de Guadalaxara 1570
13. Alonso de la Pena espadero n del Romeral en el Reyno de Toledo 1574
14. Alonso Garcia marinero n y vez de la ciudad de Cadiz en el Andaluzia 1574
15. Asencio Lopez ventero n de la Villa de Belmonte 1574
16. Alvaro Fernandez arcabuçero n del Valle de Monterrey en Galizia 1575
17. Antonio de Sandoval n de Huete Obispado de Cuenca 1576
18. Ana de Figueroa n de la ciudad de Leon en Castilla estante en Mexico 1582
19. Agustin de Goz Calderon n de la Villa de Poza en Espana, residente de la Villa de Çamora Obispado de Mechuacan 1584
20. Antonio de Aseuedo y por otro nombre Luis de Azevedo n de la villa de Tordesillas en Spana tratante de Guaxaca 1584
21. Antonio Perez sastre n del Puerto de Santa Maria vez de la Parroquia en la provincia de Avalos 1592
22. Alonso de la Polla n de Lepantevedra Galizia 1592
23. Alvaro de Carrion n de Cerbera de Riopisuerga en los reynos de Castilla, rresidente de Tilquautla junto a las minas de Pachuca 1601
24. Alvaro Zambrano n de la Villa de la Parra en Extremadura 1601
25. Adrian Garcia marinero n de la çiudad de Sanlucar de Barrameda 1605
26. Augustin de San Bernardo de la orden de San Agustin de la provincia de los Reies en el Peru n de Triana 1608
27. Alonso Martin Collado architeto n de la villa de Junquilla en el Obispado de Murcia 1615
28. Antonia Tellovez de la Vera n de la villa de Alçna Alcaçar en el aljarafe de Sevilla 1626

29. Beatriz Gomez muger de Alvaro Matheos sastre vez de Mexico n del Almendral 1539
30. Bernardo de Arenillas n de fuente de don Bermudo 1567
31. Bartolome de Scobar carpintero n de Sanlucar de Barrameda vez de Mexico 1574
32. Bartolome Sanchez herrero n del Puerto de Santa Maria 1575
33. Bartolome de Altube y por otro nombre Olaçava cuchillero vizcaino n de San Sebastian 1576
34. Bernabe Galan n de Almodovar del Campo en Castilla vez del lugar de Yçucar en la Nueva Espana 1596
35. Bartolome Alfonso n de Cangas de Gines en Asturias 1596
36. Bartholome Gonçalez n de la villa de Guia en Canaria vez de la villa de Valladolid 1601
37. Beatriz de Morales por otro nombre Beatriz de Ribera muger de Juan Martin de Garnica n de Sanlucar de Alpechin 1603
38. Fray Buenabentura de Ayarçe de la orden de San Francisco n de los caserios llamados de Ayarçe en la provincia de Guipuzcoa 200 leguas de la villa de Azpitia 1612
39. Christoval Ruiz harriero n de las minas de Valdeiglesias 1537
40. Catalina de Vargas beata n de Xerez de la Frontera 1557
41. Catalina Muniz n de la Villa de Moguer en el Condado de Niebla 1566
42. Christobal Lobo n del puerto de Sancta Maria en los Reynos de Castilla 1598
43. Clara Gonçalez n de Fuenteovejuna muger de Andres de Molina çapatero vez de Mexico 1589
44. Christoval de Castro Verde n de Sevilla vez de las minas de Pachuca 1621
45. Doctor Pedro de la Torre medico stante en la Veracruz n de Logrono 1538
46. Diego Leal n de la Rambla aldea de Cordova calçetero, stante en Guatemala 1567
47. Dona Marina de Peralta biuda vez de Mexico n de Granada 1576
48. Doctor Pedro de Santander medico de Veracruz n de Çija 1561
49. Diego Lopez Mesonero n del Puerto Maria 1562
50. Domingo Garcia labrador n de Mejorada arçobispado de Toledo 1583
51. Diego de Peramato n de ciudad Rodrigo 1570
52. Diego de Cordoba çapatero n de Sta. Olalla en el Reyno de Toledo 1575
53. Diego Gomez Flores n de Guarena aldea de Medellin vez de Toluca 1575
54. Diego Arias de Rivera n de Sevilla y procurador en las minas de Guanajuato 1576
55. Diego Madero y por otro nombre de Montesinos n de Villanueva de los Ynfantes vez de Zonquitlan obispado de Guaxaca 1577
56. Diego Munoz labrador n de la villa Azuaga en Extremadura 1577
57. Dona Margarita Pacheco biuda n de Barcelona 1577
58. Domingo de Torres cuchillero n de la Villa de Azpeitia en Guiposcoa stante en Mexico 1589
59. Diego de Monrroy n de Granada clerigo presbitero Ben(eficia)do de Tutupeque 1593
60. Domingo de Arguila scrivano publico de Queretaro n de la villa de Larrio en el Senorio de Biscaya 1626
61. Diego Alonso Cepero soldado de la China de la compania del capitan don Fernando de Silva n de la villa de la Gineta en La Mancha en el Obispado de Murcia 1609
62. Dionysio de Torres Cabeça de Moro cirujano vez de las Minas de San Luis n de la çiudad de Sevilla 1610
63. Diego Hernandez n del pueblo de Garachico en la Ysla de Tenerife vez de Chalco 1610
64. Don Francisco Enrriquez de Ribera n de la ciudad de Zara en el Reyno de Granada 1610
65. Diego Gonçalez Carmona n de Araçena en el arçobispado de Sevilla 1615
66. Diego Jimenez Minino n de Alcaçar de Cons[u]egra en el arçobispado de Toledo 1603

67. Don Guillen de Gabazos n de Sevilla 1579
68. Duarte Rodriguez n dela c. de Valencia 1642
69. Doña Ysabel Tristán n de Sevilla viuda de Luis Fernandez Tristan vez desta ciudad 1642
70. Domingo de Arguila scrivano publico de Queretaro n de la villa de Larrio en el Senorio de Biscaya 1626
71. Esperança Valenciana n de la çiudad de Valencia, stante en Mexico 1539
72. El Bachiller Bartolome Barriga clerigo del Obispado de Nicaragua n de Caçalla 1598
73. Francisco Ximenez n de Guadalcanal blasfemo 1537
74. Francisco de Soto n del hospital del Rey de Burgos, Receptor de la Audiencia Real 1577
75. Fray Miguel de Oropeza de la Orden de San Francisco n de la Puebla de la Calzada en Extremadura 1577
76. Francisco Marino clerigo presbitero de Nicaragua n de Araçena arçobispado de Sevilla 1577
77. Fray Pedro de Onate n de la Villa de Oñate 1583
78. Francisco Garcia harriero vez del pueblo de Atrisco, n de Fonseca junto a Toledo 1603
79. Francisco Rodriguez de Ledesma n de la Villa de Barrueco de Salamanca que va y viene a Cartagena 1603
80. Francisco Lopez Bermudez sastre y hotelano naçido en la çiudad de Sanlucar de Barrameda vez de la çiudad de Puebla 1612
81. Gonzalo de Morales tendero n de Sevilla vez de Mexico 1528
82. Gonçalo Avila minero vez de Çacatecas n de Almodovar del Campo 1574
83. Gonçalo Hernandez de Hermosillo n de la çiudad de Antequera en el Reino de Granada, residente en las minas de Tasco arçobispado de Mexico 1590
84. Gregorio Ruis çapatero n de Triana en Sevilla vez de las minas de Sanct Luis 1596
85. Gaspar de Villafranca n de la ciudad de Horiguela en el Reyno de Valencia 1596
86. Lorenço Gutierrez vez de las minas de Guaxacatlan n de Cervera de Aragon 1568
87. Luis Martin ortelano n de Ayamonte residente en la Guerta de los Espindolas junto a Tacuba 1605
88. Lucia Ponce de Leon n de la çiudad de Sevilla vez de Mexico 1617
89. Leonardo Pardo n de la çiudad de Cordoba vez de la nueva Veracruz 1621
90. Luis de Castro fraile religioso sacerdote de la orden de Santo Domingo en la nueva España n de la çiudad de Sevilla 1626
91. Miguel de Armillas y mudado el nombre Gonçalo de Herrera n de la çiudad de Çaracoça en el Reyno de Aragon vez de la çiudad de la vieja Guatemala 1609
92. Nicolas de Espindola n de Xerez de la Frontera 1635
93. Pedro Garcia lario ressidente en las minas de Guautle n de Torrezilla de los Cameros junto a la ciudad de Logrono 1596
94. Rodrigo del Campo escribano publico y del rumbo de Mexico n de la villa de Quintanar de la orden en el obispado de Cuenca 1603
95. Rodrigo Lorenço n de la villa de Guelba en el condado en los Reynos de Castilla 1620
96. Fray Sebastian Ruiz sacerdote religioso de la orden de Santo Domingo de la provincia de Guatemala n de la Villa de Villajermosa en el Reino de Toledo 1620
97. Anton Martin n de Valdetorres vez de Granada de la Provincia de Nicaragua 1567
98. Gonzalo Hernandez de Hermosillo n de la ciudad de Antequera en el Reyno de Granada 1590
99. Beatriz de Morales por otro nombre Beatriz de Ribera muger de Juan Martin de Garica n de S[an]lucar de Alpechin [Sevilla] 1603

100. Tomas Trevino de sobremonte vez dela ciudad de Antequera deel Valle de Guajaca n de la Villa de Medina de Rioseco en Castilla la vieja 1649
101. Andres Ortiz n de Durango [Nueva Vizcaya] 1567
102. Andres Vazquez de Granada moço soltero n de la çiudad de Mexico 1598
103. Antonio de Cabrera Hespañol n de la çiudad de Guayangares en la provincia de Mechoacan 1603
104. Bartolome Hernandez castizo harriero n de la ciudad de los Angeles 1576
105. Beatriz Fernandez mestiça n de Ocotepex Arçobispado de Mexico vez de Tasco 1574
106. Bartolome Rodriguez mestizo n del valle de Toluca residente en el pueblo de Ijilyotla 1621
107. Domingo Rodríguez mestizo de la Puebla de los Angeles 1615
108. Diego de Heredia soldado mestiço n de la ciudad de Antequera 1569
109. Fray Juan de Saldaña n de la ciudad de Guadalaxara en el Nuevo Reino de Galizia 1584
110. Francisco Hernandez n de la çiudad de Puebla de los Angeles mestiço 1605
111. Andres Mexia clerigo del Obispado de Yucatan n de la ciudad de los Angeles 1590
112. Maria Leonor mestiza n de la çiudad de Mexico vez de la Puebla de los Angeles 1613
113. Francisco de Rojas mestizo residente en el pueblo de Xaltepec n de Guayangares 1610
114. Francisco Hernandez mestizo n del pueblo de Tecamachalco 1610
115. Elena de la Cruz monja professa del monastrio de la conçebiçion n de Mexico 1568
116. Elvira de Lares mestiza n de la Villa de San Ildefonso 1569
117. El alferez Sebastian de bargas vez de la çiudad de Manila n de la de Mexico 1620
118. Fray Pedro de Cuellar sacerdote de la Orden de Santo Domingo n de Mexico 1577
119. Franco. Hernandez n de la ciudad de Puebla de los Angeles mestiço 1605
120. Gaspar de los Reyes ressidente en las minas de San Luis n de Mexico mercader tratante 1602
121. Gaspar Perez mestiço çapatero n de Guatemala vez de Lerena obispado de Guadalaxara simple fornicación auto publico açotes y destierro 1574
122. Marcos Ruiz mestiço harriero n de Guaxaca 1583
123. Maria Leonor mestiza n de la ciudad de Mexico vez de la Puebla de los Angeles 1613
124. Nicolas Pacheco mestiço n de Merida de Campeche 1646
125. Pero Sanchez de Reyna n de la villa de San Ildefonso en los çapotecas 1569
126. Anton Sanchez Gavilan tratante que reside en Guaxutla 1595
127. Alonso de Ruuio harriero vez de Guaxaca 1561
128. Francisco de Castellon vez de la ciudad de San Salvador Obispado de Guatimala 1566
129. Alonso de Toledo scrivano de Mechoacan 1570
130. Anna Maria muger de Bartolome Garcia calafate vez de la Vera Cruz hechizera 1596
131. Gonzalo de Salazar mestizo vez de la ciudad de Mexico 1596
132. Anton de Castilla clerigo beneficiado del pueblo de Nacaxuxuca en la provincia de Yucatan 1600
133. Bartolome Perez blasfemo 1563
134. Cathalina Bermudez muger de Spinossa vez barbero de la Vera Cruz 1596
135. Doña Juana de Aguirre muger de Juan Ramirez vez de Puebla de los Angeles 1596
136. Doña Leonor Maldonado mujer de Bernardo franquez vez dela ciudad de Veracruz 1596
137. Diego de Porras Vellerias vez de Mexico estudiante en la facultad de Leyes 1598
138. Fran(co) Sanchez harriero vez de Jacona Obispado de Mechuacan 1571
139. Fray Dionisio de la Cruz clerigo del obispado de Tlaxcala 1590
140. Franco. de Vallejo hijo de Pedro de Vallejo vez del pueblo de Sanct Simon 1603

141. Franco. Lopez del Salto presbitero de los pueblos de Huitepec y Estetla en los peñones en el Obispado de Guadalajara 1611
142. Gaspar de la Tapia vez de Guadalaxara 1561
143. Geronimo de Spinossa ressidente en Mexico 1596
144. Hernan de Alvarez clerigo del Obispado de Guatemala 1567
145. Lucia de Alcala biuda vez de la ciudad de Veracruz 1596
146. Alonso Amado portugues n de Huelva palabras malsonantes 1540
147. Alonso Delgado n de Cumbres Baxas a la Raya de Portugal 1541
148. Antonio Mexia n de Campomayor en Portugal 1559
149. Andres Rodriguez n del Fondon en Portugal mercader ressidente en Tezcuco 1596
150. Antonio Rodriguez difunto portugues moço soltero vez dela ciudad de Mexico n dela Villa de Mogadouro 1601
151. Antonio Gomez portugues n del Fondon vez de Mexico, tratante 1601
152. Alvaro Rodriguez abogado portugues vez de Mexico 1601
153. Doña Ana Xuarez n de Mexico hija de Gaspar Xuarez n de Lamega en Portugal 1648
154. Antonio Vaz Tirado Alias capitan Castelo Blanco n de Castelo Blanco en el Reino de Portugal residente en Mexico por judaizante 1649
155. Doña Blanca Enriquez n de Lisboa vez de la Nueva Veracruz de hedad de 50 años 1644
156. Catalina Enriquez muger de Manuel de Lucona portugues vez de las minas de Pachuca 1596
157. Constança Rodriguez muger de Sebastian Rodriguez portugues tratante en mercadurias 1596
158. doña Felipa de Atayde portuguesa n de Lisboa vez de Mexico 1577
159. Domingo Rodriguez portugues tratante residente en la ciudad de Manila de las Philipinas 1593
160. Domingo Cuello portugues tratante en la provincia de Mechoacan n de la ciudad de la Braga en Portugal 1596
161. dona Francisca Nunez de Carvajal n de la Villa de Mogadoro en la Raya de Portugal vez de Mexico judaizante relapsa relaxada en persona 1596
162. dona Isabel Rodriguez de Adrada su hija n de Benavente en Castilla viuda de Gabriel de Herrera vez de Mexico 1596
163. dona Catalina de Leon tambien su hija n de la Villa de Benavente muger de Antonio Diaz de Caceres vez de Mexico judaizante relapsa en persona 1596
164. dona Leonor de Andrada tambien su hija de la dicha Villa de Benavente 1596
165. Duarte Rodriguez n de Cuvillana en Portugal 1596
166. Dona Mariana de Carvajal donzella hija de Francisco Rodriguez de Matos portugues relaxado en estatua por el Santo Officio por la guarda y observancia de la Ley Muerta de Moyssen n de Benavente en los Reynos de Castilla, y de dona Francisca de Carvajal, muger relapsa relaxada en persona por judaizante 1601
167. Dona Anna de Carvajal donzella n de Benavente hija de Francisco Rodriguez de Matos relaxado en estatua por judaizante 1601
168. Jorge Rodriguez portugues moço soltero n de la çiudad de Sevilla 1601
169. Diego Lopez Regalon n del Fondon en el Reyno de Portugal vez de Mexico 1601
170. Ruy Diez Nieto n de la ciudad de Oporto en el Reyno de Portugal 1601
171. Diego Hernandez Vitoria difunto vez de la ciudad de Manila sospechoso judio 1610
172. Domingo Diez alias Domingo Rodriguez portugues n de esta ciudad de Mexico vez de la Puebla de los Angeles 1615

173. Diego de Losada portugues n de la Villa de Lemos en el Reino de Galizia 1625
174. Domingo de Sosa Donado de la Orden de San Francisco de nacion portugues n de la çiudad de Lisboa 1626
175. Diego Perez de Alburquerque portugues vez de la Puebla de los Angeles n de la çiudad de Burdeos en Francia 1630
176. Mariana de Lemos alias Mariana Gomez portuguesa n de la Villa del Fuyal en las Islas de las Terceras 1626
177. Simon Montero Portuges n de Castelo Blanco mercader vez de Sevilla residente en Mexico 1635
178. Ana Cavallero mulata vez de Mexico 1575
179. Ana Perez negra libre n de Valencia de Aragon 1577
180. Anton de Arenas mulato portuguee n de Telmoz 1578
181. Diego negro criollo esclavo de Diego Cano obragero de Mexico 1610
182. Domingo Vaca esclavo de Sebastian Vaca vez de Mexico 1610
183. Anton negro criollo n de la ciudad de Cartagena esclavo de Alvaro de la Rosa tavernero, vez de Mexico 1601
184. Agustin mulato esclavo de Andres Bueno Batihoja vez de Mexico 1601
185. Anton de Cartagena negro esclavo de Hernando Alvarez en los altos de Tlalnepantla 1600
186. Andres de Loya negro esclavo de Fran(co) Alvarez obragero vez de la Villa de Cuyoacan 1605
187. Ana de Vega mulata curandera n de la Puebla de los Angeles 1649
188. Anton de la Cruz negro de Santa Benguela [Angola] esclavo de Gabriel 1652
189. Agustina de Zevallos alias la cumba mulata n de Cartagena de Indias vez de la nueva Veracruz 1655
190. Beatriz de Padilla mulata libre n dela villa de los Lagos [Nueva Galicia] 1652
191. Christobal negro criollo esclavo de Joan Hernandez de Gamboa 1659
192. Domingo negro criollo esclavo de Gaspar de los Reyes 1596
193. Diego Hernandez mulato libre de la ciudad de Guadalaxara en la Nueva Galizia que mudado el nombre se llama Diego Hernandez Valades y Diego Hernandez Coleto 1607
194. Diego de la Cruz negro desta ciudad esclavo de Bartolome Valfermoso clerigo presvitero vez de la ciudad de Tescuco 1650
195. Esperança Rodriguez mulata n de Sevilla viuda de Joan Baptista del Bosque aleman vez desta ciudad 1642
196. Franco. Granados mulato libre n de Mexico 1571
197. Francisco de Castañeda mulato libre n de Mexico 1610
198. Franco. mulato criollo n de la ciudad de Mexico esclavo de Pedro Lopez de Rivera vez della 1610
199. Franco. de Santiago mulato libre n de Abrantes en Portugal 1613
200. Luis negro ladino esclavo de don Juan de Saavedra vez de Mexico 1596
201. Andrea de Rodas Griego marinero de Cozon de la Ysla de Rodas, stante en Mexico 1528
202. Andres Morab aleman lapidario n de Bruna en la Provinçia Morab [Moravia] vez de Mexico 1536
203. Andrea Jacome n de Bergamo en Lombardia 1563
204. Anton de Niça n de Villafranca de Niças tierras del Duque de Saboya 1577
205. Alberto de Meyo n de la Villa de Eclo en Flandes tonelero en la calle de Tacuba 1601
206. Adrian Cornelius n de la ciudad de Hitanclaz en los estados de Olanda 1601
207. Charles de Salignate barbero frances 1561

208. Cornelius Adriano Cessar n de la ciudad de Arlem en Holanda 1601
209. Christoval Miguel n de la ciudad de Nimeguen en el Ducado de Gueldres en Flandes 1601
210. David Alexandro Yngles n de Souixx 1574
211. Daniel Borgoñon (Bretaña) n de la ciudad de Damcie, rresidente en Tecamachalco, sospechoso de herege luterano y luego judaizante en su prision 1569
212. Duarte Olander alias Rodrigo Jacobo n del lugar de Estenuis en los estados de Flandes por herege Calvino reconciliado y que no salga de esta nueva Hespaña sin licencia 1601
213. Diego del Valle flamenco de la ciudad de Midelburg por herege Calvino reconciliado que este recluso en la parte que se le señalare 1601
214. Enrique de Olanda çapatero n de la ciudad de Amçerdama en la provincia de Olanda en Alemania la Baxa vez de la villa de Campeche 1569
215. Fray Cornelio de Vie n de la Haya en la Isla de Olanda en los estados de Flandes, sacerdote profeso de la orden de San Agustin 1583
216. Guillermo Corniels yrlandes barbero n de Corço vez de la villa de la Trinidad, Obispado de Guatemala 1575
217. Lorenço Gueset frances n de Ave de Gracia en Normandia 1560
218. Martin Cornu barbero frances n de Roan 1574
219. Marcelo Miraelo n de la ciudad de Amancia, Napoles 1601
220. Simon de Santiago n del pueblo de Vildesbussen junto a la ciudad de Bremen en Alemania la baxa, residente en Mexico por herege Calvino relaxado en persona 1601
221. Simon Canobloch apartador del oro de la plata n de la ciudad de Greinfemberg en Alemania la Alta 1603

References

Abecedario de relaxados, reconciliados y penitenciados en la Nueva España: 1571-1700 (Henry E. Huntington Library HM 35096). Mexico City: Santo Officio.

Acevedo, Rebeca. 1997. *El español del Altiplano central mexicano durante la época colonial. Reducción del paradigma verbal*. University of Michigan Ph.D. dissertation.

Aguilar Moreno, Manuel. 2002 The *indio ladino* as a cultural mediator in the colonial society. *Estudios de Cultura Náhuatl* 33: 149-184.

Aguirre Beltrán, Gonzalo. 1972. *La población negra de México. Estudio etnohistórico*. Mexico: Fondo de Cultura Económica.

Alarcos Llorach, Emilio. 1968. *Fonología española*, 4th edn. Madrid: Gredos.

Alberrro, Solange. 1988. *Inquisición y sociedad en México: 1571-1700*. Mexico: Fondo de Cultura Económica.

Alonso, Amado. 1953/1961. *Estudios lingüísticos. Temas hispanoamericanos*. Madrid: Gredos.

Althoff, Francis Daniel. 1998. *The Afro-Hispanic Speech of the Municipio of Cuajinicuilapa, Guerrero*. University of Florida Ph. D. dissertation.

Altman, Ida. 2000. *Transtlantic ties in the Spanish Empire. Birhuega, Spain and Puebla, Mexico: 1560-1620*. Stanford, CA: Stanford University Press.

Álvarez Nazario, Manuel. 1982. *Orígenes y desarrollo del español en Puerto Rico (siglos XVI y XVII)*. Río Piedras: Universidad de Puerto Rico.

Arias Álvarez, Beatriz. 1996a. *El español de México en el siglo XVI. Estudio filológico de quince documentos*. Mexico: Universidad Nacional Autónoma de México.

Arias Álvarez, Beatriz. 1996b. Motivación de la alternancia *les/los* en documentos novohispanos del siglo XVI. *Contextos* 16 (27-28): 49-64.

Arias Álvarez, Beatriz. 1996c. El orden de colocación de los clíticos pronominales durante la primera mitad del siglo XVI. *Revista de Humanidades* 1: 128-137.

Arias Álvarez, Beatriz. 1997. Nuevamente sobre las sibilantes. *Anuario de Letras* 35: 43-59.

Arias Álvarez, Beatriz. 2004/2005. Caracterización de los sonidos sibilantes del castellano. El origen de las dento-alveolares medievales. *Anuario de Letras* 42: 33-49.

Arias Álvarez, Beatriz (coord.). 2014. *Documentos públicos y privados del siglo XVI: textos para la historia del español colonial mexicano* I. Mexico: Universidad Nacional Autónoma de México.

Arias Álvarez, Beatriz and Gloria Estela Báez. 1996. Reconstrucción del sistema de sibilantes del español a través de la transliteración de nahuatlismos. *Estudios de Lingüística Aplicada* 23-24: 15-28.

Asratian, Arucia. 2007. Variación –RA / –SE en el español hablado en Caracas. *Boletín de Lingüística* 19 (27): 5-41.

Assadourian, Carlos Sempat. 1989. La despoblación indígena en el Perú y Nueva España durante el siglo XVI y la formación de la economía colonial. *Historia Mexicana* 38/(3): 419-453.

Assadourian, Carlos Sempat. 2006. Agriculture and land tenure in pre-and post-conquest. In Victor Bulmer-Thomas, John B. Coastworth and Roberto Cortés Conde (eds.), *The Cambridge Economic History of Latin America*, Vol. 1, 275-341. Cambridge University Press.

Aureliano, Ramón, Ana C. Castro and Susana López Sánchez. 1996. *Índice de Las gacetas de literatura de México de José Antonio Alzate y Ramírez*. Mexico: Instituto Mora.

Bakewell, Peter J. 1971. *Silver Mining and Society in Colonial Mexico. Zacatecas: 1546-1700*. Cambridge University Press.
Bakewell, Peter J. 1997a. *A history of Latin America. Empires and sequels: 1450-1930*. Oxford: Blackwell.
Bakewell, Peter J. 1997b. Introduction. In Peter J. Bakewell (ed.), *Mines of Silver and Gold in the Americas* (An Expanding World 19), xiii-xxiv. Aldershot and Brookfield: Variorum.
Bakewell, Peter J. 1997c. Notes on the Mexican silver mining industry in the 1590's. In Peter J. Bakewell (ed.), *Mines of Silver and Gold in the Americas* (An Expanding World 19), 171-198. Aldershot and Brookfield: Variorum.
Bakewell, Peter J. (ed.). 1997. *Mines of Silver and Gold in the Americas* (An Expanding World 19). Aldershot and Brookfield: Variorum.
Bello, Andrés. 1847/1857. *Gramática de la lengua castellana destinada al uso de los americanos*. Santiago de Chile. (Reprinted in Bogota in 1860 by Echavarría Hermanos).
Bello, Andrés. 1954. *Gramática de la lengua castellana destinada al uso de los americanos*. Buenos Aires: Editorial Sopena.
Bello, Andrés and Rufino J. Cuervo. 1874/1881/1954. *Gramática de la lengua castellana*. Edited, revised, and annotated by Niceto Alcalá-Zamora y Torres. Buenos Aires: Editorial Sopena.
Benítez, Fernando 1953/1985. *Los primeros mexicanos. La vida criolla en México en el siglo XVI*. Mexico: Fondo de Cultura Económica.
Bermúdez Plata, Cristóbal. 1940-1986. *Catálogo de pasajeros a Indias durante los siglos XVI, XVII y XVIII*. Seville: Archivo General de Indias.
Blackburn, Robin. 1998. *The Making of New World Slavery: from Baroque to the Modern (1492-1800)*. London: Verso.
Blanco, José Joaquín. 1989. *La literatura en la Nueva España. Conquista y Nuevo Mundo*. Mexico: Cal y Arena.
Boyd-Bowman, Peter. 1964. *Índice geobiográfico de cuarenta mil pobladores españoles de América en el siglo XVI: 1493-1519*. Vol.1. Bogota: Instituto Caro y Cuervo.
Boyd-Bowman, Peter. 1968. *Índice geobiográfico de cuarenta mil pobladores españoles de América en el siglo XVI: 1520-1539* (Academia Mexicana de Genealogía y Heráldica). Vol. 2. Mexico: Editorial Jus.
Boyd-Bowman, Peter. 1976. Patterns of Spanish Emigration to the Indies until 1600. *Hispanic American Historical Review* 56: 580-604.
Boyd-Bowman, Peter. 1985. *Indice geobiográfico de más de 56 mil pobladores de la América Hispánica*. Mexico: Fondo de Cultura Económica.
Brading, David A. 1971. *Miners and Merchants in Bourbon Mexico: 1763-1810*. Cambridge University Press.
Brown, Cecil H. 2011. The Role of Nahuatl in the Formation of Mesoamerica as a Linguistic Area. *Language Dynamics and Change* 1 (2): 171-204.
Calvet, Louis-Jean. 1999. *Puor une écologie des langues du monde*. Paris: Plon.
Carrera de la Red, Micaela. 1998. Grafías y grafemas representativos de sibilantes en documentos dominicanos de los siglos XVI y XVII. Propuesta de análisis. In José M. Blecua, Juan Gutiérrez and Lidia Sala (eds.), *Estudios de grafemática en el dominio hispánico*, 25-36. Salamanca: Universidad de Salamanca/Instituto Caro y Cuervo.
Carroll, Patrick J. 1991. *Blacks in Colonial Veracruz: Race, Ethnicity and Regional Development*. Austin, TX: University of Texas Press.

Castillo, Norma A. 2005. La pérdida de la población de origen africano en la región de Puebla. In María E. Velázquez Gutiérrez and Ethel Correa Duró (eds.), *Pobalciones y culturas de origen africano en México*, 299-325. Mexico: Instituto Nacional de Antropología e Historia.

Castro Aranda, Hugo. 2010. *Primer Censo de la Nueva España 1790. Censo de Revillagigedo: "Un censo condenado"*. Mexico: Instituto Nacional de Geografía y Estadística.

Catalán, Diego. 1956-1957. El çeçeo-zezeo al comenzar la expansión atlántica de Castilla. *Botetim de Filología* 16: 306-334.

Catalán, Diego. 1957. The end of the phoneme /z/ in Spanish. *Word* 13: 283-322.

Cebrián, José. 2003. *Desde el siglo Ilustrado. Sobre periodismo y crítica en el Siglo XVIII*. Seville: Universidad de Sevilla.

Cervantes de Salazar, Francisco. 1554/1988. *México en 1554. Tres diálogos latinos*. Introduction by Margarita Peña. Mexico: Trillas. (Translated from Latin by Joaquín García Icazbalceta)

Cervantes de Salazar, Francisco. 1560. *Túmulo Imperial de la gran ciudad de México*. Mexico: Casa de Antonio de Espinosa.

Cohen, Martin A. 2001. *The Martyr Luis de Carvajal. A Secret Jew in Sixteenth Century Mexico*. Albuquerque, NM: University of New Mexico Press.

Company Company, Concepción. 1994. *Documentos lingüísticos de la Nueva España: El Altiplano Central*. Mexico: Universidad Nacional Autónoma de México.

Company Company, Concepción. 1994a. Semántica y sintaxis de los posesivos duplicados en el español de los siglos XV y XVI. *Romance Philology* 48 (3): 111-135.

Company Company, Concepción. 1997. El costo gramatical de las cortesías en el español americano. Las consecuencias sintácticas de la pérdida de *vosotros*. *Anuario de Letras* 35: 167-191.

Company Company, Concepción. 2002a. Reanálisis en cadena y gramaticalización. Dativos problemáticos en la historia del español. *VERBA* 29: 31-69.

Company Company, Concepción. 2002b. Gramaticalización y dialectología comparada: Una isoglosa semántico-sintáctica del español. *DICENDA. Cuadernos de Filología Hispánica* 20: 39-71.

Company Company, Concepción. 2004. ¿Gramaticalización o desgramaticalización? Reanálisis y subjetivización de verbos como marcadores discursivos en la historia del español. *Revista de Filología Española* 84 (1): 29-66.

Company Company, Concepción. 2008. The directionality of grammaticalization in Spanish. *Journal of Historical Pragmatics* 9 (2): 200-224.

Company Company, Concepción. 2012. El español del siglo XVIII. Un parteaguas lingüístico entre España y México. In María T. García Godoy (ed.), 255-291. *Cambios diacrónicos en el primer español moderno*. Bern: Peter Lang.

Conde-Silvestre, Juan C. 2007. *Sociolingüística histórica*. Madrid: Gredos.

Consejo Nacional de Población (ed.) 1993. *El poblamiento de México*, Vol.2. Mexico: Consejo Nacional de Población.

Cortés, Eladio. 1992. *Dictionary of Mexican Literature*. Westport: Greenwood Press.

Cortés, Hernán. 1520/1866. *Cartas y relaciones de Hernán Cortés al Emperador Carlos V*. (Introduction, collection and illustrations by Don Pascual de Gayangos). Paris: Imprenta Central de los Ferrocarriles.

Cortés, Hernán. 1520/2007. *Cartas de relación*. Mexico: Porrúa.

Cortés, Hernán. 1522. *Carta de relación embiada a su Santa Majestad del Emperador nuestro señor* (Henry E. Huntington Library RB 108651). Seville: Casa de Jacobo Cromberger.

Cortés, Hernán. 1523. *Carta tercera de relacion embiada por Fernando Cortes* (Henry E. Huntington Library RB 108652). Seville: Casa de Jacobo Cromberger.
Cuervo, Rufino J. 1893/1954. Las segundas personas de plural en la conjugación castellana, In *Obras II*, 138-166. Bogota: Instituto Caro y Cuervo.
Cuervo, Rufino J. 1895. Los casos enclíticos y proclíticos del pronombre de tercera persona en castellano. *Romania* 24: 96-113, 220-263.
Cuervo, Rufino J. 1895/1954. Los casos enclíticos y proclíticos del pronombre de tercera persona en castellano, In *Obras II*, 167-239.
Cuervo, Rufino J. 1898/1954. Disquisiciones sobre antigua ortografía y pronunciación castellanas, In *Obras II*, 240-476.
Cuervo, Rufino J. 1901. El castellano en América. *Bulletin Hispanique* 3: 35-62.
Cuervo, Rufino J. 1901/1954. El castellano en América, In *Obras II*, 518-562.
Cuervo, Rufino J. 1902/1954. Lindo, In *Obras II*, 591-597.
Cuervo, Rufino J. 1907. *Apuntaciones críticas sobre el lenguaje bogotano con frecuente referencia al de los países de Hispano-América, 5th edn*. Paris: A. & R. Roger and F. Chernoviz.
Cuervo, Rufino J. 1914/1954. Apuntaciones críticas sobre el lenguaje bogotano, In *Obras I*, 1-906. Bogota: Instituto Caro y Cuervo.
Cuervo, Rufino J. 1944/1954. Castellano popular y castellano literario, In *Obras I*, 1321-1660.
Chevalier, Francois. 1952/1963. *Land and Society in Colonial Mexico. The Great Hacienda*. (Translated from French by Alvin Eustis). Berkeley: University of California Press.
Chuchiak, John F. 2012. *The Inquisition in New Spain, 1536-1820: A Documentary History*. Baltimore: Johns Hopkins University Press.
DeMello, George. 1993. –Ra vs. –Se subjunctive. A new look at an old topic. *Hispania* 76(2): 235-244.
DeMello, George. 2002. Leísmo in contemporary Spanish American educated Spanish. *Linguistics* 40 (2): 282-263.
Díaz Collazos, Ana M. 2015. *Desarrollo sociolingüístico del voseo en la región andina de Colombia (1555-1976)*. In Claudia Polzin-Haumann and Wolfgang Schweicard (eds.), *Beihefte zur Zeitschrift für romanische Philologie* 392.
Díaz del Castillo, Bernal. 1571/1969. *Historia verdadera de la conquista de la Nueva España*, 7th edn. Introduction and notes by Joaquín Ramírez Cabañas. Mexico: Porrúa.
Douglas, Thomas R. 1982. Notes on the spelling of Philip II. *Hispania* 65 (3): 418-424.
Duverger, Christian. 2007. *El primer mestizaje. La clave para entender el pasado mesoamericano*. Mexico: Taurus.
Entwistle, William J. 1936/1951. *The Spanish Language together with Portuguese, Catalan and Basque*. Cambridge University Press.
Erauso, Catalina de. 1652/2008. *Historia de la Monja Alférez, Catalina de Erauso, escrita por ella misma*. Edited by Ángel Esteban. Madrid: Cátedra.
Espinosa, Aurelio M. 1911. *The Spanish Language in New Mexico and Southern Colorado*. Santa Fe: New Mexican Print (Historical Society of New Mexico).
Farrar, Kimberley and Mari C. Jones. 2002. "Introduction". In Mari C. Jones and Edith Esch (eds.), 1-18. *Language Change: The interplay of Internal, External and Extra-linguistic Factors* (Contributions to the Sociology of Language 86). Berlin: Mouton de Gruyter.
Ferguson, Charles. 1959. Diglossia. *Word* 15: 325-40.

Fernández Christlieb, Federico and Pedro Urquijo Torres. 2006. Los espacios del pueblo de indios tras el proceso de Congregación, 1550-1625. *Investigaciones Geográficas* 60: 145-158.

Fishman, Joshua A. 1972a. *The Sociology of Language. An Interdisciplinary Social Science Approach to Language in Society*. Rowley: Newbury House.

Fishman, Joshua A. 1972b. *Language in Sociocultural Change*. Selection and introduction by Anwar S. Dil. Stanford, CA: Stanford University Press.

Flores Cervantes, Marcela. 1999. Leísmo, laísmo y loísmo en español antiguo. Caso, transitividad y valoraciones pragmáticas. *Romance Philology* 55: 41-74.

Flores Cervantes, Marcela. 2002. *Leísmo, laísmo y loísmo. Sus orígenes y evolución*. Mexico: Universidad Nacional Autónoma de México.

Flórez, Luis. 1973. *Las "Apuntaciones críticas" de Cuervo y el español bogotano cien años después*. Bogota: Instituto Caro y Cuervo.

Fontanella de Weinberg, María Beatriz (ed.) 1993. *Documentos para la historia lingüística de Hispanoamérica. Siglos XVI a XVII*. Madrid: Boletín de la Real Academia Española. Anejo 53.

Forti, Carla. 1989. Letture di Bartolome de las Casas: uno specchio della cosienza, e della falsa coscienza, dell'Occidente attraverso quattro secoli. *Critica Storica* 26: 2-52.

Frago Gracia, Juan A. 1987. Una introducción filológica a la documentación del Archivo General de Indias. *Anuario de Lingüística Hispánica* 3: 67-98.

Frago Gracia, Juan A. 1993. *Historia de las hablas andaluzas*. Madrid: Arcos Libros.

Frago Gracia, Juan A. 1994. *Andaluz y español de América: Historia de un parentesco lingüístico*. Seville: Junta de Andalucía.

Frago Gracia, Juan A. 1999. *Historia del español de América*. Madrid: Gredos.

Francis Soriano, Susana. 1960. *Habla y literatura popular en la antigua capital chiapaneca*. Mexico: Instituto Nacional Indigenista.

Franco, John K. 2004. Blacks in Northern New Spain. *The Journal of Big Bend Studies* 16: 47-58.

García Añoveros, Jesús María. 2000. Carlos V y la abolición de la esclavitud de los indios. Causas, evolución y circunstancias. *Revista de Indias* 60 (218): 57-84.

García Fajardo, Josefina. 1984. *Fonética del español de Valladolid, Yucatán*. Mexico: Universidad Nacional Autónoma de México.

García Fuentes, Lutgardo. 1980. *El comercio español con América: 1650-1700*. Seville: Escuela de Estudios Hispanoamericanos de Sevilla.

García Icazbalceta, Joaquín. 1858-1866. *Colección de documentos para la historia de México*. Mexico: Librería de J. M. Andrade.

García Icazbalceta, Joaquín. 1886. *Bibliografía mexicana del siglo XVI. Primera parte. Catálogo razonado de libros impresos en México de 1539 a 1600 con biografías de autores y otras ilustraciones*. Mexico: Imprenta de Francisco Díaz de León.

García Icazbalceta, Joaquín. 1898/1968. La fiesta del Pendón en México, In *Obras II*, 443-452. New York: Burt Franklin.

Garner, Richard. 1997. Long-term silver mining trends in Spanish America: A comparative analysis of Peru and Mexico. In Peter J. Bakewell (ed.), *Mines of Silver and Gold in the Americas*, 225-262. Aldershot and Brookfield: Variorum.

Garrido Asperó, José María. 1998. Las fiestas celebradas en la ciudad de México. De capital de la Nueva España a capital del Imperio de Agustín I. Permanencias y cambios en la legislación festiva. *Cuadernos del Instituto de Historia del Derecho* 2: 185-201.

Garrido Asperó, José María. 2006. *Fiestas cívicas históricas en la ciudad de México: 1765-1823.* Mexico: Instituto Mora.

Garza Cuarón, Beatriz and Georges Baudot. 1996. *Historia de la literatura mexicana desde sus orígenes hasta nuestros días.* Vol. 1. Mexico: Editorial Siglo XXI.

Gayangos, Pascual. 1866. "Introducción" in *Cartas de Relación de Hernán Cortés al Emperador Carlos V.* Paris: Imprenta Central de los Ferrocarrileros.

Gerhard, Peter. 1977. Congregaciones de indios en la Nueva España antes de 1570. *Historia Mexicana* 26 (13): 347-395.

Gerhard, Peter. 1993. *A Guide to the Historical Geography of New Spain (Revised edn.).* Norman, OK/London: University of Oklahoma Press.

Gibson, Charles. 1964. *The Aztecs under Spanish Rule. A History of the Indians of the Valley of Mexico: 1519-1810.* Stanford, CA: Stanford University Press.

Gonzalbo Aizpuru, Pilar. 1990. *Historia de la educación en la época colonial. El mundo criollo y la vida urbana.* Mexico: El Colegio de México.

González Jiménez, Manuel. 1997. La repoblación de Andalucía: Siglos XIII-XV. *Relaciones. Estudios de Historia y Sociedad* 18 (69): 22-40.

González Peña, Carlos. 1968. *History of Mexican Literature.* Translated from Spanish by G. Barfield Nance and F. Johnson Dunstan. Dallas: Southern Methodist University Press.

Granda, Germán de. 1978. Velarización de Ř en el español de Puerto Rico. In Germán de Granda (ed.), *Estudios Lingüísticos hispánicos, afrohispánicos y criollos,* 11-68. Madrid: Gredos.

Granda, Germán de. 1994. Formación y evolución del español de América. Época colonial. In Germán de Granda (ed.) *Español de América, español de África y hablas criollas hispánicas. Cambios, contactos y contextos,* 49-92. Madrid: Gredos.

Granda, Germán de. 1999. Observaciones metodológicas sobre la investigación lingüística en Hispanoamérica. In Germán de Granda (ed.), *Español y lenguas indoamericanas en Hispanoamérica,* 7-18. Valladolid: Universidad de Valladolid.

Granda, Germán de. 2007. Hacia la diacronía de una forma de tratamiento en el español: *su merced. Lexis* 31 (1-2): 165-175.

Gruzinski, Serge. 1988/1991. *La colonización de lo imaginario. Sociedades indígenas en el México español: Siglos XVI-XVII.* Translated from French by Jorge Ferreiro. Mexico: Fondo de Cultura Económica.

Guirado, Krístel. 2007. La alternancia *para~pa* en tres comunidades de habla de Venezuela. *Interlingüística* 17: 455-464.

Guirado, Krístel. 2011. Allá yo iba pa' estudiar. Un estudio de variación en el habla de jóvenes universitarios caraqueños. *Boletín de Lingüística* 23 (35-36): 57-80.

Guitarte, Guillermo L. and Rafael Torres-Quintero. 1974. Linguistic correctness and the role of the Academies in Latin America. In Joshua A. Fishman (ed.), *Advances in Language Planning,* 315-368. Berlin: Mouton de Gruyter.

Hamilton, Michelle M. 2000. La poesía de Leonor de Carvajal y la tradición de los criptojudíos en Nueva España. *Sefarad. Revista de Estudios Hebraicos, Sefardíes y de Oriente Próximo* 60 (1): 75-93.

Hanke, Lewis. 1949/2002. *The Spanish Struggle for Justice in the Conquest of America.* New Introduction by Susan Scafidi and Peter Bakewell. Dallas: Southern Methodist University Press.

Hanke, Lewis. 1959. *Aristotle and the American Indians: A Study in Race Prejudice in the Modern World.* Chicago: Henry Regnery Co.

Henríquez Ureña, Pedro (ed.). 1938. *El español en Méjico, los Estados Unidos y América Central*. Buenos Aires: Biblioteca de Dialectología Hispanoamericana 4.

Hernández-Campoy, Juan M. and Juan C. Conde-Silvestre (eds.). 2012. *The Handbook of Historical Sociolinguistics*. Malden, MA: Wiley-Blackwell.

Hernández de León-Portilla, Ascención. 1999. Un prólogo en náhuatl suscrito por Bernardino de Sahagún y Alonso de Molina. *Estudios de Cultura Náhuatl* 29: 199-208.

Hernández de León-Portilla, Ascención. 2007. Fray Alonso de Molina y el proyecto indigenista de la Orden Seráfica. *Estudios de Cultura Náhuatl* 36: 63-81.

Hernández Hernández, Esther. 1996. *Vocabulario en lengua castellana y mexicana de fray Alonso de Molina: Estudio de los indigenismos léxicos y registro de las voces españolas internas* (Biblioteca de Filología Hispanica 15). Madrid: Consejo Superior de Investigaciones Científicas.

Hidalgo, Margarita. 1990. The Emergence of Standard Spanish in the American Continent. *Language Problems and Language Planning* 14 (1): 47-63.

Hidalgo, Margarita. 2001a. One century of study in New World Spanish. *International Journal of the Sociology of Language* 149: 9-32.

Hidalgo, Margarita. 2001b. Sociolinguistic stratification in New Spain. *International Journal of the Sociology of Language* 149: 55-78.

Hidalgo, Margarita. 2002. Review of Germán de Granda. *Español y lenguas indoamericanas en Hispanoamérica: Estructuas, variaciones y transferencias* (1999). *Language in Society* 31(1): 137-142.

Hidalgo, Margarita. 2006a. The multiple dimensions of language maintenance and shift in colonial Mexico. In Margarita Hidalgo (ed.) *Mexican Indigenous Languages at the Dawn of the Twenty-First Century* (Contributions to the Sociology of Language 91). 53-86. Berlin: Mouton de Gruyter.

Hidalgo, Margarita. 2006b. Language policy. Past, present, and future. In Margarita Hidalgo (ed.), *Mexican Indigenous Languages at the Dawn of the Twenty-First Century* (Contributions to the Sociology of Language 91). 357-376. Berlin: Mouton de Gruyter.

Hidalgo, Margarita.2008. Language contact in South America. *International Journal of the Sociology of Language* 189: 165-169.

Hidalgo, Margarita. 2011. El español de América en los archivos de la Inquisición. Nueva España (1527-1635). *Anuario de Lingüística Hispánica* 27: 71-94.

Hidalgo, Margarita. 2013. Estratificación sociolingüística y koineización en Nueva España. Siglo XVI. *Anuario de Lingüística Hispánica* 29: 33-56.

Himmerich y Valencia. 1991. *The encomenderos of New Spain, 1521-1555*. Austin: University of Texas Press.

Holler, Jacqueline. 2007. Conquered spaces, colonial skirmishes: Spatial contestation in sixteenth century Mexico City. *Radical History Review* 99: 107-120.

Hordes, Stanley M. 2007. Between toleration and persecution: The relationship between the Inquisition and Crypto-Jews on the northern frontier. In Susan Schroeder and Stafford Poole (eds.), *Religion in New Spain*, 218-237. Albuquerque, NM: University of New Mexico Press.

Hummel, Martin, Bettina Kluge and María E. Vázquez Laslop (eds.). 2010. *Formas y fórmulas de tratamiento en el mundo hispánico*. Mexico and Graz: El Colegio de México and Karl Franzens Universität Graz.

Illades, Lilián. 2008. Los espacios del pregón. *Nuevo Mundo/Mundos Nuevos*. Puebla: Benemérita Universidad Autónoma de Puebla. (Online document retrieved January 2, 2008).
Jaksić, Ivan. 2001. *Andrés Bello. Scholarship and Nation-building in Nineteenth-century Latin America* (Latin American Studies 87). Cambridge University Press.
Jones, Mari C. and Edith Esch (eds.) 2002. *Language Change. The interplay of Internal, External and Extra-linguistic Factors* (Contributions to the Socioloogy of Language 86). Berlin: Mouton de Gruyter.
Kany, Charles E. 1945. *American-Spanish Syntax*. Chicago: University of Chicago Press.
Kany, Charles E. 1960. *American-Spanish Semantics*. Chicago: University of Chicago Press.
Kerswill, Paul. 2006. Koineization and accommodation. In J. K. Chambers; Peter Trudgill and Natalie Schilling-Estetes (eds.) *The Handbook of Language Variation and Change*, 669-702. Malden, MA: Blackwell.
Kicza, John. 1990. Migration to major metropoles in colonial Mexico. In David J. Robinson (ed.), *Migration to Colonial Spanish America*, 193-211. Cambridge University Press.
Konetzke, Richard. 1972/2001. *América Latina II. Epoca Colonial*. Buenos Aires: Siglo XXI.
Lapesa, Rafael. 1956. Sobre el seseo y el ceceo en Hispanoamérica. *Revista Iberoamericana. (Homenaje a Pedro Henríquez Ureña 1844-1946. A diez años de su muerte)* 21 (41-42): 409-416.
Lapesa, Rafael. 1985. *Historia de la lengua española*. Madrid: Gredos.
Lara Tenorio, Blanca. 2005. La integración de los negros en la naciente sociedad poblana, 1570-1600. In María E. Velázquez Gutiérrez and Ethel Correa Duró (eds.), *Pobalciones y culturas de origen africano en México*, 285-297. Mexico: Instituto Nacional de Antropología e Historia.
las Casas, Bartolomé de. 1542/1982/2007. *Brevísima relación de la destruición de las Indias*. Edition and prologue by André Saint-Lu. Madrid: Ediciones Cátedra.
las Casas, Bartolomé de. 1547/1875/1951. *Historia de las Indias*. Preliminary study by Lewis Hanke. Mexico: Fondo de Cultura Económica.
Lathrop, Thomas A. 1984. *Curso de gramática histórica española*. Barcelona: Editorial Ariel.
Lemon, Jason E. 2000. *The encomienda in Early New Spain*. Emory University Ph. D. dissertation.
León-Portilla, Miguel. 1970. "Estudio preliminar". In Alonso de Molina. *Diccionario en lengua castellana y mexicana y mexicana y castellana*. Mexico: Porrúa Editorial.
Lerner, Victoria. 1968. Consideraciones sobre la población de la Nueva España (1793-1810), según Humboldt y Navarro y Noriega. *Historia Mexicana* 17 (3): 327-348.
Liebman, Seymour B. 1963. The Jews of Colonial Mexico. *Hispanic American Historical Review* 43 (1): 95-106.
Liebman, Seymour B. 1964. The *Abecedario* and a check-list of documents at the Henry E. Huntingon Library. *Hispanic American Historical Review* 44 (4): 554-576.
Liebman, Seymour B. 1967. *The Enlightened. The Writings of Luis de Carvajal, el Mozo*. Coral Gables, FL: University of Miami Press.
Liebman, Seymour B. 1970. *The Jews in New Spain. Faith, flame and the Inquisition*. Coral Gables: University of Miami Press.
Liebman, Seymour B. 1971. *Los judíos en México y América Central (fe, llamas e Inquisición)*. Mexico: Siglo XXI. (Translated from English by Elsa Cecilia Frost).
Liebman, Seymour B. 1974. *The Inquisitors and the Jews in the New World. Summaries of procesos, 1500-1810, and bibliographical guide*. Coral Gables: University of Miami Press.

Liss, Peggy. 1975. *Mexico Under Spain, 1521-1556: Society and the Origins of Nationality.* Chicago: University of Chicago Press.
Lockhart, James. 1991. *Nahuas and Spaniards. Postconquest Central Mexican History and Philology.* Stanford: Stanford University Press.
Lockhart, James. 1992. *The Nahuas after the Conquest. A Social and Cultural History of the Indians in Central Mexico, Sixteenth through Eighteenth Century.* Stanford: University Press.
Lockhart, James and Stuart B.Schwartz. 1983. *Early Latin America. A History of Colonial Spanish America and Brazil.* Cambridge University Press.
Lloyd, Paul M. 1987. *From Latin to Spanish. Historical Phonology and Morphology of the Spanish Language* (Memoirs of the American Philosophical Society 73). Philadelphia: American Philosophical Society.
Lope Blanch, Juan M. 1979. Antillanismos en la Nueva España. In Juan M. Lope Blanch (ed.), *Investigaciones sobre dialectología mexicana,* 161-169. Mexico: Universidad Nacional Autónoma de México.
Lope Blanch, Juan M. 1985. *El habla de Diego de Ordaz. Contribución a la historia del español americano.* Mexico: Universidad Nacional Autónoma de México.
Lope Blanch, Juan M. 1987. *Estudios sobre el español de Yucatán.* Mexico: Universidad Nacional Autónoma de México.
Lope Blanch, Juan M. 1995-1996. La toponimia amerindia en el habla de Hernán Cortés. *Boletín de Filología* 35: 231-243.
Lope Blanch, Juan M (ed.). 1977. *Estudios sobre el español hablado en las principales ciudades de América.* Mexico: Universidad Nacional Autónoma de México.
López de Gómara, Francisco. 1554/1943. *Historia de la conquista de México.* Introduction and notes by Joaquín Ramírez Cabañas. Mexico: Editorial Pedro Robredo.
López de Velasco, Juan. 1894. *Geografía y descripción universal de las Indias (desde el año 1571 al de 1574).* Boletín de la Sociedad Geográfica de Madrid. Madrid: Justo Zaragoza.
López Guzmán, Rafael. 2005. Ciudades administrativas o de españoles en México (Siglo XVI). *Atrio. Revista de Historia del Arte* 10 (11): 87-92.
Macías Domínguez, Isabelo. 1999. *La llamada del Nuevo Mundo. La emigración española a América (1701-1750).* Seville: Universidad de Sevilla.
Marín-Tamayo, Fausto. 1956. Nuño de Guzmán: el hombre y sus antecedentes. *Historia Mexicana* 1(2): 217–231.
Martinet, André. 1951-52. The unvoicing of Old Spanish sibilants. *Romance Philology* 5: 133 156.
Martinet, André. 1953. Diffusion of language and structural linguistics. *Romance Philology* 6: 5-13.
Martinez, Glenn A. 2001. Política lingüística y contacto social en el español méxico-tejano: La oposición –*ra* y –*se* Tejas durante el siglo XIX. *Hispania* 84 (1): 114-124.
Martínez, José Luis. 1983/1999. *Pasajeros de Indias. Viajes transatlánticos en el siglo XVI.* Mexico: Fondo de Cultura Económica.
Martínez, María Elena. 2006. The language, genealogy and classification of race in colonial Mexico. In Ilona Katzew and Susan Deans-Smith (eds.) *Race and classification: The case of Mexican America,* 25-42. Stanford, CA: Stanford University Press.
Martínez, María Elena. 2008. *Genealogical fictions. Limpieza de sangre, Religion and Gender in Colonial Mexico.* Stanford, CA: Stanford University Press.
Martínez Montiel, Luz M. 1994. *Presencia africana en México.* Mexico: Consejo Nacional de la Cultura y las Artes.

Martínez Shaw, Carlos. 1994. *La emigración española a América (1492-1824)*. Gijón: Fundación Archivo de Indianos.

Máynez, Pilar. 1998. Un caso de interferencia lingüística en el Confesionario Mayor de Fray Alonso de Molina. *Estudios de Cultura Náhuatl* 28: 365-379.

Máynez, Pilar. 1999. La incidencia de hispanismos en los Confesionarios Mayor y Menor de fray Alonso de Molina: Un análisis contrastivo. *Estudios de Cultura Náhuatl* 30: 275-284.

Máynez, Pilar. 2002. Las doctrinas de Molina y Sahagún. Similitudes y diferencias. *Estudios de Cultura Náhuatl* 33: 267-275.

Mejías, Hugo A. 1980. *Préstamos de lenguas indígenas en el español americano del siglo XVII*. Mexico: Universidad Nacional Autónoma de México.

Melis, Chantal; Rivero Franyutti and Beatriz Arias Álvarez. 2008. *Documentos lingüísticos de la Nueva España. Golfo de México*. Mexico: Universidad Nacional Autónoma de México.

Melville, Elinor G. K. 1994. Land-labor relations in sixteenth-century Mexico: The formation of grazing haciendas. *Journal of Slavery and Abolition* 15 (2): 26-35

Menéndez Pidal, Ramón. 1904/1977. *Manual de gramática histórica española*. Madrid: Espasa-Calpe.

Menéndez Pidal, Ramón. 1919. *Documentos lingüísticos de España I. Reino de Castilla*. Madrid: Centro de Estudios Históricos.

Menéndez Pidal, Ramón. 1968. *Orígenes del español. Estado lingüístico de la Península Ibérica hasta el siglo XI*, 6th edn. Madrid: Espasa-Calpe.

Mendieta, Jerónimo de. 1596/1870/1971. *Historia Eclesiástica Indiana*. Mexico: Porrúa.

Megenney, William. 1985. Rasgos criollos en algunos villancicos negroides de Puebla, México. *Anuario de Letras. Lingüística y Filología* 23: 161-202.

Milán, William G. 1983. Contemporary models of standardized New World Spanish: Origin, development, and use. In Juan Cobarrubias and Joshua A. Fishman (eds.) *Progress in Language Planning. International Perspectives*, 121-144. Berlin: Mouton de Gruyter.

Millán, Mónica. 2011. *Pronouns of Address in Informal Contexts. A Comparison of two Dialects of Colombian Spanish*. University of Illinois at Urbana Ph.D. dissertation.

Miño Grijalva, Manuel. 1993. *La protoindustria colonial hispanoamericana*. Mexico: El Colegio de México/Fondo de Cultura Económica.

Miño Grijalva, Manuel.1998. *Obrajes y tejedores de Nueva España. 1700-1810*. Mexico: El Colegio de México.

Molina, Alonso de. 1555/1571/1970. *Vocabulario en lengua castellana y mexicana y mexicana y castellana*. Preliminary study by Miguel León Portilla. Mexico: Editorial Porrúa.

Montesinos, Antón de. 1982. *Ego vox clamantis in deserto*. Sermón pronunciado en Sto. Domingo en 1511. *Boletín de Antropología Americana* December: 147-161.

Mörner, Magnus. 1970. *La corona española y los foráneos en los pueblos de indios de América*. Stockholm: Almqvist-Wiskell (Instituto de Estudios Ibero-Americanos).

Mörner, Magnus. 1976. Spanish migration to the New World prior to 1801: A report on the state of research. In Fredi Chiapelli; Michael J. B. Allen and Robert L. Benson (eds.) *First Images of America. The Impact of the New World on the New*, 737-782. Berkeley, CA: University of California Press.

Mott, Margaret. 2001. Leonor de Cáceres and the Mexican Inquisition. *Journal of the History of Ideas* 62 (1): 81-98.

Motta Sánchez, José A. 2005. ¿Huellas bantúes en el noroeste de Oaxaca? In María E.Velázquez Gutiérez and Ethel Correa Duró (eds.), *Pobalciones y culturas de origen africano en México*, 357-410. Mexico: Instituto Nacional de Antropología e Historia.

Muriel, Josefina. 1982. *Cultura femenina novohispana*. Mexico: Universidad Nacional Autónoma de México.
Navarro Tomás, Tomás. 1933/1975. *Capítulos de geografía lingüística de la Península Ibérica*. Bogota: Instituto Caro y Cuervo.
Nebrija, Antonio de. 1486. *Introducciones latinas contrapuesto el romance al latín*. Münster: Nodus Publikationen.
Nebrija, Antonio de. 1492/1984. *Gramática de la lengua castellana*. Introduction and edition by Antonio Quilis. Madrid: Editora Nacional.
Nevalainen, Terttu and Helena Ramoulin-Brunberg. 2012. Historical Sociolinguistics: Origins, Motivations, and Paradigms. In Juan M. Hernández-Campoy and Juan C. Conde-Silvestre (eds.) *The Handbook of Historical Sociolinguistics*, 22-40. Malden, MA: Wiley-Blackwell.
Olveda Legaspi, Jaime. 2013. La abolición de la esclavitud en México, 1810-1917. *Signos Históricos* 29: 8:34.
Osorio Romero, Igancio. 1990. *La enseñanza del latín a los indios*. Mexico: Universidad Nacional Autónoma de México.
Otero, Carlos Peregrín. 1971. *Evolución y revolución en romance*. Barcelona: Seix Barral.
Padua, Jorge. 1979. *El analfabetismo en América Latina*. Mexico: El Colegio de México.
Penny, Ralph. 1991. *A History of the Spanish Language*. Cambridge University Press.
Penny, Ralph. 2000. *Variation and Change in Spanish*. Cambridge University Press.
Penny, Ralph. 2012. *Gramática histórica de la lengua española*. Madrid: Ariel.
Peña, Margarita. 2006. El teatro novohispano en el siglo XVIII. *Bulletin of the Comediantes* 58 (1): 155-172.
Pérez, Joseph. 2005. *The Spanish Inquisition. A History*. Translated from the French by Janet Lloyd. New Haven, CT: Yale University Press.
Perissinoto, Giorgio A. 1992. El habla de "un caballero de la tierra" novohispano del siglo XVI. *Nueva Revista de Filología Hispánica* 50 (1): 29-43.
Perissinoto, Giorgio A.1994. The Spanish sibilant shift revisited: The state of seseo in sixteenth century Mexico. In Peggy Hashemipour, Ricardo Maldonado and Margret van Naerssen (eds.) *Studies in Language Learning and Spanish Linguistics in Honor of Tracy D. Terrell*, 289-301. New York: McGraw-Hill.
Pescador, Juan J. 1993. Patrones demográficos urbanos en la Nueva España. In *Consejo Nacional de Población* (ed.) Vol. 2, 108-131. Mexico: Consejo Nacional de Población.
Petrarca, Francesco. 1962. *Canzoniere*. Introduction by Roberto Antonelli and Saggio di Gianfranco Contini. Notes by Dianele Poonchiroli. Turin: Einaudi Tascabali Editors.
Post, Anita C. 1933. Some aspects of Arizona Spanish. *Hispania* 16 (1): 35-42.
Post, Anita C. 1934. Southern Arizona Spanish phonology. *Humanities Bulletin* 5 (1): 1-57.
Probert, Alan. 1997. Bartolomé de Medina: The patio process and the sixteenth century silver crisis. In Peter J. Bakewell (ed.) *Mines of Silver and Gold in the Americas*, 96-130. Aldershot and Brookfield: Variorum.
Proctor, Frank T. 2003a. *Slavery, Identity and Culture. An Afro-Mexican Counterpoint, 1640-1763*. Emory University Ph.D. dissertation.
Proctor, Frank T. 2003b. Afro-Mexican slave labor in the *obrajes de paños* of New Spain, seventeenth and eighteenth centuries. *The Americas* 60 (1): 33-58.
Proctor, Frank T. 2006. Gender and the manumission of slaves in New Spain. *Hispanic American Historical Review* 86 (2): 309-336.
Quilis, Antonio. 1984. "Estudio de la *Gramática de la lengua castellana* de Antonio de Nebrija". Madrid: Editora Nacional, 7-92.

Quiñones Melgoza, José. 1982. "Introducción". In *Bernardino de Llanos. Diálogo en la visita de los inquisidores representado en el Colegio de San Ildefonso (Siglo XVI), y otros poemas inéditos*. xv-lxv. Mexico: Universidad Nacional Autónoma de México.
Reed Torres, Luis and María del Carmen Ruiz Castañeda. 1995. *El periodismo en México. 500 años de historia*. Mexico: Edamex.
Rojas Mayer, Elena M. (ed.). 2000. *Documentos para la historia lingüística de Hispanoamérica, siglos XVI a XIX*. Madrid: Boletín de la Real Academia Española II, Anejo 58.
Romaine, Suzanne. 1982. *Socio-historical Linguistics. Its Status and Methodology*. Cambridge University Press.
Rosas Mayén, Norma. 2007. *Afro-Hispanic Linguistic Remnants in Mexico. The Case of the Costa Chica Region of Oaxaca*. Purdue University Ph.D. dissertation.
Rosenblat, Angel. 1954. *La población indígena y el mestizaje en América*. Vol. 1. Buenos Aires: Editorial Nova.
Rosenblat, Angel. 1956. *Estudios sobre el habla de Venezuela. Buenas y malas palabras*. Vol. 1. Buenos Aires: Monte Ávila Editores.
Roudil, Jean 1970. Alphonse le Savant, rédacteur de definitions lexicographiques. In Georges Matore and Jeanne Cadiot-Cueilleron (eds.), *Mélanges de linguistique et de Philologie Romanes*, 153-175. Paris: Klincksieck.
Sáez Faulhaber, María E. 1993. El mestizaje en la integración de la población colonial. In *Consejo Nacional de Población* (ed.), Vol. 2, 86-107. Mexico: Consejo Nacional de Población.
Sahagún, Bernardino de. 1950-1982. *Florentine Codex. General History of the Things of New Spain*. Edited and translated by Arthur J.O. Anderson and Charles E. Dibble. Santa Fe, NM: School of American Research.
Saint-Lu, André. 1968. *La Vera Paz. Esprit évangélique et colonisation*. Paris: Institut d'Etudes Hispaniques.
Saint-Lu, André. 1982. *Las Casas Indigéniste. Etudes sur la vie et l'oeuvre du défenseur des Indians*. Paris: L'Harmattan.
Saiz, María Dolores. 1983. *Historia del periodismo en España 1. Los orígenes. El siglo XVIII*. Madrid: Alianza Editorial.
Saussure, Ferdinand de 1915/1945. *Curso de lingüística general*. Translation from French, introduction, and notes by Amado Alonso. Buenos Aires: Losada. Published by Charles Balley, Albert Sechehaye and Albert Riedlinger.
Schell Hoberman, Louisa. 1991. *Mexico's Merchant Elite 1590-1660. Silver, State and Society*. Durham, NC and London: Duke University Press.
Silverstein, Stephen. 2015. La hibridación en las cartas de Luis de Carvajal, el Mozo. *Mexican Studies/Estudios Mexicanos* 31 (1): 1-21.
Simpson, Lesley Byrd. 1929. *The encomienda in New Spain. Forced Native Labor in the Spanish colonies, 1492-1550*. Berkeley, CA: University of California Press.
Simpson, Lesley Byrd. 1950. *The encomienda in New Spain. The Beginning of Spanish Mexico*: Berkeley, CA: University of California Press.
Suárez de Peralta, Juan. 1589/1990. *Tratado del descubrimiento de las Yndias y su conquista*. Transcription, prologue, and notes by Giorgio Perissinotto. Madrid: Alianza Editorial.
Super, John C. 1983. *La vida en Querétaro durante la colonia. 1531-1810*. Mexico: Fondo de Cultura Económica.
Swadesh, Morris. 1971. *The Origin and Diversification of Language*. Edited by Joel Sherzer. Foreword by Dell Hymes. Chicago: Aldine Atherton.

Tanck de Estrada, Dorothy. 2005. *Atlas ilustrado de los pueblos de indios. Nueva España 1800.* Mexico: El Colegio de México.

Thomason, Sarah G. and Terrence Kaufman. 1988. *Language Contact, Creolization and Genetic Linguistics.* Berkeley, CA: University of California Press.

Toro, Alfonso. 1932/1995. *Los judíos en la Nueva España.* Mexico: Fondo de Cultura Económica/ Archivo General de la Nación.

Toro, Alfonso. 1944. *La familia Carvajal. Estudio histórico sobre los judíos y la Inquisición de la Nueva España en el siglo XVI, basado en documentos originales y en su mayor parte inéditos, que se conservan en el Archivo General de la Nación de la ciudad de México.* Mexico: Editorial Patria.

Torres Quintero, Rafael (ed.). 1952. *Bello en Colombia. Homenaje a Venezuela.* Bogota: Instituto Caro y Cuervo.

Tuten, Donald E. 2003. *Koineization in Medieval Spanish* (Contributions to the Sociology of Language 88). Berlin: Mouton de Gruyter.

Uber, Diane R. 2011. Forms of Adress. The Effects of the Context. In Manuel Díaz-Campos (ed.), *The Handbook of Hispanic Sociolinguistics,* 244-262. Malden MA: Wiley-Blackwell.

Universidad Nacional Autónoma de México. 2007. *Atlas Nacional de México.* Mexico: Instituto de Geografía.

Urrutia Cárdenas, Hernán. 2003. Los clíticos de tercera persona en el País Vasco. *Cauce. Revista de Filología y su Didáctica* 26: 517-538.

Valbuena Prat, Ángel. 1937. *Historia de la literatura española.* Barcelona: Gustavo Gili Editor.

Valdés, Juan de. 1535/1964. *Diálogo de la lengua.* Edition and notes by José F. Montesinos. Madrid: Espasa-Calpe.

van Scoy, Herbert A. 1940. Alfonso X as a lexicographer. *Hispanic Review* 8 (4): 277-284.

Velasco, María del Pilar. 1993. La migración ibérica y africana: Características e impactos regionales. In *El poblamiento de México,* Vol. 2, 64-85. Mexico: Consejo Nacional de Población.

Velázquez Gutiérrez, María E. and Ethel Correa Duró (eds.). 2005. *Poblaciones y culturas de origen africano en México.* Mexico: Instituto Nacional de Antropología e Historia.

Velázquez Gutiérrez, María E. 2005. Amas de leche, cocineras y vendedoras: mujeres de origen africano, trabajo y cultura en la ciudad de México durante la época colonial. In María E. Velázquez Gutiérrez and Ethel Correa Duró (eds.), *Poblaciones y culturas de origen africano en México,* 333-356. Mexico: Instituto Nacional de Antropología e Historia.

Villa-Flores, Javier. 2002. "To lose one's soul": Blasphemy and slavery in New Spain. *Hispanic American Historical Review* 82 (3): 435-468.

Vinson, Ben III. 2000. The racial profile of a rural Mexican province in the "Costa Chica": Igualapa in 1791. *The Americas* 57: 269-282.

Viqueira, Carmen. 1985. El significado de la legislación sobre la mano de obra indígena de los obrajes de paños, 1567-1580. *Historia Mexicana* 35 (1): 33-58.

Viqueira, Carmen and José I. Urquiola. 1990. *Los obrajes en la Nueva España: 1530-1630.* Mexico: Consejo Nacional para la Cultura y las Artes.

von Mentz, Brígida. 2005. Esclavitud en centros mineros y azucareros novohispanos: algunas propuestas para el estudio de la multietnicidad en el centro de México. In María E. Velázquez Gutiérrez and Ethel Corra Duró (eds.), *Poblaciones y culturas de origen africano en México,* 259-276. Mexico: Instituto Nacional de Antropología e Historia.

Wagner, Max L. 1920/1924. *El español de América y el latín vulgar.* Buenos Aires: Instituto de Filología de la Universidad de Buenos Aires Vol. 1.

West, Robert C. 1997a. Aboriginal Metallurgy and Metalworking in Spanish America: A brief overview. In Peter J. Bakewell (ed.), *Mines of Silver and Gold in the Americas* (An Expanding World 19). 41-56 Aldershot and Brookfield: Variorum.

West, Robert C. 1997b. Early Silver Mining in New Spain, 1531-1555. In Peter J. Bakewell (ed.), *Mines of Silver and Gold in the Americas* (An Expanding World 19), 57-73. Aldershot and Brookfield: Variorum.

Wilson, Joseph M. 1983. The –ra and –se Verb Forms in Mexico. A Diachronic Examination from Non-literary Sources. Ph.D. dissertation. University of Massachusetts.

Wobeser, Giselle von. 1986. Los esclavos negros en el México colonial. Las haciendas de Cuernavaca-Cuautla. *Jarbuch für Geschichte von Staat, Wirtschaft und Gesellschaft Lateinamerikas* 23: 145-171.

Yuste, Carmen (ed.) 1991. *Comerciantes mexicanos en el siglo XVIII*. Mexico: Universidad Nacional Autónoma de México.

Zamora Vicente, Alonso. 1967. *Dialectología española*. Madrid: Editorial Gredos.

Zavala, Silvio A. 1935. *La encomienda indiana*. Madrid. Centro de Estudios Históricos.

Zavala, Silvio A. 1944/1978. *Ensayos sobre la colonización española en América*. Mexico: Porrúa.

Zavala, Silvio A. 1952. Nuño de Guzmán y la esclavitud de los indios. *Historia Mexicana* 1 (3): 411–428.

Zavala, Silvio A. 1971. *Las instituciones jurídicas en la conquista de América*. Mexico: Porrúa.

Zavala, Silvio A. 1984. *El servicio personal de los indios en la Nueva España I. 1521-1550*. Mexico: El Colegio de México.

Zavala, Silvio A. 1985. *El servicio personal de los indios en la Nueva España II. 1550-1575*. Mexico: El Colegio de México.

Zavala, Silvio A. 1987. *El servicio personal de los indios en la Nueva España III. 1576-1599*. Mexico: El Colegio de México.

Zubiría, Ramón de. 1982. Presencia y vigencia de don Andrés Bello. *Thesavrvs* 37 (1): 1-22.

Index

A

Abecedario, El xiii, 26, 30, 32, 96–101, 359
– ethnic groups in 98–99, 312, 394–400
accommodation 2, 27, 42, 61, 63, 64, 108, 245
accusative 154, 155, 156, 178, 215, 371, 379, 380
Acevedo, Rebeca 129, 161, 183, 247, 299, 300, 303, 330, 332, 353
Africa 36, 40, 58, 61, 90, 101, 104, 111, 186, 284
African languages 3, 59, 63, 70, 94, 98, 106, 144, 210, 284, 378
Afro-Hispanic varieties 378, 389, 390
Aguirre Beltrán, Gonzalo 57, 58, 102, 279, 312
Albornoz, Rodrigo de 83, 105, 148, 149, 150, 158, 159, 195, 357, 363
Alfonso X, the Learned 38, 39, 258
Álvarez Nazario, Manuel 371, 386
Alzate y Ramírez, José Antonio de 337
Amerindian languages 21, 118, 120, 223, 261, 390
Amerindian loans 29, 149, 181, 360, 376
– from Nahuatl 27, 134, 170, 338, 340
– from Taino 37, 59, 111, 150, 164, 170, 225
Andalusia 30, 37, 39, 40, 41, 42, 44, 45, 46, 47, 48, 50, 51, 52, 55, 57, 59, 72, 76, 111, 135, 146, 158, 278, 304, 311, 331
Andalusians 36, 42, 56, 57, 144
Andalusian (Spanish) 9, 21, 22, 27, 30, 34, 35, 36, 41, 42, 45–46, 47, 48, 49, 51, 53, 60, 61, 62, 63, 64, 65, 370
– regions 2, 4, 5, 6, 7, 9, 10, 23, 26, 28, 33, 36, 37, 40, 41, 42, 43, 44, 45, 46, 47, 48, 50, 51, 52, 53, 57, 54, 55, 56, 59, 60, 64, 65, 76, 278, 311
Apuntaciones 6, 7, 8, 10, 25, 370, 371
aspiration 14, 23, 24, 47, 48, 50, 52, 60, 64, 143, 145, 151, 166, 176, 181, 222, 236, 243, 362 – 364, 368, 387, 389
– of -s 177, 235
Aztec 81, 84, 85, 113, 114, 115, 116, 117, 185, 197, 249, 252, 261,
– capital 85, 113, 114, 116, 117, 136, 141, 142, 197
– Empire 55, 81, 84, 113, 116
– nobility 78, 86, 209, 250, 252, 255, 261, 270, 275, 320

B

Basque 39, 49, 304, 311
– language contact 51, 155
– region 39, 42, 46, 50, 57, 60, 61, 156
Bello, Andrés 15, 16
bilingualism 31, 106, 249, 250, 251, 258, 259, 271, 272, 276, 309, 314, 340
– and religion 13, 108, 249
– elite 5, 51, 62, 144, 204, 210, 249, 258, 260, 263, 267, 271, 276, 281, 309, 310, 317
– massive 19, 33, 104, 107, 184, 199, 250, 255, 271, 305, 309, 317, 353
Bogota 6, 15, 25, 371, 380, 381
Bourbon administration 313, 320
– Reforms 32, 341
– Bourbons 15, 337

C

Canary Islands 26, 44, 45, 47, 52, 61, 99, 311
capitales mineras 191–196, 205
Caracas 90, 331, 380, 381, 387, 388
Caribbean area 1, 2, 25, 36, 37, 47, 61, 84, 105, 108, 222, 306, 370, 388, 389
– contact 70, 106, 140, 202, 234
– islands 4, 29, 36, 37, 55, 71, 73, 74, 76, 90, 101, 106, 112, 131, 140, 146, 164, 181
Carvajal family 92, 100
Carvajal, Luis de 91, 92, 93, 100, 108, 242
– *el mozo* 93, 100
– *el viejo* 93, 216
Castile 13, 23, 37, 38, 39, 40, 41, 42, 44, 50, 51, 52, 55, 57, 61, 64, 65, 76, 85, 88, 126, 143, 146, 181, 211, 242, 252, 280, 282, 311
Castilian 7, 8, 9, 11, 12, 14, 16, 22, 23, 27, 30, 31, 35, 36, 37, 38, 39, 41, 42, 44, 45, 46, 47, 49, 50, 51, 52, 53, 61, 62, 63, 64, 65,

111, 126, 135, 140, 142, 148, 154, 155, 161, 165, 166, 168, 169, 170, 171, 174, 175, 181, 207, 226, 228, 245, 249, 256, 259, 260, 285, 288, 289, 359, 370, 374, 385, 391
Castilian and Andalusian 6, 42, 10, 62, 65, 169
Catholic Church 31, 78, 92, 254, 263, 271
Catholic faith 73, 88, 113
Catholic liturgy 59, 206, 271
ceceo 42, 45, 46, 53, 60, 135, 149, 235, 236, 244
Central America 58, 91, 234, 266, 331, 389, 390
Central Highlands 5, 26, 27, 31, 62, 135, 136, 140, 149, 159, 162, 165, 175, 176, 178, 180, 181, 182, 183, 202, 211, 212, 234, 236, 240, 244, 246, 247, 285, 286, 287, 289, 290, 291, 297, 300, 302, 303, 309, 321, 323, 324, 328, 329, 330, 333, 344, 347, 348, 349, 350, 351, 352, 353, 354, 359, 379
Cervantes de Salazar, Francisco 82, 207, 209
Chalco 77, 115, 175, 198, 225, 251, 384
Charles V 13, 79, 81, 87, 113, 114, 115, 116, 117, 148, 149, 156, 159, 209, 254
Chiapas 29, 58, 102, 279, 312, 348, 382
Christian 21, 37, 38, 39, 40, 41, 42, 70, 72, 73, 88, 96, 98, 109, 130, 170, 203, 204, 205, 249, 255, 256, 257, 258, 261, 262, 263, 265, 268, 274, 283
– doctrine 13, 170, 204, 262, 268, 283
– dominions 41, 53, 96
– faith 73, 88, 170, 225, 249, 260, 263
– mission 29, 33, 55, 70, 193, 194, 196, 203, 204, 207, 254, 255, 258, 263, 269, 280
– resistance 37, 43, 98, 107, 249, 255, 342, 377
Christianization 108, 255, 265, 266
ciudades de españoles 191, 194, 195, 196, 269, 280
Colegio de San Pedro y San Pablo 205, 280, 319
Colegio de Santa Cruz de Tlatelolco 93
Colombia 6, 16, 22, 24, 26, 135, 147, 383, 384, 389, 390

Company Company, Concepción 26, 64, 140, 287, 301, 333, 342, 359, 380, 385
conditional sentences 7, 28, 129–130, 160–161, 217, 233, 244, 303, 367
congregaciones 270, 271
Cortés, Hernán xiii, 26, 28, 30, 55, 71, 72, 74, 75, 77, 81, 83, 84, 85, 101, 105, 110 – 111, 112, 113, 114, 115, 116, 117, 118, 119, 120, 125, 126, 128, 130, 131, 132, 134, 136, 137, 147, 148, 149, 153, 154, 156, 157, 159, 160, 161, 163, 164, 165, 170, 175, 177, 178, 179, 186, 187, 208, 226, 227, 230, 231, 234, 241, 254, 338, 354, 357, 366, 368, 369
– *Cartas de Relación* 74, 110, 111, 118
– *First Letter* 110, 112–113, 119, 121, 124, 125, 131
– *Second Letter* 26, 28, 30, 110, 111, 113–118, 119, 121, 122, 123, 124, 126, 127, 128, 129, 130, 131, 132, 134, 136, 354, 355, 357, 366, 368
Cortesian texts 124, 147–164
creolization 65, 106, 108, 109, 339, 378
Cromberger, Jacobo xiii, 30, 113, 206
Cromberger, Juan xiii, 30, 113, 206
Cruz, Sor Juana Inés de la 208, 306
Cuba 24, 26, 37, 45, 55, 71, 73, 75, 76, 101, 102, 111, 112, 116, 117, 132, 137, 140, 146, 147, 156, 389
Cuervo, José Rufino 2, 6, 7, 8, 9, 10, 22, 23, 24, 25, 234, 370, 371, 374

D

dative 154, 155, 156, 228, 371, 379, 380
demographic trends 17, 32, 65
de-palatalization 43, 52, 135, 175
devoicing 14, 42, 43, 45, 52, 135, 149
Díaz del Castillo, Bernal 75, 111, 208
diffusion of Spanish 3, 15, 30, 163, 191, 196, 210
diglossia 10, 143, 370, 386
discourse markers 130, 162, 233
Disquisiciones 9, 10
diversification 1, 2–3, 4, 18, 25, 30, 31, 32, 33, 36, 64, 65, 108, 136, 184, 185, 210, 237, 273, 277, 306, 307, 309, 339, 342,

343, 374, 376, 377, 383, 384, 385, 386, 390, 392
doctrina 254, 269, 361
Documentos Lingüísticos de España 285, 286
Documentos Lingüísticos de la Nueva España 26, 140, 148, 175, 308, 343
domain(s) 1, 3, 4, 9, 10, 13, 22, 27, 29, 31, 33, 54, 62, 64, 65, 71, 83, 103, 108, 131, 135, 140, 142, 155, 163, 168, 174, 181, 182, 184, 185, 199, 207, 210, 220, 230, 237, 238, 243, 244, 249, 250, 255, 263, 264, 269, 271, 272, 273, 284, 299, 300, 301, 306, 307, 325, 327, 333, 343, 350, 360, 364, 368, 369, 371, 376, 379, 383, 384, 386
– domestic 90, 206, 273, 283, 310, 369, 386
– in education 318
– informal 3, 5, 7, 10, 26, 35, 60, 62, 63, 71, 83, 122, 131, 134, 136, 140, 143, 144, 162, 171, 182, 203, 220, 230, 237, 238, 249, 282, 299, 327, 348, 350, 358, 376, 383, 387
– in religion 260
– intra-familiar 71, 182, 220, 325
– in work 197, 199
– personal 6, 11, 53, 78, 93, 94, 106, 118, 140, 142, 148, 154, 176, 177, 179, 181, 184, 187, 212, 217, 220, 230, 246, 260, 272, 278, 300, 301, 306, 325, 338, 349, 350, 372, 373, 376, 383, 392
– semantic 28, 104, 129, 155, 168, 170, 180, 224, 256, 272, 333, 348, 350, 383, 385, 388, 392
duplicate possessives 359, 385

E

education of Spanish speakers 204, 319
emigration 1, 57, 69, 266, 278, 309, 310, 379
encomenderos 4, 30, 64, 70, 72, 73, 74, 75, 76, 77, 78, 79, 82, 83, 86, 94, 99, 107, 109, 141, 148, 176, 180, 185, 186, 197, 201, 223, 253, 264, 265, 267, 268
– *encomienda(s)* 5, 73, 74, 75, 76, 77, 83, 148, 184, 187, 211, 219, 253, 268, 269, 310
español indígena 339, 389
Ethnic groups 99, 304
– Afro-mestizos 102, 103, 276
– Afro-Mexicans 102, 103, 104, 105, 106, 109, 247
– *bozales* 104, 105, 106
– *criollos* 58, 95, 98, 101, 204, 239, 250, 259, 263, 273, 280, 282, 284, 308, 310, 314, 315, 318, 319, 320, 322, 337, 341, 353
– *gachupín(a)* 334, 335
– Indians 58, 71, 73, 74, 76, 78, 79, 80, 84, 86, 99, 102, 103, 114, 115, 141, 176, 184, 185, 186, 189, 190, 191, 192, 193, 194, 196, 197, 198, 199, 200, 201, 202, 204, 206, 234, 250, 251, 253, 254, 255, 259, 260, 262, 263, 264, 265, 266, 267, 268, 269, 270, 271, 275, 278, 279, 280, 283, 293, 312, 314, 315, 340, 355, 363
– Jews 3, 30, 39, 49, 50, 51, 87, 88, 89, 90, 92, 97, 98, 100, 107, 109, 266, 284, 363
– *ladino(s)* 51, 101, 106, 242, 250, 259, 264, 266, 268, 272, 274, 276, 294, 334, 335, 356
– *mestizo(s)* 4, 58, 78, 98, 99, 102, 103, 144, 180, 193, 194, 195, 196, 206, 223, 250, 261, 264, 265, 266, 267, 268, 269, 270, 274, 274, 275, 279, 283, 310, 312, 314, 315, 320, 334, 335, 341, 353
– *moriscos* 41
– *moros* 40, 41, 207
– *mozárabes* 39, 50
– *mudéjar(es)* 39, 41
– mulattoes 4, 58, 78, 80, 103, 108, 195, 201, 204, 250, 261, 265, 266, 267, 275, 280, 282, 283, 284, 314
– Muslims 3, 38, 40, 41, 88, 89, 99, 249, 266
– Sephardic Jews 51, 101, 108, 109, 242
– Spaniards 4, 42, 70, 72, 73, 77, 79, 80, 81, 83, 85, 86, 89, 97, 103, 105, 115, 116, 117, 141, 143, 144, 148, 185, 187, 188, 189, 191, 192, 193, 194, 195, 196, 197, 198, 200, 201, 202, 203, 204, 211, 224, 226, 234, 239, 252, 261, 264, 265, 266, 267, 268, 269, 270, 272, 275, 278, 280, 282, 283, 300, 308, 310, 314, 315, 318, 320, 331, 332, 334, 337, 339, 340, 341, 342, 376

ethnicity 2, 98, 101, 104, 108, 180, 190, 234, 242, 249, 256, 304, 306, 308, 315, 319, 334

F
Fishman, Joshua A. 33
first generation of Spanish speakers / writers 4, 31, 63, 140, 150, 161, 165, 176, 181, 209
Frago Gracia, Juan 42, 45, 53, 54, 145, 146, 147, 243

G
Gibson, Charles 77, 78, 197, 198, 199, 200, 201, 202, 250, 252, 253, 254, 262, 263, 264, 270
Golden Age 7, 9, 32, 54, 121, 208, 305, 306, 338, 346
– authors 6, 7, 9, 10, 15, 18, 19, 20, 42, 46, 53, 121, 123, 149, 152, 164, 176, 177, 178, 205, 208, 209, 212, 240, 306, 336, 337
Granda, Germán de 11, 140, 142, 383, 390
Great Tenochtitlan 77, 113, 114, 116, 142, 144
Greek 13, 15, 98, 101, 170
Guadalajara, New Spain 148, 191, 204, 267, 269, 311, 313, 314, 317, 319
Guadalajara, Spain 56, 99, 147, 148, 252
Guatemala 29, 55, 87, 90, 91, 95, 98, 268, 345, 389, 390
Gulf (the) 211, 235, 241, 246, 285, 290, 302, 323, 327, 344, 347, 348, 363, 379
Guzmán, Nuño de 147, 148, 150, 157, 159, 162, 192, 208

H
hacienda(s) 40, 72, 102, 144, 184, 188, 189, 190, 193, 194, 196, 199, 202, 236, 250, 270, 275, 283, 307, 318, 323, 356, 362, 384
Hidalgo, Margarita 1, 3, 75, 156, 178, 193, 249, 258, 378, 386, 390, 392
Hidalgo y Costilla, Miguel 75, 378
Hispanic Romance 21, 29, 38, 39
Hispaniola 37, 71, 79, 111, 112, 140
Hispanization 184, 198, 261, 265, 270, 275, 276

Historia General de las cosas de la Nueva España 146, 258
Historia verdadera de la conquista de la Nueva España 111
historical sociolinguistics 2, 18, 20, 33, 390, 391, 392
Holy Office 26, 32, 87, 88, 91, 92, 93, 94, 95, 96, 97, 106, 108, 109, 215, 284, 293, 324, 377

I
Iberian Peninsula 29, 37, 39, 89, 105, 110, 117, 249, 266
immigrants 2, 4, 27, 29, 35, 36, 39, 42, 55, 56, 59, 61, 66, 71, 76, 81, 82, 89, 94, 95, 109, 136, 146, 211, 311
imperfect subjunctive 26, 28, 31, 32, 54, 126, 128–130, 160–161, 167, 179–180, 217, 233, 244, 247–248, 288, 302–303, 328–332, 351–354, 381, 382, 392
Independence 10, 15, 27, 75, 270, 308, 332, 334, 341, 342, 345, 351, 378, 382, 384, 386
indigenous languages 21, 31, 36, 37, 59, 70, 93, 95, 107, 144, 173, 185, 191, 196, 207, 210, 249, 250, 255, 256, 263, 271, 272, 276, 281, 315, 333, 376, 378, 386, 389, 390
Inquisition 30, 32, 33, 54, 57, 59, 71, 87–101, 106, 107, 108, 140, 176, 177, 204, 210, 215, 261, 274, 291, 299, 320, 322, 338, 377
inter-dialect contact 156, 216, 245
internal change(s) 1, 10, 17, 19, 23, 33, 42, 50, 65, 134, 155, 156, 168, 169, 170, 218, 220, 376, 391, 392

J
Jesuits 80, 196, 203, 204, 205, 280, 281, 318
– education 167, 182, 185, 203, 204, 205, 319
– expulsion of 41, 50, 51, 96
– schools 31, 181, 191, 203, 204, 205, 206, 211, 279, 280, 305, 307, 318, 319
journalism 32, 335, 336, 376
Judaeo-Spanish 48, 51–52
Judaism 89, 90, 92, 93, 97, 98, 100
Jurisdictions in Revillagigedo Census (1790)

- Alta California 313, 317
- Baja California 313, 317
- Durango 313, 314, 316, 317
- Guadalajara 311, 313, 314, 317, 319
- Guanajuato 310, 313, 314, 316, 317
- Merida 313, 314, 388
- Mexico 313, 314, 317
- Nuevo Mexico 313, 317
- Oaxaca 312, 313, 314, 317, 319, 320, 331
- Puebla 313, 314, 317, 319, 331
- San Luis Potosi 311, 313
- Sinaloa 313, 316, 317
- Sonora 313, 316, 317
- Tlaxcala 313, 317
- Valladolid 311, 313, 314, 319, 320
- Veracruz 313, 331, 379
- Yucatan 312, 339, 378, 390
- Zacatecas 313, 314, 317

K

koineization 1, 2–3, 4, 11, 27, 30, 37, 39, 61, 62, 64, 65, 71, 136, 144, 181, 243, 370
koine(s) 3, 4, 5, 12, 61, 62, 64, 65, 108, 132, 135, 140, 143, 144, 150, 170, 359, 369, 389

L

laísmo 155, 216, 229, 297, 348, 371
language contact 19, 29, 31, 107, 156, 173, 184, 191, 196, 197, 198, 202, 234, 249, 265, 271, 272, 309, 376, 389
language maintenance 32, 106, 197, 254, 255, 258, 263, 270, 271
language shift 32, 106, 200, 250, 253, 254, 261, 270, 271, 390
las Casas, Bartolomé de 73, 79, 80, 208, 366, 377
Latin 7, 10, 12, 13, 14, 15, 16, 17, 20, 23, 24, 39, 43, 49, 50, 51, 52, 54, 59, 62, 90, 110, 111, 119, 126, 127, 128, 129, 131, 134, 143, 146, 153, 154, 166, 185, 203, 204, 205, 206, 210, 231, 259, 260, 262, 271, 280, 281, 285, 288, 290, 299, 319, 335, 337, 362, 363, 391
Latin American Spanish, modern 126, 130, 131, 134, 135, 136, 152, 155, 161, 163, 167, 229, 243, 308, 350, 359, 373, 374, 380, 382, 383, 384, 385, 387, 388

leísmo 2, 9, 26, 27, 29, 32, 126, 147, 154, 155, 156, 178, 182, 216, 223, 297, 307, 308, 324, 371, 379, 385
leístas 146, 216, 243, 297, 392
LE(S) and LO(S) 8, 9, 27, 31, 32, 125, 135, 146, 153, 154, 155, 156, 159, 178, 182, 215, 216, 223, 226, 227, 228, 229, 232, 240, 243, 245, 291, 292, 294, 295, 296, 297, 302, 308, 323, 324, 325, 341, 346, 347, 348, 371, 374, 379, 380, 391
literature 2, 5, 9, 32, 65, 143, 144, 207, 208, 210, 302, 305, 307, 310, 335, 336, 337, 341, 370, 376, 389
– in New Spain 32, 33, 75, 91, 92, 110, 207–208, 209, 222, 256, 259, 260, 261, 263, 267, 268, 275, 279, 281, 299, 302, 305–306, 310, 318, 335, 336, 337
– in Spain 2, 8–9, 11, 207–208, 305–306, 334, 335, 336
loísmo 155, 216, 348
Lope Blanch, Juan 26, 120, 132, 140, 143, 147, 165, 167, 168, 169, 273, 378, 387

M

Madrid 8, 9, 13, 43, 51, 56, 91, 155, 167, 209, 252, 298, 319, 335, 336, 381, 383
Medellín, Colombia 110
Medellín, Spain 110
medieval Spanish 7, 11, 23, 27, 29, 43, 44, 45, 118, 119, 121, 128, 134, 135, 136, 143, 147, 150, 151, 152, 161, 212, 215, 217, 222, 223, 233, 244, 285, 287, 288, 290, 303, 335, 348, 350, 360, 376, 379, 385
Melis, Chantal 26, 64, 140, 289
Mendieta, Jerónimo de 208, 254, 260
Menéndez Pidal, Ramón 18, 49, 285, 286, 363
merchants 4, 56, 64, 77, 82, 90, 94, 99, 101, 186, 187, 203, 204, 268, 278, 279, 284, 309, 310, 316, 317, 318, 319, 320, 331, 332, 333, 341
mergers 27, 42, 43, 52, 65, 391
– de-affrication 43, 44, 52
– de-lateralization 43, 47
– de-palatalization 43, 47, 52, 135, 175
– inter-dentalization 43

Mesoamerican area 70, 71, 81, 110, 120, 131, 143, 225, 255
– civilization 72, 84, 208, 337
– languages 1, 3, 12, 13, 16, 17, 19, 31, 36, 37, 47, 49, 59, 70, 91, 94, 95, 98, 100, 101, 106, 111, 120, 132, 142, 143, 144, 153, 154, 174, 210, 249, 250, 252, 255, 256, 257, 259, 263, 271, 272, 276, 277, 281, 284, 309, 314, 336, 342, 376, 378, 386, 390, 392
– peoples 3, 12, 21, 71, 72, 73, 89, 96, 97, 107, 113, 127, 164, 184, 192, 197, 201, 223, 252, 255, 258, 263, 377
mestizaje(s) 58, 109, 252, 271, 276, 284, 308, 320
Mexican Colonial Spanish 1, 26, 28, 106, 108, 153, 211, 243, 338, 340, 342, 360, 365, 368, 381, 385, 391, 392
Mexican colony xiii, 148
Mexican Spanish 1, 5, 22, 25, 27, 30, 37, 70, 106, 110, 118, 129, 131, 132, 134, 136, 140, 144, 148, 162, 163, 165, 170, 174, 229, 273, 323, 341, 342, 348, 351, 358, 360, 362, 368, 370, 371, 372, 377, 380, 385
Mexico City 4, 26, 56, 57, 59, 66, 74, 75, 77, 80, 83, 86, 87, 90, 91, 93, 94, 100, 104, 117, 136, 144, 148, 149, 174, 186, 187, 197, 200, 205, 209, 222, 253, 256, 262, 263, 264, 266, 275, 278, 279, 280, 282, 314, 315, 317, 318, 320, 331, 338, 359, 381
miners 64, 74, 77, 99, 102, 184, 186, 187, 188, 189, 190, 193, 195, 203, 204, 275, 283, 316, 317, 331
mining sites 5, 36, 80, 86, 102, 141, 185, 186, 187, 189, 190, 191, 196, 280
– Guanajuato 58, 102, 188, 190, 195, 205, 283, 310, 313, 314, 316, 317
– Pachuca 102, 190, 193
– Puebla 58, 84, 94, 99, 102, 103, 105, 175, 192, 194, 202, 204, 211, 266, 280, 282, 311, 313, 314, 317, 319, 331
– Queretaro 58, 194, 280, 315, 316
– San Luis Potosí 194, 313
– Sultepec 102, 186, 187, 190, 192, 193
– Taxco 99, 102, 186, 187, 190, 192, 193

– Zacatecas 76, 90, 188, 190, 191, 195, 203, 205, 275, 280, 311, 313, 314, 317
– Zumpango 187, 262
Moctezuma, Emperor 76, 82, 113, 114, 115, 116, 117, 128, 130, 134, 175, 178, 179, 226, 231
Molina, Alonso de 9, 26, 132, 133, 155, 170, 171, 172, 173, 175, 181, 256, 257, 258, 259, 260, 262, 305, 360
Montesinos, Antón de 79
Muteeçuma 113, 120, 126, 127, 128, 130, 131

N

Nahuas 79, 249, 251, 252, 258, 272, 309, 338, 339, 340
Nahuatl 27, 30, 31, 37, 59, 70, 94, 107, 111, 118, 120, 135, 136, 142, 143, 150, 164, 170, 171, 172, 173, 174, 175, 176, 180, 181, 200, 208, 223, 225, 249, 251, 252, 255, 256, 257, 259, 260, 261, 262, 263, 271, 272, 273, 276, 306, 309, 333, 338, 339, 340, 360, 377, 378
Nahuatl-accented Spanish 107, 276, 338, 378
Nahuatlismos 27, 170, 171, 174, 175, 176, 180, 223
Nahuatl language 27, 170, 255
Nahuatl sibilants 174, 175
Narváez, Pánfilo de 55, 75, 101, 116, 180, 363
Nebrija, Elio Antonio de 10, 12, 23, 37, 49, 50, 119, 174, 207, 299, 318, 363
New Laws of 1542 30, 78, 80, 101, 105, 157, 189, 253, 268
New Spain 1, 4, 5, 8, 26, 28, 30, 32, 39, 52, 55, 56, 57, 58, 63, 71, 73, 74, 75, 76, 77, 78, 80, 84, 88, 89, 90, 91, 93, 95, 97, 98, 99, 101, 102, 103, 104, 105, 106, 107, 108, 111, 117, 118, 136, 140, 141, 143, 144, 145, 148, 149, 156, 162, 170, 174, 182, 185, 188, 189, 190, 191, 192, 196, 202, 204, 205, 207, 208, 209, 211, 212, 222, 234, 243, 244, 247, 249, 250, 255, 260, 266, 267, 268, 269, 275, 276, 278, 282, 284, 306, 308, 309, 310, 312, 313, 314, 318, 319, 321, 324, 331, 332, 336, 337, 338, 341, 342, 344, 348, 346, 353, 359, 372, 383, 389

New Spanish society 59, 140, 170, 204, 273, 279, 318
New World 1, 2, 3, 5, 6, 7, 8, 9, 16, 17, 21, 22, 23, 24, 25, 26, 27, 28, 29, 30, 33, 35, 36, 37, 41, 43, 44, 45, 46, 47, 48, 51, 52, 53, 54, 55, 56, 57, 58, 59, 60, 61, 62, 63, 65, 70, 71, 72, 73, 80, 81, 82, 87, 89, 90, 93, 94, 96, 101, 105, 107, 108, 110, 125, 132, 133, 135, 136, 140, 141, 143, 144, 145, 146, 148, 161, 165, 168, 169, 181, 182, 188, 189, 208, 210, 211, 217, 220, 222, 223, 244, 247, 254, 258, 264, 266, 267, 269, 274, 278, 282, 284, 285, 286, 289, 290, 300, 301, 302, 306, 307, 308, 310, 315, 318, 323, 331, 332, 337, 338, 341, 342, 343, 348, 350, 351, 352, 357, 360, 369, 370, 371, 372, 374, 376, 378, 379, 382, 383, 384, 385, 388, 391, 392
New World Spanish 1, 2, 3, 5, 6, 8, 9, 16, 21, 22, 25, 26, 27, 28, 29, 30, 35, 36, 37, 43, 46, 48, 54, 59, 60, 61, 62, 65, 107, 110, 125, 133, 135, 141, 144, 148, 152, 163, 165, 167, 168, 169, 181, 188, 217, 220, 229, 243, 247, 285, 286, 289, 300, 301, 302, 306, 307, 343, 350, 357, 369, 370, 371, 374, 379, 384, 385, 388, 392
Nueva Galicia 102, 148, 275, 279, 312

O

obrajeros 202
obrajes 103, 184, 199, 201, 202
Old Castile 23, 37, 41, 43, 50, 57, 61, 76, 111, 146, 155, 278, 311
Old Christian lineage 3, 90, 110, 136
Old Christian(s) 3, 88, 90, 95, 110, 136, 274, 275, 280
Old Spanish 14, 23, 38, 45, 48, 51, 52, 118, 120, 146
Ordaz, Diego de 26, 140, 143, 147, 149, 165, 166, 167, 168, 169, 170, 182

P

para and pa 29, 122, 159–160 357, 388
Peninsular Spanish 48, 52
peninsular tree 21, 29, 32, 379, 384, 385, 388

Peru 25, 29, 48, 55, 80, 90, 98, 189, 202, 266, 267, 331, 384, 389
Petrarca, Francesco 208, 301
Philip II 13, 14, 15, 207
polymorphism 11, 23, 45, 123, 222, 343, 350
popularization 3, 4, 65, 71, 378
population 4, 30, 32, 57, 58, 70, 72, 77, 79, 80, 81, 88, 89, 102, 103, 108, 142, 146, 148, 184, 190, 191, 193, 194, 195, 196, 198, 200, 201, 211, 250, 251, 255, 261, 262, 265, 270, 274, 275, 278, 279, 280, 282, 283, 302, 306, 308, 309, 310, 312, 313, 314, 315, 317, 318, 319, 320, 378, 379, 386, 390
– by caste 58, 279, 312, 314, 315
– by intendancy 313, 314
– by sex and jurisdiction 313
Portugal 40, 57, 80, 89, 90, 95, 98, 283
Portuguese 12, 20, 30, 42, 52, 55, 72, 80, 89, 90, 91, 92, 93, 94, 98, 99, 100, 101, 104, 106, 108, 284, 387
Portuguese-Spanish bilinguals 99, 100
printing press 12, 13, 23, 85, 118, 146, 185, 206, 210, 318
probanzas 89, 93, 204, 274, 280, 281, 319, 320
pro-etymological variants 216
pronouns of address 6, 29, 31, 32, 133, 161, 182, 212, 217, 230, 237, 240, 246, 323, 327, 341, 350, 373, 374, 382, 383, 384
protasis and apodosis 129, 161, 217, 223, 244, 303, 329, 351, 367
proto-Mexican Spanish 5, 59, 70, 108, 118, 132, 136, 149, 173, 175, 181, 182
Puebla de los Angeles 84, 99, 103, 192, 204, 211, 266, 311, 331
pueblos de indios 191

R

Reconquista 21, 35, 37, 38, 40, 41, 43, 65, 72, 249
religion 71, 82, 90, 98, 108, 185, 206, 249, 254, 256, 258, 262, 263, 264, 272, 283
Renaissance 87, 203, 204, 208, 249, 261, 305
repartimiento 40, 83, 111, 184, 189, 190, 199, 200, 203, 249

residual variants 5, 21, 22, 26–27, 28, 32, 105, 106, 134, 136, 236, 343, 354, 360, 361, 369, 370, 374, 385
– optimal 27, 32, 236, 243, 360, 364, 374, 385, 391
– popular 4, 5, 6, 7, 10, 22, 23, 26, 28, 32, 65, 80, 105, 106, 136, 208, 233, 236, 263, 289, 299, 336, 351, 360, 365, 368, 369, 371, 374, 379, 380, 383, 385, 386, 387, 389, 392
resistance 37, 43, 98, 107, 249, 255, 342, 377
Revillagigedo Census 308, 312, 313, 314, 315

S

Sahagún, Bernardino de 146, 171, 208, 212, 256, 257, 258, 260, 364
Salamanca 51, 110, 140, 148, 207, 293
Santiago de Chile 16, 387
Santiago de Cuba 71
Santo Domingo 25, 37, 55, 56, 76, 145, 147, 188, 370, 384, 389
Schools of thought 17
second generation of Spanish speakers / writers 31, 211, 222, 234, 241, 372
Segura de la Frontera 113, 117, 175
semantic extension(s) 224, 334
seseo 9, 24, 26, 27, 29, 31, 32, 42, 45, 46, 48, 52, 53, 60, 64, 145, 146, 149, 150, 177, 181, 212, 213, 222, 235, 236, 243, 244, 287, 288, 289, 307, 308, 321, 341, 344, 345, 363, 379, 391
Seseo-P 342, 343, 379, 391
Seseo-W 322, 342, 343, 344, 346, 379
Seville xii, xiii, 21, 26, 30, 39, 40, 41, 45, 46, 48, 50, 53, 56, 60, 61, 64, 68, 110, 111, 113, 118, 120, 140, 145, 148, 206, 209, 278, 305, 311, 331, 381
sibilants 2, 9, 27, 29, 42, 43, 44, 45, 46, 47, 51, 52, 60, 61, 63, 108, 135, 145, 146, 147, 149, 174, 175, 177, 212, 213, 222, 235, 243, 244, 285, 286, 287, 290, 307, 308, 321, 335, 341, 343, 374, 379, 391
– graphemes 9, 11, 27, 31, 38, 53, 145, 174, 182, 235, 243, 244, 245, 285, 286, 288, 289, 306, 308, 321, 322, 335, 343, 344, 345, 346, 362
– voiced apico-alveolar fricative 166
– voiceless apico-alveolar fricative 233
– voiceless pre-palatal fricative 150, 171
socialization 71, 82, 87, 90, 93, 196, 199, 250
social networks 184, 196, 212, 384
social stratification 3, 4, 35, 62, 63, 70, 74, 82, 136, 142, 161
Spanish-accented Nahuatl 338
Suárez de Peralta, Juan 26, 211, 222, 223, 224, 225, 226, 228, 231, 233, 234, 369, 385
subjunctive mood 122, 160, 338
– in SI-clauses 332
su merced 29, 31, 135, 183, 237, 238, 246, 298, 299, 308, 323, 324, 325, 327, 348, 350, 383
sus mercedes 183, 237, 246
Swadesh, Mauricio 376

T

Taino 27, 37, 70, 71, 118, 131, 132, 136, 150, 164, 181, 224, 360
Tenochtitlan 55, 70, 75, 77, 81, 85, 113, 114, 115, 116, 117, 174, 175, 179, 197, 252, 254, 266
textiles 31, 184, 202, 253, 331
toledano 43, 52, 62, 63, 64, 65, 140, 142, 143, 150, 166, 174
toledano-castellano 62, 63, 64, 142, 150, 174
Toledo 11, 21, 37, 38, 39, 43, 44, 48, 52, 56, 88, 140, 143, 146, 209, 242, 252, 258
transculturation 268, 269
transplantation 1, 26, 29, 30, 35, 70, 72, 73, 388
traza 84, 85, 86, 141, 266
tú 7, 8, 28, 29, 31, 60, 123, 135, 168, 170, 182, 212, 217, 218, 220, 221, 230, 231, 237, 238, 246, 290, 298, 299, 300, 301, 306, 308, 325, 327, 341, 348, 350, 351, 359, 370, 372, 382, 383, 384, 392, 393
tuteo 230, 298, 325

U

Use of *–SE* and *–RA* 28, 29, 31, 32, 54, 147, 167, 302, 307, 308, 328, 331, 332, 341, 351, 353, 374, 381
– *see also* conditional sentences and imperfect subjunctive

Usted 28, 31, 136, 182, 298, 299, 301, 308, 325, 326, 327, 348, 350, 373, 382, 384, 392
Ustedes 28, 136, 308, 350

V

Valdés, Juan de 38, 49, 53, 293, 336
Valladolid, New Spain 55, 105, 140, 146, 179, 192, 204, 215, 280, 311, 313, 314, 319, 320
Valladolid, Spain 55, 105, 140, 146, 179, 192, 204, 215, 280, 311, 313, 314, 319, 320
variation(s) 31, 129, 156, 390
Veracruz 22, 24, 55, 75, 80, 81, 102, 105, 106, 113, 145, 175, 205, 236, 311, 313, 331, 379
verbs of perception 215, 227
verbs, spelling of common 6, 16, 28, 118, 119, 123, 149, 150, 151, 155, 157, 158, 162, 163, 168, 170, 176, 177, 215, 219, 226, 227, 228, 229, 230, 231, 290, 292, 295, 296, 323, 324, 333, 355, 366, 371, 375, 377, 379, 380
Vocabulario en lengua castellana y mexicana y mexicana y castellana 26, 256
vos 7, 8, 9, 27, 29, 31, 52, 54, 60, 134, 135, 162, 166, 167, 168, 169, 170, 179, 182, 212, 214, 217, 218, 220, 221, 230, 231, 237, 239, 246, 298, 299, 300, 301, 306, 308, 327, 348, 350, 357, 359, 372, 373, 374, 382, 384, 392, 393
voseo 8, 26, 29, 60, 135, 168, 169, 170, 182, 218, 220, 221, 230, 239, 325, 327, 348, 349, 350, 370, 382, 383, 384, 392

vosotros 28, 54, 134, 179, 183, 217, 220, 230, 231, 232, 237, 238, 239, 299, 300, 301, 306, 327, 374, 392
vuesa merced 232, 300, 383
vuesas mercedes 232
vuestra merced xiv, 28, 29, 31, 135, 162, 179, 182, 220, 221, 237, 238, 244, 246, 298, 299, 300, 301, 306, 308, 323, 325, 326, 327, 341, 348, 350, 372, 373, 382, 383, 384
vuestras mercedes 28, 135, 183, 237, 238, 239, 246, 327

W

Western(ized) civilization 84, 378
Western medicine 207
workshops 103, 199, 201, 283

X

Xalitzintla 175
Xochimilco 77, 198, 251, 252, 254, 259

Y

yeísmo 48, 52, 60, 145
Yucatán 121
Yuste, Carmen 26, 308, 331, 332

Z

Zacatecas 76, 90, 188, 190, 191, 195, 203, 205, 275, 280, 311, 313, 314, 317
Zumárraga, Juan de 81, 148, 149, 156, 157, 206, 357, 361, 367

Usted 28, 31, 136, 182, 298, 299, 301, 308, 325, 326, 327, 348, 350, 373, 382, 384, 392
Ustedes 28, 136, 308, 350

V
Valdés, Juan de 38, 49, 53, 293, 336
Valladolid, New Spain 55, 105, 140, 146, 179, 192, 204, 215, 280, 311, 313, 314, 319, 320
Valladolid, Spain 55, 105, 140, 146, 179, 192, 204, 215, 280, 311, 313, 314, 319, 320
variation(s) 31, 129, 156, 390
Veracruz 22, 24, 55, 75, 80, 81, 102, 105, 106, 113, 145, 175, 205, 236, 311, 313, 331, 379
verbs of perception 215, 227
verbs, spelling of common 6, 16, 28, 118, 119, 123, 149, 150, 151, 155, 157, 158, 162, 163, 168, 170, 176, 177, 215, 219, 226, 227, 228, 229, 230, 231, 290, 292, 295, 296, 323, 324, 333, 355, 366, 371, 375, 377, 379, 380
Vocabulario en lengua castellana y mexicana y mexicana y castellana 26, 256
vos 7, 8, 9, 27, 29, 31, 52, 54, 60, 134, 135, 162, 166, 167, 168, 169, 170, 179, 182, 212, 214, 217, 218, 220, 221, 230, 231, 237, 239, 246, 298, 299, 300, 301, 306, 308, 327, 348, 350, 357, 359, 372, 373, 374, 382, 384, 392, 393
voseo 8, 26, 29, 60, 135, 168, 169, 170, 182, 218, 220, 221, 230, 239, 325, 327, 348, 349, 350, 370, 382, 383, 384, 392

vosotros 28, 54, 134, 179, 183, 217, 220, 230, 231, 232, 237, 238, 239, 299, 300, 301, 306, 327, 374, 392
vuesa merced 232, 300, 383
vuesas mercedes 232
vuestra merced xiv, 28, 29, 31, 135, 162, 179, 182, 220, 221, 237, 238, 244, 246, 298, 299, 300, 301, 306, 308, 323, 325, 326, 327, 341, 348, 350, 372, 373, 382, 383, 384
vuestras mercedes 28, 135, 183, 237, 238, 239, 246, 327

W
Western(ized) civilization 84, 378
Western medicine 207
workshops 103, 199, 201, 283

X
Xalitzintla 175
Xochimilco 77, 198, 251, 252, 254, 259

Y
yeísmo 48, 52, 60, 145
Yucatán 121
Yuste, Carmen 26, 308, 331, 332

Z
Zacatecas 76, 90, 188, 190, 191, 195, 203, 205, 275, 280, 311, 313, 314, 317
Zumárraga, Juan de 81, 148, 149, 156, 157, 206, 357, 361, 367

www.ingramcontent.com/pod-product-compliance
Lightning Source LLC
Chambersburg PA
CBHW022103290426
44112CB00008B/536